THE GUIDANCE FUNCTION IN EDUCATION

PERCIVAL W. HUTSON
PROFESSOR OF EDUCATION
University of Pittsburgh

The Guidance Function
in Education

APPLETON-CENTURY-CROFTS, INC., New York

PRINTED IN THE UNITED STATES OF AMERICA

Preface

WHAT DO WE KNOW about the guidance function in education? In the half century that has elapsed since Frank Parsons articulated the concept of vocational guidance, an astounding body of opinion, of descriptions of practice, and of reports of research have by virtue of publication become common property. To what state of knowledge has this flood of literature brought us? It is the ambitious, indeed presumptuous, purpose of this writer to organize and present the accumulated understandings of the guidance function and of the features which implement it, in so far as that can be done within the limits of a single, manageable volume.

By way of qualification for such a project, the writer must first acknowledge his debt to an obligation. For twenty-four years, 1933 to 1956, inclusive, he prepared an annual article, "Selected References on Guidance," for the September number of the *School Review*. This yearly responsibility compelled him to canvass the output of guidance literature in order to evaluate and sift it. The process was indeed subjective, but the obligation afforded an unusual opportunity to gain such command of the field as seemed to warrant the writing of a book devoted to organizing and presenting the best thinking on the subject of guidance.

No book of readings, however, would permit the author to express *himself*—such information, values, and principles as have come to him by virtue of years of teaching courses in guidance and directing research in the field. Hence, his own appraisals and interpretations are closely integrated with the reporting of the literature.

Some readers and critics set great store by recency as the major criterion for judging the materials drawn upon for such a book as this one. But value should come first. Just because Bingham and Thorndike are no longer with us in mortal flesh, shall we assume that their ideas are outmoded? We are still and forever in debt to the creative minds of yesterday, some of whose thoughts have never been clothed in more apt phrases than those in which the original authors arrayed them. If Finney's 1928 analysis of American society helps us to understand the 1958 world in which we seek to bring about a rational matching of talents and tasks, we should drink of his wisdom. If Alltucker practiced counseling imaginatively and logically in 1924, we impoverish ourselves if we spurn her report because of its date. If Allen was building such good mousetraps in 1932 as to attract counselors from all over the country, we do well to recount his work to a generation which has grown up since his day.

Helen M. Walker* in introducing a long quotation from Galton said:

Again and again, students of science and mathematics note the extreme clarity of exposition in the writings of the man who discovered some particular idea. With a multitude of more modern presentations available, the best introduction to some topic is often provided by the paper in which it was first discussed.

Donald Paterson recently expressed similar values in a guest editorial: †

In my opinion, our younger colleagues seem to lack an intimate knowledge of the major contributions made by the pioneers [attention called to seven "classics" which were published before 1919]. . . . The term *counseling psychology* is used by some as if it came into existence as a new profession in 1952. Yet vocational counseling, marriage counseling, religious counseling, personal and emotional counseling, to mention only a few types of counseling, have been in existence for many years.

Looking for value rather than recency, this writer has selected writings which seemed to make contributions to guidance theory and practice without regard to the decade of their appearance.

In drawing upon research contributions, an effort has been made to present sufficient data from the investigator's report and enough detail from his statement of method to convey clear impressions of the research. The allusive style does not appeal to this writer.

It is hoped that the readers of this book will find helpful in their thinking about guidance the organization of the field as here presented. Chapters 1–4 define the function, show its relation to society and education, and cite surveys which evidence the need for performing the function. Chapter 5 sets forth a breakdown of the function into its basic components. The balance of the book describes the various features of the guidance program and takes up their bearing on the components of the function.

This book is for all school workers. Accepting the point of view that guidance is a pervasive function, performed in notable degree by the same activities which are carried on for growth and development, it is a responsibility of teachers and principals as well as of specialists called counselors and deans. Again, guidance is needed at all school levels. Hence, due account has been taken of its exercise in the elementary, secondary, and higher schools.

* *Elementary Statistical Methods* (New York, Holt, 1943), p. 203.
† *Journal of Counseling Psychology,* Vol. III (Summer, 1956), p. 82.

The understandings which teachers typically obtain from their undergraduate courses in education and psychology are assumed. Readers are *not* assumed to have taken graduate courses in statistics and psychological measurement. Perhaps the book is optimally suited to the first year of graduate study in education.

Since a considerable number of permissions to quote have been sought and granted, it has seemed more fitting to acknowledge the courtesy at appropriate points throughout the book than to list them here.

P. W. H.

Contents

Part I

DEFINITION AND SOCIAL ORIENTATION OF THE GUIDANCE FUNCTION

CHAPTER 1

History and Definition
of the Guidance Function

PRESENT INCIDENCE OF GUIDANCE ACTIVITY

The Individual Faces a Complex and Turbulent World

"More completely than any other single movement, vocational guidance must take for its function the *conservation of human resources.*"[1] These words, uttered by one of the seers of American education, in 1915 forecast our mid-century concern for the identification and maximum use of human talent. A deep-felt urgency is signified by the appearance of such titles of books and periodical literature as the following: "The Human Resources of the United States," "America's Resources of Specialized Talent," "Who Should Go to College?" and "A Policy for Scientific and Professional Manpower." Hot war, cold war, and uneasy peace have forced us to take account of the nature and extent of our human capital.

Viewed from the standpoint of the individual or the mass, the recent years have witnessed the most extensive social dislocation of our history. The shifts from peace to war and back to peace again, in an age when war is "total war," can only be accomplished at the price of untold shock and strain. Staggering to the imagination are the economic, social, and psychological adjustments which individuals are called upon to make. War brings about extreme subordination of the individual to the state, for the national organism responds to danger from without by summoning up all its human and material resources. This means control over the destinies of individual people, classifying them with reference to their potentialities for serving the dominant national purpose, employing power, propaganda, or the attraction of profits and high wages to achieve optimum individual placement. When the emergency of war has passed, controls are relaxed, war occupations are abolished,

[1] F. E. Spaulding, "Problems of Vocational Guidance," in Meyer Bloomfield, *Readings in Vocational Guidance* (Cambridge, Mass., Harvard University Press, 1915), p. 69.

and individuals are given their customary peacetime freedom in occupational choice. But the ending of a war economy creates new crises and therefore necessitates new adjustments, the severity of which are enhanced by the fact that the postwar world can never be a duplicate of the prewar world. How difficult for the individual amid such turbulence to find a way of existence which is settled, stable, and satisfying!

Contemplation of the abnormalities created by wars should not obscure our vision of the on-going industrial revolution as a more basic factor in the complex world which the individual faces. A commonplace story is that of the shift of our society from an agrarian to an industrial status, from a rural to an urban character, from a handicraft to a machinocraft basis, from small, simply organized industrial units to large, complex ones, from occupations which are few and general to occupations which are many and highly specialized. Yesterday, the collaboration of thousands of workers in making a shoe, a plow, or a coat; today, the mechanization of corn and cotton growing and harvesting; tomorrow, automation—"the harnessing of electronic brains to mechanical muscles." Change and increasing complexity have become the normal order. And since Thomas Edison systematized invention, stimulating the establishment of vast laboratories up and down the land, the rate of social change has sharply accelerated.

What of the individual in an environment of such instability and complication? With home, community, and other basic institutions, as well as vocation, undergoing relatively rapid modification, can he experience the sense of security, of self-realization, and of importance which seem to characterize the happy, well-adjusted person? That the situation presents grave difficulties in the attainment of such ends must be admitted. The problem will be elaborated in a later chapter.

Guidance Activity Recently Given Marked Impetus

Increasing sensitivity to the plight of the individual and also to the need of society for the maximum use of its members has recently brought widespread recognition of the value and place of guidance service as a social function. Undoubtedly its most publicized employment down to this date has been in connection with the adjustment and rehabilitation of the veterans of World War II. The need was apparent early. A year or more before V-E Day the Army and Navy established counseling services at their Separation Centers to offer vocational guidance and other types of advisement. Military education and experience were summarized, and a record—interpreted for its meaning in civilian careers—was given the dischargee as an introduction to educational authorities or prospective employers. The military authorities recognized that adjustment to civilian life presented serious problems to many dischargees, especially to those who had had no civilian occupational history and to those whose service-incurred disabilities restricted their choice of occupation. Nevertheless, these authorities acknowledged the limitations of

Separation-Center counseling, as indicated by the following statement from an authoritative description: "Counseling given at Separation Centers and at Army hospitals should be regarded as *preliminary* to the work of civilian agencies engaged in direct placement or long-term rehabilitation."[2]

The Veterans Administration, in its district, regional, and subregional offices, and through the Guidance Centers which it established in approximately 200 colleges and universities in all parts of the country, put into operation a most extensive program of counseling. Adequately financed and broadly conceived, the program constituted a demonstration which inevitably extended the public's acquaintance with the guidance function. Educational and vocational counseling are prominent in the Veterans Administration program, but full recognition is also accorded to the wide variety of emotional, physical, and social problems that frequently are obstacles to the successful pursuit of vocational or educational objectives. Correlation of the skills of the several professions represented by the counselor, physician, psychiatrist, clinical psychologist, and social worker is at times demonstrated.

Stimulated without doubt by the presence of Veterans Administration Guidance Centers in academic halls, the period since the end of the war has been one of remarkable activity among colleges in the establishment of counseling services for their students, veterans and nonveterans alike. While it is true that some colleges had long been exercising the guidance function with commendable thoroughness and that many had partially developed programs, a marked awakening to the need for guidance service carried on with modern professional tools wielded by professional personnel is undoubtedly taking place.

Secondary schools are similarly evincing a mounting interest in guidance. Tradition-bound high schools are calling for trained counselors.[3] In no small degree this growing appreciation of guidance may be attributed to the Occupational Information and Guidance Service, established as a division of the Office of Education by federal legislation in 1938, and to similar state-directed service in nearly all the states of the Union, for which federal aid was made available under the same 1938 law. Even more, the accelerating acceptance of the function may be due to such wartime experiences of the schools as the following: marked loss of enrollment as pupils left school for jobs, programs of pre-induction training, increase of maladjustment due to

[2] Colonel George R. Evans, "The Army Separation Classification and Vocational Counseling Program," *Occupations,* Vol. XXIII (November, 1944), p. 70.

[3] A recent survey of the employment of counselors is reported in Arthur J. Jones and Leonard M. Miller, "The National Picture of Pupil Personnel and Guidance Services in 1953," *Bulletin of the National Association of Secondary-School Principals,* Vol. XXXVIII (February, 1954), pp. 105–159.

From *School and Society,* Vol. 85 (June 8, 1957), comes a projection of future need, as follows: "The number of counselors employed in public schools is expected to increase about 70% by 1960–61, according to a University of Michigan study among public-school principals throughout the country. About 44,000 counselors were employed in 1955–56."

decline in home care and discipline, numerous polls of pupil opinion of their felt needs showing guidance service to be asked for in highest frequency. Such events and conditions are disturbing to complacency; they demand action.

Another sign of the sudden spurt in the growth of guidance activity was the establishment in 1945 of employment counseling as a function of the United States Employment Service (transferred to the states shortly after the war). A supervisor of employment counseling was designated for each state and one or more counselors appointed to each of the 1500 offices of the Service. The following quotation suggests the scope and purpose of guidance as it is being exercised by this agency:

The problems of occupational adjustment have been intensified and multiplied by the war but are present at all times and in all types of economy. Assistance in solving them must be a part of the normal operations of the Employment Service. . . . Early programs emphasized youth counseling; however, it became evident that problems of occupational adjustment were not confined to any age group. Experienced workers also face vocational problems since neither the individual nor his environment remain static. Thus we find that individuals must enter new fields of work because of the changes in demand that inevitably accompany technical advance; others must enter new fields of work because of the acquisition of disabilities. Many workers change their vocations either because their original choice was poor or they no longer find it satisfying.[4]

Such extensive use of guidance procedures as just related is impossible without a considerable period of experience, without a body of technical knowledge accumulated through research, and without a sizable nucleus of trained personnel. How the foundations were laid for these recent manifestations of a vigorous social service is the subject of the next section of this chapter.

BEGINNINGS AND GROWTH OF THE GUIDANCE MOVEMENT

Vocational Guidance

Among the half dozen sources from which the present concept of guidance has been derived none is more clearly related to it than the vocational-guidance movement. Credit for originating vocational guidance as a social service and for coining the term "vocational guidance" is given to Frank Parsons, a civic-minded writer and lecturer who founded the Vocation Bureau of Boston in 1908 in the Civic Service House of that city. Parsons lived only a few months after establishing the Bureau, but he fixed the pattern and the spirit of counseling for vocational choice with such wisdom that contemporary authorities pay tribute to the soundness of his analysis. In his *Choosing a*

[4] Lilian Alexander, "U.S.E.S. Appoints Employment Counselors," *Occupations,* Vol. XXIV (October, 1945), p. 5.

Vocation[5] he set forth the principles and methods as he saw them and amply illustrated his practice with "sample cases." "In the wise choice of a vocation," said Parsons,

there are three broad factors: (1) a clear understanding of yourself, your aptitudes, abilities, interests, ambitions, resources, limitations, and their causes; (2) a knowledge of the requirements and conditions of success, advantages and disadvantages, compensation, opportunities, and prospects in different lines of work; (3) true reasoning on the relations of these two groups of facts.

The Bureau operated after Parsons' death along the lines he had laid down for it—collecting and publishing occupational information, conducting the group study of occupations, carrying on individual counsel, introducing vocational guidance into the Boston schools, and training vocational counselors. In 1917 the Bureau was taken over by the Division of Education of Harvard University.

Leaders in American education very early caught the social significance of Parsons' contribution. They acclaimed the value of vocational guidance for the individual and for society. Helpful and illuminating literature in the field of vocational guidance today are the papers and addresses given between 1910 and 1915 by President Eliot and Professor Hanus of Harvard, President MacLaurin of the Massachusetts Institute of Technology, Professor Mead of the University of Chicago, F. E. Spaulding, then superintendent of schools in Minneapolis, and Professor Thorndike of Teachers College— writings included in Meyer Bloomfield's *Readings in Vocational Guidance.*[6]

The strength of the vocational-guidance movement is attested today by a vigorous professional organization originated in 1913 and having a membership of more than 5000, and also by the continuous issue since 1922 of a professional periodical—now merged in *The Personnel and Guidance Journal.*

A few highlights in the history of vocational guidance may be cited[7] as contributing to the wider acceptance of its value and to the improvement of its techniques. First, the National Occupational Conference. This was an organization, financed by the Carnegie Corporation, which from 1933 to 1939 published *Occupations* (precursor of *The Personnel and Guidance Journal*) and carried out numerous other projects of research, publication, and promotion. These activities gave vocational guidance some useful tools and made more people acquainted with the function.[8] Second, the Minnesota Employment Stabilization Research Institute. Organized in the early 1930's, this agency made detailed analyses of unemployed persons, exemplified tech-

[5] Published posthumously (Boston, Houghton Mifflin, 1909), p. 5.
[6] Cambridge, Mass., Harvard University Press, 1915.
[7] For a full account, replete with interesting details, see John M. Brewer and Others, *History of Vocational Guidance* (New York, Harper, 1942).
[8] The activities of this agency have been summarized by Edwin A. Lee in Chapter XIX of Brewer, *op. cit.*

niques of ascertaining occupational potentialities, and tested the validity of its processes.[9] Third, the Adjustment Service of New York City. This was another subsidized experiment in vocational guidance, much like the Minnesota project. It was carried out in 1933 and 1934.[10] Fourth, the work of the Research Division of the United States Employment Service. Brought into being in 1934, this agency has carried out a systematic analysis of occupations according to human abilities required. Its greatest work, the *Dictionary of Occupational Titles*,[11] contained definitions of 23,559 separate jobs and was published just in time to be of inestimable value to the Employment Service in helping to meet the crucial manpower problems of World War II.[12]

Without the contributions of the four agencies just named, the work of present-day counselors in high school and college, in Veterans Administration and Employment Service, would indeed be impoverished and gropingly uncertain. They have enabled counseling to take a long step forward in professional status. The technical knowledge and skill they represent form a sharp contrast to the early pronouncements which defined vocational guidance as "organized common sense" used to help individuals make the most of their abilities and opportunities.

Student Personnel Administration

A second important tributary to today's guidance concept is from the type of service called "student," or "pupil personnel administration." The functionary chiefly associated with this work is most commonly called "dean." The title originated in colleges and was used to designate a faculty member who was given special responsibility for dealing with the personal and disciplinary problems of students. Deans of women organized the National Association of Deans of Women (now called the National Association of Women Deans and Counselors) in 1914, a society which has come to include secondary-school as well as college functionaries, with a membership of 1500. Deans of men first met as a Conference of Deans and Advisers of Men in 1919. Together with college placement officers and other personnel workers they formed the American College Personnel Association in 1931.

The functions of personnel workers, both men and women, are not standardized, and their associations have sought clarification. For example, in 1930 Marion Brown listed the following categories of student problems as being the responsibilities of a high-school dean of girls:[13]

[9] For a partial summary of the work of the Institute, see Donald G. Paterson and John G. Darley, *Men, Women, and Jobs* (Minneapolis, University of Minnesota Press, 1936).

[10] Jerome H. Bentley, *The Adjustment Service* (New York, American Association for Adult Education, 1935).

[11] Washington, Government Printing Office, 1939. Revised in 1949.

[12] Members of the staff of this agency described its methods and accomplishments in the following reference: "Ten Years of Occupational Research," *Occupations*, Vol. XXII (April, 1944), pp. 387–446.

[13] In S. M. Sturtevant and H. Hayes, *Deans at Work* (New York, Harper, 1930), pp. 101, 103.

1. Those involved in educational and vocational guidance.

2. Discipline cases involving offenses against constituted authority, good taste, moral standards, and rights of others.

3. Social problems stressing especially relationships with other persons in the school situation.

4. Those problems of physical and mental health which affect the child's school progress.

5. Economic factors which enter into the life of the girl as a student.

At about this same time, Arch O. Heck, in a series of articles in the *Educational Research Bulletin* (1935), reported practices as determined by surveys made in 1930, '32, '33, and '34. No mention was made of deans or counselors and the inquiry was limited to the following functionaries:

Directors	School psychiatrists
Attendance officers	Clerks
Visiting teachers	Dentists
School physicians	Dental hygienists
School nurses	Specials
School psychologists	Attendance supervisors

Only the last article[14] of the series, devoted to a projected organization of a department of pupil personnel in a school system, showed some inclusion of school guidance services.

In 1937 a committee working under the auspices of the American Council on Education made a report[15] in which they proposed that the work of a college or university be considered as classifiable in the three large categories of instruction, business management, and student personnel services. The last named category included 23 activities which Lloyd-Jones and Smith, in a diagrammatic representation, compressed to the following elements as constituting the student personnel program:

Orientation	Health
Counseling	Housing
Education and	
Vocational Guidance	Financial Aid
Placement	Social Program
Discipline	Selection and Admission
Records	Religion
Research	Extra-Curricular Activities[16]

[14] "Administrative Organization," *Educational Research Bulletin,* Vol. XIV (November, 1935), pp. 214–216.

[15] *The Student Personnel Point of View,* American Council on Education Studies, Series I, Vol. I, No. 3 (June, 1937).

[16] Esther Lloyd-Jones and Margaret R. Smith, *A Student Personnel Program for Higher Education* (New York, McGraw-Hill, 1938), p. 22.

Most of these elements will be recognized as important services in a modern program for the lower schools as well as the higher. The extent to which they are "guidance" will be considered in the following section of this chapter.

Psychologists, Working as Researchers and Clinicians

The debt guidance owes to psychology should be evident without extended reporting. Without the objective instruments for measuring human behavior and potentialities—intelligence tests, special aptitude tests, achievement tests, diagnostic tests, interest inventories, and the like—it is difficult to envisage guidance as much more than "organized common sense." These tools are the products of psychological research. Frank Parsons did not have them, but a careful reading of his *Choosing a Vocation* suggests that he would have used them if they had been available. Their growth parallels in time that of vocational guidance.

Psychologists have become clinicians primarily at the college and adult levels and in child guidance clinics. Large city school systems have one or more psychologists in their central organizations for very specialized services, but individual elementary and secondary schools seldom have such a functionary on their staffs. This clinical role of the psychologist was clearly set forth and urgently pressed some years ago by Symonds,[17] and within the past decade some progress has been made toward realizing his ideal.

Personnel Work in Industry

Paralleling the history of vocational guidance is the history of personnel work in industry. The two movements stem from contrasting motives, it is true, as suggested by Thorndike in 1913:[18]

The employers, humane though they be, will by habit tend to emphasize only the suitability of a given child for a given job; whereas, the greater view of the problem is to make sure of the suitability of a given job for the child.

The employer, concerned with operating an enterprise for a profit, looks to the maximum use of manpower as he does to the maximum use of steel, wood, glass, or other material goods which he may need in his business. Accordingly, the studies of scientific management, begun by Frederick Taylor as early as 1879, were favorably received. Personnel work in industry has developed many new facets since Taylor's studies of time and motion, including the derivation of standard specifications for jobs, the creation of tests for applicants for jobs, studies of fatigue, studies of learning, and studies of motivation. Practical application of these researches has been made in the selection and administration of personnel in industry. During World War II a considerable impetus was given to employee counseling for a wide range of

[17] Percival M. Symonds, "Every School Should Have a Psychologist," *School and Society,* Vol. XXXVIII (September 9, 1933), pp. 321–329.
[18] In Bloomfield, *op. cit.,* p. 97.

problems of adjustment. These included not only adjustment to the job and to fellow workers but also assistance in meeting the problems of housing, health, family relationships, finance, and whatever might interfere with the worker's job efficiency.

The relationship of personnel work in industry to vocational guidance is attested by many joint meetings of the Personnel Research Federation, organized in 1923, with the National Vocational Guidance Association. Furthermore, personnel workers frequently cross the line from education to industry and vice versa.

Social Work

A fifth source of the present guidance concept and program is that of social work, its particular contribution being the visiting-teacher movement. This took form in 1906 and 1907 when Boston, New York City, and Hartford, Connecticut, through settlement houses or civic associations, appointed visiting teachers to work in certain schools with problem pupils and their parents.[19] From that beginning the service has grown steadily so that it is now accepted quite universally by theorists as indispensable to a sound educational program, and in practice a considerable fraction of school systems have such functionaries—preferably now called "school social workers"—on their staffs. A five-year demonstration in a number of cities in the early 1920's was financed by the Commonwealth Fund to give impetus to the movement. Several books were published by the Fund as part of its program for acquainting the public with such work.

The school social worker is steadily replacing the truant officer. The latter represents the law and punishment; the former represents diagnosis, understanding, and adjustment. Trained both for teaching and social work, the school social worker effects a liaison between home, school, and community social agencies. He signifies the conception of education as the joint responsibility of home, school, and community. He works primarily to make those institutions more effective in the case of problem children who show signs of becoming social liabilities rather than assets.

Mental Hygiene and Psychiatry

The publication of Clifford W. Beers' autobiography, *A Mind That Found Itself*,[20] furnished the stimulus for the origin of the National Committee for Mental Hygiene, an organization which has aggressively disseminated the principles of mental health. As a result, sensitivity to the various types of personality maladjustment has greatly increased; awareness of the conditions essential for good adjustment has brought about human relationships which

[19] A concise statement of the history and recent status of this service is to be found in the following pamphlet: Katherine M. Cook, *The Place of Visiting Teacher Services in the School Program*, United States Office of Education Bulletin, 1945, No. 6.

[20] (New York, Doubleday, Doran, 1908.)

signify respect for personality; and with increasing frequency it is recognized that the development of wholesome personalities is the most important purpose of education.

Treatment of the more serious mental disorders is the province of psychiatry. But beginning with the work of Dr. William Healy and Dr. Augusta Bronner, who in 1919 established a clinic for the Chicago Juvenile Court, psychiatry has been increasingly looked to as well for the combatting of juvenile delinquency. The five-year demonstration mentioned above included the setting up of "child guidance clinics" to develop the psychiatric study and treatment of problem children in the schools and juvenile courts. The staff of each clinic usually consisted of a psychiatrist as director, a psychologist, and two or three psychiatric social workers. Numerous clinics now exist over the country, usually staffed with the same specialists as the first ones. While the number of persons served by child guidance clinics is relatively very small, the influence of the clinics on the thought and action of school workers seems to have been marked. Educational literature and teacher-training curriculums have been notably enriched.

In summary of these six movements from which the guidance function has sprung, one may say that all reflect an enhanced appreciation of the worth of every individual and the necessity of helping him to bring his potentialities to actuality. They express our realization of the individual's need for help in finding his place in a complex world. They signify a determination to temper the raw winds of unfettered competition, to salvage the individual who otherwise might be wasted, to conserve all our human resources.[21]

THE GUIDANCE FUNCTION DEFINED

The Nature and Scope of Guidance

To mark out the limits of this book requires that the social service with which it is concerned should be defined. Especially is this made necessary by the fact that the definition of guidance in educational circles has been subject to some confusion and controversy. The definition here offered will be supported by such logic and authority as can be mustered.

To a considerable degree the point of view to be expounded has already been forecast in the previous section. It was there made evident that assisting pupils in sound vocational choices is one important element in the guidance function. Some authorities would limit the application of the term "guidance" to that service. For example, Kitson, after exposing and deprecating the loose use of the word, proposed[22] "that the term 'general guidance' be abandoned

---

[21] The following reference is a recent interpretation of the forces which have been bringing about the development of our present guidance concept: Ruth Barry and Beverly Wolf, "The Genesis of Guidance—Personnel Work," *Teachers College Record,* Vol. 58 (April, 1957), pp. 382–396.

[22] H. D. Kitson, "Getting Rid of a Piece of Educational Rubbish," *Teachers College Record,* Vol. XXXVI (October, 1934), p. 33.

—that the word 'guidance' be reserved to designate only vocational guidance, its point of origin." No disposition to accept such a restriction has been shown, however, and the members of the National Vocational Guidance Association maintain their broad interests, as suggested by their close liaison with the American College Personnel Association and the other organizations which together form the American Personnel and Guidance Association.

The scope of guidance as practically exercised is suggested by "the types of counseling" enumerated and described for the Veterans Administration Guidance Centers. They are as follows: (*a*) *Vocational advisement* (for veterans under Public Law 16); (*b*) *Vocational guidance* (for veterans under Public Law 346); (*c*) *Placement counseling;* (*d*) *Educational guidance;* (*e*) *Personal adjustment counseling.*

The object of this [last] type of counseling is to assist veterans who are not well adjusted emotionally and need the services of professionally trained personnel in dispassionately analyzing their problems for the purpose of providing the insight and understanding essential to overcoming or avoiding emotional disturbances, mental attitudes, social conflicts, and other conditions that cause maladjustments which interfere with the successful pursuit of vocational or educational objectives.[23]

That high-school counselors are carrying on types of guidance other than vocational is evident from Cox's analysis of the work of one hundred counselors carefully selected for their outstanding success. Table 1 shows only four of these workers to be designated as "vocational counselors." Evidently the adjective "vocational" is too restrictive to afford adequate description of the service of these guidance functionaries.

TABLE 1. Distribution of 100 Outstanding High-School Counselors According to Title Held

Title	Number
Counselor	33
Dean	18
Director of Guidance (in the single school)	14
Teacher-Counselor	9
Adviser	7
Assistant or Vice Principal	8
Vocational Counselor	4
Miscellaneous	7
Total	100

Adapted from Table VII, p. 25, in Rachel Dunaway Cox, *Counselors and Their Work* (Harrisburg, Pa., Archives Publishing Co., 1945).

23 Ira D. Scott, *Manual of Advisement and Guidance,* Prepared in Accordance with the Approved Policies of the Veterans Administration (Washington, Government Printing Office, 1945), pp. 3–5.

Cox's analysis of the work of these outstanding guidance functionaries is also illuminating:

Being a counselor, as the selected workers report it, is a varied and complicated job. . . . A counselor needs to be an educational and vocational adviser, a social worker, a teacher, an organizer, a promoter, a public speaker, and even a public relations man. At the same time he needs some of the skills of a psychologist, some of the knowledge of a physician, some of the insights of a psychiatrist. Perhaps the hardest part of this amazingly complicated function is his need to know where and when his own work properly ends and that of some other more specialized worker begins. . . .

An analysis of reported duties shows that they fall roughly into (1) Work with Pupils, (2) Work with Parents, (3) Work with Colleagues in school and community, and (4) Contact or Promotional Work. [p. 36]

As this study has found it, counseling with individuals concerns itself with educational-vocational planning and adjustment and with emotional and social adjustment. [p. 48]

Ninety-three of the hundred counselors give a substantial portion of their time to educational—or educational-vocational—guidance. [p. 49]

Only five counselors say they never deal with problems of emotional confusion growing out of conflicts with family, friends, or other human relationships. The other ninety-five consider it one of their more important duties. [p. 54]

The topic most frequently discussed between counselors and parents is educational-vocational planning. Ninety-five name this as part of their function. [p. 76]

It is in conferences with parents concerning emotional and social adjustments that counselors feel that they do some of their most crucial work. Ninety-one of this group are called upon for this type of counseling, and sixty-three of them give much time to it. [p. 77]

To Sears, writing in 1925, the guidance function meant something more than vocational guidance. After pointing to the curriculum organization and administrative machinery of the school as "guideposts," he said,[24]

The function of guidance as here conceived is that of supplementing or expanding this well-established school mechanism so that there may be less waste energy. Somehow we have not increased our guidance facilities as rapidly as we have increased the complexity of the educational maze through which an ever-increasing number of children are trying to pass, and, as a consequence, numbers of children are on the wrong path, are losing sight of their proper goals, and the result is waste. It is to meet this issue that a plan of guidance must be devised.

[24] J. B. Sears, *The School Survey* (Boston, Houghton Mifflin, 1925), p. 323.

Williamson, writing out of his experience in the exercise of guidance at the university level, emphasizes guidance as the avoidance of waste, saying,[25]

. . . effective teaching requires the selection of students in terms of their capacity to learn and the alleviation of distractions which prevent optimum learning. . . . These distractions include worries about finances and vocational choice, social and family relations, ineffective study habits, unwholesome recreations, adolescent revolt against regulations and adult restrictions, and emotional conflicts concerning religious and philosophical questions. These often result in emotional backgrounds and attitudes which will defeat the most skillful and inspiring lecturing. . . . Optimum learning is possible only when the desire to learn is fostered by sympathetic relations with teachers, by the alleviation of emotional distractions, and by selection of students capable of profiting from college courses.

Similar to Williamson's views, but more inclusive and more fully defined, is the following statement made by Koos in 1928:[26]

It will help . . . to think of guidance under such categories as discipline, social conduct, and quality of work as *adjustment,* in the sense of effecting a better adjustment of the pupil to the school situation, and guidance under such categories as curriculum guidance, vocational guidance, placement, and follow-up as *distribution,* in the sense of distributing the pupils as advantageously as possible to the curriculum and vocational opportunities at hand. . . .
. . . I should like to emphasize the great desirability of our seeing that *both* these elements of adjustment and distribution are kept in the concept of guidance that should dominate the practices in guidance in our schools.

The scope and classification of professional service indicated in Koos' statement is essentially acceptable to this writer as a definition of the guidance function, and he has followed it in his yearly sifting and classifying of guidance literature for his "Selected References on Guidance" published in the September issue of the *School Review*. It will similarly serve as the criterion for the selection of content for this book.

Guidance as thus defined stands in a clear relationship to the total task of education. One may say that the supreme purpose of education is the optimum development of the individual. Guidance consists of those distributive and adjustive services which *facilitate* development. Distribution facilitates development by helping the youth to choose from the array of educational and vocational opportunities those which correspond most nearly to his talents. Naturally, there are some areas of life in which we desire a *common* development on the part of all; distributive guidance will be exercised only with respect to those areas in which we desire or permit *differentiation* in development. Adjustive guidance facilitates development—both common

25 E. G. Williamson, "To Avoid Waste," *Journal of Higher Education,* Vol. VIII (February, 1937), p. 65.
26 Leonard V. Koos, "Guidance Practice in Secondary Schools," *Bulletin of the National Association of Secondary-School Principals,* No. 20 (March, 1928), p. 184.

and differentiated—by removing impediments to optimum progress. Perhaps the following schematic arrangement will summarize this definition:

GUIDANCE:
distributive
and   which facilitate   DEVELOPMENT
adjustive
services

The distributive aspect of guidance is not difficult to understand; perhaps the adjustive aspect may well be elaborated upon, though Williamson's statement is suggestive of some of its ramifications. For example, one of the commonest adjustment problems is presented by the student—he may be in the first grade or he may be in the graduate school—who is failing, as judged by academic standards. Counselors, deans, principals, and homeroom teachers, as well as subject teachers, are spending considerable time in trying to bring about adjustments so that such a student may pursue his studies successfully. Sometimes the problem is simple and easily solved; sometimes it is complex and baffling. Perhaps the basic impediment is poor vision or some other physical maladjustment; with its correction the student can profit by instruction. Perhaps the problem is basically one of reading disability, but complicated by one or more types of undesirable behavior induced by the frustration of failure. Perhaps the cause of the student's failure is volitional, and adjustment consists of arousing such motivation in him that he devotes sufficient time and energy to his studies.

One could go on endlessly with the possibilities of such a hypothetical case. It is not necessary; educational literature is replete with actual cases and the readers of this book have had ample experience with actual cases. Adjustive guidance would *do* something about them, whereas, as Williamson says, speaking of guidance at the college level,[27]

The traditional attitude toward problems of student adjustment, however, has been one of *laissez faire,* of assuming that genius will find its own way, that every student knows what he is capable of doing, that students are grown-up people, and other defense mechanisms of this sort. These feeble attempts to avoid responsibility for the student's adjustment have resulted in wasted effort and serious loss of morale and have directly increased the size of our scholastic graveyards.

The types of needed adjustment to come within our purview have increased as our concept of the developmental goal has been expanded to include more than intellectual attainment. The child who does not outgrow infantile reactions, the one who is shy and withdrawn, and the one who consistently alibis his failures is more and more regarded as a challenge to the ministrations of the school. For increased ability to meet such personality problems we are indebted to mental hygiene.

[27] *Op. cit.,* p. 66.

Another concept essential to grasp in understanding adjustive guidance is that adjustment means change of the environment as frequently as it means change of the individual, and perhaps more so. By way of illustration we have the oft-quoted quip that many a child whose parents take him to the child guidance clinic should be bringing his parents to the clinic. We further have the universal testimony of students of juvenile delinquency to the necessity of modification of environment to bring about adjustment in most cases. The point of this paragraph is too obvious to need further explanation, but it is necessary to include it in order to make more clear the scope of adjustive guidance.

May not adjustive guidance at times be closely akin to development, that is to say, the prime task of education? Probably so, at least in some particulars. One can think of activities that might be difficult to classify. What about remedial reading classes? The answer in this example might be that the identification of the pupils who need the remedial work should be classified as guidance, but the teaching of the class should be regarded as part of the instructional program.

The problem of differentiating guidance and development appears with reference to the distributive as well as the adjustive aspect. For example, one of the oldest activities in distributive guidance is the study of occupations for the purpose of acquiring understanding of the vocational world as a basis for vocational choice. Commonly this activity is carried on by a course in the regular instructional program and must be regarded as developmental. Or again, it is fully recognized that the pupil's experiences in such common elements of the instructional program as English, science, history, mathematics frequently perform distributive guidance, affording pupils experience on the basis of which they make educational and vocational choices.

Evidently, the same activity may be looked on as serving both the guidance and developmental functions. This concept was apparently in the minds of Jones and Hand when they offered the following definition:[28]

Guidance is coming to be regarded as that inseparable aspect of the educational process that is peculiarly concerned with helping individuals discover their needs, assess their potentialities, develop their life purposes, formulate plans of action in the service of these purposes, and proceed to their realization. The total teaching process involves both guidance and instruction as these terms have commonly been employed in the past, and as inseparable functions. Neither can be delegated in any discrete manner to separate functionaries.

This assertion does not mean, however, that specialists, such as counselors, school psychologists, mental hygienists . . . should be done away with.

[28] Arthur J. Jones and Harold C. Hand, "Guidance and Purposive Living," in *Guidance in Educational Institutions,* Thirty-seventh Yearbook, Part I, National Society for the Study of Education (Bloomington, Ill., Public School Publishing Co., 1938), Ch. I, pp. 24–25.

Accepting the point of view expressed by Jones and Hand as essentially sound, this writer feels that a clearer exposition of the guidance function and of the program by which it is performed can be written with Koos' definition as the criterion of content selection.

What Guidance Is Not

1. Not Student Personnel Work. A comparison of the positive definition of guidance just given with the brief treatment of student personnel administration in the preceding section of this chapter should make it clear that the latter is a somewhat more inclusive term than the former. Guidance is a large element in student personnel service, but the latter also includes the health service, the direction of extracurricular life, the provision of food and housing, the government of the social program, the administration of the record system, the administration of attendance, and other student services that are outside the instructional program. While these activities are not guidance, they are closely allied to it.

Under the treatment of student personnel administration in the previous section the reader will note (page 9) the inclusion of "counseling" and "educational and vocational guidance" in the list of elements cited from the work of Lloyd-Jones and Smith. What is the distinction between these two? No interpretation of the idea of these writers will be attempted, but it may well be said at this point that in the present book, "counseling" will be considered as relating to the interview for either distributive or adjustive guidance. "Guidance" will be employed as the more inclusive term, referring to other media for achieving distribution and adjustment as well as counseling.

2. Not Individualized Education. Obviously the recognition of individual differences and the according of individual treatment to each pupil are basic to guidance. They are also basic to instruction. Some writers in the field of guidance have defined guidance as all educational activity in which attention is focused upon the individual in contrast with the mass. Such a view is confusing. Accepting the distinction that has here been drawn between guidance and development, we can clearly see that individual diagnosis is fundamental for both functions. Furthermore, both functions can be served by the same diagnostic service. For example, the counselor can use the pupil's I.Q. as an aid to his understanding of the pupil's educational and vocational potentialities. At the same time, the pupil's English teacher can use the I.Q. as a guide in adapting subject matter and teaching technique to the pupil's maximum development potential through the subject of English.

3. Not the Whole of Education. The preceding paragraph hints at a state of confusion which has beset guidance for many years—namely, the view of some writers that guidance and education are synonymous. Proctor, for example, organized his book[29] to treat not only of educational and vocational

[29] W. M. Proctor, *Educational and Vocational Guidance* (Boston, Houghton Mifflin, 1925).

guidance, but also "guidance in social and civic activities," "guidance in health and physical activities," "guidance in the worthy use of leisure," "guidance in character-building activities." Certainly these latter four titles are readily recognizable as taken from the list of objectives for secondary education formulated by a famous committee of the National Education Association.[30] Pupil growth and development is quite clearly what Proctor had in mind in his treatment of these topics.

Brewer wrote a book[31] from a similar viewpoint, indicating in its title and subtitle that he conceived of guidance as education,—"good" education, perhaps. This extreme comprehensiveness of his definition of guidance is emphasized in the first two sentences of his preface, which read as follows:[32]

In spite of the elaborate nature of our present school and college machinery, most educators would agree that the final purpose of it all is simply that students may learn to live better lives. This is essentially the guidance aim.

In the early nineteen-twenties Lyman wrote a number of articles describing outstanding junior high schools. He used "guidance" as synonymous with education. His introductory sentence in one article was as follows:[33]

In junior high school literature the term "guidance" has come to stand for the principle that lies back of all worth-while teaching of adolescents, namely, the well-rounded development of the individual through the wise direction of his activities.

He proceeded in his article to describe the program of the school under the captions "personal guidance," "remedial guidance," "civic guidance," and "cultural guidance," which, he concluded, illustrate "the principle which helps make a happy and successful school community, namely, meeting the individual needs of children through agencies which stress activity as the chief means of learning."[34]

Here we have a definite clue to the cause for present confusion. For fifty years the conception of learning as the outcome of self-activity impelled by the learner's own felt purposes has been gaining acceptance. Possessed of this theory, the teacher does not *impose* purpose or activity on the pupil. Rather, he shapes the learning environment to stimulate the pupil to acquire worth-while purposes, and offers suggestions regarding activities by which the pupil can realize his purposes. Instead of being an "assigner and a hearer of lessons," the teacher is a "guide." Guidance of learning is his function.

[30] *Cardinal Principles of Secondary Education,* U.S. Bureau of Education Bulletin, No. 35, 1918.

[31] John M. Brewer, *Education as Guidance,* An Examination of the Possibilities of a Curriculum in Terms of Life Activities in Elementary and Secondary School and College (New York, Macmillan, 1932).

[32] *Ibid.,* p. vii.

[33] R. L. Lyman, "The Guidance Program of the Holmes Junior High School," *School Review,* Vol. XXXII (February, 1924), p. 93.

[34] *Ibid.,* p. 104.

We can think of no term more apt. This use of "guidance" has recently been made quite clear in William H. Burton's comprehensive work on general method, entitled *The Guidance of Learning Activities*.[35]

Guidance of learning has become merged in some minds with the concept of guidance as the services of distribution and adjustment. That is unfortunate. It causes them to give an impossibly broad and nebulous definition to "guidance." This book will not treat of the guidance of learning.

THE GUIDANCE FUNCTION IN A DEMOCRATIC SOCIETY

In What Spirit Shall Guidance Be Exercised?

The concept of guidance is not fully clarified without some consideration of the manner in which the function is performed. Benjamin Franklin was taken by his father to see various workers carrying on their occupations. The boy's interests and inclinations were carefully noted by his father. Ben's interest in seafaring occupations was a source of distress to the father, but his interest in books and reading was seized upon as the clue to the boy's vocational future. He was bound out to be a printer's apprentice. Is this example in keeping with the spirit of modern guidance?

The answer is "No," if we may judge by the writings of leaders in the field, beginning with Frank Parsons. They condemn the authoritarian role of the father; they object to any form of prescription, dictation, or compulsion. It is perhaps important, in view of a recent challenge cited in the following division of this section, to quote on this point the views of a number of writers whose names are respected in the field of guidance. For example,

No person may decide for another what occupation he should choose, but it is possible to help him so to approach the problem that he shall come to wise conclusions for himself.[36]

The counselor does not prescribe a vocation which the pupil takes. The pupil chooses his vocation after full consideration of all the factors and consequences of his choice.[37]

. . . discretion dictates that the work of vocational guidance be regarded as of purely *monitory* value. That is, it should pretend to do nothing further than to marshal facts and to point out possibilities of attainment in giving advice.[38]

There is no authority in definition, theory, or practice for prescribing vocations or classifying children; for neither activity is there any right or possibility. . . .

---

[35] (New York, Appleton-Century-Crofts, 1952.)

[36] Frank Parsons, *op. cit.,* p. 4.

[37] Reprinted by permission of the publishers from article by Paul Hanus in Meyer Bloomfield, *Readings in Vocational Guidance* (Cambridge, Mass., Harvard University Press, 1915), p. 95.

[38] Harry D. Kitson, in Bloomfield's *Readings,* p. 107.

Vocational guidance does not mean that older people will impose ideas upon the children; the business of the teacher is rather to provide the environment in which each child will make for himself the series of choices which will determine his course of life.[39]

It hardly seems necessary to discuss compulsion as a method of guidance. . . . Clearly it is no part of the purpose of guidance to choose for a person what he shall do, to prepare him for it, and to make him do it. . . . We may surround an individual with forces that will predispose him to a certain choice, we may give him the facts and experiences that should enable him to choose intelligently, but in the last analysis he must make his own choice. The purpose of guidance is intelligent self-guidance. This only is democratic, this only is educative.[40]

Do not give advice. . . . What the counselee needs is ability to handle situations, himself, not advice to follow.[41]

A further component of the concept of guidance should be mentioned, namely, its monitory character. Guidance and arbitrary compulsion are incompatible. Guidance implies counsel, and the only compulsion possible in counsel is the coercion of judgment by pertinent facts that point the way to proper decision.[42]

Self-knowledge is a gradual growth. To gain a clear understanding of one's aptitudes is an achievement of years rather than of hours. . . . During this period of self-discovery it is a counselor's privilege not to do a person's thinking for him or to tell him what to do; but rather to facilitate his growth in understanding of himself and of the working world. Then his informed decisions are his own.[43]

Is the function of the counselor to advise the child or to assist him in making his own decision? The English lean to the former view and the Americans to the latter. . . . The difference of opinion [as to whether responsibility shall rest with the Ministry of Labour or with the schools] lies in the question as to who shall *tell* the child what to do. The American answer would be, Nobody, in which case he could probably do his deciding better in the school.[44]

These quotations signify firm adherence to the doctrine of respect for the individual. The counselor is not a person who exercises authority or one who assumes responsibility for the counselee's course of action. Perhaps, in view

[39] John M. Brewer, *The Vocational-Guidance Movement* (New York, Macmillan, 1918), pp. 11–12.

[40] Arthur J. Jones, "Vocational Guidance and Education," *Educational Review,* Vol. LXII (June, 1921), p. 20.

[41] Goodwin B. Watson and Ralph B. Spence, *Educational Problems for Psychological Study* (New York, Macmillan, 1930), p. 340.

[42] Leonard V. Koos and Grayson N. Kefauver, "The Concept of Guidance," *School Review,* Vol. XL (March, 1932), p. 206.

[43] Walter V. Bingham, *Aptitudes and Aptitude Testing* (New York, Harper, 1937), p. 12.

[44] Reprinted from *Vocational Guidance Throughout the World,* by Franklin J. Keller and Morris S. Viteles, by permission of W. W. Norton & Co., Inc. Copyright 1937 by the publishers.

of these statements of principle, "guidance" is the word that expresses the great shift that has come about in our conception of the ideal relationship of parents and teachers to children—the shift from authoritarianism to reason. Guidance will foster such insights in the individual as will enable him wisely to accomplish self-distribution and self-adjustment. Such a purpose is bold— a nation at war does not accept it—but it *is* democratic.

Do We Fail to Practice Guidance in Accordance with Democratic Principles?

Is it possible that in actual counseling we pay only lip service to the viewpoint expressed by Parsons, Hanus, and the rest? An affirmative answer to this question is implied in Carl Rogers' exposition of "nondirective counseling."[45] The antithesis of this term is "directive" counseling; the relationships which "directive" denotes are alien to those which are advocated in the quotations above. Yet the contrasts continually drawn by Rogers indicate his belief that the precepts of guidance leaders frequently have not been followed. He refers to the "client-centered counselor" in contrast to the "counselor of the traditional diagnostic-prescriptive viewpoint."[46] Quite possibly, as he says, the counselor has too often posed as an expert who solves problems, as one who has the answers and passes them out freely. Therefore, in order to set forth the characteristics of valid counseling, Rogers has felt it necessary to draw the distinction between "directive" and "nondirective" counseling. "It should be apparent," he says,

that there is a close relation between nondirective counseling and democracy as a way of life. All the characteristics of this type of counseling are also tenets of democracy. The client's participation is voluntary, self-initiated. The counseling atmosphere is built upon respect for the person, tolerance, and acceptance of differences, faith in the person's ability to accept responsibility for his own conduct, and freedom for growth toward maturity. It is perhaps no accident that this emphasis in counseling has reached its fruition in America.[47]

These views are not essentially different from those quoted above from a long line of guidance leaders. We may seem not to act in accordance with these principles, but the contrast between vocational guidance in the United States and in many other countries, as illuminated by Keller and Viteles,[48] suggests we are at least relatively democratic in our performance of guidance. And if it seems we have far to go in achieving the ideal, it must be remembered also that we are far from having attained the goal of democracy in the

[45] See especially *Counseling and Psychotherapy* (Boston, Houghton Mifflin, 1942).
[46] Carl Rogers, "Psychometric Tests and Client-Centered Counseling," *Educational and Psychological Measurement*, Vol. VI (Spring, 1946), p. 139.
[47] Reprinted by permission from *Counseling with Returned Servicemen*, by Carl R. Rogers and J. L. Wallen, pp. 22–23. Copyrighted 1946 by McGraw-Hill Book Co., Inc.
[48] *Op. cit.*

relations of pupils and teachers and of teachers and school administrators. Rogers' contribution, which will be canvassed in a later chapter, lies in the refinement of our ways of employing democratic principles in counseling.

QUESTIONS, PROBLEMS, AND INVESTIGATIONS

1. Examine one year's numbers of *The Personnel and Guidance Journal*. Note the several departments of the magazine. Make a rough classification of the articles according to subjects treated.

2. Examine one year's numbers of the *Journal of the National Association of Deans of Women*. List the articles that treat primarily of distributive and those that treat primarily of adjustive guidance.

3. Make a canvass of the article entitled "Selected References on Guidance" in the September, 1956, number of the *School Review*. Note the scope of the guidance function as indicated by the references. Classify the references as educational periodicals, psychological periodicals, books, government pamphlets, etc. Insofar as the titles and annotations enable you to do so, classify the items into (1) works of opinion, (2) descriptions of practice, (3) scientific investigations.

4. Examine Schedule G of the *Evaluative Criteria* of the Cooperative Study of Secondary School Standards and take notes for class discussion of the scope of guidance service for high schools indicated in that publication.

5. In the educational institution (of whatever level) with which you are most closely associated, identify as many activities as you can which may be classified as guidance according to the definition and scope indicated in this chapter.

SELECTED REFERENCES

BARRY, Ruth, and WOLF, Beverly, "The Genesis of Guidance—Personnel Work," *Teachers College Record,* Vol. 58 (April, 1957), pp. 382–396.

BLOOMFIELD, Meyer, *Readings in Vocational Guidance* (Cambridge, Mass., Harvard University Press, 1915).

BRADSHAW, F. F., "The Scope and Aim of a Personnel Program," *Educational Record,* Vol. XVII (January, 1936), pp. 120–128.

BREWER, John M., and others, *History of Vocational Guidance* (New York, Harper, 1942).

COWLEY, W. H., "The Nature of Student Personnel Work," *Educational Record,* Vol. XVII (January, 1936), pp. 198–226.

COX, Rachel Dunaway, *Counselors and Their Work* (Harrisburg, Pa., Archives Publishing Co., 1945).

HAWKES, Herbert E., and HAWKES, Anna L. R., *Through a Dean's Open Door* (New York, McGraw-Hill, 1945).

JONES, Arthur J., and HAND, Harold C., "Guidance and Purposive Living," in *Guidance in Educational Institutions,* Thirty-seventh Yearbook, Part I, National Society for the Study of Education (Bloomington, Ill., Public School Publishing Co., 1938), Ch. I.

JONES, Arthur J., and MILLER, Leonard M., "The National Picture of Pupil Personnel and Guidance Services in 1953," *Bulletin of the National Association of Secondary-School Principals,* Vol. XXXVIII (February, 1954), pp. 105–159.

KELLER, Franklin J., and VITELES, Morris S., *Vocational Guidance Throughout the World* (New York, Norton, 1937).

KITSON, H. D., "Getting Rid of a Piece of Educational Rubbish," *Teachers College Record,* Vol. XXXVI (October, 1934), pp. 30–34.

KOOS, Leonard V., "Guidance Practice in Secondary Schools," *Bulletin of the National Association of Secondary-School Principals,* No. 20 (March, 1928), pp. 178–185.

KOOS, Leonard V., and KEFAUVER, Grayson, "The Concept of Guidance," *School Review,* Vol. XL (March, 1932), pp. 204–212.

LLOYD-JONES, Esther, and SMITH, Margaret R., *A Student Personnel Program for Higher Education* (New York, McGraw-Hill, 1938), Chs. I–III.

NATIONAL MANPOWER COUNCIL, *A Policy for Scientific and Professional Manpower* (New York, Columbia University Press, 1953).

PATERSON, D. G., "The Genesis of Modern Guidance," *Educational Record,* Vol. XIX (January, 1938), pp. 36–46.

SCOTT, Ira D., *Manual of Advisement and Guidance,* Prepared in Accordance with the Approved Policies of the Veterans Administration (Washington, Government Printing Office, 1945).

SEARS, Jesse B., *The School Survey* (Boston, Houghton Mifflin, 1925), Ch. XLII.

SMITH, Charles M., "The History of Vocational and Educational Guidance in New York City Schools," *High Points in the Work of the High Schools of New York City,* Vol. XXVI (March, 1944), pp. 5–15.

SUPER, Donald E., "Transition: from Vocational Guidance to Counseling Psychology," *Journal of Counseling Psychology,* Vol. II (Spring, 1955), pp. 3–9.

SYMONDS, Percival M., "Every School Should Have a Psychologist," *School and Society,* Vol. XXXVIII (September 9, 1933), pp. 321–329.

———, "A Plea for the Integration of School Guidance Activities," *Teachers College Record,* Vol. XXXVIII (May, 1937), pp. 686–710.

"A Symposium Regarding Change of Name and Statement of Purpose of the National Vocational Guidance Association," *Occupations,* Vol. XX (October, November, 1941), pp. 27–44, 131–137.

THORNDIKE, Edward L., "Vocational Guidance a Function of Public Education," (address given in 1913), *Occupations,* XIX (December, 1940), pp. 163–167.

UHL, Willis L., *Principles of Secondary Education* (Morristown, N.J., Silver, Burdett, 1925), pp. 379–384 (article by Virgil E. Dickson) and 409–419 (article by Arthur J. Jones).

WILLIAMSON, E. G., "To Avoid Waste," *Journal of Higher Education,* Vol. VIII (February, 1937), pp. 64–70.

CHAPTER 2

The Social Scene in Which

Guidance Operates

GUIDANCE—VOCATIONAL GUIDANCE—assumes that the world has worthwhile vocations for all its citizens to engage in, vocations which challenge their varied abilities and interests, vocations which they can voluntarily choose for the rational reasons of their fitness for the work and their vision of the work as a way of life. The individual differences of people and the varied requirements of jobs are harmoniously united by the intelligent, reasoned decisions of the workers themselves—this to the end that society may be best served and that the individual may be engaged in satisfying activity.

How does this social process accord with the social actualities of American life? Are our social institutions, our social ideas, our values and attitudes such as will help or hinder this process? What kind of a world do we have in which to perform this guidance function? The service is desired. The need for it is widely recognized. Is our society geared to the fundamental assumptions of guidance?

Some answer to these questions must be rendered if counselors and other guidance workers are to make an intelligent attack in the discharge of their function. Counseling is not carried on in a social vacuum. Every act of counsel, every feature of the guidance program, exists in a certain social climate, must reckon with certain social forces, must cope with a certain social psychology. Justifiable, therefore, is the devotion of this chapter to the description of the social scene in which guidance operates.

AN OPEN-CLASS SOCIETY

The Heritage of the Frontier

We are the product of our own past. In the past of the American people a factor which has contributed mightily to our philosophy of life is the experience of conquering a continent in less than three centuries. As a result of this experience, one of the elements of our philosophy is the conviction that a good society is one which allows the fullest opportunity for the individual to exercise his powers and which exalts the ideal of individual responsibility and self-dependence. The negative expression of such worship of individualism is seen in Jefferson's statement that the best government is the one that governs least, and in Thomas Paine's conviction that government is but a necessary evil. Direct descendant of these views of the founding fathers is the expressed resentment against wartime and postwar controls, the outcry against a planned economy.

To the vast, open continent of America came people who chafed at the restraints of the crowded, tradition-bound little countries of Europe. They pushed into the untamed wilderness and wrested the elements of existence from rawest nature. Through individual resourcefulness, courage, and strength, homes were built, farms established, clothing and food obtained, civilization extended. The success achieved by some was greater than that of others; it seemed that each was rewarded according to his efforts and his ability. To the frontier came men of varying background, some of distinguished families and some of the humblest origins. That did not matter. Frontier conditions were such as to level off all such distinctions; it was the man himself that counted. In this process innumerable individuals rose from obscurity to positions of responsibility and leadership. We came to possess an unshakable belief in the responsibility of the individual for his own career and his own fortune. We achieved "a culture stressing 'Every tub on its own bottom,' 'You win if you're any good and your winnings are caused by you and belong to you,' and 'If a man doesn't make good it's his own fault.' . . ."[1]

The concept of the good society as the one which offers the maximum of individual opportunity has been described most appealingly by James Truslow Adams as

the *American Dream,* that dream of a land in which life should be better and richer and fuller for every man, with opportunity for each according to his ability or achievement. . . . [It] has not been a dream of merely material plenty, though that has doubtless counted heavily. It has been much more than that. It has been a dream of being able to grow to fullest development as man and woman, unhampered by the barriers which had slowly been erected in older civilizations, unrepressed by social orders which had developed for the benefit of classes rather than for the simple human being of any and every class.[2]

Contemplation of the frontier experience of our forefathers, an experience repeatedly undergone for eight or ten generations, clarifies the current insistence that guidance shall involve no coercion in vocational choice, as was made clear in the last chapter.

[1] Robert S. Lynd and Helen M. Lynd, *Middletown in Transition* (New York, Harcourt, Brace, 1937), p. 24.
[2] *The Epic of America* (Boston, Little, Brown, 1931), pp. 404–405.

But the part played by environment in the development of this individualistic outlook cannot be overemphasized. The population was sparse. Virgin lands, forests, and minerals were abundant and unappropriated. Enormous natural resources invited human exploitation.

Nature seemed to make equal opportunity for all a reality; it was easy to suppose that, barring illness and accident, individuals won or lost in the industrial race according to their own industry and ability. . . . Because of the abundance of unused natural wealth, the economic struggle of individuals was not so much against one another as with nature itself.[3]

Our ideal of human equality, expressed in our most fundamental political documents and institutions, seemed not to call for any curb on strident or greedy individualism, because the bounties of nature were so extraordinary. If the strong ones seemed to grab more than their share in a given community, those who were beaten could go on to new lands, forests, and minerals. Thus, all through the nineteenth century, while industrialization was changing the character of the country, any and all who felt that the conditions of Eastern cities were such as to deny them the full opportunity of American life, could go to the West and its still unexhausted riches.

Said an elderly Texan whom John Dos Passos met in his travels:[4]

When we used to have all the room in the world in this country it didn't matter what any one man did. He could go off on the range and get drunk and do any damn thing he liked in his own way. There was still plenty of room. If you wanted to put on a phoney land boom you hurt nobody but yourself and a few suckers. It was devil take the hindmost. What I try to tell people now is that we can't be free that way any more in this country. There ain't the margin for error. We've got to learn to co-operate. . . .

Our Society One of Open Classes

As suggested in the Texan's last three sentences, we have left the frontier society behind. The twentieth century finds us in a different world. Coincident with our conquest of the continent was the great change known as the industrial revolution. In frontier days a little capital or a new idea was enough to start a man in business for himself—especially when Nature lent so generous a hand—and the workingman of one year was the employer of the next. There was no hard and fast line between the two classes. By contrast the post-frontier industrial order is characterized by large business and industrial units, mass production methods, an extreme degree of interdependence, and innumerable other revolutionary changes which need not be listed here.

[3] John Dewey and John L. Childs, "The Social-Economic Situation and Education," Chapter II in W. H. Kilpatrick, ed., *The Educational Frontier,* Yearbook Number XXI of the National Society of College Teachers of Education (Chicago, University of Chicago Press, 1933), p. 40.

[4] *State of the Nation* (New York, Houghton Mifflin, 1944), p. 119.

The significant point to be made is this: While we have left the frontier life behind, we have carried over into this different world important elements of frontier ideology. To understand the kind of society such a contradiction has given us, we can do no better than to draw upon the interpretations of Ross L. Finney, educational sociologist, for an extended quotation: [5]

It all goes back to a rather fundamental misconception of what constitutes a good society. To present this prevalent misconception let us say that there are three kinds of societies: first, a caste society, second, a society of open classes, and third, a cultural democracy. Every reader understands what is meant by caste, and cordially disapproves of such a rock-layered social order. . . . By an open-class society is meant a social organization in which there is opportunity to rise from the lower to the higher classes; and in which, conversely, the unworthy members of the upper classes are always in imminent danger of falling into the lower classes. It is the kind of society which the old aphorism is intended to describe, that there are only three generations from shirt sleeves to shirt sleeves. This is the kind of social organization that we are supposed to have in America. . . . To it the popular faith is accordingly committed; and it the prevailing ratiocination justifies. (We are naturally as hypnotized with it as Plato was with Athenian slavery!) Nevertheless it is only a halfway station in the evolution of a good society: the cultural democracy. In the really good society of the future the lower classes will have escaped *en masse* from a status of poverty, ignorance, and cultural deprivation, into a really humanizing condition of living. Such is a society from which will have disappeared both the squalid misery of the present lower classes and the sordid luxury of the so-called upper classes; and in which all will be middle class together, sharing equitably in the cultural resources of civilization. . . . democracy will never be contented to rest short of such a society, because only in such an order can its objectives be achieved. . . .

The so-called open-class society of the present is a sort of impossible compromise based upon fundamental principles that are self-contradictory. It assumes equal opportunity for all; but as a matter of fact the very class distinctions that furnish its motivation are themselves the result of artificial privileges and handicaps arising chiefly out of the organization of our economic system. Without discounting the reasons for private property and the inheritance thereof, one need be no socialist to realize that the children of the prosperous classes have opportunities for getting a start in life that the children of the poor do not have. . . . Our system is a class system based upon economic achievement; but a system in which one's achievements—except in exceptional cases—are predetermined only in part by innate abilities, but in part also by artificially inherited handicaps and advantages. It is an open-class system in which the classes are *not* really open to all alike. It contains within it the remnants of caste. It is, therefore, a compromise of inherent contradictions.

In this connection one is reminded of the old fable of the fish pond. This pond was populated mostly by minnows, who were ruled over by a small school of pike, who, in turn, fed upon the minnows. It appears that once upon a time agitators arose among the minnows who led them into a long hard struggle for liberty,

[5] *A Sociological Philosophy of Education* (New York, Macmillan, 1928), pp. 374–381.

equality, and fraternity. At last the struggle was settled by a compromise to the effect that hereafter the one minnow out of every ten thousand who should prove himself most worthy might himself become a pike. Thereafter the ambitions of the minnows were absorbed in the competitive struggle among themselves, and those who did not succeed in becoming pikes were constrained to regard the fault as their own. And nobody noticed that the ratio of pike to minnows was the same as always, that the minnows remained after all nothing but minnows, and that the pike continued to feed on them as before.

It would appear that a democracy, according to the popular conception, is a society in which every democrat aspires confidently to become an aristocrat. Accordingly, it is a society in which education is for the purpose of lifting over-alls boys into white-collared jobs. . . . [The] competitive struggle does not modify the *percentages* of the population in the various classes; these *percentages* being determined by the techniques and organization of industry. To borrow a meta-phor from the fertile pen of Professor Ross, the upper classes are like full rafts, from which, if anybody struggles on, somebody else must be pushed off—and contemporaneous civilization is obsessed with no dearer delusion than that this is not so. Our so-called open-class democracy is a society that hardens its heart toward the poverty and ignorance of the laboring classes *as a whole*, anesthetizing its conscience instead with the illusion that anybody (and therefore presumably everybody!) can climb out of that class if he has individual ability.

. . . the white-collar objective of education, with its social correlate, the every-democrat-a-potential-aristocrat idea, is a grand illusion, except in a period of rapid industrial expansion.

. . . an "open-class" society is in unstable equilibrium. It is predestined to shift its weight either to the right foot or to the left. If the privileges and handi-caps inherent in the economic order are allowed to remain, the classes will become increasingly hereditary, until the illusion of open classes is finally frankly aban-doned. But if those privileges and handicaps are gradually abolished, or canceled by a really adequate public education, then there is no place for stopping such reforms short of a cultural democracy, in which the over-alls boys (whose per-centages will of course remain relatively static) will lead white-collared lives, along with all the other economic functionaries, when they are off duty. Neither this nor any other society can stand, half privilege and half opportunity; it tends always to become either the one or the other. As wealth becomes more and more concentrated, and population more and more dense, the tendency will of course be toward privilege—unless a new vision takes possession of the souls of edu-cators.[6]

It is in this society, embodying an ideal out of harmony with the actualities of its structure, that we are commissioned to perform vocational guidance, to bring about a rational distribution of workers among the many vocations, and to do it through the workers' own intelligent choosing. The actual prob-

[6] The extent to which Finney's 1928 analysis of American society holds true today can only be speculated upon. It is at least highly useful as a point of departure for this chapter.

lem posed for the counselor will be illuminated in concrete detail in a following section.

Our Pride in the Open-Class Society

The tenets of the frontier ideology are strenuously inculcated. Animated by admiration for our earlier society and its accomplishments, "eminent statesmen and university presidents, as well as more humble citizens vie with each other in praising the social order which permits individuals to rise above the station into which they are born."[7] Schools assiduously implant the ideal of individual success, making much use of biography to acquaint their pupils with all the crooks and turns of the highway from the log cabin to the White House. The courses in history, civics, and literature, and the library reading lists, convey to impressionable minds the success stories of citizens who have "risen" from humble surroundings to positions of affluence and power. The textbooks in occupations, designed to assist in the process of vocational guidance, employ "biographies of successful workers" as an important medium of occupational information. Frequently they show the "line of promotion" or "vocational ladder"—for example, from wrapper girl to buyer in the department store.

Popular magazines and newspapers consciously and unconsciously indoctrinate their readers with the concept of American opportunity for individual success. Mainly, they employ a bombardment of biographies in which the modal beginning wage of the subjects may be estimated at $3 a week. The headlines of a few years ago were reading,

> MILLSOP, EX-LABORER, MADE HEAD
> OF WEIRTON STEEL
> ROY FAULKNER FINDS SUCCESS BY
> LEAVING CITY FOR STICKS
> FROM MILL HAND TO MILL HEAD—
> THAT'S STORY OF JOHN L. PERRY
> MEN YOU SHOULD KNOW [daily feature
> for a period]

Sometimes an article includes several biographies, as the *Saturday Evening Post* of May 2, 1936, under the caption, "Horatio Alger at the Bridge," presented interviews with J. C. Penney, Vincent Bendix, and other leaders of business and industry. (Incidentally, this article was primarily propaganda to defeat the Child Labor Amendment by pointing out how early in life these leaders began their careers.)

Occasionally an advertisement is used to convey the story of America's open-class society, as in the following example:[8]

---

[7] George S. Counts, *The American Road to Culture* (New York, John Day, 1930), p. 60.

[8] *Life* (January 20, 1947), pp. 108–109.

Up from the Ranks

These are presidents of operating telephone companies of the Bell System. They all started at the bottom of the ladder. . . . Nine years ago the Bell System first published an advertisement like this, except that there are now thirteen new faces in the picture. These new presidents also started at the bottom. The Bell System aims to keep the opportunity for advancement open to all. One of its traditions is that its executives come up from the ranks.

With this message were shown the pictures of seventeen presidents, bearing the biographic facts that they had "started as" clerks, ground men, office boys, installers, and so on.

In 1928 Herbert Hoover's telegram accepting the nomination for the presidency included the following paragraph:

You convey too great a compliment when you say that I have earned the right to the presidential nomination. No man can establish an obligation upon any part of the American people. My country owes me no debt. It gave me, as it gives every boy and girl, a chance. It gave me schooling, independence of action, opportunity for service and honor. In no other land could a boy from a country village, without inheritance or influential friends, look forward with unbounded hope.

The same pride in the open-class society was expressed in 1955 by the editor of a metropolitan daily newspaper.[9] Visiting the small Midwest town of his youth, he reported a conversation with an old resident who brought the editor up-to-date with the success stories of individuals who had grown up and left the little town.

Our informant himself had done pretty well, he thought. He'd come to town from Europe, years and years ago. Started a little junk collecting business.

"I got this house. . . . I own some income property around town, too, so there's enough to take care of me and my wife." . . .

One son is head of a department in a big state university out West, one is an army officer—a career military man—and the third is a big figure in a large mercantile corporation. . . .

We came away feeling well inside, as one does after a pleasant warming experience. And we congratulated ourselves on being Americans, for where but in this country would you be likely to stumble on such a story? And where else could you find such incidents repeated over and over again, in every quiet town in the land?

Individual success stories make dramatic reading. The public wants them. They "help sell the papers." Very commonly they teach the desirable individual traits of industry, frugality, honesty. Our objection to them is essentially stated in the quotation from Finney, namely, that they instill in the reader the idea that if some can go up the ladder, all can do so. Success simply depends on the individual's ability and diligence. Accepting that philosophy,

[9] Andrew Bernhard, *Pittsburgh Post-Gazette* (April 18, 1955), p. 2.

those who remain at the bottom of the ladder deem it their own fault and those who have gone up agree with them. However important the social service rendered in those vocations at the bottom of the ladder, there is slight motive to make them a worthy and honored way of life because the open-class society presumably makes it unnecessary for anyone to remain in those posts.

The basis for our pride in the open-class society is our assumption that its opportunities for the individual are a symbol of democracy. We overlook the fact that the economic organization is such that only a few can enjoy much individualism. The bulk of people can have very little of it. Their lives are narrowly circumscribed, highly regimented. They are required to punch time clocks; their time is not their own; they are subject to the beck and call of others. They take their narrow places in large and complex organizations, each one a small cog in a large wheel.

Some Realities of the Social and Occupational Structure

The thought just expressed needs further elaboration and factual support. For, as Hilgard has pointed out,[10]

Even if we managed to send everyone to college, we should still be up against the stubborn facts of the census; namely, the distribution of available jobs for the products of our schools. So long as a large proportion of workers engage in unskilled labor and in personal services, we must see a corresponding proportion of our youth entering such jobs, unless some unforeseen upheaval greatly changes the complexion of our productive processes.

Perhaps the most comprehensive view of our open-class society in actual operation is to be had from a look at the facts of the distribution of income. Table 2[11] shows pertinent data on this point for the year 1952. An illustrative reading of the table is as follows: The income group receiving less than $1,000 before taxes included ten per cent of the family units; their income was one per cent of the income received by all the family units; this group had five per cent of the liquid assets possessed by all the family units. Summarizing those family units who received less than $5,000 before taxes, one finds 67 per cent of the family units included in this category, that they received 39 per cent of the total money income, and that they had 37 per cent of the liquid assets. A computation of the median income of the family units yields the figure of $3,875.

The year 1952 was one of full employment; wages were rising and so was the cost of living; the Korean War and heavy expenditures for the upbuilding

[10] Ernest R. Hilgard, "Success in Relation to Level of Aspiration," *School and Society*, Vol. LV (April 11, 1942), p. 427.

[11] *Statistical Abstract of the United States, 1954,* Table No. 338. Bureau of the Census, United States Department of Commerce, 1954, p. 307.

of the national defense buoyed up industrial activity. Without attempting to interpret what $1,000, $2,000, or $5,000 would buy in 1952, the meaning of Table 2 is first of all the fact that economic rewards in the open-class society vary extremely. There are ladders to favored positions in the economic scale, but the bulk of the workers are on the lower rungs, carrying on in occupations which are essential to society.

The truth is that in these occupational ladders the sidepieces are not parallel as we think of a ladder, but are far apart at the bottom and close together at the top.

TABLE 2. Family Units, Income Before Taxes, and Liquid Assets—Per Cent Distribution by Income Groups: 1952

Annual 1952 Money Income Before Taxes	Family Units	Total Money Income	Liquid Assets
All income groups	100	100	100
Under $1,000	10	1	5
$1,000–1,999	12	4	6
$2,000–2,999	14	7	7
$3,000–3,999	16	12	10
$4,000–4,999	15	15	9
$5,000–7,499	21	28	23
$7,500 and over	12	33	40

As Gardner says,[12]
the structure [of industry] forms a pyramid with fewer and fewer people at each higher level. This means that it is impossible for everyone at one level to rise to the next, and this is especially true for the non-supervisory or worker level, where there are at least ten workers for every foreman or supervisor and there may be fifty or more in some types of work.

The Lynds in their first visit to "Middletown" gathered some pertinent facts in concrete illustration of our point. They reported as follows:[13]

The traditional social philosophy assumes that each person has a large degree of freedom to climb the ladder to ever wider responsibility, independence, and money income. As a matter of fact, in six Middletown plants employing an average of 4,240 workers during the first six months of 1923 there were ten vacancies for foremen over the period of twenty-one months from January 1, 1923, to October 1, 1924. This means that in a year and three-fourths there was a chance for one man in 424 to be promoted. The total number of men estimated

12 Burleigh B. Gardner, *Human Relations in Industry* (Chicago, Richard D. Irwin, Inc., 1945), p. 186.
13 R. S. Lynd and H. M. Lynd, *Middletown* (New York, Harcourt, Brace, 1929), pp. 65–66.

by the plants as of sufficient experience on January 1, 1923, to be eligible for consideration for promotion to foremanship was 531. Of this picked group one man in fifty-three got his chance in twenty-one months.

In 1935, the Lynds examined the ladder again and reported it to be changing as follows:[14]

The ladder has lost some rungs, with the disappearance of apprenticeship and the large measure of blurring of the distinction between unskilled and skilled labor.

The step up to the first rung where the foremen stand appears to be getting higher and therefore harder for the mass on the floor to make.

Above the foreman's rung the whole aspect of the ladder has changed in three notable respects since 1890 and especially since the World War:

It is more difficult for the enterprising mechanic to find an alternative way up the ladder by launching out with a plant of his own in competition with the existing productive structure of large-unit plants.

Above the foreman's rung, the ladder is ceasing to be one ladder: there have virtually ceased to be rungs between the foreman and a higher section of the ladder beyond his reach where an entirely new set of personnel usually not recruited from working-class personnel begins.

And, finally, the ladder has lengthened with the relative increase of "absentee ownership" of local plants as units of national corporations, and the increasing absorption of formerly independent local manufacturers into the payrolls of these national corporations.[15]

The open-class society was studied in San Jose, California, to determine the degree and direction of occupational mobility—vertical mobility—from one generation to the next.[16] The authors compared the occupations of sons with the occupations of their fathers, classifying occupations in the following six categories: professional workers, proprietors (including farm tenants and owners), clerical workers, skilled workers, semi-skilled workers, and unskilled workers. A difficulty in making a valid comparison arose from the fact that the professional, clerical, and semi-skilled classes have notably increased in recent years, while there has been a decided decrease in the number of proprietors (including farmers). Nevertheless, these investigators showed that there is a marked tendency for sons to achieve occupational

---

[14] *Middletown in Transition* (New York, Harcourt, Brace, 1937), p. 71.

[15] The "ladder" has been more recently illuminated by studies cited by Simon Olshansky in "The Concept of Success in Our Culture," *Personnel and Guidance Journal,* Vol. XXXII (February, 1954), pp. 355–356. One study was a canvass by *Fortune* (November, 1952) of 900 top executives, which revealed that only 2.5 per cent had fathers who were laborers, while 15 per cent had fathers who were professional men, and 26 per cent had fathers who were founders or executives of companies. So many of the remainder came from the business class as to cause *Fortune* to conclude that "The typical big company top executive was born the son of a business man."

[16] P. E. Davidson and H. D. Anderson, *Occupational Mobility in an American Community* (Stanford, Cal., Stanford University Press, 1937).

affiliation at a level which is the same as or adjacent to that of the fathers
For example, of the 242 sons whose fathers were in unskilled occupations,
the following percentages were in the categories indicated: 41.7, unskilled;
16.5, semi-skilled; 13.7, skilled; 13.7, clerical; 10.3, proprietary; 4.1, professional. The authors' conclusion from their data was as follows:[17]

It would thus seem that a fraction somewhere between two-thirds and three-
quarters of the workers of the sample came from the level of the father or from
the adjacent levels, perhaps without greatly altering their essential status. Real
"climbers" and those seriously degraded in comparison with their fathers apparently constitute a minor fraction.

Occasionally one who has climbed the ladder is sensitive to the reality of
its structure, as indicated by the following excerpt:

This morning I attended a buyers' meeting of the large Fifth Avenue department store in which I work. As we came away I stopped at the second floor long
enough to make a hasty purchase. Passing her salesbook over for my signature,
the salesgirl remarked, "I'm going to be in on those buyers' meetings one of these
days."
"There's no reason why you shouldn't," said I as I signed my name. "And you
will too if you feel that way about it."
I like that girl. She is good at her job and I wish her well. I'll do anything I
can to help her get ahead. But actually, I put the question to myself as I entered
the elevator again, would the quick words of encouragement that had come automatically out of my mouth be, in the long run, a help to her? Or would they—
and the fear was strong within me—lay but another faggot on the fire of her
ambition the more quickly to consume her?

For I knew, as the parrotlike words emerged from my mouth, that they lied.
I knew I had encouraged her to hope for a success that statistics show she has
not one chance in ten—maybe not even one in fifty—of achieving. And I knew
too (and here was the unpleasant rub on my conscience) that I no longer believe
the hooey that pseudo-psychologists have preached at us until we in our turn
have become nothing but hypnotized parrots repeating it—this hooey that young
people should be reared on the spinach that There's Always Room at the Top,
and if they work hard enough and with intelligence they'll get there.[18]
Perhaps the supreme need of our chaotic times is the replacement of outworn and irrelevant ideas of competitive economic individualism with those
concepts of co-operation and true democracy which are consistent with the
extreme economic interdependence now existent. The bearing of the existing
contradiction on the performance of the guidance function has been made
evident. To define more clearly the social scene in which guidance operates,
let us look critically at our economic system.

[17] *Ibid.*, pp. 164–165.
[18] A Fifth Avenue Buyer, "Tell the Girls the Truth," *Harper's Magazine,* Vol. 174
(January, 1937), p. 203.

THE PROFITS MOTIVE, MODERN TECHNOLOGY, AND VOCATION

Basic Assumptions of Our Economy

Until the middle of the eighteenth century the Western world accepted the view that it was natural and desirable for government to regulate the economic life of the people. The spirit of individual liberty then taking more complete possession of men's minds than before, the theory was advanced that the *general* well-being would best be realized if men were given the fullest opportunity to seek their *individual* well-being. Let individuals acquire property with utmost freedom, let them produce that which advantages them most, and let them distribute without external regulation. Such is the laissez-faire doctrine.

Flexible prices, arrived at by bargaining, move up or down to bring adjustment whenever supply and demand for any product fail to balance. Competition acts as a stimulus to improve production by driving out the inefficient. Urged on by the profits motive, individual initiative may be depended on to achieve the constant improvement of the quality of goods at a steadily declining cost. The public buys where it can get the most for the least.

Labor, also, is a commodity that is bought and sold in accordance with laissez-faire principles. Free bargaining sets the price. The laborer sells it as dearly as possible, the employer purchases it as cheaply as possible and no more of it than he can use with profit. The smaller the labor costs of the producer, the lower the price at which he may sell to make a profit. Thus the social good is promoted by individual self-seeking.

The Profits Motive in Contemporary Society

The laissez-faire principle worked best in the simple society familiar to Adam Smith. Manufacturing was carried on in small shops. Trade engaged few people. Among these producers and distributors competition was keen. Most of the population consisted of subsistence farmers, producing according to their needs and consuming most of their own product. They had only minor use for the market.

But the industrial revolution was born at the same time as laissez-faire and has brought us to a world that Adam Smith would not know. Individual acquisitiveness undoubtedly has largely furnished the motive power for producing the change, for competition has forced men to exercise their ingenuity in the production and distribution of goods. Men have also, however, exercised their ingenuity in stifling competition and in other ways limiting the operation of laissez-faire, because they have found the profits thereby to be larger than under competition.

While the automatic adjustments never did work as smoothly as laissez-faire theory would indicate, the economy of the present day operates in such fashion as frequently to control the adjustments for strictly anti-social ends. For example, with our very large corporate units (in 1954, 135 corporations in America owned 45 per cent of the industrial assets of the nation), prices are frequently established by administrative decision of corporation executives; such prices are relatively rigid and they do not move up and down to bring adjustment when supply and demand are out of balance. Instead, adjustments are made through changes in the volume of production. A much publicized example was the inaction of the price of steel rails during the Big Depression. They remained high despite the decline in the general price level. Railroads needed the rails but could not afford to buy them at the price asked, so the mills completely ceased production. The workers who manned the mills were laid off.

Competition is frequently controlled when large corporate units dominate an industry, for competition constantly promotes combination. As George Soule reminds us, "Can we rely on an individualistic society to pursue self-interest with competition and ingenuity and hard work, and to stop pursuing it by combinations, restrictions, demands for handouts and special favors?"[19] Naturally the best assurance of profits is to suppress competition through the attainment of a monopolistic position.

Larger profits may often be had from relatively high prices and with only partial production, so the profit-seeking producer follows this policy, regardless of the workers who would be employed and the consumers who would be supplied by fuller production at a lower price. Workers thus unemployed are unable to spend, and hence the demand for other products declines. If the manufacturers of those products also maintain price rigidity, the vicious downward spiral of declining industrial and business activity is in full swing. Naturally, every group hopes that other groups will not be able to maintain price control but will have to let prices decline, maintaining the economy from collapse.

The failure of the automatic adjustments to operate is contributed to by rigidity in the price of labor. Workers through their union organizations are continually seeking the advantage of monopoly instead of being content to compete with each other. For example, in the 1930's the scale of wages of workers in the building trades was maintained at a relatively high level, contributing to the decline in building activity and the consequent unemployment of many building tradesmen. Labor legislation of the '30's greatly increased the bargaining power of the worker and the possibility of labor's maintaining a rigid wage structure.

The thwarting of demand-supply control of wages and prices is again illustrated in 1958 as the low level of activity in the manufacture of steel and autos does not result in the reduction of prices or wages.

The prices of farm products perhaps respond most freely to the automatic control of supply and demand. In the 1930's while the price of steel rails and

[19] *New Republic,* Vol. 115 (August 19, 1946), p. 205.

the wage of a plasterer remained close to 1929 levels, hogs dropped to three cents a pound. The government took action to help farmers limit production. Many citizens were extremely vocal in condemnation of such procedure although they had no word of criticism for the steelmakers who cut their production to 13 per cent.

No comprehensive exposition of the economic system can be or should be attempted here. Its general adequacy for serving mankind cannot be canvassed. We have merely sought to outline its outstanding characteristics insofar as necessary to aid us in getting a clear picture of vocation, for we must understand vocation if we are to understand vocation choosing.

Vocation and Profits

Modern industrial society is equipped with elaborate instruments of production. A small group of individuals employ the great mass of workers to use these instruments in the production of the goods that people desire. The laborer in such a situation has no permanent association with the instruments of production (in fact, he might well be thought of as an instrument of production himself), and he owns no equity in the property with which he works. Since he is given a job in order that his employer may make a profit on his labor, it may well be said that his vocation is a means of exploiting him. Just as the entrepreneur exploits materials, such as steel, lumber, glass, or oil for the profit that he may derive, so also he exploits manpower. He goes into the market and buys the labor of machine operatives, shipping clerks, and engineers, and he uses that labor as fully and efficiently as he knows how. Profits depend, for one important factor, on the effective use of labor. The exploitation may be callous and inhumane, or it may be tempered with justice and kindness, but nevertheless it is exploitation. The department stores are advertising for salespersons, the steel mills are calling for draftsmen. They do not want these workers for the purpose of giving them the opportunity for creative, developmental experience, or to serve society, but they want them because they think that their labor in selling goods or making steel will net a profit. Even the foreman, superintendent, and manager are being exploited, although their relation to the entrepreneur is so close that for all practical purposes they join him in the exploitation of human labor.

Vocation is a means of exploiting the worker in small businesses as well as large. Lewisohn says,[20]

It is certain that the worst exploitation today and some of the most troublesome forms of unrest are associated with small-scale . . . industry, where boss and wage earner work side by side. . . . Closeness of the employer to the worker is not necessarily a healthier condition.

[20] Sam A. Lewisohn, *Human Leadership in Industry* (New York, Harper, 1945), p. 13.

The clothing industry in New York City, with its many small employers, was an example of the most vicious exploitation before Sidney Hillman led the Amalgamated Clothing Workers in their noteworthy feat of reorganizing the industry.

Vocation as a means of exploitation has a long history, and its cost in human wastage forms one of the most shameful chapters in human relations. We need here only recall to the reader's memory a few examples from the last hundred years. A century ago England was the supreme industrial country. English hearts were wrung when the exploitative conditions finally came to be known, and Parliament imposed limitations upon laissez-faire. H. G. Wells has related the story of the barbarities perpetrated upon the natives of the Congo and Amazon valleys only sixty years ago by white men ruthlessly pursuing profits in rubber.[21] That the veneer of civilization, of Christian ethics, could be so thin is hardly conceivable. We may judge by the following passage that Wells was not too sure of the future:[22]

King Leopold . . . is only a crowned and glorified symbol of a world-wide undisciplined spirit of acquisitiveness. The new economic life has come upon mankind unheralded and unpremeditated, and first it caught and enslaved the poor and the children of Great Britain and western Europe, and now it has spread throughout the earth. The old traditions of trade and gain and government are insufficient to control it, and we are still struggling to discover new forms and methods of control. It feeds and expands the life of hundreds of millions which could never have come into existence without it, but also there are those other millions it crushes and torments.

A half century ago when F. W. Woolworth was founding the chain of five-and-ten-cent stores which have made retailing history and a fortune for the founder, he wrote to his managers,[23]

We must have cheap help or we cannot sell cheap goods. When a clerk gets so good she can get better wages elsewhere, let her go, for it does not require skilled and experienced salesladies to sell our goods. You can get good honest girls at from $2 to $3 per week. . . . It may look hard to some of you to pay such small wages, but there are lots of girls that live at home . . . too proud to work in a factory or do housework. They are glad of a chance to get in a store for experience, if nothing more. . . .

In the Big Depression John Steinbeck printed indelibly in the American consciousness the exploitation of our migrant fruit and vegetable pickers. His great work of fiction[24] was documented by Carey McWilliams' work of fact.[25] Another sordid story of exploitation was that of the pecan shellers of

---

[21] *The Work, Wealth, and Happiness of Mankind* (New York, Doubleday, Doran, 1931), pp. 290–309.
[22] *Ibid.*, pp. 308–309.
[23] John K. Winkler and Boyden Sparkes, "Dime Store," *Saturday Evening Post* (February 24, 1940), p. 80.
[24] *The Grapes of Wrath* (New York, Heritage, 1940).
[25] *Factories in the Field* (Boston, Little, Brown, 1939).

San Antonio, a group of workers whose five-cent-an-hour wage and squalid living conditions came to light in connection with hearings preceding the passage of the Fair Labor Standards Act in 1938.[26] When the Act passed, its application to these workers was vigorously opposed by the employers.

The primary explanation of such conditions is obviously the operation of the law of supply and demand in a period when labor exists in oversupply and is unorganized. President Roosevelt said during that period that he felt sure 90 per cent of cotton-mill operators *wanted* to pay a living wage, but the other 10 per cent undercut them. The 10 per cent may have been marginal producers, or they may have been simply greedy, but in either case the effect of free competition was to make the vocation of cotton-mill operative one that no one could voluntarily choose, despite the patently valuable social service which it is.

John Dos Passos gave numerous interesting sidelights on vocation in our economic order during World War II when he toured the country and reported on the "state of the nation."[27] Several excerpts are worth citing because they describe conditions following New Deal legislation, they depict a period of full employment, and the observations were made at a time when the social service rendered through vocations was sharply focused in the national consciousness. His conversation with an executive of the converted auto industry ran as follows:

". . . Well, the first thing we have to admit is that the workers' morale isn't what it should be . . . not by a long shot. . . . There's too much distrust of management on the part of labor. They don't understand what's at stake. Absenteeism is terrific, fifty per cent worse than in normal times. . . . There's too much loitering on the job."

"Are the labor-management committees amounting to anything?"

"I'll have to frankly admit that they got off to a bad start. . . . There's been too much of the attitude that anything that was good for management was bad for labor and vice versa.

". . . Another drag on production is the union premise that every man on a similar job should do the same amount of work every day. The good men quit when they've done their stint. You know the ever present fear the men have of working themselves out of a job." (pp. 41–43)

Such a picture shows workers so conscious of the traditional contest with employers that even if they do not feel underpaid they find in vocation no satisfaction of their fundamental drives and purposes. The activity is foreign and lacking in significance for them. They have a chip on the shoulder and they feel that they are being "used" or "pushed around."

Another converted auto plant presented a different concept of vocation,

[26] Selden C. Menefee and Orin C. Cassmere, *The Pecan Shellers of San Antonio*. A Special Report of the Division of Research, Work Projects Administration (Washington, D.C., Government Printing Office, 1940).

[27] *State of the Nation* (Boston, Houghton Mifflin, 1944).

as mirrored by Dos Passos in his report of his meeting with the plant labor-management committee:

The chairman is explaining patiently and carefully how their system originated and how it works. To begin with, this particular concern had a long record of good relations with its employees behind it. This plan to increase production by getting labor and management truly to pitch in and work together got under way some time before Donald Nelson suggested labor-management committees to industry as a whole.

The man in blue denim spoke up: "The first thing we think of when we're goin' over a suggestion is, will it work? Then, can it be put into operation right now? At the bottom of this whole business is that we want to get production increased by usin' our brains instead of our arms. Let the machine do the work."

"How about absenteeism?"

"Doesn't worry us."

"Loafing?"

"The others won't let a man loaf. They want to have that good looking rayon banner next month. . . . In fact, we feel that this campaign's been a great success. One reason is that we keep before every man's eye exactly how he's contributing to win the war, through posters and displays and through our paper. We feel we've got the men's confidence and that we're all in this together. Work to win. In spite of the fact that we've had to take on a great many green hands, . . . our efficiency has increased right along."

"Well, this company's never had any labor trouble anyway. One reason is that our labor relations are handled right from the top." (pp. 52–54)

Inferences concerning vocation as meaningful, purposeful experience can be drawn from this quotation. The last section of this chapter will develop such a concept at length.

Sitting in the office of the local trade-union weekly in another community, Dos Passos was presented with the following situation:

The Government Man is exploding in the middle of the floor. . . . They've given him the job single-handed of stopping the turnover of labor. He's trying to get the unions and management to pull together. He's trying to get the companies not to fire men on the whim of any foreman and guard, to get some order into their system of releases to workers who want to be released. All he gets is a dog-fight.

"None of us'll ever get anywhere," shouts the young man in the stetson hat, "until the employers'll treat labor like an equal."

"They won't see it," says the Mediator, an oldtime labor leader. . . . "They still think that when they hire a man they are doing him a personal favor and that he ought to be grateful."

"It's the oldtime feudal mentality."

"I try to tell the president of one of these concerns," says the Government Man, "that he ought to set up a modern labor relations department and he just

gives me a kind of oily grin and says, 'Oh go 'long—you get it all out of a book.'"
(pp. 96, 100)

Again Dos Passos, listening to the explanation given by the manager of one of the Farm Security Administration camps for migrants in the lower valley of the Rio Grande:

"The Mexicans go with a jefe or patron who owns the truck and gets together several families. . . . Down here in back roads along the valley they have their little villages of broken-down shacks they come back to each year. The local growers look with a jealous eye at anything that'll disturb their Mexicans. They are part of the wealth of the country which the growers feel is theirs to exploit, like the soil and the climate . . . if you talk to 'em about clearing up illiteracy and tuberculosis and venereal disease and making citizens out of these folks what it stacks up to from their point of view is high wages. . . . When I started up down here they were just about ready to ride me out of town on a rail. . . ."
(p. 110)

America is a battleground of powerful forces which are contending for economic advantage. Actually the struggle often takes the form of deciding the limits which should be set upon freedom to use vocation as a means of exploiting for profit the strength and skill of human beings. Occasionally a voice is raised among the exploiters to protest the narrowness of viewpoint and the inhumanity of his class, as in the following newspaper report of an address to fellow businessmen by Charles Luckman, then head of the nation's second largest soap-selling concern:[28]

Mr. Luckman declared that American business in the last 20 years, by and large, had "earned" its reputation of being "opposed to everything that spells greater security, well-being or peace of mind for the little guy.

"How? Well, we declared war on collective bargaining. We actually opposed increased taxes for education. We fought health and safety ordinances. The record proves that we battled child labor legislation.

"We yipped and yowled against minimum wage laws.

"We struggled against unemployment insurance. We decried Social Security, and currently we are kicking the hell out of proposals to provide universal sickness and accident insurance."

While the discussion is here devoted to an exposition of how a profits-motivated economy fosters the use of vocation as a means of exploiting manpower, it is altogether pertinent to hearken to the following questions raised by Lewisohn:[29]

Is exploitation confined to capitalism? If we eliminate private ownership, what system will we then have? If we get rid of capitalism, will we get rid of exploitation?

[28] *Pittsburgh Press* (November 7, 1946).
[29] *Op. cit.,* p. 17.

The author then compares the frequency rate of accidents in 1943 of four large corporations and four governmental departments, as follows:

Department of Commerce	10.8	DuPont Corporation	1.9
Post Office Department	10.9	United States Steel	3.2
Federal Works Agency	11.7	United States Rubber	3.3
Department of Agriculture	12.2	General Motors	4.3

As a matter of fact, an objective view of the facts frequently hurled at us concerning the position of public employees seems to lead to the conclusion that the public is interested in getting its garbage removed, its streets policed, its mail delivered, and its children taught as cheaply as possible. Taxpayers and their economy leagues are not unlike private employers in self-seeking.

Jobs and the Evolving Technology

The accelerating change of modern technology, powered by the profits motive, is pointed, first, to the abolition of jobs, the reduction in the number of workers. Workers are a source of expense; they cut down profits; ergo, mechanize the operation so as to do away with workers. This process goes on about us so continually that it needs no illustration. Only occasionally is it reversed, as in the case of the San Antonio pecan shellers whose labor became available during the depression at so low a cost as to halt the beginning trend toward mechanization. Application, in 1938, of the Fair Labor Standards Act, with its 25-cents-an-hour minimum wage, caused the trend to be resumed immediately, and it was expected at the time conditions were studied in 1939 that the labor requirement would be less than a third of the peak number employed under the system of hand labor.[30]

Financial analysts frequently issue data showing for various industries the relation between labor costs and gross sales, and their evidence is reflected in stock market values. Near the end of World War II, when Rotarians were saying that the function of business in the postwar period should be to provide jobs for workers, Sewell Avery, head of the Montgomery Ward Company, averred with emphasis that the true function of any efficient business is to get rid of as many of its employees as possible. That the country has thus far been able to absorb the technologically unemployed is not to be attributed to the altruism of the entrepreneurs.

Secondly, the effect of advancing technology is to make each worker more productive. The technique of time-and-motion study, originated by Frederick Taylor, combines with the steady flow of mechanical inventions to increase the output per worker from decade to decade. A Bedeaux system is resented as a "stretch-out," and in many industries the strength of labor organizations is arrayed against the plans of the industrial engineer. Despite such brakes on "progress," productivity continues to increase.

The third effect of technology on vocation is the continual *change* of jobs.

[30] Menefee and Cassmore, *op. cit.*

The tendency in large part is to simplify jobs by breaking down crafts. It is then possible to substitute low-priced workers for high-priced ones. This procedure results in putting many workers at the highly monotonous tasks of machine tending and of assembly line work where there is no opportunity for them to use their ingenuity or creative capacity. Industrial engineers are defining the job in minutest detail, and the worker is virtually assumed to be a machine tool designed for one purpose only. This is a condition concerning which Herbert Hoover expressed concern at the time he was Secretary of Commerce; it was the subject of Arthur Pound's *The Iron Man in Industry;* and Peter Drucker has analyzed its consequences as follows:[31]

First, the worker is confined to one motion: a fact which results in fatigue, in physiological and neurological damage (tics, headaches, deafness, neuritis), and finally in a numb resentment. Second, the worker is chained to the speed and rhythm of the slowest man on the line and is not allowed to work at his own speed and rhythm; the result is again fatigue and irritability, nervousness, and jerkiness. Finally, the worker never does a whole job, never makes anything that he can identify as his own personal product; this leads to lack of interest and to a deep sense of frustration.

The change of jobs wrought by advancing technology is, of course, much broader and more varied than the picture of routinization just drawn. The shift from heavy, back-breaking drudgery to machine operation is an important consequence. The shift of workers from the physical production of goods to occupations in the field of trade, personal service, and the professions is another. That the individual's plans for a settled occupational existence are liable to be upset is, however, the main point of this discussion. Vocations are changing—in many fields, rapidly. Automation will accelerate such changes.

Jobs and the Economic Cycle

No factor is more significant for vocation than the boom-and-depression aspect of our economy. World War II was a period of great stringency in the manpower market. It brought back to active employment old men who had retired, lured housewives from their normal jobs of caring for home and family, induced youngsters to leave school for work or work after school hours, absorbed in remunerative employment all manner of cripples and physically handicapped people. War and unemployment have been designated as the two great problems of our times. As society is presently organized it seems we must have war or preparation for war to overcome unemployment, unless we are willing to accept the implications of vast public works programs.

The swings of the economic pendulum define vocations and vocation

[31] "The Way to Industrial Peace: I. Why Men Strike," *Harper's Magazine,* Vol. 193 (November, 1946), p. 389.

choosing in serious particulars. Most obvious is the variable demand for workers. During the Big Depression it became painfully clear that "Efficient performance on the job by the worker does not insure him against unemployment."[32] The corollary to such variability in demand is the shift in standards. During the Big Depression qualifications required for relatively simple jobs were raised absurdly, as in the case of a publishing house which employed only college graduates for routine typing, for which the wage was $15 a week. By contrast it was said during World War II that in hiring workers the personnel man "merely felt of the body to see if it was warm." Some of the practical implications of the economic cycle for the function of guidance will be taken up at the beginning of the next section.

The social scene in which guidance operates, as described in these first two sections of this chapter, is of such a character as to make vocational life unstable and insecure. The result is, as Elton Mayo points out, that "whereas in an established society the emphasis is upon established skills, the emphasis for us is upon adaptable skills."[33] Essentially this means that many workers must expect not to send their roots down very deeply but to be subject to frequent transplanting. More than this, our analysis has shown that the vocational rewards vary widely and without regard for the social service rendered. The difficulty that such a condition presents to the rational matching of persons and vocations is, moreover, rendered more difficult to overcome because of a kind of gambler's pride in an outworn system of competitive economic individualism.

OBSTACLES TO VOCATIONAL GUIDANCE

Economic Depression

How to place people in jobs when there are not enough jobs to go around was a problem which gave most counselors and placement agencies feelings of futility during the '30s. The paradox of unemployed factories and unemployed workers largely nullified vocational guidance and vocational education. The counselor might help the pupil arrive at a sound vocational choice, and the student might show great promise for his chosen occupation as he trained for it, but when he was ready to take a position there was none. Facing the necessity of having to earn a living, he took the first job he could get.

Of all classes of workers, the depression was undoubtedly most severe for young people of the age group with which high school and college placement officers are most concerned. It was estimated in the late '30s that four million persons between the ages of 16 and 24 were neither in school nor employed.

[32] Ewan Clague and Webster Powell, *Ten Thousand Out of Work* (Philadelphia, University of Pennsylvania Press, 1933), p. 78.

[33] *The Social Problems of an Industrial Civilization* (Boston, Division of Research, Graduate School of Business Administration, Harvard University, 1945), p. 31.

The American Youth Commission, after five years' study of youth problems in the depression years, reported as follows:[34]

No good purpose can be served by blaming the young person who has not found a job for himself. The facts of arithmetic cannot be wished away. In the entire country a few thousand jobs probably are vacant because no competent applicant has appeared. Another few thousand chances probably exist for unusual young people to make their own jobs by starting new enterprises. But there are several million more young men and women who want to work than there are jobs available for them. The totals do not balance. The bright or the lucky get the jobs, but some will have to be left out until their elders, who control the economic conditions of the country, find some way to open the gates.

Guidance workers have sometimes shown extraordinary lack of understanding of the obstacle here presented. The twentieth annual convention of the National Vocational Guidance Association was held in Detroit in February, 1931. The following is an excerpt from the resolutions which they adopted:[35]

1. Much of the present unemployment and many other social evils are due to the fact that the persons now at work stumbled into their jobs without guidance; if we wish to avoid similar crises in the future we must provide systematic vocational guidance. It is estimated that of the forty million workers in the United States, about five millions are at present unemployed. It is certain that many of these unfortunate people lost their positions because they were in jobs for which they were not suited; others, because they were not adequately trained; still others, because they were trained for fields which were already overcrowded. A large majority of workers, both employed and unemployed, drift into their jobs by accident. This results not only in periodic recurrences in unemployment, but also in crime, low productivity, seasonal employment, exploitation of labor, particularly juvenile labor, low standards of living, poverty, misery, and unhappiness.
2. In order to avoid these evils we urge that society so organize itself that it can give to both workers and prospective workers systematic vocational guidance.

The criticism of this statement is that the "present unemployment" and the "periodic recurrences in unemployment" are due, not to the lack of vocational guidance, but to the sickness of our economic order. The basic cure for unemployment is an increase in the number of jobs. Guidance does not do this. It merely helps those who have its benefits to compete more successfully for the jobs available. In 1938 a superintendent of schools in western Pennsylvania said, "We're getting jobs for our graduates—not always the kind of jobs they'd like, but we are getting jobs for them. Our counselors have active contacts with 55 large employers." Here was a school enrolling 600 pupils and having two full-time counselors. No other school in the

[34] "A Program of Employment for Youth," *School Review,* Vol. XLVIII (January, 1940), p. 2. (Editorial quotation from a publication of the American Youth Commission.)

[35] *School and Society,* Vol. XXXIII (March 28, 1931), p. 441.

district had comparable guidance service. Employment for the graduates of that school simply meant less opportunity for the graduates of other schools.

While this chapter makes extensive reference to the period of the '30s as an example of the thwarting of vocational guidance by economic depression, the events of "economic recession" in 1958 as in 1954 and 1949 suggest that the lessons of the Big Depression are of current and recurring concern. In the early spring of 1958 it was evident that many June graduates who were applicants for positions in industry and commerce would not be placed.

Counselors and all who share responsibility for helping youth attain a normal adult life should see clearly the obstacle here discussed and play an active role in the building of a healthful economy. We should courageously align ourselves with those who seek to avert economic depressions. If our hearts are in our work, we should endeavor to create such conditions that we can render to the youth of the '60s the service we were unable to render the youth of the '30s.

The Social Status of Occupations

A second obstacle to the accomplishment of a rational distribution of workers is the extreme divergence of occupational rewards. Occupation is such a major factor in one's life that more than any other influence it determines how one lives and what his social standing is. The importance of occupation to the individual was stated as follows by Alba M. Edwards, of the Bureau of the Census:[36]

The most nearly dominant single influence in a man's life is probably his occupation. More than anything else, perhaps, a man's occupation determines his course and his contribution in life. And when life's span is ended, quite likely there is no other single set of facts that will tell so well the kind of man he was and the part he played in life as will a detailed and chronological statement of the occupation, or occupations, he pursued. Indeed, there is no other single characteristic that tells so much about a man and his status—social, intellectual, and economic—as does his occupation. A man's occupation not only tells, for each workday, what he does during one-half of his waking hours, but it indicates, with some degree of accuracy, his manner of life during the other half—the kind of associates he will have, the kind of clothes he will wear, the kind of house he will live in, and even, to some extent, the kind of food he will eat. And, usually, it indicates, in some degree, the cultural level of his family.

Counts explored the social status of occupations.[37] To several groups of people—high-school teachers, high-school seniors, trade-school senior boys, and freshmen in a college of agriculture—he submitted a list of

---

[36] *Comparative Occupation Statistics for the United States, 1870 to 1940.* Sixteenth Census of the United States: 1940, Population. (Washington, D.C., Government Printing Office, 1943), p. xi.

[37] G. S. Counts, "The Social Status of Occupations: A Problem in Vocational Guidance," *School Review*, Vol. XXXIII (January, 1925), pp. 16–27.

45 commonly known occupations from the well-paid to the poorly paid, from the complex to the simple, and so on. He asked the several groups to arrange the occupations in the order of their social standing, explaining that "There is a tendnecy for us to 'look up to' persons engaged in some occupations and 'down on' those engaged in others. We may even be ashamed or proud of our relatives because of their occupations." The composite ranking of the groups placed the banker first, the college professor second, the physician third, and the hod carrier forty-third, the street cleaner forty-fourth, the ditch digger forty-fifth. Perhaps the most significant finding of the study was the remarkable agreement among the several groups. The coefficients of correlation between their rankings were all above .90; in one instance the correlation was .97. Since the groups represented various parts of the country as well as different social backgrounds and vocational aspirations, it would suggest that the American people are rather well agreed on the social standing of occupations.[38]

Ege and Sullivan made studies to obtain some definition of social status, something of an inventory of its elements,[39] Ege studying the reactions of men and boys to men's occupations and Sullivan making a parallel study with women's occupations. To groups of graduate students they submitted lists of typical men's and women's occupations and directed them to "write one of the following designations before each occupation":

1. "Proud," if you think your family and friends would be proud and highly gratified to see you engage in it.

2. "Satisfied," if you think your family and friends would be reasonably satisfied though not particularly enthusiastic to see you engage in it.

3. "Disappointed," if you think your family and friends would be a little disappointed to see you engage in it.

4. "Ashamed," if you think many of your friends would feel ashamed of you if you were to engage in it.

After they had finished they were asked, first, to study the occupations before which they had written "Proud" and to write on a separate sheet the reasons why they thought their families and friends would experience the reaction of pride and gratification. Similarly, on separate sheets they accounted for each of the other designations which constituted the four-point scale of social standing. From these lists of reasons, check lists were drawn up for obtaining the reactions of high-school pupils.

[38] Counts's study was duplicated in 1946 and the ranking of occupations according to social standing was found to be practically the same as in 1925—an r of .97. See Maethel E. Deeg and Donald G. Paterson, "Changes in Social Status of Occupations," *Occupations,* Vol. XXV (January, 1947), pp. 205–208.

[39] Edward F. Ege, *An Analysis of the Factors Which Give Social Status to Men's Occupations.* M. A. Thesis (Pittsburgh, University of Pittsburgh Library, 1933).

V. Rebecca Sullivan, *An Analysis of the Factors Which Give Social Status to Women's Occupations.* M. A. Thesis (Pittsburgh, University of Pittsburgh Library, 1934).

The investigations showed that people—both adolescents and adults—are conscious of a wide variety of factors as contributing to the social status of occupations. These factors could be grouped into approximately seven categories of exaltation or degradation of the person. The social status of an occupation is the result of some kind of addition of the answers to the following questions: Does the occupation exalt or degrade the *physical* person? the *economic* person? the *intellectual* person? the *social* person? the *national* or *racial* person? the *moral* person? the *aesthetic* person? Obviously, individuals must vary in the evaluations which they place upon the several factors. Counts showed that individuals tended to disagree rather widely on the total quality of social status which they ascribed to occupations (though his groups agreed so closely) and that the individuals disagreed much more on some occupations than on others.[40]

The many detailed circumstances and conditions by which jobs acquire their social status are described by Gardner in his chapter on "The Factory as a Social System."[41] He points out the shop-office distinctions and the tendency of the office group to look down upon the shop workers as inferior in mind, manner, and morals. The symbols of status are numerous—the sort of clothes one wears, the desk one sits at, the machine one operates, the washroom one uses, pay by the hour or pay by the week.

These refinements are mentioned merely to illustrate social status in greater detail. Presumably young job hunters are not fully aware of them, but they do know enough about the fact of social status to make it difficult for counselors to induce them to think objectively about their qualifications and the jobs they match. They avoid consideration of those occupations which are characterized by inadequate remuneration, social stigma, dull routine, and other features which degrade the person. They aspire to those walks in life which promise creature-comforts, social distinction, self-realization, and similar elements which exalt the person. In an open-class society they feel that they are entitled to such aspirations.

One of the rare statements to come from the counseling firing line in full realization of this obstacle to guidance is in a provocative article by Prudence Bostwick.[42] This author gathered data in one of the schools which participated in the Eight-Year Study of the Relation of School and College. She canvassed those pupils from the experimental classes who did not go to college, but prefaced the report of her findings with the following remarks which illuminate the obstacle to guidance with which we are here concerned:[43]

[40] *Op. cit.,* pp. 22–25.
[41] Burleigh B. Gardner, *Human Relations in Industry.* (Chicago, Richard D. Irwin, Inc., 1945).
[42] "They Did Not Go to College," *Educational Research Bulletin* (Ohio State University), Vol. XVIII (September 13, 1939), pp. 147–162.
[43] *Ibid.,* pp. 150–152.

. . . it is difficult for us to talk with eager boys and girls, who come to us for help about the jobs for which they will be best suited and in which they will find happiness, and retain at the same time the necessary realism for coping with the situation. It is an interesting fact that much of the vocational study which was carried on in the experimental program was concerned with getting acquainted with professions. We had conferences with lawyers, engineers, doctors, nurses, teachers, and librarians, all representative of the kind of work that the class voted to learn about. We did have conferences with salesmen and with beauty operators, but the requests to learn about skilled and unskilled labor were practically non-existent. On the whole, we ignored with magnificent unconcern for reality the jobs of filling-station attendant, stenographer, waitress, filing clerk, messenger, butcher, telephone operator, and factory worker.

Helping individual pupils to meet adequately the problem of going into semi-skilled or unskilled labor has never seemed to be an appropriate concern for teachers of Latin, English grammar, ancient history, and geometry. Then, too, there has been a feeling that jobs such as piloting elevators, driving trucks, selling behind the counters of a ten-cent store, working in a bakery, and doing housework more or less took care of themselves. The human problem of adjustment to such work has not been thought of as the concern of the schools.

. . . A realistic approach to the problems of vocational adjustment is made almost impossible by the American dream of progressive improvement in status from generation to generation.

Conferences with young people that aim to discover vocational interests seldom gain from any pupil an ambition to be a waitress, or a clerk in a ten-cent store, or a factory hand. With characteristic enthusiasm and hope they see themselves in positions of prestige. The emphasis of the school program upon life values that have been largely derived from the tradition of constantly increasing status tends to turn the thought from the possibility that life must be lived in a job that lacks reputation and challenge and is "unworthy" of the application of minds that through formal education have tasted another fruit.

For these emphases the school is partly to blame. We have tended to solve the problem in one of two ways: either we have ignored the fact that our graduates would be called upon to do distasteful work, or we have recognized its presence only as a necessary evil to be lived through as best one may by the device of developing some real interests in an avocational life which would assuage the disappointment and defeat of the vocational.

To overcome this second obstacle, occupational life must ultimately undergo reconstruction. The day of such reconstruction will be brought closer if teachers and counselors will become realistic and genuinely democratic. They must know the facts about the present occupational structure. They must know that many millions of workers, rendering essential social services, are now so inadequately rewarded socially and economically that it is difficult to see how a youth can be expected voluntarily to enter those occupations. They must know that with secondary education becoming universal we have in our schools the section hands, housemaids, factory operatives, and common laborers of the future. Possessed of such knowledge, they will evince attitudes which signify respect for all workers who render socially valuable service. They will refrain from the attempt to motivate a pupil by the use of such a remark as, "You don't want to grow up to be just a truck driver, do you?" They will help their pupils to derive justifiable values from the individual success story; they will protect them from unjustifiable interpretation of the vocational ladder.

The Economic Handicap for Some Individuals

How can the rational matching of individuals with vocations be carried out for our most gifted youth when some of them cannot finance the advanced training required for entrance to the vocations to which their talents correspond? This is a third obstacle to guidance that brings a sense of defeat and helplessness to every teacher, principal, and counselor who is devoted to his pupils' welfare. Counselors have found that they cannot lightly advise the college-preparatory curriculum for every pupil whose intelligence and school record indicate college ability. How can Mary go to college when she is the oldest of three children and her mother a widow without income? We do not have equal educational opportunity in America when continuance in school depends on the economic condition of the family.

One of the most illuminating investigations of this problem is that of Helen B. Goetsch, who studied 1,023 secondary-school pupils who graduated from the public high schools of Milwaukee in February and June, 1937, and February, 1938.[44] These pupils were the ones whose scores on the state-wide testing program given in the senior year had been equal to the state percentiles of 86 to 100, or intelligence quotients of 117 to 146. Having such ability, they were assumed to be capable of doing college work successfully. During April, 1938, Miss Goetsch sent a follow-up questionnaire to these selected graduates. She found that only 35 per cent of them were full-time college students, 4 per cent were part-time college students, 19 per cent were in minor schools, and 42 per cent were not in school at all.

To ascertain the relationship between college-going and parental income, Miss Goetsch examined returns on the Wisconsin state income tax to obtain the 1936 income of the parents. Table 3[45] summarizes her essential findings, showing quite clearly how college-going depends on economic circumstances of the family. From the first three categories of parents—those having incomes of $3,000 and over—most of the children went to college; but it will also be noted that the number of students from homes of such affluence is very small—105, to be exact, or about 10 per cent of the total. That there

---

[44] *Parental Income and College Opportunities,* New York, Teachers College Contributions to Education No. 795, 1940.

See also the same author's article, "Relation of Parental Income to College Opportunity," *School Review,* Vol. XLVIII (January, 1940), pp. 26–33.

[45] *Ibid.,* p. 87, Table 26, adapted.

TABLE 3. Distribution of Students According to Parental Income

Parental Income	Number in the Income Group	Number in College Full Time	Per cent in College Full Time
$8,000 and over	10	10	100.0
5,000–7,999	25	23	92.0
3,000–4,999	70	51	72.9
2,000–2,999	205	91	44.4
1,500–1,999	225	65	28.9
1,000–1,499	161	41	25.5
500– 999	82	22	26.8
Under $500	245	50	20.4
All cases	1023	353	34.5

should be any students at all from the lower income brackets going to college is surprising, but this is in keeping with the long-time American tradition of earning one's way through college. That tradition has made us complacent about the true situation; it has blinded us to the waste of human resources and the class distinctions that actually prevail in American life. Just because some students all through our educational history have borrowed money and earned money to finance a college education, we have assumed that all could do it and that rugged individualism would answer society's need for trained technicians and leaders.

One of the cases described by Goetsch is the following:[46]

Alois K., I.Q. 126, high-school average of 89. Alois wishes to study medicine, but at present has a part-time job as a sales clerk in a shoe store and is taking one college course, in child psychology. His father earned $925.00 in 1936 as a factory stock clerk. There are two children; an older sister is working as a stenographer. The family own the home and have a telephone. Alois says: "I am very eager to continue my schooling, but I cannot afford to at the present time." If a full-time scholarship could be provided, to cover all the expense of a higher education, he would be very happy to be a full-time college student. It seems unlikely that Alois will ever complete a long medical course.

The situation of Alois calls for something more than a counselor has to offer.

Two other studies may be cited briefly in support of Goetsch's findings. One, based on data gathered from the 1937 high-school graduating class of an industrial and commercial city of 50,000 in New York State, brought the author to the conclusion that

Here and there is found a graduate who, with low financial resources, does go to college, but he or she is a distinct exception, whereas there are a goodly number

[46] *Ibid.*, p. 63.

who want to go to college and whose high-school marks indicate ability sufficient for college but who cannot attend because they cannot meet the costs.[47]

Davis[48] studied the June, 1940, graduates of Kentucky high schools. Using a half dozen measures predictive of college success, he found a Pearson co-efficient of correlation between the composite score of the predictors and first-semester standings in the University of Kentucky of $.67 \pm .031$. On the basis of the composite scores on the prediction battery, approximately 50 per cent of the students standing in the highest quarter and about 14 per cent of those standing in the lowest quarter were found to be attending college. Thus, about half the students who were without doubt excellent risks did not get to college. Davis produced some evidence indicating the dominance of the economic factor in determining college-going.

Considerable awareness of this obstacle to guidance has been in evidence during the past few years, former President Conant of Harvard being one of the most vocal of the educational leaders who have been urging upon the nation the necessity of making possible the advanced education of all its gifted youth. A prominent purpose of the National Youth Administration was to help both high-school and college students overcome the financial obstacle to the continuance of their schooling. Recently, under the G.I. Bill of Rights, we have witnessed a flood of young people catching up on the education they missed while in military service, many of whom would never have been able to pursue such advantages had it not been for the largesse of a grateful government. In spite of this experience the education of gifted youth still depends mainly upon individual economic status, although scholarship funds are steadily increasing.

The Obstacle of Ascribed Status

A society ascribes statuses to various groups in its midst, the distinctive factors being age, sex, color, inheritance, etc. Over an ascribed status the individual has no control. Thus, in American society, women, Negroes, Mexicans, and other groups have ascribed statuses which largely limit their occupational opportunities.

Ascribed status frequently constitutes a serious obstacle to the performance of vocational guidance. It seems generally to conflict with democratic principles, to be an expression of custom, which is in turn the expression of the dominant, ruling group of a society. Ascribed status is frequently the instrument with which a dominant group preserves certain privileges and a preferred position for its own members. By contrast, vocational guidance would decide on the rational grounds of the individual's productive useful-

---

[47] Raymond B. Stevens, "Experience of High-School Pupils after Graduation," *School Review*, Vol. L (January, 1942), p. 28.

[48] Horace L. Davis, *The Utilization of Potential College Ability Found in the June, 1940, Graduates of Kentucky High Schools,* Bulletin of the Bureau of School Service, College of Education, University of Kentucky, Vol. XV (September, 1942).

ness what his occupational role shall be, and thereby largely determine his status.

The status ascription of women operates to confine them to certain job areas, and that is what accounts for their lower wages as compared with men doing the same work: they compete heavily in the few fields open to them. Woman's ascribed status is steadily broadening, and when we take account of the history of the past one hundred years we are encouraged with the widening opportunity for vocational guidance to function. One hundred years ago the opportunity for women to study at the college level was just beginning to be grudgingly granted by the dominant male; seventy years ago the first daring women were taking up office occupations; thousands donned the welder's mask and took up his torch in the manpower stringency of World War II.

Ascribed status continually operates, though in lessening degree, as a stricture in the vocational advisement of girls. To a greater or lesser degree it limits freedom of thought about occupational affiliation on the part of the girl and her parents. More unfortunately, it sometimes inhibits the sound reasoning of the counselor to the extent that he will not adequately assess the specialized capacities of girls, or that he will not freely accept the vocational implications of the knowledge that he has about them. If the counselor would be true to his responsibility in exercising the guidance function, it seems that he should *know* the ascribed status of the counselee and should *inform* him of what it involves for the choice and pursuit of a vocation, just as he will also help the counselee to understand his vocational potentialities. Thus, if a girl wants to become a doctor, engineer, or an expert in automotive repair, she should be helped to come into a full understanding of the handicaps imposed by ascribed status as well as of the degree to which her qualifications in ability justify her aspiration.

One of the groups most handicapped in vocational choice by ascribed status is the entire Negro race. Still in the shadow of the slave tradition, Negroes are ascribed a status which largely limits them to low-paying jobs in hard physical labor or menial service. Recognition on the basis of their individual ability is being fought for on many fronts and by many organizations of both white and colored people. Of the greatest significance in the struggle have been the Fair Employment Practices laws, measures which would release the Negro from the shackle of ascribed occupational status, insofar as that can be accomplished by the passage of a law.

The Lynds drew a picture of the Negro's occupational position in a northern city in the middle '30s, as follows:[49]

Business-class Middletown tolerates the Negro population complacently as a convenient instrument for getting certain types of dirty work done for low wages. According to the head of Middletown's local branch of the State Employment

[49] *Middletown in Transition* (New York, Harcourt, Brace, 1937), p. 463.

Service office, "Negro labor in Middletown has fairly steady employment at the harder, meaner type of job in certain of Middletown's factories, as hod carriers and similar unskilled labor in the building trades, on road gangs, and, in exceptional cases where a Negro's character is above question, as janitors. But the only thing a Negro can do beyond that is a long step up from there to the professional class serving his own race. There are no intermediate steps—a Negro cannot, for instance, become a machinist." An officer in a large automobile plant stated simply, "We don't have any Negroes at all. It's degrading to a white man to have Negroes doing the same type of work."

Table 4 suggests that these restrictions on occupational opportunity for Negroes underwent noteworthy change in the 1940s.[50] In that decade the percentages of Negro men in clerical and kindred occupations, in sales work, in the crafts, and in operatives' jobs increased markedly, being drawn from the ranks of servants, service workers, and common labor. When the nine categories are grouped as "upper stratum" and "lower stratum" occupations, it is seen that the decade was one of large gains in admission to the more favored occupational fields. At both time points, however, the white workers held a marked advantage.

The occupational shifts of Negro women border on the spectacular, the percentage in upper stratum occupations almost doubling in the ten-year period, and the category of "private household workers" losing much of its predominance. White women shifted, also, to upper stratum occupations, their gain being especially out of private household work and into clerical work.

TABLE 4. Percentage Distribution of Non-Agricultural Employed Men and Women, by Major Occupational Group, by Color, United States, 1950 and 1940

| | Per cent Employed | | | | Per cent Change | |
| | 1950 | | 1940 | | 1940 to 1950 | |
Major Occupational Group	Non-White	White	Non-White	White	Non-White	White
MALE						
Total Employed Men	99.99	99.99	100.00	99.99		
1. Profess., Tech., and Kindred ..	2.98	9.44	3.17	8.39	−.19	1.05
2. Mgrs., Officials, and Prop.	2.71	13.83	2.82	13.58	−.11	.25
3. Clerical and Kindred	4.61	8.11	2.10	8.29	2.51	−.18
4. Salesworkers ...	2.09	7.92	1.65	8.75	.44	−.83
5. Craftsmen, Foremen, and Kindred ..	10.23	23.02	7.51	20.40	2.72	2.62

[50] John Hope II, "The Employment of Negroes in the United States by Major Occupation and Industry," *Journal of Negro Education*, Vol. XXII (Summer, 1953), p. 309, Table I.

TABLE 4. Percentage Distribution of Non-Agricultural Employed Men and Women, by Major Occupational Group, by Color, United States, 1950 and 1940 (continued)

6. Operatives and Kindred	28.18	23.78	21.27	23.97	6.91	−.19
UPPER STRATUM (1–6)	50.80	86.10	38.52	83.38	12.28	2.72
7. Private Household Workers	1.05	.15	3.88	.16	−2.83	−.01
8. Service Workers, Exc. Private ..	16.90	5.89	21.06	6.67	−4.16	−.78
9. Labor, Exc. Farm and Mine	31.24	7.85	36.54	9.78	−5.30	−1.93
LOWER STRATUM (7–9)	49.19	13.89	61.48	16.61	−12.29	−2.72
FEMALE Total Employed Women	99.99	99.98	100.00	99.99		
1. Profess., Tech., and Kindred ..	6.96	14.15	5.14	15.40	1.82	−1.25
2. Mgrs., Officials, and Prop.	.60	5.04	.93	4.46	−.33	.58
3. Clerical and Kindred	4.48	31.44	1.15	25.40	3.33	6.04
4. Salesworkers ...	1.45	9.36	.73	8.37	.72	.99
5. Craftsmen, Foremen, and Kindred ..	1.15	1.80	.20	1.14	.95	.66
6. Operatives and Kindred	16.51	20.86	7.94	21.05	8.57	−.19
UPPER STRATUM (1–6)	31.15	82.65	16.09	75.82	15.06	6.83
7. Private Household Workers	47.49	4.61	70.42	11.34	−22.93	−6.73
8. Service Workers, Exc. Private ..	20.08	11.99	12.48	11.91	7.60	.08
9. Labor, Exc. Farm and Mine	1.27	.73	1.01	.92	.26	−.19
LOWER STRATUM (7–9)	68.84	17.33	83.91	24.17	−15.07	−6.84

In December, 1935, the National Occupational Conference called a meeting of colored and white leaders at Atlanta University for several days' discussion of the problem of vocational guidance and education for Negroes. The following lines from Keller's statement in the issue of *Occupations* which reported this meeting may be selected to reflect the conclusions reached by the group:[51]

One of the oldest queries in the field of vocational education for Negroes is, "Shall we train colored boys and girls for the jobs that are available to them, or, in the hope that they may be lucky, shall we also train them for jobs that are now held only by whites?" There can be only one answer. Train individuals for jobs which, in the light of their interests, aptitudes, and capacities, they will be likely to fill acceptably. *But,* at the same time, assist the young person in every possible way, to understand what the chances of employment are, and insist that he also train for some job that, as a Negro, he is likely to obtain. He must be armed with skills and fortified with emotional resistance. He must know what he wants, but must realize what he can get. He must aim for the best, but be willing to take the next best rather than be idle or neurotic or both. He must be ready to fight ever to advance the frontier of Negro occupational life and to destroy that most undemocratic concept of all, "a Negro occupation."

With the census data of 1940 and 1950 now before us, as presented in Table 4, Keller's statement clearly presents a sound course for the counselor to pursue. The Negro can only escape from the limits imposed by his ascribed status if he is ready, when opportunity knocks, to render service in the occupational role to which his ability entitles him. Counselors can materially aid the continuance of Negro progress, but they must do so in the light of a balanced view of the counselee's ability and his opportunity.

Two additional factors have pertinency for our understanding of this obstacle of ascribed status. One is the attempt on the part of the dominant group to justify and explain the limits imposed by ascription on the grounds of limited ability on the part of the members of the group whose opportunity is restricted. Thus, it was long held (by men) that women were, by inborn characteristics, inferior to men in reasoning power, in mechanical ability, in mathematics, and in various other abilities essential to occupations from which they were proscribed. Objective tests and the experimental proof of women's occupational abilities have pretty well undermined this rationalization of women's ascribed status. Similar arguments have been offered in support of the limitation of Negroes' opportunity. The arguments have been similarly refuted. Where cultural opportunities have approached equality Negroes have approximately the same average and the same spread of general intelligence as whites. Perhaps the most widely cited bit of evidence on the relative intelligence of the two races was the finding in World War I that the Negro draftees from New York State excelled in scores on the Army Alpha Mental Test the white draftees from Alabama. The false evaluation of Negro ability has been further dispelled in recent years by the publicizing of the findings of the anthropologists, who, from their wide study of races, have

[51] Franklin J. Keller, "The Purpose, the Story, and the Spirit," *Occupations,* Vol. XIV (March, 1936) p. 486.

brought us to an appreciation of the great scope of social heredity as a determinant of human behavior.

The other factor bearing on ascribed status is the expansion and contraction of the labor market. In times of labor shortage members of groups accorded only limited vocational opportunity are admitted to vocations ordinarily closed to them; in times of excessive labor supply they are pushed back into their ascribed status, and some of their normal vocational fields may be invaded by members of the dominant group. Thus, during the war women gained access to many occupations calling for mechanical skill; during the depression '30s men competed with women for positions as rural school teachers. Such oscillations of the labor market tend to break down the boundaries of ascribed status. Submerged groups get a chance to prove themselves in new fields in a boom period, and some of their members continue in them when depression comes. The counselor should give a proper evaluation to this phenomenon.

THE SOCIAL SCENE AND PERSONAL ADJUSTMENT

Adjustment Affected by Instability of Occupation

This chapter has thus far been devoted to the bearing of the social and economic order on distributive guidance. In this section we shall examine its relationship to adjustive guidance. The question is, how does our open-class, profits-motivated economy affect the individual in his development and maintenance of a wholesome personality? How does it affect personal, social, emotional adjustment?

Section II of this chapter has pointed out how occupations are constantly being modified or abolished by the advancement of technology and also how workers are at the mercy of the economic cycle. Since 1942 the percentage of unemployment has been very low. Furthermore, unemployment compensation and other cushions have been established to absorb some of the shock of lay-offs. Under these circumstances the feeling of security and of confidence in the future has been so general as to minimize concern over such slight dips in the general diffusion of prosperity as occurred in 1949, 1954, and 1958. The absence of apprehension concerning the future was reflected in the mounting mortgage debt—"5 per cent down and a thirty-year mortgage"—and in the rising level of installment debt—"nothing down and three years to pay." But if the man in the street blandly assumed a secure future, some economists, having longer memories and more expertness in testing the economic currents, were saying, "Boom perils mount," "Three years is a long time to assume stability," and "What if peace should break out!"

And that no millennium of job security is likely to exist in the near future is suggested by three items on pages 1 and 2 of a single day's issue of a city newspaper, briefed as follows:[52]

[52] *The Pittsburgh Post-Gazette,* August 31, 1955.

(1) The basic steel industry will be asked for some sort of a guaranteed annual wage next year. . . . "It is our contention that companies could very well space their work out over a year's time so there would be no peaks or dips in production."

(2) An electrical manufacturing workers' union striking to protest management's plans for a time study of certain categories of workers, charged management with wanting to "reduce the number of day workers employed and create additional unemployment in this company, where already there are many, many thousands of workers now walking the streets."

(3) "Agents of Southern communities are trying to persuade mill owners in flood stricken areas of the Northeast to move South rather than attempt to rebuild in their Pennsylvania or New England locations. . . . removal of mills would only aggravate the already high unemployment in the Northeast."

Unemployment and the consequent necessity for adjustment is no respecter of social classes. At one end of the scale we read that "New equipment is bringing costs down, with 205,000 miners producing more coal today than nearly 230,000 produced a year ago."[53] At the other end of the scale, a news story is headlined, "Displaced Bosses: Merger Wave Tosses Many Top Executives onto the Job Market."[54]

One cannot doubt that unemployment and the fear of unemployment constitute a strain on mental health that leaves its mark on many people. In the years of the Big Depression statistics showed that young people of the ages 16 to 24 were unemployed with higher frequency than any other group. Mark A. May presented the problems of boys growing up in those years when the normal sequence of "school, then employment, then marriage and a new family" was broken.[55] Fedder described the plight of out-of-school girls during the depression—no place for them in the world of employment, friction at home because of this, feelings of helplessness, frustration, apathy, and dejection—then loss of pride.[56]

While unemployment may never return on such a scale as in the '30s, it is a scourge for whatever percentage it afflicts. It saps the sense of security which is so essential to the well-integrated personality. It frustrates teen-age youth in the normal drive toward emancipation from home ties. It enhances an unwholesome fear motivation in the meeting of personal economic and social problems. If economic society could become stabilized at the level which modern technology has made possible, and with valuable work contributions from all its members, adjustive guidance would be relieved of many of its problems—problems which often cannot be solved otherwise.

[53] *Wall Street Journal* (May 20, 1955).
[54] *Wall Street Journal* (August 25, 1955).
[55] Mark A. May, "The Dilemma of Youth," *Progressive Education,* Vol. XII (January, 1935), pp. 5–11.
[56] Ruth Fedder, "The World Is Laying for You," *Progressive Education,* Vol. XII (December, 1935), pp. 518–524.

Emotional Strain from Variations in Status

The struggle to rise in the social scale and so attain social preferment and a higher standard of living creates a competitive atmosphere which breeds feelings of envy and anxiety. Using a fictional medium, *Point of No Return,* John Marquand has created a vivid impression of the emotional strain of such striving, his chief characters being junior bank executives. From Gardner the following paragraph may be quoted for its portrayal of the varied manifestations and the intensity of this aspect of occupational life:[57]

. . . "Status anxiety" is a kind of individual disturbance found frequently at all levels in industry. In these cases an individual expresses concern over his position relative to others. He is disturbed if someone else gets more recognition from the boss than he does; he worries over status symbols; he is concerned if others do not recognize his proper status; and he is worried about advancement and especially about his rate of progress relative to others. This is a common development among those mobile people whose progress has been blocked. Their anxieties may become so extreme that they develop into severe neuroses accompanied by feelings of persecution, insomnia, inability to concentrate, and other nervous disorders.

Thus Gardner sets forth some of the reactions of workers to an open-class, competitive society. With the existent divergence in economic and social rewards, with the possibility of moving "up" the occupational scale (the true shape of the ladder being disregarded), the individual has an urgent invitation always to strive for a higher rung. Looking "up" at more exalted stations, his present post may seem mean and inadequate and unchallenging. Sometimes it is that way with teachers, a profession in which Counts found decided status differentials. The composite judgment of his groups ranked the college professor second in social status among 45 occupations, the superintendent of schools seventh, the high-school teacher tenth, the elementary-school teacher thirteenth, and the rural-school teacher nineteenth.[58] Hence the spectacle of elementary-school teachers qualifying for and obtaining junior-high positions while junior-high teachers are moving on to senior-high positions, sometimes disregarding their own inmost interests.

"Fortunately," says Gardner,[59]

everyone in industry does not have a strong mobility drive. Many people make good adjustment at even the bottom levels and are able to get satisfaction out of their jobs. This does not mean that they would not want better jobs, or that they will admit to a lack of ambition; but actually many are sufficiently well adjusted that they will not make the effort or take the chances necessary for going on to something better. . . .

To be well adjusted in the lower-status positions or even the lowest-status

[57] *Op. cit.,* p. 181.
[58] G. S. Counts, *op. cit.,* pp. 20–21.
[59] *Op. cit.,* pp. 194–195.

position in a work group does not mean that the individual is insensitive to status differences. In fact, we continually meet with disturbances due to minor shifts in status relationships and with cases of anxiety over relative status. . . . Sometimes an individual will quit his job entirely, even if it means taking an even worse job elsewhere, rather than face a loss of status within the same work group.

Piece-work wage systems, calculated to create incentive in the workers, and also to pay each worker according to his productivity, frequently result in such irritability and tensions that the workers informally band together and agree not to respond to the incentive. They resist the corrosive emotional influence of competition by not competing; they agree upon a common standard of accomplishment which all can meet. It is true, however, that other reasons for such restriction of production exist. One is the fear that if enough of their members attained what the management might consider an inordinately high income, the rate of pay would be cut. Another is the fear that the faster they work, the sooner they may work themselves out of a job. All of these factors were found to figure in the feelings of the bank wiring group of workers observed by Roethlisberger and Dickson in their research at the Hawthorne Works of the Western Electric Company, a group whose thought on the matter was as follows: [60]

"If we exceed our day's work by any appreciable amount, something will happen. The 'rate' might be cut, the 'rate' might be raised, the 'bogy' might be raised, someone might be laid off, or the supervisor might 'bawl out' the slower men."

Perhaps the most crucial single element in status is that of wages. Reading Gardner's fifty-page chapter on "Wages and Wage Systems," which reveals how very complicated is the whole matter of determining the differentiated monetary rewards for labor, how profoundly people's feelings are involved, and how impossible it is to work out scales which bring general satisfaction, one can appreciate why Bellamy had no money in his Utopia but simplified the matter of distributing the product of industry by issuing ration cards to all members of society. [61]

In this abbreviated treatment, the grave problems of emotional and social adjustment which our society raises can only be suggested. That many of our youth must take places in the economic order which will raise within them feelings of fear, envy, or inferiority, that many must work at jobs which are so unreal and so foreign to their purposes that they can experience no self-realization in working hours, and that many must serve society in economic autocracies operated for private gain—these are some of the "facts of life" which counselors must understand as they encounter problems of adjustment

[60] F. J. Roethlisberger and William J. Dickson, *Management and the Worker* (Cambridge, Mass., Harvard University Press, 1942), p. 417.

[61] Most provocative reading in connection with this chapter is Edward Bellamy, *Looking Backward, 2000–1887* (Boston, Houghton Mifflin, 1888). (Re-published, Cleveland, The World Publishing Company, 1945.)

and as they prepare youth to meet the emotional stress and strain of their work lives.

THE RECONSTRUCTION OF OCCUPATIONAL LIFE

What Criteria Should Guide Occupational Evolution?

While occupations have been changed by the forces which the industrial revolution, combined with the spirit of gain, have loosed among us, they have also been changed and are continually being changed by the driving power of democratic humanism. Our history is replete with evidence that we do harken to the conscience which Edwin Markham has made to say:

> We are blind until we see
> That in the human plan
> Nothing is worth the making
> If it does not make the man.
>
> Why build these cities glorious
> If man unbuilded goes?
> In vain we build the world
> Unless the builder also grows.

We do not fairly depict the social scene in which guidance operates unless we show the positive forces which are at work in the reconstruction of occupational life, and give examples of the steps that have been taken, the lines which reform is following. First, however, we may well ask ourselves, what are the elements of satisfaction which one should find in his vocation? If we are to reconstruct occupational life, what are the architectural specifications which should guide us?

In his initial study of job satisfaction Hoppock identified six major components.[62] Instead of citing them here, the "factors in job satisfaction" found in a survey of a medium-sized New England manufacturing center will be drawn upon.[63] They may be summarized as follows:

1. Independence and control, especially meaning freedom from close supervision and the right to voice one's opinion.

2. Relationships with fellow workers. The "happy family" atmosphere, smooth teamwork, respect of co-workers.

3. Fairness of treatment. An equitable system of rewards, resting on two

[62] Robert Hoppock, *Job Satisfaction* (New York, Harper, 1935), pp. 279–283. This work includes an excellent bibliography. It has been followed by a series of articles, published at approximately two-year intervals, by Hoppock and associates, in *Occupations* and its successor, the *Personnel and Guidance Journal*. These articles are discriminating and evaluative summaries, with bibliographies, of the stream of literature on job satisfaction.

[63] Lloyd G. Reynolds and Joseph Shister, *Job Horizons: A Study of Job Satisfaction and Labor Mobility* (New York, Harper, 1949), pp. 6–34.

main bases, namely, length of service with the firm, and quality of performance on the job.

4. Job interest—extent to which the job is intrinsically interesting to the worker. Most common elements are variety in the work, contact with people, and the opportunity to use one's skill completely.

5. Physical characteristics of the job: (a) nature of the job itself—clean or dirty, light or heavy, safe or dangerous; (b) the physical plant conditions—cleanliness, lighting, ventilation, toilet facilities; (c) the type of machinery—modern or obsolete, in good or bad condition.

6. Wages. Are they adequate for the worker's standard of living? Are they decided on an equitable basis?

7. Job security. A guarantee of steady work was preferred by 73 per cent over a wage increase.

Lewisohn's simplified statement of these satisfactions is as follows:[64]

I should roughly classify the more important desires of the workman as the desire for *justice*, the desire for *status*, the desire to have *his job made a career*, and the desire for *security*.

Perhaps a good way to state the criteria which should govern the reconstruction of occupational life is to accept democracy as the basic principle to which occupational life should conform and then see more specifically how the various aspects of democracy contribute the satisfactions which a vocation should offer. "Democracy," says Counts,[65]

is far more than a government. Indeed in order to place its stamp upon government it must prevail beyond the bounds of politics. It is an attitude of mind to which the exploitation of man by man is abhorrent; it is a way of life in which human personality is judged of supreme, of measureless, worth; it is an order of social relationships dedicated to the promotion of the individual and collective interests of common folk; it is, in a word, a society in which ordinary men and women may grow to their full stature—a *society* 'of the people, by the people, and for the people.'

It is indeed the way of least resistance in a mass-production industry to treat the individual worker as a mere economic automaton, but many examples could be cited to show how he reacts with a glow of pleasure which he translates into heightened productivity when he sees the purpose of the small routine task he carries on. The reason is that he feels a sense of his worth, he feels that he has a share in a large job. Drucker tells[66] of an aircraft manufacturer in whose plant the workers' morale was low despite high wages and much attention to the workers' welfare. Finally it was found that none of the employees had seen any of the planes they were producing and

[64] *Op. cit.,* p. 91.

[65] George S. Counts, *The Prospects of American Democracy* (New York, Day, 1938), p. 430.

[66] Peter Drucker, *Concept of the Corporation* (New York, Day, 1946), pp. 157–158.

had no idea of the function of the parts on which they worked. When a big bomber was brought in and the workers were shown just what their work had to do with it,

the bad morale and unrest disappeared at once. What had happened was that the worker was shown his status and function in the war effort as a responsible and valuable member of society and of the nation at war.

In another writing Drucker described[67] the definite program of orientation of workers which was carried on in a plant converted to the production of carbines for the Army. Here the worker was taken out to a shooting range by an instructor and allowed to fire a few rounds. The carbine was then taken to pieces and the worker was shown the part on which he was to work. Following this, he was shown a carbine in which the part was too large or too small; the need for manufacturing precision was convincingly demonstrated. Aided by the instructor, the worker analyzed the steps in his own job and summarized his conclusions on a chart. The management found that the workers invariably set higher standards for themselves than the time-motion engineers had worked out for the job, and that in actual work they even tended to better these higher standards.

We have illustrated the mainspring of the "mainsprings of men," which Whiting Williams calls "the wish for worth." People do not like to be "pushed around"; they feel inferior and irritated if they are "master-minded"; they hate the jobs in which they have no status. With complicated organizations built up and controlled by the owners or the managers of the instruments of production, the autocratic definition of jobs seems the easy, natural way; but the democratic method employs all the brains of the organization and enlists whole-hearted interest in the success of the enterprise.

An incident in the life of Frances Perkins, former Secretary of Labor, illustrates the sort of respect for the worker which makes his job assume its true significance. Partnership is indeed the heart of democracy.

When her admirers gave a luncheon in her honor she made a speech in which she expressed her thanks . . . to the women who had helped her bring up her daughter. Attending that luncheon were her cook and her maid and the scrubwoman who cleaned her office.[68]

In Counts' definition of democracy we can see also the gratification of the worker's craving for security. A democracy is a sharing society—a society in which all share in responsibility, controls, rights, and benefits. Not in harmony with such a society is a policy of exploiting workers for gain, then unceremoniously setting them adrift when the exploitation is no longer profitable. Neither are the ideals of democracy satisfied when "relief" is accorded to the unemployed. The "reliefer" knows full well that he is not

[67] "The Way to Industrial Peace. II. Citizenship in the Plant," *Harper's Magazine,* Vol. 193 (December, 1946), pp. 517–518.
[68] *The New York Times Magazine* (March 6, 1938), p. 21.

a member of society, but only its ward. The torch bearers of democracy in America are bent upon such reconstruction of occupational life that we shall never again witness the humiliation of millions of our citizens as in the '30s. Can this be done within the framework of a society which operates on the principle of private gain? The following divisions of this section will offer some evidence in answer to this question.

Some Examples of Occupational Reconstruction.

The experimentation with the democratization of industry which was carried on a number of years ago in the Columbia Conserve Company of Indianapolis[69] is an example of the rebuilding of occupations in accordance with democratic specifications. Under the leadership of William P. Hapgood, head of the business, an advisory council was first established to participate in management. The council consisted of three representatives of the owners and seven of the workers. Encouraged by Hapgood, the workers assumed a more and more active role in the management of the business, and gradually a number of innovations were introduced. The time clock was abolished and so were wages, for all regular workers were put on a salary basis. These steps were revolutionary. Time-honored practice has held manual workers to an hourly or daily wage, with deductions for any time lost, as evidenced by the time card. Salaries are the monthly payment of white-collar workers; they do not punch a time clock, and if they miss an hour or a day, salary deductions are seldom imposed. The wiping out of this discrimination against one class of workers greatly improved the status of their jobs. The distinction between white-collar and manual workers was further eradicated by the adoption of a policy that when work was slack in one department, the workers should lend a hand in departments that were overburdened. Practically, this meant that in the heavy rush of the canning season white-collar workers went out to the kitchen and the packing rooms to help out wherever they could. A few of the office people couldn't "take it" and quit, but the practice became established and morale rose with the acceptance of the idea that the workers were one big family. Space cannot here be taken to recount the story of financial success, the profits in which the workers shared, and the provision which Hapgood made for the employees to come into ownership of the business.

Colorado had for many years been a bloody battleground for coal miners and coal operators when Josephine Roche came into control of the Rocky Mountain Fuel Company in 1927. She found the sawed-off shotguns, the tear-gas bombs, and the other paraphernalia of industrial warfare in the Company's offices, as well as the evidences of heavy expenditures for detectives and mine guards. Having ideas radically different from other operators', Miss Roche invited her employees to organize locals of the

[69] Described in Devere Allen, *Adventurous Americans* (New York, Farrar & Rinehart, 1932), pp. 217–232.

United Mine Workers and to enter into collective bargaining with the Company. The articles of agreement which were signed were introduced with a statement of purpose which breathed the spirit of co-operation and mutual respect between management and labor. Through their committees on audit, sales, production, grievances, and personnel the miners participated in the management of the mines. Productivity per man improved notably and was reflected in the pay envelope. Turnover almost disappeared. When unfair competition resulted in a drastic reduction in the selling price of coal, the miners themselves met the emergency by lending, without interest, half their wages to the Company for a period of several months. Thus, one of the humbler occupations became a road to self-realization for Miss Roche's miners because they were not exploited for gain but were *participants in an enterprise.*[70]

Of many other examples of large industrial organizations whose employees have found justice, status, and security in their jobs, mention may be made of the Standard Oil Company of New Jersey, the American Rolling Mill Company, and the Pacific pulp and paper industry. "Thirty Years of Labor Peace" is the title under which *Fortune* for November, 1946, told the story of Standard Oil of New Jersey. It is an account of plant unions, of adequate plans for security for the workers, of steady employment, of confidence and good will between top management and workers. Close co-operation between employees and executives of the American Rolling Mill Company has been a characteristic of that organization since its founding just after the turn of the century. It was the first steel company to put its employees under group insurance, first to adopt the eight-hour day, and it pioneered in granting "separation allowances" to men displaced by machines. An adequate system of employee respresentation has assured prompt attention to grievances. As regards the Pacific coast pulp and paper industry,

Joint responsibility for all contract matters is the central plank on which this industry has built a structure of exceptionally good industrial relations . . . there are joint committees to handle rules, firing, grievances, and promotions. . . . Wage differentials are worked out by a joint management-union job analysis board for the whole industry. . . . grievances must be settled immediately. . . . This provision forces managements to take grievances as seriously as the worker does.[71]

In the men's and women's clothing industries the measurable reconstruction of occupations has been forced by two strong unions—the Amalgamated Clothing Workers and the International Ladies' Garment Workers Union. The conditions of degradation and vicious exploitation under which these workers formerly lived have been replaced by a respectable status char-

[70] Mary Van Kleeck, *Miners and Management* (New York, Russell Sage Foundation, 1934).

[71] Peter Drucker, "The Way to Industrial Peace. I. Why Men Strike," *Harper's Magazine,* Vol. 193 (November, 1946), pp. 388–389.

acterized by good wages, union-established educational programs and recreational facilities, financial and technical assistance to employers, and
generally stabilized employment.[72]

In the search for security, workers look for jobs that are characterized by
steady employment and steady income. The seasonal layoff—of more or
less indefinite duration—is the curse of many occupations. Labor leaders
and citizens with high interest in social and economic justice are insisting
that socially serviceable occupations should not be so characterized. The
remedy they seek is the guaranteed annual wage. A decade ago there were
a few scattered examples of this practice, the best known employers being
the George A. Hormel Company, the Nunn-Bush Shoe Company, and
Proctor and Gamble.[73] The recent winning of such contracts by the United
Automobile Workers presages extensive adoption of this plan for assured
yearly income. Members of the teaching profession, accustomed to the
guaranteed annual wage, should be able to appreciate the improved status
which such a feature contributes to an occupation.

Most of these examples of occupational reconstruction have represented
the enlightened attitude of some employer, frequently combined with genuine humanitarianism. Can we depend upon the spread of such enlightenment and such humane impulses eventually to make all occupations sufficiently attractive so that they will be voluntarily chosen by the right
numbers of qualified people? It seems doubtful, considering the fundamentals
of our social and economic structure as set forth in this chapter. The examples, however, are highly suggestive for collective action in modifying
that structure. Such collective action we shall examine presently, but first,
the Hawthorne studies.

What the Hawthorne Studies Teach Us About Occupation

In 1924 the Western Electric Company began an experiment in industrial
engineering at its Hawthorne plant in Chicago to find out what degree of
lighting would enable workers to do the most and best work. The results appeared so contradictory that the research was pushed into other phases
of working conditions, and in 1927 a group from the Harvard Graduate
School of Business Administration took up the conduct of the research program, terminating the work in 1932.[74] The first experiment was with a group
of girls assembling telephone relays. It was carried on, in its first phase, for
more than a year and a half through a dozen periods of from four to twelve
weeks each, the periods presenting a variety in working conditions, such as

[72] Fortune (November, 1946), tells the story of the International Ladies' Garment
Workers Union.

[73] Jack Chernick and George C. Hellickson, Guaranteed Annual Wages (Minneapolis, University of Minnesota Press, 1945).

[74] The most complete report on this research program is Roethlisberger and Dickson, op. cit.

rest pauses, longer and shorter hours, a hot snack at company expense in mid-forenoon, Saturday off, and so on. Similar experimentation was carried on with a group of girls in the mica-splitting room. A third study was the observation, for six months, of a group of men engaged in bank wiring under standard conditions. A fourth project was the holding of interviews with 21,000 workers under conditions which permitted completest release of thought and feeling.

From all of these studies it became apparent that physical conditions were of far less importance than morale in the determination of production. Morale rose when the group participated in planning their conditions of work, when the working atmosphere was friendly rather than autocratic, and when the group developed a team-consciousness. Morale was improved by variety in work; it was higher under group incentives than under individual rewards; it was built more easily in groups which enjoyed being together socially than in groups too divergent in age.

What impressed management most . . . were the stores of latent energy and productive co-operation which clearly could be obtained from its working force under the right conditions. And among the factors making for these conditions the attitudes of the employees stood out as being of predominant importance.[75]

That satisfactory social living in the work situation means much to the worker is a deduction to be drawn frequently from the pages of this report. Plenty of evidence pointed to the need for taking into account the employee as a social person rather than as one who acts entirely from economic motives.

The value of the Hawthorne studies lies in the use of scientific method, rather than opinion and uncontrolled observation for establishing those characteristics considered desirable in an occupation. The analysis of job satisfactions and dissatisfactions, of the motives and feelings of individuals and groups, and of the elements of status, contributes a realistic picture full of meaning for the work of refashioning occupations.

Occupational Reconstruction by Collective Action Through Government

Edward Bellamy, in explaining how the distribution of workers was accomplished in his Utopia, has Dr. Leete, citizen of 2000 A.D., conversing as follows with Julian West, recently aroused from his 113-year-long trance:[76]

". . . the principle on which our industrial army is organized is that a man's natural endowments, mental and physical, determine what he can work at most

[75] *Ibid.*, p. 185.
[76] *Op. cit.*, pp. 70–71.

profitably to the nation and most satisfactorily to himself. While the obligation to service in some form is not to be evaded, voluntary election, subject only to necessary regulation, is depended on to determine the particular sort of service every man is to render. As an individual's satisfaction during his term of service depends on his having an occupation to his taste, parents and teachers watch from early years for indications of special aptitudes in children. . . ."

"Surely," I said, "it can hardly be that the number of volunteers for any trade is exactly the number needed in that trade. It must be generally either under or over the demand."

"The supply of volunteers is always expected to fully equal the demand," replied Dr. Leete. ". . . It is the business of the administration to seek constantly to equalize the attractions of the trades, so far as the conditions of labor in them are concerned, so that all trades shall be equally attractive to persons having natural tastes for them. . . ."

What progress, if any, are we making toward Bellamy's ideal? To what extent is government assuming the role which he predicates for it? While space does not permit an adequate answer to these questions, brief attention should be given to evidence that with increasing frequency people are acting collectively through government to see that essential occupations do not exact social or economic deprivation on the part of the workers engaged in them. Exhortation to employers is not enough. Appeals to the altruism of those private individuals who control jobs may not be heard. But government, conceived as the people's own instrument of social justice, has undoubted power to create occupational patterns.

For the marked degree to which factory occupations are today carried on in light, airy, sanitary buildings, with machinery guarded and with many other provisions for the safety, health, and comfort of the workers we can thank the legislatures and the administrative agencies of government which have built up the factory codes and enforced compliance. Socially conscious leaders see much yet to be done and are especially concerned over conditions in backward states; nevertheless factory occupations have been vastly improved by collective action through government.[77]

Workmen's compensation acts, generally adopted since 1910, represent society's conviction that the occupation which injures or destroys the worker should not thereby cease to be an instrument of livelihood for the worker

[77] The following two noteworthy biographies illuminate governmental action of the past few decades in occupational reconstruction:

Woman at Work: The Autobiography of Mary Anderson, as Told to Mary N. Winslow (Minneapolis, University of Minnesota Press, 1951). Miss Anderson's career as director of the Women's Bureau of the United States Department of Labor for twenty-five years encompassed a period of rapid evolution in vocational life.

Impatient Crusader, by Josephine Goldmark (Chicago, University of Illinois Press, 1953), is a biography of Florence Kelley, forceful champion of governmental action for the protection of women and children workers, her career spanning the four decades from 1890 to 1930.

and his dependents. The ruthless exploitation which formerly left the victims of industrial accidents to the mercies of their own rugged individualism was held to be intolerable.

Noteworthy legislation in the reconstruction of occupations has often had its origin in some disastrous event which punishes the social conscience until corrective action is taken. It was the Triangle fire in New York in 1911 which furnished the impetus to improve factory occupations. So the depression of the '30s stimulated the enactment of a series of measures which have contributed new respectability to many occupations. That women should be engaged in making shirts in a Pennsylvania shirt factory for $2.00 a week and paying for their own ice water, was a state of occupational degradation abhorrent to the American conscience. The story of such conditions among essential workers inspired the National Industrial Recovery Act, later declared unconstitutional but largely replaced as far as labor is concerned by the Fair Labor Standards Act. Already mentioned in this chapter, this law protects millions of workers by establishing minimum wages and maximum hours. It is a significant step toward the assurance of a decent way of life in connection with an occupation. It sets limits upon the exploitation of labor. Another law, the National Labor Relations Act, was enacted to strengthen the worker in bargaining with the employer for the sale of his labor, by making collective bargaining legal and compelling employers and unions alike to accept it as the method for settling their differences.[78] Undoubtedly this measure was passed because of the ruthless killing of workers in the Memorial Day incident at the Republic Steel Works in Chicago and because of other evidence of physical intimidation of workers. It has served greatly to improve the status of many of those occupations in which the worker is a hireling.[79] The Social Security Act of 1935, by providing unem-

[78] Operation of this law in the reconstruction of occupational life is significantly described in *Causes of Industrial Peace under Collective Bargaining*, edited by Clinton S. Golden and Virginia D. Parker (New York, Harper, 1955).

[79] The measures taken in the Roosevelt administration have not resolved the industrial conflict. Rather, their net effect has been to strengthen one party to the conflict. The physical goods essential to our lives seem often to be produced as a mere incident to that conflict. As society becomes increasingly interdependent, and as capital and labor both increase their monopolistic power, the position of the public becomes increasingly precarious. The bitter struggles of the contending groups threaten the national economy with collapse whenever the production of some basic commodity such as coal or steel is thereby stopped. Local struggles which stop the production or flow of goods and services frequently cost the by-standing public millions and cause intolerable inconvenience. As this development of society becomes more clear—and more menacing—it seems likely that some new definitions will have to be created. A job will have to be conceived as a responsibility, not just a right, and the ownership of productive property will have to be regarded as the holding of a public trust. Strikes by either labor or capital will be considered as blows at the public and violative of the social function the offending party is charged with performing. Occupation, then, whether of manager or of worker, will first be defined as it always should have been, namely, as social function.

ployment insurance and old age and survivor benefits in industry and commerce, has gone far toward giving occupations the characteristic of security, something which economic individualism could not do.[80]

Agricultural occupations also have benefited by governmental action. The Agricultural Adjustment Act of 1933, overthrown by the Supreme Court in 1936, was a determined effort to rescue farming from the deplorable state to which it had been reduced, not merely by the 1929 economic crash but also by its own depression that had started in 1921. The Soil Conservation Act and the Farm Security Administration, as also the provisions for governmental support of the prices of farm products, were established for the same purpose. Some steps have been taken to improve the way of life of migrant farm workers by providing camps for them and employment information to give intelligent direction to their migrations. However, a million of these necessary workers still exist in such a state of extreme deprivation that their occupation cannot come within the purview of vocational guidance. Another agency, created by the national government, which is making farming occupations and farm life very different from the drab, harsh existence portrayed by Hamlin Garland, in his *Son of the Middle Border,* is the Rural Electrification Administration.

If we seem in these last paragraphs to be merely recounting events of recent American history, it is because these events should be looked upon as significant for the performance of the guidance function. These examples of collective action in the reconstruction of occupational life, together with the examples of individual action related in the first part of this section, suggest progress from the open-class society toward cultural democracy; they suggest the possibilities of social control to offset and restrain laissez-faire and the profits motive; they suggest growth in our understanding of the criteria of a desirable vocation.

Counselors are inevitably humanitarians. It is in the very nature of their function that they should be. The purpose of this chapter is to help them to see beyond the immediate counselee to whom they are ministering, to the world for which they are counseling him, and then to employ their humanitarianism on a broader scale in the rectification of conditions now facing their clients. The ideal of guidance and our obligation to *all* youth compel us to understand the social forces, trends, institutions, and attitudes in which we work, to know the realities, favorable and unfavorable, and to discharge our guardianship in the light of such intelligence.

[80] A summary of many changes in occupational life appeared in a special section of the *Monthly Labor Review,* Vol. 71 (July, 1950), under the title "Fifty Years' Progress of American Labor."

Several of the "selected references" at the end of this chapter have not been drawn upon directly for the chapter but are listed because they reflect the growth in recognition of the human relations factor in industry; thus they illuminate the current reconstruction of occupational life.

QUESTIONS, PROBLEMS, AND INVESTIGATIONS

1. Make a study of the powers, organization, and activities of the department of labor or industrial commission in your state. Survey the publications which it has issued. Compare it with the criteria for such an agency as you may find them in a political science textbook on state government.

2. Canvass the publications of the Women's Bureau of the United States Department of Labor. What light do they throw on the ascribed status of women?

3. Conduct a follow-up study of the pupils who graduated from high school last year. Make the study on whatever scale you are able and especially for the purpose of ascertaining their present occupations and wages. Look up Prudence Bostwick's article, cited in this chapter, as a pattern to follow.

4. Survey those members of a ninth-grade class who stand in the upper quarter in scholarship to ascertain as well as possible the degrees to which their families can assist them in getting college education.

5. Look up the literature on occupations in the field of household service. What steps are being taken or recommended for the raising of their social status?

6. Construct a ladder for department-store occupations (or any other broad field which appeals to you), showing the number of workers at each level and ascertaining their salaries as best you can.

7. Analyze a junior high school reading list for items which are notably individual success stories.

8. Study the problem of incentives. What are the present prevailing incentives to work? Criticize. Can other and sounder incentives be found?

9. Read Edward Bellamy's *Looking Backward*. How did he meet the problems raised in this chapter?

10. Read Marquis Childs' *Sweden, the Middle Way*. What patterns do you find which are useful for the guidance of American social evolution?

SELECTED REFERENCES

ALLEN, Devere, ed., *Adventurous Americans* (New York, Farrar & Rinehart, 1932).

BEARD, Charles A., and BEARD, Mary R., *The American Spirit* (New York, Macmillan, 1942).

BELLAMY, Edward, *Looking Backward* (Boston, Houghton Mifflin, 1888). (Reprinted, Cleveland, The World Publishing Co., 1945.)

BOSTWICK, Prudence, "They Did Not Go To College," *Educational Research Bulletin* (Ohio State University), Vol. XVIII (September 13, 1939), pp. 147–162.

CAPLOW, Theodore, *The Sociology of Work* (Minneapolis, University of Minnesota Press, 1954).

COUNTS, George S., *The American Road to Culture* (New York, Day, 1930).

———, "The Social Status of Occupations: A Problem in Vocational Guidance," *School Review*, Vol. XXXIII (January, 1925), pp. 16–27.

DAVIDSON, P. E., ANDERSON, H. D., and SCHLAUDEMAN, K. W., *Occupational Mobility in an American Community* (Stanford, Cal., Stanford University Press, 1937).

DAVIS, Jerome, *Capitalism and Its Culture* (New York, Farrar & Rinehart, 1935).

DEEG, Maethel E., and PATERSON, Donald G., "Changes in Social Status of Occupations," *Occupations,* Vol. XXV (January, 1947), pp. 205–208.

DEWEY, John, *Individualism Old and New* (New York, Minton, Balch, 1930).

DEWEY, John, and CHILDS, John L., "The Social-Economic Situation and Education," Chapter II in W. H. Kilpatrick, ed., *The Educational Frontier,* Yearbook Number XXI of the National Society of College Teachers of Education (Chicago, University of Chicago Press, 1933).

DIX, Lester, "The School Counselor at Work on Occupational Discrimination," *Occupations,* Vol. XXIV (February, 1946), pp. 261–265.

DOS PASSOS, John, *State of the Nation* (Boston, Houghton Mifflin, 1944).

DRUCKER, Peter, *Concept of the Corporation* (New York, Day, 1946).

————, "The Way to Industrial Peace. I. Why Men Strike; II. Citizenship in the Plant; III. Can We Get Around the Roadblocks?" *Harper's Magazine,* Vol. 193 (November and December, 1946), pp. 387–395, 511–520, and Vol. 194 (January, 1947), pp. 85–92.

A Fifth Avenue Buyer, "Tell the Girls the Truth," *Harper's Magazine,* Vol. 174 (January, 1937), pp. 203–207.

"50 Years' Progress of American Labor," *Monthly Labor Review,* Vol. 71 (July, 1950), pp. 3–103.

FINNEY, Ross L., *A Sociological Philosophy of Education* (New York, Macmillan, 1929).

GARDNER, Burleigh B., *Human Relations in Industry* (Chicago, Richard D. Irwin, Inc., 1945).

GOETSCH, Helen B., *Parental Income and College Opportunities* (New York, Teachers College Contributions to Education, No. 795, 1940).

GOLDEN, Clinton S., and PARKER, Virginia D., eds., *Causes of Industrial Peace under Collective Bargaining* (New York, Harper, 1955).

HOPE, John, II, "The Employment of Negroes in the United States by Major Occupation and Industry," *Journal of Negro Education,* Vol. XXII (Summer, 1953), pp. 307–321.

HOPPOCK, Robert, *Job Satisfaction* (New York, Harper, 1935).

KELLER, Franklin J., ed., "Vocational Guidance and Education for Negroes," *Occupations,* Vol. XIV (March, 1936), pp. 485–576.

LEWISOHN, Sam A., *Human Leadership in Industry: The Challenge of Tomorrow* (New York, Harper, 1945).

LYND, Robert S., and LYND, Helen Merrell, *Middletown* (New York, Harcourt, Brace, 1929), Chs. IV–VIII.

————, and ————, *Middletown in Transition* (New York, Harcourt, Brace, 1937), Chap. II.

MAY, Mark A., "The Dilemma of Youth," *Progressive Education,* Vol. XII (January, 1935), pp. 5–11.

NIETZ, John A., "The Depression and the Social Status of Occupations," *Elementary School Journal,* Vol. XXXV (February, 1935), pp. 454–461.

OVERSTREET, Harry, *We Move in New Directions* (New York, Norton, 1933).

REYNOLDS, Lloyd G., and SHISTER, Joseph, *Job Horizons: A Study of Job Satisfaction and Labor Mobility* (New York, Harper, 1949).

ROETHLISBERGER, F. J., and DICKSON, W. J., *Management and the Worker* (Cambridge, Mass., Harvard University Press, 1939).

STEVENS, Raymond B., "Experience of High-School Pupils after Graduation," *School Review,* Vol. L (January, 1942), pp. 24–31.

TAWNEY, R.H., *The Acquisitive Society* (New York, Holt, 1920).

THOMAS, Lawrence, *The Occupational Structure and Education* (Englewood Cliffs, N.J., Prentice-Hall, 1956), Chs. 8, 9, 10.

TUGWELL, Rexford G., *The Industrial Discipline and the Governmental Arts* (New York, Columbia University Press, 1933).

WALKER, Charles R., *Steeltown* (New York, Harper, 1950).

WALKER, Charles R., and GUEST, Robert H., *The Man on the Assembly Line* (Cambridge, Mass., *Harvard University Press*, 1952).

WARE, Caroline, and MEANS, Gardiner C., *The Modern Economy in Action* (New York, Harcourt, Brace, 1936).

WARNER, W. Lloyd, and Low, J. O., *The Social System of the Modern Factory* (New Haven, Yale University Press, 1946).

WATSON, Goodwin, "The Surprising Discovery of Morale," *Progressive Education,* Vol. XIX (January, 1942), pp. 33–41.

WELLS, H. G., *The Work, Wealth, and Happiness of Mankind.* 2 vol. (New York, Doubleday, Doran, & Co., 1931).

WHYTE, William F., *Pattern for Industrial Peace* (New York, Harper, 1951).

———, ed., *Industry and Society* (New York, McGraw-Hill, 1946).

WILLIAMS, Whiting, *Mainsprings of Men* (New York, Scribner's, 1925).

CHAPTER 3

The Educational Scene in Which

Guidance Operates

WHILE GUIDANCE IS BEING PERFORMED by agencies other than the school, it is obvious that the school is the institution predominantly charged with the function. It is, then, the school which largely conditions the exercise of guidance. Not only is this true for the pupils who are being guided while in school or college, but also for those adults who have been molded by the school before they seek the ministrations of non-school guidance agencies. It is therefore particularly appropriate to this exposition that educational institutions, philosophies (actual and ideal), practices, and personnel be examined with a view to understanding the educational climate in which guidance is being carried on. Does the school constitute an environment which is in harmony with the fundamental purposes of guidance? Does the life and work of the school contribute to or detract from the smooth, efficient performance of guidance?

Superficially, one might ask, Why raise these questions? Is not the school dedicated to the highest good of the pupils and of society? Analysis will demonstrate, however, that the school provides something less than a perfect channel for guidance. Guidance workers must know those imperfections and work for their removal.

In the characterizations which follow, no universality of application can be claimed. The schools of America vary widely and for reasons well known. Some are narrow and tradition bound; others have responded to modern conceptions of childhood and of educational purposes; the great mass of them are changing slowly and unevenly. In recent years the schools have been the object of heated attack and warm defense, of evaluations which are sometimes ill-founded and ill-tempered, sometimes sound and constructive. From the agitation and debate, stronger schools may well emerge, but sweeping conclusions about the educational scene are difficult to formulate.

THE SCHOOL PREPARES FOR THE SOCIETY OF OPEN CLASSES AND ECONOMIC INDIVIDUALISM

Education an Instrument of Personal Advancement

Inevitably the educational system must reflect the prevailing conception of society. The American competitive order, with its "ladders" from humble, underprivileged social stations to the richer, fuller life, not only condones, but demands, the use of education to aid individuals in improving their status. Finney says,[1]

It is probably safe to assert that [the prevalent ambition to rise in the social scale] is the objective which motivates ninety per cent of the registrants in American high schools and colleges. On the upper social levels advanced schooling is a conventional necessity of the class; among the middle classes, especially in the absence of heritable wealth, it is regarded as the most easily accessible social ladder available, if not the only one. A high school or college education is thought of as a sort of social fulcrum on which one can rest the lever of personal effort; with that fulcrum one's chances of rising in life are supposed to be greatly enhanced. And by the poor, education is regarded as the only means of escaping out of their class—except by some lucky but highly improbable chance.

Reflective of this purpose of schooling was the final message penciled by an entombed coal miner to his wife—"and give the boys a good education so they won't have to go into the mines." From their contacts with working class parents, the authors of *Middletown* reported that

For many, the magic symbol of education takes the place of any definite plans for vocation: "We want them to have a good education so they can get along easier than their father;" and, "If they don't have a good education, they'll never know anything but hard work."[2]

Such expressions of simple faith in education as the means of obtaining creature-comforts, freedom from physical labor, and economic security have been supported by investigations purporting to show the dollar-and-cents value of advanced schooling. Forty years ago, A. Caswell Ellis, a professor of the philosophy of education, prepared a bulletin summarizing a number of such studies showing that every day spent in high school or college increased one's income by so many dollars and cents.[3] A positive relationship between length of school attendance and earning power was demonstrated, and the relationship was assumed to be causal, overlooking the fact that selection on the basis of native ability and social advantage determines who

[1] Ross L. Finney, *A Sociological Philosophy of Education* (New York, Macmillan, 1928), pp. 373–374.

[2] *Op. cit.*, p. 49.

[3] *The Money Value of Education,* United States Bureau of Education Bulletin, 1917, No. 22. Specific data as of the year 1949 will be found in Chapter 16, Figure 18.

shall attend higher schools—factors which also determine earning power. As Counts sees it,[4]

The point of major interest here, however, is not that the American people generally accepted the economics of this analysis, but rather that they accepted its ethics. The assumption that educational opportunities, provided at public expense, should be judged in terms of their money value to the person receiving them reveals the extent to which the new pecuniary order and the ideal of individual success have come to dominate their theory of education. . . . That public education, even at those levels where attendance is highly restricted, should be regarded essentially as an individual right can perhaps be understood only in terms of that social philosophy which teaches that the general good is best conserved by permitting and even encouraging all men to pursue their own selfish interests.

Not only parents and the public at large look to education as an instrument for personal advancement, but principals, counselors, and teachers freely employ the argument of individual economic gain to motivate pupils in their studies. They endeavor to spur the laggards to continue in school by showing them how helpless they will be in the economic race unless they get a good education. Sometimes the subjects that are intended basically to serve broad social-civic purposes are smeared over with a substantial coating of the individual-success motive to help make them palatable. For example, the English teacher: "What kind of an engineer do you want to be —the kind that is left in the ditch or the kind the boss invites home to dinner?" (In other words, if you are wise, young fellow, you'll buckle down to this English; the ability to quote Shakespeare has value in the labor market that you can't afford to overlook.) The history teacher must feel the necessity for using similar tactics when she explains her unwilling and disinterested class to the visitor with the whispered remark that "These people are mostly commercials; they think that stenography and typewriting are the only worth-while subjects."

Closely allied to the vocational motive because it contributes in another sense to personal advancement, is the motive of social prestige. Unquestionably, such value attaches to college education, and in some minds it is a most important consideration. To be admitted to the society of the "right" people gives a much coveted status. Although high-school attendance and graduation do not carry the social prestige of the former years when few reached such educational levels, the social events and academic ceremonies of the senior year afford a prideful experience to the masses of the people. Whatever may be the modifications in the student's behavior because of the school experience, they are likely to figure as of small consequence when compared with the social distinction that high-school graduation brings. Social prestige not only serves as a motive impelling persistence in school

---

[4] George S. Counts, *The American Road to Culture* (New York, Day, 1930), pp. 68–69.

until high-school graduation, but it is also a factor in the relatively large enrollments in the college-preparatory curriculum. Many pupils pursue that curriculum with no intention of going to college, and one of the reasons is that they are thus enabled to associate with the "right" people.

Intrinsic Motivation Obstructed

With education so committed to the service of the concept of a progressive improvement of status—from year to year, from decade to decade, and from generation to generation—we have pupils engaging in their educational activity under the impulse of a motivation which is alien to that activity. They are not powered by impulses which are inherent in and essential to the thing they are doing. Such a hiatus between purpose and activity is disorganizing and unhealthful. If teachers are insensitive to the unsoundness of such a cleavage, and if they openly encourage such extraneous motivation, they obviously fail at the most critical point in the educative process. For no function of the teacher is clearer than that of stimulating his pupils to engage in an activity with which they can identify themselves and which they pursue with oneness of mind and emotion.

Attempting to approximate the truth of the situation, we may doubtless venture the view that most teachers condemn the extraneous motivation which stems from the desire to extract a social-prestige value from education. As regards the disposition to employ education as an instrument for personal advancement toward a preferred position in the competitive order, teachers presumably reflect the confusion inherent in the generally possessed assumption that if every person seeks his own advantage the social good will be served. Some teachers there are who lean so heavily upon the extraneous motivation we have described that they willingly put pupils through stereotyped and meaningless activities. Some teachers, on the other hand, convinced that the soundest learning is achieved through intrinsic motivation, establish learning situations which afford their pupils such present satisfactions that their more remote and unrelated motivations recede over the horizon of consciousness. May the teachers of this latter type increase!

SUBJECT-CENTERED VS. CHILD-CENTERED

Is School Life and Work Real, Functional, and in Satisfaction of Pupil Purposes?

The main educational battles of the twentieth century have been fought over the concepts and practices which the title of this section denotes and connotes. While the struggle continues, it can certainly be said that whereas the dawn of the century found education highly subject-centered, the half-way mark finds educational theory markedly child-centered and educational practice moving hesitantly in the same direction. Currently accepted ideas about the nature of educational objectives and of educative experience are bringing about the use of activities which fulfill pupil purposes; they are helping to displace teacher-dominated textbook lessons which assume education to be the memorization of a body of subject matter.

Inevitably, those who have promoted this educational revolution aroused opposition, not only because their activity was disturbing, but because some honest and competent thinkers felt that there were desirable elements in the older education of which the reformers were not sufficiently appreciative. Accordingly, to check the Progressive Education Association, chief organization of the apostles of reform, Bagley named and led an opposition group, the Essentialists. In the '30s these two bodies engaged in some warm discussions. Their relative quiescence in recent years prompted Buswell to propose that it is time to establish unity in the profession so that the drive for educational improvement may be more effective. Buswell stated the platform on which he thought harmony might be achieved, as follows:[5]

From both the divergent groups in education there have been gains which any sensible view must recognize. Educators, by and large, regardless of their particular school of thought, now accept the view that a child is an organic whole; that he learns what he does and by doing it; that motivation and purpose are essential to learning; that education must have meaning and that real problems are more stimulating than artificial ones; that there is a psychological order and sequence in the learning process which is just as valid as any logical order of subject matter; that personality development is an obligation of education; and that, in general, the activity of the learner must be free rather than dictated by authoritarian control.

On the other hand, there is likewise a recognition that education must have a content; that racial experience is a solid reality that must be interpreted and transmitted to each new generation; that whatever content there is must be organized in some coherent fashion if it is to be learned with readiness; that there is a valid logical organization of content which is just as real as the psychological organization in terms of the learner; that freedom can be carried to excess; and that there is a discipline of generalized habits which is not likely to be achieved by undirected pupil effort.

This statement has value here as a summary of criteria of educational experience and activity by which the counselor may measure his school. Coming from one who is a scientific student of education and not identified with either Essentialists or Progressives, the statement may well serve as a pronouncement of educational theory generally acceptable. The actualities of the educational scene form a considerable contrast with Buswell's platform, if we may judge by Spaulding's summary of his investigation of secondary education in New York State, three paragraphs of which read as follows:[6]

[5] G. T. Buswell, "Educational Change and Opportunity" (editorial), *Elementary School Journal,* Vol. XLVII (January, 1946), p. 241.

[6] Reprinted by permission from *High School and Life* (The Regents' Inquiry), by Francis T. Spaulding, Copyrighted, 1938, by McGraw-Hill Book Co., Inc., p. 252.

The average New York State high school is now geared to do one kind of job, and only one. It takes the boys and girls who are fed into it from the elementary schools, lets them sort themselves crudely according to their ability to master academic subject matter, and starts them on a four-year round of drill and memorization. Some pupils rebel against that round, or cannot keep up with its academic demands. These the school lets go as soon as the law will allow and as soon as they take it into their heads to leave. The rest it prepares for final examinations.

The examinations have little to do—directly, at least—with the abilities which boys and girls need outside of school. For the most part they consist of tests of the amount of academic subject matter which pupils remember well enough to use in response to written questions. Nor does the school's method of preparing for the examinations have any direct relation to out-of-school matters. The school does not, in fact, know much about its pupils' out-of-school concerns, nor does it look to see what happens to most of its leaving pupils after they have ended their school work.

Thus the average high school provides an educational mechanism which is unadjustable and relentless. The school does its work almost wholly within its own four walls. It fixes its attention on a kind of performance which has little meaning except in academic circles, and which is tested without reference to out-of-school standards.

Spaulding attributed this depressing state in part to certain outside factors, such as the system of Regents' Examinations, but his findings are nevertheless somewhat shocking, especially in view of the common judgment that New York has one of the best of state school systems.

Although Spaulding's report depicted the conditions of twenty years ago, it may well be doubted if great changes in practice have occurred in the intervening period. Paul Mort and his associates have been investigating the rate and character of educational change and have found two periods of protracted lag, as follows: (1) between the recognition of a need and the invention and introduction of a means of meeting that need, (2) between the first introduction of the new practice and its general diffusion throughout the country. One of these researches pertained to the rate of change in the laboratory schools of state teachers colleges and brought the author to the conclusion that almost fifty years is required for general acceptance of a new practice.[7]

More recently, in an independent study, Hooker and Lindvall reported an analysis of practice in 318 classrooms and found the major activities to be oral quiz by the teacher, teacher lecturing, pupils reading text at their seats, class engaged in discussion.[8] If the medical profession changed practice no faster than the teaching profession, we'd all be dead now!

[7] Thomas M. Barrington, *The Introduction of Selected Educational Practices into Teachers Colleges and Their Laboratory Schools* (New York, Teachers College, Columbia University, 1953).

[8] C. P. Hooker and C. M. Lindvall, "The Student's Day Hasn't Changed Much—or Enough, Either," *Nation's Schools,* Vol. 59 (June, 1957), pp. 48–49.

Another teacher, in 1946, stated with force, cogency, and some evidence of frustration the reasons she saw for the gap between theory and practice. Essentially her argument is that the conditions under which teachers typically work are such as to block the employment of progressive practices. Large classes and many of them, marked individual differences among pupils, inadequate equipment, rigidly prescribed curriculums—these are the chief conditions which she named as balking the teacher in applying the principles she has been taught.[9]

Implications for Guidance

If the school environment is artificial, with the pupil forced to find his real life outside, if the activities required of the pupil do not bear on the purposes which are meaningful to him—in short, if such conditions prevail as Spaulding reported from New York—a psychic atmosphere is created which is unfavorable to the integration characteristic of well-adjusted personalities. Problems arise. Pupils express rebellion or boredom or seek the earliest opportunity for withdrawal. Thus the guidance workers have to cope with adjustive problems created right in the school.

Just as it was shown in the last chapter that the morale of workers improved when they grasped the purpose of their work, when they participated in planning it, and when they found satisfactory social living on the job, so a parallel course is required with pupils if we wish to obtain the same results. Problems of adjustment will be less prevalent if teachers recognize and act on the principle that pupils need realistic experience instead of verbalisms, if pupils' interests are accepted as a central consideration in determining learning activity, and if all school workers will cease to worship traditional, organized subject matter as such.

THE COMPETITIVE INDIVIDUALISM OF THE BIG SOCIETY HAS ITS REPLICA IN THE SCHOOL SOCIETY

The Marking System

The prevalent system of evaluation of the progress of pupils reflects in noteworthy degree the spirit of competition characterizing the adult economic society. Just as adults compete for economic prizes, pupils are stimulated to strive against each other for academic rewards. They are expected to attempt to outdo each other in the retention of subject matter, and the system of credits and marks is so central in their consciousness that it dominates their thought and conversation to the nearly total exclusion of any intrinsic interest in subject matter.

Most schools follow one of two marking systems. The older one, gradually

[9] Evelyn Gibbs Rogers, "Progressive Ideals in Practice: the Teacher's Dilemma," *Educational Research Bulletin* (Ohio State University), Vol. XXV (October 16, 1946), pp. 178–182.

declining in popularity, may be called the absolute system, because each pupil is measured in terms of the percentage which he has earned of an absolute established by the teacher or some outside examiner, such as the Board of Regents. Obviously, the determination of the absolute is a very subjective matter, depending as it does on the predilection of the measurer to be lenient or exacting, simple or complex, in the tasks he assigns or the questions he asks. Pupils are not required to reach the absolute, but must attain a specified minimum percentage—most commonly 70—to be considered as having earned credit for the course. Thus, education is defined as partial learning or the partial memorization of an assorted body of subject matter. Under the exceptional teacher, who looks for actual modification in his pupils' behavior, the pupil's mark might mean that he had attained a certain level in a skill or that he had acquired a certain percentage of the abilities which the teacher considered to be the goals of the course.

The second marking system—one which seems to be winning adherents—is the relative system. It derives its name from the fact that pupils' accomplishments are compared one with another, irrespective of any absolute or possible score. More than the absolute system, it puts pupils in competition with each other to determine which one stands first, which one second, which one last. With it is usually combined the idea of the normal curve of distribution and a five-point scale, teachers being expected to award a mark of A to the highest five to ten per cent and the mark of F to a similar per cent. Whether the class as a whole does well or poorly with reference to a possible score does not matter; it is their standing in relation to each other which counts. Presumably this system derived its impetus largely from the intelligence-testing movement. Educators have assumed that good educational measurement should have the same characteristics as the authorities on intelligence measurement have required for an intelligence test, namely, enough easy items so that the slowest minds can register on it, enough hard items so that the most brilliant cannot make a perfect score, and such a "spread" of a group as fairly to distinguish the members from each other.

Theoretically, the relative system is a most potent stimulator for the competitive impulses. It is, for some pupils; and some of its outcomes will be reported in the final section of this chapter. But for others it has no terrors or attractions. They are represented by the boy who surveyed his report card with satisfaction, saying, "The grades aren't so low that Dad will cut off my allowance, and not high enough to make me unpopular with my friends—a perfect report card!" Like the workers in the bank wiring room of the Hawthorne works, as reported in chapter two, this boy and his friends had an informal agreement on what constituted a fair day's work, and they declined to sacrifice friendly associations in a race for individualistic advantage. The analogy is not exact—the boys had to satisfy fathers as well as themselves!

Objections to Employment of the Competitive Motive

Educational theorists and reformers have long held that the practices which tend to throw pupils into competition with each other are inimical to sound education. The motivation is extraneous. It focuses the attention of pupils, teachers, and parents on that competition instead of on growth and the activities by which growth is accomplished. And since many forms of growth are difficult to measure or to measure with sufficient accuracy to make distinctions between pupils, the measurements are applied to content memorized, though such may have little relationship to the valid goals of the subject or curriculum. As Finney said, the system "stresses the kind of subject matter that might be called 'cramable,' "[10] no doubt particularly well illustrated in New York State, if we may judge by the quotation from Spaulding in the section immediately preceding.

Years ago Thorndike voiced the fallacy in the school's imitation of the competitive individualism existent in economic society. He said,[11]

The most frequent race in life has been to get ahead of somebody rather than to get ahead in and for itself. The common interpretation of excellence is excelling another, leaving him below or behind. Now this custom of judging by relative superiority has been carried over from the individual's struggle for advancement to the notions of the aims of public education. But it is meaningless there. It makes no difference to the world *who* is the most gifted one of ten million children—who gains most, next, third, and least. To the world the only matter of importance is that the gains should be great. The race of civilization and welfare is not run to see who can go furthest, but to make all go as far as may be.

In similar vein, but in greater length and vehemence, Morrison castigated the principle of appraisal by rank in class, saying at one point,[12]

Thus arises the stereotype of rank-in-class and the doctrine that a pupil's education is to be judged, not by his actual development, but by comparison of his deeds with those of his fellows. Thus arises, too, the self-glorification of fond parents over the competitive qualities of their offspring and the bitter disappointment of others, not in their son's failure to grow, but in his failure to surpass the neighbor's son. Thus arises the popular conception of the highly educated man as the victor in a cultural jungle.

But, if competition is the rule of life outside the school, should not the school prepare pupils realistically for the adult world by having them experience the competitive principle? The answer is that the competitive principle and the educative principle simply cannot live together. We establish schools to *develop* pupils, each one as fully as is possible. Considering the

---

[10] *Op. cit.,* p. 367.

[11] Edward L. Thorndike, *Education* (New York, Macmillan, 1914), p. 51.

[12] H. C. Morrison, *The Practice of Teaching in the Secondary School,* rev. ed. (Chicago, University of Chicago Press, 1931), p. 71.

variation in innate ability, differences in achievement will be wide. But each pupil should find satisfaction in observing the expansion of his own powers, and that should be the satisfaction of the teacher, also.

A few school systems recognize the inadequacy and inappropriateness of traditional marking systems and have developed plans for reporting the pupil's progress in terms of his capacity; for emphasizing skills, habits, understandings, and psychological goals rather than subjects; and for taking account of all phases of pupil growth—social, emotional, and physical, as well as intellectual. Characteristics of such report cards are summarized and some facsimiles are shown by Burton.[13] Among the principles of reporting at which Evans arrives as the result of his careful analysis is one entitled "Prevention of Emotional Disturbance and Disintegration," from the development of which the following statements may be extracted as of particular significance to this section:[14]

No plan of communication aimed at the advancement of the welfare of the child can tolerate any technique, device, instrument, or medium that creates negative, emotionalized attitudes toward learning or toward members of the child's social group, his teacher, his parents, his school, his home, or himself.

The principle of respect for individual personality leaves no place for comparative appraisals of which the child is made conscious. Such information should be confined to records kept in the central office and should never be given to the child. Upon request, such information should be given to the parents verbally, but even then with emphasis upon the analysis of the child's success as a whole.

Appraisals of child success should be in terms of ability of the individual child. Competition should be confined to the child's competition against his own record. . . . Any instrument based on the idea of rank in class or relative standing is an instrument for failure. In reality, only one child in a "rated" group escapes failure in some degree. When a child is doing all that the school has a reasonable right to expect of him, it is illogical to expect more. It is undesirable that the child should attempt more. No one considers an individual a failure physically when he develops into a short rather than a tall man.

Plainly enough, the marking and reporting system constitutes an important element of the educational scene in which guidance operates. When, as in most schools, it is fabricated in the image of the competitive economic order, it creates or aggravates guidance problems. Sounder practices have been suggested.

---

[13] William H. Burton, *The Guidance of Learning Activities,* 2nd ed. (New York, Appleton-Century-Crofts, 1952), Ch. 21.

See also *Records and Reports: Trends in Making and Using Them* (Washington, D.C., The Association for Childhood Education, 1942).

[14] Robert O. Evans, *Practices, Trends, and Issues in Reporting to Parents on the Welfare of the Child in School* (New York, Teachers College, Columbia University, 1938), pp. 83–85.

THE PERSONAL FACTOR IN THE EDUCATIONAL SCENE

The Teacher Is the Pre-eminent Factor

"To paraphrase a dictum of Locke's, the school that has good teachers needs little else, and the school that is without good teachers will be little better for anything else."[15] Certainly it can be said that if schools emphasize a corroding competitive relationship betwen pupils, the individual teacher must bear some responsibility for that anti-social climate. For there are teachers who play down that emphasis and obtain a considerable degree of community feeling in their classes despite a marking system based on the normal curve. Similarly, there are master teachers who see through and beyond subjects and textbooks to desirable modifications of behavior as their real goals, and who stimulate their pupils to engage in life-like experience in the attainment of those goals. That the philosophy and the professional and personal character of the individual teacher is the pre-eminent factor in the educational scene cannot be gainsaid.

Parents are conscious of the personal influence of the teacher. They desire to have persons of good character and wholesome personality presiding over the classrooms of the school. The citizenry of New York City was decidedly shocked a number of years ago when the medical examiner responsible for checking the health of the city's teachers estimated that 1,500 of the teachers were perceptibly maladjusted in their personalities. Another observer highlighted the story by asserting that one group of such teachers made their home at a sanitarium in or near the city, daily journeying from there to their schools. In the discussion of the disclosure, it was pointed out that 1,500 was was only 4 percent of the public-school teaching personnel of the city and that the corresponding percentage of the general population who were in that state of aberration but not institutionalized was about the same. Parents are sufficiently conscious, however, of the crucial position of the teacher that they are not satisfied to have teachers who are merely representative of the population at large. They desire *every* teacher to be a well-adjusted personality. And, in truth, no one can legitimately object to that criterion.

Educational literature has been enriched by the analytical testimony of pupils themselves concerning the influence of teachers. One of the most noteworthy of such studies is Hart's report[16] of the descriptions which ten thousand high-school seniors wrote of the teacher liked best and of the teacher liked least. While Hart summarized the characteristics of teachers in the order of the frequency of mention, a large number of quotations from the pupils' responses give his work the character of a moving human document

[15] B. R. Buckingham, *The Supply and Demand in Teacher Training,* p. 3. The Ohio State University Studies, Vol. II, No. 15, 1926.

[16] Frank W. Hart, *Teachers and Teaching* (New York, Macmillan, 1934).

which should be required reading for every school worker or aspirant for the teaching profession.

A psychiatrist, formerly a teacher, in discussions with delinquent boys at a training school compiled the following list of characteristics or ways of behavior of teachers which they did not like:[17]

[1] *"Hollering."* . . . "We didn't like her. She always hollered at us."

[2] *Being ridiculed*—Children keenly resent being called crazy, dumb, awkward, sleeping beauty. . . .

[3] *Ridicule of the family*—To say, "What kind of bringing up have you had?" is to reflect against the child's mother. . . . Teachers have been known to suffer physical injury from having made such comments.

[4] *Having too much expected of them.* . . .

[5] *Grudges*—Let each day have a fresh start. "I know I done wrong, but she don't need to keep bringing it up every day. It makes me mad."

[6] *Threatening*—A child quickly loses confidence in a teacher who threatens and "gets out on a limb," or makes idle threats without intending to follow through. . . .

[7] *"Talking all the time.".* . .

[8] *Criticism of other teachers.* . . . "She would always talk against other teachers even when we could hear. She wasn't so hot herself."

This investigator also compiled the following list of characteristics or ways of behavior of teachers which the boys did like:

[1] *The teacher who is for the child.* . . . "I know I'll get a square deal. Miss Smith is handling it for me."

[2] *Loyalty.* . . .

[3] *Honesty.* . . . "You can tell her. She won't let you down."

[4] *Frankness.* . . . Many times it is quite a comfort to the child to know just where he stands with the teacher.

[5] *Willingness to listen*—Each child wants and deserves a chance to tell his own story to someone who has an open mind as to what occurred. . . .

[6] *Protection of his property.* . . . We cannot teach the child to respect the property of others if we do not respect his property.

[7] *Trust*—Within reasonable limits of the child's capacity, he wants to be trusted. "I liked the probationary school. They trusted me more."

[8] *The outgoing teacher*—Children like the teacher who "does things" and tells about the places she has been. This is proof of acceptance as fellow human beings, altho it can be overdone. . . .

[9] *The teacher who isn't "snooty."* . . .

[10] *Direct evidence of being liked.* . . .

[11] *The teacher who is strict.* . . . "She is strict but she lets you tell what happened." "Gee, we don't even *want* to be bad in her class."

[17] Florence Swanson and R. L. Jenkins, "From the Other Side of the Teacher's Desk," *Journal of the National Education Association,* Vol. XXXI (October, 1942), pp. 215–216.

While these traits, good and bad, may seem obvious, they weigh heavily in establishing the character of the educational scene.

Autocratic or Democratic Relationships

Basic to the personal factor in the educational scene is whether the traits of the teacher, principal, or counselor add up to autocratic or democratic relationships with pupils. Certainly the school has been traditionally autocratic, and although verbal acceptance is being given to the proposition that a democratic school is essential to preparation for democratic living outside the school, tradition is not easily overcome. Faculties are seldom democratic; principals "run" their schools. Teachers are not accustomed to operate as legislative bodies in their schools; they have no acknowledged sphere for such action. It is not strange, then, if the spirit and method of the classroom is prevailingly authoritarian. Sometimes the authority is exercised considerately and benevolently; sometimes with an I-plan-the-work-you-do-it-or-else attitude.

In a unique attempt to discover the effects on personality and social behavior resulting from autocratic and democratic environments, three investigators some years ago experimented with groups of ten-year-old boys in artificially created social climates.[18] Twenty boys were organized in four clubs of five boys each to engage in minor handicraft activities, of which the making of masks was one. Each club spent a few weeks under a democratic, an autocratic, and a laissez-faire regime. The leaders of the clubs were men, carefully coached to play their roles in creating the contrasting social environments. Trained observers took up such positions or attitudes that the boys were either unaware of or inattentive to their presence.

No radically autocratic methods, such as threats or the instilling of fear could be used, because the participation was voluntary. The co-operation of parents and school sysems had been obtained. The autocratic leader told the boys what to do, dictated activities step by step so that the boys never knew what the next step was, and arbitrarily assigned work tasks and the members of the teams to work on them. The leader remained aloof from the group—not actively hostile, but impersonal—being personal only when he praised or criticized each boy's work.

In the democratic groups the leader made all matters of policy and program subject to group discussion and decision. The division of tasks was made by the group. The group leader was objective or "fact-minded" in his praise or criticism. He tried to be a regular group member without doing too much of the boys' work for them.

In the laissez-faire groups there was complete freedom for group or individual decision without participation by the leader. He was available to supply

[18] Kurt Lewin, Ronald Lippitt, and R. K. White, "Patterns of Aggressive Behavior in Experimentally Created Social Climates," *Journal of Social Psychology,* Vol. X (May, 1939), pp. 271–299.

materials or information when asked, but he took no part in discussions. He did not participate in or interfere with activities and commented infrequently on activities unless questioned.

The observers found that one of the five autocracies showed aggressive action, while the other four exhibited an extremely nonaggressive, apathetic pattern of behavior which was definitely attributable to the repressive influence of the autocrat. But on the days when the boys were transferred from the repressed, autocratic atmosphere to the freer atmosphere of democracy or laissez-faire they "cut loose" in an exhibition of marked aggression, an apparent demonstration of release from repression. Analysis of the language used in the groups showed 73 per cent of the language of the autocracies to be of ego-involved types—hostility, resistance, demands for attention, hostile criticism, expressions of competition—whereas the comparable percentage for the democratic groups was 31. The observers' data indicated a more marked feeling of "we-ness" in the democratic groups than in the autocratic. The quality and quantity of work done by the democratic groups was decidedly superior to that of the autocratic groups. The democracies were characterized by more smiling and joking. Observers characterized the two laissez-faire groups as dull, lifeless, submissive, apathetic, and unsmiling. Of the 20 boys, 19 said they liked their democratic leader better than their autocratic leader, and of the 10 who experienced the laissez-faire climate, 7 liked the laissez-faire leader better than their autocratic leader.

While this experiment is related as bearing on the importance of the teacher in the educational scene, it may also be taken as showing the significance of the social milieu. The same teachers created two or three contrasting social climates; studies of the results indicate either that the teachers' personalities were not the dominant factor or that the teachers were very successful in transforming their personalities.

Administrative Officers, too, Determine the Character of the Educational Scene

While this section has been devoted thus far to the teacher as the personal factor in the educational scene, brief mention should be made of the principal as obviously an important element. It may be his autocracy or democracy that largely determines the social climate of the school. His conception of that word of many meanings—discipline—may give pupils the sense of security, of justice, and of personal worth which is demanded for the sound development of their personalities; or it may breed the fears and frustrations which create maladjustments. This writer has often thought how interesting it might be to inventory the feelings of pupils as they go to the office to ask for a change of section or in answer to a summons. Do they experience sensations of fear and anxiety? Are they bristling and ready to protect themselves? Or are they calm and undisturbed, sure of a fair hearing, of a helpful attitude, and of friendly respect?

The educational scene, too, will indeed be reflective of all the other educational insights of the principal. He may be a "mechanical" principal, keeping the school in a rut of tradition for ease of administration. Or he may be creative, quick to grasp educational needs, competent in marshalling educational forces, gifted in leading teachers in the modification of curriculum and method to the end of a sounder functionality. These are factors which profoundly affect the operation of the guidance service.

SOCIAL RECREATION IN THE SCHOOL

Educational Significance

Pressey, Janney, and Kuhlen recommend that[19] "A school should have a social as well as an educational program—and with such direction that those who most lack social experience do get it." It is unfortunate that the recommendation seems to draw a contrast between social and educational programs, because clearly the reason for the recommendation is the fact of the educational value in a social program. Efficiency in a host of social relationships being the major educational objective which it is today, practical social experience is naturally demanded as a major feature of the educational program, if we believe in learning by doing.

Social experience is of many types, but this section will be confined to the consideration of social recreation, a form of educational activity on the play level. Social recreation is of vital importance in adolescent years for bringing about social and emotional maturity. Frankwood Williams pointed out that the two major problems of the adolescent are, "first, emancipation from the home, second, the establishment of hetero-sexuality. Everything in the future depends upon the success of the boy or girl in solving these two problems."[20] Thoughtful attention to the social recreation of adolescent youth is justified because of its bearing on these two major problems of maturation cited by Williams. With or without faculty sanction, encouragement, or government, the natural groupings which school associations foster seek expression in play activities. With the onset of adolescence, this recreation tends to assume adult modes and the freedom of action characteristic of adulthood, thus signifying the attempt to be rid of the parental apron strings. At the same time the character of the events shows with increasing frequency the rising tide of interest in the opposite sex, which is the essence of heterosexuality. So normal for the teen age are these manifestations that the mental hygienist regards as unhealthy and abnormal the individual who comes to the end of the teens without having evinced such tendencies.

Are school workers fostering and guiding this development? Are they as

[19] Sidney L. Pressey, J. Elliott Janney, and Raymond G. Kuhlen, *Life: A Psychological Survey* (New York, Harper, 1939), p. 305.

[20] *Adolescence—Studies in Mental Hygiene* (New York, Farrar & Rinehart, 1930), p. 102.

conscious of the goals to be attained through social recreation as they are of the goals to be attained through English composition, and of the necessity of realizing in *all* pupils the former set of goals as well as the latter? Thirty years ago the answer was No. The analysis of literature on the extracurriculum made by Koos in 1925[21] revealed no sufficient sensitivity to the possible values of social recreation. Indeed, nine of the forty writings analyzed recognized "Higher aim than sociability only" as one "principle to be observed in organizing, administering, and supervising extracurricular activities." While this principle may have been inspired by experience with high-school fraternities and sororities, which typically militate against democracy in the school, it nevertheless relegates to a secondary position the activity which is primary in its contribution to the mental hygienist's aim.

There are signs that school people have advanced in their appreciation of social recreation since 1925. For example, some joint sessions of boys' and girls' classes in physical education are held in some schools. "Co-recreation" is the name given this innovation, which is devoted to cultivation of specific techniques for establishing successful social contacts and to creating an environment which facilitates the exercise of such techniques. A program of co-recreation reaches all pupils, as strictly voluntary social recreation may not. Further evidence of appreciation of social recreation is the helpful part played by school authorities in many communities in the establishment of youth canteens during World War II.

Practices and Problems in Social Recreation

Isolated examples of school social events that have been brought to this writer's attention have frequently included discouraging news of pupil participation—important events being attended, for example, by only a third or a fourth of the pupils eligible to attend. Objective surveys of practices, however, are few and inadequate. Brown's canvass of the social activities of students at the University of Minnesota is one investigation which revealed that the glamorous campus social life was participated in by only a minority of students, that at the other extreme were many students who led very lonely lives. Her survey brought out clearly the need of some university students for an opportunity to learn such social conventions as dancing and bridge, together with informal, inexpensive opportunities for social recreation.[22]

At the high-school level, Burger[23] canvassed 6,695 pupils of the secondary schools of Erie, Pennsylvania, to obtain an inventory of their participation in school social events in a given school year. Girls averaged six or seven

[21] L. V. Koos, "Analysis of the General Literature on Extra-Curricular Activities," Chapter II of *Extra-Curricular Activities,* Part II of the Twenty-fifth Yearbook of the National Society for the Study of Education, 1926.

[22] Clara M. Brown, "A Social Activities Survey," *Journal of Higher Education,* Vol. VIII (May, 1937), pp. 257–264.

[23] Florence Burger, *Pupil Participation in School Social Events,* Ph.D. Thesis, University of Pittsburgh Library, 1944.

social events a year, boys, four or five, with the medians somewhat lower because large numbers attended none, one, or two events, while a scattering of pupils led a flourishing social life, attending as many as twenty-five functions. For example, of the 781 boys surveyed in one high school, 146 attended no social events, 123 attended one, and 118 attended two. The three categories account for practically half of the boys.

Senior high-school pupils attended more events than did those of the junior high level, but pupils in the three separate junior high schools attended notably more events than did the junior-high pupils in the three six-year schools. The latter fact suggests that the needs of pupils of Grades VII, VIII, and IX can be and are more adequately met when they are in separate junior high schools than when they are in six-year schools.

The record of the teachers in Erie was not unlike that of the students. The survey showed that 104 men teachers averaged 3.9 school social events attended; 184 women teachers averaged 4.5 events. While 4 men and 7 women reported attendance at more than 15 events, 20 men and 32 women recorded no participation in school social life.

These data from a single city school system do not afford a refined picture, but they do suggest a situation in which the social recreation of the school is viewed rather casually by the faculty, allowed to grow, like wild blackberries, without cultivation and considered as yielding a crop of no vital importance. Each reader can estimate from his own experience how representative the data are.

Hutson and Kovar[24] obtained data from 2,163 pupils of the tenth and twelfth grades in ten high schools of Western Pennsylvania, in response to a questionnaire seeking light on their problems in social recreation. One section of the inquiry invited those who had not attended school dances to state their reasons. Their answers are given in Table 5,[25] the first twelve items being responses to a check list, and items 13-22 being the summary of their free responses. A study of this table suggests that school dances pose some serious problems to pupils at the senior high level. The obstacles listed were checked or named with much greater frequency by the tenth graders than by the twelfth graders. For example, the first item was designated by 62.9 per cent of the responding sophomores and by 48.5 per cent of the responding seniors; item 6 was checked by 21.1 per cent of the sophomores and by 10.3 per cent of the seniors. The differences between the two grade groups on these two items alone suggest how social recreation in the teen age is conditioned by variations in maturity. More of the older pupils know how to dance; more of them have gained relative freedom from parental control.

Another section of the questionnaire sought to learn the degree of social

24 P. W. Hutson and Dan R. Kovar, "Some Problems of Senior High School Pupils in Their Social Recreation," *Educational Administration and Supervision,* Vol. XXVIII (October, 1942), pp. 503–519.

25 *Ibid.,* p. 507, Table I.

TABLE 5. Reasons Given for Not Attending School Dances

Reasons	Percentage of Pupils Indicating Each Reason		
	Boys (694)	Girls (676)	Total (1370)
1. I do not know how to dance.	74.1	38.5	56.5
2. I do not approve of dancing.	10.8	5.9	8.4
3. Parents object to my dancing.	5.5	10.0	7.7
4. I felt that my clothing was not good enough	8.4	12.0	10.1
5. I did not have the money.	25.4	17.9	· 21.7
6. I would be out late at night, and my parents disapprove of that.	11.4	21.3	16.3
7. Only those who are paired off with a member of the opposite sex really have a good time.	16.1	25.7	20.9
8. I would only sit or stand around and not have a good time.	36.0	30.3	33.2
9. To girls: I did not have a special boy friend to escort me.	x	41.6	20.5
10. To boys: I did not have a special girl that I wished to take.	30.4	x	15.4
11. To boys: I lack the nerve to ask a girl.	25.2	x	12.8
12. To boys: I could not take a girl because I had no good way of getting her there and back.	35.9	6.8*	21.5
13. I would be out too late at night and would be tired at school the next day.	.3	1.3	.8
14. The one with whom I should like to attend is not a member of the group permitted to attend.	.3	3.4	1.8
15. Favored partner does not dance.	.3	1.3	.8
16. Feelings of inferiority, inadequacy, of not belonging.	5.8	18.3	12.0
17. Misconduct at or after dances.	1.3	.9	1.1
18. Complaints that boys are too bashful.	2.9	1.1	2.0
19. Conflicts with gainful work.	2.2	1.1	1.7
20. Racial barrier.	.1	.9	.5
21. Health—temporary and permanent.	.7	1.0	.9
22. Miscellaneous.	3.5	2.5	3.0

* A few girls stated that lack of transportation was a reason.

poise which these pupils had acquired, by asking them such questions as, "Do you feel at ease in introducing people?" "In general, is it difficult for you to carry on a conversation with the opposite sex?" "Are you afraid lest you make a mistake at a social affair?" and "Are there some members of your class whose competency and fearlessness in social affairs make you feel inferior and inadequate?" On these questions pupils divided approximately half and half. Invited to tell freely how they had achieved the goal of social poise in situations in which they formerly felt ill at ease, about 750 pupils wrote of their experiences, a few describing how they had screwed up courage to try the new and fearsome, many attesting the value of practice, and a considerable group acknowledging various sources of influence, such as friends, relatives, books on etiquette, and club experiences. Just two pupils mentioned the example of teachers, an outcome of the inquiry which must be considered an indictment of school policy as strangely unconcerned over this vitally important phase of development.

The evidence from this survey of pupils' problems in social recreation indicated that the evening dancing party is too advanced a recreational form for large numbers of high-school pupils. It imposes barriers in the form of money costs, transportation facilities, expensive clothing, pairing, skill in dancing, and parental jitters. If social recreation is to enrich the pupil's experience in the school community in accordance with its possibilities, the schools must encourage social events which may be attended and enjoyed by all pupils, they must teach social skills and conventions, they must create an atmosphere of kindliness, thoughtfulness, and high regard, so that the clumsiest learner may feel secure in his right and opportunity to learn. If unnoticed and unguided, social recreation in the school is too often governed by the law of the jungle, with a few socially assertive pupils determining its scale, activities, and quality. Results, then, are a combination of snobbery, pecuniary exhibitionism, and undemocratic attitudes on the part of some pupils, and feelings of frustration, dejection, and inferiority on the part of others. Social recreation is truly a frontier of democracy and an aspect of school life of greater significance to the pupil and to the adult society for which he is preparing than school workers now appreciate.

MASS-PRODUCTION METHODS IN EDUCATION

Departmentalization—the Factory Principle

With their increasing size, American schools have assumed many of the aspects which characterize large business and industrial organizations—each worker (teacher) a specialist, and the pupils moving along corridors, as on a conveying belt, from specialist to specialist. Instead of making many and intimate contacts with a few pupils, the specialist makes a limited contact with many pupils—perhaps 200 for academic teachers and often much larger numbers for teachers of nonacademic subjects. Viewed from the angle of the pupil, this plan means that responsibility for his education is much divided. The assumption behind it is that education can be performed more expertly if broken down along subject matter lines. Actually, this practice enhances the tendency to focus educational energy on subjects rather than on the pupil. The loss of intimate contact between teacher and pupil was recognized as a peril thirty-five years ago and spoken of at that time as "depersonalization."

Citation of some analyses of school organizations and schedules will illuminate this aspect of the educational scene. Departmentalization has long been a characteristic of the high school, and when the junior high school was in its formative state thirty or more years ago, departmentalization was instituted in all its grades and hailed as one of the beneficent features of the new school unit. At that time this writer analyzed the teaching load of teachers in the three junior high schools of Johnstown, Pennsylvania. A summary of the essential data yielded is shown in Table 6.[26] By dividing the teachers into three groups according to their subject fields, some interesting contrasts were presented. For example, by the most common instrument for measuring teaching load—pupil-recitation hours—the teachers of academic subjects had nearly twice as heavy a load as did the teachers of Group II and a slightly heavier load than the teachers of Group III. According to the

TABLE 6. Medians of Four Distributions of Junior High School Teachers

	Group I (83 teachers of academic subjects)	Group II (37 teachers of commercial subjects, home economics, and shop)	Group III (25 teachers of penmanship, physical education, fine arts, guidance, and dramatics)
Median Number of Weekly Pupil-Recitation Hours	831.3	445.8	775.0
Median Number of Different Pupils Taught	171.3	167.5	445.0
Median Number of Pupils in Classes	32.4	16.9	32.7
Median Number of Times a Week That Teachers Meet Pupils in Classes	5.03	2.58	1.68

number of different pupils met, the teachers of Groups I and II had approximately equal loads, while those of Group III had more than two and a half times as heavy a load. These contrasts are explained by other medians shown in the table. The teachers of Group II averaged half as many pupils to the class as did the teachers of Groups I and III, and the classes of teachers in Group I met twice as often as did the classes represented in Group II and three times as often as those of Group III.

The analysis may be clarified by showing these elements in the loads of three teachers in the same school. These data are presented in Table 7.[27] The

26 P. W. Hutson, "A Neglected Factor in the Teaching Load," *School Review,* Vol. XL (March, 1932), pp. 192–203.

27 *Ibid.,* p. 197, Table IV.

last column shows how nearly identical were the loads of these teachers when measured by the number of weekly pupil-recitation hours taught; yet the teacher of art taught almost ten times as many pupils as the teacher of stenography and typewriting and had one-tenth as many contacts with his pupils. Insofar as knowing the pupil is essential to educating him, the loads of these teachers stand in marked contrast.

TABLE 7. Instructional Loads of Three Teachers

Subject Taught	Number of Different Pupils in Classes	Number of Times a Week Pupils Are Met	Number of Weekly Pupil-Recitation Hours
Art	557	1	557
Mathematics	120	5	600
*Stenography and Typewriting	61	10	610

* Subjects in Grade X; Johnstown junior high schools include Grades VII–X.

Tables 6 and 7 show a factor in organization which is less evident in the typical four-year or senior high school. In the latter, practically all subjects are taught on the five-days-a-week basis. Tradition, and the necessity for fulfilling the requirements of the Carnegie unit—in terms of which college entrance requirements are stated—are responsible. The junior high school, on the other hand, being relatively free from both of these compulsions, has organized its educational program with many classes meeting, one, two, three, or four times a week, and with the pupil scheduled for many more subjects than is true of the pupil of the senior high school.

Other investigations support the findings of the analysis of the Johnstown junior high schools and lend additional clarification. For example, Steinmetz studied the organization of the instructional program of the junior high schools of Chicago and stated the following points in conclusion:[28]

1. Pupils of all grades, except in one class in one school, had a different teacher in every subject.
2. The junior high schools were committed to the highest possible degree of subject departmentalization.
3. The proportion of teachers who gave instruction in a single subject varied according to the size of the school and the skill of the schedule-maker.

Hutson and Keifer analyzed the schedule cards of pupils in twenty-four Western Pennsylvania junior high schools with enrollments ranging from 300 to 1,500 and found the number of subjects being carried by the pupils to be

[28] Kathryn E. Steinmetz, "Departmentalization in the Junior High Schools of Chicago," *School Review,* Vol. XL (December, 1932), p. 169.

as shown in Table 8.[29] Considerable variation within each grade is shown in the table, but the medians suggest that typically the pupil carries a number of subjects for which the classes meet less than five times a week. Under the influence of college-entrance requirements ninth-grade pupils carry fewer subjects, doubtless because four of the subjects are scheduled for five days a week.

TABLE 8. Percentage Distribution of Pupils in Grades VII, VIII, and IX According to Number of Subjects Being Carried

| Number of Subjects | Percentage of Pupils | | |
	Grade VII (234 Pupils)	Grade VIII (234 Pupils)	Grade IX (236 Pupils)
14	1.7	. . . .	. . . .
13	2.1	4.3	. . . .
12	9.8	15.4	5.5
11	27.4	21.4	14.4
10	16.2	15.4	6.8
9	33.8	26.9	16.9
8	8.5	13.2	20.3
7	0.4	3.0	16.9
6	. . . .	. . . .	12.7
5	. . . .	0.4	6.4
Median number of subjects	10.5	10.4	8.7

The data that have been presented are believed to be representative of the mechanism of American secondary schools. This prevailing organization has some critics; their views and atypical organizations which have been created will be taken up briefly in concluding paragraphs of this section.

How Well Do Teachers Know Their Pupils?

With this question in mind Baker queried 27 teachers in five representative high schools concerning a sampling of 250 pupils in their classes.[30] He submitted to them a long list of items classified under eight headings—items which he had found that educational psychologists, guidance specialists, and educators deemed important to know about pupils in order to make suitable provision for their education. Table 9 is a summary of the extent to which the teachers possessed the information about their pupils.[31] While we do not have in Baker's article the detailed list of items nor the full procedure by which he arrived at them, it is shocking to note that these teachers knew less

[29] P. W. Hutson and J. C. Keifer, "Schedules of Junior High School Pupils," *School Review,* Vol. XLVI (November, 1938), p. 673, Table 3.

[30] Harry Leigh Baker, "High-School Teachers' Knowledge of Their Pupils," *School Review,* Vol. XLVI (March, 1938), pp. 175–190.

[31] *Ibid.,* p. 181, Table 2, adapted.

than one-fourth of the facts about their pupils which it was deemed advisable that they should know. Baker sought to ascertain the factors associated with teachers' knowledge of their pupils and found, as might be expected, that contacts in connection with extracurricular activities, associations with pupils in previous semesters, and classes of moderate rather than large size were associated with greater knowledge of pupils.

More than a generation ago two teachers in large high schools expressed effectively their anxiety over the conditions which were fostering depersonalization in their schools. Said Lillian Herstein, of the Crane Technical High School, Chicago.[32]

TABLE 9. Extent to Which Twenty-seven Teachers Possessed Knowledge of a Sampling of Their Pupils

Categories of Items	Percentage of Possible Score
General ability to learn	78.9
Physical status and health	50.0
Personal adjustment	29.7
Present educational status and learning difficulties	22.2
General personality	16.8
Home and educational background	15.7
Special abilities	13.7
Interests and hobbies	11.3
Entire schedule	22.9

There is nothing particularly new about the personal phase of the teacher's job. It permeates all her contacts with her pupils. And there were teachers who got into personal touch with their students long before the subject began to trickle into the discussions of teachers' institutes and pedagogic journals. There have always been teachers with the eye to discern and the will to help the pupil struggling with the burden of straitened circumstances, ill health, or adverse home conditions. To these teachers have come, from time to time, the boy who needed to be reconciled to the new stepmother, the girl with educational aspirations beyond the family's purse or vision, the youngster who had to leave school because Father had lost his job.

And just when we have gathered into our high schools the children from almost every walk of life, and when, therefore, the personal contact is of special importance, the mania for larger and larger schools is rendering association of teacher and pupil less and less possible. . . . A high school boy of foreign birth put the case tersely: "When I was in the old country, I used to hear how in America everybody went to school, the tailor's boy in the same school with the banker's and the doctor's. And it thrilled me. Now I am here, I see it is true. The

[32] "What *Is* the High School Teacher's Job?" *New Republic* (Educational Supplement, *The American High School*) (November 7, 1923), pp. 12–13.

tailor's boy does go to school with the banker's and the doctor's, but I wonder if any of us is learning much. It is all so big and noisy and quick-moving."

And from Agnes M. Conklin, of the Girls Commercial High School, Brooklyn,[33]

One of the worst features of the present crowded high-school conditions and double sessions is the lack of contact between teacher and child. Hundreds of boys and girls slip through schools every year and their teachers know little about them personally and still less about their plans. . . . No individual teacher has time for this personal contact; the most that is known about many of the students is a hated clerical record that shunts them into some convenient pigeon-hole. . . .
Mere size of school will cost enormously if we lose sight of the child.

We need not turn back to the little red schoolhouse (or need we?) to help teachers like those just quoted to satisfy their deep professional urge to know their pupils as persons, but on reading Willis Stork's account of his two years experience in a rural two-teacher, ten-grade school, one must find infectious his exultation over a situation which enabled teacher and pupils to know each other intimately and to form fast friendships.[34] With every paragraph beginning "This couldn't happen in a large school," Stork described the rich experiences of teaching in a small school, experiences made real by his own vision of possibilities. One of his last paragraphs is the following:

This couldn't happen in a large school . . . During the entire school year the teacher of the rural school is besieged with requests of the youngsters to come home and stay all night with them. Especially is this true toward the close of the school year. It is then that one really learns to know his student and why he is what he is. If one gets up at six in the morning and goes out to "help" do the chores, one can learn much about a boy. No matter how intimate you may be with the lad at school, you will learn new things as you sit on the barn doorsill and visit with him as he milks six or seven cows.

Here is something precious that cannot be realized with mass-production methods!

The Function of Guidance Rests on a Knowledge of Pupils

The automobile industry operates on the principle of interchangeable parts. The piston rings for a given model will fit any car of that model. Minute specialization of labor and machine tools are chief factors in making possible such precision manufacture. The schools have been greatly influenced by the example of modern industry. Their workers are specialized on a horizontal basis (grade level) and on a vertical basis (subject matter). A single course of study and uniform textbooks are the tools with which they work, endeavoring to turn out products which come within the tolerances permitted.

[33] "The Parent and the Grade Adviser," *New Republic* (Educational Supplement, *The American High School*), (November 7, 1923), pp. 16–17.
[34] "It Can't Happen in a Large School," *Phi Delta Kappan*, Vol. XIX (April, 1937), pp. 265–266.

The parallelism is not intentional, but some people are aware of it and feel its inappropriateness. Hence—guidance. For guidance is conceived of as the study of individuals and the according of individualized treatment to them. Depersonalization being recognized in the educational factory, guidance functionaries are established as specialists in pupils to offset the limitations of the specialists in subject matter. Guidance workers are to envisage the *whole pupil* and to see that the potential service of the school is utilized to his individual advantage. This role of guidance in compensating for the impersonality of the school factory is evident in the following quotations cited in a city superintendent's annual report on the operation of the guidance program:[35]

"Mrs. O. . . . telephoned to thank the teachers for their efforts with her son, an outstanding case of a boy who had been unable to succeed in three previous schools."

"Mr. G. . . . called in person to thank the school for what it had done for his son. He said he once thought the boy was a hopeless case; the school had not agreed with him—the boy only needed adjustment."

"I am perfectly astounded to find in this large school that you are able to give my child all this attention. I was under the impression that the children at high school were herded together in a mass and no one knew anything about them personally."

It should impress us as very strange that we have ever allowed the idea to acquire a hold upon the public mind that the school is an impersonal agency.

Guidance workers ought to be conscious of the factory principle operating in their schools. They ought also to be aware of alternatives to that principle, aware of other methods of organizing the instructional program which obviate depersonalization. The factory principle is part and parcel of subject-centeredness. It operates without regard for pupil purposes and with no respect for the essential unity of educative experience. It therefore builds up problems of pupil maladjustment for guidance to solve.

The inadequacy of education by subject specialists has been realized by elementary-school teachers and administrators. In the 1920s the trend toward specialization of the teacher's load in the elementary school was marked. Specialists in reading, specialists in arithmetic, specialists in handwriting—that was the way to efficiency in education. Departmentalization came to prevail in perhaps the majority of city schools in the middle grades, and in many schools it was established in the primary grades. But about 1930 the tide turned. Experience had demonstrated that children did not thrive when responsibility for their education was divided among so many teachers. At present, prevailing practice seems to assign the pupils of a given grade to one teacher for all their work except some special subjects. In most schools teaching is by subjects—though the activities curriculum has gained some accept-

[35] *The Entire School as an Advisory Agency,* Report of the Superintendent of Schools (Milton C. Potter), Milwaukee, Wisconsin, prepared by F. C. Rosecrance, 1933, p. 83.

ance—but the teacher, having fewer pupils to know and more contacts with them than under departmentalization, comes to know each one as a unique personality.

At the secondary-school level the most promising innovation bearing on the problem of depersonalization is perhaps the core curriculum. Two publications of the Office of Education[36] afford some assessment of the extent and character of this development, the acceptance of which is apparently still gaining momentum. The core curriculum is variously designated as "unified studies," "common learnings," "integrated program," "general education," and "core." It aims most commonly to achieve the objectives generally held for the subjects of English and social studies; sometimes other goals are those traditionally charged to such subjects as art, music, science, geography. Core programs vary as regards their respect for the identity of the subject fields. The more conservative merely provide for some correlations between subjects; the more radical ignore subject matter lines altogether and focus upon the study of problems which originate in the felt needs and interests of the pupils.

The possibilities of the core curriculum organization for the performance of the guidance function has been widely noted and will be presented with some fullness in Chapter 7. It is briefly referred to here because it is an alternative to the factory type of educational organization described in this section. By having two or three hours of contact with a group of pupils every day, a teacher is better enabled to know them as individuals than can be the case under typical departmentalization. Furthermore, the teacher carries a smaller pupil-personality load. He may meet one core group in the forenoon and another in the afternoon—a total of 50–70 pupils. Thus, instead of planning for guidance activity as necessary to *counterbalance* departmentalization, core organization may be planned to *reduce* departmentalization and thereby reduce depersonalization.

No plan of organization will make it certain that teachers have full knowledge of their pupils. Too much depends upon the individual teacher. It can be said, however, that some plans of organization facilitate that outcome while others hinder it. Guidance workers will certainly desire the former.

THE SCHOOL CONTRIBUTING TO MALADJUSTMENT

Studies Showing the Personality Effects of Failure in School

If the reader has read the first six sections of this chapter he should not be shocked at the title of this, the seventh section. While habitually we think of the school as affording a sheltered environment, calculated to protect children and youth from the chill winds of adversity, the picture of actual conditions

---

[36] Grace S. Wright, *Core Curriculum in Public High Schools: An Inquiry into Practices, 1949,* Bulletin 1950, No. 5.

Grace S. Wright, *Core Curriculum Development: Problems and Practices,* Bulletin 1952, No. 5.

shows many of them to be subjected to a regime in which they see no valid purpose in their activity, they experience feelings of insecurity and injustice, and they are not accorded the sense of worth and personal importance essential to happiness. This section will present some data to indicate the outcome of these conditions and their bearing on the guidance function.

Hilgard has described an experiment comparing the level of aspiration, under laboratory conditions, of two groups of children of the middle grades, one group having had a history of satisfactory results in school in both reading and arithmetic, and the other group having had a history of unsuccessful work in these two subjects.[37] The two groups were matched in respect to age, intelligence, and socio-economic status. Given reading and arithmetic tasks to perform, the pupils were asked to set time goals for themselves. With noteworthy uniformity the children with a past history of success tended to try for scores close to but slightly better than those they had just achieved. The children with a past history of failure, on the other hand, tended to deviate widely in one or the other direction. "Some, as a consequence of experienced failure, appeared to be so afraid of further failure that they set their goals below present achievement," thereby protecting themselves from the possibility of further failure. Others (of the failure group) set their goals so high as to be definitely unrealistic. Hilgard points out that both of these reactions are indicative of an unsatisfactory state of mental health, concluding that "It is not wholesome for the child to be so beaten down by failure as to cease expecting anything of himself, or to be so inured to failure that what he expects of himself no longer corresponds to reality."

Sandin compared 139 "slow progress pupils" with 227 pupils of normal progress in a well-controlled investigation,[38] with a view to determining the effects of nonpromotion on social and emotional adjustments. He obtained a variety of evidence through the school year 1940-41 showing noteworthy or perceptible differences on many counts in the behavior, attitudes, and social adjustments of the two categories of children. Both at school and at home the nonpromoted pupils were under pressure for their shortcomings. With considerable frequency they indicated that their preferred companions were in grades above them. Their outlook toward school and school life, as variously appraised, was not as indicative of a happy adjustment as that of their regularly promoted classmates. In short, this study adds significantly to the evidence that repeating a grade imposes a severe personality strain.

Less restrained in their judgments are Gates and Bond, who, from their studies of reading disabilities, conclude that[39]

[37] Ernest R. Hilgard, "Success in Relation to Level of Aspiration," *School and Society,* Vol. LV (April 11, 1942), pp. 425–426.

[38] Adolph A. Sandin, *Social and Emotional Adjustments of Regularly Promoted and Non-Promoted Pupils,* Child Development Monographs No. 32 (New York, Teachers College, Columbia University, 1944).

[39] Arthur I. Gates and Guy L. Bond, "Failure in Reading and Social Maladjustment," *Journal of the National Education Association,* Vol. XXV (October, 1936), p. 205.

If serious difficulty in reading disrupts a pupil's school career, it may be expected that it will disturb his personal and social adjustment. There is much evidence that failure in school is a major catastrophe to many children and that general maladjustment is a frequent consequence.

In one hundred cases selected at random from a list of pupils with reading disabilities, the authors reported unfortunate reactions as follows, some children being listed in more than one category:

[1] Nervous tensions and habits such as stuttering, nail-biting, restlessness, insomnia, and pathological illnesses—10 cases

[2] Putting up a bold front as a defence reaction, loud talk, defiant conduct, sullenness—16 cases

[3] Retreat reactions such as withdrawal from ordinary association, joining outside gangs, and truancy—14 cases

[4] Counter-attack; such as making mischief in school, playing practical jokes, thefts, destructiveness, cruelty, bullying—18 cases

[5] Withdrawing reactions; including mind-wandering and daydreaming—26 cases

[6] Extreme self-consciousness; becoming easily injured, blushing, developing peculiar fads and frills and eccentricities, inferiority feelings—35 cases

[7] Give-up or submissive judgments, as shown by inattentiveness, indifference, apparent laziness—33 cases

That failure in reading may be a factor in causing maladjustment so serious as to result in delinquency is suggested by these authors' testimony that of 187 delinquent boys between 16 and 19 years of age in a New York State reformatory, not one could read as well as the average person of his mental age.

Pupils Who Are Socially and Academically Frustrated Leave School

No attempt to summarize the vast literature on elimination is here intended, but merely enough evidence will be presented to suggest that experiences in the school itself may cause pupils to drop out. As a first example, the Lynds, probing for the explanation of human behavior in Middletown, offer the following illuminative paragraph on social life at the high school:[40]

A number of mothers who said that a child had left school because he "didn't like it" finally explained with great reluctance, "We couldn't dress him like we'd ought to and he felt out of it," or "The two boys and the oldest girl all quit because they hated Central High School. They all loved the Junior High School down here, but up there they're so snobbish. If you don't dress right you haven't any friends." "My two girls and the oldest boy have all stopped school," said another mother. "My oldest girl stopped because we couldn't give her no money for the right kind of clothes. The boy begged and begged to go on through high school, but his father wouldn't give him no help. Now the youngest girl has left 10B this year. She was doing just fine, but she was too proud to go to school

[40] *Middletown*, pp. 185–186.

unless she could have clothes like the other girls." The marked hesitation of mothers in mentioning these distasteful social distinctions only emphasizes the likelihood that the reasons for their children's leaving school summarized above understate the real situation in this respect.

That such reasons for dropping out of school may seldom appear in statistics on elimination is suggested by a personal canvass of 100 former San Francisco Junior College students who had dropped out although doing satisfactory academic work. An interview technique was employed and in many cases the interviewer talked to relatives as well as to the subjects themselves. These former students had all filled out blanks on withdrawal, and the summary of their signed reasons compared with their real reasons is as follows:[41]

	Signed	Real
Work	75	30
Illness in family . .	16	2
Health	6	2
Transfer	2	10
Marriage	1	4
Discontent		52
Totals . . .	100	100

Reasons classified as "discontent" were related to curriculum faults (10), instructors (3), other students (3), home conditions (6), lack of interest (12), and unhappiness (18). The disparity between the signed and the real reasons is not difficult to understand: students write down answers which they will not be called on to explain further.

Lack of success in school—failure and consequent retardation—is probably the most common characteristic of the pupils who drop out of school early. Such a finding is indicated by the comparison of pupils who were eliminated from Minneapolis junior high schools with those who were retained through Grade IX, a study made by Douglass and Wind.[42] Table 10 shows

TABLE 10.* Distribution of Withdrawing Pupils and Retained Pupils According to Age-Grade Status

Age-Grade Status	Withdrawing Pupils		Retained Pupils	
	Number	Per cent	Number	Per cent
Normal	0	0.0	655	54.0
Retarded	1,086	100.0	155	12.8
Accelerated	0	0.0	403	33.2
Totals	1,086	100.0	1,213	100.0

* Douglas and Wind, p. 376, Table I.

[41] Joseph A. Amori, "Why Junior College Students Withdraw," *Junior College Journal,* Vol. XII (September, 1941), p. 19.
[42] Harl R. Douglass and Kate Wind, "Factors Related to Withdrawal from Junior High Schools in Minneapolis," *Elementary School Journal,* Vol. XXXVII (January, 1937), pp. 375–380.

100 per cent retardation among the withdrawing pupils, an outcome which the authors attribute to a well-enforced statute requiring attendance until the age of 16. Naturally, pupils who are of normal age-grade status have passed through the junior high school before they become 16.

A comparison of the two groups according to marks earned in junior high school is shown in Table 11. While the data are generally in harmony with those of Table 10, the number of withdrawing pupils with average failing grades is relatively small, suggesting that their retardation had been largely brought about before they reached the junior high school.

TABLE 11.* **Average School Marks Received in Junior High School by With-drawing and Retained Pupils**

| Mark | Withdrawing Pupils | | Retained Pupils | |
	Number	Per cent	Number	Per cent
A or B	14	1.2	240	19.8
C	580	52.0	836	68.9
D	470	42.2	136	11.2
F	51	4.6	1	0.1
	1,115	100.0	1,213	100.0

* Douglas and Wind, p. 377, Table III.

Other factors brought out by these authors were the lower intelligence and the lower socio-economic status of the withdrawing pupils as compared with the retained pupils.

Delinquency Related to School Experience

Frustration, say Dollard and his collaborators,[43] always leads to aggression. The aggression may take various forms, among which are those classified as juvenile delinquency. Since this chapter, devoted to analysis of the educational scene, has shown that from various angles school life, work, and play bring frustration to some pupils, the implication of the school as a causative factor in juvenile delinquency must be accepted as altogether probable. Let us explore this unpleasant probability.

Kvaraceus, in a study of 761 delinquents—563 boys and 198 girls—handled by the Passaic (New Jersey) Children's Bureau over a five-year period, compared their school adjustments with those of the general school population of the city and found the delinquent sample to be characterized by many school frustrations.[44] The mean I.Q. for the delinquent group was 89 in contrast to a mean I.Q. of 103 for the general school population. This handicap may be taken as largely responsible for the fact that 44 per cent

[43] John Dollard and Others, *Frustration and Aggression* (New Haven, Yale University Press, 1939).

[44] W. C. Kvaraceus, "Delinquency—a By-Product of the School?" *School and Society,* Vol. LIX (May 13, 1944), pp. 350–351.

of the delinquents had repeated one or more terms as against 17 per cent of the general school population. Similarly, it also affords an explanation for the fact that less than two per cent of the school marks received by the delinquent sample fell in the upper three categories of a five-point marking system, whereas 64 per cent of the marks received by all boys and girls in Grades VII–XII fell in the same span. With this record of unsatisfactory academic experience it is small wonder that most of the delinquents left school at the age of sixteen—as soon as the law would permit—and that 60 per cent of them expressed a marked dislike for school or some person connected with the school or classroom.[45]

Similar data depicting the delinquents' lost academic battles have been amassed by the Gluecks. In one of their studies they found that "Of 935 cases [boys] in which the extent of school retardation was known, *only 145 boys (15.5 per cent) were not retarded in school.* [46]

A juvenile court judge of long experience and excellent standing has contributed to an educational journal an article with the following thought-provoking title: "Some Tested Techniques in Teaching Delinquency."[47] From his hearings and his study of the cases that came to his court he said that he had learned of the following "techniques": name-calling; ridiculing the child; embarrassing him; comparing him unfavorably with another; shaming him publicly; unduly mistrusting him; allowing the other children to make fun or take advantage of him; repeatedly imposing tasks too difficult for him or unsuited for his capacities; failing to provide at least an occasional opportunity for him to achieve, create, and if possible, excel; providing inadequate opportunities for friendships, self-expression, recreation, adventure; impairing his sense of security, of belonging; laxity or inconsistency in maintaining discipline; regarding the maintenance of discipline as an adversary proceeding, "Teacher vs. Pupil," instead of a joint enterprise.

Writing on the basis of twenty years of experience equally divided between public and prison educational work, another author gives the following examples of the employment of some of Judge Alexander's "techniques," as he gleaned them from boys in correctional institutions:[48]

(1) "The teacher tried to make me wear better clothes like the other children. I finally told her to go to hell and walked out. I swore then that I would have better clothes if I had to steal them and I did."

[45] Kvaraceus has presented a more complete report of his study and also of the unusual organization and utilization of Passaic's community forces for combatting juvenile delinquency, in his *Juvenile Delinquency and the School* (Yonkers, N.Y., World Book, 1945).

[46] Sheldon Glueck and Eleanor T. Glueck, *One Thousand Delinquents* (Cambridge, Mass., Harvard University Press, 1934), p. 87.

[47] Paul W. Alexander, in *Educational Forum,* Vol. VIII (November, 1943), pp. 17–21.

[48] Arthur C. Johnson, Jr., "Our Schools Make Criminals," *Journal of Criminal Law and Criminology,* Vol. XXXIII (November-December, 1942), p. 311.

(2) "I had a stutter. I was put in a class with a lot of screwballs. My pals kidded me and I quit."

(3) "My mother was going nuts and I was worried about her. One day the teacher called me crazy too. I never went to school regular after that."

(4) "I was fired from school because I wouldn't study my history. When they brought me back and tried to make me study history again, I started to skip school."

(5) "I just couldn't recite in class. The teacher nagged at me and to avoid trouble I left school."

(6) "I don't know why I ran away from school. I couldn't get along in a crowd, that's all."

(7) "I was put in a class with a lot of dumb clucks. It was too much for me and I quit."

(8) "One day I got to school late and was told that if I couldn't get there on time, not to come at all, just to spoil the class record. I took them at their word."

It is axiomatic that causation in juvenile delinquency is almost invariably multiple. Many forces impinge upon the child and account for his behavior. The school is one of these forces, along with home, neighborhood, business, and other social institutions.[49]

Society certainly intends the school to serve as a meliorative influence. If its ministrations do not always correspond to that ideal, it is basically because of imperfect understanding of children, of human nature, of the principles of growth. This chapter offers no positive program for the improvement of school functioning. It does not even propose a stand on the failure or no-failure dilemma. It is intended to be descriptive, as its title implies, with a view to helping guidance workers understand the conditions under which they work.

QUESTIONS, PROBLEMS, AND INVESTIGATIONS

1. Make a study of the educational motives of pupils of junior or senior high school age. Perhaps, with the collaboration of an English teacher, you may obtain from a few classes papers written on the values they see in their school subjects. Use other means—perhaps casual questioning, or just listening to student chatter and making notes over the course of a semester.

2. Re-list the items of Buswell's platform, cited in this chapter, in enumerative form, and in two parallel columns—one for the items of each paragraph. Then discuss the extent to which education in practice is realizing these criteria, each member contributing out of his experience and observations.

3. Canvass periodical literature of the past five years for articles dealing with new-type report cards. How do they meet the criticism of traditional report cards?

4. Suggest a program for cultivating democratic teacher-pupil relationships.

[49] A well-balanced treatment, which takes up the influence of all forces and factors in the environment as well as the school, is William Kvaraceus' *The Community and the Delinquent* (Yonkers, N.Y., World Book, 1954).

5. In view of the section on the personal factor in the educational scene, what kind of a teacher are you?

6. Various fruitful investigations of the program of social recreation may be made in junior high schools, senior high schools, or at the college level. They may be large or small in scale. For example, get a complete list of those who attend that sophomore class party. Then, by comparison with the complete class roll, find out who did not attend. Study those people. Find out why they did not attend.

7. Debate the merits and disadvantages of departmentalization, being particularly careful to examine the criteria by which you praise and condemn.

8. Select a dozen items pertaining to home environment which teachers ought to know if they really know their pupils. Have some teachers, without opportunity for preparation, see how many of the items they can supply on each of the first ten pupils in their rollbooks.

9. Debate the no-failure policy, being careful to examine the criteria by which you praise and condemn.

10. Make a canvass of some present-day junior high school schedules to see if practice differs from that shown in this chapter, as, for example, in Table 8.

SELECTED REFERENCES

ALEXANDER, Paul W., "Some Tested Techniques in Teaching Delinquency," *Educational Forum,* Vol. VIII (November, 1943), pp. 17–21.

ALTMAN, Emil, "Our Mentally Unbalanced Teachers," *American Mercury,* Vol. LII (April, 1941), pp. 391–401.

AMORI, Joseph A., "Why Junior College Students Withdraw," *Junior College Journal,* Vol. XII (September, 1941), pp. 18–24.

BAKER, Harry Leigh, "High-School Teachers' Knowledge of Their Pupils," *School Review,* Vol. XLVI (March, 1938), pp. 175–190.

BARRINGTON, Thomas M., *The Introduction of Selected Educational Practices into Teachers Colleges and Their Laboratory Schools* (New York, Teachers College, Columbia University, 1953).

BROWN, Clara M., "A Social Activities Survey," *Journal of Higher Education,* Vol. VIII (May, 1937), pp. 259–264.

BURTON, William H., *The Guidance of Learning Activities,* 2nd ed. (New York, Appleton-Century-Crofts, 1952).

BUTTERFIELD, Oliver M., *Love Problems of Adolescence* (New York, Teachers College Contributions to Education, No. 768, 1939).

COUNTS, George S., *The American Road to Culture* (New York, Day, 1930).

———, *The Schools Can Teach Democracy* (New York, Day, 1939).

DEWEY, John, *Experience and Education,* The Kappa Delta Pi Lecture Series (New York, Macmillan, 1938).

DOLLARD, John, and others, *Frustration and Aggression* (New Haven, Yale University Press, 1939).

DOUGLASS, Harl R., and WIND, Kate, "Factors Related to Withdrawal from Junior High Schools in Minneapolis," *Elementary School Journal,* Vol. XXXVII (January, 1937), pp. 375–380.

EVANS, Robert O., *Practices, Trends, and Issues in Reporting to Parents on the Welfare of the Child in School* (New York, Teachers College, Columbia University, 1938).

FINNEY, Ross L., *A Sociological Philosophy of Education,* especially Ch. 19 (New York, Macmillan, 1928).

Fostering Mental Health in Our Schools, 1950 Yearbook, Association for Supervision and Curriculum Development, National Education Association, Washington, D.C.

GATES, Arthur I., and BOND, Guy L., "Failure in Reading and Social Adjustment," *Journal of the National Education Association,* Vol. XXV (October, 1936), pp. 205–206.

GLUECK, Sheldon, and GLUECK, Eleanor T., *One Thousand Delinquents* (Cambridge, Mass., Harvard University Press, 1934).

GOULD, George, "Practices in Marking and Examination," *School Review,* Vol. XL (February, 1932), pp. 142–146.

HART, Frank W., *Teachers and Teaching* (New York, Macmillan, 1934).

HEALY, William, and BRONNER, Augusta, "How Does the School Produce or Prevent Delinquency?" *Journal of Educational Sociology,* Vol. VI (April, 1933), pp. 450–470.

Helping Teachers Understand Children, by the Staff of the Division on Child Development and Teacher Personnel. Prepared for the Commission on Teacher Education (Washington, D.C., American Council on Education, 1945).

HILGARD, Ernest R., "Success in Relation to Level of Aspiration," *School and Society,* Vol. LV (April 11, 1942), pp. 423–428.

HOOKER, C. P., and LINDVALL, C. M., "The Student's Day Hasn't Changed Much —or Enough, Either," *Nation's Schools,* Vol. 59 (June, 1957), pp. 48–49.

HUTSON, P. W., "A Neglected Factor in the Teaching Load," *School Review,* Vol. XL (March, 1932), pp. 192–203.

———, and KEIFER, J. C., "Schedules of Junior High School Pupils," *School Review,* Vol. XLVI (November, 1938), pp. 667–678.

HUTSON, P. W., and KOVAR, D. R., "Some Problems of Senior High School Pupils in Their Social Recreation," *Educational Administration and Supervision,* Vol. XXVIII (October, 1942), pp. 503–519.

KVARACEUS, W. C., *The Community and the Delinquent* (Yonkers, N. Y., World Book, 1954).

———, "Delinquency—a By-Product of the School?" *School and Society,* Vol. LIX (May 13, 1944), pp. 350–351.

———, *Juvenile Delinquency and the School* (Yonkers, N.Y., World Book, 1945).

LEWIN, Kurt, LIPPITT, Ronald, and WHITE, R. K., "Patterns of Aggressive Behavior in Experimentally Created Social Climates," *Journal of Social Psychology,* Vol. X (May, 1939), pp. 271–299.

LYND, Robert S., and LYND, Helen M., *Middletown* (New York, Harcourt, Brace, 1929), Chs. 13–16.

MORRISON, H. C., *The Practice of Teaching in the Secondary School,* rev. ed., (Chicago, University of Chicago Press, 1931), especially Chs. 3, 4, 5.

NORDAU, Leon, "Education and the Competitive Motive," *School Review,* Vol. LV (March, 1947), pp. 154–160.

ROGERS, Evelyn Gibbs, "Progressive Ideals in Practice: The Teacher's Dilemma," *Educational Research Bulletin* (Ohio State University), Vol. XXV (October 16, 1946), pp. 175–182.

SANDIN, Adolph A., *Social and Emotional Adjustments of Regularly Promoted and Non-Promoted Pupils,* Child Development Monographs No. 32 (New York, Teachers College, Columbia University, 1944).

SCHOTT, E. L., "School Maladjustments of Some Mentally Superior Patients in a Psychiatric Clinic," *Psychological Clinic,* Vol. XXI (September–November, 1932), pp. 202–207.

SNYDER, W. U., "Do Teachers Cause Maladjustment?" *Journal of Exceptional Children,* Vol. XIV (November and December, 1947), pp. 40–46, 63, 73–78.

SPAULDING, Francis T., *High School and Life,* Report of the Regents' Inquiry (New York, McGraw-Hill, 1938).

STEINMETZ, Kathryn E., "Departmentalization in the Junior High Schools of Chicago," *School Review,* Vol. XL (December, 1932), pp. 760–771.

WILLIAMS, Frankwood, *Adolescence—Studies in Mental Hygiene* (New York, Farrar & Rinehart, 1930).

CHAPTER 4

Evidence of the Need for Guidance

THE SERVICE TO BE RENDERED by the guidance program can be seen more clearly if the need for it is outlined. Have we substantial evidence that special guidance service is necessary? What are the facts concerning the educational and vocational choices of people? Are such choices out of harmony with the abilities of the choosers? What are the facts concerning the kinds and extent of existing maladjustment? With what frequency are individuals impeded in their development or in the full utilization of their powers by remediable defects in their personalities, physiques, or home surroundings?

A substantial literature exists in answer to these questions. This chapter will offer a sampling of the evidence afforded by various types of surveys bearing on the need for guidance. While the evidence is being reviewed, the reader is asked to bear in mind that the same techniques of research which reveal the *need for guidance* may be employed to *measure the effectiveness* of guidance. In such observation he will have a forecast of the final chapter of this book.

EDUCATIONAL OR CURRICULUM MALADJUSTMENT

Pupil Failure

No more immediate question faces us than that of how well our pupils are adjusted within the school. In the '20s many studies were being made to show the incidence and the causation of pupil failure. Perhaps none was as comprehensive as that of J. F. Montague[1] based on data from 304 widely scattered high schools. The summary of his survey showed that the following percentages of pupils failed one or more subjects: Grade IX, 30 per cent; Grade X, 29 per cent; Grade XI, 24 per cent; Grade XII, 11 per cent; all pupils (234,854), 25 per cent. Montague estimated that 10.2 per cent of all the work attempted by the pupils was failed.

Margaret Walker's somewhat detailed analysis of failure among tenth-

[1] Reported by E. E. Windes in *Trends in the Development of Secondary Education* (U.S. Office of Education Bulletin No. 26, 1927), p. 11.

grade pupils of a typical Philadelphia high school brought out the fact that in the fall term of 1932, 24 per cent failed in one or more subjects.[2]

Would a widespread survey like that of Montague yield comparable evidence today? One cannot say. While pupil "failure" is looked upon differently today than thirty years ago, perhaps the modification of practice is so far limited mainly to elementary grades. At that level, Rogers has given us the evidence of striking change in one large school system—Chicago.[3] Whereas in 1924, in January, 32,549 pupils in Grades I–VIII did not pass, in June, 1946, only 8,294 failed. Promotion by age has gained considerable acceptance in elementary schools, and seems in some degree to have been adopted in junior high schools.

Useful detail in the study of failure at the high-school level is afforded by Landry's analysis of the figures on failure in the academic high schools of New York City for the year 1941–42.[4] He reported that there were 300,000 end term subject failures—10.1 per cent of all the subjects studied—a figure remarkably close to the 10.2 per cent cited above as reported by Montague. Landry pointed out that his figures did not include the pupils who left school during the term with failure staring at them. The rate of 10.1 per cent failure of all subjects studied compared with a rate of 14.3 per cent for the year 1932-33, thus indicating a substantial decline in the incidence of failure.

Landry reported the per cent of failures by subject fields to be as follows:

English	9.0	Music	4.6
Mathematics	18.6	Vocational and trade	9.7
Languages	14.8	Health and hygiene	7.7
Social sciences	8.5	Home economics	7.1
Sciences	13.1	Fine arts	6.2
Commercial	14.9		

Percentages quite similar to these may be found in surveys made in the 1920s.[5]

Contrasts in the percentages of pupils failing some specific subjects were given by Landry, as follows:

English, Term 1	12.2	Advanced Biology, Term 1	16.3
Term 8	3.3	Term 2	11.2
French, Term 1	18.5	American History, Term 1	11.2
Term 8	0.4	Term 2	3.6
Algebra, Elementary	25.2	Stenography, Term 1	25.0
Advanced	7.8	Term 4	12.2

[2] *A Study of High School Failures* (Scottdale, Pa., Mennonite Press, 1935), p. 37.

[3] Don C. Rogers, "Success or Failure in School," *American School Board Journal,* Vol. CXIII (October, 1946), p. 46.

[4] Herbert A. Landry, "Subject Failure in the Academic High Schools," *High Points in the Work of the High Schools of New York City,* Vol. XXV (October, 1943), pp. 27–33.

[5] W. C. Reavis, *Pupil Adjustment* (Boston, Heath, 1926), Ch. 1.

From the high failure rates in the first terms of French, algebra, and stenography, one might judge curriculum guidance in the New York City schools to be on the trial-and-error basis, for those subjects are among the variables of the curriculum. Presumably they should be elected only by pupils who have aptitude for them. American history and English, on the other hand, are constants in the curriculum, and they should therefore be so adapted to the pupils that all can pass them. The failure rates in the first term may indicate that such adaptation was not made.

Landry further pointed out that the failure rates of the high schools varied widely, ranging from 3.5 to 26 per cent. Analysis of the intelligence of pupils in the schools showed a considerable variation also, median I.Q.'s ranging from 93 to 114, but the failure rates seemed to have little or no relation to the variation in ability. To illustrate variation in failure rates, Landry gave the following data for specific subjects:

	Failure Rate in Individual Schools	
	Lowest	Highest
English, first term	0.0	43.2
Algebra, first term	7.2	54.7
Plane geometry, first term	5.1	46.7
Physics, first term	0.0	45.8
Stenography, first term	7.5	44.2
Typewriting, first term	2.2	32.6

These extremes in failure rates are so marked as to suggest that the high-school faculties represented must have widely contrasting philosophies of education.

A New York teacher commented at some length on Landry's figures in a later issue of *High Points,* and concerning the drop in the percentage of failures from 14.3 in 1932-33 to 10.1 in 1941-42, he raised the following question:[6] "Does the decrease in failures over the last ten years represent (*a*) changes in curricula to meet the needs of the students or (*b*) a general watering down of courses of study or (*c*) pressure on the part of supervisors?" He did not ask if the decrease in the failure rate might be due to improvement in the guidance service—thoughtful study of each individual to achieve rational distribution and a better scholastic adjustment.

As regards the first of the possible explanations offered by Weinstein, this is perhaps the appropriate point at which to make it plain that pupil failure is not always or solely a challenge to the guidance function. Unquestionably pupil failure is often and largely due to rigid and ill-suited curriculums, and as such is a challenge to curriculum construction rather than to guidance. This is particularly true at the secondary-school level where the main task is to administer liberal education to raise the general level of civic intelligence.

[6] Aaron Weinstein, "Some Thoughts on the Reorganization of Our Academic High Schools," *High Points in the Work of the High Schools of New York City,* Vol. XXVI (January, 1944), p. 24.

In attempting to achieve this purpose we too frequently have a common cur-riculum in such fields as English, social studies, and natural science, and this common curriculum is viewed as serving the purpose of college preparation as well as general education, a factor which enhances its difficulty for the less able members of the class. Basically, curriculum content and learning ex-periences must be geared to the variations among the pupils. When fitted primarily to the abilities, the needs, and the interests of the superior half of the class, the slower minds find the course to be "over their heads"; naturally their interest lags, and some quit trying. By the standards of almost any teacher, the achievements of some fraction of these pupils will not merit credit for the course. The basic remedy for such a situation is not guidance but curriculum construction.

Let us illustrate the respective roles of curriculum constructor and guider in order that we may more fully understand their responsibility for pupil success and failure. Occasionally there comes to this writer's attention a school in which all ninth-grade pupils are required to take algebra. If there is a counselor in the school, he finds his hands tied. For while the counselor is not a curriculum constructor, he is first to become aware of the need for curriculum making. Assuming that the counselor arouses the principal to the need for alternatives to algebra in the ninth grade, we will suppose that someone trained in curriculum making is called in to remedy the situation. Taking stock of the abilities, interests, and needs of the entire ninth-grade class, he may decide that some pupils can profit by a course in algebra, that the needs of others may best be satisfied with a course in gen-eral mathematics, while still others should be freed from any further require-ment in mathematics. After he has made these revisions in the school's cur-riculum, his work is done, and the counselor's work begins. It is the business of the latter to counsel with each pupil and help all to make wise choices from the opportunities before them. He may use the same data of pupil-analysis which the curriculum constructor gathered, but for the purpose of understanding individuals. After the pupils have distributed themselves to the courses for which they have adequate ability, the counselor continues to guard them against maladjustments which may arise to impede their progress and prevent them from realizing on their true capacities.

Returning to Weinstein's thoughtful question (p. 112), could the decline in the failure rate be due to a "general watering down of courses of study?" If this be a reason, it can only mean that in order to help pupils in the lower ability ranges attain success, the courses are being adjusted to those pupils. This, in turn, must mean that the courses are being made too easy for the pupils in the upper ability ranges. But because such a curriculum crime does not show up in pupil failures, are we so shallow in our thinking as to be satisfied with this solution of the failure problem?

Weinstein's third suggested explanation for the decline in the failure rate was "pressure on the part of supervisors." The implication is that supervisors inform teachers that a failure rate of 50 per cent or 25 per cent or whatever figure they may specify, is too high. What happens then? Teachers comply. Desiring to avoid the supervisor's disfavor, they ascertain the approximate maximum percentage of failures permitted and are careful not to exceed that figure. Instructional practice is not modified. Pupils learn no more than before. They simply find that the hurdle has been lowered.

And why should supervisors be exercising "pressure"? Essentially, for two reasons. One is the money cost of repeaters. Over the past three or four decades much has been said about this factor, and in many large city systems it has been figured quite definitely. The other reason is the growing acknowledgment that the experience of success is essential to mental health. Presumably, supervisors are better trained than teachers and feel more responsibility for the observance of this principle. But if results are achieved by the superficial means mentioned in the preceding paragraph, it is difficult to believe that mental health has been served. Does the child experience a lasting glow of satisfaction to find that he has "passed" at the end of the semester, when throughout the semester he experienced feelings of confusion, frustration, and defeat?

It will be evident from this discussion that failure rates are difficult to interpret. That the school with a low failure rate has curricular requirements and opportunities suited to the variation in its pupils, and that it has an efficient guidance program, are by no means certain. Guidance workers will be disturbed by the recorded academic failures of pupils, but they will also study the relationships of pupils and curriculum by much more penetrating means.

Counselors and homeroom teachers will properly be challenged by the case of any pupil whose achievement is not as high as his ability warrants. And such "failures" are legion. Barber's analysis of 111 graduates of Erie, Pennsylvania, high schools—all having I.Q.'s of 115 and higher—showed that

52 per cent graduated in the upper third of their classes, 33 per cent in the middle third, and 15 per cent in the lower third. On the basis of ability, all should have graduated in the upper third.[7]

This is more valid evidence of the need for guidance than report-card failures.

Elimination

Forty years and more ago we were shocked at the evidences of early school-leaving disclosed by the surveys of Thorndike, Ayres, and Strayer. Conditions have been greatly altered in the intervening years, but large numbers of pupils still do not avail themselves of the full period of schooling

[7] Leroy E. Barber, "Why Some Able High-School Graduates Do Not Go to College," *School Review*, Vol. LIX (February, 1951), p. 94.

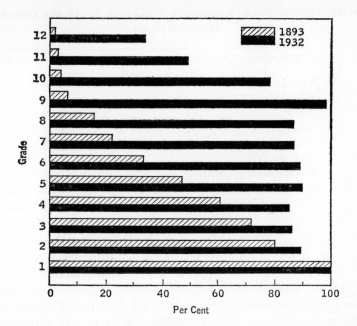

FIG. 1. Holding power of Chicago schools in 1893 and in 1932, as indicated by the number of pupils in each succeeding grade for every 100 pupils in the first grade.

offered at public expense. Figure 1[8] shows that whereas in 1893 pupils apparently began dropping out in large numbers after the primary grades, in 1932 elimination was deferred until the senior high school years. Other studies in more recent years have yielded a similar picture. In 1936–37 the Regents' Inquiry found that in one group of schools which they investigated the median grade completed by those pupils who left school before high-school graduation was the tenth; in another group of schools it was the ninth.[9] In the study of Maryland youth between the ages of 16 and 24 conducted by the American Youth Commission the distribution of the subjects according to extent of schooling was found to be as shown in Table 12.[10] In these data the median eliminate may be figured as dropping out of school in the eighth grade.

National statistics in the early '50s show, for the country as a whole, a slightly higher level of pupil retention than is evident in Table 12, a common statement being that about 50 per cent of all pupils who enter high school

[8] *Report of the Survey of the Schools of Chicago,* George D. Strayer, Director, Vol. II (New York, Teachers College, Columbia University, 1932), p. 149 (adapted).

[9] Ruth E. Eckert and Thomas O. Marshall, *When Youth Leave School,* The Regents' Inquiry (New York, McGraw-Hill, 1938), p. 40, Table III.

[10] Howard M. Bell, *Youth Tell Their Story,* (Washington, D.C., American Council on Education, 1938), p. 56, Table 13 (adapted).

TABLE 12. Highest Grade Successfully Completed by 10,898 Out-of-School Maryland Youth

School Grade Completed	Percentage of Youth
Less than 6th	6.8
6th	6.8
7th	14.0
8th	11.5
9th	9.8
10th or 11th	13.9
High school graduate	26.5
Beyond high school	10.7
Total	100.0

as freshmen (9th grade) remain to graduate. Essentially, three reasons account for this degree of improvement in the schooling level, namely: (1) a growing appreciation of schooling as an important determinant of individual success, (2) the upward extension of the period of compulsory school attendance (this being society's demand for an educated citizenry), and (3) the growing reluctance of industry and commerce to give employment to children and adolescent youth.

While the age for school leaving has advanced for these reasons, some of the factors which enter into the elimination of half or more of our pupils before high-school graduation seem not dissimilar to those which Inglis reported,[11] except that we now measure some factors, as intelligence, which could only be inferred in the earlier investigations. The Regents' Inquiry indirectly showed the characteristic retardation of eliminates by pointing out that their median age at withdrawal was only four months less than that of graduating students at graduation.[12] (Retardation and lack of success in school studies was shown in the concluding pages of Chapter 3 to be prominently associated with elimination.)

The New York State investigation compared the general intelligence of students who graduated from high school with that of those who withdrew, concluding that "The average graduate surpasses about 85 per cent of withdrawing pupils with respect to academic potentiality."[13] They canvassed the factor of socio-economic status, also, and demonstrated that the withdrawing pupils came from homes lower in the scale than did the pupils who were retained. There was, furthermore, a higher incidence of foreign-language speaking in the homes of the withdrawing pupils.[14]

[11] Alexander Inglis, *Principles of Secondary Education* (Boston, Houghton Mifflin, 1918), pp. 118–145.
[12] Eckert and Marshall, *op. cit.*, p. 43, Table IV.
[13] *Ibid.*, pp. 50–51.
[14] *Ibid.*, Ch. VI.

Ekstrom carried out an accounting for the pupils who completed Grade VIII in rural schools of two Minnesota counties in the years 1941 to 1944 inclusive.[15] He reported that

Nearly all graduates from public elementary schools located in towns of the two counties and in the city of Little Falls entered high school, whereas only 57 per cent of the graduates from rural schools and 67.1 per cent of the graduates from parochial schools proceeded beyond Grade VIII.[16]

The break between elementary and secondary education is especially sharp for the farm children; children in the towns are in school districts which have both elementary and high schools under the same school administration, and they live relatively close to a high school. Ekstrom stated in his conclusions that

The principal reasons why more farm boys and girls do not go to high school are (a) lack of encouragement on the part of parents and other adults in the community, (b) inaccessibility to high school because of distance or lack of transportation, (c) lack of school prestige, and (d) lack of an orientation program in the elementary school.

. . . Except for isolated cases, the lack of finances and the shortage of help on farms normally do not keep pupils from going to high school.[17]

Ekstrom made some study of withdrawals after entering high school, showing that in September, 1941, of the farm children who entered high school, 37.3 per cent had withdrawn before reaching Grade XII, the principal reasons being ascertained to be a lack of interest and a lack of parental encouragement. To the mind of this writer another probable reason for the withdrawal of farm children is their difficulty in adjusting to the social environment. Frequently they come to the high school quite alone from one-room country schools. The farm children in the freshman class are strangers to each other. They are also strangers to the group of children from the village or city elementary schools who enter high school with friendly associations already well established. This special problem of school articulation might well be the subject of thoughtful investigation.

One of the reasons given above for the advance in the level of schooling was the reluctance of employers to give work to youth. The years of World War II witnessed a considerable modification of that attitude. Labor shortages caused employers to bid freely for the services of young workers, with the result that the national enrollment of pupils in secondary schools declined quickly by somewhat more than a million. The rise in the issuance of general employment certificates in a single city is shown for Pittsburgh in Figure 2. If space had permitted, the figure could have been drawn to show

[15] G. F. Ekstrom, "Why Farm Children Leave School," *School Review,* Vol. LIV (April, 1946), pp. 231–237.

[16] *Ibid.,* p. 232.

[17] *Ibid.,* p. 236.

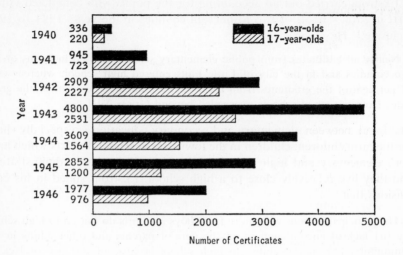

FIG. 2. Number of general employment certificates issued (first issues) by the Department of Guidance and Child Accounting of the Pittsburgh Public Schools (data furnished by courtesy of the Department).

the preceding twenty years. In the '20s large numbers of general employment certificates were issued each year, although they were then obtainable at the age of 14. In 1935 the law was changed to make 16 the minimum age required for obtaining the certificate,[18] but it had no appreciable effect on the number granted. The average number granted per year in the 1930s was approximately the number shown in the figure for the year 1940.

The industrial boom which followed the onset of the war in Korea again brought an increase in high-school dropouts. "According to the National Child Labor Committee, the number of sixteen- and seventeen-year-olds engaged in non-agricultural full-time and part-time employment increased 31.3 per cent from March, 1950, to March, 1951."[19] Thus, the evidence from the four decades is that in periods of high employment a great many pupils leave school as early as the law will permit. In times of depression but few can leave school early, because they cannot obtain the employment which is a condition necessary to the granting of the certificate. While elimination now takes place later than was the case a quarter century and more ago, the improvement is not of a kind that can afford unmixed satisfaction to school authorities.

George Melcher, superintendent emeritus of the Kansas City (Mo.)

[18] In Pennsylvania, general employment certificates are required for minors between the ages of 16 and 18 for full-time employment. The applicant must present a signed statement from an employer, promising employment, before the certificate will be issued. A minor must have a new permit for each new job.

[19] Robert C. Woellner, Editorial in *School Review,* Vol. LIX (December, 1951), p. 511.

schools, followed up a group of the wartime "dropouts" to find out what they were doing a year or more after withdrawing from school and how they fared. In his report[20] he pictured a fine record of employment at wages that would be considered excellent. Most of these young people were happy in their work. Classifying them on the basis of the reasons they gave for withdrawing from school, Melcher said,

> The twenty-four pupils who left for military service, the thirteen who left on account of poor health, and the seven who left for marriage are not the responsibility of the school. The remaining seventy-three who left because of teachers, failing grades, dislike of school, and various miscellaneous reasons are the responsibility of the school. Smaller classes, more counseling, better teaching techniques, and more interested and sympathetic teachers would probably have saved from failure and withdrawal from school the major part of these seventy-three pupils.

In deploring the early withdrawal of these pupils, presumably Melcher was not thinking so much of their individual economic future as he was of the general social contribution they might make.

Apropos of Melcher's statement that "more counseling ... more interested and sympathetic teachers" might have prevented the withdrawal of these pupils, Eckert and Marshall in their investigation of New York State high schools found that school officials and teachers knew much less about the home conditions of withdrawing pupils than of those who graduated, and that systematic plans for becoming acquainted with home environment were lacking.

> When a pupil's out-of-school life is known, the present findings suggest that it is because parents or pupils bring the information to the school. . . . Those who are the flower of the traditional academic system are those whom the school really comes to know as individuals. It knows least those who will have no further school contacts and who come from the most handicapped homes.[21]

Recent studies of withdrawing pupils have been somewhat more penetrating than the earlier ones. Researchers have learned, for example, that causes of school leaving cannot be reliably ascertained by the use of a questionnaire, so they have turned to the interview. Thus, Amori's study, cited in the last section of Chapter 3, showed the contrast in the findings obtained by these two methods. Dillon's study[22] was made in the late '40s by interview with representative samplings of school leavers in Cleveland, Cincinnati, Indianapolis, Lansing, and small towns of Jackson County, Michigan. The interviewers—school personnel selected on the basis of their knowledge of young people and their problems—were given preliminary training in the objectives

---

[20] Quoted editorially in the *School Review*, Vol. LIV (May, 1946), pp. 255–256.
[21] Eckert and Marshall, *op. cit.*, p. 85.
[22] Harold J. Dillon, *Early School Leavers: A Major Educational Problem* (New York 16 [419 Fourth Ave.], National Child Labor Committee, 1949).

and methods of the study. As to findings, Table 13[23] shows that 16 years was decidedly the modal age for school leaving in those communities; the modal grade of school leaving was the tenth; and more than half of the leavers were retarded by one or more grades. The reasons for leaving school, as ascertained by Dillon's interviewers, were classified as shown in Table 14. While

TABLE 13. Age-Grade Distribution of 1,171 School Leavers

Age	Grade 7	Grade 8	Grade 9	Grade 10	Grade 11	Grade 12	Totals No.	Per cent
14	0	4	2	1	0	0	7	1
15	9	17	30	27	9	0	92	9
16	19	81	212	227	83	7	629	54
17	1	17	55	140	98	20	331	26
18 and over	0	2	6	34	37	33	112	10
Total	29	121	305	429	227	60	1171	100

many of the earlier studies of elimination stated or implied that pupils dropped out of school primarily because their earnings were needed for the support of themselves and their families, Table 14 shows this to be a minor

TABLE 14. Frequency of Reasons Given by 957 Youth as of First Importance in Decision to Leave School

Reasons	Frequency No.	Per cent
REASONS RELATING TO SCHOOL		
Preferred work to school	342	36
Was not interested in school work	104	11
Could not learn and was discouraged	66	7
Was failing and didn't want to repeat grade	55	6
Disliked a certain teacher	47	5
Disliked a certain subject	30	3
Could learn more out of school than in school	16	1
FINANCIAL REASONS		
Needed money to buy clothes and help at home	144	15
Wanted spending money	55	6
PERSONAL REASONS		
Ill-health	49	5
Friends had left school	29	3
Parents wanted youth to leave school	20	2
Total	957	100

[23] *Ibid.*, Table 10, p. 27.

cause. Almost 70 per cent of these primary reasons reflected upon the school and indicated that it did not afford a satisfying way of life for these pupils.

Dillon's study, the Louisville study,[24] and the studies cited in the last section of Chapter 3 show that early withdrawal from school, like pupil failure, must be regarded as a challenge to curriculum construction and to teaching techniques as well as to guidance. To sizable fractions of their enrollments a great many schools have little to offer—in fact, evidence has been submitted that the offering for some pupils is frustration, defeat, and feelings of inferiority—and the counselor has little to sell. But in the exercise of distributive guidance the counselor seeks the best matching of individuals with curriculum opportunities, and in the exercise of adjustive guidance he seeks by all possible means the adaptation of school and home to the pupil's needs. He will not discharge his function by the utterance of little homilies on a nebulous advantage of "staying in school," but will work with principal and teachers to create a school the worth of which the pupil himself can see. This "worth" need not be in terms of future economic value to the individual; it is more important that it be in terms of present satisfactions. We cannot hope that by keeping all pupils in school long enough none of them will have to fill an unskilled job. And it is dishonest to give them that sort of sales talk. A study of the incidence of elimination, its causes and concomitants, in any particular school, will go far toward defining the job of curriculum construction as well as that of guidance, and action on the findings should not be superficial.[25]

Studies of College and University Entrants

One of the important decisions with which distributive guidance is especially concerned during the secondary-school years is the decision to continue schooling at college or university. The choice between college and work involves an increasing number of high-school graduates.

College graduates of 1900 equalled 1.7 per cent of all persons reaching age 22 in that year. College graduates of 1920 equalled 2.6 per cent and those of 1940 equalled 8.1 per cent of the 22-year-olds of those years. Since 1940 the actual percentages have fluctuated widely, but a continuation of the 1920–1940 trend indicates a *normal* graduation figure of 12.0 per cent for 1953 . . . the non-veteran portion of that class was reasonably close to the normal 12.0 per cent.[26]

[24] Elizabeth S. Johnson and Caroline E. Legg, "Why Young People Leave School," *Bulletin of the National Association of Secondary-School Principals,* Vol. XXXII (November, 1948), pp. 14–24.

[25] Such an analysis has been reported for the high schools of Evansville, Indiana, in the following reference: Daniel W. Snepp, "Can We Salvage the Dropouts?" *Clearing House,* Vol. XXXI (September, 1956), pp. 49–54.

[26] Dael Wolfle, *America's Resources of Specialized Talent,* Report of the Commission on Human Resources and Advanced Training (New York, Harper, 1954), p. 25.

The college decision is the more important because it is usually bound up with intention to enter an occupation on the higher levels, especially the professions. In seeking out the evidence of the need for guidance, we may therefore raise the question, How thoughtfully and rationally is the college decision being made? Beyond college entrance additional questions test the effectiveness of distributive and adjustive guidance. Do students select the curriculums in higher education which correspond to their talents? Do they advance in higher education as far as their talents warrant, or does irrational elimination occur?

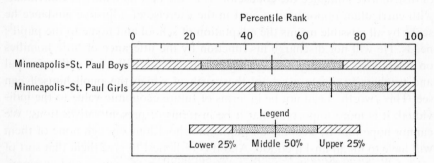

FIG. 3. University of Minnesota entrants (1922, 1923, 1924) distributed according to percentile rank in high-school graduating class.

Minnesota Studies. In the '20s Johnston[27] made numerous studies of college selection at the University of Minnesota and concluded that rank in high-school class afforded the best single index to college success, a finding which has been supported by later studies. (These are reported in Chapter 12.) He then showed how well and how poorly students were being selected by this criterion for the University of Minnesota. Figure 3 summarizes the evidence for those graduates of the high schools of Minneapolis and St. Paul who entered the University in 1922, 1923, and 1924.[28] The figure shows that the lowest 25 per cent of the boys entering the University came from the lowest 24 per cent of their classes; that the highest 25 per cent ranged upward from the 74th percentile of their classes; and that the median of the group was at the 49th percentile of their classes. Thus, the college-entering boys were almost exactly a random sampling of their high-school graduating classes. The girls, on the other hand, represented a considerable degree of selection. Because the University was required to accept any graduate of a state accredited high school, because there were no tuition charges to operate as a barrier, and because the proximity of the University invited the gradu-

[27] J. B. Johnston, "Vocational and Educational Guidance in the High School and Its Relation to Higher Education," *Vocational Guidance Magazine,* Vol. VII (October, 1928), pp. 15–25.

[28] Exact data essential for the construction of Figure 3 were made available to the writer through the courtesy of Dean Johnston in 1930.

ates of Minneapolis-St. Paul high schools, the need for a program of advisement in the high schools was most marked.

A follow-up study of the 2,807 pupils who graduated from the high schools of Minneapolis in June, 1936, showed the following percentages from each scholastic fifth to have enrolled in degree-granting institutions:[29]

Highest fifth	46.88
Second fifth	31.33
Third fifth	19.81
Fourth fifth	15.01
Fifth fifth	10.32

At the time this study was made the Minneapolis school system had had counselors in each of the high schools and a central supervisor of guidance for approximately a decade. While the figures indicate an improvement over the situation revealed in Johnston's study, and one would like to believe that guidance service had made the difference, actually no valid comparison can be made, because St. Paul pupils were included in one study and not in the other, and because the 1936 follow-up included the graduates going to all colleges, not just the ones enrolling at the University of Minnesota.

A Pittsburgh Study. Beginning in September, 1928, as a part of the Pennsylvania Study, conducted by the Carnegie Foundation for the Advancement of Teaching, extensive data were gathered on the pupils of the class which was then entering the seventh grade in the Pittsburgh public schools. In 1936 their educational achievement was summarized by Billhartz.[30] By that date practically all of those who were going to college had entered and had demonstrated their level of college achievement. Figure 4, drawn from Billhartz' study, shows the positive relationship of junior high school scholarship level to length of stay in school and to college success. The figure also shows how some youth were being eliminated from school at all levels before they had been developed to serve society in roles which correspond to their abilities. Thus, a fifth or a quarter of the pupils in the highest fifth of junior high school scholarship did not finish high school, while only about a third of the boys and a fifth of the girls at that level entered college. Guidance is challenged to conserve and develop these human resources.

A Study at Erie, Pennsylvania. Why don't they go to college? Havighurst[31] has claimed that his studies in several Midwestern communities show lack of motivation to be the main reason why many able youth do not go to college,

[29] Barbara H. Wright, *When Pupils Leave School:* Studies of Pupils' High School Progress and Post High School Adjustments (adapted from Table VIII) (Division of Instruction, Minneapolis Public Schools, October, 1937), p. 11.

[30] W. H. Billhartz, *An Attempt to Predict College Success from Junior High School Records.* Ph.D. Thesis (Pittsburgh, University of Pittsburgh Library, 1938).

[31] Robert J. Havighurst, "Social Implications of the Report of the President's Commission on Higher Education," *School and Society,* Vol. LXVII (April 3, 1948), p. 259.

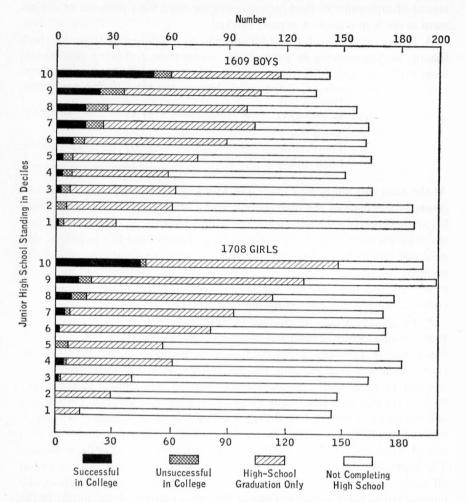

FIG. 4. Distribution, according to junior high school scholarship level attained, and according to later school achievement, of 3,317 pupils who entered the seventh grade of Pittsburgh Public Schools in 1928.

that the "motivational barrier is at least as important as the economic barrier." To take inventory of the reasons why able youth in his own city of Erie, Pennsylvania, did not go to college, Barber canvassed the 1948 graduates of the three academic high schools of the city.[32] Of the 763 graduates, 183, or 24 per cent, had intelligence quotients of 115 or higher. These were assumed to have the ability to do college work. Fifty-six of these 183—or 30.6 per cent—had entered college. Barber interviewed the remaining 127

[32] Leroy E. Barber, "Why Some Able High-School Graduates Do Not Go to College," *School Review*, Vol. LIX (February, 1951), pp. 93–96.

(except for eleven who had moved away and five who were in the armed forces), studied their high-school records, and made observations of their family, home, and job situations to ascertain as accurately as possible why they had not gone to college. Table 15[33] shows the reasons he found. He identified a major reason in every case, a secondary reason in 66 of the cases, and a third reason in 18 of the cases. Hence, the total of the percentage

TABLE 15. Reasons Why 111 Able High-School Graduates Did Not Enter College

Reason	Per Cent
Lack of finances	50
Lack of academic interests	38
Lack of serious purpose	18
Lack of college requirements	4
Preference for work experience	24
Preference for more challenging work	5
Preference for nursing	4
Preference for entering business with father	2
Preference for engagement or marriage	9
Preference for freedom from parental control	7
Feeling that marks were too low	3
Feeling of social inferiority	2
Feeling that sister should receive degree first	1
Indecision	6
Personal illness	2
Illness at home	1
Total	176

column is 176 instead of 100. While "lack of finances" is the reason appearing with highest frequency, if one groups together as "motivational" the reasons listed as "Lack of academic interests," "Lack of serious purpose," and the several designated as "Preference for . . . ," he finds them totaling somewhat larger than the economic reason.

Barber's analysis marks out with greater clarity than the previously cited evidence the dimensions and the nature of the task of guiding talented youth in the selection of goals commensurate with their powers. It should not seem strange that in many instances academic interests should be subordinate to physical, social, or practical interests, and that years of book study should be shunned. As Barber says,[34]

to many high-school Seniors, college looms up as four long years of denial and deferment—postponement of marriage, of emancipation from parental control, and of getting started in a vocation and in financial independence. College is a

[33] *Ibid.,* p. 95, Table 1 (adapted).
[34] *Ibid.,* p. 96.

prolongation of infancy, and such an expenditure of the years runs counter to some fundamental urges of the post-adolescent.

Studies of the Commission on Human Resources and Advanced Training

Alarmed by serious shortages of highly trained specialists in many fields, four national research councils created a commission to gather pertinent data concerning the trends in production of college graduates, the supply and demand in the various specialized fields, the potential supply, and the utilization of talent. From the extensive array of facts assembled, many of which represented the nation-wide situation, Tables 16 and 17 have been selected as especially pointing up the need for guidance.[35]

TABLE 16. Percentage of Youth of High Intelligence Graduating from College

Ability Level	AGCT Score	Per cent Graduating from College
Top 0.1%	160 and higher	69
Top 1%	147 and higher	59
Top 5%	133 and higher	49
Top 10%	126 and higher	42
Top 20%	117 and higher	34

TABLE 17. Percentage Rank in High School Graduating Class and Probability of Entering and Graduating from College

Percentile Rank in High School Graduating Class	Percentage of High School Graduates Who Enter College	Percentage of College Entrants Who Graduate	Percentage of High School Graduates Who Graduate from College
81–100	53	82	43
61– 80	44	68	30
41– 60	35	54	19
21– 40	26	40	10
1– 20	17	26	4

The Army General Classification Test (AGCT) score used as the measure of intelligence in Table 16 is roughly comparable to the I.Q. All of the ability levels shown in this table may be assumed to represent individuals who are capable of earning a college degree. The considerable numbers at each of the levels who do not do so, signify the serious loss to society which it is the function of guidance to prevent.

Table 17 shows college selection from the standpoint of rank in high-school class. This is indeed a sorry picture, for not only does it show that many able youth are not being developed to the extent of their capacity, but it also shows that many of those attempting college are not capable of profit-

[35] Dael Wolfle, *op. cit.,* p. 149, Table VI.1; and p. 150, Table VI.2.

ing by education at that level. Thus, guidance is challenged to *dis*suade as well as *per*suade.

With this sketchy portrayal, by a sampling of the extensive pertinent literature, the need for guidance in making the college decision has been demonstrated to be most demanding. The problem is highly complex, involving financial and motivational factors which vary in every case. To bring about a more rational matching of individuals with opportunities in higher education and to do so by the methods permissible in democratic guidance, calls for more energy and skill in guidance than we presently muster.

MALADJUSTMENT IN OCCUPATIONAL CHOICES

The Vocational Choices of High-School Pupils Viewed in Relation to Social Need

One of the tasks of vocational guidance is to bring about the distribution of workers in accordance with social need. This criterion is not easy to define; most researchers in this field have assumed that the actual distribution of those gainfully employed, as shown by the decennial census, is a satisfactory approximation to social need. Admitting that such a yardstick probably has its limitations, we shall nevertheless use it here.

Shown in Table 18 are the vocational choices of 2,773 pupils in Western Pennsylvania secondary schools, the pupils being about evenly divided between junior and senior high school levels and randomly representing 20 different school systems.[36] The pupils were asked to name the occupation they were planning to enter, or at least the occupation they were most seriously considering. The table presents percentage distributions of their choices, with the pupils divided by sex and by school level. In parentheses at the head of each column is the number of pupils in each group. If the occupations from "engineering" down to and including "miscellaneous professions" are classified as *professions,* the percentage of pupils in each group falling in that category would be found to be as follows, reading across the columns from left to right: 42.1, 42.2, 50.0, 56.9. Thus, nearly half of these pupils chose to enter the professions. Nearly one fourth of the boys elected to take up engineering, a figure which has been closely paralleled in a number of other studies. Approximately 85 per cent of the girls here canvassed chose teaching, nursing, or clerical service. Other researches have disclosed the same tendency for girls to crowd into those three fields.

The divergence of these pupils' occupational choices from the actual distribution of workers is shown clearly in Table 19, which telescopes the data of Table 18 so as to make them comparable with a census summary of em-

[36] P. W. Hutson, "Measuring the Need for Guidance in Western Pennsylvania," *University of Pittsburgh School of Education Journal,* Vol. VI (May, 1931), p. 127, Table I.

TABLE 18. Percentage Distributions of Secondary-School Pupils According to Their Choice of Occupation

	BOYS		GIRLS	
	Junior High School (793)	Senior High School (735)	Junior High School (741)	Senior High School (504)
Engineering	23.5	23.5	.3	.6
Law	1.9	1.2	.4	.2
Medicine	5.2	3.1	....	.6
Teaching:				
Secondary	3.7	5.0	9.2	11.5
Elementary	1.0	.1	16.7	12.7
Undefined	.6	.7	3.2	2.4
Total	5.3	5.8	29.1	26.6
Library	....	....	.8	1.2
Nursing	....	....	11.7	18.7
Journalism	.1	1.6	.5	.2
Art and music	2.6	2.9	3.8	5.4
Pharmacy	1.8	.8	.4	.6
Stage	.3	.4	1.8	.6
Miscellaneous pro-				
fessions	1.4	2.9	1.2	2.2
Farming and forestry	3.2	1.8	.1	....
Trade	3.7	4.6	.7	2.2
Clerical	4.3	11.8	44.4	38.5
Skilled manufacturing and mechanical work:				
Mechanic	5.8	2.2	....	....
Auto mechanic ...	4.8	1.0	....	....
Airplane mechanic	1.8	1.2	....	....
Machinist	2.8	2.2	....	....
Printer	.5	.4	....	....
Draftsman	3.3	3.1	....	....
Patternmaker	.5	2.4	....	....
Electrician	3.7	11.2	....	....
Carpenter	2.0	.8	....	....
Dressmaker and milliner	....	....	.8	.4
Other	1.6	1.1	.1	.4
Total	26.8	25.6	.9	.8
Skilled transportation work:				
Aviator	11.9	7.5	.4	.4
Other	1.6	.1	....	....
Total	13.5	7.6	.4	.4
Miscellaneous	3.9	3.4	1.9	1.2
No choice	2.8	3.0	1.5	.2
Grand total	100.3	100.0	99.9	100.2

ployed men and women over eighteen years of age. The percentage of boys proposing to enter engineering is more than thirty times as great as the percentage of employed men engaged in that profession. Similarly, about 26 per cent of employed women are engaged in teaching, nursing, and clerical work, in contrast to the 85 per cent of girls who desire to enter those fields. On the other hand, the table shows complementary shortages of pupils' choices in other fields. The comparisons shown in Table 19 should be taken with at least two reservations in mind: first, the pupils canvassed represent, we know, some degree of selection from the general population and therefore the proportions aspiring to the professions may justifiably be a little larger than the number of workers so engaged; second, since the census figures are for the country as a whole, they are not exactly representative of the vocational opportunities of Western Pennsylvania, as, for example, in the field of agriculture.

TABLE 19. Percentage Distributions of Pupils According to Occupational Choice and of All Employed Persons over Eighteen Years of Age According to Occupations (1920 Census)

| | BOYS | | | GIRLS | | |
Occupation	Junior High School	Senior High School	EM-PLOYED MEN	Junior High School	Senior High School	EM-PLOYED WOMEN
Clerical work	4.3	11.8	4.3	44.4	38.5	14.7
Engineering	23.5	23.5	.7	.3	.6	.1
Farming and forestry	3.2	1.8	28.8	.1	....	10.7
Law	1.9	1.2	.4	.4	.2	.02
Medicine and nursing	5.2	3.1	.7	11.7	19.3	2.3
Skilled manufacturing and mechanical work	26.7	25.6	25.0	.9	.8	19.6
Skilled transportation work	13.5	7.6	6.8	.4	.4	2.3
Teaching	5.3	5.8	.6	29.1	26.6	9.0
Trade	3.7	4.6	10.9	.7	2.2	10.0
Miscellaneous professions	6.2	8.6	1.2	8.5	10.2	1.9
Miscellaneous	6.7	6.3	20.6	3.4	1.4	29.4
Total	100.2	100.0	100.0	99.9	100.2	100.02

A study made in the agricultural state of Nebraska, in which a comparison was made between the vocational choices of all the high-school pupils of the state with the distribution of the workers of the state, is summarized in Table

20.[37] While the percentage of pupils proposing to enter agriculture is larger than in the Western Pennsylvania study, it is far out of line with the number of workers engaged in agriculture. The disproportion of pupils planning to enter the professions is comparable to that found in Western Pennsylvania.

Similar evidence of the need for guidance in occupational choice to meet the criterion of social need is evident in the reports of studies made in connection with state-wide testing programs of high-school seniors in Minnesota[38] and Missouri.[39]

TABLE 20. Relation of Occupational Interest of Nebraska High-School Students in 1936 to Worker Distribution in Nebraska According to the 1930 Census

Occupational Division	Distribution of Nebraska Workers	Interest of High-School Students
Agriculture	38.89	14.32
Clerical	5.98	14.45
Domestic and personal service	8.43	5.27
Extraction of minerals	.11	.03
Forestry and fishing	.03	.29
Manufacturing and mechanical industries . .	15.97	4.59
Professional, semi-professional, and recreational pursuits	7.82	43.77
Government and public service	1.24	1.99
Trade	13.27	4.56
Transportation and communication	8.24	10.57
Miscellaneous	. . . .	.12
Total	99.98	99.96

The statistical treatment accorded this problem by Lehman and Witty, as evidenced by Table 21,[40] adds further illumination. These authors obtained the occupational choices of more than 10,000 boys in Topeka, Kansas, and in Kansas City, Missouri; they reduced the number of occupations to 138 so as to get rid of occupations having little meaning for city boys in the states of Kansas and Missouri; then they found the coefficients of correlation between the numbers of white workers engaged in each of the occupations and

[37] Adapted from *Vocational Education in the Years Ahead*, Chart 35 (U.S. Office of Education, Vocational Division Bulletin No. 234, 1945), p. 310.

[38] E. G. Williamson and J. G. Darley, "Trends in the Occupational Choices of High School Seniors," *Journal of Applied Psychology*, Vol. XIX (August, 1935), pp. 361–370.

[39] A. B. Smith, *Occupational Choice, Educational Intention, and General Ability: A Study of High School Seniors from the Point of View of Guidance*. Ed.D. Thesis (Columbia, Mo., University of Missouri Library, 1936).

[40] Harvey C. Lehman and Paul A. Witty, "Vocational Guidance: Some Basic Considerations," *Journal of Educational Sociology*, Vol. VIII (November, 1934), p. 181 (adapted from Table IV).

TABLE 21. Coefficients of Correlation between Numbers of White Workers in Each of 138 Occupations and Numbers of Boys Expecting to Enter Each Occupation

Ages of Boys	Number of Boys	Coefficient
9 and 10	2317	−.01
11 and 12	2735	−.009
13 and 14	2443	−.009
15 and 16	1832	−.007
17 and 18	644	+.0003

the numbers of boys choosing each. The table indicates a complete absence of relationship, and since the older boys are not making choices in accord with social need any more than the younger boys, it would appear that the school was having no effect on choice.

More recently, Myers has reported surveys of the vocational choices of the seniors of the Eastern High School, Washington, D.C., in 1940 and 1946.[41] He concluded that these groups were planning to distribute themselves among occupations considerably out of line with social need. Likewise, Lawrence's recent survey of the vocational choices of tenth-grade Negro students in eleven California high schools showed them to be concentrating their choices on occupations which offer a maximum of social prestige but need only small numbers of workers.[42] Shosteck, reporting studies of the vocational choices of high-school seniors in Philadelphia and New Haven, found that approximately four out of every ten chose a professional occupation and that four out of every ten selected clerical or sales fields. He estimated "that only 17 per cent of all Philadelphians and 22 per cent of New Haven workers, 25 years of age or older with 4 years of high school or more education, either employed or seeking work, are classified in professional or semi-professional work."[43] Thus, the later studies substantiate the findings of the earlier study of Western Pennsylvania with which this subject of vocational choice in reference to social need was opened. Is it the nature of the American social structure that constantly creates this problem of occupational distribution?

The Vocational Choices of High-School Pupils in Relation to Ability

How well do the vocational choices of high-school pupils correspond to their abilities? To ask this question is to apply the oldest criterion—the one

[41] William E. Myers, "High School Graduates Choose Vocations Unrealistically," *Occupations,* Vol. XXV (March, 1947), pp. 332–333.

[42] Paul F. Lawrence, "Vocational Aspirations of Negro Youth of California," *Journal of Negro Education,* Vol. XIX (Winter, 1950), pp. 47–56.

[43] Robert Shosteck, "How Well Are We Putting Across Occupational Information?" *Personnel and Guidance Journal,* Vol. XXXIII (January, 1955), p. 266.

with which Frank Parsons was primarily concerned—to test the soundness of vocational choice. The measure cannot be easily made, because success in a vocation depends on so many factors existing in various combinations and weightings. And some of the factors are exceedingly intangible. Nevertheless, the counselor must be continually applying this criterion as best he can. That is the heart of counseling for vocational decision.

Figure 5, from the study of Western Pennsylvania high schools,[44] offers a single coarse measurement in answer to the question of how well pupils' choices match their abilities. The data in the upper part of the figure show the intelligence quotients of three occupational classes in the army white draft, World War I. These have been adapted from Proctor's monograph[45] in which he gave Army Alpha scores of these groups. Using Proctor's table of mental-age equivalents for Alpha scores, intelligence quotients were

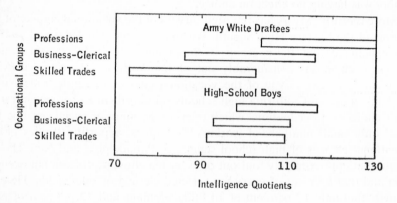

FIG. 5. Ranges of middle 50 per cent of intelligence quotients of three occupational groups and three groups of high-school boys who plan to enter corresponding occupations.

computed for the quartile scores, assuming that mental growth ceases at sixteen years. The procedure was arbitrary, but the purpose was to obtain a measure of intelligence of adult occupational groups which was comparable to that available for the pupils. The lower part of Figure 5 shows the intelligence (range of middle fifty per cent of intelligence quotients) of those high-school boys of Western Pennsylvania who chose to enter the three occupational fields indicated. The point of greatest significance is that the groups of boys overlap much more than do the groups of men. For example, the first and third bars for the boys overlap by two thirds their length. In

[44] P. W. Hutson, *op. cit.*, p. 139, Figure 7.
[45] W. M. Proctor, *Use of Psychological Tests in the Educational and Vocational Guidance of High School Pupils, Journal of Educational Research*, Monograph No. 1 (Bloomington, Ill., Public School Publishing Co., June, 1921), pp. 39–41, 67.

contrast, the first and third bars for the men do not overlap at all. One is justified in concluding that high-school boys choose an occupation without much regard for their general intelligence or the requirements of the occupation for that trait.

Williamson and Darley, in their study of the need for guidance among Minnesota high-school seniors, found similar evidence of slight regard for ability in making a choice of occupation. This is indicated in Table 22,[46] which is merely suggestive of the extensive data that these authors gathered. The college aptitude rating (C.A.R.) was obtained for each boy by averaging his percentile rank in scholarship in his high-school class. Since the boys in the highest category of occupational choices had a mean college aptitude rating of 50.1, it is evident that they were practically a random sampling of the class. Furthermore, the size of the standard deviation—24.7—suggests a wide scatter of these boys over the entire scale of ability represented by the class. While the mean C.A.R. of 50.1 for this group of boys is also the mean for the class as a whole, it is above the mean for the boys of the class. High-school girls, by virtue of higher average scholarship (Take note of the relative scholarship of boys and girls in Figure 4), achieve a mean C.A.R. somewhat above 50, and the mean for the boys of the class is correspondingly below 50. Table 22 shows a decline in mean C.A.R. from one occupational group to another corresponding to the decline in ability requirements which the sequence of the groups represents, but, as pointed out in connection with Figure 5, the decline is slight, the overlapping is marked, and the groups are more to be noted for their identity than for their difference.

From a more recent canvass of the occupational choices of 533 pupils in

TABLE 22. Mean College Aptitude Ratings of High-School Senior Boys of the Class of 1933 Classified According to Their Occupational Choices

Occupational Choice	Number of Boys	Mean C.A.R.	Standard Deviation
I. High professional and executive occupations	1799	50.1	24.7
II. Lower professional and large business occupations	1465	41.8	23.9
III. Technical, clerical, and supervisory occupations	1005	37.1	22.6
IV. Skilled tradesmen and low grade clerical work	856	32.4	20.9
V. Semi-skilled occupations	77	37.8	26.0
VI. Unskilled labor	. . . .	. . . .	. . . .
No choice given	3369	36.8	23.4

[46] E. G. Williamson and J. G. Darley, "Matching Abilities to Jobs," *Personnel Journal,* Vol. XIII (April, 1935), p. 350, data from Table III.

two junior-senior high schools in New York State, Fleege and Malone reach the following conclusion:[47]

Examining occupational choice in the light of native intelligence as reflected by the I.Q., we find little correlation between ability and the intellectual challenge of an occupation. . . . An analysis of our data suggests that both boys and girls, at all grade levels, tend to choose occupations without sufficient consideration of their ability to do the work of their choice.

Data presented by Fryer and shown here as Table 23[48] shed additional light on the problem of incorrect vocational choice. In finding the percentages (third column) at each mental-age level who made vocational choices in keeping with their intelligence, he considered individuals with mentality not more than one and a half mental ages above or below the average mental level of chosen vocations as having the approximate intelligence required. His interpretation of his data is that

TABLE 23. Relation between Intelligence and Requirements of Vocational Ambitions in Various Intelligence Groups

Intelligence Groups in Mental Age	Number of Cases	Per cent Making Correct Vocational Choices on Basis of Intelligence
18 and above	333	39
17 to 17–11	269	63
16 to 16–11	310	72
15 to 15–11	302	52
14 to 14–11	226	54
13 to 13–11	149	11
12 to 12–11	49	10
9 to 11–11	10	0
All intelligence groups	1816	49

With the exception of the decrease at the upper intelligence levels, *higher intellectual ability* appears to be correlated with *correct vocational choices*. . . . The explanation of [the exception] would seem to lie in the difficulty that high grade ability has in finding satisfactory outlet in the occupations. . . . The lower an individual is in degrees of mentality the greater he is likely to be in error in vocational interests.

We can now make additions or amendments to Fryer's interpretations as follows: The reason why so many of his subjects of low mental age made incorrect vocational choices was probably not because they lacked intelligence for choosing, but because they could not debase themselves by choos-

[47] Urban H. Fleege and Helen J. Malone, "Motivation in Occupational Choice among Junior-Senior High School Students," *Journal of Educational Psychology*, Vol. XXXVII (February, 1946), p. 80.

[48] Douglas Fryer, "Predicting Abilities from Interests," *Journal of Applied Psychology*, Vol. XI, No. 3 (1927), p. 219, Table 4.

ing the unskilled, low-paying, routine jobs to which their abilities corresponded. As to the exception in the highest mental-age brackets, it is clear that those subjects should have chosen the learned professions. But the long, expensive training required put such occupations out of reach of many who should have chosen them. Quite possibly, too, some could not endure the long postponement of financial independence and marriage imposed by this extended period of training. Hence, many of these people chose an occupation one or two mental levels lower than their intelligence warranted, but still an occupation which gave them considerable status.

The Vocational Choices of College Students

Only two studies will be cited to show the need for vocational guidance of college students. In one, Sparling[49] made a canvass of freshmen, sophomores, and juniors at Long Island University and found that 87.8 per cent of the students had selected vocations. Of these, 94.8 per cent had made their choices in the four fields of medicine, teaching, dentistry, and law— 84.0 per cent of the women choosing teaching, and 53.9 per cent of the men choosing medicine.

Women expect to earn twice as much and men four times as much as workers now engaged in the vocations they have selected. This suggests that "expected earnings" is playing an important part in their choice of a vocation.[50]

Sisson[51] tabulated the vocational choices as given upon entrance to Wesleyan University (a liberal arts college) by the classes of 1937 and 1939 and found that 83 per cent planned to enter the professions, 16 per cent looking forward to medicine. After three years in college, 67 per cent of the members of the class of 1937 still planned on the professions; after one year in college, 70 per cent of the class of 1939 had similar plans. By contrast, a tally of the occupations being pursued in 1931 by the classes of 1905, 1910, 1915, 1920, and 1925 showed only 47 per cent to be engaged in professions —2.05 per cent in medicine. Sisson concludes that even though college students are a selected group their ambitions need to be scaled down.

The Vocational Choices of Trade-School Pupils

In the studies of high-school and college students thus far reported, most of the individuals on whom the studies were based were pursuing general education and had not yet entered upon training to prepare themselves for the occupations they had chosen. By contrast, boys in a Smith-Hughes cur-

49 Edward J. Sparling, *Do College Students Choose Vocations Wisely?* (New York, Teachers College, Columbia University, Contributions to Education, No. 561, 1933).
50 *Ibid.,* p. 39.
51 E. Donald Sisson, "Vocational Choices of College Students," *School and Society,* Vol. XLVI (December 11, 1937), pp. 765–768.

riculum are actively preparing for the vocation of their choice. How sound, how well-advised, are the choices of such boys? While a direct answer to this question is not available, data with some bearing on it have been gathered and will here be cited.

A mimeographed *Survey of Graduates of Day Trade and Industrial Classes, 1938–39,* prepared by the United States Office of Education, was cited in a printed publication from the same source as reporting that[52] " 'Of the 5,761 graduates, 1,826, or 31.7 per cent, entered the trade for which they prepared . . . 498, or 8.7 per cent, entered allied occupations.' " The survey quoted covered ten states of the Midwest. The 59.6 per cent of the graduates unaccounted for in this brief quotation were either in nonrelated work, unemployed, or continuing their education. While on the face of it this situation would seem to signify a great need for guidance, we must reckon with the fact that the time of the survey was one of extensive unemployment, especially harsh on youth of the ages 16 to 24. It was a period when plenty of trained workers could not find jobs for which they were trained, and after a period of search they took whatever employment they could get.

The publication just quoted, however, continues the discussion by pointing to the heavy drop-out rate often found in trade schools. "In a certain trade school, for instance, the ratio is 100 beginners for every 25 finishers."[53] Such a figure plainly suggests that many pupils who enter trade school should never do so. They should never attempt the training. Serious waste of educational resources is involved when a faculty devotes time to the instruction of students who never complete the training sequence.

A study of the occupational affiliation achieved by trade school graduates in a period of full employment also yielded evidence of need for vocational guidance—either guidance in choice of curriculum pursued or guidance in placement. Leonard interviewed the June, 1947, graduates of Pittsburgh vocational high schools for boys about a year after graduation and found 43 per cent working in the trades or trade fields for which they were trained, 19 per cent working in trades or trade fields other than the ones for which they were trained, 31 per cent working in definitely nonrelated occupations, and 6 per cent unemployed.[54]

Reasoning in Vocational Choice

What are the reasons that people give for their choice of occupations? Fischer endeavored to obtain some answer to that question when he gathered

[52] *Vocational Education in the Years Ahead* (U.S. Office of Education, Vocational Division, Bulletin No. 234, 1945), p. 302.

[53] *Ibid.,* p. 303.

[54] Regis J. Leonard, "Occupational Experiences of Trade School Graduates," *Occupations,* Vol. XXVIII (October, 1949), pp. 28–31.

the responses summarized in Table 24 from 631 students enrolled in a general curriculum in the College of Arts and Sciences of the University of Illinois.[55] What value should be attached to the first of the "Reasons Given," namely, "Interest in work?" It has been shown that a professed interest in

TABLE 24. Percentage Distribution of the Answers Given by College Students to the Question, "What Made You Decide on the Vocation You Selected?"

Reasons Given	Per cent
Interest in work	51
Expected ability	11
Actual experience	8
Available opportunities	6
Advice from others	6
Interest in people	5
Infrequently stated reasons	12
Total	99

an occupation, undefined and not analytical, bears little relation to the possession of the essential ability-requirements for the field. The next two reasons, "Expected ability," and "Actual experience," are suggestive of the kind of thinking that vocational guidance seeks to promote.

In the Western Pennsylvania study already cited the pupils were directed on their blanks of inquiry to "List the main reasons for your choice," and were allowed three lines, numbered 1, 2, and 3, on which to write. Most pupils gave two reasons; many gave three. Table 25,[56] giving the classification of their responses, shows that most prominent in the pupils' minds were various self-advantages. They were mindful of what the occupation might contribute to them in the way of immediate and future creature-comforts. This is human, but it is not indicative of any tendency to make the occupational decision hinge upon a comparison of personal competency and occupational requirements. Neither is this kind of thinking evident in the second category of reasons which is the rubric under which were classified the expressions, "I like it" and "Am interested in it." Glancing at the columns of frequencies the reader will note that more than three fourths of the reasons fell into these first two categories, that junior and senior high school pupils do not vary markedly with regard to them, and that the percentage of boys slightly favors the first category while the percentage of girls slightly favors the second.

Table 25 is highly suggestive of the problems we meet in vocational guid-

[55] Robert P. Fischer, "Need for Vocational Information," *Journal of Higher Education,* Vol. XVI (January, 1945), p. 34, Table I (adapted).

[56] P. W. Hutson, *op. cit.,* p. 141, Table IV.

TABLE 25. Percentage Distributions of the Reasons Given by Boys and Girls for Their Occupational Choices

Reasons	BOYS		GIRLS	
	Junior High School	Senior High School	Junior High School	Senior High School
Self-advantages:				
A. Financial rewards	19.9	13.0	12.7	9.6
B. Possibilities for advancement	6.3	8.0	3.6	8.0
C. Promising future of the industry	3.2	6.1	1.3	.3
D. Easy work	3.0	.8	3.2	.7
E. Affords steady employment .	2.2	3.0	1.4	2.1
F. Field not crowded	2.3	5.3	.4	3.4
G. Others, as, health, social status, opportunity for travel, ease of learning	14.2	10.0	9.8	6.6
Total	51.1	46.2	32.4	30.7
Expressing like for, or interest in, the occupation (unanalyzed) . .	31.6	35.3	41.5	46.2
Expressed like for, or interest in, some aspect of the work, as, "I like mathematics" or "I am fond of little children"	1.3	1.3	2.1	2.1
To help my family	.1	. . . .	1.1	.6
Influence of parents or other members of family, through advice, dictation, or example	3.3	2.4	3.1	2.6
Having some qualifications for the work (general and specific mentions of capacity and experience)	6.4	8.4	10.8	8.0
The occupation is socially serviceable	2.7	2.3	3.1	3.9
Mention of source of knowledge of the occupation, as, "Learned about it from reading"	1.4	1.6	4.0	2.4
Restrictions or obstacles forcing the choice	.5	.5	.5	1.6
Affording outlet for, or challenge to, one's powers	1.5	1.5	1.1	1.5
Having opportunity to enter the vocation	.4	.5	.4	.5
Total	99.9	100.0	100.1	100.1

ance. Such data, procured by a free-response inquiry, probably have much higher validity than would have been the case if a check list had been used. For a check list would most certainly have contained such items as "Because I believe I am fitted for it" and "Because I think I can render society a service"—items which the pupils would have checked with a high degree of unanimity, but which taken together in Table 25 received no more than 10 or 12 per cent of the responses. Later studies which have employed check lists have borne out this interpretation.

Some of the authors whose studies have been cited in this section as showing vocational choices out of harmony with ability and with social need, have asserted that their data were evidence of the need for wider and more thorough dissemination of occupational information. Counts would disagree with them. He said, in interpreting his exposition of the social status of occupations (briefly described in Chapter 2, page 48),[57]

The present investigation would suggest that high-school students know a great deal about this world. They look forward to the professional occupations because they are sensitive to the social judgment and because they recognize the prestige which is attached to these callings. The difficulty, perhaps, is that they know too much rather than too little about the world into which they are going.

If the study of occupations focuses pupils' attention on "Advantages" and "Disadvantages," "Remuneration," and similar topics, it seems altogether probable that we shall be promoting the sort of thinking shown in Table 25, for the practice of self-seeking is particularly strong in individualistic America. We strike into issues and problems here that will be taken up in Chapter 9.

The canvass of the studies of occupational choice suggests to this writer that there must be a marked downward shift in vocational aspiration for a great many young people as they drop out of high school or graduate. Is this a sudden and rude awakening? Or are there *some* boys and girls who in their hearts have never really expected to reach those occupations of exalted status which they have written down in their questionnaires, but have squeezed such prestige value out of the ambition as they could during school days?[58] Perhaps, too, they have pursued the college-preparatory curriculum because of its immediate prestige value and have not had any sincere plans for entering any college. With such questions in mind, this writer must conclude that the research into occupational choice has been extensive but relatively superficial. The field is open for more intensive and more penetrating investigation.

[57] George S. Counts, "The Social Status of Occupations: A Problem in Vocational Guidance," *School Review,* Vol. XXXIII (January, 1925), p. 27.

[58] Some verification of this suspicion is afforded by the unstatistical report of the practical experience of a competent practitioner in guidance. See the following reference: Katharine W. Dresden, "Vocational Choices of Secondary Pupils," *Occupations,* Vol. XXVII (November, 1948), pp. 104–106.

EVIDENCE OF MALADJUSTMENT—PHYSICAL, SOCIAL, EMOTIONAL

Physical Maladjustment

The growth of health services in the schools over recent decades is sufficient evidence of our acknowledgment that the removal of physical maladjustments of pupils is in part a school responsibility. Guidance is concerned with the removal of all manner of impediments to pupil development —physical, emotional, scholastic, etc. While guidance organization does not include the health service, the two must work in close co-operation if the welfare of pupils is to be most adequately served. The health service through its routine examination or routine screening tests is continually contributing information which guidance workers need in order to understand children. Teachers and counselors for their part are using this information to obtain parental co-operation in the improvement of children's health, or they are adapting instruction, curriculum, and advisement to children's physical handicaps.

Various surveys have been made to show the incidence of physical maladjustments among children, but only one will be cited here. Dr. Thomas H. Eames reported the data shown in Table 26.[59] This was gathered primarily from public schools in New England in communities which were predominantly Anglo-Saxon in origin. The strikingly higher frequency of physical

TABLE 26. Frequency of Physical Defects and Diseases in a Group of 1,000 Children Who Were Failing in School Subjects and in a Group of 500 Children Who Were Not Failing

Physical Handicap	Percentage of Group Having Physical Defect or Disease	
	Children Who Were Failing	Children Who Were Not Failing
DEFECTS AND DISEASES OF:		
Eyes	59.0	21.0
Ear, nose, and throat	28.6	3.6
Circulatory system	8.0	2.0
Gastro-intestinal tract	3.0	0.2
Nervous system	3.2	1.2
Endocrine system	3.2	2.6
Skin	4.1	2.2
CONDITIONS OF:		
Allergy	2.0	0.6
Malnutrition	10.0	3.0

[59] "The Relation of Undiscovered or Disregarded Physical Handicaps to Learning," *Elementary School Journal*, Vol. XLV (May, 1945), p. 519, Table 1.

defects and diseases among the failing pupils than among those who were not failing is indeed an example of the interrelatedness of different forms of maladjustment. It bears out the soundness of the injunction, "Never overlook the physical," in seeking the explanation for scholastic inadequacy, emotional instability, anti-social conduct, or any other problem in pupil behavior.

Problems of Delinquency and of Mental Health Among Public-School Children

From the extensive literature bearing on the evidence of social and emotional maladjustment, sometimes resulting in delinquency, two studies will be drawn upon, primarily for their value in creating techniques for the discovery of such problems. The first is Ludden's search for indexes to possible delinquency.[60] He was moved to make his investigation by his observation of the mounting incidence of juvenile delinquency and the high cost of attempted rehabilitation only after the child is in trouble. His method was to compare a group of 345 delinquents on the basis of certain items of data taken from school records for the term preceding their appearance in court, with a control group of non-delinquents in the same school system. The significance of the differences between the two groups was stated in terms of the critical ratio, and in Table 27[61] are given the critical ratios which were higher than 2.0. Six of the items in the table are related to the home and eight are related to school environment. (Other items not in the school

TABLE 27. Facts on Record, Indicative of Possible Delinquency

	Critical Ratio
1. Living in a delinquency area	9.10
2. Chronological overageness—any amount	8.88
3. Living in a low-rent area—average under $20 per month	8.40
4. Living in a broken home	7.50
5. Different homes lived in, if more than one	6.76
6. Poor school attendance—over five absences	6.43
7. Terms repeated in school—over one	6.40
8. School failures—more than one subject	6.19
9. Terms with failing marks—two or more	5.61
10. Intelligence below 90 in Otis test	4 to 6
11. Low employment status of father	4.72
12. Times tardy at school—any number	4.65
13. Illegal absences from school—over five	4.32
14. Intermediate position in sibling group	2.10

[60] Wallace Ludden, "Anticipating Cases of Juvenile Delinquency," *School and Society*, Vol. LIX (February 12, 1944), pp. 123–126.
[61] *Ibid.*, p. 125, Table I.

record might have proven more crucial, as, for example, Hill's finding that "type and quality of parental discipline" had the highest critical ratio of any of 55 items on which his trained case workers gathered information.[62]) When the data sheets for each member of the delinquent and control groups were scored on the basis of one point for each of the factors which had a significant critical ratio, it was found that 68.7 per cent of the delinquents scored three or more, to 25.9 per cent of the control group. Despite the coarseness and the too-simple character of Ludden's device, the inadequacy of which he clearly admitted, it could undoubtedly be used advantageously at the sixth or seventh-grade level, thus bringing potential delinquents to the attention of guidance workers who could then take preventive measures.

A second study, by Rogers,[63] presents a method of locating school children who are socially and emotionally maladjusted, and shows the results achieved by applying this method. He drew up ten indexes of maladjustment, objective and feasible to apply, and resting on the assumptions that maladjustment may be judged in part by behavior and in part by taking account of known causative factors in poor mental health. He admits that his criteria do not take adequate account of elements in the home environment which figure importantly in causing poor mental health. The ten criteria, omitting the author's statements of description and justification, are as follows:[64]

1. The child is considered a chronological misfit if his age differs from the median age of his classroom group by more than one year.

2. A child is regarded as an intellectual misfit if his mental age is more than one year below or more than two years above the median for his own classroom.

3. A child is regarded as an academic misfit if his reading achievement is more than one year below or more than two years above the median of his classroom.

4. A child is regarded as having a reading disability if his reading age is more than one year below his mental age.

5. A child is regarded as a school failure if he is at the time of this study repeating his grade (or half-grade).

6. A child is regarded as a truant if he has been a truant from school during the current term.

7. A child for purposes of this study is regarded as a behavior or personality problem in the teacher's judgment if he received a score of more than 150 in the teacher's rating of his behavior on the Behavior Scale.

8. A child is regarded as maladjusted according to standardized tests if he made a score of more than 40 on the Personal Index [by Loofbourow and Keys] or less than 96 on the California Personality Test.

[62] A. S. Hill, "A Statistical Analysis of Significant Factors in Pupil Maladjustment," *Journal of Educational Sociology,* Vol. IX (December, 1935), pp. 219–230.

[63] Carl Rogers, "The Criteria Used in a Study of Mental-Health Problems," and "Mental-Health Findings in Three Elementary Schools," *Educational Research Bulletin* (Ohio State University), Vol. XXI (February 18 and March 18, 1942), pp. 29–40, 69–79, 86.

[64] *Ibid.,* pp. 31–34.

9. A child is regarded as maladjusted according to his companions' judgments if one seventh or more of the class wrote in his name in one or more of the significant items of the "Guess Who Game."

10. A child is regarded as maladjusted according to observers' ratings if he was rated as showing moderately serious or serious maladjustment.

The criteria were employed in a survey of the mental health of 1,524 children in three six-year elementary schools of Columbus, Ohio, the schools being chosen as representative of the different socio-economic levels of the city. Criteria 1 to 9 inclusive were employed with the fourth, fifth, and sixth grades. Criteria 8 and 9 could not be employed with the first two grades because the children were too young for such co-operation; therefore these children were observed for several hours by trained observers employing the tenth criterion. The third grade was not included in the study.

For each child a maladjustment score was arrived at simply by adding up the number of criteria on which he showed up as maladjusted. With thumbnail sketches of a few cases Rogers demonstrates that

when a child is maladjusted according to four or more indexes, he is not merely a statistical score, but an individual with a long and often tragic history of unhappiness and unfortunate life circumstances. The children with high scores have neither the sense of security nor the sense of adequacy in achievement which together are regarded as basic to good mental health. They are sufficiently maladjusted to make them excellent candidates for our jails and state hospitals, our divorce courts, and our relief agencies in another few years.[65]

Turning to the results found in the employment of the criteria with the three Columbus schools, Table 28[66] shows the percentage of the pupils of

TABLE 28. Types of Maladjustment Distributed by Percentages According to Grades in These Three Schools

Criteria	First	Second	Fourth	Fifth	Sixth
Chronological misfit	3	9	13	15	11
Intellectual misfit	12	25	17	27	32
Academic misfit	14	18	12	23	36
Reading disability	2	12	24	35	30
School failure	11	10	3	4	1
Truant	1	2	5	3	1
Maladjusted—					
Teacher's rating	30	29	31	42	26
Personality test	...*	...*	14	16	19
Children's rating	...*	...*	18	24	15
Observer's rating	24	11	...†	...†	...†

* Not given in Grades I and II.
† Not given in Grades IV, V, VI.

65 *Ibid.*, p. 40.
66 *Ibid.*, p. 73, Table III, adapted slightly.

each grade located by each of the criteria as maladjusted. In addition to showing the relative frequency with which each of the criteria was operative, the table gives a general impression of an increase from the first grade to the sixth in the number of pupils who are maladjusted. This latter point is made more clear in Table 29[67] in which it is evident that the increase comes among the moderately maladjusted. Rogers defined the "relatively well-adjusted" as those pupils who were picked out by one criterion or none. "Seriously" mal-

TABLE 29. Percentage Relationship of Maladjustment of Each Grade-Level in These Three Schools

Grade-Level	Serious	Moderate	Relatively Well-Adjusted
I	11	18	71
II	13	19	70
IV	9	24	67
V	15	44	41
VI	12	39	49
All grades	12	30	58

adjusted were those pupils of the upper three grades who were picked out by four or more criteria, and of the first two grades who were picked out by three or more criteria. The total for all grades, as shown in the last line of Table 29 is 12 per cent, or nearly one eighth, seriously maladjusted. If these schools are representative of the city, it would mean, says Rogers, that there are five thousand seriously maladjusted children in the Columbus schools.

Additional points concerning the incidence of maladjustment, as developed by this investigation, are the following: 18 per cent of the boys rated as seriously maladjusted compared to only 7 per cent of the girls; the more favored the neighborhood the fewer the number of seriously maladjusted pupils; the more a child deviates either way from the median intelligence quotient of his group the greater the likelihood of his being maladjusted.

This study is filled with meaning for all school workers. Not only does it give the evidence concerning the extent of maladjustment, but it offers an instrument with which the general run of elementary schools can locate the pupils who need help. Rogers points out the following implications of his study:[68]

Changes in school administration, school personnel, and educational policy are needed if we are to meet the problems here presented. In planning such changes it is essential that thought be given to preventive policies in connection with the well-adjusted group, and remedial policies which will improve the adjustment of the 30 per cent with moderate problems, as well as more specialized assistance and treatment for the 12 per cent of seriously maladjusted.

[67] *Ibid.*, p. 72, Table II, adapted.
[68] *Ibid.*, p. 86.

Adjustment Problems of College Students

While college students are a select group, representing for the most part the higher levels of intelligence, and representing also those who want to go to school rather than those who are by law compelled to, they present problems of adjustment the solutions of which are beneficial to the individual and to society just as in the case of pupils in the lower schools. Some idea of what the problems are and their frequency of appearance may be gathered from Table 30, an inventory compiled from the study of one hundred freshmen at the University of Chicago who were encountering difficulties in their courses, who were poor readers, and who were given remedial-reading training during the school years 1939–42.[69] The problems were discovered because the author, who was the remedial-reading teacher, found that for the effective performance of his work he had to consider the student as a whole, having due regard for both reading and nonreading problems. The total number of problems, shown at the foot of the table as 372, indicates that these students with reading difficulties averaged nearly four nonreading problems each.

L. C. Pressey, in describing her experiences in doing work similar to that of McCaul, was likewise impressed with the importance of problems other than ineffective reading or study.[70] Many probation students knew how to study but were failing their work for reasons other than personal efficiency, among which family difficulties or problems were among the most important. The author estimated that difficulties in the home, widely varying in character, were solely responsible for the failure of one tenth of probation students and were contributing factors for at least another three tenths. These problems of the home environment did not operate solely in the case of students who were living at home. Many students whose homes were at a distance were unfortunately and disadvantageously controlled or affected by their families.

Tyler, in recently reviewing the increasing importance of the guidance function at the level of higher education, pointed out that[71]

With the improvement of methods of testing college aptitude and with the exercise of greater care in the selection of students, we have reached the point in many institutions where the largest number of failures result not from lack of intellectual ability but from causes that can be dealt with through guidance procedures. In an analysis of failures in the College of the University of Chicago made this past year, we find the largest percentage apparently attributable to lack of intelligent use of the freedom of the College and the second largest percentage attributable

[69] Robert L. McCaul, "Student Personnel Opportunities for the College Remedial-Reading Teacher," *School Review,* Vol. LI (March, 1943), p. 159, Table 1.

[70] Luella Cole Pressey, "Some Serious Maladjustments among College Students," *Social Forces,* Vol. X (December, 1931), pp. 236–242.

[71] Ralph W. Tyler, "Extension of Responsibilities for Counseling and Guidance in Higher Institutions," *School Review,* Vol. LIII (September, 1945), p. 395.

TABLE 30. Problems Associated with Reading Difficulties of 100 College Freshmen Given Remedial-Reading Training

Nature of Problem	Frequency of Occurrence
Educational:	
Ineffective study habits	58
Too heavy or too light course program	35
Insufficient time devoted to study	29
Poor attitude toward study	21
Inadequate pre-college training	10
Conflicts with instructors	2
Total	155
Physical:	
Visual distress	42
Fatigue	21
Poor health	8
Hearing defects	8
Speech defects	4
Physical handicaps	3
Total	86
Environmental:	
In the home	28
In dormitory, fraternity, or sorority	10
Commuting to school	6
Total	44
Emotional:	
Fears	13
Inferiority complex	13
Sex	8
Indecision	5
Homesickness	3
Psychoses	2
Total	44
Social:	
Isolated	22
Oversocial	8
Overaggressive	1
Total	31
Financial:	
Too heavy burden of outside work	8
Inability to get scholarship, loan, or job	2
Total	10
Vocational:	
Lack of vocational objective	2
Total	2
Total number of problems	372

to emotional disturbances. Very few failures can properly be charged to lack of the intellectual ability necessary to carry on college work. Both of these chief difficulties can be reduced by counseling methods.

The evidence cited in this chapter points to the need for guidance service which is many-sided and well-integrated with the total educational program. The work to be done challenges not only specially trained personnel but all teachers and administrators in their daily contacts with pupils. In the light of the problems here described, we arrive at a clearer comprehension of guidance as rooted in the sources named in the second section of Chapter 1, namely, vocational guidance, student personnel administration, psychology, personnel work in industry, social work, mental hygiene, and psychiatry. The techniques and advanced understandings which have been developed in these fields are all needed in the work of human conservation which we have here outlined.

QUESTIONS, PROBLEMS, AND INVESTIGATIONS

1. For any high school that you know, compile failure statistics for a given school year.

2. Formulate criteria for detecting the pupils who will withdraw from school at the earliest age the law permits. Apply the criteria to a body of pupils in the seventh or eighth grades.

3. In many high schools the graduates have been ranked according to scholarship and an adequate record kept of the ones who entered college. In such a school compile the data in such a form as that of Figure 4, using the graduating classes for several years back and perhaps dividing them into fifths instead of tenths.

4. Assume that you are principal of a high school in which very little thought has been given to the guidance function. You suspect that guidance is needed. Draw up exact plans for several practical research projects to yield objective evidence by which you can inform yourself on this score and by which you can inform teachers, superintendent, and board of education.

5. From the records of medical examinations make an inventory of the physical maladjustments, permanent and remediable, of the pupils of your homeroom group or in one of your classes.

6. Survey the vocational choices of one hundred or more pupils of junior or senior high-school age and evaluate in the light of ability and social need, employing the techniques illustrated in similar studies cited in this chapter.

7. In some high school of your acquaintance, ascertain how wisely the pupils choose Latin, algebra, stenography, or some other elective subject. What cues do you gain from this chapter on technique for such a study?

8. Search out the full descriptions of Rogers' criteria for a survey of mental-health problems and apply them to a class or school.

9. Canvass several books on mental hygiene to find out what the authors say about failure in school.

10. Study a trade school of your acquaintance to ascertain the need for guidance, both distributive and adjustive.

SELECTED REFERENCES

BARBER, Leroy E., "Why Some Able High-School Graduates Do Not Go to College," School Review, Vol. LIX (February, 1951), pp. 93–96.

BERDIE, Ralph F., After High School—What? (Minneapolis, Minn., University of Minnesota Press, 1954).

BYRNS, Ruth, "Relation of Vocational Choice to Mental Ability and Occupational Opportunity," School Review, Vol. XLVII (February, 1939), pp. 101–109.

DAVIS, Horace L., The Utilization of Potential College Ability Found in the June, 1940, Graduates of Kentucky High Schools, Bulletin of the Bureau of School Service, Vol. XV, No. 1 (Lexington, Ky., College of Education, University of Kentucky, 1942).

DILLON, Harold J., Early School Leavers: A Major Educational Problem (New York 16 [419 Fourth Ave.], National Child Labor Committee, 1949).

EAMES, Thomas H., "The Relation of Undiscovered or Disregarded Physical Handicaps to Learning," Elementary School Journal, Vol. XLV (May, 1945), pp. 516–519.

ECKERT, Ruth E., and MARSHALL, Thomas O., When Youth Leave School, The Regents' Inquiry into the Character and Cost of Public Education in the State of New York (New York, McGraw-Hill, 1938).

EKSTROM, G. F., "Why Farm Children Leave School," School Review, Vol. LIV (April, 1946), pp. 231–237.

EMME, Earle E., "The Adjustment Problems of College Freshmen and Contributory Factors," Journal of Applied Psychology, Vol. XX (February, 1936), pp. 60–76.

FISCHER, Robert P., "Need for Vocational Information," Journal of Higher Education, Vol. XVI (January, 1945), pp. 33–36.

FLEEGE, Urban H., and MALONE, Helen J., "Motivation in Occupational Choice among Junior-Senior High School Students," Journal of Educational Psychology, Vol. XXXVII (February, 1946), pp. 77–86.

HAVIGHURST, Robert J., "Social Implications of the Report of the President's Commission on Higher Education," School and Society, Vol. LXVII (April 3, 1948), pp. 257–261.

HUTSON, P. W., "Measuring the Need for Guidance in Western Pennsylvania," University of Pittsburgh School of Education Journal, Vol. VI (May, 1931), pp. 115–154.

IFFERT, Robert E., Retention and Withdrawal of College Students (U.S. Office of Education Bulletin No. 1, 1958).

JOHNSON, Elizabeth S., and LEGG, Caroline E., "Why Young People Leave School," Bulletin of the National Association of Secondary-School Principals, Vol. XXXII (November, 1948), pp. 14–24.

JOHNSTON, J. B., "Predicting College Success for the High-School Senior," Vocational Guidance Magazine (now Personnel and Guidance Journal), Vol. VI (April, 1928), pp. 289–294.

JONES, Edward S., "Relation of Ability to Preferred and Probable Occupation,"

Educational Administration and Supervision, Vol. XXVI (March, 1940), pp. 220–226.

LANDRY, Herbert A., "Subject Failure in the Academic High Schools," *High Points in the Work of the High Schools of New York City,* Vol. XXV (October, 1943), pp. 27–33.

LAWRENCE, Paul F., "Vocational Aspirations of Negro Youth in California," *Journal of Negro Education,* Vol. XIX (Winter, 1950), pp. 47–56.

LEHMAN, Harvey C., and WITTY, Paul A., "Vocational Guidance: Some Basic Considerations," *Journal of Educational Sociology,* Vol. VIII (November, 1934), pp. 174–184.

LUDDEN, Wallace, "Anticipating Cases of Juvenile Delinquency," *School and Society,* Vol. LIX (February 12, 1944), pp. 123–126.

McCAUL, Robert L., "Student Personnel Opportunities for the College Remedial-Reading Teacher," *School Review,* Vol. LI (March, 1943), pp. 158–163.

MORNEWECK, Carl D., "Occupational Patterns of Employed Minors in Pennsylvania during the Past Five Years," *American School Board Journal,* Vol. CIX (October, 1944), pp. 39–41.

PRESSEY, Luella Cole, "Some Serious Maladjustments among College Students," *Social Forces,* Vol. X (December, 1931), pp. 236–242.

PUNKE, Harold H., "Factors Affecting the Proportion of High School Graduates Who Enter College," *Bulletin of the National Association of Secondary-School Principals,* Vol. XXXVIII (November, 1954), pp. 6–27.

RICHARDSON, H. D., "The Selective Function of the Secondary School," *School Review,* Vol. XLI (November, 1933), pp. 685–692.

ROGERS, Carl R., "The Criteria Used in a Study of Mental-Health Problems," *Educational Research Bulletin* (Ohio State University), Vol. XXI (February 18, 1942), pp. 29–40.

————, "Mental-Health Findings in Three Elementary Schools," *Educational Research Bulletin* (Ohio State University), Vol. XXI (March 18, 1942), pp. 69–79, 86.

ROGERS, Don C., "Success or Failure in School," *American School Board Journal,* Vol. CXIII (October, 1946), p. 46.

SEGEL, David, and SCHWARM, Oscar J., *Retention in High Schools in Large Cities* (U.S. Office of Education Bulletin No. 15, 1957).

SHOSTECK, Robert, "How Well Are We Putting Across Occupational Information?" *Personnel and Guidance Journal,* Vol. XXXIII (January, 1955), pp. 265–269.

SISSON, E. Donald, "Vocational Choices of College Students," *School and Society,* Vol. XLVI (December 11, 1937), pp. 765–768.

SNEPP, Daniel W., "Can We Salvage the Dropouts?" *Clearing House,* Vol. XXXI (September, 1956), pp. 49–54.

SPARLING, Edward J., *Do College Students Choose Vocations Wisely?* (New York, Teachers College Contributions to Education, No. 561, 1933).

STARRAK, J. A., "Matching Ability with Achievement," *Journal of Higher Education,* Vol. VIII (June, 1937), pp. 315–320.

TYLER, Ralph W., "Extension of Responsibilities for Counseling and Guidance in Higher Institutions," *School Review,* Vol. LIII (September, 1945), pp. 391–400.

Vocational Education in the Years Ahead, Ch. 9 (U.S. Office of Education, Vocational Division Bulletin No. 234, 1945).

WILLIAMSON, E. G., and DARLEY, J. G., "Matching Abilities to Jobs," *Personnel Journal,* Vol. XIII (April, 1935), pp. 344–352.

————, "Trends in the Occupational Choices of High School Seniors," *Journal of Applied Psychology,* Vol. XIX (August, 1935), pp. 361–370.

WOLFLE, Dael, *America's Resources of Specialized Talent* (Report of the Commission on Human Resources and Advanced Training), (New York, Harper, 1954).

CHAPTER 5

The Components of the

Guidance Function

ANALYSIS OF THE GUIDANCE FUNCTION into its components is now feasible after the preceding four chapters of definition and orientation. Such analysis is a necessary step preliminary to the development of a logical and well-rounded guidance service. As a further step in definition, it shows more specifically what must be done to discharge the guidance function and therefore serves to establish the main criteria by which a guidance program should be formulated.

THE COMPONENTS OF DISTRIBUTIVE GUIDANCE

To Acquaint the Pupil with the Educational and Vocational Opportunities of the World

The purpose of this component is to lay a sound basis for choice. Choice cannot well be made intelligently unless one has seen the full array from which a choice is to be made. The concept of freedom to choose we have seen to be a prized privilege of American life. It is part and parcel of our democratic ideal. Respect for the individual and for all individuals permits no authoritative pigeonholing of some to be hewers of wood and drawers of water, no ready-made assumptions that others by virtue of birth, position, or affluence are vested with preferred rights in posts which carry a favored status.

Perhaps we add complexity to the guidance process when we assume the burden of helping each pupil to see the full range of educational and vocational opportunity. In a highly stratified society the function must be easier to perform because each child is born into a certain social level and he must find his opportunities on that level. So, too, in a dictatorship, imposed classification of individuals makes unnecessary and uncalled-for any program to acquaint people with opportunities. But these are simply not the ways of democracy. And though the method of democracy is involved and cumbersome we are conscious that the end is deserving of the means.

No single, narrow activity will suffice for the realization of this component. To gain true acquaintance with educational and vocational opportunities means much more than merely reading about them. Some observation of them in actuality and some actual trial of them will clearly be necessary if one is to perceive them. As the child grows, he progressively expands his horizon of experience. If we accept Dewey's injunction "to make each one of our schools an embryonic community life, active with types of occupations that reflect the life of the larger society," we shall be most fully performing this component of guidance. In the canvass of features of guidance which comprises the following chapters of this book, there will be numerous points at which guidance practice bearing upon this component will be detailed.

To Acquaint the Pupil with His Own Powers, Interests, and Limitations

As distributive guidance is the process of matching the individual with the opportunity for which he is best fitted, it follows that the pupil must know himself as he knows opportunities. From wide-ranging experiences he learns what he likes to do, what he has ability to do, and what he does not like to do or cannot do. Self-testing is as much an indispensable preliminary of reasoned choice as is opportunity-testing.

Components 1 and 2 will evidently both be served by the same experiences, bearing to each other an obverse and reverse relationship. If the pupil's experience is rich, vivid, and life-like, he will learn much about himself and about the world; if it is artificial and shallow, he will learn little of either.

To Keep the School Fully and Continuously Acquainted with Educational and Vocational Opportunities

This component, as also the next one, follows logically if the school is to play a part in the pupil's choices. The school must know what the world is made of in order to assist the pupil in his analysis of opportunity. He is indeed dependent on the school's willingness to offer him the types of realistic experience he needs for significant job-analysis and self-analysis. Apparently the school too generally falls short of such functioning. The reader is referred back to Chapter 3, page 80 for the sweeping statements from the report of the Regents' Inquiry which condemned the high schools of New York State as academic, verbalistic, and devoted to ornamental scholarship. The college-preparatory tradition lingers on, and so the school reflects only, or too largely, the white-collar occupations and education. One has only to look at the typical personnel of high-school faculties to sense the handicap that must be overcome if schools are adequately to reflect the world. Composed largely of women with liberal-arts training and with a career of teaching academic subjects as their own most vivid experience, it is difficult to see how the general range of vocational and educational opportunity can be represented. The school must recognize the implications of this component of the guidance function not only for a wise and broadly experienced faculty, but also for a life-like curriculum and a plant and equipment which afford breadth of opportunity for contacts with the world of vocation and education.

To Acquaint the School with the Pupil's Powers, Interests, and Limitations

If the school is to assist the pupil in his choices, it must be a close observer of his reactions to the experiences which test him and reveal him. The pupil himself may not know the meaning for educational and vocational choice of his responses to mathematics, to the group life of the school, to participation in the school orchestra, or to the other manifold experiences of school life, but the school should cherish and record all such revelations for their aid in understanding him. To know the pupil the school must build up a cumulative record of his reactions through the years so as to have capital for aiding him in interpreting his potentialities for different types of education and vocation. In the realization of this component the school will not only learn what it can from the daily contacts of teachers and pupils, but it will also employ those special instruments which psychology has developed for the measurement of human abilities and potentialities, such as tests of intelligence, of aptitude, and of interests. For the pupil the experience of responding to such tests will be relatively meaningless until the counselor explains them.

Chapter 3 has made it clear that the machinery of large-scale education has raised ponderous obstacles to the close acquaintance of teachers with pupils. The obstacles must be removed, or in some way offset. Human resources cannot be advantageously utilized unless the individual person is a known quantity.

To Help the Child at Times of Selection and Decision

It will be apparent that the first four components of distributive guidance should be thought of as bearing on the *preparation* of the pupil and the school for the occasions when choice of studies or choice of occupation must be made. Successful completion of this preparation depends upon the guidance-mindedness of the entire school staff. Guidance values must pervade the entire educational program, and the activities by which pupils are trained and developed will also be recognized as performing guidance by serving one or more of the four components. Curriculum and extracurriculum from the kindergarten up cannot avoid guidance duty, but they will perform it more effectively if all school workers appreciate their relationship to guidance. It is in connection with the four preparatory components of distributive guidance that we sense the soundness of Jones and Hand's concept of guidance as an "inseparable aspect of the educational process."

In the early days of the guidance movement, attention was focused primarily on the fifth component; but as the guidance function has come to be seen in more adequate perspective, it has become evident that the largest contribution to the child at times of selection and decision comes through increased attention to the first four components. The reason is simply that thoroughgoing preparation renders less critical the moments of decision.

Nevertheless, such moments come, and they call for a focusing of all the wisdom which the school and the pupil have been accumulating for the occasion. The principal problem in connection with the performance of this component is to preserve the democratic method; namely, to avoid the counselor's imposition of a choice, to encourage objective, critical thinking on the part of the counselee, to strengthen the counselee's self-reliance and disposition to accept responsibility. The concluding section of Chapter 1 was devoted to the elaboration of this point.

THE COMPONENTS OF ADJUSTIVE GUIDANCE

To Prevent Maladjustment

A substantial argument might be made to the effect that the realization of this component is a task of far too great dimensions to be undertaken by a guidance program as a whole or through any of its parts. When one thinks of the responsibility of the economic order, the home influence, and the school environment, for maladjustment, it seems that agencies far more powerful than school guidance activities are challenged. The point is well taken. Nevertheless, overwhelming as this problem appears to be, any logical analysis must list it as a constituent part of adjustive guidance. If adjustive guidance is equipped with specialized skills and knowledge for restoring maladjusted people to a state of normality, it can also save them from becoming maladjusted. And the old adage, "An ounce of prevention is worth a pound of cure," surely never was more applicable than to this delineation of the guidance function. Guidance, like health service, can be and should be something more than trouble-shooting.

Surely the first function of the guidance specialist in the school is to sensitize teachers and principal to the conditions that breed maladjustment, so that they will shape the school environment with a view to minimizing frustration and maximizing satisfactory social living for each child. The work which the specially trained counselor carries on with pupils as individuals or in groups ought to be a continual source of education for the school faculty. A guidance-minded faculty, by formulating and carrying out school policies conducive to mental health, can reduce the number of serious cases which demand the specialist's attention. Any counselor will recognize that the true test of a guidance program is not the number of serious cases handled, but the number of children who are developing wholesomely and with ever-increasing capacity for self-guidance.

To Identify Cases of Maladjustment of Various Types and Identify them in Their Incipiency, if Possible

The techniques devised by Ludden and by Rogers, as described in the final section of Chapter 4, constitute efforts to create scientific instruments for the performance of this component. Clearly, the identification of maladjusted individuals is necessary before anything can be done about them. Even if a school is relatively well staffed with experts in various forms of maladjustment, there must be some means of locating the cases which they should study. Commonly the experts do not have sufficient contact with pupils to do this. Aside from the employment of such survey techniques as those of Ludden and Rogers, they must depend upon the reports of the teachers who are in continuous touch with pupils. Teachers have shown decided awareness of pupils whose aberrant behavior is aggressive and disturbing to the teacher and the class, but too commonly teachers have little awareness of maladjustment which asserts itself as withdrawing behavior. Therefore this step in the process of adjustive guidance calls first of all for the training of teachers to be keener observers.

To Diagnose Cases of Maladjustment

This is the next manifest step in performing adjustive guidance. Cases vary in difficulty of solution. Some tax the best trained experts; others may be solved by the common sense of an understanding teacher or principal. Many of the same resources mentioned on page 153 on distributive guidance will be useful here. Additional instruments for understanding the pupil will be employed. Co-operation from social agencies, medical examiners, psychiatrists, and other resources of the community may be needed. The testimony of teachers who daily observe the pupil's behavior under the varied circumstances of school activity will be extremely important. Often found to be a source of great value is the historical record of the pupil as represented in an adequate cumulative record folder, and this, too, is evidence, in part, of the service that is rendered to diagnosis by teachers who have been trained to make significant observations.

To Arrive at Remedial Treatment, Administer It, and Follow It Through

It will be seen that the components of adjustive guidance are derived simply by a logical breakdown of the process into the sequence of steps essential to its performance. This fourth component may require the co-ordinated effort of guidance specialist, teachers, and parents. It may require an extended period of time and a change of environment.

As stated, the component perhaps suggests a too authoritarian settlement of adjustive problems. Certainly it is important that the counselee shall achieve insight into his problem and that he shall participate actively in finding his new course of conduct. Since, however, his problem is frequently in part at least a resultant of factors and personalities which impinge upon him, one remedy, or part of the remedy, is the control or modification of these pertinent environmental elements. Here the counselee usually needs help. Adequate guidance provides that help and maintains its guardianship until adjustment has been accomplished.

If this presentation of the components of the guidance function has too frequently assumed the presence of specialized guidance personnel, it has been done for the sake of clarification. Of course, many schools have no specialists. The function of guidance, however, in all its several components, is there to be performed for the children, whether they are in a one-room country school presided over by one teacher or in a city high school staffed with deans, counselors, nurses, home visitors, and measurement experts.

The following chapters will set forth the features of a guidance program. *The features are the means of discharging the guidance function.* As no one feature can be expected to perform guidance totally, its contribution will stand out more clearly than it otherwise would, if we look for its bearing on one or more of the components of the guidance function. While the real test of a guidance program is the extent to which boys and girls are growing into wholesome personalities, with aspirations and abilities brought into harmony, there can be little doubt that the chances of attaining this goal are heightened by fashioning a program that bears adequately on all the components of the guidance function. We shall, then, accept the components as the criteria for judging the features.

To preview the relation of features to components the reader may turn to Figure 22 at the conclusion of Chapter 18.

Part II

THE FEATURES OF
THE GUIDANCE PROGRAM

CHAPTER 6

School Publications to
Orient and Inform

To HELP PUPILS at various rungs on the educational ladder acquire the information which is necessary to the making of wise choices and easy adjustments, publications have been found useful. Schools have become complex mechanisms in order to serve a complex society. They offer education in varied forms to serve the differentiated needs of society. In addition to the perpendicular lines of cleavage in secondary and in higher education, there are also the horizontal breaks in the school system between institutions of elementary, secondary, and higher education. To move with poise across these breaks and to make the best use of the varied opportunity of the school, the individual must have information. This chapter will be devoted to an examination of the principal types of printed information that have been issued by the schools themselves for purposes of information and orientation.

THE PRINTED PROGRAM OF STUDIES

General Practice as to Content and Form

At the secondary-school level the most generally published instrument for guidance purposes is the program of studies. While varying so widely in form and total content that not many aspects can be set forth as typical, the feature which is quite universal is a concise, schematic arrangement of the courses offered by the school. The arrangement shows the courses distributed by curriculums (if the program is of the multiple-curriculum type), by grade, and as required or elective. Not all curricular requirements, regulations, and opportunities can be shown with such concise enumeration, and therefore footnotes are often appended to the chart. Other information is given outside the chart, the most frequently appearing title perhaps being "Graduation Requirements." Additional content very commonly presented has to do with regulations governing the election of studies, "general information" about such matters as pupil load required and permitted, the definition of such terms as "unit," "solids," "prerequisite," and "sequence," which are essential to understanding curriculum discussions.

Many of these documents give information about college entrance requirements, but not following any common pattern. Sometimes the information is little more than a listing of high-school units commonly required by colleges. Again, the requirements of specific local higher institutions are set forth. With more projection into the individual's guidance problem, advice is sometimes given concerning the decision to go or not to go to college, the necessity for early decision and early application, the importance of demonstrating ability to carry academic studies with better than average success.

A statement of the aims or values of secondary education appears in some programs of studies, as if in recognition of the undoubted fact that many pupils and parents have little idea of the significance of education at that level in the life of the individual, the community, and the nation. Frequently, too, a paragraph is devoted to explaining the purposes and values of each of the curriculums. At this as at many other points in the program of studies, one feels that this instrument is prepared for the orientation and information of parents as well as pupils, as indeed it should be.

A number of the publications in this category that have come to the writer's attention offer a brief but pointed overview of the program of extra-curricular activities, thus bringing this aspect of school life to the attention of pupils and patrons as an educational medium alongside the school studies. Perhaps a larger number of programs of studies include a brief section explaining the marking system. Further characterizations of content are hardly possible, because the additional subjects presented, though numerous, appear infrequently.

Printed programs of studies show much variation in form. Many schools issue them only in mimeographed sheets stapled together, a relatively impermanent form. Many have them printed on paper of excellent wearing qualities in folders of four, six, or eight pages, the folders representing no common practice as to size. Bound 6 by 9-inch pamphlets of from 12 to 40 pages each have come to the writer's desk from Hartford, East Orange, Minneapolis, and Oak Park.

Some Examples

In examining the printed program of studies of any school, judgment concerning its adequacy must be reserved, for the reason that items of information that do not appear may be presented in other publications of the types that are described in this chapter. The categories under which publications are taken up are by no means clear-cut; many publications represent such overlapping that it is difficult to classify them. Not unless one could see all printed publications and mimeographed bulletins of a school could an evalu-

ation be ventured concerning the adequacy with which the school is employing this guidance feature.

"Program of Studies" is the title of a 20-page pamphlet issued by the Oak
Park and River Forest Township High School of Illinois. It contains no designated section of information or advice about college entrance requirements,
no statement about the aims or values of secondary education, and no mention of the extracurriculum. It is limited quite completely to the exposition
of its title. As the program is of the constants-with-variables type, studies required of all are listed, as are also graduation requirements, and the bulk of
the pamphlet is given to brief statements of the offering of each of the departments. These departmental descriptions make clear to the reader how
the courses of the department may be used to satisfy the major and minor
sequences of graduation requirements, their general bearing on college entrance requirements, and something of other values. In this main feature the
Oak Park pamphlet closely resembles a college catalogue. This type of publication has been issued by a number of high schools. The last page of this
pamphlet is a form entitled "Your Proposed High School Program," in which
the pupil lists for each of the eight semesters the studies he plans to pursue.
From time to time the writer has found high schools employing such a form
in their guidance programs, but usually as a separate card, sometimes to be
filled out in duplicate by the pupil, with one copy for the school and one for
himself. It serves well to bring curricular guidance to a focus.

A publication of size and character similar to that of Oak Park is "The
Senior High Schools in Minneapolis, 1945–1947." It begins with a glossary
of "Terms that May Not Be Understood," such as "tentative high school
plan," "prerequisites," and "electives." It continues with several pages organized in catechetical form to provide concise information about the opportunities and requirements of the senior high schools. A section on college
entrance requirements gives a tabular arrangement of the pertinent data for
each of the colleges of the University of Minnesota and also for the other
institutions of higher education in Minnesota. A dozen pages of this pamphlet are devoted to a description of courses.

Less detailed and less permanent is the mimeographed "Pupils' and Parents' Guide for the Selection of High School Courses" issued by the Lorain
(Ohio) High School in 1952. Still more concise is a one-page graphic representation of the program of studies of the Pittsburgh high schools issued by
the Division of Guidance in 1955. This sheet, however, is but a helpful summary of part of the guidance information contained in an extended booklet
for educational and vocational orientation which will be described in the next
section.

On a 12 by 15-inch sheet of special-stock, gaily-colored paper, folded to
make sixteen pages, the John Hay High School of Cleveland in 1946 published its program of studies in an attractive printing job done by the printing classes of the school. Since this school is a specialized high school for

business training and therefore serves pupils from all parts of the city, a map showing its location, together with a statement of the transportation facilities serving it, is an appropriate feature of this orientation literature. In addition to the program of studies, a considerable section is devoted to "Your Course and Your Job," which offers some pertinent curricular and vocational guidance. The character of another section is indicated by its title: "Life at John Hay, Not All Work—There's Fun, Too." In contrast with most printed programs of studies, this example could be considered mildly promotional.

MORE EXPANSIVE PUBLICATIONS

Bearing considerable resemblance in content and format to a college catalogue is *Your New Trier, 1952–1953: A Handbook of Information for Students and Teachers,* issued by the New Trier Township High School, of Winnetka, Illinois. The contents are as follows:

Part I—Organization, Administration, and General Information
Part II—Departments and Divisions of the School
    1. Faculty
    2. Courses
    3. Departmental Notes
Part III—Student Activities
Part IV—Scholarships and Awards
Part V—Addenda

Compact but interestingly written, this publication brings together the most essential information to help pupils make the most of their school life and to help teachers be effective in their guidance of pupils. One of the items taken up under Part I is the counseling plan of the school, described under the subtitles "Your Adviser," "Your Adviser Room," "Your Folder," "Your Adviser Chairman." The plan is of such merit that it will be found quoted at some length in Chapter 10. Perhaps *Your New Trier* should be classified as a handbook and presented in the next section, but it is far more comprehensive than the documents we commonly consider as student handbooks.

Less comprehensive in purpose and in scope, but thoroughgoing in what it attempts, is the *Academic Handbook, 1955–1957,* of the Mt. Lebanon High School in the suburban area of Pittsburgh. This 8½ by 11-inch, 40-page, two-column, pleasingly printed publication aims to help the pupil derive the greatest possible benefit from his curricular experiences in high school. It acquaints him with the academic rules, organization, and opportunity of the school; it offers useful advice on how to live a successful academic life; and sixteen of its pages are devoted to "Training Beyond High School." This latter section includes a comprehensive and well-organized list of questions which one should answer in selecting his college, a practical explanation of procedures in college admission, and sample high-school programs to prepare for institutions with different types of entrance requirements.

Canton, Ohio, with three general high schools and one vocational high school, a few years ago issued a 65-page, 9 by 12-inch description of its secondary schools, which is a guidance document of unusual attractiveness and comprehensiveness. While copiously illustrated, its text is also ample and well chosen to help pupils and their parents know educational opportunities and how to choose from them. The curriculums of the general high schools are succinctly set forth together with extensive notes concerning curriculum regulations and values. "Sixteen Pathways to Lifework through Timken Vocational High School" are described by word and picture, then summarized by the outlined program of studies. Fourteen pages are devoted to "Growing through Extracurricular Activities," a message entirely conveyed by pictures. "Suggestions for Educational Preparation for Some of the More Common Occupations" are uniquely set forth in a five-column tabular arrangement under the following headings: "Occupations," "Preparatory Schools," "Suggested Curriculums and Subjects," "Must Have Good Record in These Subjects," and "Comments." Approximately one hundred occupations are covered in this four-page section. The book is concluded with neat tabulations showing "General Facts about Ohio Colleges," their "main curriculums," and their "requirements for admission." The 9 by 12-inch page lends itself especially well to complex tabular presentations. This beautiful and serviceable book, prepared by I. W. Delp, Director of High Schools and Research, and produced in the print shop of Timken Vocational High School, is an outstanding example of guidance literature issued within a school system for the advantage of its own pupils.

A recently issued guidance manual is *Guideposts to Careers,* the work of the Pittsburgh division of guidance and child accounting.[1] A shift in the curricular organization of the senior high schools of the city created guidance needs which occasioned the issuance of this new medium for the orientation and information of pupils, teachers, and parents. One feature of the publication is an extended double-entry form showing by check marks "A Representative List of Vocations [147] with Recommended Curriculums and Post High School Training." Given extended description with tabular arrangements are the programs of the comprehensive high schools and the vocational high schools. Information concerning college entrance and college selection is given in considerable detail, but without special reference to Pittsburgh youth and without naming any higher institutions.

The Pittsburgh manual shows that the city has four boys' vocational high schools offering training in a total of twenty-one trades, and three girls' vocational high schools offering seven trade curriculums. This opportunity poses a critical guidance problem at the ninth-grade level. Should the pupil enter the comprehensive high school which serves the district in which he lives, or

[1] Made available through the courtesy of O. J. Schwarm, director.

should he enter one of the vocational schools to prepare himself for one of the trades? The latter choice will frequently entail his daily travel to another section of the city from that in which he lives.

Many cities have as much or even more differentiation in their secondary schools, and they find published descriptions of their varied educational opportunities to be useful guidance devices. In recent years several of these publications have come to this writers' desk. One, from Cincinnati, is a 32-page, 6 by 9-inch pamphlet which describes the Central Vocational High School with well-chosen text, pictures of school activity in various departments, and a number of informal drawings and diagrammatic representations. Forty-three questions with accompanying answers sharpen the style and heighten the interest of this practical brochure in vocational and educational guidance.

A booklet from Boston, entitled *A Guide to the Choice of a Secondary School,* is 60 pages in length. Following an introduction which sets forth the value of high-school education and briefly describes the main curriculums available in the city, a page or two is devoted to descriptions of the programs and services of each of the city's twenty-four "Latin, High, and Trade Schools." In a city in which secondary education is administered largely through specialized schools, and with two thirds of them accepting only one sex, the choice of school is a most critical occasion in the life of the child. Pupils, parents, and teachers need the basic information conveyed by this booklet as a starting point for the exercise of guidance.

Sometimes a school district issues a publication which is designed primarily for the purpose of informing the public about its schools and the services they render—that is, it is a "public-relations" instrument. But significant guidance values are also presented and should not be underestimated. Such a school document, brought out a few years ago, was *Opportunities in the Pittsburgh Public Schools,* a 9 by 12-inch book of 60 pages, largely pictorial, and including elementary schools and adult classes as well as secondary education. The writer was interested to hear how this expensive book was distributed and circulated. One teacher in a junior high school said: "I have a copy in my homeroom. The pupils have access to it during the day and may borrow it for overnight use. I encourage them to take it home for their parents to see it. At the end of about a month it is pretty well worn, so I turn it in to the office and get another one."

While publications of the type here discussed are particularly essential in large city school systems where more specialized educational facilities exist, some individual high schools in one-school districts have followed the same practice. For example, Highland Park High School, of the Deerfield-Shields Township High-School District, Illinois, published a booklet of sixteen 8½ by 11-inch pages which is designed to acquaint pupils and patrons with the purposes, values, and activities of each department, using the medium of both text and pictures. More informal is *Here's Your High*

School, a brochure compiled and issued by the Parent-Teachers' Association of the Evanston Township High School, Illinois, to bring to the parents of the district a graphic representation of the curricular and extracurricular life of the school.

A publication of a somewhat different character, yet meriting mention in this section is a 110-page, paper-bound book entitled *A Study of Lafayette and Other Fayette County Schools.* This is a description of the innovating school program which has developed in Lexington, Kentucky, and in Fayette County. The book was prepared by the teachers of the schools involved, with aid from the Southern Association of Colleges and Secondary Schools, and it is designated as "For the children and patrons and friends of the Fayette County Community." Most of the volume is devoted to the Lafayette High School. The rather solid textual content is illuminated by numerous half-tone prints which show the unusually wide range of curricular activities engaged in by the pupils.

Manuals of administration have appeared with increasing frequency in recent years. These are prepared in mimeographed form (occasionally printed) by high-school principals primarily to acquaint teachers with administrative routine. If the school has a guidance program, the manual will tell teachers how to play their part in it. Certainly the manual presents an opportunity for the orientation of teachers with reference to the guidance service of the school, an opportunity which should be fully employed. A variation in this publication is the teachers' manual which is solely devoted to the guidance program. An example is the *Guidance Manual for Ottawa Hills High School* (Toledo), a 32-page mimeographed pamphlet which presents a "Guidance Calendar" for the year, explains "The Meaning of Guidance," states "Specific Purposes of Our Guidance Program," charts the guidance "Organization," lists "Basic Functions of the Homeroom," describes techniques for "Studying Our Pupils," enumerates thirteen "Suggestions for Counseling," sets forth procedure for "Helping Pupils Plan Their Program of Studies," and otherwise defines the role of the teachers in guidance. Such a well-planned manual will be far more effective than oral directions at a faculty meeting or hit-and-miss, piecemeal pointers in the principal's daily bulletins.

Homeroom manuals—sometimes for teachers only, sometimes for teachers and pupils—have been prepared in many high schools and in city school systems to indicate the content and activities of homeroom group guidance programs. Sometimes they have been drawn up in virtually the form of a graded curriculum. These publications will be discussed more fully and some evaluation of their worth offered in Chapter 10.

Possibilities of the school paper as a medium of orientation and information are capitalized in a few schools. One such example to come to the writer's desk was a special issue of *The Mountaineer,* bi-weekly student paper of the Montclair (N.J.) High School, which was issued in the first week of the school year for the orientation of the incoming class. Much of its content is typical of the handbook. Written in a breezy style, with light touches of adolescent humor, its entire eight pages could hardly fail to be read by newcomers, yet the content is substantial and thoughtfully selected with reference to its purpose.

While this discussion of publications has been confined to those which are issued by secondary schools, college students, particularly at the junior-college level, have need for orientation and information similar to that of junior and senior high-school pupils. Colleges recognize this need in varying and in generally increasing degree. All of them publish annual or biennial catalogues which, on the whole, represent much faculty thought. Many publish freshman handbooks. They also put forth elaborate recruiting literature which is of dubious guidance value. Not to be underrated, however, are the pamphlets and folders which various institutions have prepared with scientific objectivity for the description of professional occupations. Many of these documents bear little or no evidence of the recruiting purpose. For liberal arts students who have not yet selected a life career, this literature has decided value. A unique example of a guidance publication issued by a university primarily to be helpful for its own students is *Ohio State and Occupations*,[2] a work of two hundred pages which lists for each department of Ohio State University "occupations appropriate to majors" in that department. Each occupation is given a concise, appropriate definition. Since other colleges and universities all over the land have departmental organizations more or less paralleling those of Ohio State, it is apparent that this publication has national as well as local usefulness, and in the libraries of high schools as well as those of higher institutions.

"Career Opportunities for Majors in English" is the title of a 20-page pamphlet coming from Indiana University in 1955. It is informative and attractive, as one might expect from a department devoted to the art of communication.

"Looking Toward College" is a pamphlet issued by the Ohio College Association as "A Guide for High School Students, Counselors, and Parents" for the purpose of giving "accurate and unbiassed information concerning the member colleges of the Association." The pamphlet is brief, concluding with a tabular arrangement of "General Facts" concerning the 47 members. It refers its readers to a book, *To College in Ohio,* "prepared by the Ohio College Association and the Ohio High School Principals Association" and sent to every high school in the state.

What Would You Like to Study is the title of a 90-page, mimeographed booklet of curricular advisement for high-school and college students issued

---

[2] Prepared by the Occupational Opportunities Service, with the co-operation of the Faculty of the Ohio State University (Columbus, Ohio, The Ohio State University Press, 1945).

recently by the Bureau of Testing and Guidance of the University of Hawaii.[3]

An example of a specialized bulletin, tailored to the needs of pupils of a given school district, is a 1956 mimeographed publication of the Providence schools, entitled *Scholarships and Student Aid: A Guide for Students and Counselors.* This sizable book is so soundly helpful for informing pupils and counselors about sources of financial assistance for all sorts of post-secondary education that it is described in Chapter 16 in the section devoted to counseling for college-going.

It is appropriate at this point in our discourse to call attention to the extensive array of publications devoted to school and college information which are intended for a nation-wide or state-wide audience, in contrast to the literature for local consumption with which this chapter is mainly concerned. These works include (1) the general indexes of institutions of higher education, such as the well-known *College Blue Book,* (2) the directories of a wide range of specialized schools (many of which are published by associations of professional workers), and (3) the publications which describe educational opportunities in states or other geographical areas. The following two references list this literature and annotate it generously:

Ruth E. Anderson, "A Bibliography of School and College Information," *Bulletin of the National Association of Secondary-School Principals,* Vol. XXXII (November, 1948), pp. 90–115. (Mainly confined to publications appearing in 1944–48.)

Ruth E. Anderson, "An Annotated Bibliography of School and College Information," *Bulletin of the National Association of Secondary-School Principals,* Vol. XXXVI (October, 1952), pp. 170–208. (Mainly confined to publications appearing in 1949–52.)

In the second of these articles Anderson has added to the three categories of literature named above the following sections: "Publications for Use in Post-Secondary School Guidance"—typified by such titles as *Choosing the Right College, Should You Go to College,* and *Predicting Success in Professional Schools;* and "Information on Student Aid—Scholarships, Fellowship Loans, Self-Help"—typified by such titles as *Scholarships and Fellowships Available at Institutions of Higher Education* and *Working Your Way through College.*

Judicious selection from this literature for the shelves of the school library and the counselor's office is a task worthy of the continued attention of librarian and counselor.[4]

---

[3] Arthur A. Dole, "Educational Information on a Shoestring," *Vocational Guidance Quarterly,* Vol. V (Spring, 1957), pp. 107–110.

[4] A recent major contribution to this literature is Lloyd E. Blauch, ed., *Education for the Professions* (Washington, D.C., Department of Health, Education, and Welfare, 1955), pp. vi, 318.

THE STUDENT'S HANDBOOK

Content and Purpose

Handbooks for the student are issued by many colleges and universities, but the present discussion will be confined to practice in secondary schools. The significance of the handbook as a potential instrument of guidance and of school administration was brought to the public attention some years ago by the analytical studies of McKown[5] and of Kershaw and Carback.[6] They collected large numbers of handbooks and analyzed them for format, authorship, contents, and in regard to other factors. Their data showed a decided lack of common standards, and they criticized the handbooks as frequently lacking systematic organization of the materials presented.

A more recent analysis is that of Curtis,[7] based on 33 handbooks from high schools of varied size in Ohio. Table 31[8] shows the major items of content, together with Curtis' comparison of his findings with those of McKown, as indicated by the use of asterisks to designate the items which McKown found in at least a third of the handbooks he examined. One studies this table and is puzzled to understand why no topic was presented in all 33 handbooks, why such an absence of unanimity prevails. "Conduct regulations," for example, exist in every school, and every pupil should clearly understand them, yet only two thirds of these schools use the handbook for such orientation. Did the other schools prefer to employ some other medium for giving pupils this information, or did they simply overlook it when deciding on the contents of the handbook? We do not have the answer. Curtis' comment on the divergence in content is this:[9]

The fact . . . that only forty-two of several hundred items were discussed in as many as a third or more of these modern handbooks would suggest either that the handbook is still in a tentative and formative stage of development or that topics of local appeal are far more numerous in such books than are those of common, or general, importance.

It is difficult to pass judgment on a handbook without knowing the problems of the individual school or the other media of publication (or communication) employed.

Table 31 shows that the handbook commonly includes some items that are characteristic of the printed program of studies, namely, graduation requirements, the marking system and reports to parents, college-entrance require-

[5] Harry C. McKown, "The High-School Handbook," *School Review,* Vol. XXXII (November, 1924), pp. 667–681.
[6] William L. Kershaw and Clarence H. Carback, "The High-School Student Handbook," *School Review,* Vol. XXXII (October, 1924), pp. 587–597.
[7] Francis D. Curtis, "A Study of High-School Handbooks," *School Review,* Vol. LI (December, 1943), pp. 614–618.
[8] *Ibid.,* adapted from Table 1, p. 617.
[9] *Ibid.,* p. 616.

TABLE 31. Distribution of Topics Discussed in Eleven or More of Thirty-three High-School Handbooks

Topic	Frequency
ADMINISTRATION:	
*Absences and excuses	32
Assemblies	23
*Cafeteria and lunchroom regulations	23
*Classification of pupils	12
Conduct regulations	22
Faculty advisers	22
*Fire-drill regulations	27
*Graduation requirements	23
Home-room organization	19
Lunch-period regulations	14
*Marking system and reports to parents	29
Noon recreation	13
*Schedule for the school day	26
Student council	19
Tardiness regulations	25
Work permits	11
INSTRUCTION:	
*College-entrance requirements	16
*Program of studies	32
Pupil load	16
Textbooks	15
EXTRACURRICULAR ACTIVITIES:	
Activities calendar	15
Athletic awards	31
*Athletic eligibility	16
Athletic-events schedule	13
Honors awards	23
Intramural sports	17
Parties and dances	16
Point merit-system	13
Student publications	20
GENERAL:	
Board of education	23
*Date of publication of handbook	30
*Directory of building	14
*Faculty roster	29
Handbook staff	20
*Index	16
*Pupil's schedule blank	13

Table 31. Distribution of Topics Discussed in Eleven or More of Thirty-three High-School Handbooks (continued)

	Frequency
Purposes of the handbook	25
*School calendar	19
*School history	19
*School songs and yells	23
School traditions	14
Use of the telephone	13

* Items which appeared in at least a third of the handbooks analyzed by McKown.

ments, and the program of studies. Inasmuch as many more schools publish the program of studies than publish a student's handbook, this must mean duplication within the school, because it is probable that virtually all schools which issue a handbook also issue a printed program of studies.

Whereas McKown found "Pupil organizations" to be an item in 96 of 110 handbooks, Curtis' classification in Table 31 does not show it at all, though "Extracurricular activities" is one of the four main divisions under which he lists items. A canvass of 27 handbooks which have recently come to the writer's desk shows 24 devoting considerable space to extracurricular organizations, life, and activity. This content is of such character and appears so commonly as to make it plain that handbook publishers generally feel that orientation to the extracurricular is one of the purposes they are trying to accomplish.

Friendly and sometimes quite detailed suggestions in regard to manners is a feature of a number of handbooks. Examples of this feature are the handbooks of the Appleton (Wis.) Senior High School and the Riverside High School of Milwaukee, which suggest proper etiquette in the auditorium, in the cafeteria, in the corridor, in the classroom, at the dance. Along these lines, *The Yankee Guide,* attractive handbook of the Alexander Hamilton High School of Los Angeles, has one of its sections entitled "Code of Common Sense and Courtesy."

Most handbooks are devoid of illustrations, and often except for a bright cover they must be described as drab. An exception to come to this writer's attention is the handbook last mentioned in the preceding paragraph, which is rendered attractive by artistic halftone cuts of the school and of the life within it as well as by the dignified division of its sections. *How Our School Wheels Turn,* handbook of the John Hay High School, Cleveland, is featured by a dozen halftones unusually effective in portraying curricular and extracurricular life in a business high school.

Concerning the organization of handbook content, the writer finds himself, on the basis of his none too adequate observations, in agreement with McKown's comment that

Few of the handbooks studied exhibit any great attempt at a systematic organization of the materials presented. . . . Nearly all of the books . . . look as if the material had been hurriedly put together.[10]

Curtis had a similarly disparaging comment, saying

Apparently no great progress toward excellence of organization is manifest in recent handbooks in comparison with older ones. In the present study, as in McKown's, a logical and systematic organization of materials was found to be the exception rather than the rule.[11]

Classification of content is sometimes inaccurate, and more frequently the printer's art is inadequately employed to show major and minor elements in the outline. This latter defect is probably due to the inadequate preparation of copy for the printer's guidance.

The potentialities of the handbook are such that it should be prepared with a great deal of thought. It is more than an instrument of guidance. It is calculated to develop the pupil's school citizenship, to cultivate in him a sense of belonging, a feeling of pride in his membership in the school. It can greatly accelerate his assimilation into the student body. There are a host of adjustments for the pupil to make on coming into a new school. These problems and needs of the newcomer should be inventoried carefully and detailed plans drawn for meeting them. The handbook may well be the principal element in the orientation program. In black-on-white it offers authoritative answers to the entering stranger. If well prepared, it acquaints him with the choice of curricular and extracurricular opportunities which the school offers. It acquaints him with faculty personnel, organization, and functions, so that he knows where to go with his problems.

Some Administrative Details

Curtis reported an absence of uniformity in the size of handbooks,[12] which is also the impression gained by this writer. Many, however, are of a handy pocket size—3 or 4-inch by 5 or 6-inch. The variation in the number of pages is marked, McKown reporting that 13 of the 110 handbooks he examined had less than 20 pages, while 16 had more than 100 pages.[13]

Perhaps the important reason for the lack of a norm in handbook size is the lack of norms in financial support and in sponsorship. In many schools the handbook is looked upon as a student activity, and the responsibility for its preparation and issue is taken by the student council, the honor society, a journalism class, or some other student group. Such student sponsorship is evident in about half the handbooks recently to come to the writer's attention. Responsibility for the other half was generally not clear, but they

[10] *Op. cit.,* p. 673.
[11] *Op. cit.,* p. 618.
[12] *Op. cit.,* p. 616.
[13] *Op. cit.,* p. 677, Table IV.

seemed to emanate from the principal's office or a faculty committee. No relationship between sponsorship and quality was apparent.

No common practice in the financing of handbooks seems to prevail. McKown says that[14]

Nearly every school makes a charge for the book, the prices ranging from ten to twenty-five cents. . . .

Another method of financing the book is for the student council, English club, senior class, or other student organization sponsoring it to raise funds by means of fairs, shows, . . . etc., and so give the book to all students. The sponsoring organization then pays any deficit incurred or takes any profit made. In a variation of this procedure the student becomes a member of the general organization or student association by paying a small fee and the book is given to him. . . .

In some schools—we know not how many—the board of education assumes part or all of the expense. If complete public financing were to prevail, as in the case of such other educational media as algebra and European history, better standards might generally be attained, though such an outcome would certainly not be automatically achieved.

How frequently is the handbook published? With what frequency *should* it be published? Some schools publish it every year, others, every two or three years. A yearly issue enables the editors to insert much current data, such as the faculty roster, the student officers of various organizations, and the calendar of events. The schools which want this advantage typically publish their handbooks the first of September. Other schools omit such matter and effect a considerable saving by publishing only once in three years. They argue that much of the content appropriate for a handbook does not change every year. But this attitude would be deplorable in the eyes of Paul Pierce, formerly leader in dynamic education at Wells High School, Chicago. In describing the development of his program, Pierce wrote as follows:[15]

Another contemplated enterprise [of the student council] was the publishing of a handbook [but] the rapid extension of the curriculum and resulting changes in routine necessitated so many revisions of the manuscript that printing it appeared out of the question. As time passed, our experience led us to a significant conclusion, namely, that printed handbooks are not practicable in a flexible high-school program. Necessary changes in school living occur too rapidly to permit printing a handbook; worse yet, if one has been printed, needed changes may have to be postponed to avoid outmoding it!

Perhaps most school workers would dislike to think of school life as so turbulent and unstable as Pierce seems to assume to be desirable. Nevertheless, they will admit that he has voiced a real danger which applies to all school publications. These are but the *instruments* of policy, not the makers

[14] Harry C. McKown, *Extra-Curricular Activities* (rev. ed.) (New York, Macmillan, 1937), pp. 497–498.
[15] Paul R. Pierce, *Developing a High-School Curriculum* (New York, American Book, 1942), p. 97.

of it, and should be used accordingly. The yearly handbook can be highly effective in orientation, but its content should be thoughtfully determined each year to avoid making it a stereotyped imitation of last year's handbook or the handbook of some other school.

Distribution of the handbook must be planned with full reference to its use and purposes. Since it is primarily intended to achieve orientation, a copy should be given—not sold—to every new student. This policy should prevail not only with new entering students but also with transfer students. Reliance on a selling campaign to get the book into the hands of new members would almost certainly fail to reach the pupils who need it most—those who are introvertive, anti-social, underprivileged, lacking educational traditions in their homes. If the book is a true reflection of a dynamic educational environment, if it contains the current year's calendar of events together with current faculty roster and assignments, if it includes information which shows that the school has been growing and changing since last year's handbook was published, every pupil, old as well as new, should have his own copy. This implies free distribution to the entire student body. Older pupils need it for reference, as new pupils study it in detail.

PLANNING THE USE OF THESE PUBLICATIONS

Planning Is Needed

Merely passing out copies of the printed program of studies, the student's handbook, or elaborate booklets on school opportunities will not realize their values. Definite plans must be made for study and discussion of this literature; high-school students cannot be depended upon to engage in such study of their own volition and in the pursuit of their own best interests. McLaughlin's recent investigation of the extent to which seniors know the colleges which they plan to enter illustrates the need for directing pupils' study.[16] From his experience in counseling high-school seniors, McLaughlin found that many students were choosing their colleges in a lamentable state of ignorance, and he therefore planned a research to measure the extent of such ignorance.

Assuming that the college catalogue should contain all the items of information about a school which a pupil should know in deliberating his choice of a college, McLaughlin analyzed a representative list of 25 catalogues for their content items. The similarity of the catalogues was found to be such as to make it possible to be very objective in the selection of items, and virtually no new items were found after analyzing the first eight catalogues. The final list of 87 items was reacted to by a jury composed of 28 high-school counselors and 29 college directors of admission. They were directed to label each

[16] John M. McLaughlin, Jr., *Extent to Which Pittsburgh High-School Seniors Possess Essential Information about the Colleges They Plan to Attend.* Ed.D. Thesis (Pittsburgh, University of Pittsburgh Library, 1953).

item "E" if they thought it to be essential information which a prospective college student should have for making a college choice, "I" if they thought the item to be important but not necessarily essential before college entrance, or "G" if they thought the item to be merely general information—of interest, but not vital for making a choice between schools. Two thirds or more of the jury designated 34 of the items as essential information, and on these a questionnaire, or test, composed of 65 items, was prepared, after adequate trial usage, for testing high-school seniors' knowledge of the colleges they planned to enter.

The test was administered in the spring to 461 seniors in Pittsburgh high schools who said they had made plans for entering 81 different degree-granting institutions. As 43 of these institutions were chosen by only one student each, the task of scoring was lightened by dropping these cases. Even so, to score the papers on the remaining 38 institutions required the preparation of 54 separate scoring keys.

These seniors proved to be very poorly informed about the colleges they planned to attend. The median percentages of acceptable responses made by pupils selecting the various types of schools for higher education were as follows: fine arts, 43; liberal arts, 41; education, 35; engineering, 31; business administration, 23; all schools, 36. Many admitted to having made application to a school without first examining its catalogue. Most pupils were quite ignorant of the plan of organization of institutions of higher education. Many had very inaccurate ideas of the cost of college education. Most of the pupils felt that they had met the subject requirements for entrance, but very few knew what the requirements were. They did not understand the meaning of the word "curricula" as it is applied to educational programs at the college level. They were unfamiliar with the "student personnel services" at the various schools. They had not investigated the school's accreditation.

McLaughlin's study affords convincing evidence of the need for planning the use of the publications which are intended to orient and inform. It is not enough to stock a library alcove with college catalogues. Just to give each pupil a copy of the student handbook affords no assurance of his sudden orientation to the school. A carefully planned and edited document setting forth the program of studies will not automatically create in the pupil's mind adequate impressions of his educational opportunities.

Methods of Use

Homeroom group guidance programs are envisaged by many school workers as concerned in part with the subjects which constitute the content of these publications. Chapter 10 will examine this guidance feature. In some schools there are classes in "guidance," organized to meet once or twice a week, in which effective school living and educational choosing are major themes.

The employment of another medium—one which is available in every school—has been described by Elizabeth Whalen, English teacher.[17] In her school it was decided to cope with the problem of orientation by making it the content of the first two weeks in English. The English teachers prepared a syllabus of some eighty mimeographed pages (with cartoons, ornamental cover, etc.) explaining practical matters necessary for knowing how to get along in high school. She stated four reasons for having the English department assume this responsibility, as follows: (1) the English teachers had worked up the syllabus and were enthusiastic about it; (2) it was easier to carry out this project through a small number of teachers accustomed to close co-operation; (3) if it had been done through homerooms, it would have necessitated extra-long homeroom periods, thus interfering with the regular program; (4) this method avoided giving the plan the flavor of being just one more administrative detail foisted upon busy homeroom teachers.

A further advantage of such a plan is that orientation is hastened; it is worked at intensively the first ten school days of the year. Also, by virtue of using the comprehensive syllabus as a guide, all pupils were exposed to the same content, thus contributing to the unification of the student body. And why should the English department assume this responsibility? Because it contributes to English objectives. On what better content could pupils practice oral and written expression than over the problems of their own adjustment to a new school?

Another appropriate medium for the direct study of orientation problems might, in some schools, be the civics classes. In four-year high schools, where civics may be a subject required of all ninth graders, the most suitable introductory unit might well be one on school citizenship, using a good school handbook as the text. The earlier the pupil understands his school, and his own responsibilities and opportunities, the sooner he becomes an effective member.

Schools which send relatively few graduates on to higher education find it inappropriate to devote the time of such heterogeneous groups as homerooms to the consideration of college choosing. A meritorious alternative found in some schools is the sponsoring of one or more college clubs. The guidance department may well play an active role in promoting such clubs and in stimulating the right pupils to become members. Effective media of this sort might well dissipate the blind choosing revealed by McLaughlin's investigation.

In concluding this chapter, it seems desirable to point out that the more serious the problems of articulation the greater is the need for carefully prepared publications to orient and inform. For example, thousands of American high schools are receiving considerable fractions of their enrollments from school districts which do not have high schools—often from one-room

[17] "English Classes Handle Newcomers' Orientation," *Clearing House,* Vol. XXI (September, 1946), pp. 27–30.

district schools. Articulation is a serious problem for these "tuition" pupils. Ekstrom's study, cited on page 117 in Chapter 4, shows that many farm children do not enter high school at all and that elimination is relatively high among those who do enter. Attractive publications for pupils and parents might well improve this situation.

It is to be hoped that this chapter makes clear the desirability of expending some of the school's resources of guidance energy in the publication of information. Authenticity, exactness, and uniformity are usually advantages of the printed word over the oral. Economy of time in dissemination is a further reason for committing information to print.

QUESTIONS, PROBLEMS, AND INVESTIGATIONS*

1. From a dozen high schools of comparable size and clientele, obtain all of their publications designed to orient and inform. Try to rank the schools according to their adequacy on this feature of a guidance program.

2. For a high school with which you have intimate acquaintance, plan homeroom group guidance lessons on the program of studies with a ninth-grade group.

3. In a senior high school, direct a tenth-grade group in the preparation of a handbook for next year's incoming class.

4. Debate the merits of a handbook prepared by one or more teachers as compared with one prepared by a group of pupils under teacher sponsorship.

5. Conduct a discussion of the high-school program of studies with a class of eighth graders and make note of the questions they ask concerning the vocational bearings of high-school studies and curriculum patterns.

6. Prepare a brief to convince a board of education that the district should finance all publications to orient and inform.

SELECTED REFERENCES

ANDERSON, Ruth E., "A Bibliography of School and College Information," *Bulletin of the National Association of Secondary-School Principals,* Vol. XXXII (November, 1948), pp. 90–115.

———, "An Annotated Bibliography of School and College Information," *Bulletin of the National Association of Secondary-School Principals,* Vol. XXXVI (October, 1952), pp. 170–208.

CURTIS, Francis D., "A Study of High-School Handbooks," *School Review,* Vol. LI (December, 1943), pp. 614–618.

DOLE, Arthur A., "Educational Information on a Shoestring," *Vocational Guidance Quarterly,* Vol. V (Spring, 1957), pp. 107–110.

KALUGER, George, "Developing an Informative Student Handbook," *Clearing House,* Vol. XXIV (September, 1949), pp. 17–20.

KERSHAW, William L., and CARBACK, Clarence H., "The High-School Student Handbook," *School Review,* Vol. XXXII (October, 1924), pp. 587–597.

---

* The instructor will do well to have available for student examination a generous collection of the materials described in this chapter. His supply should be constantly reinforced with the new and pruned of the old.

McKown, Harry C., "The High-School Handbook," *School Review,* Vol. XXXII (November, 1924), pp. 667–681.

Ohio State and Occupations, prepared by the Occupational Opportunities Service, with the co-operation of the Faculty of the Ohio State University (Columbus, Ohio, The Ohio State University Press, 1945).

Whalen, Elizabeth, "English Classes Handle Newcomers' Orientation," *Clearing House,* Vol. XXI (September, 1946), pp. 27–30.

Youngert, Eugene, "A Letter to High School Graduates Entering College," *Bulletin of the National Association of Secondary-School Principals,* Vol. XXXIX (February, 1955), pp. 89–90.

CHAPTER 7

Organization of the School
and of the Offering

CONCEIVING GUIDANCE AS A FUNCTION which is inextricably bound up with the educative process, it follows that the performance of guidance is conditioned by the organization of educational institutions. Recognition of this relationship compels the creation of such organizational forms as will meet guidance specifications. The administrator must be aware of these specifications and bear them in mind when he organizes the school system, the individual school unit, and the curricular offering. Adequate provision for guidance cannot be made by merely attaching certain features and certain personnel to a school which reflects no recognition of guidance in its fundamental structure.

The purpose of this chapter is to consider the following questions:

What form of school organization presents the most favorable setting for the exercise of guidance?

What organization of the curricular offering makes the largest contribution to guidance?

How shall the problems of articulating school units be met so as to promote sound distribution and adjustment of students?

The discussion of these questions will lead to a consideration of forms which are not ordinarily thought of as features of a *guidance* program. Their facilitation of guidance, however, is of such import in the performance of the function that the builder of a guidance program must take them fully into account.

SIGNIFICANCE OF THE EXTENDED SECONDARY SCHOOL

Time for Both Guidance and Specialization

Approximately fifty years have elapsed since the establishment of the first junior high school. The first public junior college was organized in 1902.

The story of the rapid growth and steadily increasing acceptance of these two institutions is well known. Their incorporation into the American educational ladder, bringing about a reconstruction of the school units in the educational sequence, is commonly spoken of as "the reorganization movement in secondary education." The junior high school is regarded as a two-year downward extension of secondary education; the junior college, as a two-year upward extension. While it is true that the numbers of both of the new units have increased remarkably, decade by decade, the downward extension has been adopted far more universally than the upward and with a far closer articulation with the unit from which it extends. Where the junior college exists, it commonly exists apart from the high school and is not regarded as secondary education. The pioneers who are spreading the gospel of the eight-year secondary school, organized in two units of four years each, are making progress,[1] but they are strongly opposed by tradition and vested interests.

Therefore, in exploring the significance, for guidance, of the extended secondary school, attention here will be focused primarily on the widely accepted six-year period of secondary education, organized either as separate junior and senior high schools or as a single school. The extent to which the reorganization movement has modified the institutions of secondary education is indicated roughly by Table 32,[2] which shows that by 1952 three fourths of public high-school pupils were being educated in reorganized schools, with the six-year schools growing most rapidly.

TABLE 32. Percentages of Public High School Pupils Enrolled in Regular and Reorganized School Systems, 1920–52

| | | High Schools | | |
| | | Jr.-Sr. or | | |
Year	Junior	Undivided	Senior	Regular
1920	1.9	13.8	0.9	83.4
1930	19.9	18.8	10.4	50.9
1938	19.0	24.4	13.1	43.5
1946	18.6	26.1	16.8	38.5
1952	19.8	35.1	19.9	25.2

In the period when the junior high school was new, numerous statements were isued by educational authorities listing its advantages. Superintendents of schools and boards of education, too, in establishing junior high schools felt called upon to justify their action by citing the benefits anticipated from this reorganization of their school systems. Koos summarized these claims,

[1] L. V. Koos, *Integrating High School and College* (New York, Harper, 1946).
[2] Adapted from Walter H. Gaumnitz and others, "Junior High School Facts—A Graphic Analysis," Misc. No. 21 (November, 1954), U.S. Office of Education, p. 16, Chart 6.

designated them as the "peculiar functions" of the junior high school, and explained them at length.[3] As time has passed, some of these peculiar functions, such as "economy of time," seem not to have been realized; others, such as offering the "beginnings of vocational education," seem no longer applicable; still others, such as "recognition of individual differences," seem quite as important to realize in other educational units as in the junior high school.

One of the peculiar functions given great prominence in the pronouncements of the 1920s was that of "exploration and guidance." As we see it now, and as this book will interpret it, this function is not peculiar to the junior high school. Nevertheless, there seems today sound reason to thank the junior high school movement for giving noteworthy impetus to the guidance function and for altering school organization in a manner calculated to facilitate its exercise. The bearing of the junior high school on guidance was stated by the Commission on the Reorganization of Secondary Education in 1918 in the following paragraph:[4]

> The six years to be devoted to secondary education may well be divided into two periods which may be designated as the junior and senior periods. In the junior period emphasis should be placed upon the attempt to help the pupil to explore his own aptitudes and to make at least provisional choice of the kinds of work to which he will devote himself. In the senior period emphasis should be given to training in the fields thus chosen. This distinction lies at the basis of the organization of junior and senior high schools.

James M. Glass, who pioneered in organizing the Washington Junior High School in Rochester, New York, graphically represented the distinctive roles of the two levels of secondary education, as well as the articulation with elementary education, with a figure from which Figure 6 is adapted.[5] He envisaged the junior high school as a unit which bridges the gap between elementary and secondary education and provides the breadth of experience essential to the pupil's exploration of himself and the world prior to his choice of a channel of specialized training in the senior high school. This he contrasted with the traditional 8–4 organization by which the pupil on completing elementary education was confronted immediately with the necessity of choosing his path of differentiated education, usually involving studies he had never sampled.

There can be little doubt that this theory, stated by many others in addition to Glass, has given marked impetus to the reorganization movement. Communities in which the 8–4 organization still prevails have been moved to modify the program of their seventh, eighth, and ninth grades the better

[3] L. V. Koos, *The Junior High School*, enlarged ed., (Boston, Ginn, 1927), Chs. II, III.

[4] *Cardinal Principles of Secondary Education* (Washington, D.C., Bureau of Education Bulletin, No. 35, 1918), p. 18.

[5] "The Junior High School," *New Republic*, Vol. XXXVI, Part II (November 7, 1923), p. 20, Chart 4.

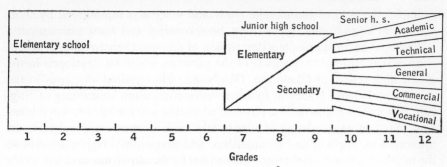

FIG. 6. The reorganized school system.

to recognize the functions of exploration and guidance. The assertion that some unreorganized school systems are more progressive in actuality than some reorganized systems can be granted, but it still does not detract from the fact that the extension of the secondary school to include Grades VII and VIII greatly facilitates the incorporation of features which bear on the guidance function. That the features actually are being incorporated in the six-year secondary school was found to be true by the National Survey of Secondary Education in their painstaking comparison of reorganized and unreorganized schools. A paragraph from their summary read as follows:[6]

In guidance the differences all favor the reorganized schools. The most important differences are two: The junior-senior high schools frequently employ a special guidance counselor, whereas a special counselor is rarely found in the conventional schools; and the junior-senior schools employ a greater number of different methods and materials in guidance. Certain not wholly reliable differences appear also, to the advantage of the reorganized schools, in the number of different problems dealt with in guidance.

One accomplishment of reorganization, in which the North Central Association of Colleges and Secondary Schools has played a leading part, is the release of the ninth grade from domination or control by college-preparation objectives. By thus deferring this type of specialization, a year is gained for education which is broadly developmental and exploratory.

The Rise and Decline of Tryout Courses

An early expression of the principle of exploration for guidance in the junior high school was the establishment of tryout courses. In the early nineteen twenties short unit courses designed to help pupils sample the educational opportunities of the senior high school and the occupational opportunities of the outside world appeared in many junior high schools. For

[6] Francis T. Spaulding, O. I. Frederick, and Leonard V. Koos, *The Reorganization of Secondary Education,* National Survey of Secondary Education, Monograph No. 5. (Washington, D.C., Office of Education Bulletin, No. 17, 1932), p. 195.

example, the field of commercial study and work was represented by short courses in stenography, typewriting, bookkeeping, and even comptometry.

Perhaps the most complete description of a comprehensive plan of tryout courses was Bruner's exposition of the program which he developed in the junior high school at Okmulgee, Oklahoma.[7] He required all pupils in the seventh and eighth grades to follow a "core curriculum" consisting of English, citizenship, mathematics, physical education and health, and a combination year course consisting of nine weeks each of music appreciation, art appreciation, spelling and penmanship, and geography. Tryout courses to the number of twenty-eight were worked out by the departments of the senior high school to afford the pupils glimpses of future studies and possible occupations. These were nine and eighteen weeks in length. Pupils in the seventh grade chose four of the nine-weeks courses, while pupils in the eighth grade chose two, three, or four of the nine-weeks or the eighteen-weeks courses. One of the courses in each year had to be science. Bruner said,[8]

These courses have been called *broadening and finding* courses, for (1) through them many of the pupils *find* the later courses for which they seem to be best fitted, and in which their interest seems to lie; (2) in some instances they *find* also their life-work, although this happens less frequently; and (3) whatever the finding, the school authorities claim that the pupils are profitably *broadened* by coming in contact with these different fields.

Among the courses offered were thirteen in home and industrial arts (fields not represented in the required core), four in fine arts, and English-Latin, pre-modern languages, journalism, and typewriting. Classes in all subjects were held one period daily.

Bruner attempted to measure the effectiveness of the Latin tryout course. Reasoning that the course would be valuable to the degree that it encouraged abler pupils to elect the regular Latin course in the ninth grade and discouraged the less able from doing so, he compiled the following data:[9]

21 who took the tryout course and avoided further study of Latin had an average I.Q. of 100

46 who took the tryout course and continued with Latin had an average I.Q. of 107; 9 per cent failed Latin in the ninth or tenth grades

69 who did not take the tryout course, but elected high-school Latin had an average I.Q. of 103; 23 per cent failed in the ninth or tenth grades

While these figures seem to indicate the value of the tryout course for both positive and negative screening, the number of cases involved is so small that one can ascribe no validity to the finding. The data are presented here because they are suggestive of the proper test for a guidance instrument.

Bruner's program represented what was, perhaps, the crest of the tryout

[7] Herbert B. Bruner, *The Junior High School at Work* (New York, Teachers College Contributions to Education, No. 177, 1925).

[8] *Ibid.,* p. 19.

[9] *Ibid.,* p. 90, from Table XII.

wave. Cline found tryout courses decreasing in frequency when he addressed an inquiry to junior high school principals of the North Central Association in 1931. He reported[10]

As far as theory is concerned, the principals seemed to be in full accord with the principles laid down by the experts. Exploration is accepted as an important function of the junior high school, and the aims of exploration are to (1) explore the interests and capacities of pupils and (2) to reveal the nature and opportunities of future school and life activities. Exploratory units are recognized as valid means of exploration and every school has one or more such units.

. . . there are relatively few exploratory units in existence. . . . Despite this lack of exploratory units, 50 per cent of the schools have made no additions in the past five years, while 25 per cent have actually either dropped one or more exploratory units without replacement or have substituted therefor 'old-line' subjects, such as Latin for general language, algebra for general mathematics, biology for general science.

In addition to the paucity of exploratory units, a strange anomaly occurs in the matter of the prescription of exploratory units. Theory is not clear on the point as to whether such units should be required of all pupils or not. In practice these units are required in only 60 per cent of the cases. An elective exploratory unit seems necessarily to be a contradiction of terms. How can a unit explore pupils who do not elect it? One might intelligently elect after having an exploratory unit but not before he has had it.

The chief mechanical difficulty to making exploratory units constant is the number of the exploratory units offered, and this is tied up with the hopeless confusion as to the nature of the contents of the units.

Examination of Bruner's program shows how the employment of the elective principle defeats the tryout purpose. His data on the value of the Latin tryout course, just cited on page 182, indicate that whereas 67 pupils took the course, 69 did not take it but entered ninth-grade Latin. The object of the course is to help pupils find out through a sampling experience whether or not they like Latin or have aptitude for it. Further examination of Bruner's program reveals that experience with the practical arts was to be had only through the tryout courses. Since these were electives, it was altogether possible for pupils to complete the junior high school without any experience in practical arts, thus missing a field important both for its developmental and exploratory values.

There is reason to believe that tryout courses have largely disappeared because it was difficult to manage and administer many short courses. There was disappointment, also, because some that were tried were so barren of "broadening" value as not to be justified for the pupils who explored them with negative results. Authorities agree that broadening or developmental value should characterize every tryout course, whatever its exploratory value for a particular pupil. Finally, it seems likely that the tryout courses have

[10] E. C. Cline, "Junior-High-School Exploratory Units in Practice," *Clearing House,* Vol. VII (November, 1932), p. 154.

been in large measure absorbed in the general courses which have grown up in junior high schools as broad approaches to the main areas of human activity. As these general courses are required of all pupils, such exploratory values as they represent are denied to no one. Their significance for guidance will be examined in the next chapter. Unquestionably the extension of the secondary school has offered a more hospitable climate for their development just as it afforded the opportunity to experiment with tryout courses.

ORGANIZATION OF THE CURRICULAR OFFERING

Characteristics of Curricular Organization Demanded by Guidance

Before exploring various curricular arrangements to evaluate them for their worth to guidance, brief attention may well be given to the characteristics most beneficial to guidance. Perhaps first among the desired attributes is *breadth of opportunity* afforded. If the realization of this quality makes for complexity in the curriculum and difficulty of administration, that price must be paid. The variation in pupils is such that if they are to be distributed properly curriculum opportunities must be numerous and varied. Typically, this means the provision of curriculums involving different levels of ability as well as different kinds of ability. There are many who recognize that work experience has something to contribute to curricular breadth and believe it should be provided. The significance of these two types of curriculum arrangement will be discussed in the latter part of this section.

Breadth is a characteristic which is difficult for the small high school to achieve in its curriculum. For a number of years, however, enterprising workers in small schools have successfully supplemented their offering with correspondence study courses. They have guided their pupils in the choice of courses and have supervised them in the study of the courses chosen. The considerable literature bearing on this extension of the high-school curriculum will not be referred to here, but if guidance workers will read a single article which appeared in the official organ of the National Vocational Guidance Association, they will have a glimpse of the way correspondence study may be employed to facilitate the exercise of guidance.[11]

A second characteristic of curricular organization which is vital to guidance is *flexibility*. In the first place, the interests, needs, and abilities of pupils vary so widely that, beyond the limited requirements of education needed by all, a wealth of variety in the combination of curriculum experiences is demanded. Such provision is consistent, also, with society's need for workers of widely differentiated training. Rigidity of organization, whether it rests on tradition, inertia, or prejudice, defeats the exercise of guidance, both distributive and adjustive.

[11] The reference is as follows: T. W. Thordarson, "Enriching the Small High School Curriculum," *Occupations,* Vol. XIX (October, 1940), pp. 29–32. It describes supervised correspondence study in North Dakota.

In the second place, flexibility of curricular organization is demanded by the process of guidance as well as by its goal. As the process is dominantly that of self-finding through exploration and experimentation, the individual needs the privilege of trying many things. Flexibility means that so far as possible *he will not be penalized for those trial experiences which show him what he cannot do or what he does not like.* An expression of this principle has been the policy of not requiring the repetition of any course of a strictly tryout character which the pupil failed. But the principle should have and does have much more extended application. Flexibility is violated by the school which organizes its offering in four-year curriculums and poses unnecessary obstacles to transfer from one curriculum to another. This applies whether the obstacles are formal rules or just the unfriendly attitude which prevails in some high-school offices to discourage pupils from asking for curriculum transfer. Facility of transfer should not, of course, be taken to mean the privilege of transferring for light and transient reasons; nor should the granting of the privilege be subject to the judgment of a clerk. Transferring is an occasion for professional counseling, just as is the first selection of curriculum or subjects.

This plea for flexibility in the curricular offering is in no sense a denial of the necessity for realizing exacting standards in occupational training. The pupil who decides late in his preparation for a career in plumbing that he has made a mistake and that he should become a bookkeeper, cannot expect the specialized training for the one field to be accepted as a substitute for the specialized training of the other field. There is, however, much opportunity to realize flexibility in the curriculum without committing absurdities.

A third characteristic of curricular organization desirable for the exercise of guidance is *vertical and horizontal articulation.* Joint planning by elementary and junior-high teachers, by junior-high teachers and senior-high teachers, and by associations of high schools and colleges, are means of acknowledging the importance of vertical articulation. The educational highway must be smooth and continuous to obviate pupil maladjustment and to facilitate distribution. Horizontal articulation calls for effective co-ordination of parallel educational opportunities at the same level, as in situations where general high schools and specialized high schools are established to serve a community. The possibility of shifting from one school to another should be worked out on as liberal terms as possible in full recognition of the fact that adolescent youths of 14 and 15 cannot with certainty choose the right school. This characteristic of articulation will be viewed at some length in the third section of this chapter.

The Main Types of Programs of Studies

The Multiple-Curriculum Type. Widely prevalent though declining in dominance among programs of studies is the multiple-curriculum type. Figure 6 represents it as the organization of the curricular offering of the senior high school. In that figure the junior high school offering might be judged to be organized as a single curriculum. A later writing of the author[12] showed that he did have in mind for the junior high school a single curriculum with a few electives in the eighth and ninth grades. It might be called a constants-with-variables type of program of studies, mostly made up of constants. In the time that Glass was writing, the junior high school was often character-ized in its upper one or two grades by multiple curriculums which were articulated with those of the senior high school.

The rigidity of the multiple-curriculum type of program of studies has been relaxed somewhat by making the curriculums partially elective. The National Survey of Secondary Education found that while a few schools organized from five to eight curriculums, modal practice was to offer four.[13] Most common titles were "academic," "commercial," "general," and "prac-tical arts." Each curriculum typically required some subjects that were com-mon to all pupils of the school, considered as bearing on general educational needs. Mainly, these were English and social studies. Second, each curricu-lum required the subjects that were peculiar to its purpose. Third came the electives, as few or as many as were permissible after requirements of the first two categories were met. The data of the National Survey were gathered about 1930, but so far as may be judged, the picture of the multiple-curricu-lum type is about the same today.

What is the worth of the multiple-curriculum type of program of studies as a guidance instrument? In the junior high school it is completely inappro-priate, for it assumes that children of that age are capable of making sound choices of education and vocation. It is equally bad in the four-year high school which is preceded by an eight-year elementary school of traditional type. For the senior high school which is preceded by a modern junior high school with a well-developed guidance program, it might at first thought seem to be the best way to organize differentiated education. Its limitation, however, is that the few educational highways which it marks out do not correspond to the great diversity of pupil interests and abilities, or to the diversity of life opportunities before them. It proves inadequate on the cri-terion of flexibility. Even the aim of preparation for college requires more flexibility than is typically provided by the college-preparatory curriculum, for college-entrance requirements vary widely, as will be made evident in the third section of this chapter.

The General Curriculum in the Multiple-Curriculum Type. It will be noticed in Figure 6 that one of the curriculums was designated by Glass as "general," and to the presence of this curriculum may perhaps be attributed the persistence of the multiple-curriculum organization of the offering. The

---

[12] James M. Glass, *Curriculum Practices in the Junior High School and in Grades V and VI* (Chicago, University of Chicago Press, 1924).

[13] A. K. Loomis, Edwin S. Lide, and B. Lamar Johnson, *The Program of Studies,* National Survey of Secondary Education, Monograph No. 19, p. 121, Table 49.

National Survey found the general curriculum to stand third in the order of frequency; among the curriculums of 96 schools they classified 158 curriculums as "college preparatory," 106 as "commercial," and 72 as "general." In contrast with other curriculums, the general curriculum is unspecialized, and by its nature and its practical employment it imparts a measure of flexibility to the entire multiple-curriculum program. It is worthy of some examination as a guidance instrument.

A study[14] of Pennsylvania high schools in third-class districts (populations of 5,000–30,000) disclosed in 1933 a median estimated age of 9.3 years for the general curriculum, a fact which suggests that this curriculum was adopted in response to the pressure of rapidly mounting pupil enrollments in the period following World War I. The subjects required in the general curriculum varied somewhat, but modal practice called for 4 units of English, 1 of mathematics, 2 of history, 1 or 2 of other social studies, and 2 of science. Approximately one fourth of all pupils were enrolled in the general curriculum, with nearly twice as many boys as girls. This disparity of the sexes in the general curriculum was found to be complemented by a large excess of girls over boys in the commercial curriculum. The percentage of pupils in the general curriculum increased considerably from the ninth grade to the twelfth, indicating that pupils were transferring into it from the specialized curriculums.

The principals from whom these data were obtained were asked also to check the conditions or circumstances under which they advised pupils to elect the general curriculum or to transfer into it. The numerous specific reasons which the principals checked with high frequency can be classified in the following categories: first, lack of capacity for, or interest in, some required subjects of the more specialized curriculums; second, the pupil's uncertainty with respect to vocational and educational plans; third, the pupil's adherence to definite and valid plans for the realization of which the general curriculum gives him the best opportunity.

A companion study[15] involved the collection of certain data from 250 high-school seniors and an analysis of their high-school records. These students were completing the general curriculum and were about to graduate from nineteen of the Pennsylvania high schools included in the study just described. The first step was to obtain the pupils' appraisal of the general curriculum by inquiring into their reasons for electing that curriculum when they entered the high school or for transferring to it during their high-school careers. Of the 250 pupils, 114 fell in the first category and 136 in the second. The reasons for their presence in the general curriculum by original election or by transfer were similar to those stated by the principals and

[14] William M. Bryson and Percival W. Hutson, "The General Curriculum," *School Review,* Vol. XLIII (January, 1935), pp. 17–27.
[15] Harry E. Brumbaugh and Percival W. Hutson, "How High-School Pupils Use the General Curriculum," *School Review,* Vol. XLIII (February, 1935), pp. 119–131.

summarized in the preceding paragraph. Many found that the greater liberty of electing their subjects enabled them to prepare for their specific goals better than could be done through any of the specialized curriculums. Of the 250 pupils, 40.4 per cent stated occupational choices which require education to the extent of four years or more beyond high school; 10.0 per cent required two or three years beyond high school; 7.6 per cent, less than two years beyond high school; 14.4 per cent, no further institutional education; 27.6 per cent gave no occupational choice. Thus, considerable numbers of these pupils were using the general curriculum as preparation for college, university, teachers college, or technical school. In order fully to understand the thinking of these pupils with regard to the general curriculum, one would need to know the alternative choices before each pupil. If, for example, the college-preparatory curriculum in a given school requires two units in a foreign language and three units of mathematics, many pupils will discover that reputable institutions of higher learning are open to them without the necessity of clearing such hurdles. The more rigid and traditional the college-preparatory curriculum the larger the number of college-going pupils who will be found in the general curriculum.

Many pupils reported finding the required subjects of a specialized curriculum too difficult or too uninteresting, and so they had transferred to the general curriculum. They reported bookkeeping and shorthand as distasteful or difficult with about the same frequency as they reported Latin and algebra. It can be truly said that they had explored with negative results; the general curriculum was their haven of refuge. The single unit of Latin or shorthand which they had earned with a grade of C or D was acceptable in that curriculum toward graduation.

A considerable number of pupils elected the general curriculum because they did not know what vocation they wished to prepare for, because they did not want to take commercial subjects, or because they did not want to go to college. The general curriculum gave them freedom to explore and locate their goals.

What kind of pupils are sifted into the general curriculum by the various "screening" influences which have been indicated as being at work? The analysis of the scholastic records earned by the 250 students of this study showed that the average number of units they had earned in four academic fields was as follows: English, 3.73; mathematics, 2.26; science, 2.75; social studies, 3.27. As the total of these averages is 12.01 units, these pupils seem to be more academic than would perhaps have been expected. Their scholarship is indicated by Table 33.[16] As letter marking systems prevailed in their schools, numerical values were assigned to the letter marks on the following basis: A was valued at 4, B at 3, C at 2, and D at 1. The marks earned by a pupil in each field were averaged. No failing marks were included for the

[16] *Ibid.*, p. 128, Table VIII.

reason that it seemed desirable to consider merely the work on which the pupil was accepted for graduation.

The subjects in which the lowest medians in Table 33 were achieved are those in which most of the work of the pupils was taken. All medians, however, are above the mark of C. Study of this table suggests that these pupils were by no means students of a low order who barely accomplish high-school graduation. It must be remembered that most of their work was taken in classes in which they competed with pupils in the academic curriculum, as there was practically no segregation on the basis of ability or curriculum in English, social studies, science, and mathematics. As a group these pupils were not the type for whom a simplified curriculum should be provided,

TABLE 33. Summary of the Percentage Distributions of Scholarship Marks Achieved by General-Curriculum Seniors

Subject	Number of Pupils	Third Quartile	Median	First Quartile
Music	55	3.40	3.16	2.38
Industrial arts	62	3.25	2.80	2.22
Home economics	103	3.22	2.56	2.13
Art	70	3.18	2.46	2.14
Health and physical education	163	2.78	2.42	2.07
Latin	102	3.10	2.38	2.01
French	110	3.09	2.30	1.60
Commercial subjects . . .	159	2.62	2.27	1.99
Mathematics	215	2.58	2.20	1.75
Science	250	2.48	2.11	1.64
Social studies	250	2.43	2.11	1.66
English	250	2.43	2.03	1.61

though some members undoubtedly would have found such intellectual fare more palatable and more digestible.

The kind of pupils who are found pursuing the general curriculum will depend on many elements of guidance policy, positive and negative, direct and indirect, intentional and accidental, and these factors were not inventoried in the Pennsylvania study. Nor is much evidence on these factors given in the study of the abilities of Oakland, California, high-school pupils, which yielded the evidence shown in Table 34.[17] In this city pupils of the general curriculum have a median intelligence quotient almost fifteen points lower than that of the college-preparatory pupils, and each of these groups accounts for slightly more than a third of the total number of students. The standard deviation of each of the four groups shown in the table may be considered relatively large, signifying a wide range of ability in each cur-

[17] Richard E. Rutledge and Allen Fowler, "The Changing Senior High School Population and the Curriculum Problem," *School Review*, Vol. XL (February, 1932), p. 110, Table I.

riculum. The authors attribute the considerable difference between the medians of the college-preparatory and the general groups to an effective counseling program in the junior high schools. Reference will be made in the third section of this chapter to evidence that Oakland junior high schools have long been giving their pupils detailed educational counsel for senior high school work.

TABLE 34. Number and Percentage of Pupils and Mean Intelligence Quotient of Pupils in Each of Four Curriculums in Oakland High Schools

Curriculum	Number of Pupils	Percentage of Pupils	Mean Intelligence Quotient	Standard Deviation
College-preparatory .	1,941	34.50	111.32	12.87
General	1,915	34.04	96.70	12.55
Commercial . . .	1,323	23.51	99.01	12.09
Trade-preparatory .	447	7.95	92.63	12.46
All curriculums	5,626	100.00	102.21	13.69

In summary, the general curriculum is a recognition of the inadequacy of the specialized curriculums. The needs of pupils call for widely varying combinations of studies, and the general curriculum has the flexibility necessary for meeting such needs. The general curriculum also constitutes a recognition of the fact that some pupils need more exploratory opportunity than junior high school years afford. Investigations of interests tell us that the decisions of a fourteen-year-old boy or girl with regard to educational and vocational plans must be regarded as tentative and subject to revision. The pupil who makes an error in his choice of a specialized curriculum can usually transfer to the general curriculum without being penalized in his progress toward high-school graduation. Thus an exploratory character is imparted to the whole program of studies.

Despite the improvement which a general curriculum contributes to a multiple-curriculum program of studies, it must be labeled as patchwork on an inadequate curriculum organization. It is misnamed—although no better name comes to mind—because it does not stand for general education. Doubtless it sometimes brings the pupil to the end of his high-school career with a too miscellaneous assortment of credits. This regrettable misuse of educational opportunity may, however, be avoided if the pupil's explorations are accompanied by skilled individual counsel.

The Constants-With-Variables Type. This name is given to a program of studies in which the subjects deemed necessary for the education of all pupils are required—these being the constants—and the rest of the offering is open to choice with relatively little restriction. An example of such a program of studies is the one recommended by the Pennsylvania Department of Public Instruction for senior high schools. It stipulates that "A minimum of thirteen units in the 10th, 11th, and 12th years shall be required for graduation. Of these thirteen units, nine shall be satisfied by sequences, including one three-unit sequence. . . . Two units of English shall be required. Three units are recommended. . . . Two units of social studies shall be required. Three are recommended." "These proposals will necessitate educational guidance, rather than vertically differentiated curriculums, as the determining factor in the pupil's selection of his program of studies."[18]

An example of this type of program of studies is that of the John Marshall High School, Richmond, Virginia, reproduced in a recent work on curriculum, and essentially illustrating the Pennsylvania recommendations.[19]

Another example of the constants-with-variables type of program of studies is that of Wichita (Kansas) High School East. From the printed program of this high school the following curriculum requirements are quoted:

1. Two majors of three units each:
   The first major in English . . . . 3 units
   The second major from one of the remaining groups . . . . . 3 units
2. Two minors of two units each:
   First minor in social studies (unless social studies
     has been selected as a second major) including
     one-half of U.S. government and one unit of
     American history . . . . 2 units
   Second minor from one of the remaining groups . . . . . . 2 units
3. The two majors and two minors must be selected
   from any four of the eight groups [of studies] . . . .
4. One unit of mathematics . . . .
5. One unit of laboratory science . . . .

The sequence requirements in this Wichita program are softened somewhat by the statement that "In counting majors and minors subjects taken in the ninth grade of the intermediate school should be included." The program would permit a girl, for example, to take three units each of home economics and of art; it would permit a boy to complete three-year sequences of mathematics and science and also take two years of shop. Widely varying combinations are possible, as well as some leeway for exploration.

There can be no doubt that the constants-with-variables program of studies invites educational guidance; in fact, it compels guidance—provision for the individual counseling of each pupil. Possibly that is one reason why its adoption does not progress more rapidly. Do principals fear that the guid-

[18] Lester K. Ade, *Graduation Standards for Secondary Schools,* mimeographed (Harrisburg. Department of Public Instruction, 1938). (These standards were amended in 1958 to require three units of English, three units of social studies, one unit of science, and one unit of mathematics except for students who elect a program of foreign languages. Thus the freedom for choosing variables has been somewhat reduced.)

[19] J. G. Saylor and W. M. Alexander, *Curriculum Planning* (New York, Rinehart, 1954), pp. 6–7.

ance resources of their schools are insufficient? Or are they loath to leave behind the time-honored classification of their pupils as "academic," "commercial," etc., in favor of a situation in which there would be no vertical classification of their pupils?

Admittedly, this flexible program does impose a heavy responsibility on the school. If the burden of advisement of pupils is widely diffused through the whole faculty they will need various aids, of which one of the most important is a publication of numerous *suggested* curriculums.

The flexibility and the breadth of opportunity afforded by the constants-with-variables program of studies makes it much better adapted to serve the guidance function than the multiple-curriculum type, even when the latter includes a general curriculum. It compels close study of the individual pupil and knowledge of the educational routes to a wide range of occupational terminals. These responsibilities should not be a cause for complaint. In the effective performance of the task of education we should not expect any short-cut substitute for these essential elements of guidance.

The Core Curriculum

An innovation in curriculum organization at the secondary-school level which has been gaining increasing attention over the past two decades is the "core curriculum." It was given noteworthy impetus by the experimental programs carried out by the Thirty Schools of the Eight-Year Study. While there are wide variations in its definition, in most formulations it seems to comprehend the constants of a constants-with-variables program of studies. In varying degree the traditional content of the constants is reconstructed and unified. Major characteristics of the core curriculum, as idealized, may be stated as follows:

1. It utilizes the problems of personal and social development common to all youth, and learning activity springs from felt needs.
2. Learning experiences develop without reference to traditional subject-matter lines.
3. There is much use of problem-solving techniques, in contrast to the emphasis on memorization which is characteristic of subject-matter mastery.
4. There is much leeway for pupil initiative in planning the activity of the group.
5. Extended provision for group and individual guidance prevails.

The fifth characteristic is the one with which we are especially concerned, for it represents an organization of the school which is in decided contrast to the traditional educational scene as depicted in certain sections of Chapter 3. There it was pointed out that the typical factory organization makes it easy for teachers to be ignorant of their pupils. With teachers meeting 150–250 pupils in classes once a day, it is assumed that it is not important for the teacher to have an intimate knowledge of his pupils. He is supposed to teach the pupils the subject matter of a course. Guidance, under such organization, is likely to be another specialized service provided and performed by an "expert" who has even less contact with the pupil than does the teacher.

The core organization, by contrast, gives more opportunity for the teacher to study each pupil as a unique personality. This aspect is keenly appreciated by the principal who knows how individual attention and understanding contribute to the pupil's fullest development. This advantage of the core is especially well stated by Malcolm B. Keck, principal of the Folwell Junior High School, of Minneapolis.[20] He does not designate the program of his school a core curriculum program but simply as a "double-period" program in which certain teachers teach English and social studies to the same pupils in a double period. Whereas the typical single-period teacher in his school meets five classes and has a homeroom, with a total of approximately 210 pupils, the double-period teacher meets one class for a double period in the morning and another in the afternoon, a total of 70 pupils. A fifth period every day is devoted to three types of activity: guidance conferences with students, conferences with parents, and weekly meetings with other double-period teachers. This teacher also directs a once-a-week folk-dancing session for each of his groups. (What an opportunity for promoting mutual acquaintance and warmth of relationship!) He keeps a folder of personal information on each of his 70 students.

Of the nine important values which Principal Keck sees in this organization, the first four are as follows:

1. The teacher has fewer students and is associated with them for a longer period of time each day than would otherwise be the case.

2. The teacher is provided with time and space in which to counsel students.

3. The teacher is provided with time and space in which to hold conferences with parents.

4. At least one teacher in the school gets to know and understand each individual student. No youngster remains semi-anonymous.

The core curriculum is known under different titles. As the program of the Eagle Rock High School, Los Angeles, was described a few years ago, it was known as the "Basic Course." This six-year school—one of the Thirty Schools—was organized in three two-year cycles, with a general policy of having teachers continue with their class personnel for two years. The guidance values are set forth with clarity in the following paragraph:[21]

The program of each student at Eagle Rock High School is unified through what is known as the Basic Course, in which the instructor of the class remains with his group during the two-year cycle and becomes in a very personal way the adviser and interpreter of the individual children in his class. To him come

[20] "We Get to Know Joe," *NEA Journal,* Vol. XLI (December, 1952), pp. 562–563.

[21] Helen Babson, "Progress at Eagle Rock High School," *California Journal of Secondary Education,* Vol. XVI (May, 1941), p. 301.

all records, all information, all recommendations; and his contacts with the parents are frequent. Regularly he meets other instructors of the grade in a grade curriculum committee so that the continuity of the child's experience may be clear in the consciousness of all his teachers as together they plan the general sequence of units of work and the materials necessary for their accomplishment. It is this particular instructor who aids the pupil in deciding upon his interests, major and general. . . . In the final analysis, the instructor combines in this capacity the homeroom and the guidance functions.

At Eagle Rock the Basic Course is three hours in length in the 7th and 8th grades, two hours in the 9th and 10th, and two hours in the 11th and 12th, though with some breaking down in the third cycle. Personnel data and all evidence revealing the pupil are kept in an individual folder and summarized at the end of each cycle.

The principal of a Philadelphia junior high school, in describing a core including homeroom, English, and social studies—with science included in some grades—remarks that

Inasmuch as the time for homeroom is included in general education, guidance is no longer a superimposed program but becomes part of the daily activities and is inherent in the pupil-teacher relationships that are established.[22]

In the senior high school at Eugene, Oregon, it is related that

teachers and principal set to work studying guidance and its implications for curriculum planning. We found that much of the material ordinarily placed in the guidance compartment of many schools belonged in the curricular offerings of the school. We also came to the conclusion that effective guidance is not done when one group of teachers is set aside as those interested in the personal lives of the pupils and another group as the pourers-in-of-subject-matter-content. After much study we finally have been able to agree that guidance, classroom instruction, and all activities of the school are more or less of a unitary nature. . . .

When a tenth-grade pupil enters, he is assigned to a social-living class, which is a two-hour class under one teacher. The theme of the year is "The Personal and Social Problems of the High-School Pupil." Here he is oriented to the school, has his language experiences, is given direction in his reading, gains contact with the cultures of other peoples. In a carefully planned unit on personality he is helped along lines of mental health, and the year usually closes with a unit on Safety in Driving which concludes with a driver's test given under regular state traffic division auspices.[23]

One principal of a junior high school, cautious about abandoning subject-matter lines, and describing his plans as midway between progressivism and traditionalism, cut down departmentalization and reduced by almost one half the number of teachers whom pupils in the seventh and eighth grades

[22] Gertrude A. Noar, "The Junior High School in Transition," *Bulletin of the National Association of Secondary-School Principals,* Vol. XXVIII (March, 1944), pp. 15–24.

[23] Harry B. Johnson, "What, No Homeroom!" *Clearing House,* Vol. XIV (May, 1940), pp. 534–535.

have to meet. He was evidently thinking of the advantage to guidance when he said,[24]

All these teachers have their homeroom pupils for a little over two hours every day of the school week. In that time they teach two related subjects, social studies and English, or mathematics and science, or health and science, and in one or two cases, English and mathematics.

This program is quite far removed from the core curriculum. It is primarily an organization of the schedule, contributing to guidance, mentioned here as a first step away from extreme departmentalization—a step which some principals may feel is within the immediate possibility of their faculties. That this step is being taken in more and more junior high schools is reported in a chapter entitled "Retreat from Departmentalization" in a recent survey of "trends."[25]

Any account of the development of the core curriculum, however brief, must include some mention of the creative work of Paul Pierce and the faculty of the Wells High School, Chicago. This group is intensely aware of the implications of curriculum organization for guidance, as is indicated by the following quotation from Pierce:[26]

. . . it was regarded as basic that problems which conventionally call for guidance should be anticipated and eliminated through development of a curriculum fitted to pupil's interests, abilities, and needs. This would care for such matters as subject failures and truancy, which traditionally consume guidance time and efforts. Our principle was thus equivalent to saying that curriculum improvement is the chief vehicle of guidance. A second principle was that guidance should be concerned not so much with determining a given niche for the student and then fitting him into it as with training him to meet realistic problems here and now, that he might effectively meet the complex problems of later life. . . . A third principle was that guidance should be an integral part of the curriculum conducted in the student's actual learning situations and not involve specialized personnel and instructional machinery.

Considering the character of his student body—practically none college-bound—Pierce organized the curriculum around a strong core. He had his codirectors of guidance devote themselves to "servicing the classroom and homeroom teachers," by giving tests of intelligence and aptitude, by training teachers in the collection of data essential to the understanding of pupils, and in other ways. An important element in Pierce's philosophy of guidance he states as follows:[27]

Another deterring factor in the counseling situation has been the idea, prevalent among many administrators, that only gifted teachers are equipped to counsel pupils regarding classroom and other problems of a personal nature. Just why

[24] Merrill F. Norlin, "Accenting the 'Junior' in Junior High School," *School Executive,* Vol. LIX (May, 1940), p. 11.

[25] L. V. Koos, *Junior High School Trends* (New York, Harper, 1955), Ch. V.

[26] Paul R. Pierce, *Developing a High-School Curriculum* (New York, American Book, 1942), pp. 217–218.

[27] *Ibid.,* p. 231.

some teachers are good for certain phases of teaching and not other phases it is difficult to see, but the policy is undoubtedly a remnant of the specialization conception of teaching so prevalent in traditional high-school circles. Our policy with respect to counseling was the same from the start as that regarding the core curriculum—all teachers had to assume the main responsibilities connected with well-rounded development of pupils, not merely to teach a particular subject.

In internal organization and scheduling, Pierce developed a unique plan, calculated to utilize the special qualifications of his teachers and also bring about conditions most conducive to the exercise of guidance. Each homeroom group was blocked to attend classes as a unit, and their chief personnel data were supplied to each core-curriculum teacher. In order further to facilitate teacher planning with regard to individual pupils, teachers and pupils were scheduled in co-operative planning and working groups.

Our first group of this kind consisted of four teachers, one in each of the core fields of English arts, science, social studies, and art, and their four homeroom divisions. Each teacher had the others' homeroom divisions, as their classes and schedules were so arranged that the teachers and their groups had classes, study sessions, lunch periods, and auditorium arts simultaneously, thus permitting teachers to get together conveniently to plan; permitting pupils to be assembled readily for large-group activities, field-trips, and the like; and allowing teachers and pupils to hold extraclass conferences.[28]

The school has been largely organized with three-teacher and four-teacher teams, keeping their respective homeroom and class groups for two or three years. Pierce avers that these procedures in organization have greatly stimulated "our sometimes laggard turning from subjects to youth as the hub of our attention."

From this brief survey of the core curriculum it is evident that this form of curricular organization is full of promise for the guidance function. Studied in the light of the components of the guidance function as they were set forth in Chapter 5, the core curriculum can be seen as a guidance feature of prime importance. In its ideal it is indeed the employment of the educative process for the attainment of the goals of adjustment and distribution.

Provision for Instruction at Different Levels

An aspect of curriculum organization which means much to guidance is the provision for pupils of different levels of ability. Just as breadth and flexibility of the offering is necessary in order to enable pupils to prepare for the types of adult activity which correspond to their varied interests and kinds of ability, so also depth is essential to serve different degrees of ability. Especially is this curricular characteristic necessary in the constants. The counselor is faced with few situations more baffling than the adjustment of the pupil who is failing in a required subject which is taught at only one level

[28] *Ibid.,* p. 243.

of ability, and that too high for him. Junior high schools have attempted to meet this problem by ability grouping, but after a quarter century of experience with this solution, it is still a highly controversial subject and will not be presented here. Rather, two or three examples of other practice will be described.

E. C. Cline, for a number of years principal of the senior high school at Richmond, Indiana, during the 1930s led his faculty in the development of two distinct groups of courses. The 1947 *Pupils' Handbook* of the school (not prepared by pupils) contains the following statement concerning the offering (p. 14):

The Richmond Senior High School offers three types of courses: the "A" courses, the "G" courses, and the Prevocational courses. The "A" courses are those for which arbitrary passing standards are set by agencies outside the schools: industry, business, or colleges; these standards must be met if the pupil is to pass. Such courses are English "A," physics, chemistry, geometry, algebra, trigonometry, foreign language, economics, sociology, stenography, bookkeeping, vocational shop work, typewriting (for stenographers), office practice, and any other courses classified as "A" courses. All others are "G" or Prevocational courses in which pupils may receive credit by doing their best. An "A" course may always be substituted for a corresponding "G" course—English "A" for English "G," for example—but "G" or Prevocational courses may not be substituted for required "A" courses.

Besides the different passing regulations, the "A," "G," and Prevocational courses also differ in kinds of material studied. The "A" courses contain material that will enable pupils to satisfy a certain requirement after they leave school; for example, English "A" emphasizes the literature, composition, and grammar that colleges expect their students to know, and stenography contains material that will enable stenographers to meet the expectations of employers. The "G" courses, on the other hand, contain the kind of training we all need and use in everyday living; English "G," for example, helps one to enjoy better reading, to know what magazines are most helpful, to write letters to friends or to employers, and the like. There is no distinction made as to which of these two kinds of courses is easier or better; any course is best for a particular pupil if it best gives him what he needs.

The Prevocational courses offer opportunities for pupils with non-academic and manual abilities to find satisfactory adjustments in the high school and to graduate on established levels of achievement, interest, and effort. . . .

This excerpt[29] expresses substantially the point of view developed by Cline in articles in educational periodicals.[30] While such a plan would be of

[29] Shortened and slightly revised but not materially changed in the 1955 Handbook.
[30] E. C. Cline, "Differentiating Secondary Education," *School Review*, Vol. XLII (June, 1934), pp. 431–439.
———, "Differentiation in English on Senior High School Level," *English Journal*, Vol. XXIV (January, 1935), pp. 17–21.
———, "Curriculum Making for Non-Academic Pupils," *School and Society*, Vol. XLV (April 10, 1937), pp. 519–522.

great aid to the exercise of guidance, it would also assume a thoroughgoing guidance program, helping pupils assuredly and advisedly to find their goals and thus to know in which areas they should meet arbitrary standards and in which effort standards would do.

Another meritorious program providing instruction at different levels has been developed in Central High School, St. Paul.[31] The school has three curriculums—college-preparatory, commercial, and general. When experimentation was begun, a large majority of the pupils were in the college-preparatory curriculum, though relatively few went to college, and the percentage of failures and elimination was relatively high. To meet this situation new subjects were created for the general curriculum and an effort standard established, while high standards, based on achievement, were maintained for the college-preparatory and commercial curriculums. The authors reasoned that the general curriculum has as its object not technical preparation but the training of pupils for useful citizenship. Thus the functions of elimination and selection should not operate in the general curriculum, but the work should be adjusted to the abilities of all the pupils found in it. "The standard of work required depends upon the level of potential achievement of each pupil and the teachers' marks are based upon the relation between each pupil's abilities and his achievement."

To administer this program the pupils have to be studied as individuals to help them choose their curriculums. Enrollment in the proper curriculum, it was agreed, must not be arbitrary but must allow pupils to try themselves out in the specialized curriculums without too much loss of time if they want to. A grade of P is given to pupils in subjects in the college-preparatory and commercial curriculums when their work and test results indicate to the teacher that the pupil does not have appropriate ability to justify continuance. That means he has done as well as his ability enables him to do, and it means that he has earned a credit in the general curriculum. It is the pupil's privilege to try over again to see if he can make a regular grade, but in general this device operates to shift pupils gradually over into the general curriculum. The P grade is used with special effectiveness in English, mathematics, and stenography, but if a pupil has high ability and doesn't use it he is not given the P grade but is failed. In order that justice may surely be served, the guidance department must make certain that the pupil's aptitude is known.

The authors state that in building new courses for the general curriculum they are not satisfied with merely watering down college-preparatory courses. Thus we have in St. Paul, as in Richmond, Indiana, definite provision for instruction at different levels. It is a far more fundamental adaptation to the realities of individual differences than is the typical general curriculum which, while flexible, is made up of pieces from the specialized curriculums.

[31] James E. Marshall and Glenn F. Varner, "Our 3 Curriculums Provide for Individual Differences," *Clearing House,* Vol. XV (March, 1941), pp. 428–431.

An apparent difference between the St. Paul and Richmond programs is that while St. Paul maintains the multiple-curricular form, the Richmond organization is on the constants-with-variables basis, though with constants on two levels.

The bearing of this curricular differentiation on guidance is plain. The outcomes, as stated by Marshall and Varner, are those at which guidance aims.

The gross effect of this differentiated curriculum is that the number of failures and subsequent eliminations from school are being materially reduced, and many pupils are able to make satisfactory adjustments to the school. We thereby avoid discouragement, elimination, and the emotional disturbances that are so common in the traditional high school. . . .[32]

St. Paul and Richmond have evidently pioneered the kind of differentiation in secondary education which has recently been advocated by James B. Conant, former president of Harvard University, as the result of his study of American public high schools. His statements indicate his full awareness of the key role of guidance in the operation of such curricular organization.

Work Experience

Though difficult to estimate, guidance values of great consequence undoubtedly lie in the work-experience programs that some secondary schools have developed in recent years. Biographies have indicated, times unnumbered, the importance of work-sampling in helping individuals in self-finding. Not long ago Brewer gave the following statement of opinion on this point:[33] "It seems doubtful . . . that any real substitute can be found for actual trial of tasks, in exploratory courses under school auspices and in work experiences of diversified kinds."

Before World War II began to create manpower shortages the desire to incorporate work experience as part of the educational program was already being expressed. A canvass of the *Education Index* for July, 1938–June, 1941, under the titles "Work" and "Work Camps" shows extended lists of writings. Bulletin No. 90 (April, 1940) of the National Association of Secondary-School Principals devoted its 158 pages to "Youth and Work Opportunities." A canvass of this bulletin shows that the experience of the depression years with the Civilian Conservation Corps and the National Youth Administration was stirring secondary-school leaders to an awareness of work experience as an important avenue to educational goals.

Then came the war. The demand for labor reached into senior high schools, then into junior high schools. High-school enrollments dropped by a million or more as pupils severed connection from the school entirely for the purpose of taking jobs. An additional unknown number took jobs—

[32] *Ibid.*, p. 431.
[33] John M. Brewer, "Classification of Items in Interest Inventories," *Occupations,* Vol. XXI (February, 1943), p. 451.

part-time or full-time—and continued their schooling. While the truth is not known, there is little reason to believe that most schools controlled the work activities of their pupils further than was involved in the issue of work permits. Certainly chaotic and exploitative conditions prevailed in many communities and interfered seriously with the education of some pupils both within the school and without.

One of the school systems, however, which had a detailed plan to make as educational as possible the work experience which pupils were going to get anyway, was that of Oakland, California. In that city a combined study-work plan, called the Four-Four Plan, was developed for students sixteen years of age and over by which they could work without sacrificing high-school graduation and without violating state or federal laws governing school attendance and child labor. As described by Marion Brown, director of guidance,[34] the Four-Four Plan was established by the schools in co-operation with the Junior Division of the United States Employment Service, parents, employer groups, and employee organizations. The following guiding principles governed the program:

1. Work experience was considered a course in school and regular counseling procedures were used in planning and selecting it.

2. Students were admitted only if they were sixteen years of age or older and had the approval of both the parents and the school.

3. Placement was handled only through the Junior Division of the United States Employment Service.

4. In each school certified teachers were appointed as work-experience co-ordinators to supervise students at work.

5. Students were instructed about general standards and ethics involved in accepting employment.

6. Upon accepting employment, the student was required to stay with the employer for at least one school semester, providing conditions of employment remained the same as when he took the job. Likewise, employers were expected to keep students in their employ for a full semester unless the student's work proved to be unsatisfactory.

7. School credit was granted equal to that earned by the satisfactory completion of two subjects.

The article gives many of the details of the administration of the plan, including numerous forms, bulletins, and letters used in communicating with pupils, parents, and employers. These convey a marked impression of how the plan was controlled by educational purposes.

Although the plan has been described in the past tense, it apparently should not be thought of as merely a wartime phenomenon, but as a standard and continuous element in the curricular organization of Oakland high schools. Marion Brown's mimeographed Bulletin No. 35, 1947 Series, May

[34] "The Work-Experience Program in the Oakland Public Schools," *Journal of the National Association of Deans of Women,* Vol. VIII (October, 1944), pp. 4–26.

1, 1947, is a report to her co-workers on the "Status of the Work-Experience Course, Spring Semester, 1947." She states that 189 students were then enrolled in the course and were working in 135 establishments. "Employers have raised their standards, but well-qualified students can still be placed."

But the idea that a work-experience course should be regarded as part of the curriculum in normal times encounters strong opposition from at least one source. Frazier says,[35] "To make a virtue out of an expediency in wartime, then, is one thing, human enough and understandable. To make a virtue out of the same expediency, for whatever reasons, in peacetime can be unforgiveable." He deplores the tendency to extol the value of work experience to the extent of having pupils give up so much of the rich life that we have worked hard to bring about in school.

From 3 o'clock on in most schools across the country, pupils who are free from the necessity of working for money gather on the athletic fields, in the workshops and laboratories, on the stages, in the offices of school publications, and in the rooms of the teachers who sponsor clubs. And there they talk and work together while taking part in the endless variety of activities that even the most hidebound of secondary schools now provide.

Frazier thinks it unfortunate that in normal times some pupils have to carry a part-time job and miss the rich experience of after-school life. Perhaps, he says, we fail to recognize that the reason pupils took up work so eagerly when wartime labor shortages brought it to them was the unpalatability of much that was going on in school. "But we have not bowed our heads in shame before this fact. We have chosen to dignify rather than to deplore it."

Frazier's article is in effect a plea to make the school what our ideals tell us it can be. There is no question but that in the tense days of the war many schools came to represent a lean and insubstantial fare of bare academic bones. Clubs died. Most activities except athletics lost much of their vitality. Teachers were busy with social service occasioned by the war or with part-time work in war plants, so that they had little time for extracurricular sponsorships. Pupils attended classes and rushed out of the building to their jobs. Frazier believes we should restore the full life of the school and focus our energies on making it as rich an environment as possible. He has a point. It does not, however, demolish the substantial values of work experience for exploration, for self-finding, and for development. It is a caution to seek those values in a temperate, tolerant spirit, fully conscious of other elements of curricular and extracurricular life.[36]

[35] Alexander Frazier, "The Case against Work Experience," *Nation's Schools,* Vol. XXXVIII (October, 1946), pp. 20–21.

[36] The more detailed meaning of work experience in the economic and psychological life of the individual has been spelled out in a research by Scales and Hutson which is cited and described in Chapter 11. The evidence that its educational values are becoming more widely noticed and accepted is to be found in the following recent publication: DeWitt Hunt, *Work Experience Education Programs in American Secondary Schools* (Washington, D.C., U.S. Office of Education Bulletin, No. 5, 1957).

ARTICULATION OF SCHOOL UNITS

The Typical College-Preparatory Curriculum Inadequate as an Instrument of Guidance

It is not the object of this section to take up in any complete manner what is being done to achieve the vertical articulation of school units, but rather to consider the subject just from the angle of organization of the school and the offering. Such steps to achieve articulation as are embodied in orientation programs will be touched on in Chapters 10 and 11.

Examining first the articulation of high school and college, it may be well at the outset to point out that as high school and college are commonly organized, the building of a smooth and adequate bridge from one of these units to the next one is very difficult. Typical academic high-school education ends without completing anything. High-school graduation finds the student right in the middle of general education. When he goes on to an institution of higher education he continues his general education for one, two, or more years before he will be admitted to a professional school. The smooth joining of high-school and college education is further rendered difficult by the elective system in both institutions. That is, general education is not satisfactorily defined. Students who intend to go to college arrive at high-school graduation with such varied assortments of credits that it is difficult to say just what stage has been reached in their general education. The college does not attempt systematically to ascertain the student's status and then prescribe studies which will supplement and complement his present attainments so that he completes general education. The college simply administers to all students certain constants, certain options, and free electives to complete the schedule for one, two, or more years prior to admission to professional specialization.

Progress toward the more rational organization of school units, as typified in the 6–4–4 plan,[37] which would reduce the problem of articulation, is currently making no headway. And the present agitation over "general education" in the first two years of college includes no concern over articulation with the high school. Therefore, principal and counselor face the traditional gap between 12th and 13th grades.

The gap is to be bridged for a growing percentage of all high school graduates, but the variation from school to school is very great. The tendency in the past has been to overemphasize this articulation, most high schools teaching all academic subjects for the fulfillment of the college-preparatory objective, regardless of the variation in pupils' future plans.

The college-preparatory curriculum being the principal instrument for achieving the articulation of high school and college, it is appropriate to

[37] Given extended description in L. V. Koos, *Integrating High School and College* (New York, Harper, 1946).

analyze it for its adequacy. To make this analysis Harriger[38] obtained from the principals of 487 high schools in Delaware, Maryland, New Jersey, Ohio, Pennsylvania, and West Virginia the exact descriptions of the college-preparatory curriculums in their schools—required subjects and electives. The schools were small schools, having enrollments of from 50 to 500, thus representing some degree of homogeneity in that all would find it more difficult to provide for varied pupil needs than would larger schools. Harriger further obtained from the principals the numbers of pupils graduating from their schools in each of the five years from 1940–41 to 1944–45, the numbers from each class entering college, and lists of the universities, colleges, and teachers colleges which they entered. It was found that the median percentage of the graduates entering degree-granting institutions was about 14 and that the percentage was about the same each year, despite the fact that eighteen-year-old boys were subject to call for military service the last three years. From the 233 higher institutions which enrolled five or more of these high-school graduates catalogues were requested. From the catalogues the college-entrance requirements of the institutions were obtained and analyzed. Thus it was possible to compare the college-preparatory curriculums of a group of high schools with the entrance requirements of the colleges their graduates entered.

Table 35[39] shows the comparison for required units in five academic fields. The data on colleges for 1913 and 1922 are taken from McKown's study[40] of more than five hundred liberal arts colleges, representing the whole country. The 1946 data on colleges represents the 104 liberal arts colleges in Harriger's study—universities, teachers colleges, and technical institutes being omitted in order to clarify the comparison with McKown's data. The percentages for 1913 and 1922 show no decimal point because they are listed just as McKown showed them. The totals for the distributions are not shown. Practically all of them fall a little short of 100.0 per cent for the reason that the few cases which call for 4½, 3½, and similar unusual numbers of units were omitted in order to reduce the size of the table.

Table 35 merits careful study. Attention is called, first, to the evidence that the specific unit requirements for college entrance show a steady decline from 1913 to 1922 to 1946. In fact, looking at the percentages of colleges which require 0 units in each of the subject fields, the decline is precipitous from 1922 to 1946.[41] That 60.6 per cent of Harriger's list of colleges should

---

[38] Guy N. Harriger, "The College-Preparatory Curriculum as an Instrument of Educational Guidance," *School Review,* Vol. LVI (March, 1948), pp. 163–167.

[39] *Ibid.,* p. 165, Table 1 (adapted).

[40] Harry C. McKown, *The Trend of College Entrance Requirements, 1913–1922* (Washington, D.C., Bureau of Education Bulletin, No. 35, 1924), Tables 21, 23, 31, 35, 46.

[41] This trend is substantiated by the following study: Richard A. Mumma, "Further Modifications in College-Entrance Requirements," *School Review,* Vol. LVII (January, 1950), pp. 24–28.

TABLE 35. Percentage Distributions of Colleges according to Number of High-School Units Required for College Entrance, Compared with Percentage Distributions of High Schools According to Number of Units Required by Their College-Preparatory Curriculums

	Colleges			College-Preparatory
Units	1913	1922	1946	Curriculums, 1946
(English)				
4	..	..	20.2	92.8
3	89	89	36.5	5.1
2	8	5	....	....
1	..	..	1.0	....
var.	..	..	1.0	....
0	2	4	41.4	1.8
(Social Studies)				
4	..	..	....	44.8
3	..	..	....	32.9
2	14	10	3.8	12.5
1	58	57	27.9	6.6
var.	..	..	1.9	....
0	26	31	63.4	3.1
(Sciences)				
4	..	..	....	30.2
3	..	..	....	15.4
2	7	6	1.0	24.4
1	41	39	27.9	21.6
var.	..	..	3.8	....
0	48	54	67.3	8.4
(Mathematics)				
4	..	..	1.0	19.5
3	21	11	1.0	25.7
2½	52	33	5.8	7.2
2	21	48	33.7	26.1
1	..	..	2.9	13.3
var.	..	..	6.7	....
0	4	6	48.1	7.8
(Foreign Language)				
7	7	2	....	.2
6	11	5	....	.6
5	7	5	1.0	....
4	23	12	1.9	7.6
3	13	10	2.9	11.5
2	27	33	25.0	35.1
1	..	..	....	.4
var.	..	..	8.7	....
0	11	30	60.6	44.6

in 1946 be requiring 0 units of foreign language may indeed be surprising. And that 48.1 per cent should be requiring 0 units of mathematics may be no less surprising. The meaning of the large percentages of colleges which in 1946 had no specific unit requirements is that the studies of Thorndike, Yates, and others, showing that no subjects have special merit as instruments of college preparation, are being more and more accepted by the colleges as determinants of admissions policy. Other facts gathered by Harriger showed the colleges to be calling for evidence of the applicant's general level of scholarship, his character, promise, etc.

The high schools, on the other hand, in their college-preparatory curriculums tend to require 4 units of English, 3 or 4 of social studies, from 1 to 4 of sciences, from 2 to 4 of mathematics, and 0 or 2 of foreign language. The comparison of these data with the facts of college-entrance requirements seems to stamp the high schools as unnecessarily rigid, as adhering to tradition when new viewpoints are coming into control. The contrast is especially marked in the case of mathematics and science, in which fields 45 per cent of the high schools require three or four units, a number required by no colleges in science and by only 2 per cent in mathematics. The high requirements of the high schools in English and the social studies—going far beyond college-entrance requirements—may not only reflect ideas of college preparation but also a responsibility for general education, since those two fields are so largely regarded as the core of secondary education.

The data of Table 35 signify the inadequacy of the college-preparatory curriculum as an instrument of guidance. It is far too coarse in its application, for in large degree it assumes relative uniformity in college-entrance requirements. It is sometimes constructed on the assumption of contingencies which are more or less remote. How can one explain the requirement of three or four units of mathematics by nearly half of these high schools except on the principal's reasoning that because an occasional graduate may want to enter a school of engineering, all college-preparatory pupils must take that mathematics hurdle? The point is illustrated by a high school which the writer recently helped to evaluate. The college-preparatory curriculum called for two units of algebra, one of geometry, and two of foreign language. Yet two thirds of the graduates who entered higher institutions entered either a teachers college which had no requirements of mathematics or language, or a nearby university which required only one unit of mathematics (except for its engineering school) and two units of foreign language.

The high schools should give up the college-preparatory curriculum, as ill-adapted to its purpose, institute the more flexible organizational features already described in this chapter, and give each pupil individual advisement. Printed advice for parents and pupils on how to use a constants-with-variables program of studies for meeting the requirements of various colleges is an important aid. An example is a printed bulletin issued by the senior high schools of Minneapolis, which clearly sets forth the requirements for entrance to the University of Minnesota and its various divisions, to the colleges, and to the teachers colleges of the state. The best preparation for college is accomplished by helping the pupil to select courses which correspond to the degree and type of talent he possesses. It will usually be found that he has then met the entrance requirements of the college to which he is best adapted.

Articulation of Lower Schools

As set forth in the first pages of this chapter, a basic idea in the promotion of the junior high school was that it would serve to articulate elementary and secondary education. Such an objective is not reached, however, by any automatic process. It must be clearly defined and striven for, or instead of one break in the school system, between the eighth and ninth grades, two will be created, one between the sixth and seventh grades and the other between the ninth and tenth.

Admittedly, articulating the sixth and seventh grades is easier if the two are in the same building and the same organization than if they are in separate buildings and different organizations. The Gary system, much publicized forty years ago, represented unusual steps in articulation by having all pupils from Grade I to Grade XII in the same building and organization. Despite expressions of admiration from many leaders in educational thought, the Gary plan was not accepted; perhaps the tradition of separate school units for elementary and secondary education was simply too strong to be broken. At any rate, even in small towns where the entire school system is housed in one building, elementary and secondary education are sharply separated, thus creating a problem of articulation.

If we acknowledge that the growth of children is gradual and continuous, then the junior high school must be accepted as one level in a continuous, unified system of education. The organization and activities of the seventh grade should not represent a radical contrast with those of the sixth grade. To make the transition smooth, so that problems of pupil adjustment may be obviated, it will be necessary for the junior high school administrator to study closely the educational regime to which his incoming pupils have been accustomed and shape his own organization so as to effect an adequate junction of the two school units. Teachers of the sixth and seventh grades will need to maintain such contacts as will enable them to join their courses of study without gaps or overlapping. Adequate personnel data must accompany pupils entering the junior high school so that the staff of the latter school has as its working capital the knowledge of the pupils which has been gained by their elementary-school teachers. Too often in the past this last matter has had no more attention than that described in the following report which the writer prepared in simple statement of the facts found from a survey of the junior high school in a New England school system of good repute:

Elementary-school principals send to the junior high school principal a roster of the pupils they are promoting to the junior high school. There is no indication that any have failed the work of the sixth grade, but opposite each name is given a rating of the pupil by use of the symbol A, B, C, D, or E. No detailed record of the pupil's achievement, abilities, or traits is sent. In addition to the roster and rating, a simple card of transfer is sent for each pupil, bearing name, parent, and date of birth.

Such an absence of liaison seems to signify two independent educational principalities. If there can be such inadequate articulation in a single school system, how much more serious it must be in those situations where elementary and secondary schools have separate governing boards!

Articulation between junior and senior high schools is also a problem in the organization of the school system. It is naturally more difficult to solve when the units are in separate buildings under separate administrations. Concluding an intensive study of articulation in four school systems under these latter conditions, Richardson said:[42]

Efforts to improve articulation were concerned, to a large extent, with helping pupils to adjust themselves to the difficulties of their new experiences after they had entered the senior high school. . . . Co-operative action, on the part of the sending- and receiving-school units for the promotion of articulation, was not extensive. The junior high school organization seemed to be chiefly concerned with its own educational program. The senior high school organization busied itself with the orientation of the new pupils after they entered.

By contrast, the practice described by Alltucker[43] a generation ago has much to recommend it today. She reported that the first step in "bridging the gap" in Berkeley was to have the junior high school counselor aid the pupil in selecting his senior high school studies. The reason for poor articulation before the inauguration of this plan had been that the senior high school advisers had attempted, on "registration day," to make up programs for several hundred incoming pupils whom they did not know. The new plan was worked out painstakingly. The junior high school counselor had extensive data on the ability, accomplishments, interests, and attitudes of his pupils, and he studied these for each individual. He conferred with the senior high school counselor to obtain understanding of that school. He helped every pupil and his parents to make a careful study of the bulletin, "What the Senior High School Has to Offer," and to select a program for the tenth grade. When the final choice was made, after individual advisement by the counselor, the pupil was given an "Introduction Card," listing the

[42] James W. Richardson, *Problems of Articulation between the Units of Secondary Education* (New York, Teachers College Contributions to Education, No. 804, 1940), p. 170.

[43] Margaret M. Alltucker, "A Counseling Plan for Bridging the Gap between the Junior and Senior High Schools," *School Review,* Vol. XXXII (January, 1924), pp. 60–66.

recommended program and signed by the counselor, which was his admission card to the senior high school. The introduction cards for a given class were sent to the senior high school several weeks before the close of the term previous to the students' entrance. After each report period in the first semester of the tenth grade the senior high school counselor held a conference with the principal, counselor, and ninth-grade teachers of each junior high school concerning failing pupils. Space precludes the presentation of further details of the Berkeley plan, a plan which was interestingly paralleled by a report from Oakland in 1935.[44]

It becomes apparent from whatever angle the problem of articulation is viewed that it is a guidance problem, that the steps taken to organize curriculum and school so as to achieve articulation are designed to achieve the goals of guidance. It follows that if a school system is to be well articulated, procedures must be decided in the light of guidance methods and objectives. Authority to carry them out must come from the superintendent's office, so that all schools—elementary, secondary, vocational—will act in harmony.

QUESTIONS, PROBLEMS, AND INVESTIGATIONS

1. As a class project, gather evidence on a number of the secondary schools in your area in answer to the following questions:

   a. What is the prevailing type of program of studies in the junior high schools?

   b. Among four-year and senior high schools, what is the relative frequency with which the different types of programs of studies are found?

   c. In the multiple-curriculum type, what are the requirements of the college-preparatory curriculums? What are the requirements of the general curriculums?

   d. What has been done to establish instruction in the senior high school on two levels, as in the St. Paul and Richmond, Indiana, examples?

2. Create a tabular arrangement of the entrance requirements of the higher institutions of your state or of the area which includes the institutions receiving most of your college-going high-school graduates.

3. Study the high-school units completed by some college students, either from one high school or several. Compare with the entrance requirements of the colleges they entered. Had the students taken more foreign language and mathematics than necessary to meet entrance requirements?

4. Investigate the status of work-experience courses in the high schools of your section. Where such courses are going forward, talk with teachers and pupils in them with a view to finding the extent to which guidance values are being realized.

5. In the secondary schools of your section, to what extent is the work of the

---

[44] Marion Brown and Vibella Martin, "Toward Better Articulation," *Progressive Education,* Vol. XII (December, 1935), pp. 533–542.

ninth grade free from the domination of the college-preparatory objective? What is the evidence?

6. Analyze the schedule of one or more junior high schools with a view to determining the extent of departmentalization. How many different subjects and how many different teachers do the pupils of each grade have?

7. Look up references which describe the organization of the University of Chicago and its laboratory schools for elementary and secondary pupils. What do you learn explicitly and implicitly about provision for guidance?

SELECTED REFERENCES

ALBERTY, Harold, *Reorganizing the High School Curriculum,* rev. ed. (New York, Macmillan, 1953).

ALLTUCKER, Margaret M., "A Counseling Plan for Bridging the Gap between the Junior and Senior High Schools," *School Review,* Vol. XXXII (January, 1924), pp. 60–66.

BABSON, Helen, "Progress at Eagle Rock High School," *California Journal of Secondary Education,* Vol. XVI (May, 1941), pp. 299–303.

BRAMMELL, P. Roy, *Articulation of High School and College.* National Survey of Secondary Education, Monograph No. 10 (Washington, D.C., U.S. Office of Education Bulletin, No. 17, 1932).

BROWN, Marion, "The Work-Experience Program in the Oakland Public Schools," *Journal of the National Association of Deans of Women,* Vol. VIII (October, 1944), pp. 4–26.

———, and MARTIN, Vibella, "Toward Better Articulation," *Progressive Education,* Vol. XII (December, 1935), pp. 533–542.

BRUMBAUGH, Harry E., and HUTSON, Percival W., "How High-School Pupils Use the General Curriculum," *School Review,* Vol. XLIII (February, 1935), pp. 119–131.

BRUNER, Herbert B., *The Junior High School at Work* (New York, Teachers College Contributions to Education, No. 177, 1925).

BRYSON, William M., and HUTSON, Percival W., "The General Curriculum," *School Review,* Vol. XLIII (January, 1935), pp. 17–27.

CLINE, E. C., "Differentiating Secondary Education," *School Review,* Vol. XLII (June, 1934), pp. 431–439.

———, "Junior High School Exploratory Units in Practice," *Clearing House,* Vol. VII (November, 1932), pp. 152–156.

———, "Some Problems Relating to Exploratory Courses," *School Review,* Vol. XXXVIII (March, 1930), pp. 206–210.

FRAZIER, Alexander, "The Case Against Work Experience," *Nation's Schools,* Vol. XXXVIII (October, 1946), pp. 20–21.

"From High School to College," *Research Bulletin of the National Education Association,* Vol. XVI (March, 1938), pp. 63–122.

GOLD, Milton J., *Working to Learn* (New York, Teachers College, Columbia University, 1951).

HARRIGER, Guy N., "The College-Preparatory Curriculum as an Instrument of Educational Guidance," *School Review,* Vol. LVI (March, 1948), pp. 163–167.

HUNT, DeWitt, *Work Experience Education Programs in American Secondary Schools* (Washington, D.C., U.S. Office of Education Bulletin, No. 5, 1957).

HUTSON, P. W., and KEIFER, J. C., "Schedules of Junior High School Pupils," *School Review,* Vol. XLVI (November, 1938), pp. 667–678.

JOHNSON, Harry B., "What, No Homeroom!" *Clearing House,* Vol. XIV (May, 1940), pp. 534–535.

KAULFERS, Walter V., "The Curriculum Maker's Responsibility for Guidance," *Curriculum Journal,* Vol. IX (May, 1938), pp. 213–217.

KECK, Malcolm B., "We Get to Know Joe," *NEA Journal,* Vol. XLI (December, 1952), pp. 562–563.

KOOS, Leonard V., *Integrating High School and College* (New York, Harper, 1946).

———, *Junior High School Trends* (New York, Harper, 1955).

LEONARD, J. Paul, *Developing the Secondary School Curriculum,* rev. ed. (New York, Rinehart, 1953).

LOOMIS, A. K., LIDE, Edwin S., and JOHNSON, B. Lamar, *The Program of Studies.* National Survey of Secondary Education, Monograph No. 19 (Washington, D.C., U.S. Office of Education Bulletin, No. 17, 1932).

MARSHALL, James E., and VARNER, Glenn F., "Our 3 Curriculums Provide for Individual Differences," *Clearing House,* Vol. XV (March, 1941), pp. 428–431.

NOAR, Gertrude A., *The Junior High School—Today and Tomorrow* (Englewood Cliffs, N.J., Prentice-Hall, 1953).

NORLIN, Merrill F., "Accenting the 'Junior' in Junior High School," *School Executive,* Vol. LIX (May, 1940), pp. 10–11.

PIERCE, Paul B., *Developing a High-School Curriculum* (New York, American Book, 1942).

RICHARDSON, James W., *Problems of Articulation between the Units of Secondary Education* (New York, Teachers College Contributions to Education, No. 804, 1940).

SPAULDING, Francis T., FREDERICK, O. I., and KOOS, Leonard V., *The Reorganization of Secondary Education.* National Survey of Secondary Education, Monograph No. 5 (Washington, D.C., U.S. Office of Education Bulletin, No. 17, 1932).

THORDARSON, T. W., "Enriching the Small High School Curriculum," *Occupations,* Vol. XIX (October, 1940), pp. 29–32.

TRAXLER, Arthur E., and TOWNSEND, Agatha, eds., *Improving Transition from School to College* (New York, Harper, 1953).

YATES, James A., *The Type of High-School Curriculum Which Gives the Best Preparation for College.* Bulletin of the Bureau of School Service, Vol. 2, No. 1 (Lexington, Ky., University of Kentucky, September, 1929).

CHAPTER 8

Curricular and Extracurricular

Experience

STRANGE, INDEED, WOULD BE the school in which those daily activities of the pupil—the curriculum and the extracurriculum—would have no bearing on guidance. In all truth, there could not be such a school, for any experience must influence the individual in his choices and adjustments. Unfortunately, however, some schools in their heart processes are so little reflective of the larger society that the pupil's experience is too restricted and too remote from actuality to afford a basis for sound choices. Again, looking at the adjustive side, there are schools, as pointed out in Chapter 3, which give experiences that contribute to *mal*adjustment rather than to adjustment.

From our basic assumption that *the goals of guidance in a democratic society are reached through education,* it follows that curricular and extracurricular experiences are main features of the guidance program. If we have failed to utilize them it is because we have thought of guidance as something *done to* or *for* a person through special media which exist apart from the main currents of school life. If we have failed to utilize them it is probably due, also, to such complete absorption in their developmental values that we have been blind to their guidance values. Through analysis and illustration this chapter will show how curriculum and extracurriculum bear on the guidance function, and how, therefore, the classroom teacher is responsible for the guidance of his pupils.

HOW THE CURRICULUM CONTRIBUTES TO DISTRIBUTIVE GUIDANCE

Components of Distributive Guidance on Which Curricular Experience Bears

Useful in clarification of the role of the school subjects in guidance is recall of the pertinent components of distributive guidance from Chapter 5. The subjects should be viewed as helping to realize the following of those components:

1. To acquaint the pupil with the educational and vocational opportunities of the world.
2. To acquaint the pupil with his own powers, interests, and limitations.
3. To acquaint the school with the pupil's powers, interests, and limitations.

Teachers must accept these components as valid objectives in planning their courses. They must realize that the teacher's function is not solely to *develop* certain skills, attitudes, abilities, and so on, in his pupils, but also to *test* and *explore* the human material before him and to give his pupils rich opportunities for testing and exploring the world and themselves. There need be no conflict between developmental and guidance values. The same activities should contribute to both.

Various writers have from time to time shown awareness of some one of the three components listed above, as outcomes of curricular experience, but have usually overlooked the other two. For example, in an article with a title broad enough to comprehend all three components, Kitson[1] a number of years ago gave extensive illumination of the bearing of the school subjects on the first component but did not mention their significance for the other two components. He was concerned with the dissemination of vocational information. The following passage is indicative of Kitson's thinking:[2]

It will be noted that several methods may be employed in introducing vocations. The teacher may select one vocation and make a number of applications of the subject to it. Or he may take one fact or principle of the subject matter and show its relation to several vocations. He may study one vocation intensively over a period of several days or he may touch lightly on a number of vocations in one day. One teacher may wish to begin a course by showing the vocational implications in the subject; another may prefer to close the course in that way. For the most part it is likely that the teacher will prefer to discuss vocations whenever they can be introduced spontaneously and naturally.

The bulk of Kitson's article was given to illustrative lessons which involved rather complete vocational analyses. For example, he proposed to lead classes to the study of the occupation of

locomotive engineer through the study of geography
physician through the study of arithmetic
banker through the study of American history
architect through the study of ancient history
secretary through the study of Latin

His illustrative lessons represented too wide a departure from, and too tenuous a connection with, the subjects, in the opinion of this writer. For

[1] H. D. Kitson, "Vocational Guidance through School Subjects," *Teachers College Record*, Vol. XXVIII (May, 1927), pp. 900–915.
[2] *Ibid.,* p. 901.

example, while a logical place in the development of arithmetical under-standings and skills could be found for problems in the cost of preparing to become a physician or perhaps in connection with the income of physicians, children would be disturbed by dropping arithmetic for the rounded study of the medical profession. The more appropriate place for the latter activity is the course on occupations, which will be the subject of the next chapter.

Perhaps it should be made clear at this point that "to acquaint the pupil with the educational and vocational opportunities of the world" means much more than the acquisition of verbal information. It means having experience with the opportunities. It means a school in which the pupils are "active with types of occupations that reflect the life of the larger society." It means that the pupil in arithmetic will acquire some acquaintanceship with accountancy because his work with arithmetic problems is akin to the major activity of the accountant. Further clarification of this component of guidance will come from many illustrations to follow in this chapter.

The second component of distributive guidance on which curricular ex-perience bears was clearly envisioned by Johnston when he said that[3]

the studies give the pupil a means of trying himself out, they give him something to bite on, they help him to find out what kinds of things his native talents enable him to do. High-school studies are the teething rings of adolescence. They assist in the eruption of native powers and help the child to learn what his particular powers are.

The third component was the subject of an article by Bonser[4] more than forty years ago. He wrote of three methods of discovering individual dif-ferences in vocational aptitude, as follows: first, trying out individuals in various vocations and noting successes and failures, which he characterized as a long and wasteful method; second, making controlled psychological tests, which he knew to be limited in value and reliability; and third, making inferences from school performances. We should expect, said Bonser, the greatest practical revelation of individual differences from this third source. "The largest contribution the school can make to the problem of vocational guidance lies in its providing such a curriculum and such methods of work that it will both reveal and develop individual capacities or aptitudes in terms of vocational activities."

The teacher must be conscious of all three of these components, on the importance of which Kitson, Johnston, and Bonser have been quoted. En-suing divisions of this section will make their application more evident.

[3] J. B. Johnston, "Vocational and Educational Guidance in the High School and Its Relation to Higher Education," *Vocational Guidance Magazine* (now *Occupations*), Vol. VII (October, 1928), p. 16.
[4] F. E. Bonser, "The Curriculum as a Means of Revealing Vocational Aptitudes," *Education,* Vol. XXXVII (November, 1916), pp. 145–159.

The Elementary-School Curriculum

It must be obvious that the outcomes which we are here stressing may be realized throughout the school, from kindergarten to graduate school. The child's career in the elementary school should represent a series of experiences which form a sound foundation for the differentiation of training which characterizes secondary education. Even the conservative school with its emphasis on the acquisition of the organized bodies of information and the conventional skills serves in some measure to reveal the individual to himself and to his teachers. If John shows extraordinary mental acuity in his ability to acquire understandings and skill in arithmeitc, in his comprehension of language structure, and in his memorization of geographical facts, such revelation certainly has some meaning for determining his course through the high school and suggesting the occupational level to which he may properly aspire. And so with each of John's classmates.

These guidance values of the elementary school are multiplied many times as its program is broadened, rendered more flexible, grounded in children's interests, and freed from bookish artificiality. To realize these guidance values in maximum degree calls for the practical recognition of the need of children for a wealth of varied and stimulating experiences. It is not necessary to elaborate this point. The doctrine has been propounded in educational literature with steadily growing intensity and progressive refinement of definition since the time that John Dewey sought "working" furniture rather than "listening" furniture for his laboratory school. The dominant emphasis has been on developmental values, but it is safe to say that guidance values are realized in direct proportion to developmental values. The program which enables the child to observe widely, to construct and create, to employ language and number in situations which are real to him, is a program which helps him to understand himself and the world and to stand revealed to his teachers.

The direct relationship between the elementary-school curriculum and understanding the world of vocations was emphasized some years ago by the publication of a useful little book on the subject.[5] The authors made detailed suggestions on the organization of the curriculum around occupations in public service in the third grade, food production in the fourth grade, clothing production in the fifth grade, and housing in the sixth grade. The outlined program is highly suggestive of some guidance possibilities in the elementary-school curriculum.

Kobliner's recent summary of the literature on vocational guidance in the elementary school does not suggest that anyone has marked out a program comparable to that of McCracken and Lamb. Rather, other writers have

[5] T. C. McCracken and H. E. Lamb, *Occupational Information in the Elementary School* (Boston, Houghton Mifflin, 1923).

devoted their thought to values and techniques in the teaching of occupations.[6]

The General Courses of the Junior High School

Their Origin and Basis. It was pointed out in the last chapter that the tryout courses which were prominent elements in the junior high school curriculum of the early 1920s soon lost ground and that in all probability they were to some extent absorbed in the general courses which developed as broad approaches to the main areas of human activity. We shall now examine these general courses, among the best known of which are those in science, mathematics, language, and social studies, with a view to ascertaining their meaning for guidance.

These courses had their origin in the revolt against subject-centeredness; they represent an important step toward the recognition of children's needs and interests as a chief point of reference in curriculum making. In their beginnings forty years ago they were hailed as an expression of "psychological order" in subject matter in contrast to "logical order." It was being pointed out that the traditional subjects of the curriculum represent an adult classification of knowledge, a classification arrived at *after* extended experience. Since the child has not had that experience, the classification is foreign and therefore artificial to him. We must reckon with the world as he sees it, we must start with the experience that he has had. Thus, we practice the law of apperception, acknowledging that the learner acquires new ideas and abilities in terms of those which he already has.

The subjects being the creation of adults and alien to the child's mind, it follows that subject lines should be ignored in the organization of educational experience. This principle was basic to the project teaching vigorously advocated by Kilpatrick and others forty years ago, as it is to the activities curriculum, or to the "units" of today. The general courses of the junior high school are to a degree an expression of this principle. As introductions to broad fields of human activity, they ignore the fences within those fields, the boundary lines between algebra and arithmetic, between history and economics, between physics and chemistry. One may say that by grouping subjects which are naturally related and giving the child an introduction to the whole group, they constitute a first step in the abandonment of subjects.

The general courses are designed also to bring to the service of the junior high school pupil in the satisfaction of his needs and purposes some of the simpler concepts from subjects that the traditional school denied him until his later adolescence. For example, in the school system of 1910 the extreme subject compartmentalization characteristic of the times denied to the pupil any contact with principles of physics and economics until the

[6] Harold Kobliner, "Literature Dealing with Vocational Guidance in the Elementary School," *Personnel and Guidance Journal,* Vol. XXXIII (January, 1955), pp. 274–276.

eleventh or twelfth grades. Such rigidity seemed absurd and artificial to the advocates of psychological order. Their study of children indicated clearly that the junior high school pupil is aware of situations in which he can use elementary concepts from those subjects.

A corollary to the introduction of the new content which the general courses involved was the diminished emphasis on advanced details in the old subjects of the seventh and eighth grades. The exhaustive treatments of arithmetic and grammar had been such punishment that their infliction could only be justified by Mr. Dooley's educational philosophy that "It doesn't matter what you study as long as it is unpleasant."

While the general courses were thus adopted primarily because they expressed a new conception of the psychology of development, they were eagerly taken up also as contributing to the aim of exploration for guidance. Instead of intensive, repetitious striving for perfection in a few skills, the general courses represent extensive contacts with many fields of human activity. They assume that specialization is to come later and that wide-ranging experiences form an essential basis for the choice of specialization, by creating interests and revealing abilities. Ideally organized, general courses pretty well encompass the full circle of human activity—at the level of junior high school pupils to comprehend—and since common practice is to make all the courses required, all the pupils contact all the fields. As pointed out in the last chapter, tryout courses, in contrast to general courses, are frequently elective, thereby permitting pupils to miss some of the tryouts. However, general courses have not been developed with uniform satisfaction. Nor have they been uniformly accepted. Some of the difficulties and problems will be presented in the descriptions of individual courses which follow.

General Science. Perhaps the most successful and certainly the most widely adopted of the general courses is general science. At the time the course was introduced, the high-school curriculum typically presented isolated unit courses in physical geography, botany, zoology, and physiology in the ninth and tenth grades, with chemistry and physics dominant in the eleventh and twelfth grades. General science started as a tryout course in the sciences, offering samples of each of the sciences in turn. The psychological considerations just set forth soon were asserted and applied to the course. The disjointed organization around subjects was discarded, and the course was organized around aspects of the environment which have reality for the learner of junior high school age. "How we heat our homes," "How we light our homes," and "How we protect ourselves from infectious diseases" are representative topics which suggest how the course has been pointed toward the understanding and control of natural phenomena. Certainly many of the processes and occupations of civilized existence are brought before the pupil in such a course. If the activities of observation, picture-viewing, experimentation, and problem-solving are adequately employed, much can be learned about the pupil's interests and abilities, and he can test himself in significant respects.

General Social Science. The course called community civics, originating about 1910, was the first course in general social science. It organized the pupil's study around the institutions and the major problems of community life, and it sought to arouse his sense of social responsibility. Concepts from sociology, economics, and political science were drawn upon as needed, and historical backgrounds or origins were utilized in minor degree. The theory and content of the course was set forth by a special committee of the Commission on the Reorganization of Secondary Education of the National Education Association.[7] It was incorporated into a general program of social studies proposed for the six secondary-school grades by the committee on social studies of the same Commission.[8] The latter committee advocated the teaching of geography, European history, American history, and civics in close correlation in junior high school years.

In the 1920s Harold Rugg developed a fusion course in the social studies for all three junior high school years. Rugg's theory for the course and his method of deriving the content were set forth in the Twenty-Second Yearbook, Part II, of the National Society for the Study of Education.[9] In 1930–32 his course was made generally available in a series of six textbooks,[10] one for each half-grade of the junior high school. Undoubtedly it is the best example of the content of general social science. Unfortunately, in the 1930s the Rugg series was made the object of unjustifiable attacks by groups and individuals who held that some of the content was "subversive" and "un-American." While in a few communities these charges were met squarely and proven groundless, school boards and school administrators in many communities were intimidated so that they discontinued use of the books or refused to consider ordering them. The net result has been the halting of progress in this area and the preservation of outmoded, traditional subject-matter organization. There are, however, some schools which administer a general social-science course, and in the schools which have organized the core curriculum, the problems of living in social groups are commonly the major content.

General social science serves the function of guidance better than the traditional subjects because it deals with the realities of life as they impinge upon youth of the 12 to 15-year age group. The emphasis on problems of contemporary living brings up such topics as housing, distribution of wealth, labor relations, technological unemployment, and many others which help

---

[7] *The Teaching of Community Civics* (Washington, D.C., U.S. Bureau of Education Bulletin, No. 23, 1915).

[8] *The Social Studies in Secondary Education* (Washington, D.C., U.S. Bureau of Education Bulletin, No. 28, 1916).

[9] *The Social Studies in the Elementary and Secondary School* (Chicago, Distributed by the University of Chicago Press, 1923), Chs. 1, 11, 15.

[10] (Boston, Ginn).

the pupil to view the occupational life and structure of his own day. The study of people and of their problems in living and working together certainly bears strongly on our first component of distributive guidance. Indeed, general social science includes the content of the separate course in occupations, which will be the subject of discussion in the following chapter. Interests and abilities of certain types will be aroused and exercised, also, in the realistic study of society.

General Mathematics. The development of a general course in mathematics was brought about by a combination of influences. One was the analysis of seventh and eighth-grade arithmetic showing that it included much nonfunctional content which could and should be eliminated. Another was the theory behind the junior high school movement that some typically secondary-school content should be brought down into the seventh and eighth grades. Another was the advocacy by some prominent mathematicians of the abolition of the "water-tight compartments" in which it was customary to divide mathematics. They felt that there was decided advantage in teaching mathematics as one subject, using arithmetic, algebra, and geometry to illuminate each other.

Under such impulsion fusion courses became common. In 1930 the National Survey of Secondary Education found that about 60 per cent of junior high schools called their mathematics courses in the seventh and eighth grades "general mathematics" or "mathematics," while the remainder of the schools called them "arithmetic."[11] A group of textbook writers prepared a three-book series to present a well-knit fusion course through all grades of the junior high school. The content for the seventh grade was mostly arithmetic, but with the simplest concepts of algebra and trigonometry introduced, together with intuitive geometry. The arithmetical content was diminished in the eighth grade, while the supra-arithmetical content was correspondingly increased. The ninth-grade course was approximately three fourths algebra.

The three-year fusion course has not attained wide acceptance for all pupils for two principal reasons: (1) some pupils in the ninth grade need algebra to satisfy college-entrance requirements; and (2) some pupils should not be required to take any mathematics beyond the eighth grade. Accordingly, many schools offer their ninth-grade pupils the privilege of taking algebra, general mathematics, or no mathematics at all. The upshot of the reform movement has been to give pupils of the seventh and eighth grades some introduction to all the secondary-school branches of mathematics. Even the textbooks which are called arithmetics offer elements of higher mathematics. Furthermore, the emphasis on social utility has affected the content of junior high school textbooks, helping pupils to see more clearly

[11] Edwin S. Lide, *Instruction in Mathematics,* p. 22. Monograph No. 23, National Survey of Secondary Education (Washington, D.C., U.S. Office of Education Bulletin, No. 17, 1932).

the uses of mathematics. This problem of functionality is so baffling and so pressing as to cause the National Council of Teachers of Mathematics to issue as their Seventeenth Yearbook *A Source Book of Mathematical Applications*.[12]

General mathematics affords pupils experience with the varied branches of the subject. While the fusion is such that the pupil may not be aware when he is sampling algebra or trigonometry, the teacher can direct his attention to it so that he will develop an understanding of the nature of advanced, specialized courses. From the general course he can form a better estimate of his ability in mathematics and of the attraction he feels toward it than is possible from a course confined to arithmetic. Moreover, the enhanced emphasis on the practical life situations calling for ability in mathematics serves to acquaint the pupil with a qualification for, or an aspect of, many occupations.

General Language. One general course which was at first beset with confusion in its aims, content, and organization is general language. In its beginnings the course consisted of sample lessons in several foreign languages, intended to serve the tryout purpose by helping the pupil to know what foreign-language study is like and to give the school a basis for estimating his probable success in that field. The course, however, was so barren of developmental values that it did not seem worth while. Furthermore, its prognostic value was disappointing. Kaulfers found the coefficient of correlation between marks in general language and marks in later specialized courses in foreign language to be .44 and concluded that simple grades in English were more predictive of foreign-language ability.[13] It seems likely, as Cline has pointed out, that the sampling experience was misleading and not representative of foreign-language study.[14] At any rate, lacking both broadening and finding values, general language seemed discredited.

Then experimentation took a different turn. The exploratory purpose was relegated to the background, and the course was made a genuine approach to the study of language as a human institution. Objectives have been stated as follows by members of the faculty of University School, Ohio State University:[15]

The ultimate aim of the general-language course in the University School has been to awaken in the student a consciousness of the importance of language and to help him to obtain a background of linguistic principles common to the study of all languages. The student should develop an ability to attack objectively the linguistic problems latent in the intelligent use of language. He is asked to view

[12] (New York, Teachers College, Columbia University, 1942).

[13] Walter Kaulfers, "The Prognostic Value of General Language," *School and Society,* Vol. XXVIII (November 24, 1928), pp. 662–664.

[14] E. C. Cline, "Some Problems Relating to Exploratory Courses," *School Review,* Vol. XXXVIII (March, 1930), pp. 206–210.

[15] Victor Coutant, Irwin Johnson, and Lou LaBrant, "Some Preliminary Considerations," *Educational Research Bulletin* (Ohio State University), Vol. XX (January 15, 1941), p. 4.

language not merely as something he himself uses but as something which has great importance for groups of human beings—at once a means of communication and an apparent obstacle to it—a vital factor in the history of the race.

"General language," said Cline,[16] "should be not a study *in* language primarily but quite frankly a study *about* language." He proposed the following outline for the course:

1. Origin and development of language
2. Language as a social tool
3. Language as the expression of ideas
4. Language and thinking
5. Structure of language (general principles)
6. Origin and development of written language
7. Semantics
8. Comparative language
9. Historical and social background of language and languages
10. The learning of language

The course described by the above-mentioned members of the Ohio State faculty is similar in content,[17] as is also the course in Detroit, described by Lilly Lindquist.[18] The latter writer made it clear that the course concluded with a few lessons in each of the foreign languages offered in the senior high school. Cline likewise favored this element, and the Ohio State course definitely includes it.

As to administration, said Cline,[19]

the course would profit if it were administered jointly by the English and the foreign-language departments. The general-language course surely has values for both English and foreign languages, and these two fields as surely have contributions to make to the content of the course. Both departments will profit, too, if they are so directly concerned with the general-language course that they will revise and adapt their courses in the light of the contribution of the general course. Therefore, the English and the foreign-language departments should cooperate in making the general-language course.

Surveys of the status of the course, made in the 1930s, showed that it was not widely prevalent. Taylor and Tharp[20] found that modal practice was to offer the course in the eighth grade and as a two-semester, five-days-a-week course. The course was usually placed in the foreign-language department

[16] E. C. Cline, "General Language," *School Review,* Vol. XXXVI (September, 1928), p. 512.

[17] "General Language, a Study by Ninth-Grade Pupils," *Educational Research Bulletin* (Ohio State University), Vol. XX (January 15, 1941), pp. 6–21.

[18] "General Language in the Junior and Senior High Schools," *Modern Language Journal,* Vol. XXI (May, 1937), pp. 577–581.

[19] *Op. cit.,* p. 515.

[20] William M. Taylor and James B. Tharp, "An Analysis and Evaluation of General Language; the Language Arts Survey Course," *Modern Language Journal,* Vol. XXII (November, 1937), pp. 83–91.

and taught by a foreign-language teacher. The Ohio State course cited above is offered in the ninth grade, but foreign language is open only to senior high school grades.

General language has such values that, like general science, general mathematics, and general social science, it should be required of all pupils. Whether or not that is possible without crowding some other equally valuable element out of the program of studies, is a question. The suggestion that the English course in the eighth or ninth grades be reorganized to include general language is offered here as a defensible solution. English is indeed taught to increase pupils' skill in the use of language; general language has been developed for the same purpose; with English as a constant every year in the secondary school there should be no difficulty in organizing it to give the equivalent of at least a semester to the content of general language. Pupils will then be sure to have the exploratory and developmental values of this subject without robbing them of the same opportunities in other equally important fields.

Practical Arts. One of the best developed and most widely accepted of the general courses in the junior high school is the required course in industrial arts. While it does not have the qualifying adjective "general" in its title, it does represent the broad, generalized approach to a comprehensive aspect of environment and to a department of study at the senior high school level which is the major characteristic of the general courses. The usual practice is to require all boys to take the course, which is so organized as to give them contact with from four to six industrial processes, such as woodworking, mechanical drawing, metal work, electricity, auto mechanics, printing. Sometimes—usually in small schools—the several experiences are all presented in a general shop, the boys rotating in groups from one to another. Again—usually in larger schools—the boys rotate among specialized shops. In many schools the course is taught twice a week over the two-year period of the seventh and eighth grades. Others give it more intensively—five times a week in the seventh grade only. An advantage of the latter plan is that the eighth-grade boy has the opportunity to pursue an elective course for a semester or a year in one of the experiences which especially interested him in the general course.

The exploratory values in this course are highly apparent. The pupil literally "tries his hand" at a number of activities in the mechanical and industrial world. But whether his exploration yields positive or negative results, he is a better home member and citizen, a more intelligent consumer, for having had these experiences. He has acquired skill for some of the unspecialized practical activities of life and improved his capacity for intelligent buying and use of the material products of civilization.

For the most adequate accomplishment of its purposes general industrial arts should include a considerable informational element concerning the processes, tools, and materials employed in each industry sampled. Probably a shortcoming of much teaching in this course is the tendency to confine the pupils too exclusively to the working out of individual projects or jobs. The instructor must bear in mind always that the object of the course is not to cultivate marketable skills, but to help pupils explore certain industries and trades, to obtain some experience in the use of common tools, and to develop appreciation of good materials and workmanship.

Use of a general industrial arts course on a bigger scale and in a different situation from that which we have been describing is related by Lipsitz.[21] The freshman year of the four-year technical high schools of Paterson, New Jersey, was organized to rotate the pupils through six shops, spending six weeks in each. Related social-science instruction provides an overview of all industries in and near Paterson, apprenticeship possibilities, employment requirements, and similar data. At the end of the year the pupil, in consultation with his parents and the counselor, selects his shop. Since this exploratory experience was adopted, it has been found that between 50 and 60 per cent of the pupils choose a different shop at the end of the year from the one which they tentatively chose at the beginning of the year.

It would seem logical to start home economics in the junior high school with a general course designed to afford the same overview of the field as has just been described for industrial arts. It would bring to the attention of girls the wide range of occupations which are based on household crafts, together with the fact that these occupations are assuming larger and larger importance because activities within the home are being taken over by outside specialists. After the general course would come specialized courses designed to teach skills for homemaking or occupational life. This pattern, however, seems not to have been accepted widely in the '20s and '30s, and it is difficult to tell what pattern does prevail at this writing.

Fine Arts. Required courses in art and music in the junior high school now qualify as "general" art and "general" music in all but the most conservative schools. The "free-hand drawing" which was the art course of forty years ago became recognized as an absurdly narrow experience and yielded to a general introduction to the field of art, with the major emphasis on understanding and appreciation for the purpose of intelligent consumption rather than on the acquisition of skill in production. As the pupil is now led to see how we are applying artistic principles in the building industry, in the clothing industry, in interior decoration, in the production of automobiles, and in a host of other situations, the numerous occupations in the field of art are brought to his attention. And in the art class he and his fellows obtain tryout experience from the employment of varied art media instead of straining for a standard of skill in one medium.

Music once stood in the junior high school schedule as "chorus" or "singing." The required course of today seeks primarily to help the pupil become

[21] Herbert J. Lipsitz, "The Exploratory Program as a Factor in Student Choice," *Occupations,* Vol. XXIV (November, 1945), pp. 92–94.

an intelligent, discriminating consumer of music. He is introduced to the various forms and diverse media of musical expression. In that breadth of experience there is a far greater chance for the individual to find an interest which he pursues in the ensuing school and out-of-school years than could possibly occur in the old striving for skill in narrow amateur production.

Commerce. Following a short-lived and unsatisfactory experience with short-unit tryout courses in commercial subjects in the junior high school, "junior business training" was introduced and adopted widely. Its purpose at first was to acquaint the pupil with the simplest of business transactions and routine so that if he dropped out of school early he would have a little preparation for juvenile jobs in the business world. Soon it was noted that the content of the course dealt largely with matters in which every consumer needed skill and understanding. Hence it was required of all pupils. Frequently one semester was required of all pupils, and a second semester was required of pupils who elected to enter the commercial curriculum. This second semester's work, sometimes called "general business" has in part been regarded as a general introduction to commerce, valuable for both broadening and finding. It has not demonstrated its certain significance, however, for these purposes. Studies have shown that relatively few students alter their course selections because of the experience of the course, which probably means that it actually does not help the pupil to explore his capacities for commercial studies. As regards the training derived from it, many commercial teachers assert that commercial students get this content later, anyway. The upshot of this experience is that a satisfactory general course in this field has not been found.

The Senior High School Subject Fields

General Bearing. Wood, in illustrating how to interpret a pupil's cumulative record, related the story of Frank Smith.[22] Frank came to college with the settled intention of becoming a writer. This decision was in part due to the influence of an uncle who was a reporter and who had encouraged Frank to take up a similar career. The boy failed in French his first semester and earned a mediocre mark in English, but he found more pleasure in having merely passed his English than in having earned rather high marks in physics and mathematics. With much hard work he passed a make-up examination in French in the middle of the second semester. He made some improvement in his work in the subject because his counselor started him in reading articles in French on science and engineering. Under continued counsel Frank, at the end of his second year, tentatively agreed to consider engineering as a possible profession, and during his third year ceased entirely to think of a career in writing and settled definitely on electrical engineering. Wood showed that the justification for this choice was fully evident in Frank's

[22] Ben D. Wood, "Personal Record Cards for Schools and Colleges," *Educational Record Supplement,* No. 8 (July, 1928), pp. 31–39.

history in the secondary school. Prominent among the items of evidence was Frank's excellent scholastic record in mathematics and physical science, while his achievement in English and foreign language was mediocre. The point is well made that Frank could have been saved the disappointments incident to his wrong choice if he had had earlier counsel on the basis of the existing revelations of his interests and abilities. Perhaps the old adage, Experience is a great teacher, is only a half truth. Experience must be interpreted to make sure that its lessons are learned.

The extent to which Frank was an exceptional case is difficult to estimate. A few years ago 500 liberal arts freshmen in the University of Nebraska were asked to list their high-school courses which were most interesting, least interesting, easiest, and most difficult. Their responses were compared statistically with their vocational plans and found to show considerable logical and psychological relationship. For example, of 50 students who gave medicine as their vocational choice, none listed science as among the subjects least interesting to them, 46 listed science as among the subjects most interesting to them, 6 listed science as among the subjects most difficult for them, and 39 listed science as among the subjects easiest for them. Yet these students seemed to be unconscious of this relationship. When "asked to list all factors they believed exerted any influence on their plans and all factors they considered in shaping their plans," only 17 per cent referred to their interest in high-school studies or the ease or difficulty of the subjects.[23]

Another study with a slightly more mature group who were thinking, probably, of college rather than of high-school subjects, yielded a higher place to the influence of the classroom. Former students who had attended the University of Idaho in the years 1936 to 1940 were queried in 1941 as to the occupation in which they were engaged or for which they were preparing and

asked to describe the circumstances whereby they first became interested in the occupation of their choice. The most frequently cited answers were as follows: by studying various school subjects, 45; through the influence of parents, relatives, and friends, 43; by talking to and observing people in the same occupation, 36; was given an opportunity to do a little work in the occupation, liked it, and decided to make it my life work, 29; as a result of the influence of school teachers or professors, 27.[24]

There were 282 cases, but the author does not say whether the figures just quoted are numbers or percentages.

Some high schools have made special efforts to help pupils see the connection between their subjects and occupational life. For example, it is reported in *Occupations* that the faculty in each department of the Arsenal

[23] Wilbur S. Gregory, "From High School to College," *Occupations,* Vol. XVIII (December, 1939), pp. 190–198.

[24] Oscar J. Kaplan, "Age and Vocational Choice," *Journal of Genetic Psychology,* Vol. 68 (March, 1946), pp. 131–134.

Technical Schools, of Indianapolis, has prepared in mimeographed form for use with their classes a statement of the occupational values and outlets of each of the various subjects. The same article reports with an example similar practice in the Newport News High School.[25] Prepared in more permanent form are the Champaign Guidance Charts,[26] of which one is adapted here as Figure 7. Each chart is similar in that it shows the subject in a center circle from which radiate related occupations shown in their logical groupings.

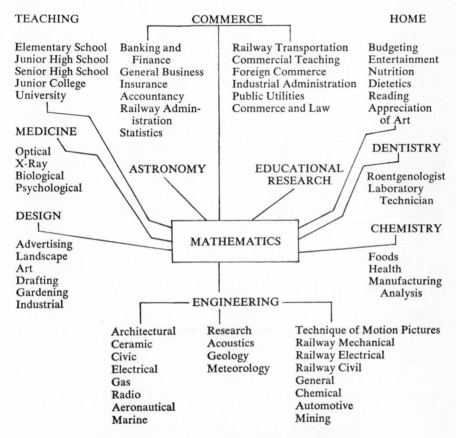

FIG. 7. Occupational relationships of mathematics.

Such activity in a school faculty is pointed out as "a legitimate and worthwhile supervisory activity" by Fahey, who feels that one of the most important contributions the classroom teacher can make to guidance

[25] Hanson H. Anderson, J. Fred Murphy, and S. D. Green, "Occupational Information through School Subjects," *Occupations,* Vol. XIX (March, 1941), pp. 409–413.
[26] (Champaign, Ill., Faculty of Champaign Senior High School, 1939)

is the application of the matter of instruction to the life-environment of the present and the future. . . . the assumption that such values will automatically be evident to the pupil is largely unfounded. Teachers often forget that the pupil's knowledge of the subject field and of the world-environment is much narrower than their own, and, in spite of the fact that ability to apply knowledge is conditioned by understanding of that knowledge, they leave the inferences of transfer to the pupil. A further difficulty is that the pupil ordinarily is not habituated by conventional school practices to look for the possibilities of applying the knowledge. Teachers themselves frequently have failed to think through the values inherent in their subject matter other than for the learning of some-more-of-the-same.[27]

A publication designed to help pupils and teachers use the school subjects for vocational and educational guidance is *School Courses and Related Careers—A Vocational Survey Plan*.[28] A section of 33 pages lists for each of the subjects occupations to which "a knowledge of and ability in [the subject] may lead." Each occupation is given a definition of from 5 to 20 words. A second section consists of a list of approximately 800 occupations, after each of which the related school subjects are indicated by simple code letters. Furthermore, the training required for each occupation is indicated by check marks as "apprentice," "college," or "special." The absence of a check mark means apparently that the occupation is learned on the job.

A similar publication at the level of higher education was described in Chapter 6—*Ohio State and Occupations,* issued by the Ohio State University Press in 1945.

English. The course of study in English has from time to time in a few communities been used as an important medium, if not the chief one, for informing pupils of occupational opportunities. Such use of the subject will be taken up in the next chapter, which is devoted to the systematic dissemination of occupational information. Here we are more concerned with the values to guidance which can be realized within the framework of the more or less customary content and activities of English.

English literature should serve to reveal many occupations to its readers, for literature is a reflection of life, and occupation is an important aspect of life. It is true, however, that to be very useful in picturing occupations to pupils, the literature ought to be modern. The ongoing industrial revolution has so altered occupations that Shakespeare, Milton, Scott, and even Dickens represent an occupational world far removed from present realities. (An example to the contrary is Shakespeare's *Merchant of Venice*. The risks accepted by that merchant surely have their parallel in the hazards which beset the entrepreneur of today!) We will not, however, recommend rejection of the classic works of English literature because they do not portray

[27] George L. Fahey, "What Every Teacher Can Do for Guidance," *School Review,* Vol. L (September, 1942), p. 517.

[28] Otto R. Bacher and George J. Berkowitz (Chicago, Science Research Associates, 1941).

modern occupational life. They have other enduring values and will surely figure in the curriculum if pupils can gain soundly educative experience from them.

For many years, however, progressive English teachers have insisted that much good literature has been written since 1892 (the death of Tennyson) and that a function of the English department is to help pupils to consume with discrimination current as well as past literature. Accordingly, such authors as Sinclair Lewis and John Steinbeck, with their realistic pictures of modern workers, have found a place in the course in English literature.

Analyses of two types of literature have suggested the extent to which they portray occupational life. Vera Morgan has classified under 133 alphabetically arranged occupations recent short stories which significantly reveal them.[29] Eleanor Lewis has listed 250 poems according to the occupations they illuminate.[30] It is not advocated that these studies be regarded as guides to curriculum making. They are presented simply as demonstrations of how the content of literature bears on vocational life.

How shall the teacher use these numerous glimpses of occupations? For the most part, it would seem wise not to make conscious use of them. Just because Richard Harding Davis' *Gallegher* conveys quite an impression of the organization of the staff of a metropolitan newspaper is no justification for requiring the pupils to chart the organization of personnel or for the teacher to build such a chart on the blackboard. Such treatment would probably reduce the pupils' interest in the story. It seems likely that the soundest policy would be to help the pupils use literature as a means of vivid experience. Let them observe workers vicariously; let them vicariously perform the workers' functions as they follow sympathetically the work lives of the characters of literature. Vocational dissection will hinder more than it will help.

Turning to English composition, the dominant guidance values would seem to be the revelation of the pupil to himself and to his teacher. In his ability to make a speech, to write a letter, to understand and practice the principles of grammar, or otherwise to employ language, the pupil may excel, he may evince average aptitude, or he may turn in a poor performance. While the teacher will not cease in his efforts to bring about the fullest development in his pupils, he cannot fail to observe the variation in their aptitudes. Who, then, is in a better position than the English teacher to start the pupils thinking about the implications for vocational choice of their interest and ability in English composition? A good beginning might be made with a class of ninth or tenth-graders by asking how many of them plan to study stenography, and proceeding from that by stimulating discussion concerning the abilities in English composition needed by the stenographer.

[29] *Vocations in Short Stories* (Chicago, American Library Association, 1938).
[30] "Odes to Occupations: Notes of an Anthological Excursion," *Occupations,* Vol. XIII (January, 1935), pp. 334–343.

Other occupations, especially those representing the vocational choices of the members of the class, could be evaluated with reference to the ability required in oral and/or written English. The illustration need not be pursued further to make clear its rich possibilities.

Mathematics. Arithmetic gives a host of glimpses of occupational life. As the pupils work the problems of Mr. Everyman, the consumer, they are constantly making vicarious contacts with producers. Algebra and geometry possess relatively little of this guidance value; while an effort has been made in the writing of textbooks to make them more reflective of practical life than formerly, they remain the most abstract subjects in the curriculum.

All branches of mathematics reveal the pupil to himself and to his teachers in particulars which bear significantly on vocational choice. The pupil's experience, however, awaits the mature interpretation of the teacher to be meaningful. A few years ago, a high-school graduating class in one of the industrial towns near Pittsburgh numbered an even hundred. Six boys in the class gave a professional career in engineering as their vocational choice. Yet none of those boys had stood in the upper third of his class in mathematics, and the general intelligence of the whole class was relatively low. Apparently the boys had not been counseled regarding the meaning of their mediocrity in mathematical power. They needed the same kind of spur to their thinking as was suggested above for pupils in English. The teacher ought to know something about the mathematics that is used by architects, engineers, statisticians, and tool-makers, and he should make that knowledge available to his pupils.

Social Studies. Developmental values of the social studies are of such supreme importance that these subjects are regarded as the core of the curriculum, undifferentiated and required of all. As much as any subject group in the curriculum, and more than most, they are designed to prepare pupils for those tasks of social living which are *common to all*. For the pupil, therefore, to approach them in any exploratory spirit is out of harmony with their scope and purpose. It would seem to be doubtful practice for the faculty to give any encouragement to such motivation. Yet the Champaign Guidance Charts show pupils the vocational bearings of each of the social studies. And another midwestern high school has recently issued to pupils and parents a small printed pamphlet entitled, *What Good Are Social Studies? or, Vocational Opportunities in the Social Studies.*

The sounder course surely is to take up the social studies under other motivation than that of individual acquisitiveness. The guidance values will still be there. The realistic study of economic principles and institutions will give the pupil glimpses of many workers in production, distribution, and exchange. The study of government should give him many vicarious and some real contacts with the army of political, professional, technical, and clerical workers who serve society through governmental agencies. In sociological study a number of types of professional workers come under observation, especially if sociological principles and processes are examined at first hand.

A day comes when the pupil is ready for assistance in interpreting his school experiences for their implications for vocational choice. If he has found special satisfaction in the social studies and if he has shown a high order of ability in their pursuit, the vocational opportunities which yield similar satisfactions and call for similar abilities can be brought to his attention.

Science. The science subjects, if taught from the standpoint of helping the pupil to understand his natural environment and gain control of it, are replete with opportunities for broadening vocational horizons, for self-testing, and for revelations of pupil talents, interests, disabilities, and dislikes to the discerning teacher. Medsker saw these opportunities plainly in biology and wrote his exposition of how biology gives experience with many occupations, especially in the following four areas: medical and health services, agriculture, conservation, and industrial processes.[31] Henius[32] made an objective analysis of the five most widely used textbooks in high-school chemistry to find all references to occupations. He found 87 occupations mentioned, some very specific and some very general. The "nature of the work" was the aspect of the occupations predominantly referred to, with 461 mentions, while "understandings needed" was second in frequency with 81 mentions, and the "health" aspect ranked third with 53 mentions.

The guidance values of chemistry have no doubt been enhanced by the tendency of recent years to "psychologize" the subject, showing it more in application and less in theory. Some textbooks now have entire chapters on such topics as the manufacture of clothing, explosives, paints, glass, and the part played by chemistry in such processes as agriculture and photography. Such departures from the traditional organization give the subject a more substantial connection with life as the pupil sees it and aid the teacher in realizing guidance components.

The pupil's interest in and aptitude for the study of the sciences has obvious meaning for his choice of study in many advanced fields—medicine, dentistry, nursing, engineering, home economics, chemistry, agriculture, etc. Likewise, his success and interest would be an important consideration for his vocational choice at less advanced levels in numerous areas, such as radio, photography, electricity, auto repair and maintenance, forestry, drycleaning.

Other Subjects. Extended exposition is not necessary for making evident the guidance values of all the remaining subject fields. The main subject fields and the types of talent and interest they reveal are as follows:

[31] L. L. Medsker, "Some Vocational Implications of Biological Subjects," *School Science and Mathematics,* Vol. XLI (June, 1941), pp. 521–528.

[32] H. H. Henius, *The Contribution of Chemistry to Vocational Guidance.* Master's Thesis (Pittsburgh, University of Pittsburgh Library, 1936).

Foreign language	linguistic
Industrial arts	mechanical
Home economics	domestic
Music	musical
Art	artistic
Commerce	clerical
Health and physical education	physical

As we shall see in a later chapter, tests have been devised for measuring the strength of most of these types of talent and interest. They are helpful—mainly to the counselor. The pupil does not learn from the tests. The *educative* way in guidance is to give the pupil the opportunity to experience widely and intensely, and by such self-testing ascertain his powers and preferences. If the guidance function is to be performed, the subject offering must be wide. Many senior high schools have not given sufficient attention to the need of their pupils for varied activity in practical and fine arts. If the smaller high schools would pay more heed to the growing liberalization of college entrance requirements, as depicted in the last section of Chapter 7, they would find it possible to strengthen their offerings in these subject fields typically considered as not college-preparatory.

HOW THE CURRICULUM CONTRIBUTES TO ADJUSTIVE GUIDANCE

General Bearing

Chapter 3 offered evidence that various aspects of the educational environment make for adjustment or maladjustment. Perhaps our main problem in employment of the curriculum as an instrument of adjustment stems from our conception of it as intellectual content to be fixed in memory, or as bodies of exercises designed to cultivate skills, primarily academic skills. We need to think of the curriculum in broader terms—think of it as comprising all the activities of a group living, working, playing together, and doing it in a spirit of such quality that each member experiences a sense of personal worth, a feeling of belonging, growth in social skills, and freedom from fear and insecurity. In the administration of such a curriculum the teacher is aware of personality development as the major goal. To attain that goal he is conscious of the necessity of making the school a wholesome place in which to live.

An atypical curriculum for an atypical group, in which the goal of the teacher was the adjustment of warped personalities, has been described by Axline.[33] In a school having six second-grade groups, the second-grade teachers were asked near the end of the first semester to submit the names of pupils in their classes who were seriously maladjusted in reading. They

[33] Virginia Mae Axline, "Nondirective Therapy for Poor Readers," *Journal of Consulting Psychology,* Vol. XI (March–April, 1947), pp. 61–69.

listed fifty pupils. The Gates Primary Reading Test was given to these children and the thirty-seven who received the lowest scores were placed in a special class, not for reading alone but for all of their work. The curriculum of this class for the second semester, planned and directed by a teacher who was expert in play therapy, was designed to give the children ample expression through the media of art materials, play materials, free dramatics, puppet plays, music, creative writing (dictating their own stories), listening to stories, taking trips, etc. Important in the therapy was the cultivation of a type of teacher-pupil relationship in which the pupils felt free to express their true feelings—whether of hate, fear, or anxiety—knowing that the teacher understood them, accepted them exactly as they were, and respected them. Freed from repression, the pupils revealed themselves as so burdened with social and emotional problems that it had not seemed worth while to learn to read. The permissive atmosphere released their tensions so that most of them joined one of the four voluntary reading groups which were formed for listening to stories and reading easy books, two hundred of which were in the room. With no remedial reading instruction, these pupils in 3.5 months made average gains of 4.7 months in the words and sentences scales and 5.8 months in the paragraphs scale of the Gates Reading Tests. Thus, through the medium of a specially designed curriculum, the impediments to development among these children were measurably dissolved. While this was the work of a highly trained specialist, it points out the value of curricular experience which is planned to build wholesome personalities.

Strang has given the following simpler illustrations of curricular experience bearing on adjustive guidance:[34] (1) how a first-grade teacher overcame a child's shyness by providing the experiences he needed; (2) how a sixth-grade teacher gained understanding of her pupils by reading their compositions on such subjects as "Why I came to school today," and "What I should like to be when I grow up;" (3) how a junior high school teacher built self-esteem as he taught social studies.

Some Examples of Progressive Thought and Practice

English. Bardwell reported that when a committee of teachers in Madison, Wisconsin, called on the elementary-school teachers of that city to report the numbers of pupils in their classes who exhibited certain types of language difficulties, they received data which is here presented as Table 36.[35] The committee pointed to the contrast in the number of pupils reported on No. 3 with the number reported on No. 7 and expressed the implication of the contrast for a shift from the traditional emphasis in language teaching.

[34] Ruth Strang, "Guidance While Teaching," *Journal of Education,* Vol. 130 (January, 1947), pp. 10–11.
[35] Richard W. Bardwell, "A New Emphasis in Language-Teaching," *Elementary School Journal,* Vol. XXXIV (October, 1933), p. 99, Table I (adapted).

TABLE 36. Number of Pupils in Elementary Schools of Madison Exhibiting Each of Ten Language Faults

Language Faults	Number Reported
1. Speech too low or too fast	112
2. Repetition or rambling talk	72
3. Grammatical errors or slang	67
4. Inability to listen	104
5. Lack of originality	56
6. Unwillingness to take part in discussion	67
7. Embarrassment in speaking before class (timidity)	243
8. Indifference to discussion	60
9. Eagerness to talk, but few ideas (aggressiveness)	119
10. Too much docility	30

It is not customary to consider problems of language-teaching from the physical and mental-hygiene viewpoint. Our study gives plenty of evidence, however, that such an attack is fundamental. . . . Obviously we are plowing in sand when we attempt to train in choice of words and in good sentence structure children who feel that the effort to talk before a group of their classmates is an ordeal. Those children must be given a feeling of security and an opportunity to grow in a satisfactory way.

Bardwell describes how this investigation and report stimulated a new emphasis in language teaching, for teachers began to use the activities of the language class to bring about personality reconstruction. The committee prepared twenty case studies of children whose language powers were improved by the intelligent treatment of physical or mental abnormalities.

Andree has recently put forward the opinion that "Teachers who are aware of the great contributions that can be made to personal and social relationships of youth through English teaching are the pioneers of today and among the really great teachers of the future."[36] He suggests how the content and activities of the English course may be shaped for the individual student who is under severe stress and strain. He cites a number of recent references which have illustrated the possibilities of the subject, especially literature, for the solving of problems of adjustment and the building of moral values on which individuals could reconstruct their lives. Perhaps these writers have helped their pupils to derive the values which Pearl Buck has said readers should derive from literature.

. . . What literature contributes to life is simply clarification of life. We ought, if we read literature and learn to love it, to know ourselves and others better, and to have some little further idea of why we behave as we do.[37]

[36] Robert G. Andree, "English—Key to Personal Adjustment," *Education,* Vol. 67 (January, 1947), p. 288.

[37] Pearl Buck, "Literature and Life," *Journal of the National Education Association,* Vol. XXVII (September, 1938), p. 174.

Numerous writers have told of the value of the autobiography or the diary, written in the English class, as a revelation of the pupil and his problems. A junior high school teacher has recently put it this way:[38]

... pupils frequently use their compositions as a way of expressing certain fears and inhibitions, and the bringing of such fears into the open is a means of overcoming them. Furthermore, compositions will give the teacher an insight into the home life of the pupil, reveal some quirk of personality, or express some hidden resentment. Such revelations may explain sullenness in one pupil, awkwardness and embarrassment in another, or a feeling of defeatism in still another.

Grover feels that the autobiography covers too wide a range to accomplish most advantageously the revelation of personality. She describes her practice in assigning more definite topics, such as "My Ideal," "An Experience I'll Never Forget," or "Things about My Home Which Annoy (or Please) Me." "Assignments for composition on any chosen mood—moods ranging from annoyance to horror, from affection to worship, from indifference to delight —prove popular with both teacher and pupils." The teacher's technique of motivation was skillful, and the responses of the pupils attested the security they felt in her friendship. The nine pupil cases described by Grover not only show how she came to know them through their compositions but also reveal her as a teacher possessed of rare understanding and of subtle skill in the use of her knowledge.

Home Economics. The emphasis in home-economics teaching has shifted from the skills of cooking and sewing to the attitudes and understandings essential to efficient and harmonious living in the family group. Or, if this is an overstatement, it can at least be said that the home economists have become keenly aware of the social and psychological aspects of home life as well as the economic and material. Their professional journals carry numerous articles bearing such titles as "Family Experience and the Development of Personality," "Personality Development for the High School Boy," and "Personal Guidance in Home Economics."

The home economists feel that problems of adjustive guidance come to them because some topics of subject matter in their field bear upon the problems and because the informal laboratory periods are conducive to the close acquaintanceship of teacher and pupils. Advice to the teacher in meeting these problems was the subject of a series of articles by two university professors of home-economics education—Jean Failing and Jessie Rhulman—which ran from September, 1945, to June, 1946, inclusive, in *Forecast for Home Economics.*

Physical Education. From time to time psychiatrists have pointed out the opportunities of teachers of physical education to make noteworthy contri-

[38] Kathleen B. Grover, "Use of English Compositions to Gain Understanding of Pupils," *School Review,* Vol. LIV (December, 1946), p. 605.

butions to the mental health of their pupils. One psychiatrist, in addressing teachers of physical education, gave this explanation: [39]

Because your work is not strictly academic or didactic it affords limitless opportunities for contacting the pupils at the physiological, psychological, and sociological levels. . . . The development of healthy, integrated, and socialized individuals is the function both of psychiatry and physical education.

Such physical factors as the following may underlie social and emotional maladjustment: personal appearance, weight, strength, glandular functions, and general physical fitness. The individual's dissatisfaction with any of these elements may cause feelings of inferiority, which are expressed in his withdrawal from his associates or indulgence in behavior designed to overcompensate for the handicap.

The psychiatrist prescribes physical education—as in the case of many veterans whose experiences brought them to a state of mental unbalance—not only for the purpose of improving the patient's general health but also because it deflects the patient's attention from himself. It is often a bridge which helps him cross over from his own subjective attitude to a more objective technique of living by supplying new interests and incentives. Evidences of an undesirable subjectivity are frequently to be found in the individuals who evade or seek to evade physical education. Some are ashamed of their bodily appearance. Others, because of insufficient exercise in the past, consider that they are not strong enough to do the work and are ashamed to have others know how weak they are. Still others are obsessed by fears—fear of fatigue, pain, or injury. Dislike for competition and fear of appearing at a disadvantage are also reasons for avoiding physical education. For all such individuals the socializing experiences of group physical play have much to offer. To induce them to participate freely, however, it may first be necessary to help them understand that their escape reactions do not constitute a satisfactory method of adjustment.

Concerning another type of individual a psychiatrist says, [40]

The over-mobilized, tense individual can often be helped by physical training. Over-mobilization and tenseness are usually expressions of emotional repressions or fear of failure. Physical educators can often teach these people how to relax physically, and similarly they need to be taught how to relax psychically and spiritually.

One of the interesting examples of the consciousness of the teachers of physical education that they have a role to fill in adjustive guidance is the account of a project carried out by a group of teachers in certain high schools

[39] Elizabeth I. Adamson, "Possibilities of Personality Development through Physical Education," *Journal of Health and Physical Education,* Vol. V (December, 1934), p. 10.

[40] William B. Terhune, "The Relationship of Physical Education and Personal Adjustment," *Journal of Health and Physical Education,* Vol. III (September, 1932), p. 61.

of Chicago and its suburbs.[41] This group assembled reports on one hundred mental-health problem cases of which they had become aware in their classes.

. . . the project suggests some obvious reasons why we, as individual teachers of health and physical education, should develop to a greater degree this guidance point of view, including, as it does, knowledge and application of the principles of mental hygiene. First, there is concrete evidence that understanding of and guidance concerning the emotional problems of such students as the chronic trouble-maker . . . not only facilitate the teaching process generally, but are essential to accomplishment of desired ends with the group. Again, there is proof of the therapeutic value of physical education activities, as demonstrated when certain activities were intentionally employed as part of the adjustment procedure in various cases. . . . In the third place, in the number and variety of problems presented appears the implication that the health and physical education program affords more opportunities for the detection of emotional and social unadjustment than does the average classroom situation. From the humanitarian standpoint, then, it should follow that with increased opportunity comes an increased sense of responsibility.

A program of physical education which is a practical example of the observance of mental-health principles was described a number of years ago as being carried on in Skokie School, a junior high school consisting of the seventh and eighth grades in Winnetka, Illinois.[42] The authors stated the aims of their program as being two-fold—first, bodily development, and second, the fostering of desirable social attitudes. In connection with the second aim they so eliminated "razzing" and other unsocial and immature attitudes from the playground that the children's own words used in a letter to incoming seventh-grade pupils were as follows:[43]

Be a good sport—play the game for the sake of the game and win if you can. If you can't win—lose like a sport. Don't crab—the other fellow is just as square as you are. Every Skokie fellow wants to do the right thing, just as you do. . . . It doesn't matter whether you have ever played before—you will never learn any younger. It doesn't matter how clumsy you think you are—there is always someone who is clumsier. If you muff the ball no one will laugh at you, because Skokie players are good sports, and everyone is ready to help everyone else. LEARN!

With such a spirit the playground was made enjoyable for children of all capacities; practically no one attempted to escape participation.

The authors gave their analysis of the following ten attitudes or qualities which they kept before the children by discussion and by example: loyalty, honesty, courtesy, modesty, reliability, cheerfulness, initiative, sociability,

---

[41] "A Project Study of Mental Hygiene," *Journal of Health and Physical Education,* Vol. XIII (February, 1942), pp. 76–77, 117.

[42] Harry P. Clarke and Willard W. Beatty, "Physical Training in the Junior High School," *School Review,* Vol. XXXIII (September, 1925), pp. 532–540.

[43] *Ibid.,* p. 534.

tenacity, pugnacity. The analysis was in terms of behavior expressed in action on the playground, as indicated in the following extract:[44]

Modesty
   a) Modest in acceptance of important position
   b) Modest in acceptance of victory
   c) Modest in acceptance of commendation
   d) Modest in acceptance of public adulation
   e) Modest in demeanor while traveling
Cheerfulness
   a) Cheerful in acceptance of group choice
   b) Cheerful in acceptance of orders
   c) Cheerful in acceptance of advice or criticism
   d) Cheerful in acceptance of minor position
   e) Cheerful in acceptance of defeat
Pugnacity
   a) Is the quality plus or minus?
   b) Is the quality constant or fluctuating?
   c) Is the quality expressed through bullying?
   d) Is the quality expressed through "picking fights"?
   e) Is the quality expressed through determined, efficient effort?

This example of practice illustrates the point made at the beginning of this section, namely, that adequate employment of the curriculum to achieve the fullest adjustment of pupil personalities demands a broad conception of what constitutes the curriculum. These Winnetka men were concerned with the quality of the relationships existing between the children, between players, leaders, coaches, and teachers. They were deeply aware of the opportunities afforded by physical education for personality development, and they planned thoughtfully for the utilization of those opportunities. Let us hope for the day when all teachers acquire a similar sensitivity and plan curricular experience in the light of such values.

HOW THE EXTRACURRICULUM BEARS ON GUIDANCE

Guidance Values

The extracurriculum bears on guidance in the same respects as does the curriculum. It gives pupils the opportunity to try out activities which are akin to the educational and vocational opportunities ahead. It reveals to teachers the interests and abilities of pupils, thus affording evidence on which to base counseling for distribution. Rich, also, are the opportunities afforded by the extracurriculum for attaining social and emotional adjustment. But the values stated in educational literature have been primarily developmental values. In the first burst of interest in the extracurriculum as an educational

[44] *Ibid.*, pp. 535–536.

medium, Koos summarized the values stated in forty writings.[45] He found twenty-five categories of values, stated in from three to thirty-seven of the writings. The categories which might be considered as bearing on the guidance function or related to it were as follows:

Recognition of interests and ambitions—10 mentions
Exploration—5 mentions
Recognition of adolescent nature—24 mentions

Perhaps this slight recognition of relationship was due to the fact that the concept of guidance was not clearly established; perhaps it was due to the conception of guidance as a kind of adjunct feature of the school. In view, however, of the slender body of writing since 1925 which has expressed the significance of the extracurriculum for guidance, we may hazard the opinion that guidance is still largely thought of as a function performed by special agencies.

In 1934 Snyder took inventory of the values of membership in the Harbor High School (Ashtabula, Ohio) band by addressing an inquiry to the 117 graduates of the years 1922 to 1933, inclusive, who had been members of the band.[46] Among the 80 per cent who replied he found recreational values accruing to the majority and vocational values accruing to a considerable number. During the depression year of 1933, 49 per cent played for pay; 16 per cent were or expected to become professional musicians.

One could, no doubt, find great numbers of journalists whose first satisfaction in their life work came in connection with experience on high-school publication staffs. Many a lawyer obtained his first taste of the arts of persuasion from participation in high-school debate. Athletic coaches and teachers of physical education probably established their life interest almost universally in connection with high-school sports. However, we can only speculate on these matters, as objective data on any considerable scale are not at hand.

A subjective analysis of the values to be derived in connection with school publications has recently been made by Merrick and Seyfert[47] of the Laboratory School of the University of Chicago. They are concerned with educational values in the broadest sense and do not recognize a distinction between guidance and developmental values, but the utility of the experience as a means of self-finding appears at numerous points in their exposition. For example,

[45] L. V. Koos, "Analysis of the General Literature on Extra-Curricular Activities," Chapter 2 of *Extra-Curricular Activities*, Twenty-fifth Yearbook of the National Society for the Study of Education, Part II (Bloomington, Ill., Public School Publishing Co., 1926), p. 11, Figure 1.

[46] Troy A. Snyder, "Recreational and Vocational Values of the School Band," *School Review*, Vol. XLII (November, 1934), pp. 694–700.

[47] Nellie L. Merrick and Warren C. Seyfert, "School Publications as a Source of Desirable Group Experiences," *School Review*, Vol. LV (January, 1947), pp. 21–28.

. . . Even children who ordinarily would consider themselves fairly capable along one line are surprised what they can do when they try another. . . .

A youngster expands his horizons and interests not only by trying different enterprises but also by working closely with others who are carrying on different undertakings.

Sometimes new and unthought-of vocational interests appear through publication work.

A marked contribution to distributive guidance can be made by a vital program of club activities. In surveying the junior high school at Wellesley, Massachusetts, in 1935 the writer found such a program.[48] Approximately twenty-five clubs were proceeding actively in this school of 575 pupils. The following is a list of some of the clubs: art, arts and crafts, bird and animal, booklovers', craft, crocheting, dancing, debating, dramatic (beginning and advanced), electrical, embroidery, model airplane and boat, musical, photography, radio, stamp, travel. That such a list of organizations would notably enhance the exploratory opportunities presented by the curriculum of the school cannot be gainsaid.

As to the adjustive phase of guidance, extracurricular life should make notable contributions, particularly to emotional and social adjustment. To a degree the authors whose writings were analyzed by Koos[49] must have had in mind something akin to this when they made claims for the extracurriculum which he classified as "Socialization," "Training for social co-operation," and "Actual experience in group life." There can be no doubt that the educational goals under discussion here are difficult to classify as developmental or guidance in its adjustive phase. And there is little to be gained by splitting hairs. Chapter III, in the section on social recreation, pointed out the vitally important form of growth—heterosexuality—to which that side of extracurricular life is intimately related, pointed out also that obstacles to the full and adequate use of social recreation often arise, and cited the mental hygienists as testifying that when that growth does not occur in adolescence, a maladjusted personality is a common resultant. Plainly enough, social and emotional adjustment is no automatic outcome of the extracurriculum. It must be worked and planned for. Sponsors, administrators, and counselors must be conscious of these values and give such direction to extracurricular life that its potentialities will be realized.

Use and Misuse of the Extracurriculum

A basic reason for the too common failure to realize the values, guidance and developmental, in the extracurriculum is the absence of an appreciation of those values by school faculties. As a consequence, the activities are controlled by *mis*educational forces. Athletics constitute the outstanding ex-

[48] *Wellesley School Survey*, C. E. Prall, Director (Wellesley, Mass., Survey Committee, 1935), p. 76.
[49] *Op. cit.*, p. 11.

ample. The tradition of the organization of athletic activity around inter-scholastic teams and contests is so entrenched in American high schools that educational leaders seem incapable of conceiving of any alternative, or too hypnotized by the on-going show to undertake the education of pupils, pub-lic, and board of education to a different ideal. For the existing system can hardly be called educational; it is essentially exploitative. It selects the few who are already most advanced in their physical development, trains them excessively in minutely specialized physical feats, and then exploits their skill for the financial success of a commercial venture. The great mass of the student body play the role of spectators for the weekly or semi-weekly con-tests. And if a boy "makes" the team one season, he is expected to return to the sport every season as long as he is eligible, no matter how much he may desire to devote his time to the acquisition of other skills, to the exploration of other fields.

The contrasting, or educational, point of view is essentially as follows: These young people—each and all of them—are entrusted to the school for the fullest development of their powers, physical, mental, social, and moral. There must be activities suitable to this manifold purpose—for all of the pupils. The school is an *educational* institution; exploitation of any of its charges for gain or glory is out of keeping with the educational ideal. Ex-ploration is essential for the finding of each pupil's talents. Curriculum and extracurriculum must be broad enough and administered with sufficient flexi-bility to allow for this. Therefore the pupil should try himself out in various activities rather than being compelled to stay in one narrow groove.

The practical working out of this viewpoint, with special reference to athletics, would call for the establishment of an after-school play period which would be made so attractive that all pupils—girls and boys—would participate in the games at least two or three times a week. (The physical-education period in the school is grossly inadequate for the physical needs of the adolescent.) Clarke and Beatty described such a program at Winnetka.[50] Other junior high schools have more recently described their programs pointed toward the same ideal.[51] Careful planning is necessary to achieve universal participation, but to the sponsor possessed of the educational ideal and convinced of the worth of physical play as an avenue to bodily develop-ment and social adjustment, the undersized and the awkward, the timid and the fearful, constitute his major challenge.

And there would be no hard words or even a frown if Bill said at the end

[50] *Op. cit.*

[51] Ray Welsh, "A Team for Everyone and Everyone on a Team," *School Activities,* Vol. XV (January, 1944), pp. 153–155.

M. J. Henly, "Every Boy Plays the Game at Our Junior High," *School Activities,* Vol. XVII (February, 1946), p. 234.

Dean F. Berkeley and W. M. Diehl, "Junior High School Athletics—A Program for All," *Bulletin of the National Association of Secondary-School Principals,* Vol. XLII (May, 1958), pp. 116–118.

of the season: "Well, fellows, don't look for me next fall. I won't be out regularly. I've learned a lot from football and I'm certainly not sorry for this season's experience at left half. But I plan to try out for the school paper and see if I'm any good at that."

The ogres of specialization and exhibitionism plague us in fields other than athletics. The typical school, whether large or small, has just one school paper. Often it is entered in state or national competition, held under the auspices of some university. When such a circumstance prevails, the opportunity for exploration is curtailed. No "greenhorns" can be permitted to jeopardize the chances of the staff to win glory for alma mater. Another activity similarly managed is that of debate. There are tryouts, but too commonly they are skimpy experiences entered into by only a few of the more assertive spirits. Faculty energy is devoted almost exclusively to the squad of six or eight who are trained with an eye toward county, district, and state championships.

These unwholesome aspects of extracurriculum administration are fostered by the necessity that these activities find their own financial support. Typically, boards of education have not been convinced of their educational value to the extent that they are willing to use public funds to support them. Hence, the public spectacles and the commercialization to raise money for more public spectacles, etc. McKown's remarks on the situation are as follows:[52]

It will be a great day for education in general and for extracurricular activities in particular when communities and schools realize that admission fees to athletic contests (and all other public "shows"—dramatic, music, forensic, etc.) are entirely illogical because of the resultant emphasis placed upon delighting the spectators rather than upon educating the participants. If a football or a basketball game is educational in general purpose and possibilities, then there is no more logic in charging a parent or adult an admission fee to it than there is in charging an admission fee to visit a class in English, algebra, or Latin. All such fees are probably illegal anyway. Once the board pays the entire bill, as it most certainly should, and abolishes all admission fees, the game will be back where it started, as a friendly, noncommercialized, properly emphasized recreational sport. Until that is done, interscholastic competition will continue to be merely a spectacle with relatively little educational value.

When a school takes a step similar to that which McKown advocates, it is news. *School Life*[53] announced that in Rochester, Minnesota, the Board of Education had voted unanimously to make all extracurricular activities a part of the regular educational program and to pay for them out of tax funds. All admissions fees are abolished for students, but the Board continues to charge them to people who are not enrolled in the school. Obviously, this falls short of McKown's recommendation, and the following remark from the

[52] H. C. McKown, *Character Education* (New York, McGraw-Hill, 1935), p. 230.
[53] Vol. XXXIX (May, 1947), p. 23.

principal of the high school may indicate that the Board has just taken over responsibility for regaling the public with its accustomed shows: "It is interesting to note that more money is being taken in at the gate now, even though all students are admitted free. Our crowds have doubled in size."

A major purpose in the extensive promotion of school clubs in the '20s was the provision of such ample opportunities in extracurricular life that all pupils would enjoy its advantages. In some schools the methods of achieving the universal participation of pupils—and teachers—were so crude and authoritarian that the plan backfired, and soon there was a "club period" with only a fraction of the pupils in clubs. The rest were herded into study halls presided over by teachers who wanted no traffic in clubs. Such a state of affairs signalizes primarily the failure of the principal to lead the faculty in a thoughtful preliminary study of pupil needs and of the nature and value of the extracurricular medium. The extracurricular spirit is a skittish thing and must be brought gently to harness. Schools which have been relatively successful in the approach to universal participation may still have a number of pupils who profess to prefer a study hall to a club. In the opinion of this writer, it is a mistake to assign those pupils to some teacher who also does not want a club. Analysis of the personalities of those pupils is likely to show that they need the club experience more than any other pupils of the school. To commit them to an anti-social teacher for the unsocial activity of individual study is about the worst thing that can be done with them. They should be given to a teacher who has superior ability in winning the confidence of pupils and great skill in counseling them. While that teacher may be much needed to sponsor a club, these pupils constitute a bigger challenge. His problem is not to accept the pupils at their own evaluation and supervise them as a study group, but to induce them to accept membership in clubs and leave the study hall. By such a procedure the extracurriculum gets its chance to accomplish adjustive guidance.

In closing this discussion of curriculum and extracurriculum as features of the guidance program, we trust that our readers are now completely convinced that guidance is an "inseparable aspect of the educational process." It has been the object of this chapter to make it clear that the pupil's choices and his adjustments are fundamentally outcomes of his experience, and that the control of that experience so that it best serves the function of guidance is entirely in harmony with its service to the function of development. The more lifelike the experience which the teacher helps the pupil to obtain, the more fully guidance as well as developmental values are realized.

QUESTIONS, PROBLEMS, AND INVESTIGATIONS

1. Analyze a modern textbook in arithmetic or general mathematics for junior high school years, to ascertain the number of occupations of which it affords glimpses. Employ this exercise in any other subject field.

2. Interview twenty or thirty high-school juniors and seniors to find out how their school subjects and extracurricular activities have influenced them positively and negatively in their vocational choices. Carry out a similar project with college students, asking them to recall both high-school and college experience.

3. Consider any liberal-arts subject. List the major activities which pupils employ in the study of the subject. List occupations which call for the exercise of the same activities, finding occupations at two or more levels of skill, if possible.

4. For each of the "general" subjects of the junior high school, prepare a blank for report by junior high school teachers on the results of a pupil's experience with the subject. Imagine the completed blank being filed in the pupil's cumulative record folder for the use of his counselor in helping him with choices of vocation and senior high school curriculum.

5. Make a survey of the language difficulties of ninth-grade pupils similar to that cited in Table 36 from Bardwell's article. Interpret your findings.

6. Look up the article by Kathleen Grover and study carefully the technique she employed. Try her procedure, if you are an English teacher.

7. Examine some up-to-date home-economics textbooks for their bearing on adjustive guidance.

8. Gather some firsthand evidence on the significance of extracurricular activities for accomplishing social and emotional adjustment; interview high-school seniors and induce them to inventory the benefits they have derived from extracurricular life.

9. Find five pupils who do not participate in athletics at all and who are classified as "fringers" by their teachers of physical education. Endeavor to find out just how these pupils feel about physical play.

10. How do the principles of mental hygiene dictate the use of curriculum and extracurriculum for the accomplishment of adjustment?

SELECTED REFERENCES

ADAMSON, Elizabeth I., "Possibilities of Personality Development through Physical Education," *Journal of Health and Physical Education,* Vol. V (December, 1934), pp. 8–10.

ANDERSON, Hanson H., MURPHY, J. Fred, and GREEN, S. D., "Occupational Information through School Subjects," *Occupations,* Vol. XIX (March, 1941), pp. 409–413.

AXLINE, Virginia Mae, "Nondirective Therapy for Poor Readers," *Journal of Consulting Psychology,* Vol. XI (March–April, 1947), pp. 61–69.

BACHER, Otto R., and BERKOWITZ, George J., *School Courses and Related Careers—A Vocational Survey Plan* (Chicago, Science Research Associates, 1941).

BAKER, G. Derwood, "Hobby Clubs in the South Pasadena Junior High School," *Clearing House,* Vol. X (February, 1936), pp. 334–337.

BARDWELL, Richard W., "A New Emphasis in Language-Teaching," *Elementary School Journal,* Vol. XXXIV (October, 1933), pp. 95–105.

BERKELEY, Dean F., and DIEHL, W. M., "Junior High School Athletics—A

Program for All," *Bulletin of the National Association of Secondary-School Principals,* Vol. XLII (May, 1958), pp. 116–118.

BONSER, F. E., "The Curriculum as a Means of Revealing Vocational Aptitudes," *Education,* Vol. XXXVII (November, 1916), pp. 145–159.

CLARKE, Harry P., and BEATTY, Willard W., "Physical Training in the Junior High School," *School Review,* Vol. XXXIII (September, 1925), pp. 532–540.

CLINE, E. C., "General Language," *School Review,* Vol. XXXVI (September, 1928), pp. 510–515.

————, "Some Problems Relating to Exploratory Courses," *School Review,* Vol. XXXVIII (March, 1930), pp. 206–210.

COUTANT, Victor, JOHNSON, Irwin, and LABRANT, Lou, "General Language, a Study by Ninth-Grade Pupils," *Educational Research Bulletin,* Vol. XX (January 15, 1941), pp. 6–21.

FAHEY, George L., "What Every Teacher Can Do for Guidance," *School Review,* Vol. L (September, 1942), pp. 516–522.

GROVER, Kathleen B., "Use of English Compositions to Gain Understanding of Pupils," *School Review,* Vol. LIV (December, 1946), pp. 605–610.

Guidance in the Curriculum. 1955 Yearbook of the Association for Supervision and Curriculum Development (Washington, D.C., National Education Association, 1955).

HUMPHREVILLE, Frances T., "Learning about Pupils through Their Written Comments on Selected Stories," *School Review,* Vol. LX (December, 1952), pp. 541–544.

KAULFERS, Walter, "The Prognostic Value of General Language," *School and Society,* Vol. XXVIII (November 24, 1928), pp. 662–664.

KITSON, Harry D., "Vocational Guidance through School Subjects," *Teachers College Record,* Vol. XXVIII (May, 1927), pp. 900–915.

KOBLINER, Harold, "Literature Dealing with Vocational Guidance in the Elementary School," *Personnel and Guidance Journal,* Vol. XXXIII (January, 1955), pp. 274–276.

LEWIS, Eleanor, "Odes to Occupations: Notes of an Anthological Excursion," *Occupations,* Vol. XIII (January, 1935), pp. 334–343.

LINDQUIST, Lilly, "General Language in the Junior and Senior High Schools," *Modern Language Journal,* Vol. XXI (May, 1937), pp. 577–581.

MCCRACKEN, T. C., and LAMB, H. E., *Occupational Information in the Elementary School* (Boston, Houghton Mifflin, 1923).

MCKOWN, H. C., *Extra-curricular Activities,* 3rd ed. (New York, Macmillan, 1952).

MEDSKER, L. L., "Some Vocational Implications of Biological Subjects," *School Science and Mathematics,* Vol. XLI (June, 1941), pp. 521–528.

Mental Health in the Classroom. Thirteenth Yearbook of the Department of Supervisors and Directors of Instruction (Washington, D.C., National Education Association, 1940).

MERRICK, Nellie L., and SEYFERT, Warren C., "School Publications as a Source of Desirable Group Experiences," *School Review,* Vol. LV (January, 1947), pp. 21–28.

MORGAN, Vera, *Vocations in Short Stories* (Chicago, American Library Association, 1938).

Ohio State and Occupations (Columbus, O., Ohio State University Press, 1945).

PIERCE, Paul R., *Developing a High-School Curriculum* (New York, American Book, 1942).

"A Project Study of Mental Hygiene," *Journal of Health and Physical Education,* Vol. XIII (February, 1942), pp. 76–77, 117.

SNYDER, Troy A., "Recreational and Vocational Values of the School Band," *School Review,* Vol. XLII (November, 1934), pp. 694–700.

A Source Book of Mathematical Applications. Seventeenth Yearbook of the National Council of Teachers of Mathematics (New York, Teachers College, Columbia University, 1942).

Stanford University Education Faculty, *The Challenge of Education* (New York, McGraw-Hill, 1937), Chs. 6–19.

TERHUNE, William B., "The Relationship of Physical Education and Personal Adjustment," *Journal of Health and Physical Education,* Vol. III (September, 1932), pp. 20–22, 61–63.

TRUMP, J. Lloyd, *High-School Extracurriculum Activities* (Chicago, University of Chicago Press, 1944).

CHAPTER 9

The Study of Occupations

THE LAST CHAPTER was an exposition of what pupils might learn about the world and about themselves through curricular and extracurricular experiences which are not specialized with reference to guidance. This chapter will be devoted to a feature of the guidance program which is more specifically created to bear on the guidance function, namely, the study of occupations. It will comprehend not only what is done in having pupils study occupations, but also what is involved in the study of occupations by the teacher and the counselor who must instruct groups and counsel individuals. The chapter will bear especially on the following two components of distributive guidance, as stated in Chapter 5:

1. To acquaint the pupil with the educational and vocational opportunities of the world.
2. To keep the school fully and continuously acquainted with educational and vocational opportunities.

HISTORY AND PRESENT STATUS OF THE COURSE IN OCCUPATIONS

Beginnings

The study of occupations is implicit in Frank Parsons' analysis of vocational choice to include as one of three factors "a knowledge of the requirements and conditions of success . . . in different lines of work." In keeping with this concept was the program of publication of pamphlets describing occupations which the Vocation Bureau of Boston began in 1911 and continued for a decade. The development of a school course in the study of occupations, however, is attributed by Brewer[1] primarily to William A. Wheatley, who, as a superintendent of schools in Connecticut, introduced

[1] John M. Brewer, *History of Vocational Guidance* (New York, Harper, 1942), pp. 124–125.

the course in the Westport High School in September, 1908. Wheatley, in collaboration with Professor E. B. Gowin, of Wesleyan University, brought out the first textbook, *Occupations,* published by Ginn and Company in 1916. It was written expressly for boys, assuming that a companion book would be written for girls.

The course in vocations was given national standing by its acceptance as an element in the program of studies recommended for secondary schools by the Committee on Social Studies of the Commission on the Reorganization of Secondary Education of the National Education Association.[2] The Committee called the course "vocational civics" and recommended it for the ninth grade. They expressed the belief that pupils of that age are ready to consider their choice of vocation and that such a course would minister to that need. They felt that it might induce pupils and parents to see the economic value of high-school education and thus influence length of stay in school. More important than its meaning for vocational guidance, however, in the minds of this committee, was its possible contribution to civic attitudes and understandings. This is a point which will be elaborated in the third section of this chapter.

Superintendent Wheatley, then at Middletown, Connecticut, was a member of the Committee. Their report cited his description of the course in "Vocational Enlightenment," which was then being taught as a half-year course in the ninth grade of the Middletown High School. The course consisted of three parts, as follows:[3]

1. Consideration of the importance of vocational information from the viewpoint of the individual and society, the characteristics of a good vocation, and how to study vocations.

2. Detailed treatment of 80 or 90 professions, trades, and occupations, grouped under agriculture, commerce. . . .

3. Practical discussion of choosing a life work, preparation for that work, securing a position, and efficient service and its reward.

In studying each of the vocations scheduled, we touch upon its healthfulness, remuneration, value to society, and social standing, as well as upon the natural qualifications, general education, and special preparation necessary for success. We investigate at first hand as many as possible of the vocations found in our city and vicinity. Each pupil is encouraged to bring from home first-hand and, as far as practicable, "inside" facts concerning his father's occupation. Local professional men, mechanics, engineers, business men, manufacturers, mechanics, and agriculturists are invited to present informally and quite personally the salient features of their various vocations.

While indicating that Wheatley's course fell somewhat short of meeting their ideals, the Committee expressed the belief that experimentation should be

[2] *The Social Studies in Secondary Education* (Washington, D.C., U.S. Bureau of Education Bulletin, No. 28, 1916), pp. 26–29.
[3] *Ibid.*, p. 28.

encouraged. Their action stamped the course as a social study and gave it grade placement.

Progress and Present Status

The recommendation of the Committee on Social Studies must have had some influence. The output of textbooks for the course on occupations was considerable during the '20s and the '30s, suggesting that a market must have developed. On the other hand, vocational civics must be reckoned the youngest member of the social studies family and the one with least prestige. It is not supported by any college department, such as history, political science, economics, or sociology. In fact, the question may well be asked, How does one prepare himself for teaching this subject? Any subject with a pedigree so obscure must have some difficulty in becoming established.

While adequate evidence concerning the prevalence of a course in the study of occupations is not available, a survey published in 1936 has some value in showing the status of the subject at that time. By inquiry addressed to a large number of school systems in all parts of the country a committee of the Department of Superintendence sought to ascertain the status of the several subjects which are classified as social studies. They found that among 234 junior high schools, community civics and vocational civics were usually taken in Grades VII, VIII, and IX in the numbers of schools indicated in the following data:[4]

	GRADES		
	VII	VIII	IX
Community civics	7	36	63
Vocational civics	6	13	25

The numbers given in Grade IX are smaller than might have been expected, said the authors, because many of the schools included in the tabulation were two-year (Grades VII and VIII) junior high schools. Nevertheless, the contrasting figures for the two courses—both recommended in 1916 by the Committee on Social Studies above cited—shows that at the end of twenty years community civics was much more widely established than vocational civics. Comparable data from the same report showed the following figures for Grade IX in 274 four-year high schools: ancient history, 67; community civics, 83; vocational civics, 35.[5] The positive factor of influential committee recommendation and the negative factor of lack of prestige—mentioned in the preceding paragraph—are thus seen as operating to give vocational civics a poor third in the competition.

In order to obtain a later sampling of evidence on the position of the study of occupations in secondary schools, the writer in the spring of 1947 ad-

[4] *The Social Studies Curriculum*, Fourteenth Yearbook of the Department of Superintendence (Washington, D.C., 1936), p. 72, Table 8.

[5] *Ibid.*, p. 76, Table 12.

dressed brief inquiries to state supervisors of occupational information and guidance and to directors of guidance in large cities. Replies were received from 38 state supervisors. Four said that their state departments of education required the teaching of occupations, while 25 said it was recommended—in some states as a separate course and in other states as an element of social studies or English. The grade placement generally recommended is ninth.

Sixty-four city directors responded to the inquiry. Following is the distribution of their answers to the question, "Is there a course in occupations in your school system?"

	Yes	No
West	4	12
Middle West . .	7	13
South	7	8
East	5	8
Total . . .	23	41

Asked to state the name of the course, 17 of the 23 gave titles which quite clearly indicated the study of occupations and occupation choosing. The remaining 6 gave such titles as "English VI," "Social Studies," or "Citizenship."

Of the 23, 14 said the course was required, 8 said it was elective, and one answer was indeterminate. Twelve cities placed the course in the ninth grade, and 5 in the eighth grade, while the remaining 6—all offering the course on an elective basis—placed it in the seventh or eighth grades or in senior high school grades. The course was a one-semester course in 13 schools, a year-course in 8 schools, and a course of 8 or 10 weeks in the other two schools. (In the latter two cases, the "course" was probably a rather definite unit in some course of semester or year length.) Seventeen of the 23 courses met five days a week.

The next question asked of the city directors was, "If no course in occupations is being taught, does the content have a place in another course?" The number answering "Yes" to this question was 36, but it included 3 who had said that they were offering a course in occupations. These three cities were Chicago, Detroit, and Kansas City. Their directors said that while they were offering the course they were also placing some content typical of such a course in other courses. Eight of the 64 cities answered "No" to both questions—they were not offering a course in occupations, nor did the content have a place in another course.

Asked to name the other course in which the content had a place, 45 responses were given, which may be classified and totaled as follows: social studies courses, 30; English courses, 6; core or general education, 3; group guidance or orientation, 6. In the great majority of cases the course was a ninth-grade course.

The number of weeks devoted to the study of occupations when it was carried on as an element of another course was described by 28 directors as being from 2 to 12, with a distinct mode at 6. The answers of eight could best be described as "variable." When the content was described as being taken up in group guidance classes—as in Providence, Syracuse, and Baltimore—it was indicated as involving an indeterminate amount of time over the pupil's years in secondary school.

To summarize and interpret these data, it seems that in 1947 about one third of these large cities had a real course in occupations, that a little more than half of them gave a place to the content—averaging perhaps six weeks —in another course, while one eighth recognized no special place in the curriculum for this field of study. Under the circumstances, it would be impossible to expect much scholarship in what Kitson calls "occupationology" on the part of the teachers in any but the first group. If the teachers in the larger group had scholarship in the content of occupations and occupation choosing, they could hardly exercise it, because the time allotted to the study was so brief as to allow for only a superficial treatment.

The findings of this survey are supported by other minor surveys or bits of information. For example, Hoy, investigating the status of occupations study in the high schools of Pennsylvania, found approximately 20 per cent to be teaching an organized course in the subject.[6] Time arrangements varied, but more than half of these courses met only once a week for a school year. Of the 281 schools replying to Hoy's inquiry 54 per cent stated that they were presenting occupational information in conjunction with some other course —most frequently as an element in ninth-grade social studies.

Hoppock and Stevens were supplied by the United States Office of Education with a list of 1,122 high schools which had reported having courses in occupations in the last previous Biennial Survey of Education.[7] They canvassed these schools for data on the courses, but the representativeness of their findings may well be open to question, since only 255 schools answered the inquiry. Indicative to this writer of the slender hold of the separate course in occupations is the fact that of the more than 23,000 high schools in the country, only 1,122 had reported to the United States Office that they were offering such a course.

Shall dissatisfaction be expressed over the small number of cities in which the study of occupations is firmly established, or should educators feel comfortable over the fact that a place of sorts is being made for the study of occupations in seven eighths of these cities? The remainder of this chapter will offer evidence on this question, but at the end it may well be that our readers will be divided in their opinion.

[6] Wayne C. Hoy, *A Survey of the Study of Occupations in Pennsylvania Secondary Schools.* Ed.D. Thesis (Pittsburgh, University of Pittsburgh Library, 1949).
[7] Robert Hoppock and Nancy Stevens, "High School Courses in Occupations," *Personnel and Guidance Journal,* Vol. XXXII (May, 1954), pp. 540–543.

OTHER AVENUES FOR THE GROUP STUDY OF OCCUPATIONS

Classes in English Composition

In 1914 Ginn and Company published a book entitled *Vocational and Moral Guidance,* by Jesse B. Davis, then principal of the high school at Grand Rapids, Michigan. The book developed an idea that Davis had been experimenting with in his high school for a number of years, namely, that the content of oral and written composition in English classes might well be vocations and the problems of vocation choosing, together with the problems of developing desirable qualities of character. Approximately one hundred pages of Davis' book are devoted to a detailed course of study, showing for each half year from 7B to 12A the outline of content about which composition work should revolve, giving the topics for themes, and providing rather extended lists of exact references for pupils to consult.

The argument for such a course is essentially two-fold—first, that the content has the guidance values which the students themselves find satisfying to their felt needs, and, second, that it furnishes much needed motivation for English composition. From personal experience this writer can attest the worth of the course in bearing on these goals. The content of occupations and of the problems of choosing an occupation offers as wide a range of opportunities for expression as can be desired. Davis reasoned that its breadth and depth and its appeal to students were such that it could be taken up in different segments and by varied approaches several times in the six-year secondary-school period. One of the advantages of taking it up in English composition is that pupils are able to take up the subject again and again in the light of their expanding experience. When reliance is placed on a specialized course in occupations, the content is taken up but once. Another advantage of utilizing English composition in this manner is that since English is required in all years of the secondary school, none will miss these recurrent experiences in guidance.

Davis' plan seems not to have been widely adopted, although it has unquestionably influenced various individuals and schools in the decades since his book was published. The report of a famous committee on the teaching of English[8] acknowledged Davis' contribution and suggested with some elaboration the subject of occupations and occupation choosing as one of several areas of content appropriate for composition in the eighth grade.

As indicated in the preceding section, the large cities of the country were, in 1947, making very little use of English as a channel for disseminating

[8] James F. Hosic, Compiler, *Reorganization of English in Secondary Schools.* Report by the National Joint Committee on English Representing the Commission on the Reorganization of Secondary Education of the National Education Association and the National Council of Teachers of English (Washington, D.C., U.S. Bureau of Education Bulletin, No. 2, 1917).

occupational information. From the director of guidance in Detroit came the comment that "English teachers in our intermediate (junior high) schools teach Occupational Information in Grades 7, 8, and 9 in connection with English." In LaCrosse, Wisconsin, the content had a place in English 12A, but the time spent on it was indefinite, depending largely on the teacher's interest. From Cincinnati came mention that the subject was supposed to receive attention in eighth-grade English, and from Chicago the more definite statement that "Our English course, also, has occupational study units."

Reliance upon the English department to assume the major responsibility for the group study of occupations is no doubt thwarted by at least two factors. First is the natural unwillingness of English teachers to accept such a chore. They feel—and, no doubt, with considerable justice—that they are often imposed upon to perform various jobs for the school just because their classes include the entire enrollment. Their sensitivity on this point was expressed a number of years ago by one of their leaders, as follows:[9]

Moral training, school spirit, patriotism, safety first, worthy home membership, vocational guidance, thrift, public health, community problems—all these and more are thrust upon the teacher of composition and must be fitted somewhere into her program. . . . Too frequently in the press of disseminating information upon a large variety of topics, the teacher of composition loses her chief function in the school, and the world wonders why our children, many of them, have a slipshod manner of expression, irrational ideas, and undeveloped powers of reflection and analysis.

The strong tradition of specialization among American high-school teachers impels the teacher of English to acknowledge allegiance only to the objectives of English, to say, in effect: "I'll teach English composition to these pupils. I know how to motivate them. And if I prefer to stimulate their expression over content other than the study of occupations, that's my business."

A second factor is the unwillingness of the guidance specialist to urge that responsibility for this feature of the guidance program be thrust upon the English department. He, too, was reared in the tradition of specialization in teaching, and he feels quite certain that English teachers are not competent to direct the study of occupations.

As the situation stands, therefore, words like "responsibility" and "specialization" may well be soft-pedaled, while "opportunity" and "co-operation" may well be emphasized. Let English teachers be helped to see that the study of vocations and vocational choosing is an opportunity to stimulate boys and girls to express themselves vigorously on subjects that are of vital interest to them. Let the counselor render the fullest co-operation by making

[9] Dora V. Smith, "The Danger of Dogma Concerning Composition Content," *English Journal*, Vol. XV (June, 1926), p. 416.

reading lists available, suggesting local observations of occupational life that might be made, offering small and large topics for investigation and report. A problem so universal as finding one's life work is surely one on which English teachers can give some help and one on which guidance specialists can render assistance by working with and through English teachers.

The Homeroom

In many secondary schools the homeroom is the principal expression of the guidance function, as we shall see in the next chapter. It is expected, among other services, to operate as the pupils' principal source of information concerning educational and vocational opportunities. The outlines that are drawn up to direct the group programs of the homerooms include the study of occupations and occupation choosing.

Some of the considerations to be brought up in evaluating the homeroom for this latter purpose are the same as were presented for classes in English composition. All pupils may be reached in the homeroom, and they may be reached every year. It is possible for the homeroom group to review the occupational problem again and again, which is frequently demanded by the steady expansion of pupil horizons. On the other hand, to spread this function out among homeroom teachers—who comprise approximately three fourths of the faculty—is to assume that there is nothing specialized about it, that all teachers have the interest and the ability essential for the proper discharge of the function.

No offhand resolution of this apparent dilemma can be or will be essayed. This book has already demonstrated the pervasive character of the guidance function, but the role of the guidance specialist and his relation to the faculty as a whole will only gradually be clarified, chapter by chapter. However, this much surely can be said now. If a group of pupils, having had a good ninth-grade course in occupations, taught by an expert, find in the eleventh or twelfth grade a compelling need to re-examine the field, they should have a right to do so. And assuming that it would be impossible to organize another course under the expert to serve them, they should have a right to expect leadership and service from their homeroom teacher, whether his *specialty* is Latin or typewriting. If this line of reasoning is sound, perhaps the reader can for the time being project his own thinking into those more numerous situations where the study of occupations is not expertly taken up in the ninth grade, and there plan the role of the homeroom teacher in the light of succeeding sections of this chapter.

Career Conferences

A medium for the dissemination of occupational information which has been consistently popular through the years is the career conference. While some colleges and universities have organized such conferences, their widest acceptance has been among senior or four-year high schools. Practice varies, but the most common characteristics of the conference are that it is an event of a single day—frequently an afternoon and evening; that a dozen or more representatives of various occupations meet classroom-size groups of pupils and talk to them about their jobs and professions; and that some expert in guidance opens and/or closes the conference with an address on general considerations in occupation choosing which are of interest to the whole student body. The main idea is to bring first-hand occupational information to the pupils and to give them a chance to ask questions of a worker in a field which interests them. Service clubs, especially Kiwanis clubs, are most co-operative in furnishing speakers for such conferences.

Forrester[10] has helpfully presented the important problems that must be considered in organizing, promoting, and conducting career conferences. One problem is the determination of what occupations are to be presented. It is commonly suggested that a questionnaire to the pupils may well be employed to answer this question, although a list so derived may well need amending by the counselor in the light of factors which the pupils could scarcely be expected to take into account. There must be a plan for preventing overcrowding at some meetings and underattendance at others. The obtaining of speakers, the issuance of suggestions and instructions to them, the entertainment and introduction of them during the conference—these and kindred details require the skillful organization of many faculty members and students.

A variation from the plan of a single yearly career day was described some years ago by Barbara Wright[11] of Minneapolis. At that time six Minneapolis high schools worked out a joint project with the Kiwanis Club for the holding of conferences during the second semester for seniors only. The number of conferences held in each school varied from six to twenty-one. Fifty-two different speakers were used, most of whom were procured by the Vocational Guidance Committee of the Kiwanis Club. Twenty-eight different occupations were discussed.

Principal points in the method used were as follows: The counselors had all 12A pupils fill out questionnaires to state the three occupations in which they were most seriously interested. Each counselor sent to the supervisor of counseling a list of the occupations which were mentioned with sufficient frequency to justify attempting to obtain a speaker. The combined lists were then taken up with the Kiwanis Club. They drew up a list of 125 Kiwanians who they thought could and would give vocational information effectively, and invited them to a dinner meeting at which vocational guidance was the

[10] Gertrude Forrester, *Methods of Vocational Guidance* (Boston, Heath, 1951), Ch. 13.

[11] "A Method of Using the Group Conference as a Guidance Device," *Vocational Guidance Magazine* (now *Personnel and Guidance Journal*), Vol. VII (October, 1928), pp. 26–33.

keynote. The plan of vocational conferences with small classroom-size groups of pupils was presented. Dr. C. A. Prosser, Director of Dunwoody Institute, and a leader well known to businessmen and school people alike, then and there briefed the speakers and handed out his terse suggestions on mimeographed sheets.

The conferences in each school were spread out over the semester, appointments being made from week to week as the school counselor notified the supervisor of counseling what conference he desired in a given week and his preference as to day and hour. The supervisor assembled the calls from the schools and sent them over to the chairman of the Kiwanis Speakers Committee, who obtained the speakers and notified the supervisor of the appointments. The supervisor in turn notified each counselor. School schedules were not broken, but each conference was held during a regular school period, and the pupils who had expressed an interest in the occupation were excused from classes to attend the conference.

This plan described by Wright has special merit as an example of the organization on a city-wide basis of a guidance feature which involves community and school co-operation.

The four senior high schools of Providence jointly hold a one-day career conference each year. The combination of student bodies makes possible their greater differentiation into audiences of classroom size. Hence, the number of occupations presented is indeed large.[12]

While the careers conference presents a severe administrative problem, and one may wonder if it is worth the hard work entailed, we have evidence that it is very influential with pupils. Shosteck[13] asked Philadelphia high-school seniors to indicate which school career-planning activities were most helpful. "Talks by people in different occupations" was checked by 53 per cent; "reading occupational materials" was checked by 25 per cent; motion pictures, 9 per cent; and the total of several other activities, 13 per cent.

Life-Career Clubs and Assembly Programs

The counselor will not fail to promote such media for the study of occupations as life-career clubs and assembly programs. The club will have to compete with other clubs and can therefore serve only a small fraction of the student body. If it builds a reputation for being helpful to those members who are quite at sea in their vocational choices, it is playing a valued role. Presumably there should be a widespread understanding in the school that the club exists for just such individuals. As there should be almost a complete turnover of membership every year, it can be seen that perhaps a hundred pupils could be profited by the activity and the association over the three-

[12] Information obtained from Mary D. Basso, supervisor of guidance and placement.
[13] Robert Shosteck, "How Well Are We Putting Across Occupational Information?" *Personnel and Guidance Journal,* Vol. XXXIII (January, 1955), p. 265.

year period of the senior high school. Any teacher for whom the growth and maturation of adolescent youth is a compelling interest and who has a wholesome breadth of outlook should be able to sponsor such a club, especially if he and his program committee can consult with a guidance specialist.

Assembly programs serve a wide range of pupil needs and interests. Inasmuch as they constitute activities which engage the entire student body, either as performers or audience, they should be planned with a view to meeting some need or interest which is universal for the audience. In the study of occupations and occupation choosing there are obviously some problems which are felt in common by all students of a given level of maturity—let us say junior high school, senior high school, or junior college. The counselor should be alert to the opportunities which assembly programs afford for the satisfaction of these common needs. A fair representation of the guidance interest on each year's programs should be one of his goals. Better than anyone else on the faculty he should know the subjects on which an assembly speaker has a chance to interest the whole audience, he should know the themes of universal interest for dramatic skits, and he should be able to supply the right motion picture for a guidance program.

In summary of this section treating of avenues for the group study of occupations other than the formal course, it should be pointed out that all the means which have been reported assume that school-age youth are interested in viewing occupational life and in pondering occupational choice over and over. They frequently feel a need for re-study of the problem. While the formal course is probably well placed in the ninth grade, because it thus contributes to a tentative vocational decision just before the pupils must make educational choices, the later opportunities for reconsideration frequently loom up importantly. The vocational decision seems more crucial as the time for decision is reduced.

On the other hand, the limitations of these devices should be plainly recognized. They do not present the balanced, organized view of the occupational world and of the problem of vocational choice that is possible in a semester course. They are fragmentary and sometimes distorted. They do not compel any adequate testing of the individual's self-planning. That they are, however, definitely in harmony with the concept of guidance goals as being reached through educational experience, cannot be denied.

Another conclusion to which this exposition clearly points is the need for a guidance specialist in the school operating as a *resource person*. He should be fertile in suggestions to English teachers, to homeroom teachers and their committees, assembly committees, and to life-career clubs. He should be helpful and interested always, but not superior or authoritarian, if he would get the highest guidance value out of these features. It is hard to see how such features can be very useful without a guidance expert to render this service.

PURPOSES

The Distributive Purpose

The purpose in the study of occupations which we emphasize in a work on guidance is that of distribution among occupations. Depending on intelligent choice to bring about the rational matching of individuals with occupations, we deem it necessary to show our young people the array from which choice is to be made. Pushing on as far as we can through group instruction toward the attainment of the goal of distribution, we seek to realize a subsidiary purpose, namely, the inculcation in each individual of certain habits of thinking in relation to occupational choice. Slender are the chances that an individual will arrive at a permanent occupational choice during the period of his formal, guided study of occupations. We know that he will come back to think of it many times. We want his thinking to be rational and well ordered. Hence, the effort to instill in him the habit of analyzing jobs in relation to aspects and criteria which are pertinent, analyzing himself for abilities, interests, shortcomings, and dislikes, and then comparing himself with jobs.

The Socializing Purpose

It was not its values as a distributive agency, however, but the socializing possibilities of the subject which gave the study of occupations lodgement in the department of social studies. The national Committee on Social Studies said in its 1918 report that[14]

As for the ninth-year study now under consideration, the committee is here interested in its vocational guidance aspect only as an incident to the broader social and civic training of the youth. . . .

The chief purpose of the phase of the ninth-year work now being emphasized should be the development of an appreciation of the social significance of all work; of the social value and interdependence of all occupations; of the social responsibility of the worker, not only for the character of his work but for the use of its fruits; of the opportunities and necessity for good citizenship in vocational life; of the duty of the community to the worker; of the necessity for social control, governmental and otherwise, of the economic activities of the community; and of the part that government actually plays in regulating the economic life of the community and of the individual.

In these lines we have a statement of purpose of such noble character that we are puzzled to know why the course has not been as universally instituted as American history or English or eighth-grade mathematics. Perhaps the course, as actually taught, has had too little bearing on this purpose to win a general vote of confidence. Perhaps the distributive purpose has dominated the course, and that purpose has seemed to be more individual than social.

Conflict or Harmony Between These Purposes?

Can both of these purposes be realized in the same course, or are they so conflicting that the teacher must accept and follow one or the other? Suppose

14 *Op. cit.*, p. 27.

a pupil in Grade 8A has learned through his homeroom orientation programs that next year he will take a course called vocational civics in which he will study the requirements and opportunities of many vocations with a view to finding *his* vocation. And when he enters the course, perhaps he finds that it is just as it was represented. In what frame of mind, then, does he look upon the various vocations as they are presented? Agricultural occupations? If he is a city resident, he is likely to think, "Well, I hope we don't spend much time on this chapter." Or, John is giving an extended report on the engineering occupations. Why should Mary and the rest of the girls attend closely? The ascribed status of women practically precludes their entrance into that field, so why consider it? (Teachers sometimes do report that sex divergence in occupational interest constitutes an obstacle to teaching occupations to mixed classes.) And why should the class as a whole consider any of the occupations which exist under a social stigma and which no one voluntarily and rationally chooses?

Enough has been said to indicate the problems which arise when the motivation of individual advantage is employed. While it is true that the distributive purpose is social as well as individual, the great divergence in occupational rewards exerts powerful pressure upon the pupil to seek a comfortable berth. Is it possible that knowledge acquired under such motivation might fail to improve such maldistribution as was reported in Chapter 4, Tables 19 and 20? If, on the other hand, the subject is approached as a social study, with the socializing objectives uppermost, will the distributive values fail to be realized? The question can be given only a theoretical answer.

To the mind of this writer, the most defensible policy is to teach the course basically as a social study. If it had taken that turn in the beginning, it probably would be well established now. Let the course be pointed toward the values cited by the Committee on Social Studies. Let the teacher remember that the cultivation of emotionalized attitudes and appreciations is at least as important to citizenship as the development of intellectual understandings. Let the pupils enter vicariously into the lives of all manner of workers and evaluate the social service they are rendering. Let them judge the rewards of the various vocations in terms of cultural living. Let their sense of values and their social ideals be given full stimulus to growth.

In the warm glow of aroused altruism, of a desire for social justice, and of a feeling of gratitude to the hosts of unsung occupational heroes, the pupil may, near the end of the course, take up the question, Where can I best fit into this complex organism? Where can my talents be most effectively employed? (The question is not, What occupation is best for me?) On such a foundation the distributive purpose has a chance of being performed in the service of society, which is as it should be. If Henry's analysis indicates that he is better suited to be an operative in a factory or a mill than to be an engineer, he has learned from the course that his job is important to society. The other members of the class, too, know the importance of Henry's job in their lives, and under the influence of such value-judgments they will exert themselves in behalf of adequate social recognition of Henry's service.[15]

Thus, this writer would accept both the socializing and distributive purposes of the course, though acknowledging their lack of harmony. He would seek to minimize the conflict between them by trying to realize them *sequentially* rather than simultaneously. If this conception of purpose is to be accepted, it will perhaps mean the development of some new teaching materials and the rearrangement of the existing materials. There should be no objection to such reconstruction, because the course as it now stands has not gained the acceptance which its originators anticipated forty years ago.

CONTENT OF THE COURSE IN OCCUPATIONS

Some Determining Factors

The content to be included in the study of occupations is obviously dependent in the first place on the amount of time available. If it is to be only a six-weeks unit in a general social-science course, the teacher must select learning experiences with a great deal of care to avoid giving the study an encyclopedic character, the quality of a dull catalogue of many facts. A course of semester length gives a far better opportunity to attain the objectives that have been described and is not unjustifiably long in view of the importance of the aspects of life to which it is devoted. In this discussion a semester course required of all pupils at the ninth-grade level will be assumed. If it were taught at the first-year college level, as in the General College of the University of Minnesota, naturally the content would be of a different character from that which is appropriate for the less mature pupils we assume.

The type of community will to a degree determine the content of the course. However, the socialization of individuals that should come from the course in occupations, as described in the preceding section, is needed by *all* pupils. The finding of one's place in the world's work is a goal common to *all* pupils. Furthermore, the numerous varieties of human talent seem to be scattered rather indiscriminately over city and country, in tenement districts and opulent suburbs. The Committee on Social Studies offered the following judgment in regard to differentiation in courses designed to cultivate common learnings:[16]

It is a fallacy, for example, to imagine that the children of native-born Americans need civic education any less than the children of immigrants; or that the pupils of a school in a purely residential suburb require instruction in industrial history

[15] Bearing on this point of view is the following reference: Harold Saxe Tuttle, "Education for Appreciation Versus Education for Efficiency," *School Review,* Vol. LIV (October, 1946), pp. 462–468.
[16] *Op. cit.,* p. 13.

or vocational civics any less than the pupils of a school in an industrial district. But the scope and emphasis of such courses may well vary in different cases.

Certainly the teacher of vocations will avail himself of community resources, will give practical recognition to the previous experience of his pupils, will take account of the currents of migration in his community, and will take stock of the magnitude of the vocational horizon before his pupils. No textbook published for the country as a whole can satisfactorily define the content of his course. Nor can a syllabus from the state department of education. We must expect the teacher to exercise judgment in the marshalling of educational forces to attain the major goals on which all are agreed.

The Occupational Structure and Trends

The reasonable way to begin the study of occupations, with the emphasis on socializing values, would seem to be the orientation of the pupil with reference to the occupational structure of society. A brief historical approach, such as is represented by Hill's chapter on "Development of Ways of Working,"[17] appeals to this writer. The sections of the chapter are "How Primitive Man Lived," "Earning a Living in the Middle Ages," and "How We Work Today." The Industrial Revolution, as it has swiftly refashioned the work life of mankind, would be viewed by the pupils so that they can better understand the present-day multiplicity of jobs. The occupations in the family economy of 150 years ago, when most families produced all but a few of their needed goods and services, would be contrasted with today's hotel economy, wherein many families produce none of the goods and services they need, but buy all of them with the salary check received by the head of the house for the minutely specialized service he renders. The major categories of workers, as defined by the United States Census, would be examined and the numbers employed in each would be noted. Classifications by degree of skill and extent of general and special education required, would be studied. The main facts of the distribution of workers by sex and by race would be analyzed, and in that connection the factor of ascribed status in occupational affiliation would be brought to light and evaluated. The proportions of manual and white-collar workers, of employees and of self-employed, would be taken into account.

The broad facts on individual income would perhaps be the next angle from which to study occupations and the occupational structure. For this purpose it would be well to put into pupils' hands tables from such agencies as the United States Department of Commerce showing the distribution of income. One such table,[18] for instance, shows the 1953 distribution of

[17] H. C. Hill, *The Life and Work of the Citizen*, Ch. XII (Boston, Ginn, 1935).
[18] "Income Distribution in the United States, 1950–53," Table 1. Office of Business Economics (Washington, D.C., U.S. Department of Commerce, 1955), p. 4.

"families and unattached individuals" by income bracket from the six per cent whose income (before income taxes) was less than $1,000 to the three per cent whose income was $15,000 and over, with a median estimated at $4,410. Thomas devotes four chapters (4–7 inclusive) of his recent work[19] to occupational income and its social meaning. Table 37, drawn from his research,[20] shows the extreme differences in incomes and how these differences have persisted through good times and bad.

To make these data more meaningful, to help pupils grasp the concept of real income, the teacher would need to have them translate the income dollars into groceries, rent, clothing, medical services, and the many other items of the family budget. The studies of family budgetary needs and living costs would necessarily be drawn upon for the making of these comparisons.[21] The rapid changes in price and wage-levels creates a problem in the accurate portrayal of occupational incomes.

TABLE 37. Portions of All Income Recipients Receiving Specified Proportions of the National Income for Selected Years

Per cent of Recipients	Percentage of National Income Received								
	1910	1918	1921	1929	1934	1937	1947	1950	1953
Top 10%	33.9	34.5	38.2	39.0	33.6	34.4	33	29	31
Top 30%	56.4	57.0	61.5	60.2	57.7	60.2	60	57	58
Middle 40%	29.8	30.5	28.7	28.9	31.1	31.8	32	34	33
Bottom 30%	13.8	12.5	9.8	10.0	11.2	8.0	8	9	9

Essential to the pupil's understanding of occupations is some comprehension of trends. Pupils need to be aware of how the ongoing industrial revolution is rendering some occupations obsolete, introducing new ones, and continually shifting the percentage of workers required in various fields. The three principal adult digests of occupational trends[22] have not been

[19] Lawrence Thomas, *The Occupational Structure and Education* (Englewood Cliffs, N.J., Prentice-Hall, 1956).

[20] Reprinted by permission from *The Occupational Structure and Education,* by Lawrence G. Thomas, p. 66. Copyright, 1956, by Prentice-Hall, Inc., Englewood Cliffs, N.J.

[21] One of the most precise and thorough of such studies is reported in the following reference: "Workers' Budgets in the United States: City Families and Single Persons, 1946 and 1947" (Washington, D.C., U.S. Department of Labor, Bureau of Labor Statistics, Bulletin 927, 1948).

[22] Ralph G. Hurlin and Meredith B. Givens, "Shifting Occupational Patterns," *Recent Social Trends,* Vol. I (New York, McGraw-Hill, 1933), pp. 268–324 (Ch. VI).

H. D. Anderson and P. E. Davidson, *Occupational Trends in the United States* (1940), and *Recent Occupational Trends in American Labor* (1945) (Stanford, Cal., Stanford University Press).

Comparative Occupation Statistics for the United States, 1870–1940. Sixteenth Census of the United States, 1940. (Prepared by Alba M. Edwards) (Washington, D.C., Government Printing Office, 1943).

rewritten for younger readers, but that fact does not excuse the teacher from helping pupils to grasp the main trends and the reasons for them. Hurlin and Givens give many comparative data for the seven censuses from 1870 to 1930 inclusive, showing such trends as the following: (1) an increasing proportion of the population gainfully employed, this being due especially to the increased employment of women and to the falling off in the relative numbers of children; (2) the decline in the percentages of the population under 16 and over 65 who are employed; (3) the decline in the number of agricultural workers, due largely to mechanization, and the increase in the percentages of workers who are engaged in trade and transportation, clerical service, domestic and personal service, public service, professional service (these shifts signifying the need for fewer workers in the production of physical goods—heart processes—and the need for more workers in exchange, distribution, and services).

The other two references cited extended the comparisons to include the 1940 Census, although they did not do so with completeness for the reason that the Standard Occupational Classification adopted for use in the 1940 Census differed considerably from that which had been employed in the 1930 and earlier censuses. However, the comparisons they were able to make showed such a continuance of 1930 trends as to suggest the continued worth of those trend studies in which 1930 is the latest date.

To afford the reader a more contemporaneous view of the distribution of workers, Figure 8 has been constructed to facilitate comparison of the country in 1940 and 1950.[23] While only two time points, a decade apart, are shown, to a notable extent they bear evidence of a continuance of earlier trends. Agricultural workers, shown in three categories, are declining rapidly, reflecting the increasing mechanization of farm work.[24] The percentage of workers in professional and technical fields increased, as, indeed, it has been increasing for some decades. The expansion of clerical work continued at a rapid pace. Craftsmen and operatives, taken together, in 1950 constituted more than a third of all employed persons, representing a perceptible increase from 1940. The precipitous decline in the number of private household workers must be attributed to the steady removal of various processes and functions from the home.

In such study of occupational structure and trends children see how new occupations are started and how they grow. They witness the decline and virtual disappearance of other occupations, but they observe that more occupations are being born than are dying, that more and more people are working in narrow specialties. This situation, they see, enhances interdependence and also enhances the responsibility of each worker for the faithful perform-

[23] Adapted from data in the *Statistical Abstract of the United States*, 1954, Table 237 (Washington, D.C., U.S. Department of Commerce, 1954), p. 208.
[24] See also *Agricultural Outlook Charts, 1956* (Washington, D.C., U.S. Department of Agriculture, 1956), pp. 24–25.

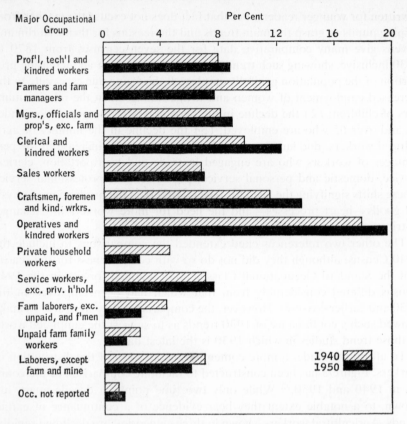

FIG. 8. Percentage distributions of employed persons, 1940 and 1950.

ance of his function. Furthermore, such data make it clear that many workers have to make occupational adjustments—they have to give up a chosen occupation and seek another, or they have to adapt to changed conditions and requirements to hold the job they have.[25]

Another occupational trend with which ninth-grade pupils should gain some acquaintance is the rapid drift toward more and more restrictions on occupational affiliation and pursuit. About 1930 Salz stated it as follows:[26]

Nor is it possible to generalize concerning freedom of access to various occupations. Whereas a generation ago it was possible to believe that there was a straight line development from a rigidly stratified occupational organization bound by tradition toward a liberal-anarchic freedom of occupational choice,

[25] A highly valuable exposition on the subject of this subdivision of the chapter is *The Occupational Structure and Education,* by Lawrence Thomas, already cited as the source of Table 37.

[26] Arthur Salz, "Occupation," *Encyclopedia of the Social Sciences,* Vol. XI, p. 434.

strong counter tendencies have since become apparent. A number of occupational groups acting independently have introduced entrance qualifications or retained them from the handicraft period; in other occupations state examinations and licensing have barred free access to newcomers.

This may come as a slight surprise to the American youth. He has been brought up in the tradition of free choice, and now he is told that barriers and restrictions and some exact specifications are being set up in connection with entrance to a number of occupations.

To obtain some precise data on the trend in one type of control, an inventory was made of all statutory restrictions on occupational affiliation and pursuit enacted by the Commonwealth of Pennsylvania from 1700 to 1938.[27] The study was narrowed to such occupations as require a state license or its equivalent and to occupations in private employment only. Analysis of the regulations showed that the great majority of them were for the benefit of the consumer, designed to protect him from malpractice or exploitation. The number of occupations licensed, by major fields, in 1938 was as follows:

Agriculture	0
Clerical occupations	1
Forestry and fishing	4
Extraction of minerals	15
Transportation and communication	26
Domestic and personal service	28
Professional service	47
Manufacturing and mechanical industries . . .	51
Trade . . , ...	137

The chronological incidence of the licensing of these occupations is shown in Figure 9. The curve rises with increasing steepness with each twenty-year

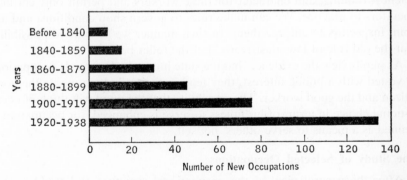

FIG. 9. Number of new occupations licensed in successive twenty-year periods (not cumulative).

27 Edgar C. Hastings and P. W. Hutson, "State Regulation of Occupational Activity." *Occupations,* Vol. XX (January, 1942), pp. 247–252.

period and shows an amazing gain in the exercise of state control over occupation since 1920. As one surveys this picture of governmental activity over the past one hundred years, he is impelled to ask, What of the future? The number of restrictions placed on licensed occupations presents a curve of even more marked concavity, with restrictions to the number of

16	enacted	before	1840
29	"	from 1840 to	1859
52	"	" 1860 to	1879
152	"	" 1880 to	1899
264	"	" 1900 to	1919
876	"	" 1920 to	1938

From such evidence we deduce that individual freedom of action in choosing and pursuing an occupation is being more and more limited. Society is concerned with the protection of its members by assuring them that only qualified practitioners shall serve them. To this degree the practice of an occupation is recognized as a social function and is required to be exercised as a social responsibility.

We may illustrate the trend in this fashion. Not so many years ago a person desiring to practice cosmetology hung out her shingle without let or hindrance. If her preparations and processes scarred milady's face instead of beautifying her, it was the client's privilege to sue and seek redress. "Let the buyer beware!"

By contrast, the modern viewpoint may be stated as follows: This occupation of cosmetology is a social service. Its proper pursuit involves skills, knowledge, and the application of materials known to be safe and beneficial. To expect each individual client to weigh the adequacy of the operator for rendering the service is absurd. But collectively we can take steps to assure the expert performance of this function. We can establish standards of competency, training, and character for these workers and permit only certified operators to practice. We can make rules to govern shop conditions and appoint inspectors to enforce them. In such manner we so shift responsibility that the old rule of law must read, "Let the seller beware!"

As pupils view the evidence that the state increasingly regards occupations as vested with a public interest, they tend in their minds to merge the good citizen and the good worker. The possibility that the pupil will think of occupational choice in terms of his fitness to serve is enhanced, for occupation is defined as a means to serve others, not self.

The Study of Selected Occupations

After the general view of the occupational structure and trends, some occupations should be taken up for detailed study. How to select them presents a problem, for they number 20,000 or more, and since each individual has a right to aspire to any of them, he ought, theoretically, to have a right to look them all over. Textbooks typically solve the problem by offering chapters on each of the major groups, frequently using the census classification or one that is similar to it. For example, a widely used text presents the following units, in a total of 26 chapters, as "Part II—Studying Representative Occupations:"[28]

Unit A—Agricultural Occupations
Unit B—Homemaking Occupations
Unit C—Manufacturing
Unit D—Transportation
Unit E—Communication
Unit F—Occupations in Business
Unit G—Skilled Trades
Unit H—Public Service Occupations
Unit I—Personal Service Occupations
Unit J—The Professions

Such a general coverage of occupations seems to be quite in harmony with both the distributive and socializing purposes. However, there remains the problem of selection within each group. Doubtless this could be done by having pupils spend part of their time in intensive type studies. Certainly the danger of a sterile, boresome uniformity of treatment is apparent to all.

It is right at this point that the unimaginative teacher is likely to be trapped by the textbook. For the textbook is written for the whole country, and perhaps it was written ten years ago. It cannot give the emphasis that is desirable for the pupils of Detropolis or Hayfield in the spring of 1960. The teacher must have in mind criteria for the selection of content.

One criterion is the probable area in which the pupils will settle to spend their adult lives. This is a difficult question to answer in migrant America. Hetzel, in May, 1941, found the locations of the twelve hundred people who had graduated from the high school at Sumner, Iowa, during the preceding forty-nine years—that is, since and including the first graduating class.[29] He found that 39.0 per cent were in the home community, 32.8 per cent were in Iowa outside the home community, and 21.8 per cent were in the United States, outside of Iowa. The small remainder were accounted for as follows: 0.7 per cent, in a foreign country; 5.2 per cent, deceased; 0.5 per cent, address unknown. Hetzel also showed that the longer the period that had elapsed since graduation, the more widely scattered the graduates were. He cited several other parallel studies, made for rural or small-town communities in Missouri, Illinois, Iowa, and Wyoming, as justifying the conclusion that about two fifths of the high-school graduates in those areas remain in

[28] Paul W. Chapman, *Occupational Guidance* (Atlanta, Georgia, Turner E. Smith & Co., 1950), pp. v–vi.
[29] Walter L. Hetzel, "Geographical Study of All Graduates of an Iowa High School," *School Review*, Vol. L (April, 1942), pp. 294–297.

the home community, and that about a third remain in the home state but not in their home community.

These data suggest that the teacher of occupations will do well, first, to emphasize local occupations, and, second, to give much attention to the occupations of the state. Other factors, however, should be taken into account in this connection. One is the cityward drift of population. The authors of *Middletown* found that this city tended to be receiving its population from nearby small towns and farms, while it was losing population to Cleveland, Chicago, Buffalo, and other large cities. The extent and the direction of the cityward drift should be estimated in every community. It follows that in large cities or metropolitan areas, the emphasis on local occupations should be more marked than in small cities and country towns: larger percentages of the high-school graduates will be taking up residence in the home community.

Another factor to be considered is that the weight to be given occupations of the state may well vary notably. Many of our state boundary lines are artificial in the extreme. It would be better for the occupations teacher to focus on the natural economic area to which his community belongs. The Inland Empire stretches over parts of three states—Oregon, Washington, and Idaho. Pittsburgh with its heavy industries has much more of kinship with Wheeling, West Virginia, and with Youngstown and Cleveland, Ohio, than it does with Philadelphia.

Another criterion to be observed in the selection of occupations to be studied is the probable occupational level for which the pupils are destined. As the introductory study of the total occupational structure makes it plain to the pupils that less than 10 per cent of workers are engaged in the professions, it ought to be clear that the great majority of the average ninth-grade class must eventually find themselves in skilled, semi-skilled, or unskilled manual labor, or in the lower levels of the white-collar occupations— selling goods or doing clerical work. To devote extended study to the professions and the more favored business occupations would, then, simply intensify longings for goals that can be attained only by the few. Will the teacher, with his white-collar tradition and his cloistered life, fall into this error?

A criterion too often followed narrowly is that of the pupil's "interest." Each pupil studies intensively the occupation he "intends to take up" or the one in which he is "most interested." Usually he carries his study through to a tangible conclusion—he makes a career book, vying with his fellows in turning out a work of art. As far as the distributive purpose goes, this practice simply begs the question. It assumes that the pupil has already made a choice of occupation, and a valid choice. There is no questioning of the choice, nor any special stimulation of the pupil to be critical. Instead of having the pupil become acquainted with the whole array of occupations so that he will have a basis for choice, it serves to concentrate his attention on a narrow sector of the vocational horizon. It is true that he will make a report to the class and that he will listen to their reports, but the learning acquired from such experience is of doubtful quantity and quality. Perhaps this criticism does not apply when no more than two weeks out of a semester are spent on such an exercise in intensive study, but in many classes a much longer time has been so spent. The practice ignores the facts of poor occupational choice among secondary-school pupils, as shown in Chapter 4.

What does it mean to study an occupation? What kinds of informational content are involved? In answer to these questions the items of an appropriate outline have been suggested by many individuals and committees over the past forty years. One agency, probably the best authority of all, which has been working on the problem for a long time, is the Occupational Research Section of the National Vocational Guidance Association. It includes the leaders in the work of gathering and publishing occupational information. In 1940 they summarized their thinking on this problem by drawing up a basic outline for a good occupational monograph. From the revised form, published in 1950, the major headings may here be cited, with minor adaptation, to indicate the scope of information involved in the study of an occupation: [30]

1. History of the occupation
2. Importance of the occupation and its relation to society
3. Duties—definition of occupation and nature of work
4. Number of workers, their distribution, the trends and outlook
5. Qualifications
6. Preparation—general education, special training, experience
7. Methods of entering
8. Time required to attain skill
9. Advancement
10. Related occupations
11. Earnings
12. Conditions of work—hours, regularity of employment, health and accident hazards
13. Organizations—employees, employers
14. Typical places of employment
15. Advantages and disadvantages not otherwise enumerated
16. Supplementary information

Concerned also with valid methods of gathering information and the readable presentation of it, the committee stated standards on these points under the following captions: "How Textual and Tabular Matter Should Be Presented," "Reporting Methods by Which the Data Were Gathered," and "Style and Format."

[30] "Standards for Use in Preparing and Evaluating Occupational Literature," *Occupations*, Vol. XXVIII (February, 1950), pp. 319–324. The article is quoted in its entirety in an appendix (pp. 431–441) to Gertrude Forrester's *Occupational Literature* (New York, H. W. Wilson Co., 1954).

Not only is the report of this committee a useful guide for those who do occupational research and reporting, but it serves as a yardstick by which the readers of this book may judge textbooks and materials ordered for the school library. The critical faculties may also be helpfully sharpened by the thoughtful study of Baer and Roeber's twenty-page chapter on "Appraising Occupational Literature."[31]

Consideration of How "to Choose an Occupation, Prepare for It, Enter Upon, and Progress in It"

Textbooks and course outlines for the course in occupations invariably include content which is calculated to help the individual find his life work. They have chapters on self-analysis and frequently include exercises which require comparison of self with various jobs. When the counselor teaches the course, he sometimes in connection with this theme administers a battery of tests and offers interpretation in helping the pupils to arrive at valid estimates of their vocational potentialities. Most widely known of the courses which strongly partake of this character is the Chicago course, "Self-Appraisal and Careers," taught as an elective for pupils of the eleventh and twelfth grades.[32] In this course the pupils are also individually counseled by the Careers teacher. This is the type of course favored by Hoppock.[33]

The value of schooling for aiding the individual in improving his qualifications for vocational life is commonly the subject of a chapter in the textbooks. Chapters on "Getting a Job" and "Successful Careers" are also commonly included.

All of these topics bear upon the distributive purpose. In keeping with what has been said in the preceding section about making the socializing purpose of the course the primary purpose, this writer believes that the topics mentioned in this division should be taken up in the latter weeks of the course. The practice of some textbooks of first focusing the pupil's attention on choosing a career is likely to create an attitude which makes it impossible for him to study occupations in the most constructive way.

PRINTED MATERIALS FOR PUPILS, TEACHERS, AND COUNSELORS

Outstanding Sources for Teacher and Counselor

The bulk of literature on occupations is overwhelming, and yet, if the few pages which may be allotted to it in this work are to contribute orienta-

---

[31] Max F. Baer and Edward C. Roeber, *Occupational Information: Its Nature and Use*, rev. ed. (Chicago, Science Research Associates, 1958), Ch. IV.

[32] Blanche B. Paulson, "A Chicago Course Called 'Careers'," *Occupations*, Vol. XXIX (May, 1951), pp. 591–594.

[33] For example, see Robert Hoppock and Norman Lowenstein, "The Teaching of Occupations in 1951," *Occupations*, Vol. XXX (January, 1952), pp. 274–276.

tion to the beginning student of guidance, the encyclopedic tendency must be avoided. This can best be done by referring the reader at the outset to a few sources which present listings and classifications of the literature.

First to be mentioned is a paper-bound book of nearly 200 pages entitled *Occupations—a Basic Course for Counselors,* by Walter J. Greenleaf. It is Bulletin No. 247, United States Office of Education, and was published in 1951. Many suggestions for teaching-and-learning activities in the study of occupations, descriptions of occupational structure and classification, and an extended appendix for the listing of source materials, are main features of this publication.

Second, Carroll Shartle's *Occupational Information: Its Development and Application,* second edition (Prentice-Hall, 1952), is noteworthy for its treatment of methods of occupational research, description, and classifica-tion. The author's extensive experience as a member of the staff of the Re-search Division, United States Employment Service, in the 1930s when the *Dictionary of Occupational Titles* was being produced, is reflected in the nature of this book. Numerous facsimiles of the forms used in obtaining oc-cupational information are shown, as well as sample pages of government descriptions of occupations.

Third, *Occupational Information: Its Nature and Use,* by Max F. Baer and Edward C. Roeber (Science Research Associates, 1958), is perhaps the most comprehensive work in this list in that it has the following purposes: orienting the reader to the occupational structure, acquainting him with the types of literature, training him to appraise sources of the literature, pre-paring him to make local occupational surveys, and educating him to the use of occupational information in group instruction and individual counseling.

Fourth, *Occupational Literature: An Annotated Bibliography,* by Ger-trude Forrester (H. W. Wilson Co., 1954), is a work of reference to serve the counselor in his office and the teacher and student in the library. Fol-lowing earlier bibliographies of occupational pamphlets, Forrester has in this work endeavored to comprehend all occupational literature that is reasonably current. Approximately 55 per cent of the items in this bibliog-raphy have been published in the 1950s. While the bibliography is classified into fourteen well-chosen categories, the most extended is the one entitled "Books and Pamphlets Listed Alphabetically by Occupations" (pp. 91–377), which begins with "Able Seaman" and is concluded with "Zoologist."

As the following divisions of this section name and characterize the several types of printed materials on occupations, Forrester's work will be referred to for its highly valuable lists.

Fifth, *Occupational Information: Where to Get It and How to Use It in Counseling and Teaching,* by Robert Hoppock (McGraw-Hill, 1957), is similar in purpose and scope to the work of Baer and Roeber cited above but with greater emphasis on methods of disseminating information about occupations and occupation choosing.

Sixth, *Books about Occupations: A Reading List for High School Students,* by M. H. Anderson, O. R. Gerakis, and O. M. Haugh (Kansas Studies in Education, Volume 7, No. 2, School of Education, University of Kansas, April, 1957) is another useful index. Works of both fiction and exposition are included, the reading level of each book is indicated, and the main classification is in the categories of the Kuder Preference Record.

Textbooks

While Forrester lists twenty titles in her bibliography entitled "Textbooks for Pupils in Classes in Occupations," only six correspond to the general pattern sketchily described in the preceding section—that is, with two thirds or more of their pages devoted to occupational content and the balance to such topics as the value of an education, self-analysis, choosing a vocation, and success on the job. A seventh book is Harry Kitson's *I Find My Vocation* (McGraw-Hill, 1954), which has gone through several editions. It does not give descriptions of occupations, but is devoted to helping pupils find occupational information, showing them the various ways of studying occupations, directing their study of their own powers and interests, and otherwise aiding them in selecting and preparing to enter upon their life work.

In 1937 Schrock analyzed the content of the six most widely used textbooks. One of his tables showed how the distribution of space to the several categories of occupations compared with the distribution of workers among the same categories. It is reproduced here as Table 38.[34] Marked disparities are evident in the table, three groups being given three or four times as high a percentage of space in the textbooks as the workers constitute among the working population. On the other hand, workers in agriculture and in domestic and personal service receive only two fifths as much space in the textbooks as their numbers apparently justify. It is difficult, however, to offer an interpretation of these data. Who is to say that the comparable percentages in the two columns should approximate equality? For example, occupations in professional service are complex and varied. They require extensive training. Surely more space will be required to describe the occupation of the plant engineer than the occupation of one of the machine operators in the plant. The illustration suggests that we do not have sufficient evidence to enable us to criticize the data of Table 38. The data of the table do tell something about the distribution of content in the textbooks.

Brayfield and Mickelson made a similar analysis of the titles listed in the *Occupational Index* and compared them with the distribution of workers in the 1940 Census, finding, for example, that 44.1 per cent of the titles dealt

[34] Archy Schrock, *An Analysis of Textbooks in Occupations,* Table III. Master's Thesis (Pittsburgh, University of Pittsburgh Library, 1937), p. 18.

TABLE 38. Percentage Distributions of Lines Descriptive of Occupations Compared with Percentage Distribution of Workers

Occupational Group	U.S. Census 1930	Average of Six Textbooks	Per cent Column 3 Is of Column 2
1	2	3	4
Agriculture	21.4	8.7	41
Forestry and fishing	0.5	1.6	320
Extraction of minerals	2.0	3.8	190
Manufacturing and mechanical industries	28.9	19.3	67
Transportation and communication	7.9	9.9	125
Trade	12.5	11.2	90
Public service	1.8	7.0	389
Professional service	6.7	27.8	415
Domestic and personal service .	10.1	4.2	41
Clerical occupations	8.2	6.5	80
Totals	100.0	100.0	

with professional occupations in contrast to the 6.5 per cent of workers so employed.[35]

A subjective examination of existing textbooks shows that some emphasize the socializing purpose; others, probably the majority, emphasize the distributive purpose. All, however, to this writer represent some degree of confusion and uncertainty which accounts in no small measure for the apparent failure to firmly establish the half-year course for which the textbooks are intended. This point was elaborated on in the two preceding sections.

Periodicals and Indexes

From time to time through the years that the vocational guidance function has been recognized, periodicals have been founded for the purpose of disseminating news about vocations to youth. For reasons unknown, but presumably financial, all but one have been discontinued. In her index to "Periodicals and Indexes" (pp. 410–411) Forrester lists one such publication, *The Career News,* an eight-page bi-monthly issued by the B'nai B'rith Vocational Service Bureau. In the 1956 "Catalog of Publications" of that agency this periodical is described as "now in its 14th year."

Three adult periodicals devoted to occupational information are issued by the United States Department of Labor, namely, *Employment Security*

[35] Arthur H. Brayfield and Grace T. Mickelson, "Disparities in Occupational Information Coverage," *Occupations,* Vol. XXIX (April, 1951), pp. 506–508.

Review, The Labor Market and Employment Security, and the *Monthly Labor Review.*

The *Personnel and Guidance Journal,* leading periodical for guidance workers, does not attempt to give occupational information or to index such materials. Outstanding publications on occupations are, however, taken up in its review columns, and its department, "Washington Flashes," conducted by Max F. Baer, is generally devoted to news of the occupational structure and trends, especially as revealed or to be revealed in government publications.

In so dynamic a field as that of occupations, a real problem of those who are engaged in vocational guidance is to keep up with the flow of new information. Forrester names four or five indexes which list and annotate such literature monthly, bi-monthly, or quarterly. The indexes are indeed duplicative, but if in every school the library subscribes for one and the counselor for another, the school probably would not be oversupplied.

A highly significant development in indexes which has occurred since the publication of Forrester's book is the issuance of the *NVGA Bibliography of Current Occupational Literature.*[36] This is a publication of the Guidance Information Review Service; it lists items appearing in the period from January, 1954, through July, 1955. Materials appearing since the latter date are being reviewed in the NVGA *Vocational Guidance Quarterly* as a continuing supplement to the *Bibliography.* The special merit of this index is that it classifies and codes materials so as to evaluate them against the NVGA *Standards for Occupational Literature.*[37]

Monographs and Pamphlets

The extent and variety of occupational materials published in pamphlet size and form is such that the teacher and counselor are hard pressed to obtain an inventory of them and to win sufficient control to use them most advantageously. Fortunately, one of the services rendered by Forrester is the listing, as Part V of her Bibliography, of "Publications Issued in Series, Arranged According to Publisher of Series." This is a section of nearly sixty pages. It lists the titles of the occupational monographs or pamphlets that have been published by the various firms or agencies making a specialty of the commercial publication of such materials. Also listed are the occupational publications of the Federal Government, which has so expanded its activities in the past two decades as to make it the most important source of occupational information. The principal issuing agencies of the Federal Government are as follows:

[36] May be ordered from NVGA Headquarters, 1534 "O" Street, N.W., Washington 5, D.C. Price, $1.00.

[37] See *Occupations,* Vol. XXVIII (February, 1950), pp. 319–324.

Department of Agriculture
Department of Labor:
  Bureau of Labor Statistics
  Employment Service
  Women's Bureau
Veterans Administration
Department of Commerce, Bureau of Foreign and Domestic Commerce
Department of Health, Education, and Welfare, Office of Education
Defense Department

Monographs and pamphlets on occupations have been published by many professional societies. Not listing their publications, Baer and Roeber give a long list of such societies, together with their addresses, ranging from the American Institute of Accountants to the American Society of Zoologists.[38] The military services, likewise, have taken account of the need for occupational information by publishing readable manuals which describe military jobs and commonly indicate their counterparts in civilian life insofar as such relationships exist.

Many other publications, widely scattered as to source, fall in this category of printed materials, though some might more fittingly be called folders, leaflets, or brochures. They appear in Forrester's main bibliography under the respective occupations which they describe.

Reference Books

Early in the vocational guidance movement books describing more than one occupation began to appear. Many were written in very popular fashion, frequently representing a very subjective choice of material, often produced by professional writers using a dramatic style. Some were compilations of short biographies of workers—successful workers—in a variety of fields. While readable, the contents of some of these books would not score well on the criteria of the NVGA for good occupational reporting. On the other hand, many of these works of reference are scholarly and fairly represent the occupations they cover.

That literature of this character forms an important category today is evidenced by Forrester's ten-page bibliography (pp. 377–387) entitled "Books and Pamphlets Describing More Than One Occupation." While the study of the titles and their annotations signify a superficial and unscientific character for many items, others are relatively penetrating and objective. A considerable number are government documents, such as *Women's Occupations through Seven Decades,* Women's Bureau Bulletin No. 218, 1947. Another type or class represented by a number of titles consists of college recruiting literature. In making selections from this bibliography for the small library, Forrester's system of single-starring the items recommended

[38] *Op. cit.,* pp. 232–250.

for first purchase and double-starring items especially recommended, singles out 10 to 15 per cent for such distinction.

Major Publications of the Federal Government

Beginning in 1934 the Research Division (later known as the Occupational Analysis Section) of the United States Employment Service has been making studies which have given us fundamental knowledge of all occupations. In comparison, the research of all other agencies appears to be sketchy, frequently superficial, and touching only small segments of the field. On the other hand, the knowledge of an occupation which has been made available by the USES does not bear upon all of the items of the NVGA Basic Outline, for it is concerned mostly with defining the exact duties of the worker and the qualifications the worker must possess for his job. The work of this agency has been described at length in a number of *Occupations* almost entirely devoted to the subject.[39]

The studies of occupations published by this agency fall into three main categories. The first is the *Dictionary of Occupational Titles,* first published in 1939, then revised in 1949. Volume I, *Definitions of Titles,* contains definitions and code numbers of 22,028 jobs. Volume II, *Occupational Classification and Industry Index,* contains all the job titles listed in groups according to their occupational code numbers. Part IV, called *Entry Occupational Classification,* was devised to aid in bringing about the occupational affiliation of young people with little or no work experience.

The second category of publications is an extended series of volumes called *Job Descriptions.* These describe occupations broken down in complete specificity, each volume centered about an industry or a class of occupations, as, *Job Descriptions for the Garment Manufacturing Industry, Job Descriptions for Hotels and Restaurants,* etc. The description of the Metal-Band-Saw Operator in *Job Descriptions for Job Machine Shops,* for example, is taken up under the following titles: Job Summary, Work Performed, Machine, Tools and Equipment, Material, Working Conditions, Relation to Other Jobs, Specialized Qualifications, and Special Information.

The third category of publications is the *Job Family Series,* an extended list of large pamphlets bearing such titles as *Occupations Related to Occupations in Printing and Publishing.* The idea of this series is to bring together occupations which require the same human abilities, regardless of their remoteness in industrial grouping. The nature and usefulness of the job family concept has been described by Shartle.[40]

The publications of this agency were not produced to promote the guidance

[39] "Ten Years of Occupational Research," *Occupations,* Vol. XXII (April, 1944), pp. 387–446.
    See also *Occupational Analysis Publications* (Washington, D.C., U.S. Employment Service, Department of Labor, November, 1945) 40 pp. Free.
    [40] *Op. cit.,* Ch. VI.

function in education, but primarily to create working tools for the 1500 or more offices of the USES, and secondarily to aid personnel departments in industry in recruitment and placement. In World War II the Armed Forces used them to great advantage.

Can schools make use of this remarkable store of occupational information? It seems doubtful if secondary-school pupils can be sent to any of these publications, except that an occasional student might be referred to one of the *Job Descriptions* volumes. But counselors must come into an appreciation of this research and learn to apply it. They must come to see that the work of this agency makes it possible for them to render professional service of higher quality than before. Beginning with Part IV of the *Dictionary* and utilizing Part I and the *Job Descriptions*, they will offer to older secondary-school pupils much more specific vocational counsel than has heretofore been feasible. To develop the technique for use of these publications is a task for extended, patient study and practice.

A few words about the character and advantages of Part IV of the *Dictionary* may be suggestive of its use. Whereas Volume I lists all occupations on a strictly alphabetical basis, without classification, in double-column pages of fine type, giving definitions and code numbers, Part IV classifies occupations according to main types of worker characteristics needed, as, professional, clerical, service work, agricultural-marine-forestry, mechanical, and manual, then subdivides these with successive degrees of refinement, showing twenty-two 3-digit classifications, 68 4-digit classifications, and on to the 5- and 6-digit classifications. Section II of Part IV gives four types of classification factors useful in ascertainment of the code numbers which should be scanned in aiding a young person to find his occupational goal. These factors are (1) personal traits, described as being involved in each of the twenty-two 3-digit job classifications, (2) leisure-time activities (more than 100 are listed), together with the code numbers of the occupations (specificity varying from 3- to 6-digit classifications) which call for similar abilities and/or interests, (3) casual work experience (more than a dozen types of occupations commonly engaged in by beginning unskilled young people—often on a part-time, after-school, vacation, or temporary basis) together with the code numbers of occupations which call for similar abilities and/or interests, and (4) training courses pursued—military and civilian.

In the section of Chapter 16 which is devoted to counseling for vocational choice will be found a description of a technique for using Part IV of the *Dictionary* in the vocational counseling of high-school seniors.[41]

A second epochal publication of the Federal Government is the *Occupational Outlook Handbook,* first issued by the Bureau of Labor Statistics in

[41] A revised edition of the *Dictionary of Occupational Titles* is scheduled for 1959, according to Max F. Baer, *Personnel and Guidance Journal,* Vol. XXXIV (March, 1956), p. 397.

1949, revised and enlarged in 1951, and again revised and brought up to date in 1957.[42] This comprehensive work gives well-organized information concerning several hundred occupations grouped according to major fields, as, professions, skilled trades, clerical jobs, service occupations, farming, etc. Each report covers the nature of the work, employment trends and outlook in the occupation, essential qualifications in native ability, training, and experience, working conditions, and earnings. Introductory sections for each group summarize the major trends in population and employment which afford useful background for understanding individual occupations. Many photographs and charts help the exposition. This work is a first-line book of reference for the counselor and for students in the upper secondary and college years.

The same agency has issued and continues to issue an extended series of comprehensive bulletins on the "employment outlook" in various occupations or fields of employment. A representative example is the *Employment Outlook in Skilled Electrical and Electronic Occupations,* December, 1955, an 8 by 10-inch booklet of fifty double-column pages. The objectivity and the authenticity of these government publications are calculated to win respect and dignity for the guidance function.

A third work of reference recently issued by a department of the federal government is *Education for the Professions*.[43] This is an oversized book of more than 300 pages, consisting mainly of thirty-four chapters "prepared by authors who have had much first-hand contact," and describing education in the various professions. In the current shortage of workers at the professional level the information gathered together in this volume should prove an invaluable aid to counselors and to those students whose abilities warrant the aspiration to be educated for a profession. The orientation provided by these chapters should afford a basis for evaluation of the contents of professional-school catalogues.

Reports of Local Surveys

The necessity for using materials which enable the pupil to see and understand the occupations of his own locality has already been made clear. Such materials must usually be gathered through original research. If, however, the research is accomplished by sound techniques, adequately reported, and mimeographed or printed in reasonably durable form, it will constitute valuable content for the study of occupations for a number of years, depending upon the tempo of change of the community.

A useful exposition of such surveys was published a few years ago by

[42] It is planned to issue biennial editions in the odd years (1959, 1961, etc.) See Seymour L. Wolfbein, "The New Occupational Outlook Program," *Vocational Guidance Quarterly,* Vol. IV (Winter, 1955–56), pp. 48–50.

[43] Edited by Lloyd E. Blauch (Washington, D.C., U.S. Department of Health, Education, and Welfare, 1955).

the United States Office of Education.[44] From this bulletin of 200 pages one may learn much about how to make such investigations. It analyzes nearly a hundred community occupational surveys, made in the decade of the 1930s, as to purposes, sponsorship, financial support, method, personnel, preparation of data, and so on. Descriptions of a number of surveys of varied character comprise Part II of the bulletin. One of these descriptions is of the survey made in a rural community of Maryland with a population of 4,200. It was directed by the counselor and carried on as a project of the 9B English classes. The details of technique and reporting are explained sufficiently to make clear what a serviceable investigation can be carried on in a small school without special funds. Other surveys of more pretentious character, involving whole states or large cities, expert help, and special financial support are individually described. An appendix of exhibits shows the forms used in gathering data in several of the surveys. Techniques are summarized by an "outline of the steps to be taken in a community occupational survey."

A more recent source of information on the gathering of local occupational information is the quite extended treatment accorded this subject by Baer and Roeber.[45] These authors report practice in many surveys, reproduce forms used, and have definite suggestions to offer for the step-by-step procedure of a survey.

Three examples of local occupational information in print are the following:

a. *Occupations in Davenport,* edited by Lawrence B. Kenyon, and published by the Independent School District of Davenport, Iowa, in January, 1951, is an 8½ by 11-inch printed book of 76 two-column pages. It includes well-chosen pictures of Davenport workers, some graphs and charts of the national scene as reproduced from publications of the Bureau of Labor Statistics, and a few significant pictographs from other national sources. The book is used in a tenth-grade course in occupations.[46]

b. *Your Career Opportunities in Evansville Industry* is a 9 by 12-inch book of 192 pages, published by a strong community effort in Evansville, Indiana,[47] and paid for by 59 companies. Job analysts from the Indiana Employment Security Division, specialists in economic research, and several writers pooled their talents to produce a book for which "The No. 1 criterion was accuracy. No. 2 was interest—words and pictures, facts and ideas that high-school students can understand."

[44] Marguerite W. Zapoleon, *Community Occupational Surveys.* Vocational Division Bulletin No. 223, Occupational Information and Guidance Series No. 10 (Washington, D.C., U.S. Office of Education, 1942).

[45] *Op. cit.,* Chs. X, XI.

[46] Lawrence B. Kenyon, "A Course in Occupations," *Bulletin of the National Association of Secondary-School Principals,* Vol. XXXII (November, 1948), pp. 131–138.

[47] The description of this book and the story of its production may be found in the following article: H. F. Williams, Jr., "The Town Tells Teens about Jobs," *Personnel and Guidance Journal,* Vol. XXXII (January, 1954), pp. 266–269.

c. An Occupational Handbook for Middletown (N.Y.), by John H. Brochard, is a publication of the Career Pattern Study, directed by Donald E. Super. It sets forth major facts about the occupations of the community in accordance with a formal outline which is followed for each occupational group. It is a straight-forward source of information, especially emphasizing the existing placement of workers between the ages of 15 and 24, and bringing together the results of a questionnaire to employers and local census data. No attempt was made to achieve such a standard of readability as characterizes the other two examples of local occupational information which have been cited.

PUPIL LEARNING ACTIVITIES[48]

Reading

So much has been said in this chapter about reading as a pupil activity in the study of occupations that perhaps excessive employment of it has been encouraged. That is indeed one of the long-time errors into which society falls when it commits the child to the school. The symbols of the printed page are necessary to short-cut the experience of the race, but we tend to forget that the symbols are but symbols, and that they can have no meaning except in terms of the child's experience with real things. Naturally, one way to avoid the excessive emphasis on reading is to keep in mind other activities of learning, such as those which will be taken up in this section. The artificiality of reading may be overcome if the teacher will accept and adhere firmly to the thought that reading must be a form of experience, that it must be a mode of observing occupations and vicariously participating in the labors and lives of workers, or that reading must mean to the pupil a way of obtaining the answers to problems which he feels to be his very own. With such criteria in mind, the teacher will select readings through which the learner can see and do; he will stimulate purposes which give the student an impetus to consult occupational literature.

Observation, First-Hand and Second-Hand

We have a course in occupations because the world is too complex for the child to observe workers after the easy fashion in which Ben Franklin's father took him around colonial Boston. But the teacher must remember that observation is one of Nature's modes of learning. When an occupational group is introduced for study, it would seem that one of the first steps taken by the teacher would be to ask the class how many members have seen such workers, where such workers may now be seen, how many have parents, relatives, or friends engaged in the occupation. Observations that have been

[48] A classic treatment of the types of learning activity is the following reference: Franklin Bobbitt, *How to Make a Curriculum* (Boston, Houghton Mifflin, 1924), Ch. IV.

made or that can be made would be employed as capital for the study. If the class can make observations as a group, certainly that is an advantage that should be grasped. There are many obstacles to the organization of a trip or excursion, and if they can be overcome there still are severe problems of preparation, organization, and review of the experience.

Rich in suggestion for the use of this activity is Forrester's chapter on "Visits to Places of Employment."[49] Some thirty years ago a unique way of doing something about the problem of pupil observation of workers was developed in a large Midwestern city. Under this plan one pupil representative of every class in occupations in each high school of the city met a guide at the City Hall each Saturday morning at nine o'clock. With advance arrangements made, the group visited some industrial or commercial establishment to observe the workers. Then each representative reported to his class on Monday morning. Such a plan seems to obviate many of the severe strictures on the use of the educational excursion and to afford a method of bringing reality into the classroom each week.

Listening to Talks by Workers

This is an activity already touched upon in connection with career conferences. The teacher will be alert to opportunities for judicious employment of this activity. The handbook of the New Trier Township High School, Winnetka, Illinois, says (p. 64): "Career Clubs—one for boys and one for girls—provide opportunities to learn about various vocations. A boy or girl who is an active member of a Career Club during the junior and senior years will hear about twenty-five or thirty different people who are authorities in their fields speak on an equal number of different vocations."

Interviewing Workers

One of the services to vocational guidance often rendered by service clubs, especially Kiwanis, is the tendering to high-school pupils of invitations to visit the members at their places of employment. Here the pupil meets the worker and talks with him under conditions which are realistic as the classroom can never be. Unfortunately, such realism is quite limited to the more favored occupations. Manual workers and the lower levels of white-collar workers are seldom members of service clubs.

Another situation in which pupils gather first-hand occupational information by interviewing workers is provided when they are used in the conduct of an occupational survey as described in the bulletin by Zapoleon referred to above. Aside from the complete community survey, field studies may be made by pupils, with noteworthy guidance advantages, said Florence E. Clark a few years ago.[50] She gave a suggested schedule and instructions by

[49] Gertrude Forrester, *Methods of Vocational Guidance* (Boston, Heath, 1951), Ch. 3.

[50] "Occupational Information in the Small Community—Part II: Field Studies," *Occupations,* Vol. XVI (December, 1937), pp. 245–251.

which pupils, after adequate preparation, could gather worth-while data by interviewing workers, preferably people who are known to them and who will co-operate with them willingly.

Picture-Viewing

Pictures enable one to observe that which is distant, remote, and inaccessible. Teachers of occupations and counselors need to be aware of this resource for educative experience and to plan the judicious use of it. The following references have recent lists of visual aids bearing on both the socializing and distributive purposes in the study of occupations:

> Gertrude Forrester, *Methods of Vocational Guidance* (Heath, 1951), Ch. 4.
> H. D. Kitson, *I Find My Vocation,* 4th ed. (McGraw-Hill, 1954).
> *Industrial Films, A Source of Occupational Information.* Occupational Analysis and Industrial Services Division, U.S. Employment Service, Department of Labor (February, 1946).

An excellent treatment of picture-viewing as a learning activity is Forrester's. She lists and describes many visual aids and succinctly states 21 suggestions for employing them. Kitson classifies his list of motion pictures according to the chapters of his book and therefore shows such titles as *Finding Your Life Work* and *How to Hunt a Job.*

Industrial Films describes 51 films representing 18 industries, selected from 175 reviewed by the Occupational Analysis Division. The films are selected primarily on the basis of their value for the training of the Division's occupational analysts, and therefore they focus especially on workers rather than on processes, which, of course, is the criterion by which to select pictures for guidance purposes. The annotations are extensive and use the titles of the workers by which they are listed in the *Dictionary of Occupational Titles.* Many of the films are produced by well-known corporations. Careful selection of materials from such sources is always necessary because the promotional purpose in their production is naturally dominant. The Division has rendered a service in making this selection.

To accompany Greenleaf's recent textbook, *Occupations and Careers,* the publishers, the McGraw-Hill Book Company, make available without charge a *Visual Aids List,* comprising almost 200 films and film strips.

The preparation of visual aids for the study of local occupations has been carried out in Racine, Wisconsin, and was interestingly reported a few years ago by Wood.[51] Finding that three out of every four children who attend school in that city later live and are employed in the city, the authorities felt the pertinency of having the children study local occupations. A well-selected committee gave thoughtful consideration to motion pictures, film strips, and slides, and chose the last as the best form of visual aid for their

[51] Harrison U. Wood, "Local Industries Help Make Film Material," *Occupations,* Vol. XIX (December, 1940), pp. 180–183.

purpose. They found the industries so enthusiastic in co-operation as to assume the financial support of the project. A five-year program was mapped out, and a science teacher, possessed of competence in photography and slide-making, started making pictures in the summer season and preparing sets of slides for each of the city's secondary schools.

A continuity, prepared by a committee of teachers, has been made available to accompany each set of material explaining every process and outlining requirements of workers in each type of job, number of workers employed locally, average number of openings per year, working conditions, machine operations, and other pertinent information. . . . The technical aspects of the material have been checked by representatives of the industries.

Wood's article deserves reading because it describes a plan which should be widely applicable.

Use of a Bulletin Board

So extensive has been the production of visual aids in connection with the output of occupational information that Forrester has a bibliography of nearly ten pages in her *Occupational Literature* (pp. 389–397) listing "Charts, Posters, and Visual Aids." They are issued by various professional societies, the military branches, large business concerns, the commercial publishers of occupational literature, and others. Individual mention will be made of the charts from only three sources: (1) The Champaign Guidance Charts. These are a series of twenty-five 12 by 18-inch charts designed to show the relationship between school subjects and vocations, published by the Senior High School, Champaign, Illinois. (2) A series of twelve charts prepared by the Women's Bureau, United States Department of Labor, presenting graphic data on the distribution of women workers by age, marital status, and major occupation group, with emphasis on trends. (3) The Wall Chart Series, from the Bureau of Labor Statistics, depicting major facts about the workers of various occupations or fields. Wall Chart No. 30, February, 1956, is devoted to "Electrical and Electronic Occupations," showing how electrical craftsmen and electronic technicians are distributed among industries.

These visual aids can do much to stimulate interest in occupations study. A plan should be made for proper filing of them when not in use and for frequent changing of those on display. The bulletin board which presents a new face every week is the one which catches the interest of students.

Taking Tests of Abilities and Interests

Occasionally one hears of a course in occupations in which tests of aptitude and inventories of interests are administered to the pupils. This activity is carried on in connection with the self-analysis which is commonly a unit in the course. The test results are made the object of discussion and interpretation to the end that the pupil will have a better understanding of his occupational potentialities. Obviously, the distributive purpose is paramount in these activities. If they are carried out under a teacher trained to the proper use of them and with due regard for the relative immaturity of the pupils, they afford highly significant learnings, but the learning lies in the results rather than in the taking of the tests. The Chicago course referred to earlier in this chapter is one of the best known for this test-taking activity.[52]

By taking due account of the several types of learning activity the teacher will far more certainly attain the objectives of the course. He must avoid the monotony that would come from simply studying each occupation or group of occupations according to the points of the Basic Outline. That was evidently in the mind of Lincoln when she wrote a chapter of 128 pages entitled "Varying the Class Procedure."[53]

FILING OCCUPATIONAL MATERIAL

Earlier in this chapter a discussion of the different types of printed materials for the study of occupations made evident the severity of the problem of classifying and filing them for ready access to pupils, teachers, and counselors. Some of the material is in book form, some is in pamphlet form, some in leaflet or folder form. Some items take up just one occupation, others take up a number of occupations. Some items do not describe occupations but portray the occupational structure and trends, discuss the choice of a life work, contribute education on how to get a job, or treat of other topics within the field.

From time to time through the years an article has appeared in a magazine or in a pamphlet giving the experience and suggested solution of some person trained to cope with this problem of filing. The writer has reviewed this literature, including the excellent series of articles which appeared in *Occupations* in the year 1943–44, the extended treatment of the subject by Baer and Roeber,[54] and the articles by Brammer and Williams,[55] Long and Worthington,[56] and Melum.[57] It will be most advantageous for the treatment of the subject in this chapter for the writer to describe the plan which has impressed him as the best one for a school or college library. That is the plan developed by Elizabeth Neal for Compton College, Compton, California

---

[52] Blanche B. Paulson, *op. cit.*

[53] Mildred E. Lincoln, *Teaching about Vocational Life* (Scranton, Pa., International Textbook Co., 1937), Ch. VI.

[54] *Op. cit.,* Ch. XII.

[55] Lawrence Brammer and Milton Williams, Jr. "Organization and Operation of a Vocational Library," *Occupations,* Vol. XXIX (December, 1950), pp. 177–181.

[56] Louis Long and Henrietta Worthington, "The Vocational Library," *Occupations,* Vol. XXX (November, 1951), pp. 115–118.

[57] Verna V. Melum, "Filing Plan for Occupational Materials," *Personnel and Guidance Journal,* Vol. XXXIV (October, 1955), pp. 106–109.

(Grades XI, XII, XIII, XIV), a school which enrolled about 3,500 students at the time of her writing.[58]

Neal describes the Vocational Guidance Alcove which she created without reference to or help from any guidance specialist. She has a four-drawer letter file with about 200 folders for as many vocations, arranged alphabetically and containing pamphlet material, clippings, and bibliographies. Inside each folder is stapled the bibliography of the occupation, listing the resources of the library on that occupation under (1) book references (about 300 books are arranged in the alcove by author), (2) monographs in series (filed separately in lower drawers of vertical file), (3) periodical references, and (4) pamphlets (which are in the folder containing the bibliography). The bibliographies in the folders are carbon copies, the original copies being assembled in one master bibliography in a ring notebook on the attendant's desk. At the end of the vertical file for vocations are five folders with the following general headings: character and personality development, choosing your life work, choosing employees, how to get a job, and success on the job.

It is Neal's belief that such a system is easiest for students to use and that it is so simple that it can be administered by clerical personnel under the direction of the librarian. Its use by the students is encouraged by the distribution among classroom groups of mimeographed, alphabetical lists of the vocations on which the library has materials. Undoubtedly the initial task of making the very useful bibliographies is onerous, but they contribute enormously to the usefulness of the library. Neal points out that space is left at the end of each bibliography for additional entries to be made as new materials come to the library. These additions are made in ink. As they become numerous, and as old entries should be removed because they represent obsolete materials, a bibliography is retyped.

Neal's system seems to be the one best devised to meet the needs of pupils and faculty in a secondary school or college. But one impression gained from the study of all the literature on filing is the desirability of some collaboration between guidance specialist and librarian in devising and maintaining the filing system. The specialist's knowledge of the field should be placed at the librarian's disposal in deciding on categories and in finding and evaluating materials for the library. The collaboration should, of course, extend to the training of pupils to understand the filing system.

As the concluding thought on this chapter, it is perhaps in point now to ask the reader some questions concerning practices revealed in the first two sections. Is group instruction in occupations and occupation choosing adequately discharged by a six-week unit in a ninth-grade civics course? Is there in this guidance feature content of such value and requiring such specialized preparation to teach, that justice cannot be done to it by English

[58] "Filing Occupational Information Alphabetically," *Occupations,* Vol. XXII (May, 1944), pp. 503–506.

teachers or homeroom teachers? If the answers to these questions signify dissatisfaction with casual or incidental teaching of occupations, we shall have to think of adequate representation for it in the curriculum, of how to obtain teachers for it who are adequately trained and disposed to accept its challenge, of gathering materials and equipment calculated to achieve the values in "occupationology."

QUESTIONS, PROBLEMS, AND INVESTIGATIONS

1. Canvass several high schools in your district to ascertain their practices in acquainting pupils with occupations. Try to estimate how adequately the practices are serving the socializing and the distributive purposes.

2. Compare three high-school textbooks in occupations for their relative emphasis on the distributive and socializing purposes.

3. Make a study of one of the monthly or quarterly indexes to current occupational materials. Trace some occupation through a year's issues to see how many references are listed as bearing on it; note the character of the references, their availability, and their usefulness to high-school pupils, teachers, and counselors.

4. Compare some of the series of commercially produced monographs listed in Part V of Forrester's *Occupational Literature.* How do they correspond to the "Standards for Use in Preparing and Evaluating Occupational Literature"?

5. Analyze the *Occupational Outlook Handbook* to check the proportions of space given to professional, business, clerical, skilled, semi-skilled, and unskilled occupations.

6. Evaluate in terms of the "Standards for . . . Occupational Literature" three of the job descriptions in the *Occupational Outlook Handbook.*

7. Define the economic area in which you teach. Ascertain the population movements which will affect the pupils of your high school after they graduate or drop out of school. In the light of this information list the occupations most appropriate for your pupils to study for performance of the distributive function, and estimate the relative emphasis to be given to them.

8. What are the occupational trends of your economic area? Assess the influence of advancing technology and of shifting demands for goods and services.

9. Plan a career conference for your school.

10. Take inventory of the occupational literature in your school library, then list the needed additions in the order of urgency of need.

SELECTED REFERENCES

Occupational Research and Information

ANDERSON, H. D., and DAVIDSON, P. E., *Occupational Trends in the United States* (1940), and *Recent Occupational Trends in American Labor* (1945) (Stanford, Cal., Stanford University Press).

CAPLOW, Theodore, *The Sociology of Work* (Minneapolis, Minn., University of Minnesota Press, 1954).

CLARK, Florence E., "Occupational Information in the Small Community," *Oc-*

cupations, Vol. XVI (November and December, 1937), pp. 117–122, 245–251.

Comparative Occupation Statistics for the United States, 1870 to 1940, Sixteenth Census of the United States, 1940 (Prepared by Alba M. Edwards) (Washington, D.C., Government Printing Office, 1943).

FORRESTER, Gertrude, *Occupational Literature: An Annotated Bibliography* (H. W. Wilson Co., 1954).

HASTINGS, Edgar C., and HUTSON, P. W., "State Regulation of Occupational Activity," *Occupations,* Vol. XX (January, 1942), pp. 247–252.

HURLIN, Ralph G., and GIVENS, Meredith B., "Shifting Occupational Patterns," *Recent Social Trends,* Vol. I (Ch. VI) (New York, McGraw-Hill, 1933), pp. 268–324.

MOORE, Louise, *Girls' and Women's Occupations: Selected References, July, 1948–September, 1954.* Vocational Division Bulletin No. 257 (Washington, D.C., U.S. Office of Education, 1955).

NVGA Bibliography of Current Occupational Literature (Washington 5, D.C., National Vocational Guidance Association, 1956).

SHARTLE, Carroll, *Occupational Information: Its Development and Application,* 2nd ed. (Englewood Cliffs, N.J., Prentice-Hall, 1952).

"Standards for Use in Preparing and Evaluating Occupational Literature," *Occupations,* Vol. XXVIII (February, 1950), pp. 319–324.

"Ten Years of Occupational Research," *Occupations,* Vol. XXII (April, 1944), pp. 387–446.

THOMAS, Lawrence, *The Occupational Structure and Education* (Englewood Cliffs, N.J., Prentice-Hall, 1956).

WILLIAMS, H. F., Jr., "The Town Tells Teens about Jobs," *Personnel and Guidance Journal,* Vol. XXXII (January, 1954), pp. 266–269.

WOOD, Harrison U., "Local Industries Help Make Film Material," *Occupations,* Vol. XIX (December, 1940), pp. 180–183.

ZAPOLEON, Marguerite W., *Community Occupational Surveys.* Vocational Division Bulletin No. 223, Occupational Information and Guidance Series No. 10 (Washington, D.C., U.S. Office of Education, 1942).

Disseminating Occupational Information

BENNETT, Margaret E., *Guidance in Groups* (New York, McGraw-Hill, 1955).

Committee on Social Studies of the Commission on the Reorganization of Secondary Education of the National Education Association. *The Social Studies in Secondary Education* (Washington, D.C., U.S. Bureau of Education Bulletin, No. 28, 1916), pp. 26–29.

FORRESTER, Gertrude, *Methods of Vocational Guidance* (Boston, Heath, 1951).

HETZEL, Walter L., "Geographical Study of All Graduates of an Iowa High School," *School Review,* Vol. L (April, 1942), pp. 294–297.

HOPPOCK, Robert, *Occupational Information: Where to Get It and How to Use It in Counseling and Teaching* (New York, McGraw-Hill, 1957).

———, and LOWENSTEIN, Norman, "The Teaching of Occupations in 1951," *Occupations,* Vol. XXX (January, 1952), pp. 274–276.

HOPPOCK, Robert, and STEVENS, Nancy, "High School Courses in Occupations," *Personnel and Guidance Journal,* Vol. XXXII (May, 1954), pp. 540–543.

KENYON, Lawrence B., "A Course in Occupations," *Bulletin of the National Association of Secondary-School Principals,* Vol. XXXII (November, 1948), pp. 131–138.

LINCOLN, Mildred E., *Teaching About Vocational Life* (Scranton, Pa., International Textbook Co., 1937).

PAULSON, Blanche B., "A Chicago Course Called 'Careers,' " *Occupations,* Vol. XXIX (May, 1951), pp. 591–594.

SHOSTECK, Robert, "How Well Are We Putting Across Occupational Information?" *Personnel and Guidance Journal,* Vol. XXXIII (January, 1955), pp. 265–269.

SINICK, Daniel, and HOPPOCK, Robert, "Research on the Teaching of Occupations, 1945–1951," *Personnel and Guidance Journal,* Vol. XXXII (November, 1953), pp. 147–150.

WEAVER, Glen L., *How, When, and Where to Provide Occupational Information* (Chicago, Science Research Associates, 1955).

WRIGHT, Barbara, "A Method of Using the Group Conference as a Guidance Device," *Vocational Guidance Magazine,* Vol. VII (October, 1928), pp. 26–33.

Filing Occupational Material

BRAMMER, Lawrence, and WILLIAMS, Milton, Jr., "Organization and Operation of a Vocational Library," *Occupations,* Vol. XXIX (December, 1950), pp. 177–181.

LONG, Louis, and WORTHINGTON, Henrietta, "The Vocational Library," *Occupations,* Vol. XXX (November, 1951), pp. 115–118.

MELUM, Verna V., "Filing Plan for Occupational Materials," *Personnel and Guidance Journal,* Vol. XXXIV (October, 1955), pp. 106–109.

NEAL, Elizabeth, "Filing Occupational Information Alphabetically," *Occupations,* Vol. XXII (May, 1944), pp. 503–506.

General and Unclassified

BAER, Max F., and ROEBER, Edward C., *Occupational Information: Its Nature and Use,* rev. ed. (Chicago, Science Research Associates, 1958).

BREWER, John M., *History of Vocational Guidance* (New York, Harper, 1942).

GREENLEAF, Walter J., *Occupations—A Basic Course for Counselors* (Washington, D.C., U.S. Office of Education Bulletin No. 247, 1951).

MAHONEY, Harold J., *Occupational Information for Counselors: The Essential Content for Training Courses* (Yonkers, N.Y., World Book Co., 1952).

Vocational Guidance Quarterly, Washington 5, D.C., National Vocational Guidance Association.

CHAPTER 10

The Homeroom and

Alternative Organizations

IN MANY SCHOOLS the homeroom is the most important feature of the guidance program, or at least the most important *recognized* feature. At the same time, it is more than a guidance feature, in terms of the definition of the guidance function stated in Chapter 1. It serves significant developmental purposes. In short, the homeroom is ideally conceived as a sort of residuary legatee to any and all services which may be needed by the individual pupil and which are not performed by other agencies of the school. In this chapter we shall have to think of the whole work of the homeroom; to disentangle the guidance from the developmental functions in this instance seems impossible and impracticable.

ORIGIN AND PURPOSES OF THE HOMEROOM

In Its Beginnings

The homeroom apparently was born as a device in high-school administration too insignificant to merit recording. No account of its origin is available. The growth of interest in the guidance movement brought about its frequent mention in educational literature in the early 1920s. An earlier account which is of interest because of its detailed definition of duties is Ballou's report on the "official teacher" in New York City high schools as he found that functionary in the 1911 survey of New York City schools:[1]

Most teachers in the high schools have also charge of an official class. Each official class teacher, as a rule, performs the following or similar functions. . . .
1. Keeping a record of the attendance of pupils. This involves (*a*) recording and reporting attendance; (*b*) computing the average monthly attendance; (*c*) keeping a list of parents and pupils, and their addresses, and notifying parents of

[1] Frank W. Ballou, *High School Organization* (Yonkers, N.Y., World Book, 1914), pp. 81–83.

pupils' absences; and (*d*) keeping an excuse book for absences. (*e*) It also involves, in some schools, issuing "admits" to classes after an absence.

2. Care and distribution of textbooks and supplies. Besides the general supervision of the proper use of books, this involves (*a*) keeping a card, or book list, of all books given out; and (*b*) receipting for the book when returned. Classroom work is seriously interfered with at times by pupils getting books when they enter late in the term, or by pupils who return books before leaving school.

3. Copying records. This means (*a*) making in duplicate (in some schools, triplicate) the promotion cards of each pupil; (*b*) copying program cards of each pupil; (*c*) copying report of each pupil for parents twice or three times each term; and (*d*) copying marks of each pupil on permanent record cards.

4. Having charge of discipline of pupils in the official class. In most schools the official class teacher has charge of the conduct of the pupils in the official class during the day.

5. Disseminating school notices and general information. The teacher in charge of an official class is the general administrative agency for that group of pupils. In some schools this includes supervising the progress of pupils, while, in others, grade advisers do that work.

6. Looking after wardrobes and lockers; issuing keys, replacing lost keys, and canceling receipts at the close of the term, or when the pupils leave school.

7. Counseling pupils about their election of studies and progress in their work, together with other general administrative duties.

The official class seems to be a necessary part of the organization of large high schools, because it brings about harmony and unity of action. It seems to be a satisfactory method of bringing the pupils into direct contact with the administrative agencies of the school. . . .

Analysis of these duties will indicate the possibility of classifying them in the following major categories:

Administrative and clerical
Disciplinary
Educational counseling

In the small high schools—enrolling, perhaps, not more than 200 pupils—these functions are the responsibility of the principal. Typically, he meets the entire student body in a combination assembly room and study hall two or four times a day. Having such immediate contact, he takes the roll, makes announcements, talks with individual students as necessary and desirable about problems of discipline or educational counsel, handles report cards and permanent record cards. Thus he makes unnecessary the "official class" teacher.

In larger schools it is impracticable if not impossible for the principal to discharge these functions. He therefore delegates them to the teachers, who, in this capacity, are called "official class" teachers, "report room" teachers, "advisers," "homeroom" teachers, or by some other name. With ever larger proportions of our adolescent youth in school, more and more schools are aggregations of pupils too large for much direct contact with the principal.

The school organized in homerooms has therefore become a common phenomenon.

No one will argue that this organization has been adopted so widely because the functions are more adequately performed than when the principal discharged them himself. In fact, the reason for the establishment of the homeroom system seems to have been purely that of expediency: the principal cannot do the work; therefore let it be distributed among the teachers. In general, there has been no compensating subtraction from other duties of the teachers; to their former load has been added this new cluster of responsibilities.

As It Is Idealized Today

In many schools of the present the homeroom is functioning at approximately the level described by Ballou. But since the early 1920s a conception of larger educational possibilities for it has been voiced with increasing frequency. Its place as an administrative agency is minimized or taken for granted, and its roles in development and guidance have been maximized.

Impetus to the advocacy and the acceptance of the modern view of the homeroom has come from the modern view of education, its values and its methods. Sensitivity to individual variation and to the need for individualized education made us conscious of the mass-production technique in our schools and of its inadequacy. Chapter 3 (pages 93–100) delineates this characteristic at some length and also touches briefly on measures taken to offset it. The homeroom is envisioned as of major importance among such measures. It is expected to bring about intimate contact between the pupil and one teacher, to give each pupil one teacher who will assume responsibility for his well-rounded development. In the eyes of the homeroom teacher the needs of the whole pupil will be paramount. The resources of the school will be thoughtfully drawn upon for each pupil according to his needs, and the teacher will himself be a general resource independent of any subject specialty.

The homeroom is regarded as an expression of the modern school's responsibility for the individual pupil. Attitudes have changed markedly in this respect. Forty years ago when John found algebra unintelligible and uninteresting and quietly dropped out of school, no one was greatly stirred. The school people complacently pursued the even tenor of their way, satisfied with their own explanation that John just wasn't made for high school. The passing years have created a new attitude concerning the school's responsibility, an attitude which may be illustrated by the following two incidents that have been described to the writer, both connected with the home-visiting program carried on in a city school system.

At the end of the school day an exasperated teacher approached the vice-principal of a junior high school which served an underprivileged section of the city, and said, "I want you to lick Tom." The request brought no surprise, for Tom was well known at the office as a disciplinary problem. But the vice-principal asked, "Have you ever visited Tom's home?" "No." "Well, wouldn't you like to do that before we apply the paddle?" The teacher agreed to the suggestion and said she would make the visit that very afternoon. The next morning before school she made a brief report to the vice-principal, concluding, "*Don't* lick that boy. Don't *ever* lick that boy."

An English teacher reported to the counselor that Sally, a member of her homeroom and also a pupil in her ninth-grade English class, had been absent for several days, but added, "I don't think we should bother to investigate her absence. She's going to be sixteen in a few days, and I'm sure she intends to drop out then." The counselor studied a school record on Sally and said, "This record indicates that Sally will soon be *fifteen*. You'd better check the matter with Sally herself and see if she has a birth certificate or a baptismal certificate to verify or correct your impression of her age." The teacher found Sally at her home in a poverty-ridden section of town. "Oh, yes," said the girl, "I'm going to be sixteen all right. I have a baptismal certificate to prove it." They visited for a few minutes in the barren, cheerless living room while the early December twilight deepened. The teacher said, "I think I ought to be going now. I'd like to see the certificate so I can tell the counselor." "Yes, I know," said Sally, with diffidence; "it's upstairs in a trunk. I just hated to remove the light bulb here and leave you in the darkness while I look for it, but this bulb is the only one we've got." While she was gone, the teacher noticed the empty socket at the end of a drop-cord in the next room. After overnight contemplation of the bleak realities of Sally's existence, the teacher reported to the counselor, "I couldn't help but think of all the things I might have taught Sally. And here I've just been trying to teach her *Ivanhoe*."

Another conception of homeroom purpose and consequent activity has grown out of the modern view of the school as an institution for the socialization of youth. Such socialization is to be brought about primarily by the experience of membership in groups, by acting in concert with others, by planning and executing group projects. As the socialization must be for democratic living, the purposes to be realized through the planned activity must be democratically arrived at rather than externally imposed.

The homeroom is conceived of as having rich potentialities for this goal and this method in learning. James Bryant Conant in a recent address has said that "if the evidence I have obtained from students is to be trusted, by far the best method of developing social cohesion among the students is by the use of the homerooms for this purpose." The subject class is too subject-centered to offer this opportunity. The school group as a whole, with its hundreds or thousands of members, is too large, too formidable, to give each one a keen experience of membership. In contrast, the homeroom group, with its number typically ranging from 25 to 40, and its broad purpose of achieving individual welfare, is well calculated to become a closely knit group in which each member can do something tangible for the group and feel himself the beneficiary of the social service rendered by all the rest. This concept of the homeroom finds expression in the well-nigh universal emphasis on organization of the group with the usual officers and with committees on program, scholarship, welfare, housekeeping, social life, etc. Thus, we have the homeroom corresponding to a club, a group of people who practice teamwork to realize a good life together. Unlike most clubs, however, no one need apply for membership. The timid, the anti-social, the "fringers"—all who have the greatest need for socializing experience—are members along with the self-assured and the socially competent.

The homeroom as thus envisioned seems to be in harmony with important elements of educational theory today extant. It represents the acquisition of the attitudes, skills, and methods of democratic citizenship by practice and experience. It acknowledges the conditioning process as a supremely important method of establishing behavior patterns. It accepts the development of wholesome personalities as the major goal of educational endeavor. Illustrative examples of the homeroom at work in this spirit will be given in the next section.

HOMEROOM ACTIVITY

Individual Counseling

In the performance of the functions of the homeroom as they have just been described, it is apparent that individual counseling must be a major activity of the teacher. The continual study of his pupils is essential to the effectiveness of this form of service. The more adequately the teacher knows the pupil's home background and environment, his curricular and extra-curricular experiences and record, his health history and needs, and the evidence yielded by standardized tests, the better he is qualified for the work of advisement. Conferences with parents and with the subject teachers of the homeroom members will frequently be necessary, both for obtaining information and for giving it. Likewise the conferences with the pupils will be held for both purposes. An indispensable tool for effective counseling is the cumulative record, which is the repository of all essential information about the pupil as gathered in the course of his successive years in the school. To place a proper value on the many items which appear in a good cumulative record requires considerable technical knowledge. The next several chapters of this book will present a summary of this knowledge and of techniques of using it.

To what extent the homeroom teacher may be expected to possess the specialized knowledge and skill essential to individual counseling is indeed problematical. Obviously, the quality and quantity of such service rendered by the members of a high-school faculty will represent a wide variation, and the average will undoubtedly seem distressingly low to anyone who is trained in the field. Daily availability to a relatively small group of counselees is the notable advantage which the homeroom teacher has as compared with the one expert counselor trying to serve hundred of pupils. In contrast to the scheduled interviews in which the counselor meets the average pupil once or twice a year, the homeroom teacher may have unnumbered casual, unscheduled interviews in which the problem of establishing rapport is non-existent. And the homeroom teacher's daily contacts may enrich his understanding of his counselees far beyond the items faithfully recorded in the cumulative record. The permissive auxiliary "may" is used advisedly in these statements of the advantages of counseling by the homeroom teacher.

Perhaps the most crucial point in the homeroom teacher's exercise of individual counsel is his knowledge of when to call for help with a problem or when to refer a case to counselor, principal, physician, nurse, or other specialist. Some schools are so staffed that many such referrals can be made; in other schools the homeroom teacher must assume almost complete responsibility. Judgment in calling on specialists depends on sensitivity to the whole range of problems and sufficient knowledge of them to recognize one's own limitations in dealing with them. This merely suggests the framework within which the homeroom teacher must carry on individual counsel.

Group Programs

Advantages. The practice of organizing the homeroom group as a club, as mentioned in the preceding section, is designed to facilitate the group attack on common problems. For the teacher solely to employ individual counsel is unnecessarily wasteful. In the solution of their problems of choosing and of adjustment, pupils need information, and much of this information can be acquired by the whole group at once instead of being repeated for each individual. Group methods are as reasonable in the study of problems of educational and vocational choice, personal appearance, or how to obtain employment as they are in the study of any school subject. Due regard for economy of time would certainly dictate the group study of problems that are common to a majority of the pupils.

If the group is relatively homogeneous, the economy of group programs is the more apparent. A homeroom of pupils just entering the junior high school have the common problem of orientation and adjustment to the new school. In the ninth grade all have the need to understand the educational opportunities of the senior high school. In the eleventh grade correct form at the junior prom is a matter of common concern. In the twelfth grade many are ripe for close consideration of how to get a job. These examples are just suggestive of the many areas of problems in which the group attack can be fruitful, provided the group is reasonably homogeneous.

Experienced guidance workers have learned that a second advantage of the group program is that many adjustments can be accomplished which would be embarrassing to take up in the individual interview. Matters of personal appearance, grooming, manners, or other areas in which some pupils have not had adequate home training may be brought up impersonally and objectively with the whole group. A knowledge of good standards is thus disseminated in such fashion that the various members can become aware of their deficiencies without experiencing individual detraction.

In the third instance, group programs widen the area in which the home-room members think and feel and act as a group. They pool their efforts in the solution of problems. The individual develops perspective on his own problems as he realizes that others have problems, some of them the same as his own. His emotional tension and worry are thereby relieved. Working together on the most immediate concerns of their lives intensifies socialization, thus contributing to a most important purpose of the homeroom.

The Problems of the Pupils as the Major Source of Group Programs. Concerning the nature of homeroom programs much confusion seems to prevail. Many teachers are more or less at sea as regards the appropriate content. Principals and even counselors are likewise uncertain. What, then, is to be expected from pupil program committees? If they devote the period to impromptu entertainment or consider the purpose to be merely the exercise of various forms of self-expression by the different members—which is often just what happens—can we rightfully chide them for such frivolous use of their time?

Some writers have suggested that programs in celebration of holidays, of the birthdays of notable personages, and of anniversaries of great historical events should have a prominent place in the yearly calendar of homeroom programs. Others have suggested the presentation of hobbies, "amateur hours," or "Professor Quiz" programs. Some of these ideas in all probability represent quite a measure of external imposition, as was the case with programs on "Pennsylvania Week" which the writer witnessed in one high school. Others are entertainment.

This writer would like to dissipate the fog of uncertainty over homeroom programs by suggesting that they be derived for the most part from the pupils' own felt needs for help in the solution of the problems of their lives, especially the problems on which they receive no aid or insufficient aid from other school sources. With such a basis, the highest type of pupil motivation should prevail. While pupils vary as to the problems they feel, this general orientation of homeroom programs should make the activity highly meaningful to the group as a whole.

What *are* the problems of youth? Many inventories have been made in recent years in answer to this question. Curriculum makers have been active in conducting investigations to ascertain pupils' problems, for their thesis is that a primary point of reference for the entire curriculum should be the interests and needs of pupils.[2] Guidance workers, likewise, have surveyed

[2] Such a research is the following: Donald C. Doane, *The Needs of Youth: An Evaluation for Curriculum Purposes* (New York, Teachers College Contributions to Education, No. 848, 1942).

groups of children and youth to compile and classify their problems. Symonds has expressed the belief that under the following fifteen headings may be fitted practically all personal problems:[3]

1. Health. Eating, drinking, exercise, posture, sleep and rest, air and temperature, sunlight, clothing, bathing, care of special parts, cleanliness and prevention of disease, excretion, elimination, use of drugs.

2. Sex Adjustments. Love, petting, courtship, marriage.

3. Safety. Avoiding accidents and injuries.

4. Money. Earning, spending, saving, etc.

5. Mental Hygiene. Fears, worries, inhibitions, compulsions, feelings of inferiority, phantasies, etc.

6. Study Habits. Skills used in study, methods of work, problem solving.

7. Recreation. Sports and games, reading, arts and crafts, fellowship and social activities, hobbies.

8. Personal and Moral Qualities. Qualities leading to success, qualities of good citizenship.

9. Home and Family Relationships. Living harmoniously with members of the family.

10. Manners and Courtesy. Etiquette.

11. Personal Attractiveness. Personal appearance, voice, clothing.

12. Daily Schedule. Planning the twenty-four hours in a day.

13. Civic Interests, Attitudes, and Responsibilities.

14. Getting Along with Other People.

15. Philosophy of Life. Personal values, ambitions, ideals, religion.

The problems of adolescents have been listed by Strang in exhaustive detail in the 1935 edition of her work, *The Role of the Teacher in Personnel Work*.[4] The eleven major categories are as follows:

Problems of health and physical development
Problems of scholarship
Financial problems
Problems of family relationships
Sex problems
Religious problems
Moral and disciplinary problems
Personality difficulties
Social problems
Problems relating to living conditions
Problems of vocational guidance

Each of the categories is broken down into several areas, and the problems are listed under the areas.

Counselors of ninth-grade pupils in the Phoenix (Arizona) Union High School recently contributed a total of 240 questions which they found their

3 P. M. Symonds, "The Principal Areas of Personal Problems," *Teachers College Record*, Vol. XXXVIII (November, 1936), pp. 144–145.
4 Ruth Strang (New York, Teachers College, Columbia University), pp. 175–186

pupils asking as individuals or in orientation groups.[5] The questions were classified under the following five headings: I. Educational problems; II. Vocational problems; III. Family problems; IV. Boy-girl problems; and V. Other personal-social problems. Examples of the problems in three areas are as follows:

I. Educational Problems
  5. *Student-teacher relationships*
    How can I get along with a teacher who I feel dislikes me?
    What should be my behavior when I feel a teacher has been unreasonable?
    Can a teacher lower your grade for chewing gum?
    If you just can't get along with a teacher, what do you have to do in order to change?
    I can't understand the way Mr. X teaches. Will you change me to Mr. Z?
    How old can you be and still teach?

III. Family Problems
  1. *Achieving increasing independence*
    Shouldn't my parents give me an allowance?
    How much allowance should I expect to get?
    How do you go about getting your allowance increased?
    If I earn money, shouldn't I be allowed to spend it the way I want to?
    Should I date a boy whom my parents don't know?
    How can I get my folks to let me go out with boys?
    What should I do when I'm in a group and I have to be home early and they don't?
    How can I make my parents stop treating me like a baby?

IV. Boy-Girl Problems
  1. *How to behave*
    How can I turn a date down without hurting his feelings?
    How do you invite a boy to a dance?
    What do you do about transportation to a dance if the boy is not old enough to drive?
    What do you talk about on dates?
    What do you do if he wants to kiss you goodnight?

Locating the problems of pupils is obviously a primary step in the use of such content for group programs. One way to do this is by means of the informal inventory in which the pupils write freely about the problems of their lives. A number of the author's students who are teachers in service have employed this technique and thereby obtained excellent statements from which they made tabulations showing the frequency with which the various problems were mentioned. Naturally, one or more main conditions must be met to get satisfactory results from this method. First, the pupils must feel a complete trust in the teacher. They must feel that their confidence will not be

5 "What Do Freshmen Want to Know?" *The Phoenix,* Vol. V (Spring, 1948), pp. 3–10.

betrayed. They must feel sure that the information will only be used to promote their own good.

Second, their powers of recall and of expression of their problems must be stimulated. A favorite device used by teachers who have had success with the informal inventory has been the introduction of the project by talking to the pupils for a half-hour or more about the problems of children or youth of the age of the group to be inventoried. Commonly they have turned to Strang's comprehensive list cited above, written the main categories on the blackboard, and talked to the pupils about the problems comprising each category. Then they have asked the pupils to write the problems of *their* lives which fall in each of the categories. Some may fear that such procedure is too suggestive of problems, that it simply puts ideas in pupils' heads. The answer is that without such stimulation the crop of problems yielded will be so slim as in no way to correspond to reality. When a teacher asks pupils to write the problems of their lives and offers no further definition, he will usually get problems mainly in the area of school duties and obligations, such as, "I get nervous when I take tests," and "It is hard for me to understand algebra." The pupil takes it for granted that the problems with which his teacher is concerned are school problems. It must be made clear to him that the scope of the inquiry is no such narrow segment but the complete circle of his life.

A second method of locating the problems of pupils is by the administration of a list of problems on which the pupil can check those that he feels are his. One of the best known of the published instruments of this kind is the Mooney Problem Check List[6] which lists in the High School Form (a College Form and a Junior High School Form are also available), 330 problems, classified in the following 11 areas with 30 problems in each area:

> Health and physical development
> Finances, living conditions, and employment
> Social and recreational activities
> Courtship, sex, and marriage
> Social-psychological relations
> Personal-psychological relations
> Morals and religion
> Home and family
> The future: vocational and educational
> Adjustment to school work
> Curriculum and teaching procedures

The subject is directed to read through the list and underline the problems which are troubling him. On completion he is directed to look back over the items he has underlined and circle the numbers in front of the problems which are troubling him most.

[6] By Ross L. Mooney, Bureau of Educational Research (Columbus, Ohio, Ohio State University, 1941).

Mooney has described, for individuals and for the group, the data which were obtained by the application of the Check List to 603 high-school students.[7] In this survey he found that pupils varied widely in the number of problems they checked and that the median number checked was 20. To the question, "Have you enjoyed filling out the List?" 94 per cent of the pupils responded affirmatively; 84 per cent asked particularly for an individual conference with someone to talk about their problems.

In the use of such an instrument a factor not to be ignored is the extent to which truthful responses will be obtained. Will the subject admit his problems and admit all of them? No easy check of such validity can be obtained. The difference in responses when the subjects are anonymous and when they identify themselves has, however, been ascertained. Fischer had his psychology classes—all women—take the College Form of the Mooney Problem Check List at the time they were studying personality and its measurement.[8] By his own estimate he had achieved excellent rapport and individual acquaintanceship with his students. He pointed out to them when he introduced the List that the taking of it could serve two purposes, namely, to acquaint them with an instrument for psychological study, and to make available to him an inventory of their individual problems on the basis of which he might counsel them individually. Their papers, he said, would be held in complete confidence.

A week later he had them take the List again, asking them not to sign their names, so that he could turn the papers over to his assistant who would find frequencies, general trends, etc., for the entire group.

From these two administrations of the List the median numbers of problems disclosed were as follows:

	Unsigned papers	Signed papers
Problems checked	36.00	34.37
Problems underlined	11.32	8.11

The study thus showed that the use of signatures had some inhibitory effect on honesty and frankness, especially as regards the admission of the more serious personal problems.

This limitation would not apply if the List were employed solely to form a basis for group discussions and counsel, because signatures would not then be necessary. And it is with the group program that we are here concerned. Whatever the means employed to ascertain the pupils' problems and to bring about serious, helpful study of the problems, it is apparent that the

[7] Ross L. Mooney, "Surveying High School Students' Problems by Means of a Problem Check List," *Educational Research Bulletin,* Vol. XXI (March 18, 1942), pp. 57–69.

[8] Robert P. Fischer, "Signed Versus Unsigned Personal Questionnaires," *Journal of Applied Psychology,* Vol. XXX (June, 1946), pp. 220–225.

factor of personal relations between pupils and between the pupils and the teacher are the major determinant of the effectiveness of group programs.

Other Group Activity

If a homeroom group is to carry on most vigorously its functions of guidance and socialization, it will engage in many group activities other than that of discussion. The members will work together and play together. They will plan and they will create in accordance with their felt needs. Of the many illustrative examples that might be given, space permits citation of only two.

Strang describes the activities of an unusual homeroom group in the Bloom Junior High School of Cincinnati.[9] The group consisted of twenty-five boys of low ability and considerable retardation. "The members . . . started with the worst truancy and tardiness record in the school and ended with the best attendance and punctuality rating of any homeroom." Responsibility for these matters was assumed by the boys themselves and carried out by a committee of three of their own election. These boys had not cared a "hang" about their personal appearance but in the course of a year "came to have the most brightly shined shoes and the best-cleaned and pressed clothes of all the pupils in the school." To bring about this change they did some very practical things. They built a shoe-shining stand in their homeroom. They set up simple cobbling equipment and a washtub and steam pressing board purchased by the Board of Education. They performed services for other pupils and teachers of the school and established a homeroom treasury.

Finding they had a surplus in their treasury, they decided to have a banquet in the school. The home economics department agreed to serve it. When the problem of table manners came up, the boys met it in their usual direct way. They asked the home economics teacher to give them instruction and elected a committee of three to check on the manners of the group during a two-week period. They learned techniques necessary for feeling at ease in social situations. Needless to say, the banquet was a great success.

These boys developed the keen sense of membership and the feeling of individual worth which were necessary to stem their drift toward juvenile delinquency.

A sixth-grade homeroom group of 15 boys and 20 girls chose as their major purpose "To learn to get along better with other people"; adopted as their name, "The Golden Rule Club"; and voted that each member should make a pledge to live up to the Golden Rule.[10]

[9] Ruth Strang, "Prevention of Delinquency through Guided Group Experience," Ch. 4 of *Juvenile Delinquency and the Schools,* Forty-seventh Yearbook, Part I, National Society for the Study of Education (Chicago, University of Chicago Press, 1948), pp. 88–90.

[10] This example was reported in an unpublished paper by Katherine Chomosh, a teacher in the Jefferson School, Monessen, Pa.

With the coming of Easter the pupils began making plans for a party. Several meetings were devoted to the planning of the program, refreshments, decorations, etc. Of course, there wasn't a pupil who wasn't vitally interested in the most minute detail. It was during my absence a few weeks before the party that some decisions were made concerning the party which were not satisfactory to several of the boys. They stated flatly that they wished to "quit the club" because the girls got to do everything, and all decisions were in their favor. Again it was necessary to spend a meeting in discussion and study of parliamentary procedure and to point out the fact that although the girls had a majority, every person, boy or girl, had a voice in the government of his club and had every right to express his opinions and objections. Another meeting was spent in discussion of the meaning of the democratic philosophy, the greatest good to the greatest number. Both the boys and girls stated their viewpoints and both decided that they were being selfish and were not living up to their pledge to observe the Golden Rule. The boys were told that they were welcome in the club and would receive every consideration, but the final decision as to whether they wished to be members must be their own. Membership in the club was voluntary, not forced. When the vote of the eight boys was taken as to whether or not they wished to continue with their club membership, four voted "Yes" and four "No."

Club activities returned to normal then, with the four nonmembers listening but not taking part in any meetings. Plans for the Easter party headed the list of business activities and every decision was the result of cooperative group planning of both boys and girls. A few weeks later the four nonmembers expressed the desire to be reinstated in the club. A special meeting was called to consider the matter. It was the most interesting meeting of the year, a real test of the pupils' ability to get along with each other. The president was remarkable in her power of leadership and foresight. Upon opening the meeting she asked each boy to express his reason for wanting to become a member of the club again.

"We don't get to do anything with the class," one said.

"I feel lost without the club," said another.

The class pondered.

The president's next question was, "How can we be sure you aren't just joining the club so that you can take part in the Easter party?" (It was only a few days before the party.)

The boys' spokesman replied, "If that's the way you feel, why don't you wait until after the party to accept us? We'll still want to be members then, even if we don't take part in the party."

That was convincing enough for the class. They voted unanimously in favor of accepting the four new members, who became the most active, most cooperative ones in the group.

In my opinion, the chief value of this particular homeroom program lay, not in the material presented in the planned dramatizations, discussions, and writing activities, but rather in the participation in the activities of the club organization —the doing of things together, sharing responsibilities, planning activities, making decisions, and just being a part of the social group.

Miss Chomosh's final statement of evaluation suggests that whatever may be the activities of the homeroom group, it is the quality of their group living that is of greatest consequence in socializing the members and in bringing about fundamental personality adjustments. The most noteworthy growth, we may assume, comes from rich experiences as participants in democratic enterprises.

PLANNING HOMEROOM GROUP ACTIVITY

Contrasting Methods of Planning

The examples of homeroom activity just described suggest the importance of a discussion of the planning for such activity. Of the numerous schools which are scheduling homeroom group programs—usually once a week— many are finding them unpalatable to pupils and to teachers. Pupils some-times resent the programs because they prefer to use the period for study; teachers frequently are so uncertain, confused, and insecure in the presence of the homeroom group that they prefer to have the pupils study. Some-times in anguish teachers have been heard to say, "I'd rather have another class any day than this homeroom job." Let us list and examine the various methods of deciding what the group activity of the homeroom shall be.

Employing a Commercially Published Outline, Manual, or Textbook. This seems to be the easy solution to the problem. It appeals to the executive. The principal who wants his school to have homeroom programs because that is "the progressive thing to do," who wants to be sure that something is going on in the homeroom period, and to know *what* is going on, finds satisfaction in the selection of a "textbook," or a series of them. Plenty of such aids (?) are on the market today, as may be judged by the list with which this section is concluded. One of these books can be genuinely helpful if rightly employed. But the teacher commonly uses it as he uses the text-book in a class in English or chemistry (a sad commentary on traditional teaching!). He uses it to determine the pupils' activity instead of allowing their activity to spring from their own purposes and felt needs. Textbook-centered! The formula works surprisingly well with the school subjects, because the pupils have, through long usage, come to accept it, and because *credit* is involved. They are quite sensitive, however, to the fact that there is no credit for the homeroom program, and frequently they stand on their rights! Why work if they are not to be paid for it?

Similar short-cut planning is represented in the acceptance and following of an outline or syllabus issued by a state department of education. The principle of imposed activity is still dominant; the satisfaction of the pupil's felt need is but incidental.

Mimeographed Plans Drawn Up by the Principal, Counselor, or Guid-ance Committee of the School. These plans are sometimes issued piecemeal, as each week's period for the homeroom program comes around. Under these circumstances all grades of the school commonly have the same program. The planners frequently pass from this stage to the creation of a mimeographed manual which presents a graded curriculum. The writer knows of a city school system in which hard-working committees of teachers produced neat manuals for the junior high schools and the senior high schools. For each grade a separate series of lessons was outlined. The problem of the guidance period seemed to be settled, but a year's trial of the manual made "guidance" a hated word among both teachers and pupils. The basic difficulty was undoubtedly the result of taking up content which was extraneous to the present felt needs of the pupils. In a noncredit experience they resented having their activities determined by a mimeographed outline.

The outline makers frequently evince some recognition of the possibility that their planning will be received in a hostile spirit. They caution the teacher against "slavish adherence" to their sequence; they urge in all modesty that their work be regarded as merely suggestive. Too often, however, such cautions go unheeded, as the teacher finds it easier to proceed in his accustomed textbook groove rather than to help the pupils start with their own direct experience.

Genovese obtained an inventory of pupil opinion concerning homeroom programs carried on under this kind of planning.[11] He canvassed nearly 3,500 pupils of Grades 10, 11, and 12 in four high schools of Western Pennsylvania in which counselors or faculty committees had developed mimeographed homeroom manuals. His inquiry, administered in the month of May, called on each pupil to designate by topic the program of that school year which had been *most valuable* to him, the one which was *second most valuable,* and one which had had *little or no value* for him. Concerning each of the three programs the pupil was asked "What did the teacher do?" and "What did the students do?" The object was to find out how well the various homeroom themes were appreciated and to find out what teacher activities and what pupil activities were commonly associated with favored programs and with programs considered to be lacking in value. The results were confusing and contradictory. No theme, no teacher activity, and no pupil activity assured successful programs. As one might expect, no formula for conducting homeroom programs emerged, suggesting that teaching is indeed an art rather than a science.

The concluding direction in Genovese's inquiry was as follows: "Think over your homeroom programs as a whole for the present school year. Were they interesting or dull? Were they helpful or a waste of time?" A percentage summary of the pupils' responses is indicated in the following tabulation:

[11] Clarence T. Genovese, *A Consensus of Senior High School Pupils Concerning Group Guidance Programs in the Homeroom.* Ph.D. Thesis (Pittsburgh, University of Pittsburgh Library, 1941).

General Opinion	School A	School B	School C	School D
Interesting—helpful	30	43	67	49
Dull—waste of time	55	37	16	32
Indeterminate	15	19	17	18

The programs were evidently not very successful except in School C. That was a school in which the superintendent of schools was keenly interested in the guidance function and whose leadership was enthusiastically accepted by the staff. To point out other qualitative differences was impossible.

The free responses of the pupils included in Genovese's study showed a wide range of reasons for their favorable and unfavorable reactions, but basically their remarks indicated that the teachers either went beyond the manual to help the pupils come to grips with the actual problems of their lives, or they followed the outline of the manual in a dry and unimaginative fashion.

Plans Made by the Individual Homeroom Teacher. Kefauver and Scott found in their survey of some years ago that most commonly the responsibility for developing homeroom programs rested in "each homeroom teacher working independently."[12] Doubtless this policy is followed in many schools today. It is probably very ineffective. Homeroom teachers are subject teachers, and they very easily shrug off the homeroom group program, saying that they just don't know what they are supposed to do.

Plans Made by the Homeroom Group, Acting Collectively or through a Program Committee. This is the complete hands-off policy which results when the principal becomes determined that the homeroom program shall be a pupil activity which teachers must not dominate. He informs the faculty that the homeroom period is the pupils' own period. Teachers are then afraid to impose or even to suggest, and pupils are left to their own devices. Generally speaking, this results in an opportunistic determination of activity, uninfluenced by stimuli from teachers or office. Oftentimes the outcome is that pupils begin to think of the period as a time for entertainment and amusement or as an occasion for self-expression. The programs become very impromptu and lose the respect of the pupils themselves. Perhaps the teacher is eventually disgusted, defies the office, reverts to an authoritarian role, says "We'll have a study period today." The pupils may feel relieved, being tired of a laissez-faire regime as was the little girl in the "progressive" school who said, "Teacher, do we have to do what we want to do today?"

Co-operative Teacher-Pupil Planning in Each Homeroom Group, with Consultative Assistance from the School Counselor or Guidance Department. This is the method of planning which is consistent with the philosophy of the homeroom. The pupils will formulate purposes which are meaningful

[12] Grayson N. Kefauver and Robert E. Scott, "The Home Room in the Administration of Secondary Schools," *Teachers College Record,* Vol. XXXI (April, 1930), p. 628.

to them, the teacher influencing the environment of stimuli from which the pupils derive their purposes. While the pupils will plan their activities in pursuit of their purposes, the teacher will be such a fruitful source of suggestion that pupils will naturally turn to him. As the group carry out their activities and arrive at conclusions, the teacher will be an interested bystander, ready with suggestions as needed but not dominating the situation. In other words, the relationship desired is one in which the teacher is a real participating member of the group, and one who is respected as being more mature and experienced and thereby gifted with understandings superior to those of the other members. The teacher's attitudes are those of a counselor and friend.

The school counselor's relationship to the teachers will be similar to that of the teacher to his pupils. He will not issue edicts or ukases. He will be on guard against the assumption of the "director" complex. On the positive side, he will be the available expert on pupil problems. He will have in his files useful materials for the illumination and analysis of problems in the various areas, concise bibliographies for the convenience of pupils and teachers, helpful suggestions for group activities.

An Example of Homeroom Planning

A recital of the evolution of homeroom program planning over a ten-year period in the Appalachian State Teachers College Demonstration High School at Boone, North Carolina, offers a corroborative illustration of the contrasting methods of planning just described. An extract from this report, given by Herbert Wey, the principal, is as follows:[13]

The inauguration of the first phase of this program consisted of only two steps. The first was the setting up of a homeroom period in the regular daily schedule. . . . The second step was to choose one of the available textbooks, suitable for use in a group guidance program. This was the extent of planning for the beginning of the group guidance program in the first phase.

The program was received with an indifferent attitude on the part of the students. The author of this article was a homeroom teacher at that time and was met on the first day with this very discouraging question: "How much credit toward graduation are we going to get from this?" It seemed that the students were not interested in vocational guidance or in any other type of guidance that came out of a textbook. The homeroom program looked to them like just another course to be studied. Because of this the program got off to a very bad start. However, due to the fact that educators are often more determined than students, the program was continued over a two-year period. By the end of the second year, most of the homeroom teachers had given up the idea of group guidance and were using the homeroom period for a study period.

[13] "An Experiment in Group Guidance," *Bulletin of the National Association of Secondary-School Principals,* Vol. XXXII (May, 1948), pp. 124–128.

The faculty discussed this problem at one of their general meetings and concluded that the school was still very much in need of a guidance program. They decided at this meeting to set up a guidance committee composed of four faculty members who would decide the topics to be discussed during the homeroom guidance period. . . .

This second phase of the group guidance continued through a four-year period, but again the success of the program was very doubtful. The topics decided upon by the guidance committee were not always of interest to the students, and the success of the guidance period depended largely upon the initiative of the individual homeroom teachers. Approximately half of the teachers were preparing materials for discussion on the topic assigned to them by the guidance committee, and the other half were doing very little. The teachers who were doing very little gave as their reason that they did not have time to spare from their other duties to prepare for this type of work.

In succeeding meetings the faculty decided that the group guidance program was still not meeting the needs for which it was introduced. They believed it would be necessary to drop the program or revise it in such a way that it would meet its objectives. Their decision was in favor of retaining the program. The responsibility was then placed in the hands of a revised guidance committee . . . [which] had six years of mistakes from which to profit. . . . The committee decided that the program had failed in the past because of the following reasons:

1. The group guidance programs had consisted of only what teachers thought students need to know. To a large extent they had failed to consider the interests of the ones for whom the program was planned.
2. All teachers were not able and some did not have the initiative to plan and follow through on a topic for group guidance discussion.

4. The idea of the textbook study lesson which was first used was contrary to the purposes of a group guidance discussion in which the students should be allowed to discover and solve the problems that are of the greatest and most immediate interest to the group.
5. The topics decided on for group discussion were not always of interest to students on different grade levels; for example, the ninth-grade homeroom boys might not be at all interested in that which would be of vital importance to the senior homeroom girls.
6. Not all of the faculty and very few of the student body had come to sense the real need of a guidance program.

With these factors in mind, the guidance committee entered the third phase of development and first requested that students be added to the committee. Students were added and the committee, now composed of four faculty members and four students, made a thorough study of the field of guidance. The inclusion of the ideas and planning ability of the students was undoubtedly the most important aspect of the third revision of the program. The committee . . . discussed the program with the student body as a whole. The following recommendations were then made:

1. To be successful the group guidance program would have to make use of the planning and interest of the student body as a whole.

2. The guidance committee should be headed by a co-ordinator who should be relieved of at least part of his classwork in order to work with the student body and faculty in planning and preparing the topics for discussion.

3. The group guidance co-ordinator should be a person who could also do individual counseling for those pupils who sought his help and for those students who were referred to him by homeroom sponsors. At least two other people should be designated to assist him with this phase of the program.

These recommendations were adopted by the faculty and put into effect. The lengthened homeroom period was used by the students under the supervision of the sponsor to decide which areas were of the greatest need and interest for discussion and research during their guidance period. From these discussions the guidance co-ordinator with the help of the guidance committee, which was now composed of students as well as teachers, chose the areas of most interest and importance.

Using the areas of interests as a basis, a questionnaire was prepared listing the number of topics for discussion under each area. This questionnaire was then given to the students in each home room for them to fill out. All topics that were of interest to all of the homerooms were put into the first group. The second group was composed of those topics that were of interest to individual homerooms or to a certain grade level. From these two groups of topics, the guidance committee prepared a calendar for each homeroom. The topics which were of school-wide interest were placed on each homeroom calendar at the same date. This was done to place school-wide emphasis on these topics at the same time.

The guidance committee under the direction of the co-ordinator assumed the responsibility for the preparation or collection of the guidance bulletins. Upon completion, the guidance bulletins were mimeographed and made available to the various home rooms.

The guidance committee took charge of several general faculty meetings at which they discussed the importance and some of the better methods of conducting a group guidance meeting.

The revised guidance program was met with an entirely different attitude by the student body as a whole, the reason being that the students were beginning to feel that the program was theirs. Also, the topics were ones in which they were interested. The homeroom officers were encouraged to take over the leadership in the discussion of any topic that could be handled satisfactorily by them. Today they are accepting this responsibility more and more, especially in the upper grades.

One could wish that more faculties would persist in thoughtful experimentation such as this extended quotation reveals.

The Role of the Teacher Further Clarified

While the function of the teacher in group guidance activity has already been defined in the preceding discussion, a more exact statement of the basic principles involved in the teacher's relation to the group is appropriate at this point. John Dewey saw it as follows:[14]

Because the kind of advance planning heretofore engaged in has been so routine as to leave little room for the free play of individual thinking or for contributions due to distinctive individual experience, it does not follow that all planning must be rejected. On the contrary, there is incumbent on the educator the duty of instituting a much more intelligent, and consequently more difficult, kind of planning. He must survey the capacities and needs of the particular set of individuals with whom he is dealing and must at the same time arrange the conditions which provide the subject matter or content for experiences that satisfy these needs and develop these capacities. The planning must be flexible enough to permit free play for individuality of experience and yet firm enough to give direction towards continuous development of power.

The present occasion is a suitable one to say something about the province and office of the teacher. The principle that development of experience comes about through interaction means that education is essentially a social process. This quality is realized in the degree in which individuals form a community group. It is absurd to exclude the teacher from membership in the group. As the most mature member of the group he has a peculiar responsibility for the conduct of the interactions and intercommunications which are the very life of the group as a community. That children are individuals whose freedom should be respected while the more mature person should have no freedom as an individual is an idea too absurd to require refutation. The tendency to exclude the teacher from a positive and leading share in the direction of the activities of the community of which he is a member is another instance of reaction from one extreme to another. When pupils were a class rather than a social group, the teacher necessarily acted largely from the outside, not as a director of processes of exchange in which all had a share. When education is based upon experience and educative experience is seen to be a social process, the situation changes radically. The teacher loses the position of external boss or dictator but takes on that of leader of group activities.

While Dewey had in mind teacher-pupil relationships in all learning situations and he voiced the same concept of the class and teacher as a social group which he expressed in *The School and Society* sixty years ago, the applicability of his doctrine to the relation of teacher and homeroom should appear compulsive to all but the most rigid of educational formalists.

Slavson calls attention to the loss of morale and efficiency in a group which is without adequate functioning leadership, saying,[15]

[14] *Experience and Education* (The Kappa Delta Pi Lecture Series) (New York, Macmillan, 1938), pp. 64–66.
[15] S. R. Slavson, *Creative Group Education* (New York, Association Press, 1937), pp. 24–25.

The leader's presence, even when he remains comparatively inactive, has the effect of integrating the group into a working whole. The differences in personalities and strivings of individual members are sources of potential discord and conflict. . . . One of the primary characteristics of a group is its need of an integrating person—someone who will hold it together as a structural and functioning unit. Leadership, therefore, is a socializing influence if it is exerted indirectly and with restraint. Direct and overt domination arouses hostility, which not only defeats the group process but increases friction and prevents constructive effort and social development.

It is quite clear from the role of the group leader indicated above that he must possess such qualities as a socialized personality, emotional maturity, love for people, humor, cheerfulness, and an even temper. Without such qualities, it is quite impossible for him to supply to the group the stability that it needs.

Although the prime need of every group is leadership, such leadership is not confined entirely to the adult. It may also be supplied by one or more members of the group, who may supplement the adult. Ideally, leaders in self-directed groups arise from the groups themselves. Actually, this usually does not happen. Young people, in their immaturity, require the guidance of an adult. But, since the aim of modern group education is to develop self-reliance, leadership must be shared by adults and group members, with the former playing an increasingly recessive role. The leader stimulates the group into worth-while activity, and as soon as the activity is on the way, he withdraws and turns over all the initiative to the members themselves. He again resumes the role of a stimulator directly the resources of the members are spent, only to efface himself as soon as the impetus has taken root. This is *the principle of alternate assertiveness and withdrawal.*

Slavson's "principle" seems particularly in keeping with the purposes and the method of the homeroom. It signifies an attitude of acceptance toward youth—acceptance of youth's right to self-expression, to individual aggressiveness, to participation in group decisions and management. This involves deep-down respect for every pupil's personality and the absence of any authoritarian complex.

One of the great obstacles to the exercise of the kind of flexible, democratic leadership here described is the teacher's subject-matter obsession. From his own experience education has come to mean the mastery of verbalistic content as set forth in textbooks. Being swamped in his own erudition, he typically finds his security in subject matter. For the successful leadership of a homeroom—a social group whose main concern is properly the creation of a good society, the growth of wholesome personalities, and the resolution of personal problems—a different orientation is needed. He must find his security in good relationships with his pupils and in satisfactions over his opportunity to participate in the ever-marvelous phenomena of human growth and change. Having achieved that orientation, the homeroom no longer oppresses him as a burden.

Reading Materials Which Are Helpful in Homeroom Planning

Specialized reading materials for the homeroom—textbooks, in fact—have appeared in recent years. So, also, have works of practical psychology for high-school pupils, books designed to acquaint them with the common mental mechanisms, to help them use their mental powers to the best advantage, to aid them in acquiring adult ways of behavior. The vast literature on occupations and occupation choosing was described in Chapter 9. The volume of literature bearing on the problems of educational choice and adjustments is hard to estimate. The extent of reading matter on all the other categories of personal problems quoted from Symonds and from Strang in earlier pages of this chapter, reaches out indefinitely.

Within the limitations of this book it is possible to present only a sampling of this varied reading material. The following list is alphabetically arranged and not classified, but the titles will suggest the categories represented. Books primarily for pupils are designated with a **P**; those for teachers, with a **T**.

T *The Adolescent in Your Family* (Washington, D.C., U.S. Department of Health, Education, and Welfare, 1954).

T ALLEN, Richard D., *Common Problems in Group Guidance* and *Case-Conference Problems in Group Guidance* (New York 3—207 Fourth Ave.—Inor Publishing Co., 1952).

P BAILARD, Virginia, and STRANG, Ruth, *Ways to Improve Your Personality* (New York, McGraw-Hill, 1951).

P BECKER, Esther R., and LAWRENCE, Richard L., *Success and Satisfaction in Your Office Job* (New York, Harper, 1954).

P BEERY, Mary, *Manners Made Easy,* rev. ed. (New York, McGraw-Hill, 1954).

P *Better Start with Good Grooming Unit* (New York 20—45 Rockefeller Plaza —Educational Service Dept. C, Bristol-Myers Co., 1954).

P BILLETT, Roy O., and YEO, J. Wendell, *Growing Up* (Boston, Heath, 1951).

P BOYKIN, Eleanor, *This Way, Please: A Book of Manners,* rev. ed. (New York, Macmillan, 1948).

P BOYNTON, P. W., *6 Ways to Get a Job* (New York, Harper, 1945).

P CANER, G. Colket, *It's How You Take It* (New York, Coward-McCann, 1946).

T *Career Plans of High School Seniors* (Washington 9, D.C.—1761 R St., N.W. —B'nai B'rith Vocational Service Bureau, 1954).

P *The College Finder* (Washington 9, D.C.—1761 R St., N.W.—B'nai B'rith Vocational Service Bureau, 1954).

P DICKERSON, Roy E., *Into Manhood* (New York 7—291 Broadway—Association Press, 1954).

P DUVALL, Evelyn M., *Facts of Life and Love for Teenagers* (New York, Association Press, 1950).

P EDLUND, Sidney, and EDLUND, Mary, *Pick Your Job and Land It,* rev. ed. (Englewood Cliffs, N.J., Prentice-Hall, 1954).

P FALK, R. D., *Your High School Record—Does It Count?* rev. ed. (Pierre, S.D., South Dakota Press, 1943).

P FEDDER, Ruth, *A Girl Grows Up* (New York, McGraw-Hill, 1948).

T FLANDERS, Ned A., and others, *Teaching with Groups* (Minneapolis 15— 426 S. 6th St.—Burgess Publishing Co., 1954).

T FOSHAY, Arthur W., WANN, Kenneth D., and associates, *Children's Social Values, An Action Research Study* (New York 27, Bureau of Publications, Teachers College, Columbia University, 1954).

P GAVIAN, Ruth Wood, *Understanding Juvenile Delinquency* (New York 3— 222 Fourth Ave.—Oxford Book Co., 1954).

P GEISEL, John B., *Personal Problems* (Boston, Houghton Mifflin, 1949).

P GOESSL, Verna, ed., *Money Management for Young Moderns* (Chicago— 919 N. Michigan Ave.—Consumer Education Dept., Household Finance Corp., 1954).

P GOODMAN, David, *Who's Delinquent?* Socio-Guidrama No. 10 (New York 17 —489 Fifth Ave.—Occu-press, 1954).

P GRUENBERG, Sidonie M., and KRECH, Hilda S., *The Many Lives of Modern Woman* (New York, Doubleday, 1952).

P *How to Visit Colleges* (Washington 5, D.C.—1534 "O" St., N.W.—National Vocational Guidance Association, 1954).

P JENKINS, Gladys, BAUER, William, and SHACTER, Helen, *Teen-Agers* (Chicago, Scott, Foresman, 1954).

Junior Life Adjustment Booklets, Life Adjustment Booklets, and *Better Living Booklets* (Chicago, Science Research Associates). These three sets of booklets are intended for junior high school pupils, for senior high school pupils, and for parents, teachers, and counselors, respectively. They offer treatments of the wide range of problems of youth which have been described earlier in this chapter as properly the concern of the homeroom.

P LANDIS, Paul H., *This Is College* (New York, McGraw-Hill, 1954).

P ———, *Your Dating Days: Looking Forward to Happy Marriage* (New York, McGraw-Hill, 1954).

T LEONARD, Edith M., and others, *Counseling with Parents in Early Childhood Education* (New York, Macmillan, 1954).

P LOEB, Robert H., Jr., *He-Manners* (New York, Association Press, 1954).

P McKOWN, Harry C., *A Boy Grows Up,* 2nd ed. (New York, McGraw-Hill, 1949).

P ———, and BAILARD, Virginia, *So You Were Elected!* (New York, McGraw-Hill, 1946).

P MAHONEY, Harold J., and ENGLE, T. L., *Points for Decision* (New York, World Book Co., 1957).

P MENNINGER, Wm. C., and others, *How to Be a Successful Teen-Ager* (New York 16—215 E. 37th St.—Sterling Publishing Co., 1954).

T MORRIS, C. Eugene, *Counseling with Young People* (New York 7—291 Broadway—Association Press, 1954).

P NEUGARTEN, Bernice L., and others, *National Forum Guidance Series* (Chicago, National Forum, Inc., 1946) Six books for Grades 7–12, with accompanying charts, comprehending the range of adolescent problems.

P NEWSOM, N. William, DOUGLASS, Harl R., and DOTSON, Harry L., *Living and Planning Your Life* (New York, Harper, 1952).

P NEWTON, Roy, and NICHOLS, F. G., *How to Improve Your Personality,* 2nd ed. (New York, McGraw-Hill, 1954).

P OVERTON, Grace S., *Living with Parents* (Nashville, Tenn.—161 Eighth Ave. N.—Broadman Press, 1954).

P REILLY, William J., *Career Planning for High School Students* (New York, Harper, 1953).

T RICHARDSON, Frank H., *How to Get Along with Children* (Atlanta, Ga.—1090 Capitol Ave., S.E., P.O. Box 5109—Tupper & Love, Inc., 1954).

P ROBINSON, Clark, *Making the Most of School and Life* (New York, Macmillan, 1952).

P SCHERF, C. H., *Do Your Own Thinking* (New York, McGraw-Hill, 1948).

P SPLAVER, Sarah, *High School Wedding Bells,* Socio-Guidrama No. 3 (New York 17—489 Fifth Ave.—Occu-press, 1954).

P STRAUSS, Bert, and STRAUSS, Frances, *New Ways to Better Meetings* (New York, Viking Press, 1952).

T TRAXLER, Arthur E., *The Improvement of Study Habits and Skills,* Bulletin No. 41 (New York 32—21 Audubon Ave.—Educational Records Bureau, 1954).

P WARTERS, Jane, *Achieving Maturity* (New York, McGraw-Hill, 1949).

P WILLING, Jules Z., *How to Land the Job You Want* (New York 22—501 Madison Ave.—The New American Library of World Literature, 1954).

P WOODWORTH, Robert S., and SHEEHAN, Mary R., *First Course in Psychology* (New York, Holt, 1951).

In connection with these reading materials the school counselor has a major function to perform. He will continuously evaluate new publications as they appear, he will keep the library adequately stocked, and he will judiciously build up shelves of materials in the homerooms. Perhaps the most helpful thing he can do in this connection is to make and mimeograph annotated bibliographies for each of the major problems that homeroom groups take up. With such aids available, the committee that is preparing a program on "Dating manners" or "How to budget one's time" will be able quickly to tap the resources of the library for ideas. Naturally, this project will be given the close co-operation of the librarian.

Planning homeroom group activity along the lines laid down in this section may well have a beneficent influence on the curriculum and method of the school. Wey pointed out that as a result of the group guidance experimentation in his school, "The two factors of pupil interest and pupil planning, which to some extent were brought to life by the guidance program, are spreading to other phases of the school curriculum."[16] If the homeroom program serves as a pilot plant for the testing of a kind of education that is more meaningful to boys and girls, it will be all to the good for the guidance function.

[16] *Op. cit.,* p. 129.

ORGANIZING AND ADMINISTERING THE SCHOOL FOR HOMEROOM FUNCTIONING

On What Basis Shall Pupils Be Distributed to Homeroom Groups?

The criterion to be employed in answering this question is obviously the attainment of homeroom objectives. The best basis for classifying pupils into homeroom groups is that which will contribute most to the realization of the ideals which we have cited for the homeroom. The question is not easy to answer. As the circumstances surrounding schools differ widely, each school must decide the matter for itself.

No research exists which will aid in making this decision. The best that can be done is to list the various bases and state the subjective arguments for and against them. We have no dependable data showing the frequencies with which the several bases are now employed in practice, and it is hard to see how such data would be helpful if they were available.

By Grade. One of the most common practices is to group pupils by grade. When a class enters it is divided into as many homerooms as are necessary to accommodate it. Sometimes the members are assigned alphabetically to each homeroom, and sometimes each group is just a random sampling. The homeroom so formed presents a considerable degree of homogeneity; the members have similar problems at each stage of their progress through school; group discussions can therefore be employed to meet many of their guidance problems. Furthermore, since the group is homogeneous in state of maturity, there are marked possibilities of molding them into a strong social unit. Another advantage that comes from having the whole school organized on this basis is the possibility of holding assemblies of a single grade without disturbing the rest of the school. For example, all senior homeroom groups may very likely be interested in how to apply for a job. They can be taken to the auditorium to view a film or hear a talk by a personnel manager on the subject, while the remaining homerooms of the school continue with their own programs.

By Sex. There probably are not many high schools in which homerooms are segregated by sex. An example is that of the New Trier Township High School, Winnetka, Illinois, where pupils are distributed to homerooms by grade and sex, and, naturally, with men sponsors for the boys and women sponsors for the girls. Presumably, the advocates of sex segregation feel that the problems of each sex can thus be taken up more freely. Those who prefer to have both sexes in each homeroom doubtless urge the advantage of having a more normal social situation in the group.

It has come to the attention of the writer that some schools have a few homeroom groups that are entirely of one sex. For example, if shop and home economics teachers are used as sponsors, and their classrooms have to be used, it may be regarded as desirable to assign only boys to the drafting room and only girls to the sewing laboratory.

By Ability Grouping. This basis of distribution apparently has no strong proponents. Its application is infrequent. It is used in a few of the many junior high schools in which pupils are classified by ability for general instructional purposes. Frequently one hears expression of the thought that if pupils are grouped homogeneously for their curricular experiences they should be grouped heterogeneously for the homeroom. If the homeroom groups of the school are to be social units (and political units, in the student government of the school) classification of the pupils according to academic ability seems out of place.

By Curriculum. Classification of pupils according to curriculum being followed would seem to bring together pupils who have common interests. As has already been pointed out, though, the secondary school should give every pupil adequate opportunity to *change* his curriculum, because he frequently does not know his interests. Better practice, as shown in Chapter 7, is the employment of the constants-with-variables type of program of studies, by which pupils are not put into any restricted curriculums.

Be that as it may, of the many schools which do have the multiple-curriculum type of program of studies, probably very few segregate pupils in homerooms according to curriculum. It is feared that such practice would enhance invidious social distinctions, that the "college-preps," the "commercials," and others, would develop a group consciousness that would be detrimental to school unity.

By First-Period Class. The practice of letting the classes of the first period or any other period be the homerooms of the school probably exists only in schools where the "report-room" idea still prevails. The ideals of the homeroom can hardly be realized when pupils are grouped on such a casual and transient basis.

By Previous Schools Attended. The idea behind this basis of distribution is to keep together pupils who have already formed friendly associations in their previous schools. The plan has its merits, but it also presents hazards. Is it advantageous or disadvantageous thus to keep separate the children from Nob Hill and those from "across the tracks?" Will old loyalties be preserved unfortunately? In Johnstown, Pennsylvania—a 6-4-2 school system—the faculty of the two-year senior high school feel very keenly the difficulty of building up a school loyalty after the three tributary junior high schools have had the pupils for four years. Systematically they scatter their incoming pupils so that each homeroom has each junior high school proportionately represented. Another school—a four-year high school—of the writer's acquaintance is accustomed to receiving sizable increments from three-year and four-year junior high schools. When the newcomers were kept to themselves in homerooms, the faculty felt that they were undigested lumps in the student body. There may be a few schools in which the benefits of distributing pupils to homerooms on the basis of previous school attended outweigh the evils, but on the whole the reverse is probably true.

By Vertical Cross Section of the School. This method of forming homeroom groups assigns to each group a representative number of pupils from each grade. The plan usually carries with it the principle of permanency. As the pupils of the highest grade are promoted to senior high school, or as they graduate from senior high school, their places in the group are taken by pupils from the next incoming class. Thus the sponsor has only a few new pupils each year with whom to become acquainted. In addition to this advantage it is held that the vertical cross section speeds up the orientation of new pupils in the school, that close association with the older pupils insures quick assimilation of the new members into the student body.

To find the objections to this plan the reader need but turn back to the first described of these bases for distribution—"by grade." The diversity of interests and maturity of a vertical cross section of a junior or a senior high school is so great as to impose marked limits on the number of topics suitable for group programs. As a matter of fact, homeroom teachers of such groups tell the writer that group guidance programs are hardly attempted in their schools. It seems that the homeroom as pictured in this chapter could be only partially realized if each group were such a representative sampling of the whole school.

How Frequently Should Homeroom Groups Be Formed?

In schools where the homeroom is still mainly an administrative expedient, pupils are distributed to homerooms annually or semiannually, that is, at promotion time. As the importance of the guidance function has become more apparent, practice has swung to the permanent homeroom. When the pupil enters a junior high school he is assigned to a homeroom and remains in that homeroom until he is promoted to senior high school. In the senior high school he has the same homeroom from the time he enters until he graduates. Six-year high schools which have established the permanent homeroom almost invariably change the pupil's homeroom between the ninth and tenth grades. The six-year Eagle Rock High School, of Los Angeles, as described on pages 193–194, carries the pupil through two-year cycles, the homeroom functions being taken care of by the core teacher.

There are many arguments in favor of the permanent homeroom. In the first place, the sponsor has a real chance to become well acquainted with his pupils. Knowing that he will have the same pupils for three or four years, he is encouraged to study his charges, to take note of their aptitudes, interests, weaknesses, dislikes, and limitations. He takes note of their success and failure with the various school subjects, of their standing on the tests and inventories administered by the school, and of their participation in school organizations and activities. He visits the homes of his pupils and establishes a co-operative relationship with the parents. Building up a thorough acquaintanceship with his pupils in his first year with them, the sponsor has some capital to enable him to carry on far more effectively the next two or three years than if he had to start each year with a new group.

In the second place, responsibility for advisement is definitely fixed when the homeroom is permanent. The principal, on assigning a teacher a ninth-grade group just entering the school, can say, "This is your family. You will be their school parent, counselor, and friend until they graduate. We'll be helping you all we can from the office, but they're your responsibility." There can be no "passing of the buck" if at graduation time it develops that Mary Ellen was obviously misadvised in her elections, or if no attention has been paid to some serious maladjustment in Henry. On the other hand, parents and principal know definitely to whom credit is due when pupils give evidence of being well advised and well adjusted.

A third advantage arises out of the characteristics of continuity and responsibility just depicted. It is the advantage of economy. With the group continuously under one sponsor there need be no duplication of programs. The group may want to take up a problem two or three times as they progress through the school, but each succeeding time it will be treated in the light of what was learned before.

A fourth advantage of permanence in the homeroom is the larger opportunity it gives to attain the socializing objective. To build up enthusiasm among pupils and teachers over their membership in a group which they know has only a year to live, is indeed difficult. When teacher and pupils know that their group is permanent, they will want to make it a good society, they will want to make it function effectively, they will want it to be a group of which they feel proud to be members.

Many school administrators who recognize the desirability of obtaining the benefits just cited are fearful of instituting the permanent homeroom because they sense certain disadvantages, which, indeed, must be frankly faced. First, the wide variation in the capacities of teachers for homeroom leadership must be reckoned with. Some have the personal qualifications of good counselors; others do not. Some have a gift for easy, democratic leadership; others are authoritarian and strained in their relations with pupils. Some are naturally interested in their pupils as persons; others have their major interest in subject matter. With such differences in sponsors, it is certain that some pupils would be fortunate and others would be less fortunate. With the permanent homeroom, their good or ill fortune would be permanent, too. The annual homeroom is more likely to give all pupils an even break as regards sponsors—they may share the good, bad, and indifferent.

The permanent homeroom system, it is urged, does not take account of the fact that some teachers are more gifted in the leadership of older pupils, others, of younger pupils. A teacher who is quite acceptable to the ninth

grade may be laughed at by twelfth-graders. A teacher who is greatly irritated by the juvenility of ninth-grade pupils may find the relative maturity
of a twelfth-grade group a welcome challenge. Closely related to this point
is the idea that some advantage derives from a teacher's constant experience with pupils of a given grade—he becomes expert in the problems most
characteristic of that grade.

For such reasons the permanent homeroom can hardly be considered an
unmixed good. Thoughtful administration in the high-school principal's
office may, however, largely reduce these disadvantages of the permanent
homeroom. Suggestions in the paragraphs immediately following bear on
this point.

Selection of Homeroom Sponsors

The major objection to extended reliance on homeroom teachers for the
counseling of pupils is that the function calls for a degree of specialized talent and training which the rank and file of teachers cannot be expected to
have. The answer to the objection is partly given in the quotation from Paul
Pierce on page 196, "all teachers had to assume the main responsibilities
connected with well-rounded development of pupils, not merely to teach a
particular subject." The reality of variation in teacher capacity remains,
however, and one way to reckon with it and to meet the objection to the
dependence on homeroom teachers for counseling, is to exercise much
greater discrimination in the selection of teachers for homeroom duty than
is commonly done.

Not all of the teachers of the school are homeroom teachers. On the average, probably 70 to 75 per cent of a faculty are needed for this function.
They should be selected thoughtfully on the basis of fitness for the work.
There is some evidence that extraneous criteria now prevail in determining
which teachers are given homeroom assignments, such as the subject taught
or the kind of classroom the teacher has. Typically, this means that all
academic-subject teachers are homeroom teachers and that most teachers
in the practical and fine arts and in physical education do not have homeroom groups.

In contrast with this practice, it is proposed that the qualifications of all
members of the faculty for the homeroom responsibility be carefully as-
sessed and that selection be made on the basis of fitness. If such procedure
disqualifies an English teacher because she is formal and distant with pupils,
unable to work in the democratic framework of the homeroom, or congenitally out of sympathy with homeroom objectives, well and good. Let her
classroom be taken for the homeroom period by that shop teacher who is
interested in adolescent youth and knows how to win their confidence. That
does not, however, complete the principal's work of job assignment. He
must be sure that the English teacher has such duties as will give her a full

load. When teachers see ineptitude rewarded by a lightened load they feel that efficiency and competency are penalized.

At the senior high school level another possibility of allowing for variation in the capacity of teachers for homeroom sponsorship presents itself. Elimination brings about a progressive decline in enrollment from Grades 10 to 12, so that a school which needs 10 homerooms in the tenth grade may need only 8 in the eleventh grade and 7 in the twelfth. By breaking up the homeroom groups of the weakest sponsors each year and distributing their members among the remaining groups, a disadvantage of the permanent homeroom system may be reduced.

Scheduling the Homeroom

Questions in connection with this subject are: For what time of the day and week should the homeroom period be scheduled? How long should homeroom periods be? How many per week or per month? The answers to these questions can only be given in terms of opinion and existing practice. Many schools establish an "activities period" in the daily schedule in which they take care of events that they wish to have occurring once or twice a week, such as assemblies, club meetings, and homeroom programs. This avoids interference with or irregularity in subject-class meetings. Such a plan was followed by Wey, in whose school the activities period was used for homeroom programs on Mondays and Wednesdays, for clubs on Tuesdays and Thursdays, and for assemblies on Fridays.[17] Probably the majority of schools schedule the homeroom program once a week.

When the weekly homeroom program is thus fitted into a daily activities period, it is obvious that the length of the period and the time of day it comes will be determined by many factors in addition to the welfare of the homeroom. Schools apparently vary widely in their practice.

That the period of the homeroom program should not be interrupted seems too obvious to mention. It is a fact not to be overlooked, however, that the failure of the homeroom in many high schools is to be largely attributed to the permission of interruptions for a variety of administrative and extracurricular purposes. Sometimes these interruptions take the form of "excusing" various individuals for other activities that are permitted to go on at the same time. Does the principal consider that homeroom programs are not very important because they carry no credit? If he regards them so casually it will be difficult to get teachers and pupils to take them seriously. Wey's committee, in preparing for the third phase of his experiment, recommended that "The home-room period should be lengthened to fifty minutes, and the administrative activities should be stopped by the ringing of a bell ten minutes after the homeroom period started."[18] They were determined to prevent encroachments on the time needed for homeroom programs.

[17] *Op. cit.*, p. 125.
[18] *Op. cit.*, p. 127.

That attitude must be generally accepted if the objectives of the homeroom are to be realized.

The New Trier Homeroom Plan

As an example of well-developed homeroom organization, the plan of the New Trier Township High School, Winnetka, Illinois, may well be described at some length. Figure 10[19] is a chart of the organization. Noteworthy in the chart is the provision for the use of varying degrees of expertness in guidance—the deans as trained specialists, the eight chairmen as teachers possessed of unusually keen interest in the problems of pupils of a given grade and endowed with some qualities of leadership, the adviserroom teachers to meet the pupils daily in class-size groups and counsel them individually and collectively. The presence of the chairmen makes it possible to administer a program with greater accuracy and efficiency in a large school than can be done where there are no intermediate officers between the counselor or principal and 50 to 100 homeroom teachers. The New Trier grouping of pupils according to class and sex brings together those who have common problems.

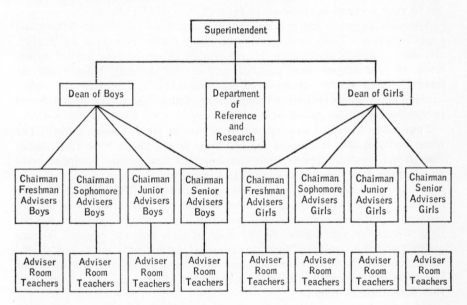

FIG. 10. Organization of the faculty for adviser work in the New Trier Township High School, Winnetka, Illinois.

[19] Adapted from a mimeographed chart obtained in 1927 through the courtesy of F. E. Clerk, at the time superintendent of the New Trier Township High School, Winnetka, Illinois.

As pointed out in Chapter 6, New Trier issues an unusually comprehensive students' handbook. From the 1952–1953 edition the following paragraphs are quoted for their portrayal of the homeroom system:[20]

The first and the most important member of the faculty you will come to know is your adviser. Your adviser will soon know you better than does any other teacher. Your adviser will meet you the first thing each morning, will read to you the student bulletin, will handle matters regarding your records in attendance, punctuality, and scholarship. If you are a freshman or a new student at New Trier, your adviser will soon visit your home and become acquainted with your parents and will discuss freely with them and with you any plans or difficulties you may have. Notes from your home to the school should be addressed to your adviser, and, in any emergency, your adviser is the first to whom you should turn. A good slogan would be, "When in doubt or difficulties, see your adviser!" or "Whatever it is—tell your adviser."

Your adviser is your friend in the truest sense. As such, he will not overlook your shortcomings. No real friend would. Rather, he will strive to remedy your faults in the most effective way even though such attempts should seem unpleasant at the time. He is directly concerned with your development during your high-school career and is expected to further your highest interests regardless of your personal convenience or his own.

Your adviser group has been selected and organized for certain definite and specific purposes. These include not merely such routine matters as punctuality, attendance, reports, registration, etc., but many others of even greater importance. In your adviser room you hear and discuss the daily bulletin and the reports of your various adviser-room representatives. You consider the significance of many school policies or changes in regulation. The adviser period should be the most profitable period of the whole day.

Your adviser keeps a detailed record of you in your "adviser folder." The folder contains data relating to you and your school life at New Trier. Notes from home, permits, reports from your teachers, test results, discipline complaints, records of any offices you hold or teams you may make, are filed in it. It is a complete record of your progress or the reverse. The contents of these folders are strictly confidential. No other student has access to your folder. No teacher, except your adviser, adviser chairman, dean, or superintendent, has the right to examine your folder. At the close of each year the material is summarized and the significant facts are recorded permanently on record sheets. Your record is, of course, your own affair. Whether it speaks well for you or not is entirely in your own hands. Make a record of which you, your parents, and your school will be proud.

Your class has two adviser chairmen, one for the boys and one for the girls. These chairmen are the faculty sponsors of your class. They have charge of all class affairs, such as elections, parties, collections of class dues, appointments of class committees, etc. They also direct the program of your adviser-room work throughout the year. Your chairman will visit your adviser room frequently and is ready at all times to consult with you on class matters.

[20] *Your New Trier, 1952–1953: A Handbook for Students and Parents,* pp. 24–25.

Your chairman has another important role. Whenever any difficulty arises which, in the judgment of your adviser, should be considered by the administration, such situations are frequently referred to the chairman. Perhaps some irregularity in registration or college preparation demands more attention than the adviser feels he should give. In such situations your adviser chairman is called into conference.

You might consider your chairman as a link between your adviser and the dean. Your adviser chairman does not progress with your class each year as your adviser does. You should, then, have a different one each year of your course, but always the same adviser.

This account depicts major reliance on the homeroom as the key feature of the guidance program. The pupil's attention is indeed focused on his homeroom teacher as his guide and counselor. Chairmen of groups of homeroom teachers there are, but their concern is not with the individual pupil; they are not pupil counselors except in problem cases that are too involved for the adviser. The directions concerning the cumulative record folder and the making of home contacts signify a high degree of responsibility reposed in the homeroom teacher.

Time for Homeroom Duties

In the majority of schools not much thought has been given to this subject. No survey data are at hand to indicate practice; studies of teaching load have not taken account of this element. Does the principal blithely plan to activate a homeroom guidance program without planning the reduction of other responsibilities of teachers to allow time for it? Certainly that has happened in many schools, and it is difficult to see how really strong programs can be developed under such circumstances. In contrast with this common practice, we have the statement of Principal Matthew P. Gaffney of the New Trier Township High School that teaching load in that school is distributed "so that each person acting in the [adviser] system is assigned one less class. . . ."[21] As the 1952–1953 students' handbook of New Trier shows 80 "adviser room teachers," it seems that 80 classes must have been subtracted from their loads. Assuming an average of five classes as a full teaching load, that would mean an additional sixteen teachers in the school. Relatively few school administrators and boards of education have thought seriously about paying such a price for a homeroom system. Yet it is hard to make bricks without straw. In all fairness, it must be recognized that it is impossible to expect the teacher to be the effective counselor of 30 or 35 pupils according to the New Trier standard without allowing time for it. And that such a standard pays dividends in human happiness and efficiency is something for guiders and school administrators to prove. The public needs and deserves facts, figures, and a wealth of objective data to show

[21] Quoted in Clifford E. Erickson and Marion C. Happ, *Guidance Practices at Work* (New York, McGraw-Hill, 1946), p. 25.

that the expenditure of professional energy on such a homeroom system as that of New Trier yields worthwhile results.

ALTERNATIVES TO THE HOMEROOM

"Small Schools" Within the Large School

Quite a number of years ago a few brief notes in educational literature called attention to an organization of the student body in a few large high schools known as the *house principal plan*. The general idea of this plan was the division of the school into "houses" of 200–300 pupils each for purposes of administration, guidance, and study supervision. Each house had its principal who carried out those functions and was expected to be an expert in them. Generally speaking, the teachers had little to do with such responsibilities.

For many years the Evanston Township High School, Illinois, with a dozen large rooms of the study-hall type—each with 250 to 300 desks—was organized on this plan. Beginning in the fall of 1958, however, this school is embarking upon an organization which is designed not only to bring guidance expertness to the service of the pupils, but also to bring about an integration of the whole staff in the performance of the guidance function. The school is to be divided into four divisions, each composed of about 650 pupils—a quarter of the school's enrollment—each a vertical cross section of the four grades, and each staffed with its own principal, assistants, counselors, teacher associates, and clerical worker. Each division will occupy three of the large study halls. Each division will probably be staffed with four half-time counselors, one for each grade, and it will generally be expected that the counselor will serve his group of pupils throughout their four-year high school career. This latter organizational feature, it will be noted, is substantially like that of the Providence class-counselor plan described below, although the provision for group guidance is not as clearly set forth as in the Providence plan.

Each division will have a faculty composed of approximately one fourth of the teachers of each department. Insofar as is practicable, each teacher will do all of his teaching with the pupils of his division. Divisional faculty meetings and informal divisional associations are expected to be planned for the attainment of a better understanding of the individual pupil.

The report of the committee of consultants who drew up the plan for Evanston expresses well the concept of guidance and the responsibility for the function which is advocated in this book.[22]

A somewhat different pattern of small schools within the large school was described in Chapter 7, namely, the organization developed at Wells

[22] This report, prepared by Frank S. Endicott, Camilla M. Low, Van Miller, and C. W. Sanford, was made available to the writer by the courtesy of L. S. Michael, Superintendent of the Evanston Township High School.

High School in Chicago twenty years ago. Occasionally one hears of other schools which have adopted such a plan, but no evidence of rapidly rising acceptance is at hand.

The Providence Class Counselor Plan

Widely known and emulated is the guidance organization developed in the secondary schools of Providence, Rhode Island, by the late Richard D. Allen.[23] In this school system of separate junior and senior high schools, each school is staffed with six class counselors, one for each semester-grade. As each class enters the school, it is associated with one of the counselors, and that counselor is continuously in charge of the class until it is graduated. Twice a week the pupils meet in class-size groups with their counselors for instruction in occupations, for educational orientation, and for consideration of problems in adjustment which may be effectively handled by group discussion.[24] The size of the total group assigned to each counselor is generally from 200 to 300 pupils. In addition to the group counseling, the counselor does individual counseling and is allowed time for that purpose.

While the Providence plan includes the homeroom, it is apparently in the main an administrative agency. Since the class counselors meet their pupils only twice a week, the homeroom is needed for taking the attendance, making daily announcements, and for such other purposes as make it necessary for the administration to contact pupils daily. The Providence plan thus puts guidance mainly in the hands of specialists, and through the group meetings twice a week makes it possible for the counselor to become acquainted with his counselees and keep quite continuously in contact with them.

An Experimental Evaluation of the Homeroom Plan and the Providence Plan of Class Counselors

What are the relative merits of the homeroom organization and of such a plan as that in Providence? Georgia May Sachs has attempted to answer this question by research carried on in two Pasadena junior high schools.[25]

---

[23] For a brief description, see W. C. Reavis, *Programs of Guidance,* Ch. 6, National Survey of Secondary Education, Monograph No. 14 (Washington, D.C., U.S. Office of Education, Bulletin No. 17, 1932). For a more extended account, see R. D. Allen, *Organization and Supervision of Guidance in Public Education,* Vol. IV of Inor Group Guidance Series (New York, Inor Publishing Co., 1937). A visit to Providence in 1957 revealed that the pattern of organization established by Allen is still substantially intact.

[24] The content and method of this "course" were set forth by Allen in Volumes I, II, and III of the Inor Group Guidance Series, entitled, respectively, *Common Problems in Group Guidance, Case-Conference Problems in Group Guidance,* and *Self-Measurement Projects in Group Guidance* (New York, Inor Publishing Co., 1952).

[25] *Evaluation of Group Guidance Work in Secondary Schools.* Southern California Education Monographs No. 14 (Los Angeles, University of Southern California Press, 1945).

Both schools included Grades 7–10 and had much in common. Both had had well-established guidance programs for a number of years, developed on the same basic philosophy and with similar instructional materials. The principals of both schools actively supported their group guidance programs.

School A used the guidance-teacher plan, which was similar to the Providence class-counselor plan. There were four guidance teachers, one for each grade, selected because of special interest and training. Each teacher had about 300 pupils and met them in ten groups—half of them three times a week and half twice a week. The pupils averaged 125 minutes a week in group guidance through the year. The remainder of the guidance teacher's day was for individual counseling.

School B used the homeroom plan, the homeroom period being one of twenty minutes at the beginning of each day. The teacher followed his 30 to 35 pupils through the four years of junior high school. In the seventh grade the homeroom teacher was also the core teacher, meeting his homeroom pupils in a three-period core of English, social studies, and arithmetic. His contact through classes with his homeroom pupils in the remaining three grades was only slight. "Homeroom teachers met regularly (every month or six weeks) with the guidance worker who sponsored their grade level in order to pool suggestions concerning group guidance work. Pupils participated to an unusual degree in the planning of activities. . . ."[26]

Sachs measured the two systems on 27 criteria, organized under 8 areas of study. She took steps to pair the pupils carefully, using the bases of sex, grade, expected achievement age, socio-economic status of the home, and educational quotient. Nonwhite pupils and pupils who had attended other junior high schools were eliminated. This left 371 pairs.

As one of the steps in evaluation, guidance teachers and homeroom teachers were required in faculty meeting and without warning to fill out "Personal Data Blanks" for a sampling of their pupils. The results showed no significant differences with respect to information concerning pupils' level of school achievement and level of general intelligence, but homeroom teachers on the average had more adequate information than did guidance teachers concerning the health of pupils and concerning home situations. Asked for any additional comments on pupils, the homeroom teachers scored somewhat higher than the guidance teachers.

Measurements of teacher-pupil relationships showed that the pupils of School B felt much closer to their homeroom teachers than did the pupils of School A toward their guidance teachers.

A comparison of value derived from content taken up during a semester under guidance teachers and homeroom teachers showed pupil reactions to favor the homeroom system. Interest was compared by having pupils rate their guidance periods on a five-point scale from "very interesting" to "very uninteresting." To compute mean ratings, numerical values of 2, 1,

[26] *Ibid.,* p. 7.

0, −1, and −2 were assigned to these ratings. The following tabulation shows the means derived:[27]

Grade	7–1	7–2	8–1	8–2	9–1	9–2	10–1	10–2	All
School A	.14	−.55	−.98	−1.53	−1.28	−.91	−1.07	−.38	−.85
School B	1.16	1.12	1.42	.40	1.25	.51	.50	.22	.85

The difference is markedly in favor of School B (homeroom plan).

Concerning the strong points of each plan Sachs reported the following findings:[28]

1. Analysis of [teacher] reactions to the School A guidance-teacher program revealed certain strong points not evidenced in the homeroom program: (a) the fact that the School A guidance teacher was charged with the responsibility for both the group and individual guidance of a group of pupils, (b) the fact that sufficient time was available in a fifty-minute period for adequate development of many group guidance topics which could not be handled effectively in a twenty-minute period, and (c) the fact that group guidance was not considered just an addition to a full load of subject-matter teaching.

2. Study of reactions to the homeroom program revealed certain strong points not evidenced in the guidance-teacher program: (a) opportunity for really knowing pupils and building up close pupil-teacher relationships, (b) a higher degree of pupil participation, (c) development of a strong group feeling in the homeroom group, and (d) closer relationships between homeroom teachers and the parents of pupils.

It is indeed a complex problem which Sachs made the object of scientific investigation, and space does not permit an adequate statement of her techniques or findings, or a summary of the limitations of her research, of which she evinced a full awareness. The homeroom is itself a complex organism with objectives that are involved and hard to analyze or define. It is difficult to say that a youth's behavior is to be attributed to his homeroom experience as distinguished from the many other forces that play upon him. Nevertheless, the schools which rely on the homeroom as a major feature in the guidance program must be continuously weighing its effectiveness by objective or subjective means. It has been the purpose of this chapter to clarify the potentialities of the homeroom and to illuminate the conditions under which its ideals may most likely be attained.

QUESTIONS, PROBLEMS, INVESTIGATIONS

1. As learned from literature or from direct contacts, describe the attitudes and activities of an ideal pupil member of a homeroom.

2. Do the same for the teacher member of a homeroom.

3. Define the role of the school counselor with reference to the homerooms of a large high school.

[27] *Ibid.*, adapted from Table XVI, p. 67.
[28] *Ibid.*, p. 83.

4. As school counselor, plan the resources you will have available for (*a*) a homeroom that wishes to raise a low scholarship average; (*b*) an eleventh-grade homeroom that wishes to canvass the employment opportunities of the community; (*c*) a twelfth-grade homeroom that wishes to study the problem of getting a job; (*d*) or for any other problem that high-school homerooms may bring up.

5. Obtain an expression of pupils' problems, using one or more of the methods suggested in this chapter.

6. In a dozen high schools ascertain the bases for selecting teachers for homeroom sponsorships.

7. Compile an annotated list of motion pictures that might be shown to student assemblies and then used as the basis of homeroom discussions.

8. In a school of your acquaintance survey the resources of the library for the support of the homeroom program, and then draw up a considered list of books and other materials that should be added.

9. Canvass the study by Georgia May Sachs, described in the last section of this chapter, and decide what it tells you about the most desirable method of administering group guidance.

10. Enumerate the aspects of the ideal homeroom which exemplify principles or practices of progressive education.

SELECTED REFERENCES

ALLEN, Richard D., and BENNETT, Margaret E., "Guidance through Group Activities," Ch. 5 of *Guidance in Educational Institutions,* Part I of Thirty-Seventh Yearbook, National Society for the Study of Education (Chicago, University of Chicago Press, 1938).

BENNETT, Margaret E., *Guidance in Groups* (New York, McGraw-Hill, 1955).

CROW, Lester D., and CROW, Alice, *Our Teen-Age Boys and Girls* (New York, McGraw-Hill, 1945).

CUPP, Marjorie, "Shall We Junk the Home Room?" *Clearing House,* Vol. 32 (April, 1958), pp. 457–460.

DEWEY, John, *Experience and Education* (The Kappa Delta Pi Lecture Series) (New York, Macmillan, 1938).

DIXON, Fred B., and THOMPSON, Orrin G., "Freshman Orientation Practices," *School Activities,* Vol. XVI (September, 1944), pp. 3–5, 20.

DUNSMOOR, Clarence C., "Desirable Features of a Homeroom Guidance Program," *Educational Method,* Vol. XX (January, 1941), pp. 186–190.

———, and MILLER, Leonard M., *Guidance Methods for Teachers in Homeroom, Classroom, Core Program* (Scranton, Pa., International Textbook Co., 1942).

FEDDER, Ruth, *Guiding Homeroom and Club Activities* (New York, McGraw-Hill, 1949).

FISCHER, Robert P., "Signed Versus Unsigned Personal Questionnaires," *Journal of Applied Psychology,* Vol. XXX (June, 1946), pp. 220–225.

FLEEGE, Urban H., *Self-Revelation of the Adolescent Boy* (Milwaukee, Wis., Bruce Publishing Co., 1945).

HOPPOCK, Robert, *Occupational Information* (New York, McGraw-Hill, 1957).

HUMPHREVILLE, Frances, "Interaction in Home Room 225," *School Review*, Vol. LVII (September, 1949), pp. 358–363.

KOILE, Earl A., "Group Guidance—A Fringe Activity," *School Review*, Vol. LXIII (December, 1955), pp. 483–485.

LEEVY, J. Roy, "Social Competence of High-School Youth," *School Review*, Vol. LI (June, 1943), pp. 342–347.

LONG, Helen Halter, "Pupil Direction Revitalizes the Homeroom Period," *Clearing House*, Vol. XXVIII (February, 1954), pp. 323–326.

McCORKLE, David B., and O'DEA, J. David, "Some Problems of Homeroom Teachers," *Personnel and Guidance Journal*, Vol. XXXII (December, 1953), pp. 206–208.

McFARLAND, John W., "Developing Effective Home Rooms," *School Review*, Vol. LXI (October, 1953), pp. 400–405.

McKOWN, Harry C., *Home Room Guidance*, 2nd ed. (New York, McGraw-Hill, 1946).

MOONEY, Ross L., "Personal Problems of Freshman Girls," *Journal of Higher Education*, Vol. XIV (February, 1943), pp. 84–90.

———, "Surveying High School Students' Problems by Means of a Problem Check List," *Educational Research Bulletin*, Vol. XXI (March 18, 1942), pp. 57–69.

NORTON, Stanley K., "Student Problems Met by the Teacher," *School Review*, Vol. LVI (September, 1948), pp. 404–409.

NOVAK, Benjamin J., "Don't Sell the Homeroom Short," *Nation's Schools*, Vol. XLVIII (October, 1951), pp. 49–51.

OHLSEN, M. M., and DeWITT, A. F., "Group Counseling: A Report on Ways and Means," *Clearing House*, Vol. XXIV (February, 1950), pp. 335–339.

RATHBUN, Jesse E., "The Functions of Group Counseling," *California Journal of Secondary Education*, Vol. XX (December, 1945), pp. 447–452.

ROSS, Jacob M., "The Home Room Period in the Senior High School," *High Points*, Vol. XXII (October, 1940), pp. 45–52.

ROSS, Vivian, *Handbook for Homeroom Guidance* (New York, Macmillan, 1954).

SACHS, Georgia May, *Evaluation of Group Guidance Work in Secondary Schools*, Southern California Education Monographs, No. 14 (Los Angeles, University of Southern California Press, 1945).

SANTAVICCA, G. G., "What Homeroom Teachers Should Know," *Occupations*, Vol. XXX (February, 1952), pp. 351–355.

SHEEDER, Franklin I., "Transition Problems of College Freshmen as Seen by the College Administrator," *Journal of Educational Sociology*, Vol. XII (October, 1938), pp. 117–125.

SLAVSON, S. R., *Creative Group Education* (New York, Association Press, 1937).

STRANG, Ruth, *Group Activities in College and Secondary School*, rev. ed. (New York, Harper, 1946).

———, "Guidance Young People Want," *School Review*, Vol. LV (September, 1947), pp. 392–401.

————, "Prevention of Delinquency through Guided Group Experience," Ch. 4 of *Juvenile Delinquency and the Schools,* Forty-Seventh Yearbook, Part I, of the National Society for the Study of Education (Chicago, University of Chicago Press, 1948).

————, *The Role of the Teacher in Personnel Work* (New York, Teachers College, Columbia University, 1953).

SYMONDS, Percival M., "The Principal Areas of Personal Problems," *Teachers College Record,* Vol. XXXVIII (November, 1936), pp. 144–151.

WATERS, E. W., "Problems of Rural Negro High School Seniors on the Eastern Shore of Maryland: A Consideration for Guidance," *Journal of Negro Education,* Vol. XXII (Spring, 1953), pp. 115–125.

WEY, Herbert, "An Experiment in Group Guidance," *Bulletin of the National Association of Secondary-School Principals,* Vol. XXXII (May, 1948), pp. 124–129.

WRIGHT, Barbara H., *Practical Handbook for Group Guidance* (Chicago, Science Research Associates, 1948).

CHAPTER 11

Analysis of the Individual: Information

Obtained by Observation and Inquiry

A FUNDAMENTAL COMPONENT of the guidance function, both distributive and adjustive, is a thorough understanding of the client. Human resources cannot be optimally employed unless the individual is a known quantity. Nor can maladjustment be combatted without knowledge of the capacity and attributes of the individual, together with the extent and character of his departure from the norm. Consequently, the guidance program must include activities calculated to bring about a complete knowledge of the individual pupil by all who are responsible for his guidance.

Research into the nature of the individual has created hundreds of instruments for the objective measurement of the person in his various phases, traits, potentialities, and accomplishments. Untold numbers of studies have been made for the purpose of testing these instruments and determining their worth. To sift through this extensive literature and report the findings which contribute permanent and practical aid in the exercise of the guidance function is a task of no mean proportions. Three chapters will be devoted to the exposition of this feature of the guidance program.

Let it be understood at the outset that analysis of the individual is quite as essential to the exercise of the broad developmental task of education as of the guidance function. As pointed out in Chapter 1, on page 17, the same program of pupil analysis can be used to serve both guidance and development. We shall in these chapters focus on the guidance uses of the instruments for analysis.

METHODS OF OBSERVATION AND INQUIRY

The Use of Observation

Simple and obvious may seem the observation of pupil behavior, but the value of it must not be minimized, and the potential extent of its employment must not be underestimated. Implicit throughout Chapter 8 is the assumption that teachers are alert in noting pupil reactions to curricular and extracurricular experiences. Independently of any tests that may be administered, the pupil is revealing himself to the observant teacher as possessing a talent or lacking it, as evincing an interest or failing to do so. Such revelations should be interpreted to the individual to afford him guideposts for educational and vocational choosing. This conception of the teacher's function implies that he promotes pupil activity which is vigorous and varied, that the pupil is primary and the subject secondary in his considerations, and that he recognizes that what he observes depends upon his own powers of perception. Primarily, the bearing of Chapter 8 was on distributive guidance.

In the service of adjustive guidance, observation of behavior always has played and apparently always will play a major role. Teachers from time immemorial have observed the activity and the conduct of their pupils. To a certain extent they have commonly observed without understanding what they saw. Perhaps the most serious limitation on their powers of observation has been rooted in their preoccupation with their pupils' mastery of subject matter. Dominated by that purpose, they have been especially observant of the forms of conduct which interfered with its attainment. Aggressive behavior—whispering, clowning, noise-making, etc.—which disturbed the accustomed class order, has disturbed the teacher more than the class. Meanwhile, the withdrawing types of behavior—fearfulness, shyness, self-consciousness, etc.—have not been observed by the teacher, although the mental hygienist considers them to be much more serious than aggressive behavior because they threaten the pupil's adequate personality development.[1]

Teachers who agree reasonably well on what they observe in a problem pupil may differ widely in their interpretation and in their proposals for remedial treatment. Naturally, this is because of the variation in knowledge of mental hygiene, in attitudes, and in values which they bring to the observation. Torgerson has effectively illustrated this factor in the observation technique by presenting the reports of three hypothetical committees of teachers who were assigned by the principal to study a problem boy and recommend a course of action. One committee recommended a program of punishment. The second committee recommended that the school authorities pay no attention to the boy's life outside of school but concentrate on rigid requirements of subject-matter mastery. The third committee supple-

[1] E. K. Wickman, *Children's Behavior and Teachers' Attitudes* (New York, The Commonwealth Fund, Division of Publications, 1929). A recent study shows that in the years which have elapsed since the Wickman investigation, teachers' attitudes toward children's behavior have changed somewhat, now contrasting less sharply with the attitudes of the mental hygienists. See George A. W. Stouffer, Jr., "Behavior Problems of Children as Viewed by Teachers and Mental Hygienists," *Mental Hygiene,* Vol. XXXVI (April, 1952), pp. 271–285.

mented their observations with inquiry and with tests in order to obtain a fuller understanding of the boy and then recommended a course of action in terms of the boy's social, emotional, physical, and intellectual needs.[2]

Teachers must be trained to use observation and to use it effectively in the study of pupils. While all gradations of guidance workers and such specialists as the psychologist and psychiatrist will use observation in the analysis of the pupil, the teacher has by far the greatest opportunity to make observations. His contacts with the pupil are so numerous and long continued that he should detect problem behavior and detect it in the incipient stage. Counselors, deans, and psychiatrists must largely depend on the observations of teachers in order to locate the cases which need their ministrations.

Accordingly, numerous authors have written helpful accounts of observation techniques designed to train teachers to effective employment of this method of understanding pupils. For example, Morrison[3] described in fine detail an appropriate technique for observation of the pupil's power of sustained application and followed with suggestions for pupil training in that power. Driscoll's monograph[4] is directly on the point of this discussion. Her discourse includes an exposition of the opportunities and methods for studying children's behavior—in classroom, on the playground, in out-of-school activities. She describes with many brief examples various types and kinds of behavior, then explains causation, effect on personality development, ways of helping. Assuming that her readers are teachers, she has sprinkled throughout her work dozens of groups of questions calculated to stimulate practical experience in observation of pupils. An example of such a group of questions is the following, taken from a section entitled "Clues for Determining Emotional Development":[5]

1. Are there children in your class who have difficulty in controlling their emotional responses?

2. Do some children resort to tantrums at home but exercise control in school?

3. Are some children regarded askance by their classmates because they express emotion vigorously? Have you found a legitimate avenue of expression for these responses?

4. Are there some children whose moods fluctuate during the day?

Another manual for child study is that of English and Raimy.[6] While it comprehends the use of tests and the gathering of all the data called for by

---

[2] Theodore L. Torgerson, *Studying Children: Diagnostic and Remedial Procedures in Teaching* (New York, Dryden, 1947), pp. 7–15.

[3] H. C. Morrison, *The Practice of Teaching in the Secondary School,* rev. ed. (Chicago, University of Chicago Press, 1931), Ch. IX.

[4] Gertrude Driscoll, *How to Study the Behavior of Children* (New York, Teachers College, Columbia University, 1941).

[5] *Ibid.,* p. 45.

[6] Horace B. English and Victor Raimy, *Studying the Individual School Child: A Manual of Guidance* (New York, Holt, 1946).

a complete case study, it delineates the techniques of observation and in a "Sample Case Study" shows the continuous employment of those techniques.

In his well-rounded recent work on the study of children, Torgerson[7] has included one extended chapter entitled "How to Identify Problem Behavior by Observation." His detailed "Behavior Inventories" show the remarkable degree to which observation can be employed to assess the child's work habits, study skills, academic progress, physical health, and social behavior.

An interesting example of the use of observation as a research technique in the identification and detailed analysis of social maladjustment is Cowell's report[8] on the comparison of a dozen junior high school boys who were selected by their physical-education teachers as "fringers," with a similar number of "actives"—spontaneous participants in physical games. Observers, without knowledge of the category in which each boy belonged, made their observations in the locker rooms and on the playground. The boys were not conscious of being observed. Resultant descriptions of specific behavior offered helpful analyses of the two types, the most frequently mentioned characterizations of the "fringers" being as follows: "If he disappeared the group would not miss him very much," "Rather clumsy and awkward," "Content to be an onlooker," "Would rather be a spectator than a participant."

Observation is basic. The scope of this book is such, however, that the reader must be referred to the manuals of Driscoll, Torgerson, and English and Raimy, already cited, for training in observation techniques.[9]

Recording Observations

Rating Scales. In order that observations may be most useful in analysis and counsel of the individual, it is indeed desirable that a record of them should be made. Among other means, several rating scales have been developed for this purpose. Two of them will be cited here. One, created by Van Alstyne,[10] presents thirteen classroom situations and lists descriptions of several forms of behavior with which the child might meet the situation. as,

[7] *Op. cit.,* Ch. 3.

[8] Charles C. Cowell, "Physical Education as Applied Social Science," *Educational Research Bulletin,* Vol. XVI (September 15, 1937), pp. 147–155.

[9] Another manual of undoubted merit for helping teachers to identify the pupils who have special abilities or special handicaps is the following: Jack Kough and Robert F. DeHaan, *Teacher's Guidance Handbook,* Part I, *Identifying Children Who Need Help* (Chicago, Science Research Associates, 1955).

[10] Dorothy Van Alstyne, "A New Rating Scale for Behavior and Attitudes in the Elementary School," *Journal of Educational Psychology,* Vol. XXVII (December, 1936), pp. 677–688.

When faced with failure

    Sees cause of failure and corrects it
    Tries to get help to overcome difficulty
    Recovers quickly and plans new activity
    Shows disappointment but continues activity
    Is apparently indifferent to failure
    Becomes discouraged easily—must succeed in order to continue activity
    Becomes irritable or angry, or cries[11]

The second scale, widely known and used, is a five-point graphic scale.[12] It raises questions about the ratee, such as, "Is he even-tempered or moody?" and for each question offers five answers on the scale, such as, "Generally even-tempered" and "Has periods of extreme elation or depression." Values ranging from 1 to 5 are given each of the answers, with the lowest value representing the most wholesome behavior. Since the arrangement of the values varies with each scale, no profile across the scales can be drawn for a pupil, but a total score can be found.

Naturally, a characteristic of these scales is that they direct observation closely and contain it within quite specific limits. Nor do they leave the observers' reports of observation to the vagaries and variations in their powers of expression. Both of the instruments here cited are the products of scientific investigation. Their value has been measured and found to be noteworthy.

A wider and more inclusive treatment of rating scales will be found in Chapter 13, but occasion may here be taken to call the attention of the reader to the reproduction of the American Council on Education Cumulative Record Card for Junior and Senior High Schools in Chapter 14. Pages 3 and 4 of the Card constitute another example of a plan for the recording of teachers' observations of pupils' conduct.

Inventories. Torgerson's inventories[13] consist of check lists of symptoms or disabilities in general scholarship, in each of the several elementary-school subjects, in vision, hearing, health, speech, and social behavior. The items do not give a rounded evaluation of the individual; they serve only to point out his inadequacies, his maladjustments, the particulars in which he fails to measure up to desirable standards of health, personality, and academic accomplishment. Some of the items are character traits which represent deductions or generalizations that the teacher makes from observed behavior, as, "un-co-operative," "irresponsible," "vindictive," and "self-ish," in the list of 50 items classified as "Social Behavior." The form in which Torgerson has cast his instrument invites the teacher to appraise each

---

[11] *Ibid.,* pp. 688–689.
[12] M. E. Haggerty, W. C. Olson, and E. K. Wickman, *Haggerty-Olson-Wickman Behavior Rating Schedules* (New York, World Book, 1930).
[13] *Op. cit.,* pp. 56–75.

pupil of his class with reference to each item in the inventories. All of the inventories, says the author, are applicable to pupils in grades 1 to 9, and all except the inventories of spelling and arithmetic are applicable to grades 10 to 12.

Such direction of observation would provide a noteworthy impetus to the teacher's growth in skill, awareness, and sensitivity in the study of his pupils. Torgerson's instrument is not the kind that the teacher would fill out some day after school and be done with. It would serve as a constant guide to observation. Tentative checks would be entered for various items and on different children from day to day as they reveal themselves. At the end of a semester many of the symptoms or disabilities exhibited by the various members of the class could be recorded with considerable assurance of their validity. Very properly, however, the author has listed for each of the sections of the inventory "Objective criteria which may be used in validating the ratings." These are diagnostic and achievement tests and examinations by such specialists as nurse, physician, psychologist, psychiatrist, and speech clinician.

Another inventory, brief and quite specialized, was drawn up jointly by the United States Office of Education and the Medical Division of the National Selective Service during World War II for the purpose of utilizing the observations of high-school teachers in detecting emotional and mental instability in older high-school boys. Use of this inventory was intended to aid military induction centers in locating inductees who should be especially studied by Selective Service psychiatrists.[14]

The Anecdotal Behavior Journal. A method of recording observations of pupils which has received much attention in educational literature in the past two decades is the anecdotal behavior journal or record. Most authorities accord to the Rochester Institute of Technology, of Rochester, New York, credit for originating this instrument and demonstrating its possibilities. As used there,

Specific entries in the Journal, described as anecdotes, were composed of objectively recorded behavior incidents, which reflected some significant item of conduct, gave a word picture of the individual in action, provided a snapshot at the moment of the incident, or recounted any event in which the student took part, in such a way as to reveal significant aspects of his personality.[15]

Admitting that not all acts of the individual can be entered in the journal, these authorities say that in selecting incidents for recording, the fundamental question should be,[16]

[14] The development and use of this instrument is described in Harry A. Jager, "Plan for Locating Emotionally Unstable Youth," *Occupations,* Vol. XXII (January, 1944), pp. 237–242.

[15] L. L. Jarvie and Mark Ellingson, *A Handbook on the Anecdotal Behavior Journal* (Chicago, University of Chicago Press, 1940), p. 1.

[16] *Ibid.,* p. 21.

Does this particular behavior episode, or series of episodes, give insight into the emerging behavior patterns of the student and consequently make possible an understanding of the degree to which his personal needs are, or are not, being satisfied?

Good writing of anecdotes involves straightforward, objective reporting of the incident or episode without any use of evaluative terms and without any generalizations concerning the character of the pupil observed. Interpretation may be offered, but it should be written in a paragraph separate from that of the anecdote. Similarly, if recommendations come to the mind of the writer, they should be written under a proper caption which distinguishes them from the anecdote and its interpretation. To write a journal from which one may with greatest assurance come to some deductions concerning the personality and character of a pupil, the dates and sequences of the behavior incidents must be clearly indicated. Then the persistence of a trait is disclosed, or the progressive development of the individual is revealed.

Many questions come to mind concerning the practical use of the anecdotal behavior journal. Teachers have to exercise selection in determining the incidents they will report. After all, the pupil is active over something or other all the time. The basis on which selection of incidents will be made is not easy to state. The admonition of protagonists of the journal is commonly to report positive and favorable incidents as well as those which are negative and unfavorable. Such a rule calls for the objectivity and open-mindedness which are desirable in an observer, but it does not help one in being selective. Again, the "significant" incidents should be reported. But what is significant to one teacher may appear insignificant to another and altogether escape the notice of a third. Certain patterns do, however, appear in the initial reporting of teachers, and these patterns may be changed as the teachers become experienced and are educated to a certain point of view. The following quotation is an example:[17]

At first teachers had difficulty in deciding what incidents to describe as they studied individual children. Their initial choices were based largely upon the following considerations: the child's success or failure in school work, the child as a disturbing or helpful element in carrying on classroom routine, the status of the child's family in the community, and the child's personal attractiveness or repulsiveness to the teacher. As time went on, however, these teachers selected incidents more and more because of their significance in connection with the children's particular developmental tasks. There was thus a definite shift in what the teachers recognized as important.

To train teachers to keep the anecdotal behavior journal effectively is, indeed, to train them to be effective and discerning observers of children in

[17] *Helping Teachers to Understand Children.* By the Staff of the Division on Child Development and Teacher Personnel. Prepared for the Commission on Teacher Education (Washington, D.C., American Council on Education, 1945), p. 41.

the light of valid educational objectives. In his experimentation with the journal, Hamalainen gave the teachers who co-operated with him a frame of reference for the selection of behavior incidents. He directed them to collect anecdotes which would indicate pupils' progress or lack of progress toward the Cardinal Objectives of Elementary Education, a formulation of objectives in terms of pupil behavior which had been generally accepted and studied by the elementary-school teachers of New York State.[18] Naturally, these objectives were very sweeping in scope, comprehending the development of the child in all particulars. Bowes, for her experiment with a second-grade group, narrowed the field of behavior to be recorded to the incidents which revealed progress in character development. She reclassified the incidents as positive and negative with reference to their bearing on that goal. By showing the numbers of plus and minus anecdotes recorded in September-October in comparison with the numbers of each recorded for December-January, she was able to arrive at quantitative evidence of what she was accomplishing in character education, just as objective tests showed progress in academic skill and knowledge.[19] It seems probable that the limiting of the field concerning which anecdotes are to be written is desirable in teachers' first experience in such activity.

Miss Bowes worked in the relatively simple situation in which one teacher observed her roomful of pupils all day, wrote the anecdotes, summarized, and interpreted them. In the departmentalized school, each pupil will be observed by several teachers. Their anecdotes must be collected and the ones on each pupil must be brought together. Presumably a counselor or the principal then studies the episodes and arrives at an interpretation of each pupil. Certainly it is most advantageous to bring together the observations made by several teachers over a period of time and made in the variety of situations with which the pupil is confronted by the subjects, the personalities, and the extracurricular life of the average school. The co-ordination of the anecdotes, however, must be managed so that the individual teacher does not feel that his role is inferior. As he is brought into the process of interpretation, he will recognize more fully the indispensable part he plays in the study of pupils and will be stimulated to grow in his capacity as a partner in this significant professional enterprise.

The anecdotal behavior journal differs markedly from the trait-rating scales described above as a means of recording observations. The anecdotes offer the raw material of behavior examples from which the traits may be deduced. The rating scales simply call upon the teacher to present the deductions, conclusions, and generalizations to which his observations lead him. The specially trained interpreter of behavior, such as the school coun-

---

[18] Arthur E. Hamalainen, *An Appraisal of Anecdotal Records* (New York, Teachers College, Columbia University, Contributions to Education No. 891, 1943), pp. 11–14.
[19] Fern H. Bowes, "The Anecdotal Behavior Record in Measuring Progress in Character," *Elementary School Journal,* Vol. XXXIX (February, 1939), pp. 431–435.

selor, has a better chance to employ his powers if a wealth of objectively described examples of behavior can be placed before him.

One is puzzled to know how so time-consuming a device as the anecdotal behavior journal can be practically employed in the typical departmentalized secondary school or college. The teacher has so many students that it is impossible for him to write anecdotes about any sizable fraction of them. In frank recognition of this situation, as also in full acknowledgment of the fact that the education of teachers to the writing of a good journal is a task of sizable proportions, a program of writing anecdotal records should not be entered upon lightly. A further consideration of practicability is the task of summarizing, interpreting, and applying the information contributed by the teachers' journals.

Professional ideals, however, impel us to judge the anecdotal behavior journal on more fundamental criteria than that of practicability. Logically, the first question ought to be: Should teachers thoughtfully observe the behavior of the individual children for whom they are responsible? They should. The second question ought to be: Should teachers keep written records of their observations? They should. Such records, or a summary of them, constitute valuable capital for succeeding teachers. The third question ought to be: Should such examples of pupils' behavior be cited as to give objective and life-like images of them? They should. With such data before him, the school counselor is unquestionably more effective in accomplishing both distributive and adjustive guidance.

Viewing the anecdotal behavior journal in such a light, the evident duty of guidance workers is to press for schools which are so organized and so staffed that the employment of this guidance feature is feasible. The core-curriculum organization is suggestive. So, also, is the New Trier Township High School, the guidance organization of which was described in Chapter 10. In the meantime, most school faculties will find it possible to take up anecdote writing in a limited way. They may agree on a few pupils each semester whose personalities they will seek to illuminate by recording observed incidents of behavior. Their own professional growth may well be the most notable outcome of the experience.

Interviewing the Pupil

The interview is sometimes employed to obtain information for diagnosis and sometimes for the purpose of influencing choices or conduct. Often the two purposes are combined in the same interview. We are here concerned with the diagnostic purpose.

The interview which is most clearly identified as diagnostic is that which is employed with all pupils soon after they become members of a school. It may be made clear to an entering class as a group that the policy of the school is to become acquainted with each individual pupil as early as possible in order that his individual needs may be given full consideration in planning his education and to help him get the most out of school. To that end, the pupils may be told, the school keeps a cumulative record folder for each pupil in which are entered semester after semester the marks he earns, his scores on standardized tests, and various other evidences of his aptitudes and growth. With such orientation the secondary-school pupil or college student should be prepared for the interview which is held for the purpose of making initial entries in his folder.

As an example of the information that will be called for in this first interview, the reader is invited to turn to Chapter 14 in which he will find a facsimile of the American Council on Education Cumulative Record Folder for Junior and Senior High Schools. A study of that folder will indicate some items of information on the entering seventh-grader, such as "Previous School Record," as usually best obtained from data sent forward by his elementary school. But the interview with the pupil may well be the primary source of information for the following items called for by the folder:

Interests
Out-of-school and summer experiences
Work experiences
Educational and occupational plans
Family and home environment
   Occupations of parents and siblings
   Education of parents and siblings
   Religion
   Names, sex, and age of siblings

Health, decease of either parent, birthplaces, citizenship, changes in type of occupation of parents, language spoken, type of community, study conditions, or other factors, such as "broken home".

In later interviews information may well be obtained on such topics as the following:

Best liked studies
Least liked studies
Favorite recreational activities
Member of what clubs or groups outside of school?
Does the pupil take lessons in music or other accomplishments outside of school?
Do boarders or relatives live in the home?
Home duties
Part-time employment

The interviewer will doubtless have a form on which he records what he learns on these topics, but it seems likely that the interview will be much more warm and friendly, and therefore much more revealing, if the recording is postponed until after the interview is over. If the pupil feels that the counselor is genuinely interested in him, he is likely to talk with freedom and ease. The counselor listens attentively, and his direction of the conversation is unobtrusive. If the pupil feels sufficiently sure that the counselor is really his friend, he may volunteer much information about circumstances which are highly influential in determining his personality and character but which the counselor would not dare to seek out by direct questioning. The following are such areas of information:

Economic status and stability of the home
Quality of the neighborhood and of community relationships in which the pupil lives
Habits and character of the parents
Type and quality of discipline exercised by father and by mother
Parental interest in and ambitions for the pupil
Parental compatibility
Relations with siblings

Perhaps the best opening wedge for the interview is the subject of the client's educational and vocational plans. In the course of such a discussion the counselor can, without impertinence, raise the question, "Well, what do your parents think of your plans?" Such a lead may precipitate a conversation which helpfully reveals many of the family attitudes and circumstances in which the pupil is growing up, or it may yield only a meager response; the counselor takes what is volunteered and pursues the subject further only as the counselee's attitude invites him.

Not to be overlooked in this brief statement concerning the interview as a means of obtaining information is the behavior of the subject during the course of the interview. Innumerable reports of case studies illustrate the value of this obvious technique. The pupil is observed to react to the interview situation with sincerity, frankness, and a helpful spirit, or he may give impressions of suspicion, self-consciousness, shame, defiance, or other feelings. The counselor makes mental note of the moods of the client which each turn of the interview elicits. Two observations reported by a psychological counselor in the Milwaukee Public Schools illustrate the somewhat obvious point of this paragraph:[20]

. . . Her reserve left her; she was no longer shy and withdrawn, but fairly sparkled as she told me of her triumphs, of the great demand for her talents, of the fun it was, and the money her mother received.

After a bit of a chat I began to wonder about that 73 I.Q. Tom was so sensible, so reasonable, so understanding in his remarks. A Wechsler-Bellevue yielded an I.Q. of 128, 133 on the verbal scale and 117 on the performance.

Interviewing Teachers

The values of interviewing teachers as a method of learning about pupils have been made somewhat plain by the preceding discussions about teacher

[20] Katharine W. Dresden, "Vocational Choices of Secondary Pupils," *Occupations*, Vol. XXVII (November, 1948), p. 105.

observation of pupils and about the writing of anecdotal behavior journals by teachers. Each teacher, of course, registers his evaluation of the pupil's academic success and progress as required by the school administration. In many schools he also gives his estimate of the pupil's possession of various character traits, such as those called for by the American Council on Education Cumulative Record Folder. But here we are concerned with the descriptions of behavior, the examples of conduct, and the revealing anecdotes which the teacher can relate, together with his own deductions and generalizations from such evidence. Teachers naturally vary widely in their disposition to observe pupils and in their ability to interpret their observations. Their opportunities for observation also vary. A number of years ago the writer said to a teacher of physical education who was unusually sensitive to her pupils, "It seems to me that you physical education teachers must know your pupils much better than the general run of academic teachers. You meet them in situations which are so free in comparison with the restraint characteristic of the academic classroom." Her reply was, "It depends on the individual teacher in physical education, as in academic subjects. Some are observant and some are not." This statement, of course, is true, but it may also be true that teachers of physical education strike a higher average in knowledge of pupils than do academic teachers. A study carried out with full respect for scientific method could answer the question. The reader is invited to turn back to Chapter 10 in which data were cited from Sachs' experiment on a parallel research. She found that guidance teachers and homeroom teachers were approximately equal in their knowledge of pupils' level of school achievement and general intelligence, but that homeroom teachers averaged higher in information of pupils' health and home situations.

Teachers in the undepartmentalized elementary school typically have much more knowledge of pupils than do teachers in the departmentalized secondary school. Some years ago a teacher of the writer's acquaintance was made counselor in his school—a large six-year high school. He expressed amazement at how much he could learn about a problem pupil by talking with the teachers in the elementary school from which the pupil had come. "They put us high-school teachers to shame."

Years ago a good practice in assembling the knowledge possessed by a pupil's previous teachers was described by Margaret Alltucker as prevailing in the Berkeley Senior High School. Concerning the failing pupil, she said,[21]

After each report period, during the student's first term in the senior high school, the senior high school counselor holds a conference with the principal, the counselor, and the ninth-grade teachers of each junior high school. Here the case record of each problem case is carefully considered. In this way the senior

---

[21] "A Counseling Plan for Bridging the Gap between the Junior and Senior High Schools," *School Review*, Vol. XXXII (January, 1924), p. 64.

high school learns what, in the estimation of those who have known, studied, and worked with him for three years previously, are the factors making for the pupil's present failure and possibly what measures can best be adopted to prevent future failures.

The lesson of acquiring information from a pupil's present teachers is well taught in the film *Learning to Understand Children*.[22] Miss Brown, in seeking to understand the apparent scholastic and social maladjustment which Ada evidenced in her English class, consulted the pupil's teachers in civics, mathematics, art, and general science. Their testimony concerning Ada's behavior in the varied situations which their subjects presented helped to clarify the child's problems.

Interview with Parents

It goes without saying that an understanding of the home environment is essential to our understanding of the pupil. This will be accomplished primarily by interviewing the parents in the school and at home, and by observing the behavior of parents and the physical circumstances of the pupil's home life. Effective guidance calls for friendly and co-operative relationships between home and school. This teamwork will be delineated in later chapters, but at this point we shall limit ourselves to the interview for acquiring information.

Kawin[23] has emphasized the importance of interviewing the parents of kindergartners. She has described the plan developed in the schools of Glencoe, Illinois, of having the kindergarten teachers interview parents shortly after the child enters school—usually at school after school hours. A Parent-Interview Blank was developed to give structure to these interviews. The teacher seeks to learn and record significant facts about the child's home background and family relationships, his developmental history, his preschool interests and experiences, the problems that he had presented at home, and what his parents hoped he might gain from his school experiences. For every child a cumulative record folder is started, and in it is filed his Parent-Interview Blank.

The "basic areas for analysis and study" through interview and observation, says Torgerson, are as follows: (1) parental relationships, (2) child training, (3) parent-child relationships, (4) child-to-child relationships, and (5) socio-economic status.[24] He presents a "Home Environment Inventory" of 43 items classified under the five areas just named. All the items represent unfavorable environment. The teacher is directed to "Check the statements which apply to each pupil. Use O if you do not know."[25] The

22 (New York, McGraw-Hill, 1946).
23 Ethel Kawin, "Guidance in the Glencoe Schools," *Journal of Educational Research,* Vol. XXXVII (March, 1944), pp. 481–492.
24 *Op. cit.,* p. 129.
25 *Ibid.,* pp. 136–139.

Inventory is well calculated to afford wise direction to the search for pertinent information.

Generally speaking, the contacts by which information is obtained from parents should hardly be designated by so formal a term as "interview." Rather, they will be home visits or informal conferences at school, characterized by a mutual sharing of information. Teacher and parent confer as equals. If the pupil presents a real problem they try to define it and solve it by pooling their resources of knowledge. The spirit of these contacts was well described by F. E. Clerk for the guidance of the teachers of the New Trier Township High School in their activity of home visiting, as follows:[26]

The object of this visit is to establish a liaison with the home on a friendly, informal basis. The adviser on this occasion represents the school and he should conduct himself with this fact in mind. This visit presents an opportunity to know the student in his home and to formulate some impressions of the nature of the home influence. This visit should be used to explain to the parent that the school is anxious to co-operate with the home for the best interests of the student. Prying questions or inquiries of an intimate nature about the home should be absolutely avoided. Observe what the parents volunteer in this connection and keep it in strictest confidence. Above all things advisers should avoid discussing at this or any other time the affairs of other students. If parents try to bring other students' affairs into the conversation, advisers should make it clear, as tactfully as possible, that it is possible to discuss the affairs of a student *only with his parents.* In arranging the home visit do it as far as possible with the co-operation of the student.

The practical problem of allowing teachers and counselors adequate time for home contacts must not be overlooked. In New Trier, homeroom teachers are assigned one less class than are the teachers not serving in the advisory system.[27] This time allowance is in consideration not merely of home visiting but of the total homeroom responsibility. Another solution for the problem of time for home contacts was found by the school system in which the Commission on Teacher Education of the American Council on Education directed the teachers in their study of children:[28]

Arrangements were made to hold only morning sessions at school during the first week of each academic year. In this way five afternoons were freed at the very beginning of school so that the teachers could accomplish more quickly their round of visits to the homes of all pupils. . . .

It is probable that the administrators were influenced to make this arrangement by the earlier experiences of the first-grade teachers. For some years the first grades had operated on a half-day schedule during the first month of school and

[26] Mimeographed bulletin for 1926–27.

[27] Clifford E. Erickson and Marion C. Happ, *Guidance Practices at Work* (New York, McGraw-Hill, 1946), p. 25.

[28] *Helping Teachers to Understand Children* (New York, American Council on Education, 1945), p. 46.

the teachers had devoted the afternoons to extended visits in the homes of their pupils.

The effectiveness of home visiting and other contacts with parents in yielding information essential to the understanding of children and youth from kindergarten to graduate school is amply attested by the extensive literature of case studies. Just how *important* it is to know that one child comes from a working-class home while another comes from a white-collar home, that one comes from a broken home while another comes from a normal home, that one is subject to stern home discipline while another has parents who are lax in their control—these and other typical differences will be given interpretation in the next section of this chapter.

Questionnaires Filled Out by Pupils

Because the individual interview is a relatively expensive and time-consuming method of gathering information, most schools employ questionnaires on which the pupil or parent can record many important items of data. At the high-school level many schools use one or two homeroom periods for gathering data in this manner. The mimeographed questionnaires are either filed in the pupils' record folders or the information is transferred from questionnaire to the folder's printed form by a clerk.

Careful thought must be given to the items called for by the questionnaire. First, the items should be significant. The tendency is to keep adding to the length of a questionnaire from year to year, including more and more queries for information of doubtful value. Second, the questionnaire must be adapted to the age-level of the pupils who are to respond to it. They must understand what is called for, be able properly to register their responses, and possess the information called for. Third, the questionnaire should be confined to areas of information in which pupils may properly be expected to be willing to respond truthfully. It may indeed be important to know if a child's father is an alcoholic, but we cannot expect to elicit such information by questionnaire.

Perhaps, in the average of secondary-school situations in which a class or homeroom is asked to fill out a blank of information, data on the following items may be called for:

Personal data on each parent—health, religious affiliation, education (extent and kind), occupation, place of birth, whether deceased
Personal data on siblings—age, schooling, occupation, whether living at home
Best and least liked studies
Favorite recreational activities
Educational and vocational plans
Summer vacation experiences
Extracurriculum experiences
Membership in organizations outside of school

The questionnaire is a time-saver for gathering the sort of factual material with which no marked feelings or attitudes are connected, but for areas of information such as are listed on page 337 in the discussion of the interview, it would be worse than useless. It would arouse ill-will and suspicion.

What dependence may be placed on data gathered by questionnaire? As one answer to this question, Bain's study may be cited.[29] This author reported giving a questionnaire calling for 61 items of personal information to 50 college freshmen, with careful directions to obtain uniformity in filling in the schedule. Two and a half months later the same questionnaire was given with the same directions. Comparison of the responses showed that more than 23 per cent had been changed—27 per cent in the area of factual family data, 18 per cent in the area of factual personal data, and 24 per cent in the area of subjective personal data. The items were in general such as are dealt with in this chapter, except that the category called "subjective personal data" included some items characteristic of an adjustment questionnaire (see Chapter 13). Care was taken not to regard a response as changed unless it was a clear case, and opportunity was given the students, at their second responding, to identify items in which the facts in truth had changed. Items falling in this latter category were not counted as changed.

A second answer to the question of validity of questionnaire responses has been given by Wiley.[30] In his study the answers given by pupils were checked by case workers going into the homes and by other objective sources. From this validation Wiley concluded that "we may rely upon the answers to a school questionnaire with a reasonably high degree of assurance. . . ."

Undoubtedly the questionnaire will greatly reduce the work of interviewing for information if, in employing it, good judgment is exercised in seeking only information which the pupils are able and willing to give.[31]

Daily and Weekly Schedules of Pupils

One method of studying the pupil is to take account of how he spends his time. The value of obtaining from the pupil a schedule of his time expenditure for the twenty-four hours a day was made especially evident by the studies of Sturtevant and Strang.[32] These authors gave specific directions to a

[29] Read Bain, "Stability in Questionnaire Response," *American Journal of Sociology*, Vol. XXXVII (November, 1931), pp. 445–453.

[30] Andrew T. Wiley, "To What Extent May We Rely Upon the Answers to a School Questionnaire?" *Journal of Educational Method*, Vol. VI (February, 1927), pp. 252–257.

[31] For many helpful suggestions, see L. V. Koos, *The Questionnaire in Education* (New York, Macmillan, 1928).

[32] Sarah M. Sturtevant and Ruth Strang, "A Study of the Twenty-four Hour Schedules of Forty High School Girls," *Teachers College Record*, Vol. XXVIII (June, 1927), pp. 994–1010; "The Daily Schedule as an Aid to Advisers," *Teachers College Record*, Vol. XXIX (October, 1927), pp. 31–45; "Activities of High School Girls," *Teachers College Record*, Vol. XXX (March, 1929), pp. 562–571.

group of girls for the sequential listing of all their daily activities, together with the number of minutes spent on each activity. They found that these schedules were remarkably revealing. The home life, the home chores, the reading habits, the music lessons, the paid employment, the socializing, the mode of transportation to and from school—all these and many more activities of daily living were so depicted as to offer much evidence for the interpretation of each individual. The schedule provided something objective on which to center counseling. It helped the pupil to analyze his own behavior and gain insights into his problems.

Another example of the use of this device for the study of the pupil is given by Hayes,[33] who had pupils fill out a time-diary each morning in the homeroom period for the previous 24-hour interval. The diary form divided the day into convenient major periods and listed certain regular or anticipated activities so as to stimulate recall. Table 37 presents Hayes' classification of activities so as to show "profiles" of eight pupils.[34] A casual canvass

TABLE 37. Profiles of Eight Pupils Showing Number of Hours Spent Weekly in Voluntary Activities of Six Types

Type of Activity	Pro-file 19	Pro-file 45	Pro-file 80	Pro-file 93	Pro-file 115	Pro-file 168	Pro-file 211	Pro-file 314
Paid employment	....	....	17.0	....	22.5	3.0	....	....
Home chores	9.0	1.5	4.0	4.5	.5	3.5	13.0	9.5
Study	6.5	7.5	10.5	6.5	4.5	3.5	8.0	1.5
School groups	13.0	....	....	19.5	3.0	6.5	3.0	9.0
Community groups	9.5	20.0	5.5	6.0	10.0	6.0	6.0	10.0
Solitary	2.5	11.0	3.0	3.0	.5	18.0	4.0	9.5

of the data of the table suggests the variety of circumstances and influences under which high-school pupils are growing up. However, for the practical purpose of understanding the individual pupil, the counselor would study the detailed time expenditure of each case, recognizing that such a classification as shown in Table 37 is not sufficiently revealing. For example, does activity in school groups mean basketball or the junior play? does activity in community groups mean a scout troop or a pool-hall gang? does solitary activity mean reading, practicing music lessons, or building a radio? The time diary, if pupils feel confident that the information will be used only for their ad-

[33] Wayland J. Hayes, "Recording the Extra-Class Activities of High-School Pupils," *School Review,* Vol. XXXIX (June, 1931), pp. 439–448.
[34] *Ibid.* Adapted from Figure 1, p. 444.

vantage, can be extremely useful for its revelation of values and interests, and, perhaps, of home circumstances.

The Autobiography

Guidance authorities are quite aware of the possibilities of the autobiography as a means of revealing the client to the counselor. From the individual's telling of his own life story, much may be learned about the physical and psychological environment in which he has been growing up. His interests, attitudes, and values are illuminated, and from the quality of his writing some evidence of his intelligence and educational achievement is obtained. The reader, of course, must be on guard against distortions, biased testimony, the tendency of the writer to justify himself. Most autobiographers fail to report themselves with rigorous objectivity. Bearing in mind such limitations, the autobiography will be checked thoughtfully and used to supplement information obtained by tests, observation, and interviews.

The form of the autobiography varies. Some users have employed a questionnaire outline which requires the subject to give information on a large number of specific points. An example of this type is to be found in the report of the Breathitt County demonstration.[35] All the elementary-school and secondary-school pupils of the county filled out an autobiographical schedule which was organized in seven sections, as follows:

First Facts about Myself
My Family
Our Home
My Education Thus Far and Plans for More
What I Like—My Interests
My Future Occupation—Occupational Preferences
Group Contacts

The detailed information under each section was called for in a form which closely resembled a completion test. Undoubtedly such detailed direction of the autobiography gives the guidance worker opportunity to request a wide range of data which he knows to be valuable, but the emphasis is on facts, and the pupil's expression of feeling and value is decidedly restricted.

Forms for the autobiography range from the type just described through simple outlines or suggestions to the narration written spontaneously by the subject. At the latter extreme, the pupil's product is likely to be characterized by omissions which are serious from the standpoint of the guidance worker. Furthermore, the organization of the paper will vary widely from pupil to pupil.

English teachers have reported experience in the use of the autobiography as a writing form which counselors will do well to consider. For example,

[35] Wilbur I. Gooch and Franklin J. Keller, "Breathitt County in the Southern Appalachians," *Occupations*, Vol. XIV (June, 1936, Section Two), pp. 1024–1025.

Preston[36] points out that oftentimes too little is made of the writing of the autobiography and that it is perfunctorily done, in which case results are poor. He suggests that children should be stimulated by the reading of autobiographies and that they be helped in organizing for the writing of their own (but not to the extent of giving them an outline). He would assure the children of the confidence in which their work will be held if they so desire, and he emphasizes the importance of the teacher having the confidence of his class.

Crouse has described her practice in having her high-school sophomores write extended autobiographies—five to eight chapters averaging 700 words each. ". . . faculty members who are in charge of guidance groups found that reading the stories of students in their groups brought about a clearer understanding through knowledge of background."[37]

A rather extended unit in autobiography in twelfth-grade English is described by Mildred Sobotka,[38] a unit which was climaxed by the pupils' thoughtful writing of their own life histories under the assurance that no eyes but their teacher's would see their work. "More important even than the improvement in the organization of material and in the mechanics of writing as a result of interest and concentration on subject matter was the revelation of student background, of character, of hopes and ideals—facts that no office records or files would ever reveal."

From the experience of English teachers, guidance workers can learn that in obtaining autobiographies as a means of understanding pupils, it is important (1) to build up fullest motivation for the writing, (2) to have pupils feel that their confidences will be respected, and (3) to manage the autobiography project through the collaboration of English teachers and guidance workers.

Sociometric Analysis

Data presented at several points in Chapters 3 and 4 showed how importantly the individual's group life figures in his adjustments. Chapter 10 treated extensively the problem of creating a healthy, vigorous group life in the homeroom. To the readers of this book there need be no elaboration of the fact that inter-pupil relationships constitute the source of many of the problems that challenge the guidance function in its adjustive phase. It is essential therefore that these relationships be understood.

While observations by perceptive subject teachers, homeroom teachers, and extracurriculum sponsors are helpful in the study of interaction among

[36] Ralph C. Preston, "Children's Autobiographies," *Elementary English Review,* Vol. XXIII (November, 1946), pp. 306–307, 310.

[37] Ruth Crouse, "Writing an Autobiography," *English Journal,* Vol. XXXIII (May, 1944), pp. 264–265.

[38] "The Autobiography in a New Guise," *English Journal,* Vol. XXX (October, 1941), pp. 663–664.

pupils, it must be borne in mind that they primarily indicate how pupils *do* associate; they do not clearly reveal how the pupils would *like* to associate. A method for the study of pupils' associational desires is the sociometric test, the results of which are commonly plotted as a sociogram.

In essence, the sociometric test is made by simply asking the pupils of a class, club, or homeroom to name their preferred companions in some venture of work or play or just proximity.

You are seated now as you happened to get seated in our homeroom, but now that we all know one another, every pupil should have the opportunity to sit near the other pupils he most wants to sit beside. Then the classroom can be arranged to suit everyone. Write your own name and under it three choices of pupils you would like to sit near in this room. Put a "1" next to your first choice, a "2" for your second, and a "3" for your third choice. I will try to fit in as many of everyone's choices as possible. But since there are many pupils and each of you may be choosing in many different ways, you can see how it is that I can only do my best to arrange the seats so everyone gets at least one choice and more only if I can figure the seats out that way.[39]

These directions illustrate the following criteria which the author states must be observed for valid sociometric testing:[40]

1. The situation should be *real* for the choosing; choices are not hypothetical; they are made for an *actual* situation, in the same terms as the action is going to be.

2. The test is not an end in itself; its results are always put into effect to change the arrangements for working or living in accordance with the choices; sociometric arrangement is only setting the stage for a better group-work situation.

3. There is an *immediacy* to the choosing: it is for right now, tomorrow, or next week, not some vague time in the future or two months later.

Quite clearly, the implication of these criteria is that sociometric testing is carried on primarily to meet the needs of the members of a pupil group. In another writing, this author, who has devoted years to the study of this instrument, asserts that a "better group work situation" does result from its employment, her conclusion being as follows:[41]

Among the many teachers who have used sociometric choices and continued their arrangements over a period of time, none have reported more than temporary disturbances, and all have found that their classroom atmosphere and working morale have increased markedly.

[39] Helen Hall Jennings, "Sociometric Grouping in Relation to Child Development," in *Fostering Mental Health in Our Schools,* 1950 Yearbook, Association for Supervision and Curriculum Development (Washington, D.C., National Education Association, 1950), p. 204.

[40] *Ibid.,* p. 205.

[41] *Sociometry in Group Relations: A Work Guide for Teachers* (Washington, D.C., American Council on Education, 1948), p. 47.

The value of sociometry for the guidance function lies in its revelation of the position of the pupil in the society of his peers. A sense of belonging, of acceptance by one's fellows, is highly important to children, and seems to increase in acuteness as they grow into adolescence. To be denied this desired status for any length of time is certain to mark the personality. Some will evince aggressive forms of behavior, such as attention-getting tactics. Others will exhibit withdrawing patterns. Both types frequently neglect their academic responsibilities, present attitudes of boredom, apathy, or preoccupation. However, a withdrawn child sometimes applies himself intensely to his studies in order to demonstrate his competence and win the praise of the teacher, as compensation for his lack of status in the group. Or, he simply cultivates the teacher, causing the teacher to misunderstand the pupil's status, as in the following instance:[42]

At first I couldn't believe that Ray had no friends. I would have said that he is very popular. After observing the class for a while I discovered that the facts shown by the friendship chart are correct. I misjudged Ray because he is always so friendly with me and goes out of his way to do nice things for me. I like him but the other children don't pay any attention to him.

Does the teacher's favorable response to such a boy actually contribute to the boy's unpopularity with his fellows?

Identifying, by means of the sociogram, the pupils who are not chosen by their fellows, does not tell why they are not chosen. The interview and other methods will be employed to find the reasons for such isolation. Then all the skill the teacher can muster will be employed to bring about the acceptance of those pupils.

Sociometry is much too complicated a technique to be used on the basis of the explanation in this abbreviated statement. Undoubtedly, the method is promising, but the individual teacher or the faculty who wish to use it must first study it at length and then practice it under skilled supervision. Otherwise, unfortunate errors will occur in the specifics of the technique, the interpretation of results, and the subsequent counseling or remedial steps.[43]

MEANINGS OF INFORMATION OBTAINED BY OBSERVATION AND INQUIRY

"The teachers said that the cumulative records currently being kept were a big chore and of little practical help. They reported that they spent a lot of time making entries on the records but seldom were able to get anything

[42] Merle Elliott, "Patterns of Friendship in the Classroom," *Progressive Education,* Vol. XVIII (November, 1941), p. 390.

[43] H. Otto Dahlke and Thomas O. Monahan, "Problems in the Application of Sociometry to Schools," *School Review,* Vol. LVII (April, 1949), pp. 223–234.

useful out of them."[44] In this quotation is criticism and challenge. To require teachers to engage in time-consuming, meaningless busywork is to do dishonor to their profession. Careful selection must rule the collection and recording of data on pupils—selection on the basis of probable value. To ascertain and record for *all* pupils every item that may be helpful in understanding *any* pupil is impossible and also wasteful. Hence, limitations must be set in accordance with the degree of contingency of value.

Concerning many items of information about pupils, scientific studies have been made. They will be drawn upon insofar as possible for the light they shed on the extent and kinds of value to be attached to the items. The logic of common sense will be called upon where scientific information is not available. The purpose of this section is to help teachers and counselors understand pupils by being able to interpret some of the information found in a good cumulative record folder.

An important word of caution should be uttered concerning the application of the findings of scientific studies to the interpretation of individual behavior. These studies derive their meanings from differences between groups. For example, highly educated parents have ambitions for their children which are different from the ambitions of parents of little education. *But only as a group.* The statistically significant difference between the two groups still allows for their extensive overlapping in the trait measured. So, the average for a group must not be considered as applicable to each member. The individual is always unique, and the counselor must ascertain the extent to which he possesses the characteristic which has been found for his group.

The Family and the Home

The modern educationist thinks of children's behavior as being caused. He sees a pupil's actions as based upon his past experience and the present forces which impinge upon him. Among these forces none is so potent as is that primary social institution, the family. Educational literature of the past quarter century attests a steadily growing appreciation of the role of home life in shaping the ideas, attitudes, and values with which a child moves into his adulthood. The significance of various aspects of home and family life for distributive and adjustive guidance will be examined.

Health of Parents. The kinds, degrees, and durations of health conditions in a child's parents are so numerous, changing, and complex as practically to preclude the measurement of their influence or the arrival at any generalization concerning their effect on children. Common sense tells us, however, that the health of the parents is a crucial factor in the home environment. Typically, the illness or invalidity of the mother affects the housekeeping; physical incapacity of the father affects the economic status of the family.

[44] *Helping Teachers to Understand Children, op. cit.,* p. 22.

Surely, the possible repercussions of this factor on the life of the child need not be detailed. A cumulative record folder cannot properly take it into account. The situation requires that each pupil have an understanding and available adviser with whom he talks freely about the changing circumstances of his life.

Religion. Cumulative record folders typically have blanks for listing the religion of father and mother. Such evaluative studies of this item of information as have been made are of uncertain usefulness. James Harvey Robinson apparently would caution the counselor against regarding church membership or affiliation as sure-fire evidence of adherence to good moral principles. He has pointed out that[45]

Bradstreet does not reckon with religion in establishing one's credit. The custom house official would not pass unexamined the luggage of one professing the Athanasian creed or submitting a certificate of good standing in the Brick Church.

Interpretation of this item of information is indeed difficult.

Birthplace of Parents. A number of years ago when the percentage of foreign-born in our population was much larger than now, studies of juvenile delinquency and criminality showed that those anti-social characteristics were definitely more common among the children of foreign-born parents than among those whose parents were native-born. This generalization is not now deemed very helpful because we have so few children of foreign-born parents and because the search for understanding of criminal tendencies has progressed to more complex and fruitful channels, as will be described in a following division of this section.

Nevertheless, it is important to know if parents are foreign-born, their ethnic origin, and at what age they came to this country. If they came to maturity before emigrating to America, the family life they establish in their adopted country may well express their native culture and thereby be at variance with the world in which their children are growing up. The freedom in her social life which the American high-school girl typically enjoys must appear scandalous to the father and mother of Greek or Italian origin and upbringing. Their own daughter may be quite unhappy and frustrated if forced to conform to old-world standards when she yearns to attend the junior prom with her schoolmates.

The point of this illustration is that if the child is caught in a conflict of cultures, he is often seriously alienated from his home. Unable to accept his home—perhaps ashamed of his parents—he lacks the steadying influence of mature advice and direction. If, on the other hand, he grows up in complete harmony with parents and home life which represent old-world ways, he is out of step at school, is dubbed queer by his classmates, and tagged as "socially maladjusted" by his teachers.

[45] *The Human Comedy* (New York, Harper, 1937), p. 327.

To a lesser degree the jostling of variant cultures right within America must be taken into account. We are a mobile people, experiencing major movements of population from country to city, from agriculture to industry, from East to West. The teacher in Detroit finds in his class a pupil whose family has just been lured to the city from the Tennessee mountain country. The teacher in Los Angeles helps a boy fresh from a Great Plains state to achieve social and academic adjustment in a large city school. As a ten-year-old, Bernard Baruch emigrated from rural South Carolina to New York City, and seventy years later paid tribute to the teacher whose kindly welcome and thoughtful orientation had smoothed his way.[46]

Truly, these paragraphs have reached out beyond their caption, "Birthplace of parents," and have suggested the importance of knowing the background of every child who, either directly, or at secondhand, is or has been subject to a culture alien to that which dominates the community.

Education and Cultural Level of Parents. A recent survey of 25,000 Minnesota high-school seniors to ascertain their plans for the future and the factors influencing those plans, led to the conclusion that

> In general, with both college aptitude and economic status held relatively constant, family attitudes and home cultural influences related to plans to attend college can be identified. . . . a home with many books. . . . A family subscribing to many magazines. . . . Parents active in community organizations, particularly those related to schools. . . . Parents who have progressed far in school. . . .[47]

These are constituents of cultural status demonstrated to be closely identified with plans for going to college. Obviously, a task for counseling is to induce youth who have college aptitude to go to college, regardless of the cultural level of their homes.

Dropping out of school at a lower level than high-school graduation is characteristic of pupils from homes of low educational tradition much more than from homes where the parents have had educational advantages. While there are indices to incipient school leaving of greater cruciality than the education of the parents, the counselor will find that this factor will frequently go far toward explaining pupils' attitudes toward schooling.

Occupation of Father. The now classic study by George S. Counts[48] was the first comprehensive exposition of the relation of father's occupation to length of pupil's stay in school. From his extensive data gathered from the pupils of four cities, Table 38[49] is a sample which may well be regarded as

[46] Bernard Baruch, "A Real Teacher," *NEA Journal,* Vol. XXXIX (September, 1950), p. 415.

[47] Ralph F. Berdie, *After High School—What?* (Minneapolis, University of Minnesota Press, 1954), p. 64.

[48] *The Selective Character of American Secondary Education,* Supplementary Educational Monographs, No. 19 (Chicago, University of Chicago Press, May, 1922).

[49] *Ibid.,* p. 40, Table 15.

illustrative of Counts' findings. The seventeen-fold classification of occupations represents the author's effort to establish a scale which would be based on a combination of social status, economic position, and intellectual outlook. The difficulties of making such a scale and the imperfections of his product were fully described by the author.

The reader will note that the first five occupational classes are primarily white-collar workers; the remaining classes are manual workers. Totaling the percentages in each grade whose fathers were white-collar workers

TABLE 38. Percentage of Children from Each Occupational Group in Each of Two School Grades. Data from 739 Children in the Sixth Grade and 136 in the Senior Year of the High School, Mt. Vernon [New York].

Parental Occupation	Sixth Grade	Senior Year of High School
Proprietors	13.1	29.4
Professional service	6.8	16.9
Managerial service	10.0	20.6
Commercial service	6.0	15.4
Clerical service	4.3	5.2
Agricultural service	2.3	.0
Artisan-proprietors	9.1	5.2
Building trades	16.5	.7
Machine trades	4.7	.7
Printing trades	.4	.0
Miscellaneous trades	5.2	2.2
Transportation service	4.2	.7
Public service	1.5	.0
Personal service	2.4	.0
Miners, lumber-workers, fishermen	.4	.0
Common labor	10.8	.0
Unknown	2.3	3.0
Total	100.0	100.0

yields 40.2 per cent of the sixth grade and 87.5 per cent of the twelfth grade. The meaning of this contrast is that as children advance up through the grades, elimination takes its toll primarily among the children of manual workers; the children of white-collar workers stay in school and thus constitute an even larger percentage of the remaining student body.

As pointed out in Chapter 4, pupil elimination does not occur as early today as at the time of Counts' research. The law and inhospitable industry combine to keep children in school longer. Perhaps school is more attractive, too. Still, less than half of our children today are graduating from high school. And the lesson of Table 38 for guidance workers is that father's occupation affords a valuable clue for early detection of potential drop-outs.

Beyond this specific interpretation of father's occupation, attention should be called to the more general and wide-sweeping importance of this item. The Lynds expressed it this way:[50]

One's job is the watershed down which the rest of one's life tends to flow in Middletown. Who one is, whom one knows, how one lives, what one aspires to be—these and many other urgent realities of living are patterned for one by what one does to get a living and the amount of living this allows one to buy.

And so a family's economic status and cultural level, its way of life, is probably indicated more surely by the father's occupation than by any other single characteristic. Knowing that fact in the pupil's background frequently helps us to understand his attitudes toward school and society, his school associations, and perhaps his social and emotional problems. The counselor must bear in mind, however, the caution stated at the beginning of this section, namely, the necessity for studying every individual and not assuming that he will surely reflect some characteristic generally found in his group.

Social Class. No cumulative record form known to this writer calls for the recording of a pupil's social class. Nevertheless, in ascertaining occupation of father and education of parents, two important constituents of social class are being defined. It seems quite possible that in the future the systematic accumulation and summarizing of the necessary data for establishing social class will be undertaken.

For an understanding of social class in American society and the techniques for determining an individual's social class, we are especially indebted since approximately 1940 to the researches made by the social anthropologist, W. Lloyd Warner, with his associates and students.[51] The novels of Sinclair Lewis and John Marquand notably delineate the classes in American society, the latter author very evidently being influenced by Warner's studies.

As Warner analyzed the population of Yankee City and found to exist in the minds and behavior of the people themselves distinctions on the basis of income, source of wealth, occupation, genealogical background, education (including prestige of college), membership in clubs, churches, and other social groups, location of home (section of city), pretentiousness of dwelling, and other factors or symbols of social position, he found six classes, as follows:[52]

[50] Robert S. Lynd and Helen Merrell Lynd, *Middletown in Transition* (New York, Harcourt, Brace, 1937), p. 7.

[51] See especially W. Lloyd Warner and Paul S. Lunt, *The Social Life of a Modern Community* ("Yankee City Series," Vol. I) (New Haven, Yale University Press, 1941); also, W. Lloyd Warner, Robert J. Havighurst, and Martin B. Loeb, *Who Shall Be Educated?* (New York, Harper, 1944).

[52] Warner and Lunt, *op. cit.,* p. 88.

	Per Cent
Upper-Upper	1.44
Lower-Upper	1.56
Upper-Middle	10.22
Lower-Middle	28.12
Upper-Lower	32.60
Lower-Lower	25.22
Unknown	.84
	100.00

In a later work[53] he has explained his Index of Status Characteristics (I.S.C.) and made clear the method of using it for determination of social class. After successive revisions and refinements, his I.S.C. is now based on four factors, namely, occupation, source of income, house type, and dwelling area. For each of these he has developed a seven-point rating scale by which the factor is rated from 1 (highest) to 7 (lowest). For example, the scale for source of income is as follows: 1—Inherited wealth; 2—Earned wealth; 3—Profits and fees; 4—Salary; 5—Wages; 6—Private relief; 7—Public relief and nonrespectable income. The four factors, or status characteristics, are also weighted, occupation being given a weight of 4, source of income, 3, house type, 3, and dwelling area, 2. Thus, an individual who is given the highest rating on each status characteristic obtains a total score of 12; the individual who is given the lowest rating on each, a score of 84. On the combined weighted scale, each social class has its interval, as, 23–37 for the upper-middle class.

While Warner identifies these classes in American society, he says, "A class system, unlike a caste or any other clearly and formally marked rank-order, is one in which movement up and down is constantly taking place in the lives of many people."[54] His works carry an abundance of illustrations of such vertical mobility and point to such causes as education, marriage, and the gain or loss of wealth.

Of what importance for guidance is a knowledge of the pupil's social class? In the first place, such knowledge goes far toward explaining the pupil's attitudes toward education and the values he seeks in education. Gardner, Gardner, and Loeb,[55] studying a community with Warner techniques, point out that the lower classes tend to look for immediate utility in schooling, especially in terms of making money or setting up a home. Oftentimes they regard earning so highly as to give it precedence over education and permit a child to stay out of school or drop out of school because of a job.

[53] W. Lloyd Warner, Marchia Meeker, and Kenneth Eells, *Social Class in America: A Manual of Procedure for the Measurement of Social Status* (Chicago, Science Research Associates, 1949).

[54] Warner and Lunt, *op. cit.,* pp. 90–91.

[55] Burleigh B. Gardner, Mary R. Gardner, and Martin B. Loeb, "Social Status and Education in a Southern Community," *School Review,* Vol. L (March, 1942), pp. 179–191.

The middle class holds education in high regard, thinking of it as the best means of "getting ahead," or leading to jobs of a managerial or professional character. The upper classes take education for granted and think of life as beginning in college. They view schooling as an avenue to "culture" and are not concerned with immediate bread-and-butter values. Of course, a practical effect of the divergence between the classes in their view of educational purposes is that their curriculum choices to a notable extent reflect class lines. For the conservation of human talent, guidance must often oppose this influence of social class.

"The Impact of Social Classes on Adolescents" is the subtitle of a sociological survey which must provoke the thinking of any secondary-school worker.[56] The author lived, for the period of the survey, in a small midwestern city, acquired a wide acquaintance with adults and adolescents, and ascertained the social class of 535 families which had a total of 735 adolescent members. In age, these youth ranged from 13 to 19, inclusive, but 84 per cent were in the 14-year to 17-year bracket.

The relationship between social class and early withdrawal from school, as shown in Table 39,[57] is most marked. In this table, as all through the

TABLE 39. Percentage Distributions of the Adolescents of Each Class According to School Status

| | Classes | | | | | |
	I	II	III	IV	V	All
(Number of cases)	(4)	(31)	(158)	(312)	(230)	(735)
In school	100.0	100.0	92.4	58.7	11.3	53.1
Out of school	0.0	0.0	7.6	41.3	88.7	46.9
Total	100.0	100.0	100.0	100.0	100.0	100.0

survey, Class I includes both of Warner's upper classes. The aggregate number of adolescents in Hollingshead's Class I and Class II is very small, and all were in school. Very few of the 158 Class III youth were out of school. By contrast, early school leaving was the rule among the youth of Class V and notable among those of Class IV. The table plainly suggests that by ascertainment of the social class of each pupil, school workers take an important step in the identification of early school leavers. In Elmtown, inadequate enforcement of the compulsory attendance laws made it possible for Class V youngsters to drop out of school as early as the age of 12, and the mean age of their withdrawal was 14.9 years.[58]

"The dynamics of withdrawal" from the Elmtown schools are given illustrative explanation by Hollingshead. Economic need was clearly one factor

[56] August B. Hollingshead, *Elmtown's Youth* (New York, Wiley, 1949).
[57] *Ibid.*, adapted from data on page 330.
[58] *Ibid.*, pp. 329–331.

in the stories told by youth, but parental neglect and low evaluation of education were also prominent. Most important, perhaps, was the social discrimination practiced by schoolmates. The bitterness and frustration in social relationships expressed by some of these early school leavers signified a lack of democracy and a deplorable consciousness of social class in both elementary school and high school. The maladjustments fostered by such a social milieu call for correction on a wider scale than can be administered by a guidance specialist, but he cannot ignore their challenge.

The influence of social class on the behavior of pupils and teachers appeared in many aspects of Elmtown school life.[59] In election of curriculum, for example, although the college preparatory curriculum carried much the greater prestige, less than ten per cent of the Class IV and V pupils elected it; they chose the general and commercial curriculums. Discipline was harsh and exacting with pupils of Class IV and V; those of Class I and II were allowed to go unpunished for infraction of rules. Participation in activities and attendance at games, dances, and parties was notably higher on the part of upper-class pupils; lower-class pupils expressed feelings of not belonging, of not being wanted.

Space does not permit further elaboration or illustration of the meaning of social class. Certainly it is a noteworthy conditioning element in both distributive and adjustive guidance.

Occupation of Mother. Less and less does the child's mother confine herself to the role of homemaker and housekeeper. More and more, she also has employment outside the home. In 1952, of the 13.3 million women workers who were or had been married, 2 million had children under 6 years of age, and 5.3 million had children under 18 years of age.[60] What is the effect upon the child when the mother attempts the dual responsibility of holding a job and maintaining a home?

The evidence offered by a high-school principal of the writer's acquaintance may shed some light on this question. During World War II, the principal's community was the scene of feverish shipbuilding activity for the production of landing ships. With labor scarce, many housewives were induced to take short-course training in welding and enter the shipyards. During the school years 1943–44 and 1944–45 the high-school office was continually crowded with disciplinary problems—youngsters who were tardy, truant, violating other school regulations, and otherwise needing corrective and counseling attention. September, 1945, brought a marked change; relative peace and quiet prevailed in the office. The principal's explanation was that the production of ships had ceased and mothers were once more giving full time to the management of home and children.

One scientific study of the significance of this factor is that reported by

[59] *Ibid.,* Ch. 8.
[60] *Women as Workers,* Women's Bureau, U.S. Department of Labor (Washington, D.C., 1954?), p. 71, Table 29.

Essig and Morgan.[61] They administered Leland Stott's adjustment scale entitled "Home Life" to 151 adolescent girls, mostly 14 and 15 years old, whose mothers had regular, full-time employment outside the home, and to 151 similar girls whose mothers did not work outside the home. No girls from broken homes were included. "Whereas almost one third of the experimental group made more than 50 per cent unfavorable responses (score of 40 or less), only 6 per cent of the control group were that low."[62] For example, daughters of employed mothers indicated with greater frequency than the daughters of mothers who did not work, that their parents expressed disapproval of their friends, that there was little time or inclination for family discussion regarding problems, that both father and mother resented the girl's disagreement with them, that their parents lacked interest in and love for them. Almost 70 per cent more of the girls of the experimental group than of the control group felt that where their affairs were concerned, "what my folks don't know won't hurt them." A similar majority said they thought, "Oh, what's the use!" after they had tried to explain their conduct to their parents.

The Essig and Morgan study is the only scientific investigation of this subject known to this writer. It seems to have been soundly designed and carried out. As the data were collected during World War II, a critic might allege that they were affected by abnormal times, but he makes only an unsupported allegation.

It is well for the guidance officer to know that on the average the home situation is adversely affected when the mother has outside employment, but with this as with other factors, each pupil's environment must be studied to ascertain the working of the factor in *his* case.

Siblings. The American Council Cumulative Record Folder calls for the following data on siblings: name, sex, age, occupation, education. What significance attaches to this information? The common answer to this question is, it will vary with every individual. No basis exists for imputing certain characteristics to the only child, the oldest child, the middle child, or the youngest child.

By inquiry among 2,204 ninth-grade and twelfth-grade pupils, Weast[63] endeavored to assess the influence of older siblings. He found, for example, that approximately 45 per cent of these pupils *planned* for more schooling and more advanced occupations than had been attained by older siblings. He found that large numbers admitted to having received admonitions from

[61] Mary Essig and D. H. Morgan, "Adjustment of Adolescent Daughters of Employed Women to Family Life," *Journal of Educational Psychology,* Vol. XXXVII (April, 1946), pp. 219–233.

[62] *Ibid.,* p. 224.

[63] Harry P. Weast, *Some Aspects of the Influence of Older Siblings on Ninth- and Twelfth-Grade Pupils.* Doctoral dissertation (Pittsburgh, University of Pittsburgh Library, 1953).

older siblings to "finish high school," and smaller numbers, "to go to college."

Because so many case studies have reported that parents and teachers have made comparisons—often invidious—between the subject and an older sibling, Weast asked the pupils, "Have your parents or any teacher tried to influence you by referring to the school record, behavior, occupation, or education of an older brother or sister?" The question was answered affirmatively for parents with much higher frequency than for teachers —no doubt partly because many of the pupils' teachers had not known older siblings. Ninth-graders attested the comparison to an older sibling much more frequently than did twelfth-graders, probably because of the selective factor. That is, the ninth grade certainly has many members who will be dropping out of school before they get to the twelfth grade, and their school leaving will be associated with poor school records, slothful and willful behavior, low educational and occupational aspirations. From 37 to 48 per cent of these ninth-grade pupils asserted that their parents had pointed to the example of an older sibling in school record, behavior, and educational attainment. Sometimes the example was good, and sometimes it was bad, as, "Mary always got A's—why can't you?" or "I hope you don't drop out of school the way Jim did."

Of course, younger siblings are also an influence and are often referred to as examples for older brothers and sisters. Weast's study was confined to the influence of older siblings. It is suggestive of the ways in which sib-lings constitute a force to be reckoned with in both distributive and adjustive guidance.

The Broken Home. The literature on this subject is voluminous. Some of the meanings of the fact of the broken home must be obvious. On average, the child has less supervision and less affection, and may therefore be more likely to develop problem behavior than is the pupil from the unbroken home. On average, also, the broken home is at a lower economic level than the unbroken home, and this reduces the child's educational opportunity.

But, first, what is the frequency of existence of this condition? Risen administered a questionnaire to the pupils of a Philadelphia junior high school, asking these questions: "(1) Is your father living? (2) Is your mother living? (3) Are you living with both parents? (4) If the answer to No. 3 is 'no,' with whom are you living?" About 90 per cent (1,625 pupils) of those present answered. The number reporting the absence of one or both parents from the home was 235, or 14.5 per cent.[64] There is some justification for thinking that this percentage would have been higher if 100 per cent had replied. It is known that some pupils are unwilling to admit the fact of their broken home, especially if the break brought feelings of shame to the child.

[64] Maurice L. Risen, "Relation of Lack of One or Both Parents to School Progress," *Elementary School Journal,* Vol. XXXIX (March, 1939), pp. 528–531.

The home situation among Risen's broken-home children is somewhat defined by the following tabulations of percentages:

Reason for lack of parent		Child lives with	
Father dead	41.3	Mother alone	50.2
Mother dead	25.1	Father alone	16.2
Father away	20.8	Father and stepmother	9.3
Both away	6.0	Mother and stepfather	7.7
Mother away	3.8	Other relatives	16.6
Both dead	3.0		
	100.0		100.0

Wallenstein studied 3,131 pupils in Grades 5-B to 8-B in metropolitan New York and found 17.6 per cent to come from homes broken either by death or separation. He cited other studies as showing 25.3, 29.0, and 25.4 per cent of broken-home cases among public-school children, and explained the lower percentage in his own study as being due to the large proportion of Jewish and Italian children in the population. These national groups typically have small percentages of broken homes.[65] Do teachers realize that in the average classroom one fifth or more of the pupils come from broken homes?

One effect of the broken home is apparently to diminish the chances of going to college. From his study of Minnesota high-school seniors Berdie reported that[66]

. . . there was a trend for the students planning on working to report more frequently than students planning on college that their fathers were dead: 10 per cent of the job-planners compared with 6 per cent of the college-planners. . . . Between 10 and 12 per cent of the students planning to get jobs had parents who were separated or divorced and between 4 and 6 per cent of the students planning to go to college had parents who were separated or divorced.

Other observable effects of the broken home are to be noted in Table 40, taken from Risen's study.[67] Pupils from broken homes achieve a lower scholastic average and a lower citizenship average than other pupils of similar intelligence; they are more frequently special cases for the counselor, and less frequently elected to positions of leadership in student life.

It must be remembered that these are group differences. Plenty of pupils attain a very wholesome adjustment despite the handicaps of a broken home. Contrariwise, some pupils from unbroken homes become seriously maladjusted. Each pupil, therefore, must be studied as an individual.

Psychological Quality of the Home. "An old truism rediscovered by modern psychiatrists, psychologists, educators, and workers with youth is

[65] Nehemiah Wallenstein, *Character and Personality of Children from Broken Homes,* Contributions to Education No. 721 (New York, Teachers College, Columbia University, 1937), pp. 37 ff.

[66] *Op. cit.,* pp. 126–127.

[67] *Op. cit.,* p. 530, Table 2.

TABLE 40. School Progress of Group A (235 Pupils Lacking One or Both Parents), of Group B (235 Pupils Matched with Pupils in Group A but Possessing Both Parents), and of Group C (Remainder of Student Body)

Item Compared	Group A	Group B	Group C
Mean intelligence quotient	109	109.5	114
Percentage of over-age pupils	24	10	14
Percentage of pupils marked "excellent" in co-operation	36	44	55
Percentage of pupils marked "good" in co-operation	41	40	27
Percentage of pupils marked "fair" in co-operation	19	14	15
Average number of failures per pupil	0.34	0.25	0.29
Percentage of pupils on honor roll	24	34	36
Percentage of pupils referred to counselor as special cases	9	4	6
Percentage of pupils elected to school-government offices	4	7	7
Average number of physical defects per pupil	2.2	1.4	1.9

that the family is the cradle, not only of most of the ideas, sentiments, and attitudes of the growing child, but also of most of his insecurities, anxieties, tensions, and other emotional distortions."[68]

Healy and Bronner, widely known for their authoritative studies and publications in the field of juvenile delinquency, tested the assumption that poverty, poor neighborhood, and other material aspects of the home environment are critical in delinquency causation and came to the conclusion that these factors are inconsequential as compared with the quality of the relationships between the child and his parents and his siblings.[69]

Two reports of research may be briefly cited to illustrate the detrimental effects on school success of homes with psychological qualities which are disturbing. In one, Axline[70] has described her experiment with a class of 37 second-grade repeaters in a large Chicago elementary school. These pupils had not been promoted because of failure to meet standards in reading. Axline's analysis of the individuals showed that most of the children were

[68] Reprinted by permission of the publishers and the Commonwealth Fund from Sheldon Glueck and Eleanor Touroff Glueck, *Unraveling Juvenile Delinquency* (Cambridge, Mass., Harvard University Press, Copyright, 1950, by the Commonwealth Fund), p. 93. This permission also applies to other citations of this work in succeeding pages of this chapter.

[69] William Healy and Augusta F. Bronner, *New Light on Delinquency and Its Treatment* (New Haven, Yale University Press, 1936), pp. 49, 122, 201 ff.

[70] Virginia Axline, "Nondirective Therapy for Poor Readers," *Journal of Consulting Psychology,* Vol. XI (March–April, 1947), pp. 61–69.

so loaded with social and emotional problems from unhappy and insecure relationships with their families that learning to read had not seemed to be important. Employing no remedial reading techniques, but creating a permissive atmosphere (described in Chapter 15 following), she brought about reading gains averaging 4½ months in 3 chronological months.

Pressey has described how college students are also subject to the home influence, even though it is remote control.[71] For eight years in charge of a course for the training of probation students in methods of study, she found from a study of some 500 case records that difficulties in the home were solely responsible for the failure of approximately one tenth of these students and were contributing factors for at least another three tenths.

The psychological quality of the home environment is especially indicated by the type and quality of discipline which the parents employ in governing the children. Hill's research showed the marked importance of this factor in the behavior of problem children.[72] He described how the Department of Adjustment in the Des Moines Public Schools developed an objective type of report of case studies to replace the usual narrative type. The form, "Report of Problem Case," consisted of 55 items considered to be important subjects of inquiry in a case study. Each item was scaled according to the degree of severity, and each value on the scale was given a numerical equivalent. Using the critical-ratio technique, the cruciality of each item was determined by an experimental use of the form with 130 chronic school behavior problem children. By this test it was found that of the 55 items the first eight in order of cruciality were as follows:

1. Record of delinquencies
2. School citizenship outside classrooms
3. Type of disciplinary measures—mother
4. Type of companions
5. Scholarship (average grades)
6. Average attendance
7. Child's acceptance of parents' interest and counsel
8. Type of disciplinary measures—father

As we are here focusing on parental discipline, it will be pertinent to quote the scale and values used for numbers 3 and 8 in the above list, as follows:

0—Extreme severity—beaten, mistreated, and subjected to extreme verbal abuse
1—Severe—frequent resort to corporal punishment—some verbal threats
Complete resort to verbal abuse and threatening

[71] Luella C. Pressey, "Some Serious Maladjustments among College Students," *Social Forces*, Vol. X (December, 1931), pp. 236–242.

[72] Arthur S. Hill, "The Use of an Objective Type of Case Study in the Analysis and Prognosis of Pupil Maladjustment Problems," *Educational Administration and Supervision*, Vol. XXI (November, 1935), pp. 611–618; "A Statistical Analysis of Significant Factors in Pupil Maladjustment," *Journal of Educational Sociology*, Vol. IX (December, 1935), pp. 219–230.

2—Frequent resort to corporal punishment—no verbal abuse
   Much "fussing" and argumentative measures
3—Probably more than necessary resort to corporal punishment
   Tendency to overdo verbal persuasion
4—Intelligent measures with minimum of corporal punishment
3—Frequent use of ineffective measures
2—Tendency to overlook need for discipline
1—Seldom punish child—noticeable lack of disciplinary measures
0—Complete protection and pampering

The scale shows, appropriately enough, that the extremity of harshness and the extremity of shielding and yielding are equally bad.

Many of the elements and characteristics of family life which bear a causative relationship to maladjustment of the child are spelled out in noteworthy detail in the most recent research of the Gluecks.[73] This investigation—most penetrating study of juvenile delinquency to date—involved a comparison of 500 delinquent boys with 500 non-delinquents matched on the basis of age, general intelligence, national (ethnico-racial) origin, and residence in underprivileged neighborhoods. With these factors held constant, the two groups were then compared with respect to home and family conditions, school and community adjustment, personality structure and temperament, physical condition and physical structure. The staff for the research represented the disciplines of psychology, psychiatry, medicine, anthropology, statistics, and social work. From the comparison of home conditions and family life, some data will be cited.

Table 41 shows the frequency with which certain conditions were found to exist among the parents of the contrasted groups. While the differences favoring the non-delinquents are noteworthy for each condition, considerable percentages of the non-delinquents were also subject to those influences; for example, there was criminality among nearly a third of their fathers and drunkenness among nearly two fifths.

TABLE 41. Percentages of Mothers and Fathers of Delinquents and Non-Delinquents Having a History of Conditions Enumerated*

	Mother		Father	
	Delin-quents	Non-Delin-quents	Delin-quents	Non-Delin-quents
Serious physical ailments	48.6	33.0	39.6	28.6
Mental retardation	32.8	9.0	18.4	5.6
Emotional disturbances	40.2	17.6	44.0	18.0
Drunkenness	23.0	7.0	62.8	39.0
Criminality	44.8	15.0	66.2	32.0

* Adapted from Table IX-10, p. 101, Sheldon and Eleanor Glueck, *op. cit.*

[73] *Op. cit.*

The work habits of the fathers were rated on a three-point scale as good, fair, poor. Fathers of non-delinquents excelled in this characteristic, 71.1 per cent being rated "good," as compared with 37.6 per cent of the fathers of the delinquents.

In their Chapter 10, "Quality of Family Life," the Gluecks presented ratings of the two groups on characteristics of the home, some of which are as follows:

Family's management of income
    Entirely planned, partially planned, haphazard
Routine of household
    Entirely planned, partially planned, haphazard
Self-respect of family
    Marked, slight, none
Ambitiousness of family
    Marked or slight, none
Conduct standards of home
    Good, fair, poor
Conjugal relations of parents
    Good, fair, poor
Supervision of children by mother
    Suitable, fair, unsuitable
Family group recreations
    Often, occasional, never
Cohesiveness of family
    Marked, some, none

All of these comparisons showed notable differences in favor of the non-delinquents. "Supervision of children by mother" was rated as "suitable" for 7.0 per cent of the delinquents and for 65.2 per cent of the non-delinquents. "Cohesiveness of family" was rated as "marked" for 16.0 per cent of the delinquents and for 61.8 per cent of the non-delinquents.

The relative instability of the home life of delinquent boys is indicated by Table 42. It requires no great stretch of the imagination to picture how such boys had been handed around among relatives, foster homes, step-parents.

TABLE 42. Percentage Distributions of Boys According to Number of Household Changes Experienced*

Changes	Delinquents	Non-delinquents
None	49.6	90.0
1–2	19.6	6.4
3–5	16.9	2.4
6 and over	13.9	1.2
Total	100.0	100.0

* Adapted from Table XI-7, p. 121, Sheldon and Eleanor Glueck, *op. cit.*

Of the delinquents, 60.4 per cent were from homes that had been broken by separation, divorce, death, or prolonged absence of a parent. For non-delinquents the corresponding percentage was 34.2.

Bearing most directly on parent-child relationships are Tables 43 and 44. Table 43 shows that these delinquent boys experienced a lack of affection

TABLE 43. Percentage Distributions of Boys According to Degree of Affection of Fathers and Mothers for the Boy*

Description	Delinquents		Non-delinquents	
	Mother	Father	Mother	Father
Warm†	72.1	40.2	95.6	80.7
Indifferent	21.2	42.9	3.4	16.0
Hostile, rejective	6.7	16.9	1.0	3.3
	100.0	100.0	100.0	100.0

 * Adapted from Tables XI-13 and XI-14, pp. 125–126, Sheldon and Eleanor Glueck, *op. cit.*

 † "Warm" includes overprotectiveness, a trait seldom found in the fathers, but ascribed to about 20 per cent of mothers.

from parents, especially the father, with high frequency. The delinquents also experienced deplorable discipline, according to Table 44, while a good majority of the non-delinquents were disciplined in a spirit that would score well on Arthur Hill's scale quoted above. The ratings on "emotional ties of boy to father," "emotional ties of boy to mother," and "boy's estimate of parents' concern for his welfare" all showed marked differences in favor of the non-delinquents.

TABLE 44. Percentage Distributions of Boys According to Characteristics of Parental Discipline*

Description of Discipline	Delinquents		Non-delinquents	
	Mother	Father	Mother	Father
Lax	56.8	26.6	11.7	17.9
Overstrict	4.4	26.1	1.6	8.7
Erratic	34.6	41.6	21.1	17.9
Firm but kindly	4.2	5.7	65.6	55.5
Total	100.0	100.0	100.0	100.0

 * Adapted from Table XI-22, p. 131, Sheldon and Eleanor Glueck, *op. cit.*

The data on parent-child relationships were obtained by the psychiatrist in his interview with the boy, from information given by the parents themselves to the home visitors, and from social workers who had known the family over long periods. From their extensive analysis which illuminated so many factors that are critical in the identification of delinquency, the authors set themselves the task of constructing prediction tables[74] that will

[74] *Ibid.,* Ch. 20.

detect the potential delinquent at entrance to school or soon after. The one most practicable for schools, as commonly staffed, to employ, is based on the following five factors of social background:

> Discipline of boy by father
> Supervision of boy by mother
> Affection of father for boy
> Affection of mother for boy
> Cohesiveness of family

Even without giving to these factors the precise values which the Gluecks' prediction table assumes, teachers of the primary grades should be able to detect unfavorable home environment in some of the factors. The pupils thus identified could be studied more closely by such a functionary as the home and school visitor. Constructive measures could be taken to head off the anti-social attitudes and behavior which carry the individual into acts of law violation.

While guidance workers are concerned with all degrees and types of maladjustment rather than confining themselves to the extreme form which is juvenile delinquency, the Glueck study is most provocative in suggesting what to look for in analyzing the psychological quality of the home. Their comparison of delinquent and non-delinquent slum dwellers shows how superficial it is just to associate delinquency with slum environment. To combat delinquency and lesser degrees of maladjustment the home life of middle-class and upper-class pupils must be understood as well as that of lower-class pupils.

The psychological quality of a *good* home is high-lighted in a recent report on children who are well adjusted.[75] The authors asked principals and teachers to name children for whom each of the following questions could be answered affirmatively:

1. Does he play well with other children?
2. Does he appear to be a happy child?
3. Does he have reasonable control over his emotions?
4. Can he be depended upon?
5. Is he achieving somewhere near his capacity?
6. Is he able to think for himself?
7. Is he kind and helpful to teachers and classmates?
8. Is he liked and respected by his peers?

They then obtained from the parents of 261 of these well-adjusted children (aged 5 to 21) answers to the question, "What in the home life accounts for your child's good adjustment?" As might be expected, the interviews uniformly brought out a picture of marked affection by parents, supervision by

[75] Grace Langdon and Irving W. Stout, *These Well-Adjusted Children* (New York, Day, 1951).

parents, and a high level of family cohesion—the antithesis of the psychological environment revealed by the Gluecks.

Parental Interest in and Ambitions for Pupil. Parents are obviously concerned with their children's choices and adjustment, and certainly they are endeavoring to influence their children. School guidance workers need to know the weight and direction of such parental influence in order to counsel intelligently. They find that parental interest ranges all the way from zero to such complete domination as to leave the child no opportunity for making his own decisions. They find, also, that parental ambitions are sometimes in harmony with the child's abilities and interests, and sometimes quite inappropriate. If the parent's ambitions are too high or too low, the counselor has the task of trying to bring about the needed correction. At any rate, knowledge of the subject of this paragraph is surely foundational for counseling and may properly lead to the employment of such co-operative techniques as have recently been described by counselors in the Huntington Beach Union High School, Huntington Beach, California.[76]

Opportunity for Home Study. In a school which operates on the assumption of home study, it is obviously important to learn how adequate the home environment is for such activity. Surveys which were made forty years ago showed that the home study of many pupils had to be carried on under the distracting conditions of family conversation, housekeeping routine, and other disturbing factors. The facts of home study as thus disclosed were used as arguments for the longer school day and supervised study at school. To the home distractions of that period must now be added the comic books, radio, and television, while the auto beckons to take one outside the home to distractions that are bigger and more overpowering. With many schools still assuming home study, it is more than ever important to identify the pupils whose home-study conditions are unfavorable. Guidance functionaries spend much time with pupils who are failing. They accept responsibility for helping pupils to be academically successful. If they are to perform this function, they must have understanding of all aspects of the pupil's life which affect his study.

Home Chores. It must be recognized that some pupils are waited on hand-and-foot by parents and/or servants, and that other pupils carry such a burden of home chores as to be veritable drudges. These extreme conditions call for counseling—mainly, the counseling of parents. If the pupil is to grow in capacity as a worthy home member he should undertake home responsibilities according to his maturity. If, by contrast, he is exploited for home routine to the exclusion of normal recreation, social life, and home study, his years of self-development are not as fruitful as they should be.

Boarders or Relatives Living in the Home. No research into the frequency or the significance of this factor is known to the writer. Certainly there are

76 Wilma Hughell and Gerald G. Lance, "Student-Parent-Counselor Conferences," *Personnel and Guidance Journal,* Vol. XXXI (May, 1953), pp. 509–512.

many family circles that include others than father, mother, and children. It seems logical that the influence of these "others" must vary so widely as to defy characterization. It is important to know of their presence and to try to assess their significance in the case of each individual pupil.

The Physical Child

The cumulative record folder for secondary schools which is published by the American Council on Education (reproduced in Chapter 14) calls for a notation each year of the pupil's "health and physical characteristics." This is a reflection of the school's continuous interest in and sense of responsibility for the physical child. Physical development and adjustment we deem to be important not only for themselves but also for their bearing on other aspects of the pupil's growth. If the reader will turn back to page 140, Chapter 4, he will see the evidence of the connection between academic success and physical defects or diseases. Knowing this relationship, the homeroom teacher or counselor will inform the subject teachers of pupils' disabilities so that such disadvantages may, insofar as possible, be overcome. Then, for example, the pupil of poor vision or hearing will be seated where he has the best opportunity for learning.

Good or poor health, physical charm or repellence, and physical skill or awkwardness, have been studied by Harold E. Jones and his associates[77] and found to have noteworthy influence on the social and emotional adjustment of adolescents. Positive correlations have been found between popularity of boys of junior high school age and their strength and physical ability. When a boy's lack of skill or his physical ineptitude makes it difficult for him to play a usual part in the physical activities of his fellows, he may experience decided social rejection, with consequent untoward behavior. Among the physically inadequate members, there are invariably, however, some who have strongly compensating personality traits which win them social acceptance and security.

The adolescent is exceedingly critical of his own developing body. One of the commonly stated developmental tasks of that age is the accepting of one's physique and learning to use the body effectively. It is not surprising, then, that the physician who periodically examined the subjects in a California eight-year study of youth reported that 31 per cent of the boys and 41 per cent of the girls were at one time or another during that period definitely disturbed concerning their physical characteristics.[78] They were anxious to stand well in the society of their peers, anxious about attaining adulthood.

The guidance worker will never overlook the possibility of a physical

[77] See especially Chs. 5 and 6 in *Adolescence,* Part I of the 43rd Yearbook of the National Society for the Study of Education (Chicago, University of Chicago Press, 1944).

[78] *Ibid.,* pp. 85–86.

explanation for academic, social, and emotional maladjustment. He will also accept as natural the sometimes exaggerated emphasis which the adolescent devotes to personal appearance. He will counsel with the pupil and his parents about needed physical corrections.

Attendance Record

While some schools no doubt treat the attendance record as a clerical chore, there are many in which guidance workers follow it closely, having learned by experience that a child's record of absences frequently signifies some form of maladjustment. Researches bear this out. For example, the Gluecks[79] found that 94.8 per cent of their delinquent group truanted, 63 per cent persistently, while of the non-delinquent group, only 10.8 per cent truanted, none persistently. This finding was in line with the high percentage of delinquents found to be disliking school and experiencing relative lack of success in school.

An inquiry into the attendance services in the schools of New York City resulted in a report[80] which showed that absence from school is symptomatic of maladjustments of various types and forms. The recommendations in this report called for integration of the treatment of attendance problems with the over-all school program for dealing with adjustment problems, acceptance by teachers of responsibility for early detection and removal of maladjustments, and the exercise of a mental-hygiene orientation in dealing with infractions of the attendance code.

In a Pennsylvania high school the counselor experimented on attendance by doing away with the written parental excuse, substituting for it her personal interview with the pupil who had been absent. The attendance record of the school was demonstrably improved, and she found in those interviews the clues to needed contacts with the home and with teachers.[81]

Favorite Recreational Interests and Activities

What does the pupil do in his spare time, and what does it mean? As scientific evaluations of the pupil's recreational pursuits do not exist, his recreations are simply taken into account as part of the rounded picture of the individual. They may afford clues that will indicate the best direction for the pupil's further education, or they may suggest a vocational choice. Certain it is that many a scientist, musician, journalist, and business man reflected in the leisure-time activities of his childhood and adolescence a predilection for the vocation of his adulthood. Interests, however, are subject to change with advancing maturity and new experiences—concepts

[79] *Op. cit.*, p. 148.
[80] *Children Absent from School,* Citizens' Committee on Children of New York City, Inc. (136 E. 57th St.; not dated, but about 1950).
[81] Mildred Van Zandt, "Please Excuse," *Educational Method,* Vol. XXII (January, 1943), pp. 179–181.

which will be developed more fully in Chapter 13. The counselor will wish to know the interests the pupil is actually exercising, as well as those which an interests test shows he possesses, but he will interpret them with caution, knowing that some interests will be superseded by others and that some may find expression in avocations.

Work Experiences

The pupil's summer employment and part-time employment during the school year have long been recognized as circumstances of interest to guidance workers. They know that through such experience the pupil is learning about his own interests and abilities, and also about the world of jobs. He is also revealing himself to his counselor as a person characterized by certain likes and dislikes, abilities and disabilities, positive and negative personality traits. It is pertinent to keep a record of the pupil's work experiences for the clues it affords for vocational counseling.

Beginning in World War II, however, this aspect of pupils' lives assumed enhanced proportions, both as to the number of pupils involved and the extent of involvement of the individual pupil. As described briefly on pages 199 ff of Chapter 7, a few schools sought to regularize and control pupil employment so as to give it educational direction. In most schools, however, the pupil's work for pay has not been controlled or influenced by the school; except for child labor laws and school attendance laws, control is vested in the pupil, his parents, and the employer. The problems that arise are numerous: How many hours a day, a week, can and should the pupil work during the school year? Is the kind of work sufficiently developmental to offset its exploitative effect? What shall he do with his earnings? Do the job or the consequent earnings bring him into conflict with his parents?

Some of these challenges to counseling were first stated by Nancy Larrick[82] during the war, as scattered evidences of youthful bad judgment came to her attention. Bateman[83] endeavored to test the effect of working experience on pupil adjustment. In a canvass of three high schools he found that approximately 60 per cent of the pupils of the 11th and 12th grades were working for pay (and with no supervision from the school). From the 60 per cent who were working and the 40 per cent who were not working he matched 263 pairs on the basis of grade, sex, father's occupation, and intelligence. Using the Bell Adjustment Inventory with both groups he found virtually no difference in home, health, social, and emotional adjustment.

In an earlier study at the junior high school level in Detroit, Gilles and

[82] "Counseling Youth on Excess Earnings," *Occupations,* Vol. XXII (May, 1944), pp. 469–471.

[83] Richard M. Bateman, "The Effect of Work Experience on High-School Students as Revealed by the Bell Adjustment Inventory," *Journal of Educational Research,* Vol. XLIII (December, 1949), pp. 261–269.

Nemzek[84] matched 250 boys who had part-time employment with 250 non-employed boys on the basis of intelligence, curriculum, grade, and age, and compared school achievement on the basis of teachers' marks. They found no appreciable differences.

Scales and Hutson[85] have reported a study in which the main object was to find out what part-time employment means to the pupil, particularly as regards the accomplishment of his developmental tasks. For this purpose, interviews were held, under permissive conditions, with 150 Negro boys of the Hill District in Pittsburgh. The boys were of the ages 14 to 17 inclusive, were enrolled in secondary schools, and had gainful employment. Approximately 90 per cent were of the lower-lower and upper-lower social classes. Two thirds were from unbroken homes, suggesting that the phenomenon of part-time employment exists pretty much independently of the marital state of parents. The boys worked mainly for small employers in the district in which they lived; the median of their earnings was $12.44 a week (range— $1.50 to $49); the median wage per hour was 67 cents; the median number of hours worked weekly was 20.9. More than 90 per cent of the boys obtained their jobs by personal application, through friends, or through their families and other relatives. Seventy per cent admitted that they did not have employment certificates, although they were supposed to.

What satisfactions did these pupils experience as a consequence of their work? How did they characterize their parents' attitudes, both before and after they got their jobs? How were they spending their money, or for what purpose were they saving some? From the conversation based on these questions, it was found that the pupils identified six developmental tasks

TABLE 45. Developmental Tasks Identified by Responses of the Pupils

Developmental Tasks	Per cent
Establishing economic independence	68.0
Achieving emotional independence of parents and other adults . . .	48.0
Acceptance of the proper sex role	20.0
New relations with peers	20.0
Accepting, desiring, and achieving socially responsible behavior . . .	3.3
Selecting and preparing for an occupation	.7
No developmental tasks identified	7.3
Total	167.3*

* This column totals more than 100 per cent because some boys indicated more than one task.

84 L. N. Gilles and C. L. Nemzek, "The Effect of Part-Time Employment on Scholastic Achievement," *Journal of Social Psychology,* Vol. XIII (May, 1941), pp. 419–422.

85 E. E. Scales and P. W. Hutson, "How Gainful Employment Affects the Accomplishment of the Developmental Tasks of Adolescent Boys," *School Review,* Vol. LXIII (January, 1955), pp. 31–37.

as being promoted by their jobs and the money they earned. These tasks are listed in Table 45[86] with the frequency of their identification.

This study shows that work experience has deep meanings for the pupil, meanings which guidance workers must understand if they are to help these young workers to make good judgments. Important as it is to prevent these adolescents from pursuing their self-exploitation at the expense of their self-development, the satisfactions which they derive from work for pay must be recognized. To youth these values seem so substantial that they are sought not only by the financially impoverished but by many whose families can well take care of their financial needs.

Educational and Vocational Plans

Cumulative record folders typically call for this item to be stated yearly. Chapter 4 presented evidence that pupils' choices were frequently out of line with their ability and with social need; hence, the guidance function. It should be clear that the pupil's statement of educational and vocational plans should be regarded primarily as a springboard which launches activity for testing and weighing the soundness of the plans. Unfortunately, in some schools guidance is bypassed at this very point. The homeroom teacher accepts as gospel the pupil's statement of plans and proceeds to help him make a schedule of studies for carrying them out. In contrast to such reliance on the pupil's own judgment, the guidance function would bring to bear upon the pupil's plans all the knowledge that we possess concerning educational and vocational opportunity plus all the knowledge of the pupil's abilities, interests, limitations, and dislikes that we have gained from observing and testing him.

Already cited in this section is the evidence that educational and vocational plans are influenced by the occupation of the father, the cultural level of the family, and the social class to which the pupil belongs. Another factor which has been shown in many studies to influence the college decision is the proximity of opportunity for higher education. Berdie[87] demonstrated this circumstance in his survey of Minnesota high-school seniors, finding that approximately 50 per cent of metropolitan boys were planning to go to college, compared with 20 per cent of the farm boys; for girls, the corresponding percentages were 40 and 24. Berdie pointed out that higher education was easily accessible to the metropolitan students but remote for most of the farm students.

The proximity of an institution of higher learning may have effects on educational plans which must be combatted. Particularly is this true when the institution is designed to give one form of specialized education, as is the case of an isolated teachers college. After taking inventory of the attitudes and interests of the student body of a Pennsylvania state teachers col-

[86] *Ibid.,* Table 2.
[87] *Op. cit.,* p. 113.

lege located in a section quite remote from other institutions of higher education, Hallisy stated as one of his conclusions,

As a majority of the students do not enter the College specifically to become teachers, but to obtain preparation for other vocations, to obtain an inexpensive college education, or because they can live at home, their attitudes toward teachers, teaching, and the teaching profession represent, in effect, the attitudes of the general population of high-school graduates entering colleges and not the attitudes desired of students preparing for the profession of teaching.[88]

The counselor of a large high school located only a half-mile from one of America's typical small colleges said to the writer: "The proximity of that college creates severe problems for me. Our graduates tend to flock over there indiscriminately; some should enter other types of institutions of higher education."

The validity of the plans of pupils who are not going to college and do not have college ability must be tested as thoroughly as guidance techniques make possible. Influential with these pupils, as with the college-going members, will be found the factor of proximity—the nearness of a certain industry, plant, or mill often being the chief determinant of vocational choice. In the chapters which follow it will become evident that better instruments for the prediction of college success are available than is the case for the prediction of occupational success.

Observation and inquiry are important methods of obtaining other information than the items which have been taken up in this chapter. Nevertheless, the major areas and the most commonly recorded information have been canvassed. Meanings have been found for both distributive and adjustive guidance.

QUESTIONS, PROBLEMS, INVESTIGATIONS

1. Select three pupils with whom you have daily contacts and make anecdotal records for a month, being careful not to include generalizations or recommendations.

2. Interview a half-dozen pupils concerning their educational and vocational plans. For each one, make a brief record of the impressions of his intelligence, character, and personality traits which you gained from the interview contact.

3. Analyze the practices of a half-dozen secondary schools in interviewing pupils for obtaining information for the cumulative record folder.

4. After adequate study of the writings of Helen Hall Jennings, make a sociometric analysis of a class or a homeroom group.

5. Find pupils whose parents represent a culture somewhat at variance with the culture which is predominant in the community.

[88] Richard G. Hallisy, *The Attitudes and Interests of the Student Body of a State Teachers College as They Relate to the Teaching Profession.* Doctoral Dissertation (Pittsburgh, University of Pittsburgh Library, 1953), p. 196.

6. In a six-year high school, classify the pupils of the seventh and twelfth grades according to occupation of the father, following Counts' technique.

7. Using a random sampling of 100 pupils in a junior high school, find the number who come from broken homes.

8. After studying *Social Class in America,* by Warner, Meeker, and Eells, ascertain the social class of several pupils and see to what extent this fact explains pupil behavior. For aid in interpretation, read Hollingshead's *Elmtown's Youth.*

9. Interview a dozen pupils who have part-time employment to find out the important facts, also to find what values the pupils feel they derive and what problems are raised by their jobs.

10. For any class or homeroom group, make a survey of the pupils' opportunity for study at home.

SELECTED REFERENCES

ALLTUCKER, Margaret, "A Counseling Plan for Bridging the Gap between the Junior and Senior High Schools," *School Review,* Vol. XXXII (January, 1924), pp. 60–66.

AXLINE, Virginia, "Nondirective Therapy for Poor Readers," *Journal of Consulting Psychology,* Vol. XI (March–April, 1947), pp. 61–69.

BERDIE, Ralph F., *After High School—What?* (Minneapolis, University of Minnesota Press, 1954).

BOWES, Fern H., "The Anecdotal Behavior Record in Measuring Progress in Character," *Elementary School Journal,* Vol. XXXIX (February, 1939), pp. 431–435.

COUNTS, George S., *The Selective Character of American Secondary Education.* Supplementary Educational Monograph No. 19 (Chicago, University of Chicago Press, May, 1922).

COWELL, Charles C., "Physical Education as Applied Social Science," *Educational Research Bulletin,* Vol. XVI (September 15, 1937), pp. 147–155.

CROUSE, Ruth, "Writing an Autobiography," *English Journal,* Vol. XXXIII (May, 1949), pp. 264–265.

DAHLKE, H. Otto, and MONAHAN, Thomas O., "Problems in the Application of Sociometry to Schools," *School Review,* Vol. LVII (April, 1949), pp. 223–234.

DANIELSON, Paul J., and ROTHNEY, J. W. M., "The Student Autobiography: Structured or Unstructured?" *Personnel and Guidance Journal,* Vol. XXXIII (September, 1954), pp. 30–33.

DRISCOLL, Gertrude, *How to Study the Behavior of Children* (New York, Teachers College, Columbia University, 1941).

ENGLISH, Horace B., and RAIMY, Victor, *Studying the Individual School Child: A Manual of Guidance* (New York, Holt, 1946).

ESSIG, Mary, and MORGAN, D. H., "Adjustment of Adolescent Daughters of Employed Women to Family Life," *Journal of Educational Psychology,* Vol. XXXVII (April, 1946), pp. 219–233.

GLUECK, Sheldon, and GLUECK, Eleanor, *Unraveling Juvenile Delinquency* (New York, Commonwealth Fund, 1950).

HAMALAINEN, Arthur E., *An Appraisal of Anecdotal Records.* Contributions to

Education No. 891 (New York, Teachers College, Columbia University, 1943).

HEALY, William, and BRONNER, Augusta F., *New Light on Delinquency and Its Treatment* (New Haven, Yale University Press, 1936).

Helping Teachers to Understand Children, By the Staff of the Division on Child Development and Teacher Personnel. Prepared for the Commission on Teacher Education (Washington, D.C., American Council on Education, 1945).

HILL, Arthur S., "A Statistical Analysis of Significant Factors in Pupil Maladjustment," *Journal of Educational Sociology,* Vol. IX (December, 1935), pp. 219–230.

————, "The Use of an Objective Type of Case Study in the Analysis and Prognosis of Pupil Maladjustment Problems," *Educational Administration and Supervision,* Vol. XXI (November, 1935), pp. 611–618.

HOLLINGSHEAD, August B., *Elmtown's Youth* (New York, Wiley, 1949).

HOYT, Kenneth B., "How Well Can Classroom Teachers Know Their Pupils?" *School Review,* Vol. LXIII (April, 1955), pp. 228–235.

HUGHELL, Wilma, and LANCE, Gerald G., "Student-Parent-Counselor Conferences," *Personnel and Guidance Journal,* Vol. XXXI (May, 1953), pp. 509–512.

JARVIE, L. L., and ELLINGSON, Mark, *A Handbook on the Anecdotal Behavior Journal* (Chicago, University of Chicago Press, 1940).

JENNINGS, Helen Hall, "Sociometric Grouping in Relation to Child Development," Ch. 13 in *Fostering Mental Health in Our Schools,* 1950 Yearbook, Association for Supervision and Curriculum Development (Washington, D.C., National Education Association, 1950).

————, *Sociometry in Group Relations: A Work Guide for Teachers* (Washington, D.C., American Council on Education, 1948).

JONES, Harold E., chairman, *Adolescence,* Part I, 43rd Yearbook of the National Society for the Study of Education (Chicago, University of Chicago Press, 1944).

KAWIN, Ethel, "Guidance in the Glencoe Schools," *Journal of Educational Research,* Vol. XXXVII (March, 1944), pp. 481–492.

KOOS, L. V., *The Questionnaire in Education* (New York, Macmillan, 1928).

KOUGH, Jack, and DeHAAN, Robert F., *Teacher's Guidance Handbook,* Part I, *Identifying Children Who Need Help* (Chicago, Science Research Associates, 1955).

LANGDON, Grace, and STOUT, Irving W., *These Well-Adjusted Children* (New York, Day, 1951).

LARRICK, Nancy, "Counseling Youth on Excess Earnings," *Occupations,* Vol. XXII (May, 1944), pp. 469–471.

MORRISON, H. C., *The Practice of Teaching in the Secondary School,* rev. ed. (Chicago, University of Chicago Press, 1931), Ch. 9.

PRESSEY, Luella C., "Some Serious Maladjustments among College Students," *Social Forces,* Vol. X (December, 1931), pp. 236–242.

PRESTON, Ralph C., "Children's Autobiographies," *Elementary English Review,* Vol. XXIII (November, 1946), pp. 306–307, 310.

RISEN, Maurice L., "Relation of Lack of One or Both Parents to School Progress," *Elementary School Journal*, Vol. XXXIX (March, 1939), pp. 528–531.

SCALES, E. E., and HUTSON, P. W., "How Gainful Employment Affects the Accomplishment of the Developmental Tasks of Adolescent Boys," *School Review*, Vol. LXIII (January, 1955), pp. 31–37.

STOUFFER, George A. W., Jr., "Behavior Problems of Children as Viewed by Teachers and Mental Hygienists," *Mental Hygiene*, Vol. XXXVI (April, 1952), pp. 271–285.

STURTEVANT, Sarah M., and STRANG, Ruth, "A Study of the Twenty-four Hour Schedules of Forty High School Girls," *Teachers College Record*, Vol. XXVIII (June, 1927), pp. 994–1010.

TOPP, Robert F., "Preadolescent Behavior Patterns Suggestive of Emotional Malfunctioning," *Elementary School Journal*, Vol. LII (February, 1952), pp. 340–343.

TORGERSON, Theodore L., *Studying Children: Diagnostic and Remedial Procedures in Teaching* (New York, Dryden, 1947).

VAN ZANDT, Mildred, "Please Excuse," *Educational Method*, Vol. XXII (January, 1943), pp. 179–181.

WALLENSTEIN, Nehemiah, *Character and Personality of Children from Broken Homes*. Contributions to Education No. 721 (New York, Teachers College, Columbia University, 1937).

WARNER, W. Lloyd, HAVIGHURST, Robert J., and LOEB, Martin B., *Who Shall Be Educated?* (New York, Harper, 1944).

WARNER, W. Lloyd, and LUNT, Paul S., *The Social Life of a Modern Community* ("Yankee City Series," Vol. I) (New Haven, Yale University Press, 1941).

WARNER, W. Lloyd, MEEKER, Marchia, and EELLS, Kenneth, *Social Class in America: A Manual of Procedure for the Measurement of Social Status* (Chicago, Science Research Associates, 1949).

CHAPTER 12

Analysis of the Individual:

Ability and Achievement

THIS CHAPTER and the one which follows will be much concerned with the tests and measurements which have proliferated since 1916 (birth date of the Stanford-Binet). Perhaps it is well at the outset to state some of the limitations with which the writer restricts the scope of his treatment of so immense and complicated a subject. Bearing in mind the purpose of this work as that of a one-volume basic treatment of the guidance function, these chapters will not include (1) a presentation of techniques of test construction and standardization, (2) a classified catalogue of tests with data from their manuals concerning reliability and validity, (3) a discourse on the administration and scoring of tests, (4) an explanation of statistical practices in the handling of test data. On the positive side, the chapters will focus on the task of aiding students in the interpretation of test data, presenting many selected researches and summaries of researches which illuminate the values of pupil measurements in the performance of distributive and adjustive guidance.

The organization of this chapter presented a problem. The writer first explored the possibility and desirability of organizing it around the main categories of measuring instruments, such as school marks, intelligence tests, special aptitude tests. He concluded that such a structure would not be as serviceable to the readers of this book as one in which the main focus of the discourse is on clear-cut guidance tasks. Hence, following an introductory section on the main characteristics of the several types of measures of ability and achievement are sections on the problems of predicting success in secondary-school subjects and curriculums, predicting success in higher education, and predicting success in occupations. The final section of the chapter points to the bearing of ability measurements on adjustive guidance.

A major advantage of this organization is that it affords a more satisfactory structure for the reporting of the existing pertinent researches. In many cases, a single research has involved the testing of several ability measures—sometimes a combination of measures—in order to find out how best to make a given prediction. Thus, with the chapter organized as it is, a research intended to find the best basis for predicting success, let us say, in algebra, can be reported in its entirety.

MEASURES OF ABILITY AND ACHIEVEMENT

School Marks

Prominent in the pupil's cumulative record folder are the marks he has earned, semester by semester, in each of the subjects he has pursued. His adviser refers continually to that section of the folder to check on the progress the pupil is making toward the fulfillment of requirements for curriculum, diploma, or degree. Fortunately, also, as will be shown by scientific studies in the following sections of this chapter, the pupil's marks have noteworthy value for the prediction of his educational future. His adviser learns how to analyze them for this purpose.

Brief descriptions of the absolute and relative marking systems were presented in Chapter 3, and they will not be repeated here. With both types, the pupil's mark frequently is arrived at by highly subjective processes, resulting in much variation from teacher to teacher, although this is probably somewhat less pronounced now than was true forty years ago. Furthermore, the variation in standards between schools is sometimes quite extreme, as was brought out by the evidence of divergence in the failure rates of the high schools of New York City (data which were submitted in the first section of Chapter 4). And while the variation in the intelligence of the New York City high schools, as there reported, is represented by the range of median I.Q.'s from 93 to 114, the failure rates seemed to bear little or no relation to the variation in ability.

What are the constituents which comprise a pupil's mark of B in mathematics or C in history? Forty years ago many teachers gave a percentage value to the pupil's "daily recitation" or daily work and averaged the daily marks at the end of the six-weeks marking period. That average was then combined with the pupil's standing on a test or tests given during the same period to arrive at the pupil's six-weeks mark, daily work usually counting as two thirds and test marks as one third. Some teachers approximate that process today, but many are very vague about placing a value on daily work—they rely mainly on the scores which pupils earn on objective tests. Other factors which sometimes enter into a mark are conduct in class, courtesy, attendance, "extra work," and good enunciation in recitation. Emphasis on the theme that "we are educating the whole child" sometimes is expressed by making the school mark an average of still more components.

The school mark is also complicated when a faculty comes to acknowledge the ideal of every child "working up to his ability" and endeavors to measure the degree of attaining that goal within the framework of the traditional marking system. The adoption of various forms of homogeneous grouping raises problems in marking. Most commonly they are answered by simply giving all marks at each level, so that pupils of a slow group can and do earn A's just the same as the pupils of a fast group, despite the contrast in their achievements. Of course, this is confusing and may generate more problems than it solves.

Despite the fact that school marks reflect so many influences which are calculated to detract from their validity as instruments of measurement, they do have noteworthy predictive significance, as the following sections of this chapter will demonstrate. Their value can be enhanced by limiting them to the role of a measurement of learning achievement and seeking to improve the accuracy with which they accomplish that purpose. The pupil's attitudes of co-operation and good citizenship, the industry and conscientiousness he evinces, and the various concomitant objectives he attains, should be accounted for separately from his actual achievement of learnings in the subject. The American Council Cumulative Record Folder shown in Chapter 14 provides for such separation by allowing space for five evaluations in connection with each subject, suggesting "work habits, ability to think logically, mastery of technique, oral and written communication, and some estimate of achievement." Furthermore, character traits are rated on another page of the folder. A trend in marking and reporting pupil progress, which has been steadily gaining acceptance over the past decade, is the issuance of descriptive statements which tell how the pupil is progressing in the various areas of growth, the possibilities and the limitations which appear to characterize him, the difficulties and obstacles he is encountering. This trend has made much greater progress in elementary than in secondary schools. A basic purpose of such a method of evaluation is to eliminate or minimize the traditional competitive marking with the objectionable mental hygiene which has been described in Chapter 3.

At this point in our consideration of marking and the marking system we face something of a dilemma. Adjustive guidance is served by the abolition of competitive marking. Distributive guidance, on the other hand, needs the ranking of students which competitive marking affords, in order that predictions may be made. Numerous studies, we shall see, use the pupil's scholastic rank in a lower school in order to predict his scholastic rank in a higher school, marks thus serving as *predictor* and as *criterion*. And the pupil's scholastic rank cannot be a counselor's secret. The principle of self-guidance demands that the pupil face the reality of his standing in class and know its meaning for the choice he is contemplating.

As long as some pupils should go to engineering school and others should not; as long as some pupils should take algebra and others should not; as long as some should be mechanics and some should be clerks—the problem of measuring fitness for various choices rests upon us, and that means that comparisons must be made. For example, the college desires to know in which fifth of his high-school class the applicant graduated. It thus appears that some type of comparative evaluation must remain. To be hoped and planned for is a marking system that does not interfere with educational purposes but facilitates their attainment. It is conceivable that the present college concern about rank in high-school class may disappear as better methods of motivation, of teaching, and of evaluating growth are practiced at both the high-school and college levels.

Standardized Achievement Tests

Following the demonstrations of the fallibility of teachers' marks—the extraordinary disagreement among teachers as to the value to be given a pupil's paper—came a demand for sounder measurements of pupil learning and growth. Hence, the past forty years have witnessed a marked development in the use of "objective" tests or "restricted-answer" examinations in schools, government, and industry. Many teachers make such tests for the measurement of learning in their classes. More important for this discussion are the many standardized tests of achievement which are commercially available and are regularly purchased as essential school supplies. These measuring instruments contribute markedly to the analysis of pupils on the basis of which distributive and adjustive guidance are performed.

First came the tests of reading ability—reading speed and comprehension —then tests of learning in arithmetic, spelling, and content subjects. With the finding of norms for each grade, it was possible to determine the grade level attained by each pupil. Because reading is a primary tool for the study of many subjects, reading tests have marked value in the guidance program; academic maladjustment—frequently attended by emotional repercussions —is also often attributable to a lack of reading skill.

Achievement test batteries, such as the California, Metropolitan, and Stanford, were designed to measure general and specific school achievement in the elementary grades. With grade and age norms calculated, it was possible to ascertain the educational age of the pupil and compare it with his mental age and chronological age. Certainly these batteries yield information which show up the problem cases needing adjustive service. When the educational age is lower than the mental age, it may be an indication that the pupil is not using his talents. When educational age is higher than mental age, it may be found that the pupil is anxious, overly conscientious, and working under pressure. The value of achievement batteries for prediction will be made evident in researches cited in the next sections.

Achievement tests in the specific subjects of the high-school program are numerous, the most extensive list produced by one publisher being the Co-operative tests now published by the Educational Testing Service. While most of the Co-operative tests are constructed to measure attainment in specific academic subjects, some are for the purpose of measuring general achievement in broad fields, such as mathematics, science, and social studies. With senior high school pupils pursuing divergent programs as they do, it is difficult to make fair comparisons of their educational achievements by the use of a broad-fields battery. For example, some will have taken three or four units of mathematics, while others will have had only a ninth-grade course in general mathematics; some will have had both physics and chemistry, while others will have had only a course in senior science or none at all.

Achievement batteries of a different type are the Iowa Tests of Educational Development (intended for Grades 9 to 13) and the Tests of General Educational Development prepared by the United States Armed Forces Institute. Authors of these tests assert that they are aiming at the measurement of ultimate educational outcomes, such as the acquisition of broad generalizations and concepts and the ability to use these learnings in life-like situations, rather than the memory of detailed facts from which the generalizations were derived. Hence, the sub-tests purport to measure the ability to do quantitative thinking, to interpret reading materials in social sciences, natural sciences, and literature, and to use correct form in written expression.

Achievement tests of all types are conceded to bear primarily upon the task of bringing about the pupil's development. The arguments concerning their value for that purpose need not be reviewed here. Their service to adjustive guidance lies in their revelation of the individual as achieving according to his ability or not doing so. Their service to distributive guidance rests upon their usefulness in affording a prediction of the pupil's future achievement based upon his past achievement. The following sections will offer some evidence on the predictive value of such tests.

General Intelligence Tests, Individual and Group

The brief discourse on achievement tests at several points stated or implied a distinction between ability and achievement, and also the guidance function of harmonizing the two. Turning now to an overview of measures of ability, the first to be mentioned is the general intelligence test. The objective measurement of intelligence may for all practical purposes be considered to have begun with the publication of the Stanford-Binet Scale of Intelligence in 1916 (revised in 1937). This instrument—a test individually administered—has been so universally accepted that subsequent test makers have frequently established the validity of their own tests for measuring intelligence by showing how their results agree with those obtained with the Stanford-Binet.

The first widely known intelligence test constructed for administration to groups was the Army Alpha, a paper-and-pencil test developed by a committee of psychologists for measuring the intelligence of soldiers in World War I. So extensive an employment of an intelligence test gave great prestige to psychological testing, and immediately after the war a number of group tests were made available for use in schools and colleges. As with the Stanford-Binet, these tests were standardized by giving them to large numbers of pupils of the ages for which they were intended, then ascertaining the average scores earned by the pupils of different ages. If the median score of 500 pupils just ten years of age was 87, that score was taken as designating a mental age of ten. If, then, an eight-year-old child scored 87 on the test, his mental age of ten was divided by his chronological age of eight to give him an intelligence quotient of 1.25, or 125. Similarly, if a twelve-year-old child scored 87, his intelligence quotient was .83, or 83, computed by translating $10/12$ to its decimal form; hence, M.A./C.A. = I.Q.

From the first, it was asserted that the I.Q. is constant and unchanging as a child grows up. Intelligence tests, it was claimed, measure mental alertness, the ability to solve problems. A person's intelligence level can be pretty accurately determined by the age of six, and he will stand at that level in comparison with his fellows as he grows up. This theory has been challenged seriously a number of times by respected scholars, but it has on the whole withstood such attacks. However, most psychologists would agree that the theory does assume relative equality in cultural opportunity. If a child is being brought up in some backwater of American civilization he will for that reason be at a loss in meeting some problems of the test. It has been authentically demonstrated that when children who have been growing up in such an environment are transferred to an area where they are in the main stream of American life, their I.Q.'s show noteworthy increase in a year's time.[1]

Teachers and counselors need to know such facts and conditions of the child's history and current life (defined in detail in Chapter 11) as will enable them to become aware of the I.Q.'s that should be questioned. Of course, they should also know that an I.Q. is sometimes spurious because of faulty administration of a test, pupil malingering, temporary indisposition, reading disability, visual defect, etc.[2] Cases of serious inaccuracy may be few but numerous enough so that no recorded I.Q. should be held in awe.

A recent study suggests that teachers now have a pretty accurate notion of the factors of intelligence, of the behavior symptoms characteristic of high, average, and low intelligence. Hubbard and Flesher described an adequately

[1] Some authorities, notably Allison Davis, of the University of Chicago, feel that most intelligence tests are unfair to children from the lower social classes, and they urge that tests should be made "culture free." See Allison Davis and others, *Intelligence and Cultural Differences* (Chicago, University of Chicago Press, 1951).

[2] The factor of anxiety has recently been given an illuminating though subjective treatment in Daniel Sinick, "Anxiety in the Testing Situation," *Personnel and Guidance Journal,* Vol. XXXI (March, 1953), pp. 384–387.

controlled plan for having 24 teachers of classes in Grades 2–8 estimate the exact I. Q. of their pupils.[3] Following the estimation, the pupils' I.Q.'s were measured by intelligence tests. Then the pupils were ranked according to their teacher-estimated I.Q.'s and also according to their test-measured I.Q.'s, and the coefficients of correlation between the rankings were determined. The median of the coefficients was .72, high enough to suggest that teachers have considerable ability to spot spurious test-determined I.Q.'s, and that they should therefore be encouraged to use their critical faculties so that discriminative retesting may be done.

The variation in I.Q.'s yielded by different tests is a disturbing factor which is hard to allow for in interpretation. Traxler[4] found correlations of approximately .60–.65 between the Binet I.Q.'s of 421 elementary-school pupils and their Kuhlmann-Anderson I.Q.'s—substantial, but not very high for two tests designed to measure the same thing. Hughes[5] reported a coefficient of .71 between I.Q.'s yielded by the Kuhlmann-Anderson and the Terman tests. As he points out, such a coefficient admits of fearfully wide distributions of one set of I.Q.'s in relation to the other. "When a Terman I.Q. between 110 and 120 corresponds to a K-A I.Q. anywhere between 90 (or below) and 130 (or above), it would be utter folly to base too much of our educational fortune telling on a single group I.Q."[6]

Will the second taking of an intelligence test yield the same I.Q. as the first? The answer to this question is a measure of the reliability of a test; it is a question that all test makers seek to answer by the test-retest method, the use of the split-half technique or other procedure. Hughes[7] reports a coefficient of correlation of .88 between the first and second tests of 707 children on a well-known group intelligence test. (Such reliability coefficients on the Revised Stanford-Binet are reported as ranging for the various ages from .85 to .95, with a median of .91.) Hughes examined the scores and found them to indicate changes in the children's I.Q.'s ranging from 25 points loss to 33 points gain, with an average change of 5.8 points.

These differences in the I.Q.'s yielded by different tests and by retakes of the same test point to the desirability of including in the testing program the administration of two forms of the same test, so that an average can be struck to yield a more precise measurement than can be derived from either

[3] Robert E. Hubbard and William R. Flesher, "Intelligent Teachers and Intelligence Tests—Do They Agree?" *Educational Research Bulletin*, Vol. XXXII (May 13, 1953), pp. 113–122, 139–140.

[4] Arthur E. Traxler, "Comparison between I.Q.'s on the New Edition of the Kuhlmann-Anderson Intelligence Tests and Binet I.Q.'s," *Educational Records Bureau Bulletin*, No. 31, 1941.

[5] W. Hardin Hughes, "Educational Fortune-Telling Is a Precarious Process," *Nation's Schools*, Vol. XII (July, 1933), pp. 49–54.

[6] If the reader is unfamiliar with the coefficient of correlation, he is invited to turn to page 388 on which appears a footnote offering some clarification of this statistical expression which is so frequently used in the literature of guidance.

[7] *Loc. cit.*

a single group test I.Q. or from trying to average, let us say, an Otis and a Henmon-Nelson. The child's record for intelligence tests ought to show the following items:

Date	Test	Form	Score	Local PR	Nat'l PR	M.A.	C.A.	I.Q.

Among these items for the record are "Local Percentile Rank" (PR) and "National Percentile Rank." These expressions of the individual's standing on the test are usually employed with tests for college students and adults, and more and more commonly for high-school pupils. The reason for their use is that the I.Q. cannot be accurately determined for some individuals beyond the elementary grades because of limitations in mental-test construction. Richardson[8] demonstrated this shortcoming of the I.Q. by giving the Terman test to 193 eighth-grade pupils in the spring, and repeating the test approximately thirty months later when those pupils were in the eleventh grade. The reliability coefficient of the two measurements (expressed as I.Q.'s), was .88, which indicates a high state of agreement in the two rankings; but the standard deviation of 14.88 on the first test dropped to 9.90 on the second test, signifying that the pupils were not nearly as widely dispersed on the scale in the second testing as in the first. What happened was that the dull pupils gained in I.Q. while the bright pupils lost. The changes are demonstrated in the following data:[9]

I.Q. in first test	79 and below	80–89	90–109	110–119	120 and above	Total
Number of pupils	2	16	90	41	44	193
Mean algebraic change shown in second test	+4.5	+4.4	−0.9	−6.3	−12.2	−4.1

When related to chronological age, it was shown that the eighteen pupils whose years were 12–0 to 12–11 at the time of the first test lost an average of 13.1 points in I.Q., while the four pupils whose years were 16–0 to 16–11 gained an average of 8.8 points.

Now, tests for persons of teen age and older commonly state their norms in terms of percentile rank. Thus, a 15-year-old who makes a given raw score will be found in the table of equivalents to stand at, let us say, the 43rd percentile of 15-year-olds. This means that his score is the score which 43 per cent of the group failed to attain, while 57 per cent exceeded it. Such an expression of the individual's standing lends itself to the ready understanding of any teacher who consults the record.

The advantage in figuring local percentiles for a given school lies in the

---

[8] H. D. Richardson, "The Intelligence Quotient and Secondary-School Guidance," *School Review*, Vol. XLIII (January, 1935), pp. 49–59.

[9] *Ibid*. Taken from Table 2, p. 53.

further clarification of a pupil's rank in case his group is somewhat different from the national group on which the test was standardized. In the case of a school which serves a community in which average intelligence is high, the 15-year-old example cited above might stand at the 33rd percentile, which would mean to his teachers that two-thirds of his age group in his own school exceeded him.

While the percentile scale is easily understood by the average person, the inequality of the units of the scale must always be kept in mind in interpretation of percentile rank. The bell-shaped curve of the normal distribution means that most of the cases will cluster about the central tendency. The middle 50 per cent of the cases—that is, those between the 25th and 75th percentiles—are packed in close to the median, while those at the extremes are spread out widely. Thus, a difference of five centiles is relatively unimportant at the center, while a difference of one or two centiles is of extreme importance at the upper and lower ends of the scale. Practically, this means that a student who stands at the 80th percentile on an intelligence test has a much greater advantage over a student at the 60th percentile than the latter has over a student standing at the 40th percentile.

To correct this feature of percentile ranking, many psychologists favor the use of standard scores to express standing on tests. The disadvantage of standard scores is that some statistical training is necessary to understand them. More promising is, perhaps, such a graphic representation as that recommended for use with the Differential Aptitude Tests and shown in this volume as Figure 12 on page 396. Such a form shows the percentile rank but keeps constantly before the reader the inequality of percentile scale units. Standard scores are also shown for those who wish to use them.

One more explanation must serve to conclude this brief statement regarding general intelligence tests, and it will also serve to introduce the following measures of ability which are comprehended in this section. Early in the history of intelligence tests, most psychologists recognized that the tests did not test a single trait, but rather, a constellation of traits. They compared a person's intelligence to a wheel with its spokes standing for various traits. The spokes vary somewhat in length, but *tend* to form a perfect circle, the radius of which is the *average* of the lengths of the spokes. Thus, some spokes do not reach out to the theoretical rim, while others go beyond it. The diameter of the wheel is the intelligence quotient, and the most noteworthy difference between individuals is in the diameter of their intelligence wheels. Contrasts in the lengths of the spokes have claimed more and more attention, however, and their importance has been signified by the provision of a report form for many intelligence tests showing the pupil's standing on each of the sub-tests as well as on the test as a whole. Such analysis will often show, for example, that a pupil stands considerably higher in an opposites test than in

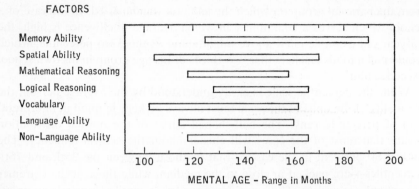

FIG. 11. Range of differences in mental factors among twenty sixth-grade pupils having identical I.Q.'s of 109 (data obtained by administration of California Test of Mental Maturity, Elementary Series).

an arithmetic test, or the reverse. Figure 11[10] shows the range of differences on sub-tests exhibited by twenty pupils of the sixth grade who had identical I.Q.'s of 109. For some of the tests the range is more than five mental years. Thus, it is quite apparent that "general intelligence" is an average of a number of more or less distinctive traits. Furthermore, it has long been apparent that the traits are mainly those used in learning the academic school subjects, that there are important human abilities which the tests do not appraise. Hence, these tests are now frequently called tests of scholastic aptitude.

Special Aptitude Tests

Mechanical Aptitude. To fill in some of the obvious gaps in ability measurement, test-makers have built tests for the measurement of aptitudes in mechanical work, music, art, clerical work, foreign languages, mathematics, and many other areas. In the field of mechanical work, considerable investigation has taken place and a number of tests of mechanical aptitude have been constructed. Common observation tells us that people vary in their degree of ability to work with tools and machinery, and the researchers have endeavored to measure such variations precisely. In 1918, Stenquist created an instrument for measuring this ability and called it the Assembling Tests of General Mechanical Ability. It consisted of a flat box containing in its ten compartments ten common mechanical devices, such as a bicycle bell, a mouse trap, and an electric push button. The articles were all disassembled and the test consisted of the task of assembling as many of them as possible

[10] Ernest W. Tiegs, "Educational Diagnosis," Educational Bulletin No. 18, California Test Bureau (Los Angeles, Cal., 1948), p. 5, Fig. 3.

in thirty minutes. This test being awkward to administer, Stenquist prepared two paper-and-pencil tests with the title of Mechanical Aptitude Tests. These were mainly pictures of common mechanical objects with questions concerning association of parts. Correlating the ranking of upper elementary-grade boys on intelligence tests with their ranking on the two types of mechanical-aptitude tests, Stenquist found coefficients of .20 to .30 for the assembling tests as compared with coefficients of .50 to .60 for the picture tests. Thus, it is evident that the assembling tests measured a trait of greater uniqueness than did the picture tests.[11]

Pioneers in the field of testing for mechanical aptitude recognized that such aptitude is not a single, unitary thing, but more likely a congeries of abilities—abilities needed in varying degrees and combinations for the various occupations. With such an assumption the MacQuarrie Test for Mechanical Ability was constructed in 1925. Its seven sub-tests are Tracing, Tapping, and Dotting (which test manual dexterity or eye-hand co-ordination), Copying, Location, and Blocks (which test spatial visualization), and Pursuit (a test of perceptual speed and accuracy). Many researches have been carried out with this test as a whole and with its several sub-tests to determine its worth, its relation to intelligence, its comparison with other tests of mechanical aptitude. So commonly, however, the descriptions of their techniques, controls, and populations have lacked precision that it is difficult to say anything conclusive about the test. Being a group test easily administered, it has been widely used, and some of its sub-tests influenced the formation of the General Aptitude Test Battery of the United States Employment Office, which will be discussed under the next topic of this section.

The most comprehensive work in the analysis and measurement of mechanical ability is a research which was carried on at the University of Minnesota in the 1920s.[12] Since this study was a thoughtful attempt to define mechanical ability or abilities and to create valid instruments for measuring it, rather than to make a predictive study with existing instruments, the project can be briefly reported here rather than in the next sections which are devoted to predictions.

The investigators first made a careful survey of existing tests and selected 26 as possible measures of mechanical ability. Some revisions were made in many of the tests, and they were then administered to boys of the seventh and eighth grades in a Minneapolis junior high school serving a middle-class population. After a few days the boys were retested in order that test reliabilities might be determined. As these boys were taking five shop courses in

[11] John L. Stenquist, *Measurements of Mechanical Ability,* Contributions to Education No. 130 (New York, Teachers College, Columbia University, 1923).

[12] Donald G. Paterson, Richard M. Elliott, and others, *Minnesota Mechanical Ability Tests* (Minneapolis, University of Minnesota Press, 1930).

sequence—woodwork, electricity, sheet metal work, mechanical drawing, and printing—with ten weeks for an hour each day devoted to each course, the criterion employed for assessing the validity of the tests was their success in the shops. Directions were given to their teachers for rating the boys as objectively as possible.

This activity was all preliminary to the experiment proper. From this trial effort it was learned that many of the tests could be eliminated, while others were extensively revised. For example, the Stenquist Assembling Test was extended from 10 items to 36, thereby raising the coefficient of reliability from .72 to .90. It was called the Minnesota Assembly, Boxes A, B, and C. A paper form board and the Link Spatial Relations Test were similarly lengthened, and entitled, respectively, the Minnesota Paper Form Board and the Minnesota Spatial Relations Test.

The experiment proper began by giving the abbreviated battery of tests to 150 boys just entering the seventh grade and with no previous school training in mechanical subjects. Their intelligence was tested with the Otis test, and they were ranked according to their success with their academic subjects based on their work in the three quarters of the seventh grade and the first two quarters of the eighth grade. A "Things Done Questionnaire" of 410 items in the nature of mechanical operations was checked by each boy; it was scored by counting the number of items checked. This is listed in Table 46 as "Son's Mechanical Operations." Data for a "Questionnaire on Cultural and Mechanical Environment" were collected by home visits. Intended to assess the influence of father's mechanical occupation or avocations on son's mechanical ability, this instrument did not show such influence.

These researchers took great care in establishing the criteria by which they evaluated the above-mentioned measures of prediction. They were not satisfied with anything so simple and unreliable as teachers' marks. And no standardized achievement tests were available. They gave thoughtful consideration to the creation of instruments for measuring the quality of mechanical work done, the quantity of mechanical work produced, creativeness shown in mechanical work, and critical appreciation of mechanical work. The principal criteria which they eventually employed were called the "quality" and the "information" criteria and are so designated in Table 46.

To obtain objective measurements of the quality of work done, the curriculum of each shop was first analyzed into the operations which were carried on, as, measuring, sawing, chiseling, gluing, in the woodshop. Each boy's work was then scored by three methods—observation; physical measuring devices and machines; and rating scales—and standards were carefully drawn up for each method. The information criterion was based on paper-and-pencil objective examinations administered in each shop during the last week of shop work. These examinations were designed to test the pupil's knowledge of tools, materials, and operations.

Table 46[13] shows the relationships between tests and criteria. Standing out as most predictive are the Minnesota Spatial Relations, the Paper Form Board, and the Minnesota Assembly—the first two of which test spatial visualization while the last one is manipulative and manual. It is worth noting that both the Spatial and the Assembly tests correlate notably higher with the quality criterion than with the information criterion. When it is also noted that the Otis and the academic grades have good correlations with the information criterion, one must conclude that the latter measures something much nearer to the trait we call general intelligence than does the quality criterion. This impression is reinforced by the r[14] of .21 between the Otis and the quality criterion. The last item in the table, Interest-Analysis Blank, refers to an interest test similar in type and purpose to the interest tests which will be taken up in the next chapter.

The Minnesota Paper Form Board, revised by Likert and Quasha, is the most widely used test to emerge from the Minnesota research project. Table 46 shows it to be predictive of both criteria. No doubt it also owes its popularity to its brevity, low cost, and ease of administration.

By combining the more predictive tests into a battery and also combining

TABLE 46. Coefficients of Correlation between Mechanical Ability Tests and Criteria for Success for 100 Seventh-Grade and Eighth-Grade Boys

Test		Criterion		
	Relia-bility of Test	Quality	Infor-mation	Quality and In-formation
Packing Blocks	.77	.26	−.04	.13
Card Sorting	.90	.19	.00	.11
Minnesota Spatial Relations, Boards A, B, C, D	.84	.53	.40	.55
Paper Form Board, Series A and B	.90	.52	.57	.65
Stenquist Picture I	.89	.24	.35	.35
Stenquist Picture II	.90	.31	.34	.39
Minnesota Assembly, Boxes A, B, and C	.94	.55	.35	.53
Otis Intelligence Quotient		.21	.67	.52
Academic Grades		.42	.54	.57
Son's Mechanical Operations		.30	.35	.39
Interest-Analysis Blank		.55	.39	.56

[13] *Ibid.* Drawn from Table 12, p. 109, Table 25, p. 204, and Table 26, p. 205.
[14] Symbol for coefficient of correlation.

the two criteria into one, a higher degree of correspondence was found, as shown in Table 47.[15]

The claim for uniqueness of mechanical ability and for the adequacy of the instruments used in this research for measuring it, seems conclusively demonstrated in the following coefficients:[16]

	Quality Criterion	Academic Grades
I.Q.	.21	.57
Mechanical-ability apparatus test battery	.61	.24

TABLE 47. Correlation between a Test Battery and Shop Success ($r = .68$)

Quality-Information Criterion	Test Battery Scores						
	F	E	D	C	B	A	Total
A						1	1
B			1	6	8		15
C		1	6	21	7		35
D		8	14	9	1		32
E	1	6	6	2			15
F	1	1					2
Total	2	16	27	38	17	0	

They show the mechanical-ability tests predicting the quality of mechanical work done fully as well as the I.Q. predicted academic grades, and the two predictors were equally weak in their relationships to the opposite criterion.

An additional test of mechanical aptitude which has been widely used since its publication in 1940 is the Bennett Test of Mechanical Comprehension. This is a paper-and-pencil test of sixty items in the form of picture

[15] Paterson, Elliott, and others, *op. cit.* Drawn from Figure 43, p. 218. The showing of this correlation table, with its coefficient of .68, may well be the occasion for making a brief explanation. The coefficient of correlation is a mathematical concept, represented by the symbol *r*, which is here applied to the comparison of the rankings of a group of people on two measurements. If the members of the group stand in exactly the same order on the two measurements, the coefficient is $+1.00$. If they stand in exactly the reverse order, the coefficient is -1.00. Looking at Table 47, we have a correlation table, sometimes called an expectancy table, which represents each testee on the two measures. For example, the figures in Column B mean that of the 17 persons of B standing on the test battery, 1 earned A standing on the criterion, 8 earned B, 7 earned C, and 1 earned D. If all the testees in the table had fallen in the diagonal line of boxed intervals—meaning that they stood in the same order on the one measure as on the other—the coefficient would have been 1.00. In Table 46 it will be noted that the correlation between card sorting and the information criterion was .00. The correlation table for that relationship would show no diagonal arrangement of cases—they would be scattered indiscriminately. To sense the degree of scatter from the diagonal line of expectancy which coefficients of various magnitude represent, the reader may look at Tables 70 and 71.

[16] Paterson, Elliott, and others, *op. cit.* Data taken from Table 45, p. 246.

problems which the subject solves according to his command of physical principles. In its demands upon the subject's powers of logical analysis the Bennett seems to be testing an aptitude of greater complexity than is involved in the mechanical-aptitude tests we have heretofore canvassed.

Traxler[17] compared the Bennett test with the Minnesota Paper Form Board by giving the two tests to 230 cadets in the United States Merchant Marine Corps, most of whom were between the ages of 18 and 22, with academic aptitude somewhat above that of the average high-school senior. The coefficient of correlation between the two tests was .393, which is low enough to suggest that to some degree the tests measure different traits. Using the partial correlation technique to hold constant the factor of general intelligence as represented in the subjects' scores on the A.C.E. Psychological Examination, the coefficient between the Bennett and the Paper Form Board was found to be .283. This is further support for the contention that the two tests measure different traits.

McElheny[18] compared the Bennett test with the Purdue Mechanical Assembly Test on 80 men students at the State University of Iowa. These men were miscellaneously chosen from various fields of specialized study. The Purdue test is like the Stenquist and the Minnesota assembly tests, except that whereas the latter two present *familiar* objects disassembled, the Purdue test has eliminated stereotyped mechanical contrivances and substituted novel mechanical problem situations with which the subject has had no chance familiarity. The coefficient of correlation was .63, large enough to suggest that to a noteworthy degree the two tests were measuring the same aptitude. Such being the case, the Bennett should be much the preferred test to use, because, as a group paper-and-pencil test, it is easy and inexpensive to administer.

Tests of mechanical aptitude will be found in the standard batteries which are presently achieving widening acceptance; some of these batteries are described on pages 394–398.

Musical Aptitude. A cluster of aptitudes in the field of music are of noteworthy uniqueness. For their identification and measurement we are especially indebted to Carl E. Seashore, who designed the Seashore Measures of Musical Talents in 1919. These instruments were thoroughly revised and much reduced in length in 1939, but most of the extensive body of research literature on the Measures was the result of research with the 1919 tests. The present battery consists of three double-faced phonograph records to which subjects listen and record their discriminations in the six capacities called Pitch, Loudness, Time, Timbre, Rhythm, and Tonal Memory. Norms are

[17] Arthur E. Traxler, "Correlations between 'Mechanical Aptitude' Scores and 'Mechanical Comprehension' Scores," *Occupations,* Vol. XXII (October, 1943), pp. 42–43.

[18] W. T. McElheny, "A Study of Two Techniques of Measuring 'Mechanical Comprehension,'" *Journal of Applied Psychology,* Vol. XXXII (December, 1948), pp. 611–617.

available for subjects from Grade 5 to adulthood. Intercorrelations between the tests are all low enough to suggest that they measure relatively independent traits. That the traits are innate and hardly subject to development by educative experience is the conclusion reached by Stanton and Koerth[19] from their research project which involved retesting children after 3, 6, and 9 years of systematic music study in the preparatory division of the Eastman School of Music.

Failure to understand the non-improvable character of these capacities may result in such an error as that reported by Seashore, as follows:[20]

One of my first experiences in talent testing was the analysis of the ability of a brother and two sisters. The occasion was the fact that the older sister had been having about ten years of musical training without making progress, and the other two children, without much attention to education, were making splendid progress through spontaneous and voluntary efforts. I found that the older sister was radically lacking in fundamental capacities, whereas the other two children were highly gifted. The action upon my findings by the parents, a minister and his wife, was to send the older daughter to the New England Conservatory of Music in order that she might be able to keep ahead of her brother and sister.

Apparently the true nature of the talents measured should be explained to parents.

These musical talents are unrelated to general intelligence. Hollingworth[21] reported that 49 pupils with I.Q.'s above 135 met the Seashore tests only as well as average children of their age. Other researchers have reported an absence of correlation between standing on the music tests and on intelligence tests.

To be able to profit by musical instruction, however, the student must have intelligence as well as the fundamental musical capacities, and truly advanced study of music requires intelligence of a high order. This was demonstrated by Stanton's extended researches at the Eastman School of Music. She worked out a cumulative key for classifying students on the two bases—musical talents as measured by the Seashore test and intelligence as measured by the Iowa Comprehension test. Table 48[22] shows the five-fold classification of students in relation to the criterion of completion of training, which is certainly an objective measure of validity. The table does indeed

[19] Hazel M. Stanton and Wilhelmine Koerth, *Musical Capacity Measures of Children Repeated after Musical Training,* Series on Aims and Progress of Research, New Series No. 259 (Iowa City, University of Iowa Studies, September 15, 1933).

[20] Carl E. Seashore, "Educational Guidance in Music," *School and Society,* Vol. XLV (March 20, 1937), p. 387.

[21] Leta S. Hollingworth, "Musical Sensitivity of Children Who Test Above 135 I.Q. (Stanford-Binet)," *Journal of Educational Psychology,* Vol. XVII (February, 1926), pp. 95–109.

[22] Hazel M. Stanton, *Measurement of Musical Talent: The Eastman Experiment,* Studies in the Psychology of Music, Vol. II (Iowa City, University of Iowa Studies, 1935), p. 72.

TABLE 48. The Annual Academic Survivors and the Graduates in Four Years, of the Five Differential Groups of the Class Which Entered Eastman School of Music in 1925

Group	Number Entering 1st Year	Per cent Continuing 2nd Year	Per cent Continuing 3rd Year	Per cent Continuing 4th Year	Per cent Graduating In 4 Years
Safe	29	89.6	72.4	55.1	55.1
Probable	40	67.5	50.0	37.5	37.5
Possible	63	65.1	52.3	39.5	31.7
Doubtful	21	57.1	42.8	19.1	19.1
Discouraged	11	18.1	0.0	0.0	0.0

show the combined predictor to be indicative of length of stay in the curriculum (which culminated in the degree of Bachelor of Music). A decided limitation on the soundness of the criterion, however, is the certain fact that students dropped out or continued because of many factors in addition to musical talent and intelligence—for example, economic resources, intensity of ambition and determination to achieve, health, family attitudes.

The fact that relatively few persons take up musical occupations probably accounts for the tendency in many schools to neglect the measurement of this special aptitude. Some schools seem to employ tests of musical talent only with those pupils who express an interest in a musical career. Such an attitude, of course, simply sidesteps guidance; it assumes that the pupils who have decided *not* to seek musical careers have made sound judgments. A valid policy requires the measurement of every pupil. Such a dragnet survey will locate some children of extraordinary musical gifts, though they and their parents and teachers have been quite unaware of such gifts. Then, discriminating counsel can begin, helping each pupil to judge what kind of musical vocation or avocation he is justified in aspiring to. The character of the field is so special that it seems to this writer preferable to have music teachers rather than general counselors do both the testing and the advisement.

Artistic Aptitude. What is the nature of artistic aptitude? Meier, who has studied this type of human ability most extensively, identifies the following six factors:[23]

    I. Manual skill
    II. Energy output and perseveration
    III. Aesthetic intelligence
    IV. Perceptual facility
    V. Creative imagination
    VI. Aesthetic judgment

[23] Norman C. Meier, "Factors in Artistic Aptitude," in *Studies in the Psychology of Art,* Psychological Monographs, Vol. 51, No. 5, 1939.

The analysis by which Meier built up this classification was subjective in considerable degree, his sources especially being the biographies of artists. "It is the thesis of this writer," says Meier,[24] "that the person with the six factors *can* bring this end about [extraordinary accomplishment in art] and that the person without these factors *cannot* bring this about to any great degree."

Aesthetic judgment is the factor that Meier considers most important in artistic competence, and it is the one which he purports to measure in his Meier Art Judgment Test. This test consists of 100 pairs of pictures, black and white prints, mostly of paintings, and all representing reputable art, though generally unfamiliar to those who take the test. One member of each pair is an exact reproduction of the original work, while the other has been slightly modified. The distinction is pointed out to the examinee, but without letting him know which is the original. He selects the picture which he prefers in each pair. Ziegfield points out that these differences involve only factors of design and that[25]

To assume that aesthetic judgment is based entirely upon the ability to respond to design is a misleading oversimplification. There are many other factors, such as expression, color materials, subject matter, and all their interrelationships, that enter into the making of an aesthetic judgment.

Norms on this test are available for junior high school students, senior high school students, and adults, but the meaning of the norms is somewhat cloudy due to the uncertain character of the populations on which they are based.

Not as much research has been carried on with the present Meier test (1940) as with the earlier edition (1929). Such validity studies as have been made are not clear-cut and convincing. Considering the wide range of occupations requiring the exercise of various artistic skills, various artistic media, and various artistic judgments, the Meier test seems very narrow in the scope of capacity which it aims to test. Since other tests of artistic aptitude have less to recommend them than the Meier test, it seems that the objective measurement of this special aptitude is relatively undeveloped. To find the youngsters who possess artistic talent, chief reliance must lie in the observation of boys and girls in the art classes of the elementary and junior high school grades.

Clerical Aptitude. The most widely used test in the field of clerical aptitude is the Minnesota Clerical Test. Originally named the Minnesota Vocational Test for Clerical Workers, its creation in 1934 was a project of the Minnesota Employment Stabilization Research Institute. The test calls for speed and accuracy in number checking and name checking. The subject is confronted with 200 pairs of numbers, ranging from three through twelve

[24] *Ibid.,* p. 158.
[25] Edwin Ziegfield, Review in Oscar Buros' *The Third Mental Measurements Yearbook* (New Brunswick, N.J., Rutgers University Press, 1949) p. 258.

digits. In some of the pairs the two members are identical; in others, the members are slightly different. The task is to mark the pairs which are identical. The name-checking test is similar.

What is the nature of the capacity which is measured by such a test? Is it distinct from other capacities, general or special? Rather simple visual perception, with a premium on speed, seems to be the faculty called upon. Perception we found was prominent in mechanical aptitude and in artistic aptitude. Perception is the heart of musical aptitude, though it is auditory rather than visual. The Minnesota test measures perception, in a very narrow area, conceived to be employed by many clerical workers.

Much research has been done on and with this test, and it is generally conceded to have some value in selecting clerical workers and students for training in clerical occupations. An example of this research literature is Ghiselli's report[26] that scores on the two elements of the Minnesota test which were included in the General Clerical Battery of the United States Employment Service correlated with the job success of 562 assorted clerical workers almost as well as did the scores on the whole battery, the coefficient of which was .42.

The manual for this test contains extensive information concerning its validity, such as the following items: (1) coefficients of correlation between standings on the two parts of the test and marks in accounting earned by university students were .47 and .49, whereas the coefficient between standing on an academic-ability test and marks in accounting was .17; (2) the test differentiated between rapid, average, and slow typists notably better than did academic-ability tests; (3) the test distinguished various categories of clerical workers—accountants and bookkeepers, for example, standing much higher than routine clerical workers or shipping and stock clerks, while the median score for the latter groups was shown to be better than the 75-percentile for the general population.

Norms are given in the manual for a number of classes of clerical workers and for school pupils in Grades 8–12. In all cases the sexes are shown separately, which is well advised in view of substantial differences in favor of women and girls.

Since clerical aptitude is a trait which figures to some degree in many occupations other than those which are clearly classifiable as clerical, a measure of this capacity in every boy and girl would be helpful in occupational counseling. The Minnesota test is an inexpensive test, easy to administer, and requiring only 15 minutes—8 for number checking and 7 for name checking. Of the many other clerical tests presently on the market, most are characterized by similarity to the Minnesota.

Other Special Aptitudes. Often referred to as special aptitudes are capacity

[26] Edwin E. Ghiselli, "A Comparison of the Minnesota Vocational Test for Clerical Workers with the General Clerical Battery of the U.S.E.S.," *Journal of Applied Psychology,* Vol. XXVI (February, 1942), pp. 75–80.

for learning in mathematics and in foreign language. Both of these fields of aptitude are more closely related to general intelligence than are the ones that have been canvassed. Substantial coefficients of correlation attest this relationship. The instruments for measuring these aptitudes will be described and evaluated in the next section, which is devoted to prediction of success in studies.

Standardized Test Batteries

From the preceding discussion of intelligence tests which pointed to them as instruments appraising special intelligences and striking an average, and from the presentation of special aptitude tests which measure mental capacities not included in general intelligence, the development of comprehensive test batteries seems logical enough. The Thurstones well stated this logic in 1941 when they said,[27]

For many years psychologists have been accustomed to the problems of special abilities and disabilities. These are, in fact, the principal concern of school psychologists who deal with children who cannot read, with children who have a blind spot for numbers, or with children who do one thing remarkably well and other things poorly. It seems strange that, with all this experience in differential psychology, we have clung so long to the practice of summarizing a child's mental endowment by a single index. . . . The error that is frequently made is that the intelligence quotient is sanctified by the assumption that it measures some basic functional unity, when it is known to be nothing more than a composite of many functional unities.

Professor Thurstone has been one of the leaders in the employment of the statistical techniques of factor analysis for the identification of psychological traits and the construction of tests for their appraisal. On the basis of such studies he constructed the series of test batteries known as the Tests of Primary Mental Abilities, now available for different age groups and distributed by Science Research Associates. What are these "primary mental abilities?" The battery for ages 11 to 17 purports to measure the following five: verbal meaning, space, reasoning, number, and word-fluency.

Test makers using factor analysis vary in the factors which they identify. Some have subdivided such traits as Thurstone has called "primary," and there is apparently no thought of isolating traits in the purity that can be achieved with chemical elements. Nor is there denial of the possibility of a general or *g* factor of intelligence which may be common to most or all of the traits identified. The existence of a general factor is clearly indicated in the intercorrelations, which are positive though not high, between the tests of Thurstone's battery.

Many researches have been carried on to determine the worth of the PMA

[27] L. L. and T. G. Thurstone, *Factorial Studies of Intelligence*, Psychometric Monographs No. 2 (Chicago, University of Chicago Press, 1941), p. 8.

tests. These have been reported and interpreted in the works of such psychologists as Anastasia, Cronbach, and Super, which are cited in the list of references at the end of this chapter. They find many grounds for criticism and express the hope for revision and further work on this battery to contribute to its practical value. Crawford and Burnham concluded their searching analysis with this remark:[28]

As judged by external criteria rather than mere self-contained data, no studies reported thus far indicate that the Primary Mental Abilities Battery serves a notably useful purpose for individual measurement and student counseling whether educational or vocational.

The PMA battery may well be regarded as a pioneer effort which has greatly influenced other test makers toward battery construction and induced test users to look with favor upon the integrated test battery. Mention should first be made, however, of an earlier feat of the Thurstones which did much to accustom test users to the idea of a breakdown of the concept of general intelligence. This was the construction of the American Council on Education Psychological Examination so as to yield a linguistic (L) score, a quantitative (Q) score, and a total score. Popularly known as the ACE test, this instrument has been used for many years, in a new form each fall, for the measurement of the freshmen entering hundreds of colleges and universities. Its predictive value corresponds fairly well to the average of intelligence tests, to be remarked upon in the third section of this chapter.

A modern test battery of practical attributes which has won favorable commendation from test authorities is the Differential Aptitude Tests (Psychological Corporation, 1947). One long-felt need that the DAT satisfies is that it brings together tests of academic, mechanical, and clerical aptitude as an integrated battery *standardized on the same population*. The norms for all the tests are based upon the same 47,000 pupils in Grades 8 to 12, tested in approximately 100 communities in 26 states. The pupil is thus compared with the same national group on each test. The norms are given in the form of percentile rank for each grade, each sex, each test. The list of tests is as follows (quotations from the manual):

Verbal Reasoning (VR) (30 min.)
"ability to understand concepts framed in words . . . analogies form. . . ."
Numerical Ability (NA) (30 min.)
"understanding of numerical relationships and facility in handling numerical concepts." Computation form to avoid the language elements of the usual arithmetic reasoning problem.
Abstract Reasoning (AR) (25 min.)
"intended as a non-verbal measure of the student's reasoning ability . . ."
Space Relations (SR) (30 min.)
"The ability to visualize a constructed object from a picture of a pattern

28 Albert B. Crawford and Paul S. Burnham, *Forecasting College Achievement* (New Haven, Yale University Press, 1946), p. 214.

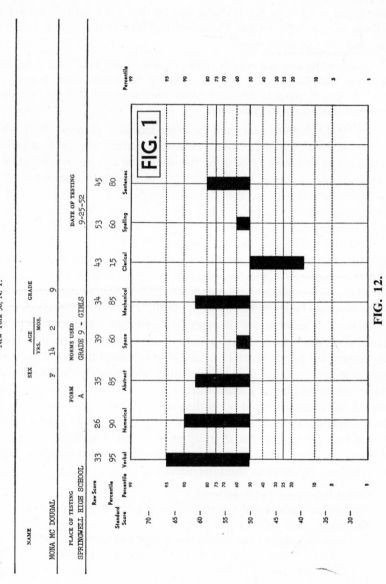

FIG. 12.

. . . [and] the ability to imagine how an object would appear if rotated in various ways. . . ."
Mechanical Reasoning (MR) (30 min.)
"Each item consists of a pictorially represented mechanical situation together with a simply worded question." Comparable to the Bennett Mechanical Comprehension Test.
Clerical Speed and Accuracy (CSA) (6 min.)
"to measure speed of response in a simple perceptual task."
Language Usage
Part I—Spelling (10 min.)
"selected from the lists in Gates' *Spelling Difficulties in 3876 Words.*"
Part II—Sentences (25 min.)
"to measure the pupil's ability to distinguish between good and bad grammar, punctuation and word usage."

The authors state that the first three tests may be thought of as measuring functions commonly associated with general intelligence, an interpretation which is borne out by correlations with several general-intelligence tests.[29] For example, most of the correlations of Verbal Reasoning with intelligence tests are in the .70's and .80's; those of the Numerical Ability average slightly above .60; and those of Abstract Reasoning, about .55.

This battery provides for reporting each individual's scores on the eight tests plotted as percentile ranks on a profile chart. Three ways of making the profile are illustrated in the manual, of which the one shown here as Figure 12[30] is favored. With bars drawn upward and downward from the median, it shows the extent and direction of the individual's variation from the average. The spacing of percentile ranks on the graph in such a way as to take into account the normal curve of distribution will help the reader to make the correction for the inequality of percentile scale units, a point which was referred to earlier in this chapter. Figure 12 shows also in the left-hand margin a scale for standard scores.

Thousands of coefficients have been figured to ascertain the predictive significance of the elements of the DAT battery. These will be reviewed in the next section of this chapter.

One other battery will be described briefly in this section; namely, the General Aptitude Test Battery (GATB), a tool of the United States Employment Service and a product of the research arm of that agency. The battery

29 George K. Bennett, Harold G. Seashore, and Alexander G. Wesman, *A Manual for the Differential Aptitude Tests* (New York, The Psychological Corporation, 1952), pp. 72–73, Tables 34 and 35.
Evidence that two other tests of this battery also test inborn ability will be found in a recently reported experiment involving the tests of Mechanical Reasoning and Space Relations. See Lorenzo Mendicino, "Mechanical Reasoning and Space Perception: Native Capacity or Experience," *Personnel and Guidance Journal,* Vol. XXXVI (January, 1958), pp. 335–338.
30 *Ibid.,* p. 22, Fig. 2.

consists of 12 tests chosen as a result of factor analysis studies of a large number of tests. It measures 9 aptitudes which in varying degrees and combinations contribute to occupational success. The aptitudes are designated as follows: G—intelligence, V—verbal aptitude, N—numerical aptitude, S—spatial aptitude, P—form perception, Q—clerical perception, K—motor co-ordination, F—finger dexterity, and M—manual dexterity. Of the 15 tests, 11 are paper-and-pencil tests and 4 are apparatus tests. The entire battery requires about 2¼ hours for administration.[31]

In contrast to the DAT, the reader will note that the latter three aptitudes named are manual and motor in character—capacities not tested by the DAT.

The GATB was constructed for the purpose of identifying the occupational potentialities of adults and older adolescents. It has been standardized on workers in various occupations. At the latest report, norms had been established for 20 fields of work representing approximately 2000 occupations. The extensive work in job analysis which had been done by the U.S.E.S. facilitated the establishment of the norms which are referred to as "Occupational Aptitude Patterns."

Much of the procedure by which this battery was constructed and standardized has not been described in fullness and clarity. The battery is not available to the public but is extensively administered to high-school seniors by members of the counseling staffs of U.S.E.S. offices co-operating with high-school counselors. When resources of the employment offices are too limited to give the tests to the entire senior class, common practice is to give them to those members who are not going to college and who have not followed the commercial curriculum—in other words, the group that is usually least well served by the school's testing and counseling program. As pointed out above, the GATB has elements for the measurement of the manual and motor capacities which many of these pupils will use in the occupational strata for which they are likely destined—hence, the importance of measuring such capacities.

A noteworthy contribution to our understanding of test batteries is afforded by the series of articles sponsored by Donald E. Super, which appeared in the nine issues of Volume XXXV (1956–57) of the *Personnel and Guidance Journal*. Following an introductory article by Super, the authors of eight well-known batteries described in turn their product in successive articles, each article being followed by Super's critical "Comments." The series presents an admirable opportunity to gain an understanding of these instruments, although the concepts acquired from courses in statistics and psychological measurements are necessary for adequate comprehension.

In closing this section, mention should be made of David Segel's *Measurement Index*, Circular No. 388, Revised, August, 1956, U.S. Office of Edu-

---

[31] *Counseling and Employment Service for Special Worker Groups* (Washington, D.C., U.S. Employment Service, Department of Labor, 1954), pp. 92–100.

cation. This pamphlet is a convenient tool which lists tests, broadly classified; publishers; and the major current books on educational and psychological testing.

PREDICTION OF SUCCESS IN THE SECONDARY SCHOOL

Homeroom teacher, counselor, and principal are faced with many questions under this rubric. "High school" means differentiation in educational opportunity, and efficient functioning of the school demands that each pupil find the opportunity which corresponds most nearly to his abilities, interests, and needs. Which curriculum shall Harry choose—college preparatory, commercial, general, practical arts? And how about the choices within each curriculum? Or, if the program is of the constants-with-variables type, which 17 of the 50 units offered are the best for Helen to take? a foreign language? shorthand? home economics? Then there are the specialized vocational schools for boys and for girls. Ninth-graders must compare the opportunities of such schools with those of the comprehensive senior high school and make a choice.

While we write here of problems primarily in the area of distributive guidance, they bear a close relationship to adjustive guidance, for sound choices of school, curriculum, and subjects contribute to social, emotional, and academic adjustments. Pupils whose differentiated abilities, needs, and interests are well served do not leave school at the first opportunity.

Predictive Value of School Marks

With marks as *predictor* and marks as *criterion,* some fairly close relationships have been shown. One of the first researches into this relationship is the often-cited dissertation of Kelley in which he found a coefficient of .789 between a composite of elementary-school marks and the average of first-year high-school (9th-grade) marks.[32] Seldom have parallel studies produced a coefficient of such magnitude. For example, Ross, a decade later, found a coefficient of .60 between the same two variables.[33] Critics explain the contrasting results of these two studies as follows: Kelley's cases had their elementary and secondary education entirely in one school in which one standard of marking prevailed; Ross' study was carried on in a school system in which the high-school students came from a number of elementary schools, the marking standards of which no doubt varied somewhat.

It is reasonable, of course, to expect that the pupil's success in the lower school will be indicative of his success in the higher school, and despite the

[32] Truman L. Kelley, *Educational Guidance,* Contributions to Education No. 71 (New York, Teachers College, Columbia University, 1914), p. 8.

[33] Clay C. Ross, *The Relation between Grade School Record and High School Achievement,* Contributions to Education No. 166 (New York, Teachers College, Columbia University, 1925), p. 15.

limitations on school marks described in the first pages of this chapter, there is much evidence of their predictive value. Ross tested many more-detailed relationships than the one mentioned above, and found, for example, that marks in seventh-grade and eighth-grade English correlated with ninth-grade English to the extent of a coefficient of .53, and with ninth-grade Latin to the extent of .54.[34]

These relationships may be made more evident by drawing upon the data from a study made by this writer a number of years ago.[35] With the aid of graduate students who were teachers and counselors in service, he gathered from a number of school systems the data presented here as Tables 49, 50, and 51.

TABLE 49. Relation between Success in Seventh- and Eighth-Grade English and in Ninth-Grade Latin

No. of Cases	English	Latin					Total (Per cent)
		F	D	C	B	A	
46	A		4.3	15.2	47.8	32.6	99.9
299	B	4.7	17.7	39.5	28.8	9.4	100.1
297	C	14.5	38.0	29.6	16.5	1.3	99.9
107	D	24.3	35.5	29.0	11.2		100.0
16	F	62.5	37.5				100.0

TABLE 50. Relation between Success in Seventh- and Eighth-Grade Mathematics and in Ninth-Grade Algebra

No. of Cases	Mathe-matics	Algebra					Total (Per cent)
		F	D	C	B	A	
65	A	1.5	1.5	7.7	49.2	40.0	99.9
377	B	4.5	11.7	37.4	37.1	9.3	100.0
507	C	8.9	33.5	38.9	16.8	2.0	100.1
206	D	24.8	38.8	24.3	12.1		100.0
20	F	45.0	20.0	35.0			100.0

In these correlation or double-entry tables the numbers of cases were changed to percentages for the sake of clarity. To understand the prediction, pupils should be taught to read across the table, as, in Table 49, of 46 pupils who earned A in English, 4.3 per cent earned D in Latin, 15.2 per cent earned C in Latin, and so on. Coefficients for the relationships shown in these tables were not computed because the writer was primarily interested in demonstrating the possibilities of correlation tables for counseling with

[34] *Ibid.*, p. 18.
[35] P. W. Hutson, "Deriving Practical Instruments for Guidance," *Vocational Guidance Magazine,* Vol. XI (March, 1933), pp. 247–254.

TABLE 51. Relation between Success in Ninth- and Tenth-Grade English and in Stenography

No. of Cases	English	Stenography					Total (Per cent)
		F	D	C	B	A	
15	A			13.3	53.3	33.3	99.9
118	B		1.7	39.8	51.7	6.8	100.0
275	C		16.7	65.8	16.7	.7	99.9
102	D		55.9	39.2	4.9		100.0
2	F		50.0	50.0			100.0

pupils, especially using the data of school marks with which pupils have great familiarity. The tables are introduced here to show the predictive significance of school marks for helping the pupil make some typical choices of the secondary school. Despite the fact that these tables present a hit-or-miss collection of data from a number of schools of varied student bodies, they bear clear evidence of predictiveness and could profitably be used now as the basis for discussion and self-examination by groups of pupils faced with the opportunity to choose Latin, algebra, or shorthand. Nevertheless, if each school were to make these correlational studies of its own marks, it would have custom-made guidance instruments which would afford a better fit for its own pupils than an imported product such as the tables above.

Intelligence and Differentiated-Ability Tests

In the 1920s a great many studies were made to find the relationship between results on tests of general intelligence and school success. Summaries of the coefficients of correlation found between intelligence and success in the individual academic subjects (as measured by school marks) showed them to be averaging in the .40's—not high enough to encourage the use of intelligence tests in counseling pupils with reference to the election of optional subjects.

Occasionally, a prediction study was made with great care and with a view to excluding subjective judgments from the criterion. Such a research was that of Hurd[36] in which he tested the value of the I.Q. for predicting success in high-school physics. The physics classes in one high school were given two group intelligence tests—the Miller and the Otis—and the I.Q.'s derived from each test were averaged, thus obtaining a better measure of general intelligence than one test alone could give. Success in physics was measured by twelve comprehensive tests corresponding to the units of the course and given throughout the year as each unit was completed. The tests were generally in two sections—subject matter information and problems for solu-

[36] A. W. Hurd, "The Intelligence Quotient as a Prognosis of Success in Physics," *School Review,* Vol. XXXIV (February, 1926), pp. 123–128.

tion. Their scoring was objective, with a total possible score for the year of 415 points. Hurd correlated the mean I.Q.'s with the total scores earned by the pupils and obtained coefficients of .76 (Pearson) or .82 (Spearman). The study illustrates how prediction can be improved when steps are taken to increase the accuracy of the predictive instrument and employ a sound, objective criterion.

Turning to the value of general intelligence tests for predicting total average scholarship in secondary schools, Feingold summarized numerous studies made in the early twenties by reporting that most of the coefficients varied between .35 and .65,[37] of which the midpoint would be .50. Serene's recent study reports coefficients of .46 for the tenth-grade class in his high school, .57 for the eleventh grade, and .55 for the twelfth grade.[38] Each class numbered about 300. Marks were determined by the sigma system.

With the trend toward differential aptitude testing, it is natural that differential prediction should follow. Thus, while the 1952 DAT manual records thousands of coefficients to show how elements of that battery predict success in the various subjects, there are none to show a prediction of average school success. To suggest the worth of the DAT in subject-success prediction, Table 52 presents a summary of the coefficients for four subject fields, as given in the manual,[39] using only the four elements of the battery which were most predictive. A study of this table brings up a number of observations and some questions. First, a comparison of the median r's for boys and for girls shows that those for the girls are slightly higher in every instance except two. The reason for this difference seems to be a subject for speculation. It could be that girls average higher in conscientiousness than boys, thus achieving more nearly in harmony with their ability. At any rate the fact of the differences justifies separation of the sexes in these validity studies, as also in the norms.

The median coefficients do show considerable correlation between the battery elements and the subject fields. The abstract-reasoning test is least predictive. As regards mathematics, three of the tests are relatively unpredictive; only Numerical Ability (NA) shows a fair amount of relationship. In the case of the other three fields, it is perhaps surprising to note that NA is practically as predictive as VR. Suppose these two tests were combined? Would notably higher coefficients result? The possibilities of getting better predictions by making varied combinations of these battery elements has been demonstrated in 1958 by the constructors of the DAT, but at this writing the data have not been released.

[37] Gustave A. Feingold, "Correlation between Intelligence and Scholarship," *School Review*, Vol. XXXII (June, 1924), p. 455.

[38] Michael F. Serene, "An Experiment in Motivational Counseling," *Personnel and Guidance Journal*, Vol. XXXI (February, 1953), p. 323.

[39] Bennett, Seashore, and Wesman, *op. cit.*, data drawn from Tables 2–9.

TABLE 52. Summary of Validity Coefficients between Scores on Four Elements of the DAT Battery and School Marks

	Boys			Girls		
	Highest r	Median r	Lowest r	Highest r	Median r	Lowest r
ENGLISH						
VR	.78	.49	.11	.78	.52	.22
NA	.74	.48	.03	.71	.48	.23
AR	.74	.32	.03	.66	.40	.09
Sentences	.76	.50	.02	.77	.53	.22
MATHEMATICS						
VR	.70	.33	.04	.63	.45	.07
NA	.65	.47	.27	.71	.52	.25
AR	.61	.32	.07	.62	.38	.00
Sentences	.65	.32	.06	.65	.40	.06
SCIENCE						
VR	.80	.54	.10	.79	.55	.06
NA	.74	.52	.10	.75	.50	.14
AR	.67	.42	−.02	.70	.45	.03
Sentences	.78	.45	.07	.77	.52	.24
SOCIAL STUDIES						
VR	.72	.48	−.01	.79	.52	.27
NA	.76	.46	.04	.74	.50	.25
AR	.74	.32	−.12	.62	.38	.17
Sentences	.73	.43	.20	.83	.49	.17

And now the puzzling question which a perusal of Table 52 inevitably raises. Why is there such an astounding range of coefficients—from practically no correlation to very marked correlation for each test and each subject? This is a characteristic of the literature of predictive studies which is distressing and discouraging to the reader who would take measurements of his pupils so that he can help them make wise choices. In bewilderment he says, How do I know if this test will do us any good? If I compare its prediction with our pupils' achievement, will it yield .03 or .74?

Since this problem of conflicting evidence comes up continually, a discussion of it should perhaps not be postponed. The Psychological Corporation, publisher of the DAT, has contributed an orderly way of thinking about this problem in an article entitled "The Three-Legged Coefficient" which appeared in their *Test Service Bulletin,* No. 40, December, 1950. The three legs, each of which must be studied in evaluating a coefficient, are the *test* (or other predictor), the *criterion,* and the *population* (the group measured).

The criterion most often used as the measure of educational success is that of school marks. Their limitations and uncertainty were set forth at some length in the first pages of this chapter, and we cannot doubt that varied methods of arriving at pupil marks account for much of the divergence of coefficients shown in Table 52, and also operate to hold down the average size of the coefficients. As an example casting doubt on the validity of marks as a criterion, *Test Service Bulletin* No. 40 relates how a numerical-ability test for the prediction of success in geometry was given to a class of boys at the beginning of the year of their study of the subject. The coefficient with the instructor's grades at the end of the year was a disappointing .30. The pupils' achievement had also been measured by a statewide examination in geometry, and the use of that criterion yielded a coefficient of .60 with the numerical-ability test. "The guidance director used the discrepancy between these two correlation coefficients to initiate discussions with the mathematics teachers as to the bases on which grades were being assigned."

The DAT manual affords another example of how coefficients are less divergent and average higher when objective criteria are used. For the Co-operative English Tests, given in Des Moines, Newark, and White Plains, eleven coefficients are shown (for boys) as representing the correlation of the Tests in their several subdivisions with the DAT Verbal Reasoning. The coefficients range from .62 to .83 and average .73. Against the Iowa Tests of Educational Development—consisting of nine tests ranging over the fields of literature, composition, social studies, natural science, and mathematics—the coefficients with Verbal Reasoning ranged from .45 to .82, averaging .67; the coefficients with Numerical Ability ranged from .40 to .85, averaging .59; and the coefficients with Abstract Reasoning ranged from .30 to .80, averaging .53. The reader may compare the data of this paragraph with those of Table 52.

Let us look at the test or predictor leg of "The Three-Legged Coefficient." *Test Service Bulletin,* No. 40, says, "A correlation coefficient is not a judgment. . . . It is not a substitute for thinking—quite the contrary, it should be the impulse which starts the thinking process going." This writer's thinking process was started when he noticed that the DAT Manual shows the coefficients of correlation of each of the DAT scores with every criterion shown in Table 52 and in all the rest of the manual. That is, for example, for every group and every subject on which the coefficient for Verbal Reasoning was figured, it was also figured for Space Relations, Mechanical Reasoning, and Clerical Speed and Accuracy. It should be evident from the very titles of these latter three tests that they are not calculated to predict success in the academic branches. Naturally, they show up in the Manual as poorly correlated with those subjects. The point of this paragraph is that judgment must be used in the choice of a predictive instrument. The limitations of school marks must be recognized when they are used as predictor as well as when they are used as criterion. If a standardized objective test is to be used as predictor, the one who selects it should by careful analytical comparison see if it exercises the same human capacities as the experience it is supposed to predict. This will not be easy. As Wesman[40] has pointed out, a course in English may mean several things—grammar and language mechanics, literary appreciation, creative writing, or speech making. Courses in other subject fields may also be characterized by considerable divergence in aims and activities. When either the predictive test or the criterion test corresponds closely to the course or curriculum we say it has curricular validity. Presumably, it is a lack of curricular validity that results in the low coefficients shown in the DAT Manual between the Clerical Speed and Accuracy test and all commercial subjects, as also between the Space Relations and Mechanical Reasoning tests and marks in industrial arts courses. Does lack of curricular validity also explain the low average coefficients with marks in foreign-language courses—VR, .34, NA, .35, AR, .25, and Sentences, .45?

The variety in populations is also a factor which produces variation in coefficients. As Crawford and Burnham say,[41] "What was determined for a certain group in a certain situation will not necessarily hold for some other group under different conditions." Was that English class for whom a coefficient was reported in a high school where pupils are sectioned by ability or curriculum, or was it a random sampling of the whole tenth grade? Was it in a school serving a city slum district, or in a school serving a suburb of professional and business people with a high percentage of college graduates? One general principle is that the more homogeneous the group the lower the coefficient is likely to be, for the reason that when the range of differences in a group is small, the test will not rank them so accurately. The widely used ACE Psychological Examination may rank quite well the heterogeneous freshman class of a large university where every graduate of a state high school must be accepted. But in one of the prestige colleges or universities which is highly selective, the median student of the class may stand at the 90th percentile on national norms. Besides the fact that the test cannot make the fine distinctions between the members of such a homogeneous group with accuracy, the differences in the achievement of such a class will not reflect differences in ability so much as differences in drive, conscientiousness, energy—a matter for consideration in the next chapter.

Many researches are reported without adequate definition of the three elements in the correlation, particularly, criterion and population. The improvement of counseling depends, in part, on the production of more thorough prediction studies.

Prognostic Tests

This is a classification of tests designed especially to forecast a pupil's success with a particular subject. The most valuable work has been done

[40] Alexander G. Wesman, "The Differential Aptitude Tests," *Personnel and Guidance Journal,* Vol. XXXI (December, 1952), pp. 167–170.

[41] *Op. cit.,* p. 73.

in constructing such tests for the fields of foreign language and mathematics. Since these subjects are now among the electives in the secondary-school curriculum, it is highly important to establish as sound a basis as possible for helping pupils to make those choices.

The Orleans-Solomon Latin Prognosis Test was based on an analysis of the study of Latin for the processes, skills, and background needed for its successful pursuit. For the measurement of those abilities or characteristics the test consists mainly of a series of short lessons to be studied, followed by tests over their content. It is valid only for pupils who have never studied Latin. For example, pupils who have had exploratory Latin in the eighth grade could not be fairly compared on this test with pupils who have not had that experience.

This test has been available since the late twenties. In 1949 Odell said of it,[42]

Although it has been more than 20 years since this test appeared, it still merits use for the prediction of probable success in Latin courses. . . . Its use indicates that a coefficient of correlation of .70 or higher can usually be secured between the scores on this test and success in beginning Latin courses.

In the field of modern foreign language the Luria-Orleans Modern Language Prognosis Test is one which is constructed along the same lines as the Orleans-Solomon. The authors obtained a correlation of .68 between scores on the test and scores on an achievement test.

Some years ago Kaulfers canvassed and summarized the studies of prognosis in foreign language, presenting a classification of 612 correlations. Extracted from his summary tables are a few outstanding items shown here as Table 53.[43] Of the several predictive factors or instruments which are evaluated it will be noted that prognostic test correlations have one of the highest median coefficients—namely, .60—but the range is from near zero to .85. Kaulfers recognized that the variation in the coefficients was due in part to varied and often inadequate criteria—in some cases, achievement tests, in others, teachers' marks. But he was also aware that variation in language courses and methods of instruction would account for high and low correlations. For example, the teacher who employs the direct method assiduously and in undiluted form in the first year would certainly have achieved very different learnings than the teacher who used the traditional grammar-translation technique. For these reasons, every school should make its own thoughtful approach to the guidance of pupils in this matter of foreign-language election. That would mean deciding on the goals to be sought in the study of the language, organizing the course to attain the

[42] C. W. Odell, Review in Oscar Buros' *The Third Mental Measurements Yearbook,* p. 207.
[43] Walter V. Kaulfers, "Present Status of Prognosis in Foreign Language," *School Review,* Vol. XXXIX (October, 1931), pp. 589–591; data drawn from Tables I–V.

TABLE 53. Summary of Correlations between Certain Predictive Factors and Achievement in Foreign Language

Factors	Number of Coefficients	Highest r	Median r	Lowest r
Individual school subjects	195	.98	.435	−.199
Prognosis tests	58	.85	.60	.055
Intelligence	117	.99	.356	−.04
Standing at previous stages in same language	70	.87	.64	.22
Record in different foreign language	29	.83	.47	.19
High-school average	6	.57	.51	.37
Elementary-school average	3	.43	.41	.34
Character traits	6	.76	.66	.32

goals, then experimenting to find the best predictor of student success in the subject.

In the field of mathematics good prognostic tests are available for both algebra and geometry, tests which are substantially more predictive than intelligence tests. A test which first appeared about 1930 and has since been revised is the Orleans Algebra Prognosis Test. It consists mainly of a number of brief lessons in algebraic content for the pupil to study, followed by questions for him to answer. Each lesson and each test is carefully timed, as, for example, Lesson 4, 2 minutes, Test 4, 4½ minutes. Orleans reported that use of the test with 250 pupils yielded a coefficient of correlation of .71 between scores on it and scores on an objective test of algebra given at the end of the first semester.[44] Later trials with 16 groups of students in 8 different high schools yielded coefficients ranging from .50 to .79 between prognosis-test scores and achievement-test marks, and from .36 to .92 between prognosis-test scores and teachers' marks.[45]

The Lee Test of Algebraic Ability is apparently about as effective an instrument for prediction as the Orleans, the authors citing coefficients of about .70. It consists of four sub-tests—arithmetic problems, number analogies, number series, and formulas. Reviewed favorably by Segel,[46] the Iowa Algebra Aptitude Test, revised in 1942, is the result of extended experimentation and compares favorably with the Orleans and Lee tests.

Tests of geometric aptitude have been constructed by the Orleanses and by

[44] Joseph B. Orleans and Jacob S. Orleans, "A Study of Prognosis in High School Algebra," *The Mathematics Teacher,* Vol. XXII (January, 1929), pp. 23–30.

[45] Joseph B. Orleans, "A Study of Prognosis of Probable Success in Algebra and in Geometry," *The Mathematics Teacher,* Vol. XXVII (April and May, 1934), pp. 165–180, 225–246.

[46] David Segel, Review in Oscar Buros' *The Third Mental Measurements Yearbook,* pp. 327–328.

the Lees, and coefficients in the .60's and .70's have been reported for their prediction of achievement in geometry. A comparison of these two tests was made in 1937 by administering them to 200 pupils of the tenth grade just before they entered upon the study of plane geometry.[47] At the same time the Terman Group Test of Mental Ability was administered and the I.Q.'s figured. At the end of the year achievement was measured by teachers' marks and the Co-operative Plane Geometry Achievement Test. The following were the coefficients between prediction and achievement:

	Teachers' Marks	Achievement Test
I.Q.	.58 ± .035	.55 ± .037
Lee Test of Geometric Aptitude	.64 ± .031	.62 ± .032
Orleans Geometry Prognosis Test	.60 ± .034	.58 ± .035

The authors admitted that the teachers' marks may have been influenced by the achievement-test results, which, however, does not alter the considerable predictive value shown by the two prognosis tests.

The evidence for the use of these specialized tests of prognosis for the fields of mathematics and foreign language is noteworthy. Segel said, in 1949,[48] "The usefulness of these tests will decrease more and more as multiple-aptitude tests, i.e., tests of various mental traits, are developed for this level. . . ." The not-so-good correlations shown in the DAT manual for algebra, geometry, and foreign languages suggests that the day envisaged by Segel has not yet arrived.

Prediction of Success in Vocational Industrial Education

One of the problems of guidance at the junior high school level is that of helping boys and girls make the right decision with reference to entering a trade school. In a large city several such schools are usually available. They are operated with support from the Federal Government and may generally be entered by pupils who are fourteen years of age and have completed the eighth grade. Who should enter? What are the qualities and aptitudes of the pupils who will have the best chance to be successful in such a school?

The best answer to these questions has been given by Joseph W. Fleming[49] who twenty years ago studied the records of boys in the C. B. Connelley Trade School, of Pittsburgh. This is a relatively large school, operating under the recommendations of the Smith-Hughes Act. At the time of Fleming's study it was offering seventeen shops in the following five trade groups: building, electrical, metal, woodwork, and graphic arts.

[47] Sister Loretta Marie Goddeyne and Claude L. Nemzek, "The Comparative Value of Two Geometry Prognosis Tests in Predicting Success in Plane Geometry," *Journal of Social Psychology,* Vol. XX (November, 1944), pp. 283–287.
[48] *Op. cit.,* p. 328.
[49] "Predicting Trade School Success," *Pittsburgh Schools,* Vol. XI (May–June, 1937), pp. 153–210 (Published also in *Industrial Arts and Vocational Education,* Vol. XXVII (October, November, December, 1938), pp. 315–318, 365–367, 422–426.

Fleming did not carry on a prognostic type of study, in which one takes various measures of a group before they enter upon a course or curriculum with the design of determining which measure or combination of measures is most predictive. Rather, he canvassed the records of graduates and former students of the school and classified them according to achievement level as determined by shop teachers' marks. He found the following three factors especially related to the pupil's success in trade school:

1. Marks earned in junior high school industrial arts (JrHSIA)
2. Marks earned in junior high school English, science, and mathematics combined (JrHSAcad)
3. I.Q.

Substituting numbers for letter grades on the basis of A = 4, B = 3, C = 2, D = 1, E = 0 in the first two selective factors, Fleming showed how four formulas combining the three predictive factors would have selected boys for the trade school. Table 54 shows the percentages of those who won each of three levels of trade school success who would have been selected.[50]

Admittedly, the formulas leave much to be desired. Formula A would have excluded 70 per cent of the boys who made A or B averages in trade school shops, and even Formula D would have excluded 40 per cent of such boys. As Fleming points out, the study lumps together the boys from all 17 shops; there were not enough cases to justify the study of the boys from each shop separately. It is probably true that the various shops do not require the same degree of intelligence or academic ability, and that the industrial arts

TABLE 54. Percentages of Boys at Three Levels of Trade School Success Who Would Have Been Selected for Trade School by Four Combinations of Selective Factors

	Selective Factors Combined			Levels of Trade School Success*		
	JrHSIA	JrHSAcad	I.Q.	A and B	C	D and E
(A)	2.50 and above	1.75 and above	95 and above	30	13	7
(B)	2.50 and above	1.75 and above	90 and above	33	15	10
(C)	2.50 and above	1.50 and above	90 and above	41	20	15
(D)	2.00 and above	1.25 and above	90 and above	60	38	31

* Shop teachers' marks

[50] *Op. cit.* Data drawn from Tables XXXIV–XXXVII, pp. 194–195.

experience bears more relationship to some shops than to others. Fleming also explored entering age and grade and found that they had some relation to success in shop work. As the boys' entering age increased and their entering school grade became higher, their marks in shop became higher. However, these differences were not large and they were not reliable. It is quite possible that they would apply to some shops more than to others.

Shop teachers in general feel keenly the need for a service of prediction and counseling so that they can have a better qualified student body. In some school systems boys who do poorly in the academic high school, or who are disciplinary problems, are sent to the vocational high school. Fleming's study should be extended and refined.

PREDICTION OF SUCCESS IN HIGHER EDUCATION

Prediction of Success in Liberal Arts

Because the liberal arts college is the basic element in higher education, it is but natural that predictive studies should have begun with it rather than with professional schools. Furthermore because the student's success in his first year of liberal arts seemed to be highly indicative of his success in later years, attention has been especially focused on predicting the first year. As a matter of fact, with marks of the first year as predictor and marks of later years as criterion, correlation studies in liberal arts, engineering, and some other schools have practically all yielded coefficients in excess of .70.

The rise of intelligence testing gave the first noteworthy impetus to studies for the prediction of success in college. In the first flush of enthusiasm over intelligence tests, many college authorities thought that the tests could be used for the selection of students, and in some instances that was done. A minimum I.Q. of 110 was popularly mentioned as a desirable standard for college applicants to meet, and in some instances it seems to have been arbitrarily employed. Counselors and admissions officers who administered the standard were confounded by having some of their rejected applicants enter their college a year later by transfer from some other accredited college to which they had been admitted and in which they had earned a freshman's credits.

Then came disillusioning researches which showed that general intelligence was not a very good predictor of success in college. As early as 1924, Feingold[51] summarized such studies by saying that in the upper three grades of elementary school the correlation between intelligence and scholarship was such as to yield coefficients mainly varying from .40 to .70; in the high school, from .35 to .65; and for college students, from .30 to .50. This decline in these coefficients as one progresses up the educational ladder is attributed by some to the fact that the more selected the population the less

[51] Gustave A. Feingold, "Correlation between Intelligence and Scholarship," *School Review*, Vol. XXXII (June, 1924), p. 455.

accurately can intelligence tests rank the individuals of a group according to intelligence. Whereas elementary-school pupils represent a cross-section of the population, college students are indeed selected. Another and more likely explanation lies in the fact that as the student goes up the educational ladder he is able to be more and more selective in his educational diet, that is, the elective system operates to permit him to pursue the studies in which he is interested and can be successful, and to avoid those not corresponding to his talents and interests. In the elementary school he must take all the subjects. If the ability to do arithmetic is a short spoke in his intelligence wheel, he must use that ability anyway, and what he accomplishes with it forms part of his record that is averaged in with all the rest, just as the spoke of quantitative intelligence is averaged in with all the other spokes to determine the radius of the wheel. In high school he will avoid mathematics; in college he will continue to avoid it.

Under the elective system the student pursues subjects which correspond to the long spokes in his intelligence wheel. Therefore, his general intelligence is a less influential factor in what he accomplishes than was true in the elementary school. The radius of the wheel (average of all spokes) counts for less while the particular spokes which correspond to the differentiated aptitudes he chooses to exercise count for more.

The relatively low correlation between intelligence-test scores and college marks induced researchers to explore anew the predictive potential of high-school marks. From their studies they reached the generalization that high-school marks—usually expressed as rank in class—constitute the best single index to college success. Segel[52] summarized many studies and found the following median coefficients:

	College Marks
Intelligence tests	.44
High-school marks	.55

An example of a research made since Segel's compilation was published is that of Garrett.[53] This author investigated the effectiveness of high-school marks and the Ohio State Psychological Examination for predicting the college scholarship of the first semester. The OSPE has been used in a different form every year for quite a number of years with high-school seniors in the entire state of Ohio. Because it is not timed, it is commonly referred to as a power test and is said by some authorities to be a better predictive instrument than the more usual timed intelligence test. Garrett's subjects (1935–40) were graduates of the senior high school at Warren, Ohio, who

[52] David Segel, *Prediction of Success in College,* Bulletin No. 15 (Washington, D.C., U.S. Office of Education, 1934).

[53] Wiley Garrett, "The Ohio State Psychological Examination," *Occupations,* Vol. XXII (May, 1944), pp. 489–495.

had gone to college—52 different colleges. The computation of correlations yielded the following coefficients:[54]

	College Grade Point Average
High school grade point average	.67
Ohio State Psychological Examination Raw Scores	.61
Multiple R	.69

These are coefficients of more than usual magnitude, with the combination of the two predictors not much superior to either one alone.

In a more practical form for use as a counseling instrument is the relationship, shown in Table 55, between high-school marks and college marks.[55] This is a correlation table for the 173 graduates of the Taylor Allderdice High School of Pittsburgh who entered the University of Pittsburgh in June and September, 1948, and February, 1949. Their work through the summer session of 1949 formed the record from which each one's QPA was figured. The reader will note the extent to which the cases diverge from the line of expectancy in a scattergram with a coficient of .68.[56] The advantages of

TABLE 55. Relation between High-School Marks and University Quality Point Average (173 Cases)

Rank in High-School Class	Quality Point Average ($A = 3,\ B = 2,\ C = 1,\ D = 0,\ F = -1$)					
	Below .5	.5– .99	1.0– 1.49	1.5– 1.99	2.0– 2.49	2.5– 3.00
First Fifth			7	10	18	13
Second Fifth		5	12	12	12	4
Third Fifth		11	11	5	5	
Fourth Fifth	6	7	13	5	1	
Fifth Fifth	6	7	3			
Total	12	30	46	32	36	17

$r = .68$

[54] *Ibid.* Adapted from Table III, p. 493.

[55] By courtesy of John M. McLaughlin, Jr. Adapted.

[56] R. P. Brimm has devised a comprehensive profile sheet to help the pupil predict his success in college. It shows the pupil his percentile rank in scholarship, academic aptitude, English expression, reading, achievement battery test, interest in school, study habits, determination to go to college. See his article, "Helping High School Students Predict Their Success in College," *Nation's Schools,* Vol. 59 (April, 1957), pp. 53–55.

such a table for counseling have already been suggested in connection with Tables 49, 50, and 51. The table makes quite apparent the justification for the practice of many colleges in accepting applicants from the highest fifth of the high-school graduating class without regard for their entrance units.

Many investigators have tried combinations of predictive measures. Dean Johnston of the University of Minnesota, one of the most persistent students in search of the soundest basis of prediction of college success, came to the conclusion from his experimentation that the combination of ranking in a psychological test with ranking in high-school class in scholarship gave the best predictive measure. To equate rankings in high-school classes of different sizes he translated numerical ranks into percentile ranks. He treated rankings on psychological (intelligence) tests in the same way, then simply averaged the two ranks for each individual. For example, the individual who stood at the 80th percentile in scholarship and at the 60th percentile on the psychological test was considered to be at the 70th percentile on the combined rating. Correlating the combined predictive rating with freshman scholarship record at the University of Minnesota, he drew up such tables as Table 56.[57] His interest at first was in trying to find a critical score on the predictive instrument. From previous trials of this combined rating he said he had found that all men who fell below the 36th percentile would not do satisfactory work at the University, and accordingly he drew a line across the table at that level, which he called "the threshold of ability." As the table shows, his prediction was correct for 143 men but not for 3 men. That may appear almost a bull's-eye prediction until study of the table brings one to notice that Dean Johnston made no prediction for 243 men whose combined ratings were at or above the 36th percentile, but whose university work was unsatisfactory—namely, the large group falling in the upper left-hand quadrant of the table and ranging from the 36th up to and including the 95th percentile.

These comments will serve to point up the relative futility of trying to find a critical score or a threshold of ability. Such practice amounts to an attempt to predict with certainty. It cannot be done, or at least it can be done only for a few at the extremes. Of the cases in Table 56 it can be said that all whose combined ratings were 15 and lower did unsatisfactory university work and all whose combined ratings were 96 and higher did satisfactory work.

In later writings Dean Johnston gave up the attempt to establish a threshold of ability and used the whole table as a table of probability, an instrument like Table 55, from which pupils can be shown the probabilities—that is, what the chances are that they will attain a given level of success in university work. A little computation in simplification of Table 56—making the intervals quartiles instead of 5-centiles—will show that of pupils stand-

[57] J. B. Johnston, "Predicting College Success for the High School Senior," *Vocational Guidance Magazine,* Vol. VI (April, 1928), p. 292.

TABLE 56. Correlation of Combined High School and Test Ratings with Freshman Scholarship, 1923, 1924, 1925 (University of Minnesota Men)

Combined Ratings	F−	F+	D−	D+	C−	C+	B−	B+	A
96–100						6	9	2	
91–95			2	1	6	8	4	2	
86–90			5	4	10	8	5	1	
81–85			4	10	12	5	3		
76–80			4	8	8	1	1		
71–75	2		1	5	12	1	2		
66–70		1	4	15	6	4	1	1	
61–65	1		8	12	6	3	2		
56–60	4	3	6	11	8	3			
51–55	3	8	10	13	4				
46–50	5	3	12	12	4	2			
41–45	4	3	14	8	6				
36–40	9	7	11	10	5			243|161	
31–35	8	5	10	8	1			143| 3	
26–30	10	6	12	7					
21–25	12	2	10	2	1				
16–20	9	4	8	1	1				
11–15	9	2	1	2					
6–10	6	2	2						
1–5	4	1							

ing in the highest quarter, 70 per cent did satisfactory university work in the freshman year, in the second quarter 30 per cent did satisfactory work, in the third quarter 10 per cent, and in the fourth quarter, 2.5 per cent. Thus, to a student whose combined rating places him at the 82nd percentile we can say, You have 7 chances out of 10 of being successful, and to the student at the 32nd percentile, You have 1 chance in 10 of being successful. Thus can be launched a discussion of what it takes to be successful in university work. Chapter 16 will delve further into the counseling process.

The coefficient of Table 56—to satisfy the reader's curiosity and enable him to compare this study with others (Dean Johnston did not compute coefficients—is .69.

Segel[58] brought together a number of these studies in which two or more predictive measures were combined, and found coefficients of correlation ranging from .58 to .81, with a median of .66. The most common elements in these combined predictors were rank in high-school class and rank in intelligence test.

A distinctive prediction of university success is that which is related by

[58] *Op. cit.,* Table XVIII, pp. 72–73.

Diederich[59] as computed at the University of Chicago, where admission does not depend on high-school units earned or rank in high-school class, but on standing on the following three objective tests: (1) a test of reading comprehension representing the major types of materials to be read in the College; (2) an objective test of writing skill; (3) ACE Psychological Examination.

When this battery of entrance tests was developed it yielded a multiple correlation of .72 with average marks in the College. Separately, the reading-comprehension test yielded a correlation of about .65; the writing-skills test, about .45; and the Psychological Examination, about .55. Since that time the College has adopted a program of placement tests which advances able students at once into the more difficult courses and requires the less able to take the easier preliminary courses and even remedial treatment. Naturally, under these conditions, all correlations with college marks have declined. . . .

If we have understood the program of the University of Chicago aright, it is probably true that "marks in the College"—Diederich's criterion—are arrived at very largely on the basis of extended objective examinations, whereas most college marks represent a more subjective and uncertain criterion.

Diederich's statement, just quoted, concerning the declining magnitude of predictive coefficients as students are matched with courses which correspond to their ability, is a point which Williamson has elaborated in an extended article.[60] He submitted data from the University of Minnesota showing a decline between 1926 and 1935 in the coefficients of correlation between measures of prediction and college achievement. He attributed the decline to certain changes in educational and personnel practices, such as the introduction of sub-freshman courses and the organization of the University Testing Bureau in 1932 which has helped students to select courses in line with their aptitudes and interests. Placement examinations, also, have been used to place students in the courses in English, mathematics, and languages which correspond to their varied levels of attainment. Since such practices violate the uniform conditions of the original predictive studies, namely, that students shall be permitted to take courses regardless of their probability of succeeding in them, correlations are lowered.

How Early Can College Success Be Predicted?

To tell a pupil just completing the twelfth grade that on the basis of his high-school record and his standing on a scholastic aptitude test he stands a good chance of being successful or of being unsuccessful in college, is unfortunately tardy counsel. He made some kind of college decision three or four years earlier. If he decided not to go to college, he elected some kind of

[59] Paul B. Diederich, "The Abolition of Subject Requirements for Admission to College," *School Review*, Vol. LVII (September, 1949), pp. 364–370.

[60] E. G. Williamson, "The Decreasing Accuracy of Scholastic Predictions," *Journal of Educational Psychology*, Vol. XXVIII (January, 1937), pp. 1–16.

terminal curriculum in high school and is therefore unprepared to be told he is good college material and ought to enter college. If, on the other hand, he has struggled with college-preparatory subjects for four years, he may well feel bitter at being so tardily advised that his chances of college success are poor.

Byrns and Henmon reported two studies[61] in which they tested the possibility of earlier prediction of college success. One was a follow-up of pupils who, in December, 1920, while enrolled in Grades 4–8 of the Madison, Wisconsin, public schools, were given the National Intelligence Tests. Of these pupils 250 later enrolled in the University of Wisconsin and completed at least a semester's work. The I.Q.'s that had been obtained in elementary school correlated with the first-semester university average to the extent of a coefficient of .45. The psychological test percentile obtained when the students entered the University yielded a coefficient of .46 with first-semester university average. The reader will note how both of these *r*'s approximate the .44 quoted above from Segel as the average of many studies. Byrns and Henmon reported a coefficient of .81 between the I.Q.'s of elementary-school years and psychological test percentiles of first-year university.

The other study reported by these authors was one in which they averaged rank in tenth-grade scholarship and rank in I.Q. and found that this combined rating predicted average university marks almost as well as did an average of four-year scholarship record and scholastic aptitude test given in the senior year.

To find how well college success could be predicted at the end of junior high school years was the objective of a study by Billhartz and Hutson.[62] They availed themselves of data gathered by the Pennsylvania Study, conducted by the Carnegie Foundation for the Advancement of Teaching. One of the projects of the Study was the gathering of extensive data on pupils who entered the seventh grade in September, 1928, and recording the data on the ACE Cumulative Record Folder. This record was kept until these pupils graduated from high school. By 1936 those who had proceeded through school at the normal rate had been graduated for two years and had had time to compile a college record. It was at that time that these authors were granted access to the folders of the Pittsburgh pupils who had been included in the project. From the folders the following items of data were taken: (1) marks earned in academic subjects in Grades 7, 8, and 9; (2) percentile scores on the Stanford Achievement Test; (3) I.Q.'s.

The pupils who had entered college were traced through the high schools from which they had graduated. To those colleges was sent a request for

[61] Ruth Byrns and V. A. C. Henmon, "Long Range Predictions of College Achievement," *School and Society*, Vol. XLI (June 29, 1935), pp. 877–880.

[62] Wm. H. Billhartz, Jr., and P. W. Hutson, "Determining College Ability during Junior-High-School Years," *School and Society*, Vol. LIII (April 26, 1941), pp. 547–552.

transcripts, and the request was granted by 48 institutions which had received 282 students. These students' transcripts showed marks for at least ten semester hours, and five-eighths of the students had completed two years of college work. Marks on most of the transcripts (as also the marks earned in the junior high schools) were expressed in letter grades on a five-point letter system. Marks from the few colleges having atypical marking systems were translated to the common system.

The three predictive measures listed above were correlated with the college grade-point average and the following coefficients resulted:

	College Grade-Point Average
Junior high school grade-point average	.56
Stanford Achievement Test	.36
I.Q.	.37

Thus, in common with the researches already cited, marks are notably more predictive of college success than are achievement or intelligence tests. Furthermore, the coefficient for marks is as high as the average coefficient in studies correlating high-school marks and college marks. The evidence of this study strongly suggests that *college success can be predicted as well at the end of junior high school years as at the end of senior high school years.* The import of this finding was stated in the first paragraph of the discussion of this topic. In addition, it may be pointed out that if a concerted effort were made to find the college-ability youth at the end of the ninth grade, the chances are that a larger fraction of them would enter college than is presently the case.

James B. Conant, currently (1958) engaged in a survey of the high schools of the nation, has said on several occasions, "The academically talented ought, in the national interest, to be identified in the eighth grade at least; they ought to be persuaded to take a tough program." Such timing seems well-advised, because able youth should not miss ninth-grade algebra.

Variation in Intellectual Level of High Schools and Colleges

The prediction of college success is greatly complicated by variation in the intellectual capacity of student bodies among high schools on the one hand, and among colleges on the other hand. The readers of this book are all aware that the median intelligence of a high school serving a slum area of a city will be found definitely lower than the median of a high school located in a suburb which is economically and socially over-privileged. Of the high schools in one large city it was found that the median I.Q. in the high school of lowest intellectual level was twenty points less than the median in the high school of highest intellectual level. At the same time, the distribution of marks—A, B, C, D, F—is probably about the same in each school. The average C pupil in the high-level school is probably as competent as the average A pupil in the low-level school. We say "average" advisedly because it is known from experience that the low-level school will frequently have a brilliant pupil who is the equal of the best in the high-level school.

How can a college which practices selective admission calculate and allow for this variability of attainment represented by the equal marks given or ranks earned in different high schools? Especially does this mean a great deal when four-year scholarships are at stake. It becomes necessary for the college to try to rank the secondary schools from which graduates are applying for admission.

L. D. Hartson, of Oberlin College, has made helpful studies of this problem using the secondary-school and college records of Oberlin students, as well as the intelligence rating of the students on the Ohio State University Psychological Examination.[63] His object was to find the best basis for rating or ranking the secondary schools which were sending students to Oberlin. He could only make the study for a small fraction of such schools, because he limited the project to the schools which had, over a period of years, sent a minimum of 10 students to Oberlin. Thus, in 1934, he found 61 schools which had, since 1923, sent a total of 10 or more students. By 1937 there were 86 such schools, 41 of which had sent at least 15 each, and 27 of which had sent at least 20 each. Hartson ranked the students of each included school according to their high-school scholarship record, their college scholarship record in the first semester, and their standing on the OSU Psychological Examination. Then he computed the means of each of these rankings, and used these means to represent each school. Ranking the schools by their means, he computed correlations as shown in Table 57.[64] The table shows near zero coefficients between mean intelligence test scores and mean secondary-school grades, as also between mean college scholarship and mean secondary-school scholarship. But the means of college scholarship correlate with the means of intelligence-test scores with coefficients of approximately .70. Thus, it can be seen that a secondary school's standing cannot be predicted from the secondary-school grades earned by its students, but can be quite well predicted by the average of the intelligence ratings of its graduates.

Hartson has clearly established the need that all colleges have for knowing the general intellectual level of each secondary school. The rational way to meet this need would be for each secondary school to furnish the information, perhaps showing for its distribution of intelligence the range, median, and quartiles. It is probable, however, that only the most favored communities would permit any dissemination of such information.

[63] "Relative Value of School Marks and Intelligence Tests as Bases for Rating Secondary Schools," *School and Society*, Vol. XLIX (March 18, 1939), pp. 354–356; "School Marks vs. Mental Tests in Rating Secondary Schools; A Second Study," *School and Society*, Vol. LVII (January 16, 1943), pp. 80–83.

[64] *School and Society*, Vol. XLIX (March 18, 1939), p. 355. Adapted from Table I.

TABLE 57. Correlations between (1) the Mean College Scholarship, (2) Mean Test Intelligence, and (3) Mean Secondary School Scholarship, of Various Groups

Groups	Number of Schools	Number of Students Minimum	Total	Median	Correlations (1) with (2)	(1) with (3)	(2) with (3)
A	61	10	1530	25.1	.706	.192	.148
B	61	10	1834	30.1	.721	.219	.129
C	86	10	2121	24.7	.716	.096	−.002
D	41	15	1596	38.9	.729	.174	.132
E	27	20	1366	50.6	.734	.319	.246

Group A: The 61 schools which, between 1923 and 1934, had sent a minimum of 10 students each to Oberlin.

Group B: The total of 1,834 students who had come to Oberlin between 1923 and 1937, from the schools in Group A.

Group C: The 86 schools which, between 1923 and 1937, had sent a minimum of 10 students each.

Group D: The 41 schools which, between 1923 and 1937, had sent a minimum of 15 students each.

Group E: The 27 schools which, between 1923 and 1937, had sent a minimum of 20 students each.

Turning to the college side of the picture, a number of studies have made it clear that colleges differ considerably in the intellectual level and intellectual capacity of their student bodies. One of the projects of the Pennsylvania Study was the taking of "An Academic Inventory of the Baccalaureate Mind"—the administering of a test in May, 1928, to the graduating seniors of 49 Pennsylvania colleges. The test was especially constructed for this project as a test of general educational achievement. A sampling of the mean scores of the institutions showing the range, median, and approximate quartiles is as follows:[65]

Institution ranking	1st	12th	25th	37th	49th
Mean score	886	566	539	499	355

While the spread among the institutions constituting the middle 50 per cent is not great, the range does indeed suggest the wide differences in what the bachelor's degree stands for. Of these 49 institutions, the mean score of the one ranking highest is 2½ times that of the one ranking lowest.

At one time the American Council on Education published in its official organ, the *Educational Record,* the median and quartile scores of students

[65] Wm. S. Learned and Ben D. Wood, *The Student and His Knowledge* (New York: The Carnegie Foundation for the Advancement of Teaching, 1938). Data taken from Chart 2, p. 78.

of each institution in which the ACE test was given.[66] This form of report, which identified institutions, was discontinued, but the picture of institutional differences in the intelligence of students may be partially viewed in the data of Table 58.[67] Here are shown the median and quartile scores for the 15 highest and 15 lowest institutions, except that the 11 institutions in which less than 100 students were examined have been omitted.

The data of Table 58 and from the Pennsylvania Study show that counseling for college is indeed not counseling for *any* college. It is a case of helping each pupil find a college which is stimulating for him and in which the competition is suitable for his level of ability. Just as the colleges need information about the general intelligence of their contributing high schools, the high schools need the same information about the colleges.

TABLE 58. Scores on the ACE Psychological Examination of Individual Colleges and Universities Represented by Code Number

Institution Code Number	Number of Students	Gross Scores		
		Q_1	Median	Q_3
2	349	105.46	118.53	132.22
5	193	100.39	114.03	126.78
6	101	104.12	113.75	127.81
7	600	98.06	113.00	127.62
8	163	102.15	112.61	123.49
10	227	95.80	112.20	123.70
11	303	98.53	112.13	125.06
12	165	98.83	111.80	123.69
13	403	97.46	111.04	124.89
15	169	95.77	108.28	121.17
341	185	48.17	66.17	85.38
342	121	53.44	65.94	87.64
345	127	50.63	64.77	85.94
348	300	45.80	61.45	78.24
350	266	47.67	60.89	74.64
351	123	45.72	60.28	76.35
352	166	47.79	60.00	75.75
353	230	44.50	58.57	76.50
354	161	45.62	58.03	73.12

Prediction in Engineering Education

Two special batteries of tests have been constructed for the measurement of aptitude for the study of engineering. One, the Engineering and Physical

[66] "The 1934 Psychological Examination," *Educational Record,* Vol. XVI (April, 1935), pp. 226–234.

[67] Drawn from L. L. Thurstone and others, "The 1938 Psychological Examination," *Educational Record,* Vol. XX (April, 1939), pp. 271, 277.

Science Aptitude Test,[68] consists of six parts, requiring a total of 72 minutes. As yet, no extensive literature has appeared to make its validity clear. The other battery, the Pre-Engineering Inventory,[69] has been more extensively employed, though it is relatively expensive and requires two three-hour periods for the administration of its seven elements. The battery is not intended for use in high schools or liberal arts colleges. It was designed for testing applicants for entrance to engineering schools, and for testing students already enrolled in those institutions. Twelve engineering schools were reported as having used the Inventory with their already admitted freshmen. The best correlation obtained with freshman grades was .60, and that was with the composite score on three of the tests, namely, "technical verbal ability," "ability to comprehend scientific materials," and "general mathematical ability." Consideration could well be given to the reduction of the Inventory to these three elements.

Pierson and Jex[70] used the Pre-Engineering Inventory and the Co-operative General Achievement Tests in English, social studies, natural science, and mathematics with 276 freshmen entering the University of Utah. They correlated the four Co-operative tests with the four elements of the Inventory with which they seemed to be most comparable, and found coefficients of .76, .80, .78, and .76. They concluded that the Co-operative tests were as useful as the specially constructed Inventory. But they found that the best prediction of engineering grade-point average in the freshman year was the high-school grade-point average, the coefficient being .57. "In any event," they concluded

we are convinced that the process of selecting and guiding engineers cannot be automatic. And we believe that the scores earned by a prospective engineering student on any battery of tests must take their place as a part of the constellation of data that he will want to consider with a qualified and responsible counselor before he decides to undertake the study of engineering.[71]

A summary of the numerous studies of this problem in prediction will be found in a 1949 publication of the American Council on Education.[72] A quotation (p. 40) from their interpretation of the research is as follows:

[68] Charles H. Griffin and Henry Borow, "An Engineering and Physical Science Aptitude Test," *Journal of Applied Psychology,* Vol. XXVIII (October, 1944), pp. 376–387.

[69] Frederick Lord, John T. Cowles, and Manuel Cynamon, "The Pre-Engineering Inventory as a Predictor of Success in Engineering Colleges," *Journal of Applied Psychology,* Vol. XXXIV (February, 1950), pp. 30–39.

[70] George A. Pierson and Frank B. Jex, "Using the Co-operative General Achievement Tests to Predict Success in Engineering," *Educational and Psychological Measurement,* Vol. XI (Autumn, 1951), pp. 397–402.

[71] *Ibid.,* p. 401.

[72] Stuit, Dewey B., chairman, *Predicting Success in Professional Schools* (Washington, D.C.), Ch. 2.

The most efficient combination of predictive indexes to be used in estimating an individual's chances for success in the study of engineering appears to be one comprising (*a*) previous scholastic record (high school or college), (*b*) scholastic aptitude test score, and (*c*) scores obtained on subject-matter achievement tests in the areas of mathematics, science, and English.

Demonstrated proficiency in mathematics (especially as revealed by high scores on mathematics achievement tests) seems to be the best single indication of the likelihood that an individual will complete engineering training successfully. Grades received in high school and/or college mathematics courses also constitute an additional source of valuable predictive data.

To the mind of this writer a serious limitation of the whole body of research in prediction of success in engineering education is that it assumes no attempt at such prediction will be made until after the pupil has graduated from high school. All the studies reported have measured the student's capacity as of June or September before or upon entering engineering school. A previous topic of this section pointed out that for the college decision in general, such a date was too late. For engineering such tardiness is particularly lamentable. Engineering colleges require either three or four units of supra-arithmetical mathematics for entrance. They *should* be taken sequentially, which means that the first course should be taken in the ninth grade. The implication of this fact is that the finding of engineering talent should earnestly begin in the eighth grade. Long-range prediction studies should be made to find the best instruments for that purpose. In the meantime, much value could be derived from going back to the junior high school records of engineering graduates, especially to the junior high schools that were doing well the functions of pupil analysis and record keeping. What capacities and what degrees of capacity did these engineering graduates evince when they were junior high school pupils?

Prediction in Other Professional Education

Summaries of the research studies which bear on the prediction of success in training for law, medicine, dentistry, nursing, and other professional fields are to be found in the American Council publication[73] by Stuit and others just referred to in the discussion of engineering. Practically all the work that has been done has been designed to serve the function of selection rather than that of counseling. Since, in the case of law, medicine, and dentistry, selection does not occur until after two or more years of college work, most of the research has been done with students who have reached that level of maturity.

Several special aptitude tests have been developed for the measurement of capacity for the study of law. Of one of these, Stuit says,[74]

---

[73] *Ibid.*
[74] *Ibid.*, p. 55.

The Yale Legal Aptitude Test, which comprises verbal comprehension questions, logical inference, analogy problems, and judgment of the applicability of certain legal principles, has yielded correlation coefficients ranging from .55 to .64 between test scores and first-year law grades, while a combination of test scores and college grades correlated .78 with law grades.

A similar test, the validity of which has been evaluated in a number of researches, is the Iowa Legal Aptitude Test, revised in 1946. It has predictive value similar to that of the Yale test. More recently, the Educational Testing Service, of Princeton, New Jersey, has developed the Law School Admission Test and is administering it four times a year at ETS-Supervised centers throughout the country as an aid to nearly fifty law schools in selecting their students.

From studies in the prediction of scholastic achievement at the University of Minnesota, it was concluded that "In the Law School, the abilities of value for the purposes of prediction are reasoning about legal material, arithmetical reasoning, and vocabulary."[75] To a considerable extent these capacities should be measurable in junior high school pupils, using instruments presently available, but we do not have norms to indicate the scores necessary for probable success in law school. One can only guess that since college students are a selected group and law school students are still more selected, a ninth-grader should stand among the highest 10 per cent of his group in the essential abilities named by Douglass or described above as elements of the Yale test.

Admission to medical training requires, for most medical schools, the taking of the Medical College Admission Test, administered twice a year by the Educational Testing Service at their supervised centers located throughout the country. Its correlation with medical school success is not known. The student's standing on it is considered by medical school admissions officers along with other data, such as biographical information, scholastic record, and recommendations. Numerous studies have been made of the predictive signficance of premedical college records as a whole and in particular subjects. Stuit shows 37 coefficients averaging .46 for the whole premedical record, and 27 coefficients averaging .41 for individual courses in the premedical record.[76]

Undoubtedly high-school pupils who aspire to the study of medicine should make an academic record of generally high quality in all the academic fields and be especially superior in the physical and biological sciences. Beyond that, they should realize that there are so many other hurdles to medical-school admission that they will be wise to have alternative careers in mind.

Dentistry is a profession which requires a combination of scholastic apti-

[75] H. R. Douglass, "Different Levels and Patterns of Ability Necessary for Success in College," *Occupations,* Vol. XXII (December, 1943), p. 184.
[76] *Op. cit.,* pp. 66, 69.

tude, mechanical aptitude, and finger dexterity. Stuit[77] cites a study which analyzed dental school curriculums, revealing that "57 per cent of a student's time is spent in activities requiring manipulative performances." At the same time, proficiency in the physical and biological sciences is necessary. These subjects figure heavily in predental programs, and predental scholarship correlates notably with the theoretical course work of the dental school.

In attempting to predict success in a dental school training program, particular attention should be paid to ability to visualize objects in three dimensions. A significantly high relationship was found to exist between dental school achievement and these factors as they were measured by the following tests: Minnesota Metal Filing Test, which involves the filing of an iron bar to specified dimensions; Mechanical Judgment Test, a part of the Iowa Dental Qualifying Examination and patterned directly after the revised Minnesota Paper Form Board; and a Manipulation and Construction Test, another sub-test of the Iowa battery which required the shaping of a plaster-of-paris block to specified dimensions.[78]

While no studies of prediction from the high-school level have been made, measures analagous to those found predictive at the college level may be found and employed by the well-trained high-school counselor.

Many studies have been made for the prediction of success in nursing schools, practically all of them taking the predictive measurements at the time of application for admission or at the time of entrance to such schools. Douglass summarized the research at the University of Minnesota School of Nursing in this paragraph:[79]

Success in the School of Nursing is predicted best by a test of high school science and one in simple fractions, and previous record of scholarship, yielding multiple coefficients in the lower seventies.

Potts[80] has described the battery of tests administered by the Nurse Testing Division of the Psychological Corporation as consisting of a scholastic aptitude test at college freshman level, two vocabulary tests, two reading tests, a test of general scientific information, and an arithmetic test involving problems and the use of decimals, fractions, and percentage. The data of Table 59[81] show a definite relationship between score on the scholastic aptitude test, failure in classwork, and graduation.

For a summary of the studies made for the purpose of predicting success in nursing education, the reader is referred to Stuit's chapter on this area of professional training.[82]

As we take account of the problem of predicting success in the professions and note how little we are presently prepared to perform this function with

[77] *Ibid.*, p. 92.
[78] *Ibid.*, p. 93.
[79] *Op. cit.*, p. 184.
[80] Edith M. Potts, "Testing Prospective Nurses," *Occupations,* Vol. XXIII (March, 1945), pp. 328–334.
[81] *Ibid.*, p. 333, Table IV (adapted).
[82] *Op. cit.,* Ch. 9.

TABLE 59. Percentages of Nursing Students at Various Levels of Scholastic Aptitude Who Were Eliminated for Classwork Failure and Who Graduated

Scholastic Aptitude Score	Number of Cases	Percentage	
		Eliminated for Classwork Failure	Graduating
190+	33	0	85
180–189	125	4	74
170–179	337	2	77
160–169	758	3	77
150–159	1,323	5	76
140–149	1,694	8	71
130–139	1,912	12	70
120–129	1,565	15	67
110–119	912	18	63
100–109	374	28	57
90–99	169	36	52
80–89	59	44	32
70–79	21	43	43
60–69	10	60	20
50–59	1	100	0
40–49	1	100	0
Total	9,294		

youngsters about to enter upon differentiated secondary education, the necessity of performing a broader kind of guidance comes to mind. That is the appraisal of the potentialities of each pupil and cultivating in him a sense of obligation to develop all his talents. Consider the case of George S. At the end of the eighth grade, George was known to his teachers as having an I.Q. of 122; he had demonstrated superior learning power in all his subjects and had been sufficiently faithful to assignments to have achieved a good academic record; in the mathematics and general science of the eighth grade George had shone brilliantly. Clearly, this boy was a good college risk; quite possibly he could become an engineer. But his father, a Czech immigrant, had been forced by an injury to leave a good-paying railroad job and take up work which paid poorly. He could give George no help for education beyond high school. Now George had already demonstrated considerable athletic prowess and found some keen satisfaction in sports. He dreamed of glory on the gridiron. Feeling certain that he could go no further in school than high-school graduation, he decided to elect the easiest subjects so that he would have plenty of time for football and other sports. Without two units of algebra and one each of geometry, physics, and chemistry, how will George be able to enter upon the engineering course that a great steel company or electric manufacturing company will be glad to help him finance, or that his future GI rights might enable him to pursue? The task of guidance is to help every pupil presently to live and to work up to his potentialities even though the future is more or less shrouded in uncertainty.

PREDICTION OF SUCCESS IN OCCUPATIONS

Difficulties, Especially in Finding Criteria

Prediction in school or in college can only be done very imperfectly. Prediction of occupational success is still more difficult. A commonly read and heard expression is this: It is easier to predict success in *training* for an occupation than to predict success in the occupation. The task and the responsibility, however, cannot be evaded. The counselor is continually making some kind of prediction of occupational success. When he counsels one pupil to take the college-preparatory curriculum, he is estimating that that pupil has the potentials for occupational success at the professional level. When he counsels another to elect the commercial curriculum, he is predicting success in some clerical or commercial occupation for that pupil. Thus, educational choices and occupational choices are bound together.

The criteria for educational success are marks, or scores on achievement tests. While we are not satisfied with them, it is much more difficult to find satisfactory criteria for occupational success. Shall it be income? That is a criterion which enjoys a high measure of popular sanction in America, but at the same time it is recognized as superficial and inadequate. Even within one occupational group, as, physicians, it is felt that the criterion of income would be a grossly unfair basis for ranking. To supply illustrative examples would be an unnecessary labor.

When a group representing a miscellany of occupations is compared on the basis of income, we may well be even more skeptical concerning the meaning of the findings. Such a study was reported a number of years ago by J. R. Shannon.[83] In following the male graduates of a certain high school, he found that a dozen years after graduation those who had been "scholars" in high school had a median annual income of $3000; those who had been "leaders" had a median annual income of $3450; a "random" group had a median of $3000. In comparing his "leaders" and "scholars" Shannon did use other criteria: he found leaders to excel perceptibly in "outstanding accomplishments" and in "evidences of community service or leadership." But to this writer so many variables in the occupational careers of these cases are unaccounted for as hardly to justify Shannon in his conclusions that

It seems that whatever it is that is necessary for success in the high school is not the factor that is requisite for success in life. . . .

Whatever is required to excel in the extracurriculum life of the high school seems to be the same thing that contributes most to success later.

[83] "The Post-School Careers of High-School Leaders and High-School Scholars," *School Review,* Vol. XXXVII (November, 1929), pp. 656–665.

Another criterion of occupational success is that of output. For salesmen of a wholesale house, that would mean dollars' worth of goods sold; for teachers, the scores of their pupils on achievement tests; for armature winders, the number of units completed. Objections can be raised to the application of this criterion in almost any field, and in many occupations output cannot be objectively measured.

Efficiency ratings by supervisors have been used in factories and mills, in offices, in the teaching profession, in the military service, and in various other occupational fields. While lacking in objectivity, they have the advantage of estimating achievement on a broader and more comprehensive basis. In such a field as teaching, where there is considerable lack of agreement as to goals, efficiency ratings, it is often said, are colored by the philosophy of the rater.

Turning to the predictor side, no doubt part of the difficulty in occupational prediction lies in the fact that success depends on other qualities than ability, such as character and personality traits, which are not so easily measured but have an importance which will be developed in the next chapter. We have tended to base our predictions on measures of ability, while one's accomplishment or output depends not only on ability but on application of ability.

This latter statement points up the fact that workers' success in most fields is accounted for by their possession or employment of varying combinations of traits, aptitudes, abilities—or varied weightings of such attributes. One offsets his weaknesses in traits C and D by his strength in traits A and B. With another, the reverse is true. That means, of course, that the population carrying on the occupation may vary widely in the amount of a given trait which they possess.

Super has lately questioned the soundness of the whole concept that "success" may properly be measured by earnings, output, and other objective criteria.[84] He says that these ignore the individual's feelings, values, and judgments. The focus of the objective criteria, says Super, is on *achievement* rather than on *adjustment*. Or, perhaps, there are such differences in the concept of achievement that to some workers a satisfying adjustment to one's job in which he feels his identity with it and with his fellow workers *is* achievement. A trend toward recognizing that success is in part, at least, a subjective matter is seen

in current *rating scales*. Whereas many of those that were used in the earlier days stressed descriptions of the worker's application, industriousness, and output, today rating scales pay more attention to the worker's relations with his fellow employees, subordinates, superiors, and customers.[85]

As pointed out in Chapter 2, in the description of the Hawthorne study,

[84] Donald E. Super, "The Criteria of Vocational Success," *Occupations,* Vol. XXX (October, 1951), pp. 5–9.

[85] *Ibid.,* p. 7.

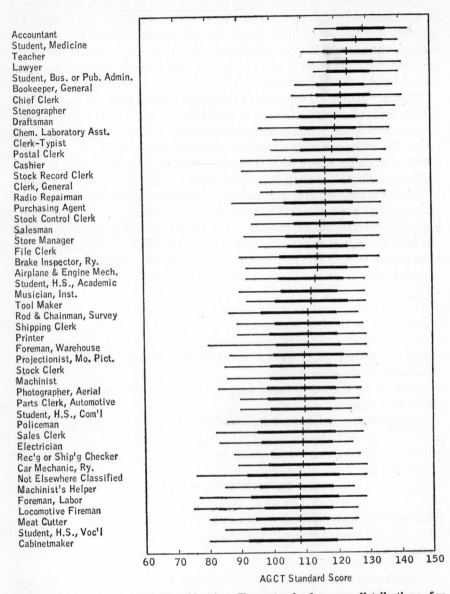

Accountant
Student, Medicine
Teacher
Lawyer
Student, Bus. or Pub. Admin.
Bookeeper, General
Chief Clerk
Stenographer
Draftsman
Chem. Laboratory Asst.
Clerk-Typist
Postal Clerk
Cashier
Stock Record Clerk
Clerk, General
Radio Repairman
Purchasing Agent
Stock Control Clerk
Salesman
Store Manager
File Clerk
Brake Inspector, Ry.
Airplane & Engine Mech.
Student, H.S., Academic
Musician, Inst.
Tool Maker
Rod & Chainman, Survey
Shipping Clerk
Printer
Foreman, Warehouse
Projectionist, Mo. Pict.
Stock Clerk
Machinist
Photographer, Aerial
Parts Clerk, Automotive
Student, H.S., Com'l
Policeman
Sales Clerk
Electrician
Rec'g or Ship'g Checker
Car Mechanic, Ry.
Not Elsewhere Classified
Machinist's Helper
Foreman, Labor
Locomotive Fireman
Meat Cutter
Student, H.S., Voc'l
Cabinetmaker

60   70   80   90   100   110   120   130   140   150

AGCT Standard Score

FIG. 13. Army General Classification Test standard score distributions for all occupations with 100 cases or more (showing medians, quartiles, and 10th and 90th percentiles).

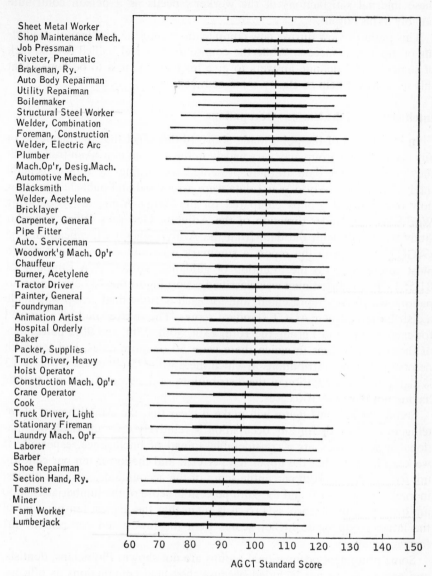

FIG. 13. (cont'd)

these internal satisfactions of the worker's needs as a person contribute notably to his output.

This point of view throws new complications into the problem of predicting occupational success. While the counselor may feel baffled for the lack of some simple, definite answers to give his charges, it is to be hoped that this section will help to clarify some complexities.

Intelligence and the Various Occupations

In illustration of the point made above to the effect that the members of any occupational group may vary widely in the amount of a given trait which they possess, some data are here presented concerning the trait of general intelligence. After World War I data were assembled and published to show how occupational groups compared on the Army Alpha test. Following World War II, under direction of the Adjutant General's Office a similar study was made with the data from the Army General Classification Test (AGCT), and from the report a summary was published where it would most surely come to the attention of guidance workers.[86] A sampling of 81,553 white enlisted men was classified according to the 227 civilian occupations which they represented, and for each occupational group was made a distribution of their AGCT standard scores. The source cited here showed for each occupational group the 10th, 25th, 50th, 75th, and 90th percentiles of those distributions in which there were 50 or more cases, and the 50th percentile for the distributions in which there were 25–49 cases.[87] Figure 13 is a graphic representation of the distributions of the 95 occupational groups having not less than 100 cases.

Some study of this figure will make it clear that the establishment of intelligence standards for any occupation is relatively difficult. Each occupational group represents a considerable spread of intelligence, especially if we keep in mind that the upper ten per cent and the lower ten per cent are not shown. As the 10th percentile score of the accountants, who are highest in intelligence, is 114, and the 90th percentile score of the lumberjacks, who are lowest in intelligence, is 116, it is plain that the highest ten per cent of the latter group made higher scores than the lowest ten per cent of the former group.

Some prominent occupational groups are not shown. Physicians, dentists, and engineers are not included because they held commissions as officers, and the study was limited to enlisted men.

No evidence as to the occupational success of these men exists. While in general it is to be supposed that a positive relation exists between intelligence and success in an occupation, the strength of the relationship varies among occupations, according to many studies in the literature of personnel work

[86] Naomi Stewart, "A.G.C.T. Scores of Army Personnel Grouped by Occupation," *Occupations*, Vol. XXVI (October, 1947), pp. 5–41.
[87] *Ibid.*, Table I, pp. 9–17.

in industry. From studies which have revealed vocational misfits, we know that some workers have too much intelligence for the jobs in which they find themselves and therefore have poor vocational adjustment, while others are hardly able to hold their own in competition because of insufficient intelligence. In those occupations in which success and intelligence are positively and significantly correlated, it seems certain that the lower a man stands in the intelligence distribution of his group, the more of something else—interest, industry, personality, conscientiousness, or maybe bluffing—he has to put into the job in order to remain in it.

Personnel Work in Industry and the Armed Forces

The title of this section, "Prediction of success in occupations," is an invitation to the study of a large segment of the literature of personnel work in industry, in the armed forces, and in the civil service. For jobs in all of these fields it is necessary to select workers. To select a worker is to make a prediction concerning his fitness for the job and the likelihood of his success in it. Turnover is expensive because it involves repetition of the processes of selection and training; hence, the constant effort to improve prediction. To classify soldiers for military training and jobs is to make predictions concerning the probabilities of their success in the various military jobs. In the complexities of modern warfare a sloppy job of prediction means military defeat.

The sequence of steps in the process is perhaps well indicated in Robert Thorndike's book[88] based on his experience in the Aviation Psychology Program. First, the job analysis to ascertain the skills, aptitudes, and abilities involved; second, the selection of promising tests and the invention of new ones; third, the estimation of reliability; fourth, the estimation of test validity; fifth, combining tests into a battery; and so on through administration, recording, and employing test results.

Post-war developments in the function of classification in the Air Force are briefly reported by Schultz and Levine.[89] They tell of the creation through extensive research of the Airman Classification Battery, designed to assess the potential of the basic trainee for each of "the following eight Aptitude Clusters: Mechanical, Craftsman, Clerical, Equipment Operator, Radio Operator, Services, Technician Specialty, and Electronics Technician." It is recognized, however, that test scores cannot be the sole basis for classifying airmen, for though good correlations have been obtained they are far from perfect. "It is now believed that a good deal of the unmeasured variance lies in the realm of personality and motivation variables." Thus, again, ability to do and doing are two different things—one good reason why predictions are imperfect.

[88] *Personnel Selection: Test and Measurement Techniques* (New York, Wiley, 1949).
[89] Irwin J. Schultz and Abraham S. Levine, "*Before* the Wild Blue Yonder: Counseling in the Classification Program for Air Force Men," *Occupations,* Vol. XXX (December, 1951), pp. 82–85.

As an example of the literature of success prediction in the field of commerce, Paterson has recently reported a canvass by questionnaire of 195 companies to ascertain what uses they are making of tests in selecting salesmen.[90] While a majority reported that they were using tests, it was evident to this eminent personnel psychologist that the selection of salesmen is a problem on which tests can best be used not directly for selection but to give useful information on applicants, thereby helping the sales executive in the exercise of his judgment.

A striking bit of evidence of the activity of industrial personnel workers in research to promote the prediction of success in occupations is the presence of a regular department called Validity Information Exchange in the magazine *Personnel Psychology*. To this department are contributed validity studies written up in concise form according to a standard outline and directions by the editor. A recent number had reports on dietitians, budget clerks, radio repairmen, maintenance mechanics, and light-bulb assemblers—each report using one or two pages.

With these intimations of an extensive literature bearing on the prediction of occupational success, the subject must here be concluded. It is plain that researchers in school guidance and in adult personnel work have much to contribute to each other and to the practitioners in each other's fields, united in the purpose of achieving maximum vocational adjustment.

THE BEARING OF ABILITY AND ACHIEVEMENT MEASURES ON ADJUSTIVE GUIDANCE

Achievement Compared to Ability

Certainly it has been made abundantly clear that when an individual's achievement is less than his ability justifies, guidance is challenged to bring about an adjustment. Thus, when a pupil is failing, we consult his folder to ascertain his standing on measurements of ability. If he has sufficient ability to meet his academic responsibilities, we look for other causes for failure. Instead of focusing our attention on the failing pupils, a more inclusive comparison of ability and achievement is desirable, so as to identify *all* the pupils who are under-achievers and *all* the pupils who are over-achievers. Serene did this in a systematic fashion so as to establish the basis for a program of academic counseling[91] which will be described in Chapter 16. He correlated an entire tenth-grade class as to general intelligence and general academic achievement, identifying every individual in the correlation table. All the under-achievers thus stood revealed and were made the object of his close study with a view to bringing about their academic adjustment. The over-achievers, also, were plainly evident. Serene did not study them, but prob-

---

[90] Donald G. Paterson, *A Survey of 195 Companies on the Use of Tests in Selecting Salesmen* (Chicago, The Dartnell Corp., 1951).

[91] Michael F. Serene, "An Experiment in Motivational Counseling," *Personnel and Guidance Journal*, Vol. XXXI (February, 1953), pp. 319–324.

ably analysis of their cases would have disclosed some who were not achieving a well-balanced development, some who were laboring under anxiety complexes, some whose excessive study was compensatory for inadequacies in nonacademic areas, and so on.

Teachers and counselors spend considerable time in seeking to overcome the maladjustments which the comparison of ability and achievement brings to light. To do this in a thoroughgoing fashion is certainly to make a noteworthy contribution to the conservation of human resources.

Maladjustments Due to Lack of Ability

When a child is reported as exhibiting untoward behavior, the wise counselor usually begins his study of the case by consulting the record of ability and achievement measures. From experience he has learned that atypical, anti-social behavior is generally caused by frustration, and that frustration is frequently due to inability to get assignments, to hold his own in competition with his fellows, and to experience the satisfactions of success. In the knowledge of the pupil's general intelligence, his differentiated aptitudes, his powers in reading, arithmetic, and study skills, may lie the explanation.

The studies which show that inability to read causes emotional and social maladjustment are legion. One such study by Gates and Bond was drawn upon at some length in Chapter 3. A somewhat condensed review of the literature on this subject has recently appeared.[92] It is based on 34 writings, many of which are reports of original investigation.

Thus, it will appear evident that many and diverse measures of ability are needed, and the counselor will have to take account of some abilities which are not measured and recorded. For example, the bravado front put up by a fat boy may be accounted for by his inability to run the bases or climb a rope in the gym hand over hand like a regular fellow. The inferiority complex which grips another lad may be due to a lack of social abilities and skills.

The counselor, bearing responsibility for the guidance function, will play a major role in deciding on the program for the measurement and recording of ability and achievement which the school carries on. Since those measurements, however, also serve the instructional function and the curriculum-making function, the co-operation of the principal and teachers will be necessary in establishing the measurement program.

QUESTIONS, PROBLEMS, AND INVESTIGATIONS

1. Draw up one or more correlation tables for practical guidance situations in your school.

2. In a junior high school which has general intelligence test records based

92 Nila Banton Smith, "Research on Reading and the Emotions," *School and Society*, Vol. 81 (January 8, 1955), pp. 8–10.

on a test for which sub-test scores as well as total-test scores are shown, find ten pupils of the same grade with identical or near-identical I.Q.'s. Then, in parallel columns, list their sub-test scores and study the contrasts.

3. Plan the program of ability and achievement tests which you consider desirable and practicable for a junior-senior high school which is known to you.

4. From the catalogues of such test publishers as the Psychological Corporation, the World Book Company, Educational Testing Service, Science Research Associates, and California Test Bureau, compile a list of competing tests in any area which interests you; then read the reviews of them in Buros' *Mental Measurements Yearbooks*.

5. Intelligence tests vary somewhat in the intelligence quotients which they yield. Canvass educational literature for scientific studies of such variation.

6. Read "Expectancies," one of the last writings of Walter Van Dyke Bingham (*Educational and Psychological Measurement,* Vol. XIII—Spring, 1953—pp. 47–53). What does it contribute to this chapter?

7. If you are in a school with generous curriculum opportunity and a strong and successful guidance program, test Williamson's claim concerning the decline of predictive coefficients under those circumstances.

8. Interview five high-school or college students who are definitely underachievers with a view to finding the reasons why they stand below the line of expectancy.

9. Interview five high-school or college students who are definitely overachievers with a view to finding the reasons why they stand above the line of expectancy.

10. In a junior high school locate a half-dozen pupils whose reading achievement is three or more years below grade level and obtain descriptions of their attitudes and behavior from their teachers.

SELECTED REFERENCES

ANASTASI, Anne, *Psychological Testing* (New York, Macmillan, 1954).

BENNETT, George K., SEASHORE, Harold G., and WESMAN, Alexander G., *A Manual for the Differential Aptitude Tests* (New York, The Psychological Corporation, 1952).

BILLHARTZ, Wm. H., Jr., and HUTSON, P. W., "Determining College Ability during Junior-High-School Years," *School and Society,* Vol. LIII (April 26, 1941), pp. 547–552.

BINGHAM, Walter V., *Aptitudes and Aptitude Testing* (New York, Harper, 1937).

BRIMM, R. P., "Helping High School Students Predict Their Success in College," *Nation's Schools,* Vol. 59 (April, 1957), pp. 53–55.

BUROS, Oscar, *The Third Mental Measurements Yearbook* (New Brunswick, N.J., Rutgers University Press, 1949).

———, *The Fourth Mental Measurements Yearbook* (Highland Park, N.J., Gryphon Press, 1953).

BYRNS, Ruth, and HENMON, V. A. C., "Long Range Predictions of College Achievement," *School and Society,* Vol. XLI (June 29, 1935), pp. 877–880.

CRAWFORD, Albert B., and BURNHAM, Paul S., *Forecasting College Achievement* (New Haven, Yale University Press, 1946).

CRONBACH, Lee J., *Essentials of Psychological Testing* (New York, Harper, 1949).

DAVIS, Allison, *et al.*, *Intelligence and Cultural Differences* (Chicago, University of Chicago Press, 1951).

DIEDERICH, Paul B., "The Abolition of Subject Requirements for Admission to College," *School Review*, Vol. LVII (September, 1949), pp. 364–370.

DOUGLASS, Harl R., "Different Levels and Patterns of Ability Necessary for Success in College," *Occupations*, Vol. XXII (December, 1943), pp. 182–186.

Counseling and Employment Service for Special Worker Groups (Washington, D.C., U.S. Employment Service, Department of Labor, 1954), pp. 92–100.

FEINGOLD, Gustave A., "Correlation between Intelligence and Scholarship," *School Review*, Vol. XXXII (June, 1924), pp. 455–467.

GARRETT, Harley F., "A Review and Interpretation of Investigations of Factors Related to Scholastic Success in Colleges of Arts and Sciences and Teachers Colleges," *Journal of Experimental Education*, Vol. XVIII (December, 1949), pp. 91–138.

GARRETT, Wiley, "The Ohio State Psychological Examination," *Occupations*, Vol. XXII (May, 1944), pp. 489–495.

GHISELLI, Edwin E., "A Comparison of the Minnesota Vocational Test for Clerical Workers with the General Clerical Battery of the U.S.E.S.," *Journal of Applied Psychology*, Vol. XXVI (February, 1942), pp. 75–80.

GODDEYNE, Sister Loretta Marie, and NEMZEK, Claude L., "The Comparative Value of Two Geometry Prognosis Tests in Predicting Success in Plane Geometry," *Journal of Social Psychology*, Vol. XX (November, 1944), pp. 283–287.

GRIFFIN, Charles H., and BOROW, Henry, "An Engineering and Physical Science Aptitude Test," *Journal of Applied Psychology*, Vol. XXVIII (October, 1944), pp. 376–387.

HARTSON, L. D., "Relative Value of School Marks and Intelligence Tests as Bases for Rating Secondary Schools," *School and Society*, Vol. XLIX (March 18, 1939), pp. 354–356.

———, "School Marks vs. Mental Tests in Rating Secondary Schools; A Second Study," *School and Society*, Vol. LVII (January 16, 1943), pp. 80–83.

HOLLINGWORTH, Leta S., "Musical Sensitivity of Children Who Test Above 135 I.Q. (Stanford-Binet)," *Journal of Educational Psychology*, Vol. XVII (February, 1926), pp. 95–109.

HUBBARD, Robert E., and FLESHER, William R., "Intelligent Teachers and Intelligence Tests—Do They Agree?" *Educational Research Bulletin*, Vol. XXXII (May 13, 1953), pp. 113–122, 139–140.

HUGHES, W. Hardin, "Educational Fortune-Telling Is a Precarious Process," *Nation's Schools*, Vol. XII (July, 1933), pp. 49–54.

HULL, Clark L., *Aptitude Testing* (Yonkers, N.Y., World Book Co., 1928).

HUTSON, P. W., "Deriving Practical Instruments for Guidance," *Vocational Guidance Magazine*, Vol. XI (March, 1933), pp. 247–254.

JOHNSTON, J. B., "Predicting College Success for the High School Senior," *Vocational Guidance Magazine*, Vol. VI (April, 1928), pp. 289–294.

KAULFERS, Walter V., "Present Status of Prognosis in Foreign Language," *School Review,* Vol. XXXIX (October, 1931), pp. 585–596.

LEARNED, Wm. S., and WOOD, Ben D., *The Student and His Knowledge* (New York, The Carnegie Foundation for the Advancement of Teaching, 1938).

MEIER, Norman C., "Factors in Artistic Aptitude," in *Studies in the Psychology of Art,* Psychological Monographs, Vol. 51, No. 5, 1939.

MENDICINO, Lorenzo, "Mechanical Reasoning and Space Perception: Native Capacity or Experience," *Personnel and Guidance Journal,* Vol. XXXVI (January, 1958), pp. 335–338.

ORLEANS, Joseph B., "A Study of Prognosis of Probable Success in Algebra and in Geometry," *Mathematics Teacher,* Vol. XXVII (April and May, 1934), pp. 165–180, 225–246.

ORLEANS, Joseph B., and Jacob S., "A Study of Prognosis in High School Algebra," *The Mathematics Teacher,* Vol. XXII (January, 1929), pp. 23–30.

PATERSON, Donald G., ELLIOTT, Richard M., and others, *Minnesota Mechanical Ability Tests* (Minneapolis, University of Minnesota Press, 1930).

PIERSON, George A., and JEX, Frank B., "Using the Co-operative General Achievement Tests to Predict Success in Engineering," *Educational and Psychological Measurement,* Vol. XI (Autumn, 1951), pp. 397–402.

POTTS, Edith M., "Testing Prospective Nurses," *Occupations,* Vol. XXIII (March, 1945), pp. 328–334.

RICHARDSON, H. D., "The Intelligence Quotient and Secondary-School Guidance," *School Review,* Vol. XLIII (January, 1935), pp. 49–59.

SCHULTZ, Irwin J., and LEVINE, Abraham S., "*Before* the Wild Blue Yonder: Counseling in the Classification Program for Air Force Men," *Occupations,* Vol. XXX (December, 1951), pp. 82–85.

SEASHORE, Carl E., "Educational Guidance in Music," *School and Society,* Vol. XLV (March 20, 1937), pp. 385–393.

SEASHORE, Harold, "Tenth Grade Tests as Predictors of Twelfth Grade Scholarship and College Entrance Status," *Journal of Counseling Psychology,* Vol. I (Summer, 1954), pp. 106–115.

SEGEL, David, *Measurement Index,* Circular No. 388, revised (Washington, D.C., U.S. Office of Education, August, 1956).

————, *Prediction of Success in College,* Bulletin No. 15 (Washington, D.C., U.S. Office of Education, 1934).

SERENE, Michael F., "An Experiment in Motivational Counseling," *Personnel and Guidance Journal,* Vol. XXXI (February, 1953), pp. 319–324.

STANTON, Hazel M., *Measurement of Musical Talent: The Eastman Experiment,* Studies in the Psychology of Music, Vol. II (Iowa City, University of Iowa Studies, 1935).

————, and KOERTH, Wilhelmine, *Musical Capacity Measures of Children Repeated after Musical Training,* Series on Aims and Progress of Research, New Series No. 259 (Iowa City, University of Iowa Studies, September 15, 1933).

STENQUIST, John L., *Measurements of Mechanical Ability* (New York, Teachers College, Columbia University, Contributions to Education No. 130, 1923).

STEWART, Naomi, "A.G.C.T. Scores of Army Personnel Grouped by Occupation," *Occupations,* Vol. XXVI (October, 1947), pp. 5–41.

STORRS, Sibyll V., "Evaluative Data on the G.A.T.B.," *Personnel and Guidance Journal,* Vol. XXXI (November, 1952), pp. 87–90.

STUIT, Dewey B., Chairman, *Predicting Success in Professional Schools* (Washington, D. C., American Council on Education, 1949).

SUPER, Donald E., *Appraising Vocational Fitness by Means of Psychological Tests* (New York, Harper, 1949).

———, "The Criteria of Vocational Success," *Occupations,* Vol. XXX (October, 1951), pp. 5–9.

———, "The Use of Multifactor Test Batteries in Guidance," *Personnel and Guidance Journal,* Vol. XXXV (September, 1956), pp. 9–15. (See also each of the remaining issues of Vol. XXXV for articles on eight multifactor test batteries, with "Comments" by Super. Then, Super's concluding article, "The Multifactor Tests: Summing Up," Vol. XXXVI (September, 1957), pp. 17–20).

———, "Vocational Adjustment: Implementing a Self-Concept," *Occupations,* Vol. XXX (November, 1951), pp. 88–92.

THORNDIKE, Robert L., and HAGEN, Elizabeth, *Measurement and Evaluation in Psychology and Education* (New York, Wiley, 1955).

THURSTONE, L. L., and T. G., *Factorial Studies of Intelligence,* Psychometric Monographs No. 2 (Chicago, University of Chicago Press, 1941).

TRAXLER, Arthur E., "Correlations between 'Mechanical Aptitude' Scores and 'Mechanical Comprehension' Scores," *Occupations,* Vol. XXII (October, 1943), pp. 42–43.

WESMAN, Alexander G., "The Differential Aptitude Tests," *Personnel and Guidance Journal,* Vol. XXXI (December, 1952), pp. 167–170.

WILLIAMSON, E. G., "The Decreasing Accuracy of Scholastic Predictions," *Journal of Educational Psychology,* Vol. XXVIII (January, 1937), pp. 1–16.

CHAPTER 13

Analysis of the Individual: Vocational Interests, Personal Adjustment, and Character Traits

THE PREDICTION STUDIES reported in Chapter 12 showed that tests of ability afford quite imperfect prediction of achievement. Factors other than ability are highly important in determining level of accomplishment. To delineate some of these factors and to describe the principal instruments that have been created for their measurement is the purpose of this chapter. Individuals vary, for example, in their likes and dislikes for different kinds of activity, and they are therefore highly motivated to pursue some activities and poorly motivated for others. Discovering these differences and knowing their meaning for different kinds of work should help to locate each individual in a vocation which affords him pleasure and satisfaction. Likewise, individuals vary in attributes of character and personality—industry, conscientiousness, tact, dependability, etc. Some of these traits are needed for practically every curricular and occupational activity; other traits are essential only to selected activities. Educational and vocational adjustment depends notably upon the possession of various traits and the strength of them.

The measuring instruments to be described in this chapter will be seen to have been created in the objective pattern established for ability testing. Responses are summed up in numerical scores. But whereas the answers in tests of ability and achievement are right or wrong, the answers in tests of interests and adjustment cannot be so classified; they are but the individual's expression of his values, feelings, attitudes, and, perhaps, a portrait of the kind of person he would like people to think him to be. The researches which reveal these limitations will be cited in sufficient detail to help the reader evaluate the instruments and know when and how to use them. Attention will be given to subjective methods, particularly character trait rating, as means of capitalizing the observations of teachers.

MEASURES OF VOCATIONAL INTERESTS

The Nature and Importance of Interests

That a person's vocation should match his make-up in interests as well as in abilities is axiomatic. Some people like routine work; others like work that has variety and gives them a chance to be creative. Some like manual work; others like mental work. Some like to work in a team; others prefer to work alone. Vocational guidance must take full account of these likes and dislikes. Hence, the extended study of interests—of how they originate and develop, of how their variety and their strength can be measured—has long been an important branch of study in the field of guidance.

In the early days of vocational guidance it became apparent that interest or interests could not be reliably ascertained by asking for the student's verbal expression of them. And when the student volunteered that he was "interested in" aviation or medicine or costume designing, the counselor was skeptical because he feared that the "interest" had no sound experiential foundation. Such choices often stemmed from dreams of prestige or opulence, from inadequate vocational information, or from family influence.

The search for the individual's true interests and the disposition to respect those interests in helping to bring about a wise vocational choice is consistent with the modern educational theory which holds to the idea of interest as the mainspring of effort in education. Increasingly, interest is acknowledged as providing the best and strongest motivation for activity in both educational and vocational pursuits. By contrast, in the beginnings of experimental psychology only a few decades ago, attention of the researchers was on the activity of the subjects, with motivation largely ignored. Rats ran mazes, and records were kept of the number of trials required for them to learn the right pathway. Children learned nonsense syllables or repeated digits, and the time and error data of their activity were compiled and analyzed. When we turned from the activity to ponder the reasons behind it, we found a complex field for research. What are the basic goals and desires that impel the organism to activity? What yearnings, what satisfactions and pleasures, furnish the motive power? While some motivating pressures have been found to be common and undifferentiated—for example, the "developmental tasks" which figure so prominently in current educational thinking—other forces, which we call "interests," notably differentiate individuals to fit them for finding satisfactions in varied types of vocational activity.

For a simple definition of interests and for a theory to explain their origin and development, we may refer to the work of Edward K. Strong, Jr., whose contributions to scholarship in this field have been pre-eminent.[1]

---

[1] Reprinted from *Vocational Interests of Men and Women,* by Edward K. Strong, Jr., with the permission of the publishers, Stanford University Press. Copyright 1943 by the Board of Trustees of Leland Stanford Junior University.

... an interest is a response of liking; an aversion is a response of disliking. (p. 6)

Since interests involve reactions to specific things, they must all be learned. Accordingly, they may be modified later on by re-education. (p. 10)

We have just said that all interests are learned, acquired. There are some interests, however, that come very close to being native, if they are not actually inherited, such as liking sugar and disliking quinine. But let us disregard these exceptional cases and consider the great majority of interests. These appear only after experience with things, after reacting to objects, including persons. After apparently the same experience, some say they like it and others that they dislike it. Whence comes the difference in response? Apparently the explanation is to be found in the varying capacities of men. (p. 12)

Are interests inherited as are physical traits? The first answer to this question must be "No." Interests are related to objects and activities in the environment in quite a different sense from height or color of eyes. Interests are learned. Liking to be an aviator and disliking gardening are reflections of experience. The second answer to this question is that interests are inherited to some degree. An interest is an expression of one's reaction to his environment. The reaction of liking-disliking is a resultant of satisfactory or unsatisfactory dealing with the object. Different people react differently to the same object. The different reactions, we suspect, arise because the individuals are different to start with. (pp. 682–683)

Thus, interests seem to emerge from the interaction of the individual with experience. To find one's enduring and deep-seated interests numerous and varied experiences must be recommended.

Are interests sufficiently stable so that they may be used as guide posts in planning for one's life work? Do vocational interests coincide with vocational aptitudes, or what is their relationship? Such questions as these will be taken up in the following portions of this section in connection with the description and evaluation of the two most widely used instruments for interest measurement.

The Strong Vocational Interest Blank[2]

This is an instrument of 400 items to which the subject is asked to react in terms of his likes, dislikes, and preferences. To a large number of occupations, he indicates if he likes that kind of work, is indifferent to it, or dislikes it (L I D). He makes the same choices among a list of amusements, school subjects, activities, and peculiarities of people. Other exercises call for an indication of the order of preference for activities; types of persons admired; choice between two paired activities; and self-ratings in specified present abilities and characteristics.

The theory behind this blank is that successful workers in a given occupation have a characteristic set of likes and dislikes which distinguishes them from other occupational groups. Acting on this assumption, Strong has used the blank on workers in forty or more occupations to find the interest patterns of such workers. In his manual he gives succinct descriptions of these

[2] Published by Stanford University Press (Stanford, Cal.).

"criterion groups," recording the number, average age, and average level of schooling of the members, together with evidence of their success or high standing in their occupations. The interest pattern of each criterion group constitutes a key against which a subject's responses are corrected. Thus, to find the occupational group to which a person's interests most nearly correspond, his blank must be compared (corrected) with each of the forty or more keys which Strong has constructed. Most users of the Blank send their students' answer sheets to one of several centers which specialize in scoring them.

Strong[3] has made extensive studies in the classification of occupations according to interests. For example, he has found a high degree of identity in the interests of mathematicians, physicists, engineers, and chemists. Thus, he has been able to classify more than thirty occupations into seven groups. Such occupations, however, as musician, production manager, and certified public accountant were so distinctive as to make it unwise to combine them with any of the groups. For each of the groups an "average" key has been created. By using the group keys instead of each occupational key, the expense of correction can be greatly reduced.

This description of occupational classification refers to research that has been done with Strong's Blank for men. Strong has also constructed a Blank for women listing 410 items on which scales are available for 18 occupations.[4] Its characteristics and value have not been investigated extensively.

In Buros' *Mental Measurements Yearbooks* are listed 273 references reporting researches on the Strong Blank. Because of its validation with successful workers, this instrument has been used to make many contributions to knowledge about vocational interests. For example, follow-up studies have demonstrated the permanence of the vocational interests which were first revealed by the use of the Blank while the subjects were college students.

Occupational interest scores of 345 college students agree with the occupation engaged in twenty years later to the extent of 86 per cent of the possible maximum. For the 230 men who did not change their occupation the agreement amounts to 91 per cent of the maximum; for the 115 men who have changed their occupations the agreement amounts to 77 per cent of the maximum.[5]

In a follow-up study based on the Vocational Interest Blanks of 306 Stanford University freshmen of 1930, many of whom were contacted for filling out the Blank again in 1931, 1939, and 1949, Strong concluded,[6]

[3] *Op. cit.,* Ch. 8.

[4] *Ibid.,* pp. 699–702.

[5] Edward K. Strong, Jr., "Interest Scores While in College of Occupations Engaged in 20 Years Later," *Educational and Psychological Measurement,* Vol. XI (Autumn, 1951), p. 335.

[6] "Nineteen-Year Followup of Engineer Interests," *Journal of Applied Psychology,* Vol. XXXVI (April, 1952), p. 74.

Considering . . . all the factors that determine occupational choice which are independent, or largely so, of interests, such as health, ability, finance, and family pressure, the over-all agreement between engineer interest scores and choice of occupation is far greater than the writer would have anticipated.

Whatever an interest test measures, whether interests, preferences, values, goals, or what have you, it measures something very stable and permanently possessed and something that contributes very greatly to occupational choice.

How important, then, to measure vocational interests and use the findings in vocational counsel!

A Minnesota study underscored the importance of interests by another approach. Sarbin and Anderson[7] found that an analysis of one hundred cases from files of the University of Minnesota Testing Bureau indicated that "adults who complain of occupational dissatisfaction show, in general, measured interest patterns which are not congruent with their present or modal occupation." Job satisfaction, of course, should be used with caution as a criterion of a vocational-interest test, for the reason that satisfaction or dissatisfaction may be due to conditions peculiar to a particular job.

How early in life does one acquire his permanent interests? Do interests change with age? To answer these questions Strong made many studies of the responses of men 15, 25, and 55 years of age. He has shown that some of the 100 occupations listed in Part I of the Blank are not sufficiently familiar to 15-year-old boys for them to express liking for them.[8] They were likewise handicapped in responding to some of the school subjects listed in Part III. Very few of them professed to like economics or sociology—subjects which they had not yet studied. In large numbers they admired Henry Ford and Thomas A. Edison, but not Charles Dana Gibson, John Wanamaker, and William H. Taft (Part VI). Could not this difference be accounted for by a difference in familiarity?

Strong puts forward two conceptions of the factor of familiarity: (1) viewed as merely the result of physical contact with the object, and (2) the comprehension or appreciation of the object after physical contact with it. He views these two conceptions as discrete and avers that the second is "the only true one." It is sounder, in this writer's opinion, to view the factor as existing in varying degrees, on a continuum, from no familiarity to very great familiarity, and determined by variation in the extent and depth of experience.

On various individual items and classes of items, Strong[9] found differences in the three age groups. The percentage of 15-year-olds who favored activities involving physical skill and daring was 50.7, compared with 48.2 per cent of 25-year-olds and 31.2 per cent of 55-year-olds. The percentages

[7] T. R. Sarbin and H. C. Anderson, "A Preliminary Study of the Relation of Measured Interest Patterns and Occupational Dissatisfaction," *Educational and Psychological Measurement*, Vol. II (Summer, 1942), p. 35.

[8] *Vocational Interests of Men and Women*, pp. 290–291.

[9] *Ibid.*, Ch. 13.

claiming the possession of present abilities were 34.8, 48.8, and 52.9 for the 15-year, 25-year, and 55-year age groups, respectively. Comparable percentages who attested their liking for "Amusements—general cultural" were 34.7, 50.0, and 52.0.

"The most noticeable difference [between 15-year-olds and 25-year-olds] is the increase in the percentage of items which are liked by 25-year-old men as compared with the younger group."[10] This fact may be taken as evidence of the difference in the experience of the two groups. That lifetime interests have not surely emerged at the age of 15 may be deduced from the following paragraph with which Strong concludes his chapter, "Change of Interests with Age:"[11]

The primary conclusion regarding interests of men between 25 and 55 years of age is that they change very little. When these slight differences over thirty years are contrasted with the differences to be found among occupational groups, or between men and women, or between unskilled and professional men, it must be realized that age and the experience that goes with age change an adult man's interests very little. At 25 years of age he is largely what he is going to be and even at 20 years of age he has acquired pretty much the interests he will have throughout life.

That the Strong Blank is adapted to and has been used primarily with college students or young adults rather than with elementary-school or high-school pupils seems to be no limitation. If these younger people have not yet had enough experience so that they can surely know what they like and dislike, there is not much point in measuring their interests. We would do better to focus on helping them to try out many kinds of activities in curriculum, extracurriculum, and community life.

A limitation of Strong's Blank is the relatively small number of the occupations of modern society for which he has ascertained interest patterns. If a person has the interests of a TV repairman, for example, they cannot stand revealed by the use of the test, because no key for that occupation has been established. The reverse limitation of the Strong Blank is that the correction of the testee's paper with the present forty occupational keys is relatively expensive.

The Kuder Preference Record[12]

This widely used inventory, first published in 1939, consists of some 500 triad test items, from each of which the subject selects the activity he likes best and the one he likes least. These yield scores for interests of the following ten types: outdoor, mechanical, computational, scientific, persuasive, artistic, literary, musical, social, and clerical. The test is easy to administer.

10 *Ibid.*, p. 298.
11 *Ibid.*, p. 313.
12 Published by Science Research Associates (Chicago).

It can be scored by the subject himself, and he can represent his scores for each of the scales on a profile chart. The manual lists occupations corresponding to each of the categories of interests and to combinations of the categories.

From the 208 references listed in Buros' *Mental Measurements Yearbooks* it is evident that the *Kuder* is a much researched instrument. A quotation from one of the reviewers is as follows:[13]

The Kuder is an instrument that went through a carefully planned and thoroughly executed developmental process. It falls short of the Strong in the thoroughness of its validation and other supporting data. One major set of validation data is the presentation in the manual of mean profiles for occupational groups largely derived from data contributed by test consumers. The author's device of soliciting validation data from test users, while a convenient way of solving a costly, time-consuming problem, is less than adequate as a rigorous demonstration that these interest scales are indeed relevant to distinguishing occupational groups in terms of interests. First, it is difficult to interpret the significance of mean test profiles for a given group without information as to the conditions under which the test was administered. Was this a study in which the subjects had no particular stake? Were they taking the tests as applicants for a job? Was it for counseling? [We must *always* be asking these questions, in view of the faking possibilities of interest inventories.] . . . A further drawback in the validation evidence is the very small number of cases on which many of the mean profiles are based. One important type of supporting data about this test that is not now available is definitive evidence about the stability of test results. Nothing approaching the long-term follow-up studies on the VIB [Strong] has been reported.

A further limitation on the value of Kuder's occupational profiles is that no evidence is offered to show that the workers are carrying on their occupations successfully, as is the case with Strong's criterion groups.

The Kuder is widely employed in high schools and even in junior high schools. In view of what has been found about the emergence and gradual stabilization of interests during the teens, the practice of measuring and interpreting interests during that period must be termed hazardous. To define the hazards, Mallinson and Crumrine conducted an investigation by comparing the scores earned on the Kuder by 250 pupils in Grade 9 and again in Grade 12.[14] They found that with 80 per cent of the students the area of interest ranking highest in the ninth grade was among the three highest ranking areas in the twelfth grade; with 70 per cent of the students the second highest ranking area in the ninth grade was among the three highest in the twelfth

[13] Edward Bordin, in *Fourth Mental Measurements Yearbook* (Highland Park, N.J., Gryphon Press, 1953), p. 737.

[14] George G. Mallinson and William M. Crumrine, "An Investigation of the Stability of Interests of High-School Students," *Journal of Educational Research*, Vol. XLV (January, 1952), pp. 369–383.

grade; with 52 per cent the third highest ranking area remained in the highest three. The implications of these findings, said the authors, are as follows:[15]

1. Students should not be counseled at the ninth-grade level on the assumption that the rankings of interest at that level will remain the same throughout high school.

2. Students may be counseled reliably on the basis of interest at the ninth grade provided that the two or three highest areas of interest and the two or three lowest areas of interest are considered in such counseling.

This evidence that the *development* of interests is still going on in the high-school years supports the more intensive and extensive research with the Strong inventory. Because of the danger that pupils, parents, and teachers will attribute an unjustified finality to results obtained by the administration of an interests test to immature pupils, it is the recommendation of this writer that such an instrument should not be employed below the eleventh grade.

Do the interest inventories agree in their measurements? A number of investigations have sought the answer to this question, and especially they have been focused on the Kuder and Strong instruments. Triggs and associates in several articles, of which one may be listed here,[16] found some agreements between Strong's groups and Kuder's types, but not enough so that the two instruments could be used interchangeably. This finding was not interpreted to the disadvantage of either inventory, but, rather, it was felt that if both were used, a more penetrating analysis of a client's interests would be afforded. Using both approaches to assess a client's vocational interests should be regarded as feasible in any college or veterans' counseling center which uses the Strong, because the Kuder is so easy to administer and score, and so inexpensive, as to involve a very little addition to the testing program.

Relation of Interests to Aptitudes

Does a person with measured clerical interests also have clerical aptitude? Does a man with mechanical interests have mechanical aptitude? It is probably true that an affirmative answer to these questions is widely assumed and often voiced. The popular conception is that one is interested in that activity which he can carry on successfully, and that therefore aptitudes can be assumed from interests. From many reports which have come to this writer, this conception prevails to the extent that many high-school pupils think of interests and aptitudes as interchangeable, and their teachers and counselors in some instances have the same idea.

[15] *Ibid.,* p. 383.

[16] J. R. Wittenborn, Frances O. Triggs, and Daniel D. Feder, "A Comparison of Interest Measurement by the Kuder Preference Record and the Strong Vocational Interest Blanks for Men and Women," *Educational and Psychological Measurement,* Vol. III (Autumn, 1943), pp. 239–257.

A number of researches have been made to ascertain the truth in this matter. Brayfield[17] studied the clerical interests and aptitude of 231 female office workers divided into six major job categories. He used the Kuder and the Minnesota Clerical Test. The relationships found were negligible.

Anderson[18] tested the relation of aptitudes to interests by comparing computational and clerical interests as measured by the Kuder, on the one hand, with the quantitative score earned on the ACE Psychological Examination and the numbers score earned on the Minnesota Clerical Test, on the other hand. The subjects were 257 male clients of the Psychological Service Center, New York City. The correlations were as follows:

	ACE Arithmetic	Minnesota Numbers
Kuder Computational	0.26	0.11
Kuder Clerical	−0.10	0.01

"The correlations present striking evidence that related supporting aptitudes cannot be assumed, but must be confirmed before strong interests can provide a basis for educational and vocational decisions."

The *Differential Aptitude Tests Manual,* Second Edition,[19] shows the coefficients of correlation between DAT scores and Kuder scores as derived from the testing of boys and girls of the 10th, 11th, and 12th grades in an Ames, Iowa, high school. Of the 432 coefficients—each DAT test against each Kuder interest category for each sex and each grade, the range was from .54 to −.51, with 218 positive and 214 negative. A quotation from the interpretation is as follows:

Only two appropriate pairings—*DAT Mechanical Reasoning* with *Kuder Mechanical Interest* and *DAT Mechanical Reasoning* with *Kuder Scientific Interest* —reveal consistent and significant relationships, in both cases for boys only. For all other pairings, relevant as well as irrelevant, the coefficients are either inconsistent or insignificant (e.g., *DAT Clerical Speed and Accuracy* and *Kuder Clerical,* or *DAT Language Usage* and *Kuder Literary*). It appears that, for the most part, Kuder interest categories have little to do with measured aptitudes.

The evidence of these three studies should be a warning to be heeded by all who administer and interpret interest inventories. Counselees should be told emphatically that such an instrument as the Kuder does not measure ability, but interests. Probably it would be unwise to try to interpret interest scores apart from ability scores, and both should be supplemented by the illumination of interests and abilities which is derived from the observation of behavior.

[17] Arthur H. Brayfield, "Clerical Interest and Clerical Aptitude," *Personnel and Guidance Journal,* Vol. XXXI (February, 1953), pp. 304–306.

[18] Rose G. Anderson, "Do Aptitudes Support Interests?" *Personnel and Guidance Journal,* Vol. XXXII (September, 1953), pp. 14–17.

[19] By George K. Bennett, Harold G. Seashore, and Alexander G. Wesman (New York, The Psychological Corporation, 1952), pp. 71, 75.

Criticisms and Evaluations

The weaknesses of interest inventories have recently been catalogued in an article by Rothney and Schmidt.[20] They attack the widespread use of these instruments as unjustified and potentially dangerous. Their criticisms may well be taken up and examined.

First, they charge that results obtained by the use of an interest inventory cannot be depended upon as constituting a true picture of the subject because he may have faked his responses. Substantial research as well as analysis of individual cases backs up this charge. Always one must ask, Under what motivation is the test being taken? Paterson[21] described the case of a client who desired transfer from his clerical position to a much better paying job in the personnel department of the same company. He knew when he took the Kuder that the results would have some bearing on his aspiration.

In spite of nine years of successful experience as an office clerk, Mr. 'X' rated low in computational and clerical interests. When queried he indicated that he had never liked clerical work but had stayed on the job because 'he liked the people he came in contact with.' When his attention was drawn to the unusually high persuasive score, he admitted he had been considering a selling job but that commissions are 'too uncertain.' He explained the high scores on mechanical interests by saying that he has always liked to tinker with autos. He could not explain the high social service score except that he believed it to be important in personnel work. Persistent questioning failed to elicit any prior activities allied with social service interests. Mr. 'X' did offer an illuminating statement by saying, after he had filled out the Kuder inventory that 'it would be easy for anyone to fake his score on the test.'

He was immediately given the Strong Blank, on which he demonstrated a primary pattern of interests in the group of occupations—accountant, office manager, and purchasing agent—having to do with office detail. A secondary pattern was in sales occupations, and a tertiary pattern in social service occupations. Paterson concluded from this case that

in a selection situation, it would appear that the Strong is to be preferred because it is more subtle and the vocational significance of liking or disliking each of the 400 items is not so readily apparent to the person taking the test. This conclusion needs to be verified by data drawn from additional cases.

Longstaff[22] ran a scientific test of "fakability" with an adult group, having them first take the two tests in good faith, then directing them to take the

[20] John W. M. Rothney and Louis G. Schmidt, "Some Limitations of Interest Inventories," *Personnel and Guidance Journal,* Vol. XXXIII (December, 1954), pp. 199–204.

[21] Donald G. Paterson, "Vocational Interest Inventories in Selection," *Occupations,* Vol. XXV (December, 1946), pp. 152–153.

[22] Howard P. Longstaff, "Fakability of the Strong Interest Blank and the Kuder Preference Record," *Journal of Applied Psychology,* Vol. XXXII (August, 1948), pp. 360–369.

tests again and fake some interests up and some down. They were able to fake as directed on both tests, "the Strong considerably more so than the Kuder on the fake upward categories and the Kuder more so than the Strong on the fake downward categories for the male subjects."[23] Longstaff's findings have been supported by an experiment which Cross carried on with high-school pupils and from which he concluded,[24]

As shown by the present study, when an applicant for a job has any idea of what job he is being considered for, his scores should be interpreted in the light of the knowledge that faking is possible *if he desires to fake*. In the properly motivated guidance situation, this problem does not arise.

A striking example of the possibility of faking and the kind of circumstance in which it may occur came to this writer's attention a few years ago. A superintendent of schools gave boys of the eighth grade a high-pressure sales talk on the advantages of electing the Smith-Hughes vocational industrial curriculum for their next year. A few days later the Kuder was administered. John, 14, without any coaching, came through with very high musical interests and very low mechanical interests. Actually, his mother explained to the writer, John had a minimum of musical interests, but decided to appear that way because he was fearful of being coerced into the vocational curriculum.

Strong recognizes the possibilities of faking his inventory by the following quotation from his "Instructions for Taking the Test:"[25]

It has been demonstrated that if students desire to, they can raise their scores quite significantly. Consequently, if the test is employed for admission purposes it should be given with maximum emphasis upon filling the blank in minimum time, in order to prevent students figuring out the proper responses. . . .
When men are really desirous of knowing what occupation they should enter, there is no danger that they will falsify their reactions. For this reason it seems preferable to give the test so that this motive is appealed to, whenever possible.

A second criticism offered by Rothney and Schmidt is that the classification of items as signifying mechanical interests, clerical interests, or some other category of interests is entirely subjective. (This process, of course, does not apply to the Strong.) They hold that many items would be classified differently by someone else. To this charge of subjectivity in the classification process, the studies of faking just cited seem to supply an answer. If clients can at will achieve high scores or low scores in any category of interests, it must be that they notably agree with the test author in his classification.

Third, Rothney and Schmidt aver that many vocabulary items in these

---

[23] *Ibid.*, p. 367.
[24] Orrin H. Cross, "A Study of Faking on the Kuder Preference Record," *Educational and Psychological Measurement*, Vol. X (Summer, 1950), p. 277.
[25] *Manual for Vocational Interest Blank for Men* (Stanford, Cal., Stanford University Press, 1945), p. 7.

tests are too difficult for pupils for whom the tests are supposed to be suitable. This allegation has been given some documentation by Christensen.[26] He made a check on 21 words found in the Kuder, using the Thorndike-Lorge Word Scale, and learned that the average occurrence of these words per million words is three. He constructed an objective test to ascertain the meanings which ninth-grade pupils assigned to certain terms and demonstrated that many members had erroneous ideas concerning the meanings of these terms. He then spent eight 40-minute periods in the study of the items of the blank, after which the pupils took the test a second time. When correlated with the first taking of the test, the coefficients for the nine scales ranged from .63 to .85. In view of the numerous reliability studies on the Kuder, all yielding r's above .90, this study shows that pupils notably altered their preferences when they understood the items.

Kuder seems to recognize the criticism of the vocabulary of his instrument by including in his 1951 manual a glossary of more than fifty words and phrases, headed by the injunction, "If you find a strange word or phrase, the list below may help you to understand it." How the testee could be expected to make use of a glossary in the test manual is something of a mystery.

Fourth, Rothney and Schmidt deplore the forced choice between alternatives of which one's knowledge is frequently not equal—of which, indeed, it is sometimes a case of knowledge versus ignorance. Closely allied to this criticism is the fifth lament of Rothney and Schmidt, namely, that *degrees* of preference cannot be shown. The difference between a lukewarm preference and a highly enthusiastic one cannot be registered, yet there can be no doubt of the importance of such a distinction for counseling.

A sixth criticism is the lack of validation of the inventories, with one exception—presumably the Strong. This is a subject already treated in this section. Finally, these critics deplore the tendency of many shallow-thinking users of interest tests to justify their use, even with junior high school pupils, on the grounds that the youngsters enjoy taking such tests. Quite clearly, the use of the tests must first of all be justified on the basis of unquestioned value.

From a review of the literature on interests and interest measurement, one must conclude that the identification of student interests calls for a wealth of experience through the curriculum and extracurriculum, as described in Chapter 8, and for the employment of the methods of observation and inquiry, as set forth in Chapter 11. The gradual, day-by-day building up of a capital of acquaintanceship with the student is even more necessary for the ascertainment of interests than for abilities. No "quickie" interest test can serve as a substitute. The counselor cannot soundly advise with a stranger concerning whose interests he knows only what appears on an interests profile sheet.

Yet one cannot overlook the long-term studies made by Strong in which

[26] Thomas E. Christensen, "Some Observations with Respect to the Kuder Preference Record," *Journal of Educational Research,* Vol. XL (October, 1946), pp. 96–107.

he has shown that college graduates who entered and followed the professions in which their interest inventories indicated the highest level of interest, achieved success and satisfaction. If interest tests are administered when the subjects have no reason for faking and when they are old enough to have had experiences from which true interests emerge, there is no doubt that they can advantageously supplement observation and inquiry. In a later chapter the judicious use of interest-test results in counseling will be discussed.

MEASURES OF PERSONALITY

Importance of Measuring Personality

That guidance workers need to be able to identify and diagnose personality problems and to be skilled in applying remedial treatment, is axiomatic. Such activity is primarily in the adjustive phase of guidance. Some people need to undergo personality adjustments if they are to accomplish in education and vocation what their abilities indicate they can. There are youth in our schools, from kindergarten to graduate school, who need help in achieving the integration of mind and emotion which is necessary to the effective employment of their powers. The child who has fears, feelings of inferiority, and an inadequate sense of worth challenges guidance to free him from such bonds. The high-school youth who clowns or cannot accept correction needs help in coming to terms with himself and society so that he becomes the citizen, the student, and the worker he has it in him to be. To remove impediments to development and to acceptability in social and employment circles, the counselor has frequent need for understanding the subject's personality.

For distributive guidance, also, an understanding of personality is necessary. Occupations have varied personality requirements. On the whole these are somewhat nebulous, and in most occupations we see persons of quite different personalities performing with apparently equal success. Nevertheless, some occupations involve a high level of emotional stability; some require a special measure of self-assurance, as in the exercise of leadership; some require that the employee like to work with people, while others require that he like to work alone. Such personality variables continually feature statements of the qualifications for jobs, as in the following quotations:[27]

For cashier:
  A neat appearance, pleasant personality, poise, and ability to meet the public are required. (p. 7)
For nurse aide, orderly:
  Should have pleasant personality, physical stamina, and great patience. A desire to be of human service is important. (p. 19)

[27] *Job Guide for Young Workers* (Washington, D.C., U.S. Employment Service, Department of Labor, 1954).

Significantly, the qualifications mentioned in this document for such occupations as bookkeeper assistant, stenographer, bricklayer helper, and radio serviceman do not mention personality characteristics, but are confined to educational level and skills and to physical attributes.

Further discourse on the importance of measuring personality for both adjustive and distributive guidance is to elaborate the obvious. The idea of *measuring* personality, or personality traits, without doubt originated in the general measurement movement and was given special impetus by the early enthusiasm generated by the success of mental testing. If a test of 30 to 60 minutes could give an objective measurement of a child's ability to learn, why not construct similar instruments for the quick appraisal of aspects or attributes of personality?

Descriptions of Some Widely Known Personality Tests

First of the paper-and-pencil personality inventories, and one which served as the prototype of the many which followed, was the Woodworth Personal Data Sheet. It consisted of questions which probed for neurotic symptoms. The first half-dozen were as follows:

1. Do you usually feel well and strong?
2. Do you usually sleep well?
3. Are you frightened in the middle of the night?
4. Are you troubled with dreams about your work?
5. Do you have nightmares?
6. Do you have too many sexual dreams?

The questions were answered "yes" or "no." Taken as a whole, the inventory was intended to approximate a standardized psychiatric interview and thereby to reveal the individuals who had abnormal fears and worries, obsessions and compulsions, tendencies to retreat into unreality, psychosomatic symptoms, and the like. The validity of the items was worked out by item-analysis procedures, and the instrument was employed to some extent with the soldiers of World War I to detect the maladjusted. After the war Mathews revised it so that it was entitled the Woodworth-Mathews Personal Data Sheet and was applicable to children as young as 12 or 13.

In 1931 appeared the Bernreuter Personality Inventory, designed for use with college students, pupils in the upper secondary years, and adults. Using the same 125 "Yes-No-?" items, Bernreuter worked out four scoring keys by assigning differential weightings to each response. The keys are for neuroticism, self-sufficiency, introversion-extroversion, and dominance-submission. Intercorrelations among the four scores are so high, however, as to indicate that the alleged traits are not at all distinctive. Nevertheless, the apparent economy of the Bernreuter, in the claim that it tests four aspects of personality with the same 125 items, has undoubtedly contributed to its popularity. The first half-dozen items are as follows:

1. Does it make you uncomfortable to be "different" or unconventional?
2. Do you daydream frequently?
3. Do you usually work things out for yourself rather than get someone to show you?
4. Have you ever crossed the street to avoid meeting some person?
5. Can you stand criticism without feeling hurt?
6. Do you ever give money to beggars?

The *Fourth Mental Measurements Yearbook* lists 259 references pertaining to this inventory, which suggests the immense amount of research that has been done on it.

Another popular self-report personality blank is The Adjustment Inventory, by Hugh M. Bell, copyrighted in 1934. One form is for adults and one is for students of high-school and college age. The student form consists of 140 items similar to those appearing in the Bernreuter and Woodworth instruments (in fact, all of these inventories have borrowed items freely from their predecessors). Four types or areas of adjustment are measured, as follows: home, health, social, and emotional. Thus, the psychological terminology of the Bernreuter scales is avoided, and the intent is to provide an instrument which can be interpreted as well as administered by counselors or teachers with minimal training in psychology. Each item applies to only one of the scales. Thus, there are really four separate scales based on 35 items each, but the items are mixed at random throughout the inventory, the subject being given no indication of the categories in which his responses will be classified. The *Fourth Mental Measurements Yearbook* lists 119 references on this test.

Some other personality inventories of the self-report type, such as the Minnesota Multiphasic Personality Inventory (MMPI), are for use only by counselors with extended psychological training. Accounts of their nature and utility will be found in the recent works of Anastasi, Cronbach, and Super which are listed at the end of this chapter.

Reliability and Validity

For a summary of the numerous researches into the soundness and worth of self-report personality inventories we are indebted to two reports by Albert Ellis, one representing a canvass of the literature down to 1946 and the other covering the period from 1946 to 1951, inclusive.[28] Following are quotations from Ellis' first report:

While the reliabilities of personality questionnaires have usually been notoriously high, their validities have remained more questionable. (p. 385)
Of nine attempts to validate personality questionnaires with groups of be-

[28] "The Validity of Personality Questionnaires," *Psychological Bulletin,* Vol. XLIII (September, 1946), pp. 385–440; "Recent Research with Personality Inventories," *Journal of Consulting Psychology,* Vol. XVII, No. 1 (1953), pp. 45–49.

havior-problem children, two have given positive, one questionably positive, and six negative results. (p. 394)

Of 34 tests of the validity of personality questionnaires in the diagnosis of delinquency, 15 have proven to be positive or mainly positive, 6 questionably positive, and 13 negative or mainly negative. (p. 398)

Of 75 attempts to validate personality questionnaires against psychiatric or psychological diagnosis, 36 have shown positive, 9 questionably positive, and 30 negative results. (p. 406)

Of 44 attempts to validate personality questionnaires against the ratings given to respondents by their teachers, friends, or associates, results have been positive in 12 cases, questionably positive in 10, and negative in 22. (p. 411)

Of 42 experimental attempts to discover whether or not respondents over-rated themselves on self-description instruments, 6 investigators found that they did not, and 36 found that they did. (p. 420)

Of 15 studies where personality tests of the conventional type were given individually, instead of in group administrations, the validity results were positive in ten cases, questionably positive in three, and negative in two. [These were mainly done with the MMPI.] (p. 422)

It is concluded that group-administered paper and pencil personality questionnaires are of dubious value in distinguishing between groups of adjusted and maladjusted individuals, and that they are of much less value in the diagnosis of individual adjustment or personality traits. (p. 426)

Ellis' second summary yielded similarly unfavorable evidence on the worth of these instruments, and only the following concluding paragraph need be quoted here:

The results of the present study, as well as of previous surveys made by the writer . . . would lead to the conclusion that although modern personality inventories, when employed for group diagnosis, have *some* degree of validity, scores obtained by individual subjects are partly or largely dependent upon (*a*) the subject's specific motivation at the time of taking the test; (*b*) the conditions under which he is tested; (*c*) his intelligence; (*d*) his degree of psychological sophistication; (*e*) his general test-taking attitudes; (*f*) his general psychological defenses; (*g*) his specific (conscious and unconscious) tendencies to lie to others and to himself; and (*h*) various other motivational and attitudinal factors. (p. 47)

As an example of these researches, one reported by Darley testing the validity of Bell's Adjustment Inventory may be drawn upon.[29] More than 800 students were tested with the Bell at the University of Minnesota counseling center. Each one was repeatedly interviewed by a counselor during the year, after which a diagnosis of the kind and extent of maladjustment was made. The Bell had identified correctly 40 students with problems of home adjustment, had missed 41, and produced 73 false positives—that is, had falsely identified 73 as having such problems. Correctly identified as emo-

29 John G. Darley, "Tested Maladjustment Related to Clinically Diagnosed Maladjustment," *Journal of Applied Psychology,* Vol. XXI (December, 1937), pp. 632–642.

tionally maladjusted were 32, but 42 were falsely identified, and 75 were missed.

Similarly, Feder and Baer tested the Bernreuter.[30] Eighty-one under-graduate girls residing in a semi-co-operative dormitory at the University of Iowa were individually tested with the Bernreuter under most favorable conditions of rapport, then observed during the course of the academic year and their behavior carefully recorded. The testing and the observing were done by the social and personnel director of the dormitory who achieved intimate knowledge of each girl and her personal problems through daily contacts and interviews, normally initiated by the girls themselves. At the end of the year the record of each girl—with identifying information omitted—was independently studied by each author, and the girls were classified by quartiles as to the nature and quality of their adjustments. The agreement of the authors was higher than 90 per cent. Comparing their clinical evaluations with Bernreuter scores, the authors gave data to support this conclusion:

A large amount of disagreement was found between the Inventory scores and the actual behavior records of maladjustment. Personality problems, arising only in the face of certain specific circumstances, were frequently obscured by the generalized type of questions contained in the Inventory. Cases which should be recommended for psychiatric treatment in terms of the norms, actually manifested problems of less seriousness than other cases given satisfactory adjustment ratings.[31]

Beyond these evidences that the paper-and-pencil inventories of personality lack validity, Darley has expressed common-sense judgments which show the insufficiency of "statistically significant" scores for practical counseling.[32] He has pointed out that whereas there is always danger in personnel work that test data will be used too mechanically and too exclusively, with attitude and adjustment scales such superficiality is even more serious.

Statistically significant measured maladjustment is an untenable concept in some fields dealing with human behavior; the problem that is worrying the individual case should be the only point of departure. Students, for example, will tell the counselor that they have "an inferiority complex." If such a statement is not accompanied by a statistically significant deviate score on a specified scale, it is not thereby neglected; the average test score itself may be used to make the student realize that this problem, of absolute magnitude and concern to him, is no greater in his case than in the cases of large numbers of people. If he is still upset, other forms of therapy are tried, and it may develop that the test definition of inferiority differs from the student's definition. In such a case, statistical maladjustment is obviously an inadequate concept. (p. 632)

[30] D. D. Feder and L. Opal Baer, "A Comparison of Test Records and Clinical Evaluations of Personality Adjustment," *Journal of Educational Psychology,* Vol. XXXII (February, 1941), pp. 133–144.
[31] *Ibid.,* pp. 143–144.
[32] *Op. cit.*

A statistically significant deviate score grows out of the additive effect of many individual test items, whereas an individual student may be excessively concerned about small items of behavior or a few specific problems. (p. 638)

Furthermore, the wise counselor, when he becomes acquainted with the student as a person, notes problems that do not show up in the score on any scale and of which the subject is not aware. An example is the student of college age who is overly dependent on one or both of his parents and does not realize it.

Alternatives to the Self-Report Inventory

The discussion to this point has made it evident that the employment of personality inventories is not recommended. What alternatives, then, are there in the measurement, analysis, or appraisal of personality or personality traits?

Presumably, at the present time, we shall have to give up the search for some neat score obtained by self-report and mainly rely upon what may be learned by some of the methods of observation and inquiry as described in the first part of Chapter 11. The use of the Mooney Problem Check List or the SRA Youth Inventory, as described in Chapter 10, may provide some analysis of personality which can afford starting points for counsel, but their weaknesses as self-report instruments must be kept constantly in mind. Carl Rogers' method of locating children who are socially and emotionally maladjusted, as described in some detail in Chapter 4, is another alternative.

The rank and file of teachers must be students of personality. Psychiatrists and psychologists will always be in short supply and therefore available for only the most aggravated cases of maladjustment. Those who meet the pupils daily, the teachers, must be able to distinguish the wholesome from the unwholesome in pupil behavior; they must understand the chief mental mechanisms; they must be competent in the creation of environment which is conducive to mental health. There is no short-cut.

CHARACTER TRAIT RATING

Nature and Importance of Trait Rating

Made abundantly evident in Chapter 12 was the limited value of tests of ability as predictors of achievement. Ability to do and doing are not the same thing. One of the first constructors of intelligence tests who recognized the predictive limitations of those instruments was Haggerty, who expressed himself as follows on this point:[33]

It is not at all probable that a perfect test or measure of intelligence would give a perfect correlation with school success or with success in later life. A more

[33] M. E. Haggerty, "Recent Developments in Measuring Human Capacity," *Journal of Educational Research*, Vol. III (April, 1921), pp. 246–247.

accurate measure of intelligence than any we now have would only render the inadequacy of intelligence more apparent, for the simple reason that success is not quantitatively coterminous with intelligence, but with intelligence in combination with other significant human traits not subject to evaluation by tests of the type currently used as measures of intelligence.

Teachers from the elementary school to the graduate school early learn from their practical experience that students of mediocre intelligence frequently surpass their more brilliant classmates by virtue of superior industry, conscientiousness, regularity, and other virtues that figure in achievement. These are the "human traits" to which Haggerty refers as not subject to objective evaluation.

That traits of character also figure prominently in occupational success is attested by observations in everyday life as well as by some extensive surveys. One of the latter is Brewer's report of the actually recorded reasons for discharges from industrial establishments in 4,375 cases.[34] He classified as *Lack of Skill* or *Technical Knowledge* four of the reasons (Incompetence, Slow, Physically unadapted, and Spoiling work), and found that they totaled 34.2 per cent. Under *Lack of Social Understanding* he listed Insubordination, General unreliability, Absenteeism, Laziness, Trouble-making, Drinking, Violation of rules, Carelessness, Fighting, Misconduct, Dishonesty, Loafing or sleeping, Dissatisfied, and Habitual lateness; these comprised 62.4 per cent of the reasons for discharge. The remaining 3.4 per cent were unclassified.

Another survey, editorially cited a number of years ago,[35] was made by questionnaire and personal interview, soliciting large employers for information regarding their office and clerical employees. Seventy-six corporations gave the causes for discharge and prevention of promotion which are listed, with frequencies, in Table 60. Here is the evidence of the importance of character traits in occupational success. Here is the challenge to guidance to take full account of a highly significant cluster of components in occupational adjustment.

Terman's long-term study of a large group of highly gifted persons offers some striking evidence of the importance of character traits. Twenty years after the initial testing and selection of the approximate 1,500 pupils, all of whom were above the 99th percentile of the general population in I.Q., they ranged in vocational success all the way from international eminence to semi-skilled labor.[36] Using as the primary criterion of success the extent to which a subject had made use of his superior intellectual ability, Terman

34 John M. Brewer, "Causes for Discharge," *Vocational Guidance Magazine,* Vol. VI (January, 1928), pp. 149–150.

35 "Why They Couldn't Hold Their Jobs," *Personnel Journal,* Vol. XIV (December, 1935), p. 227.

36 Lewis M. Terman and Melita H. Oden, *The Gifted Child Grows Up,* Vol. IV of *Genetic Studies of Genius* (Stanford, Cal., Stanford University Press, 1942), pp. 311–316.

TABLE 60. Percentage Distributions of Causes for Discharge and Prevention of Promotion

Causes	Discharge	Prevention of Promotion
Lack of specific skills (in shorthand, English, penmanship, etc.)	10.1	23.5
Character traits:		
Carelessness	14.1	7.9
Non-co-operation	10.7	6.7
Laziness	10.3	6.4
Absence for causes other than illness.	8.5	3.7
Dishonesty	8.1	1.2
Attention to outside things	7.9	5.6
Lack of initiative	7.6	10.9
Lack of ambition	7.2	9.7
Tardiness	6.7	4.6
Lack of loyalty	3.5	4.6
Lack of courtesy	2.2	3.3
Other	3.1	12.0
	89.9	76.6
Total	100.0	100.1

and Oden compared the most successful 150 (A group) out of 730 men with the least successful 150 (C group) as to occupational affiliation. Table 61 shows the distributions of these two groups. With regard to the data of this table the authors commented that the majority of the C group were in occupations which did not make heavy demands on general intelligence, and that the 25 who were in the two highest occupational categories had achieved among the least impressive records of the gifted group who were in such occupations. "Often the difference between a C and an A is little more than a difference in level of aspiration." Is this a compound of the traits of ambition and self-confidence?

These differences in occupational attainment had already been forecast by differences in educational attainment. "Of [college] graduates in the A group, 37.8 per cent were elected to Phi Beta Kappa and 26.7 per cent to Sigma Xi. The corresponding proportions for graduates in the C group were 1.8 per cent and 3.6 per cent." (p. 320)

Some of the most interesting A-C differences were brought to light by trait ratings, including self-ratings by the subjects, ratings on the same traits by their wives and parents, and ratings on certain other traits by the field workers. These ratings were all made before the A and C groups were made up. The subjects, their wives, and their parents showed remarkable agreement in rating the A's far higher than the C's on Perseverance, Self-confidence, and Integration toward goals. (p. 351)

TABLE 61.* Occupational Classification of A and C Groups (1940)

Occupational Category	Group A (per cent)	Group C (per cent)
I. Professional	68.67	9.33
II. Semiprofessional and managerial	30.67	7.33
III. Clerical, skilled trades, retail business		48.67
IV. Agriculture		1.33
V. Semiskilled occupations, minor clerical positions, and minor business		22.00
VI. Slightly skilled trades or occupations requiring little training or ability		4.00
Student	0.67	2.00
Unemployed		4.00
Incapacitated		0.67
Unclassified		0.67
Total	100.00	100.00

* Terman and Oden, Table 96 (adapted), p. 316.

Attempts have been made to construct instruments for the objective measurement of character traits. Most notable among such researches are the works of Hugh Hartshorne and Mark A. May and their associates.[37] While such labors have not met with success, and they will not be reviewed here, the interested reader will find that they contributed much to our understanding of character. Because of our inability to measure character or character traits as we do intelligence or special aptitude, we have turned to the use of rating systems for the estimation of degrees of trait possession, as illustrated above in the quotation from Terman and Oden.

For two reasons guidance workers are interested in having the character traits of their students appraised, namely:

(1) For the ascertainment of needed adjustments. If each student is to develop into the most effective person he can be, such flaws in attitude and behavior as are indicated by the character traits listed in Table 60 must be identified so that adjustive counseling may be undertaken.

(2) For purposes of prediction. If counselors and principals are to answer the questions about character which are put to them on blanks of reference by colleges and employers, they must have at hand the most accurate estimates or ratings that they can get. All who make or use trait ratings, however, must accept this admonition: they must never forget that traits of character may be changed, that, in fact, adjustive guidance operates on the principle that they *can* be changed. In this sense, these factors in achievement are unlike the relatively unmodifiable I.Q. and the special aptitudes described in Chapter 12; occasionally their changes confound prediction.

[37] *Studies in Deceit; Studies in Service and Self-Control; Studies in the Organization of Character* (New York, Macmillan, 1928, 1929, 1930).

Are we justified in assuming the existence of generalized traits—honesty, industry, punctuality—which are unfailingly operative or inoperative? Rating literature seems to accept this assumption, but the more penetrating literature of character and personality indicates that this is a moot question. Hartshorne and May said that they did not find evidence to support a theory of generalized traits, that further research might reveal them, but that on the basis of their data, honest or deceptive behavior, for example, simply consisted of specific habits learned in relation to specific situations.

In support of Hartshorne and May is the evidence reported by Krathwohl[38] from his study of industriousness of students in a college of engineering. He derived an Index of Industriousness by comparing scores on aptitude and achievement tests. To 308 students he administered, in September, 1946, aptitude tests in English, mathematics, chemistry, and physics. In May, 1948, he gave the students achievement tests in those subjects. He found such a lack of correlation between the students' indexes of industriousness in the four subjects as to cause him to conclude that a student should not be considered industrious or indolent, but as so characterized in English, or in any of the four subjects. From his data he felt that it was quite possible for a student to be industrious in mathematics, "normal" in English, and indolent in physics. Expressing his agreement with Hartshorne and May, Krathwohl said that we cannot speak of an industrious individual but of an individual who is industrious in some one area of activity.

Evidence and argument contrary to that just cited have been advanced. Many authorities hold that traits exist, but that it is not to be expected that they will operate with unvarying consistency on all occasions, that some situations may precipitate conflicts between traits (Didn't Jean Valjean steal a loaf of bread because he loved his family?). Rating assumes the existence of traits, but presumably when a rater gives a rating of "average" on perseverance, he means that sometimes the ratee perseveres and sometimes he does not. It has been found that the average of several raters' judgments gives a more valid rating than one alone. Such a reliance on consensus is an acknowledgment that the operation of a trait may vary with circumstances and stimuli. These questions of the generality or specificity of traits cannot be resolved here. There must be variation among individuals. How rating shall be done to show such variation with accuracy, regardless of the theory, must be the main issue for exposition here.

Description and Evaluation of Hughes' Experiment in Trait Rating

In the first quarter of the twentieth century, many researches into the problems and the techniques of rating were carried on. Major contributors to our knowledge of rating were Thorndike, Rugg, Knight, Franzen, Paterson, Kingsbury, Symonds, Watson, Freyd, Scott, Conklin, Shen, Cady, Fur-

---

[38] William C. Krathwohl, "Specificity of Over- and Under-Achievement in College Courses," *Journal of Applied Psychology,* Vol. XXXVI (April, 1952), pp. 103–106.

fey, and Landis. Little knowledge has been added since 1925. Of the several writers who summarized the principles of sound rating which research had revealed, perhaps no one made a more inclusive statement than did Watson in his 19 "findings."[39] Of greater value here than the reporting of such conclusions is the description of a plan of rating which employs the principles discovered by research. Such a plan was that devised by W. Hardin Hughes for experimental use in Pasadena, California, and described by him in several writings.

Figure 14[40] is the form on which Hughes had the teachers of 450 senior high school pupils and 580 junior high school pupils—in separate schools—do the rating of their pupils on twelve traits and ten special interests. The "Manual of Instructions" referred to in Figure 14 consisted mainly of definitions of the traits, the first two of which are as follows:

TRAIT CHARACTERISTICS

I. Regularity and Persistency

Lowest Rank	*Highest Rank*
1. Is seldom found in the right place at the right time.	1. Is found in the right place at the right time.
2. Works sporadically.	2. Works regularly and on time.
3. Habitually leaves job unfinished.	3. Completes job before leaving it.
4. Is discouraged by trifling obstacles.	4. Perseveres even when making little progress.
5. Is inconsistent in thought and behavior.	5. Holds tenaciously to worth-while purposes.
6. Is conspicuous for procrastinating.	6. Is generally consistent in thought and behavior.

II. Trustworthiness

Lowest Rank	*Highest Rank*
1. Does not hesitate to offer as his own the work done by another.	1. Is scrupulously honest in work.
2. Disregards own promises and other obligations.	2. Fulfills promises and other obligations.
3. Gives false impression by exaggeration.	3. Avoids exaggerations and other inaccuracies.
4. Is subject to own prejudices.	4. Is not misled by own prejudices.
5. Does not admit error even when shown to be wrong.	5. Admits error if shown to be wrong.
6. Loafs when unwatched.	6. Does not loaf when unwatched.
7. Does not "play the game" honorably.	7. "Plays the game" honorably.

[39] Goodwin B. Watson, "The Measurement of the Less Tangible Qualities," *Vocational Guidance Magazine,* Vol. IV (March, 1926), pp. 281–289.

[40] W. Hardin Hughes, "A Rating Scale for Individual Capacities, Attitudes, and Interests," *Journal of Educational Method,* Vol. III (October, 1923), p. 58.

FIG. 14. PRACTICE RATING SCALE
Individual Capacities, Attitudes and Interests
(Trait)

School. . . . . Department and Grade. . . . . . . Person Rating. . . . . . . Date. . . . . . .

Preliminary Instructions: (1) This rating sheet is to be used for only fifty students. In making up the list to be rated, take the names of all students in a single class division. Add to this list enough names from a representative class division of approximately the same grade to complete fifty. Let the latter be selected alphabetically so that they will be fairly representative. Place the list before you. Now turn to column headed HIGHEST and read everything in that column before writing in any names.

NAMES OF STUDENTS ACCORDING TO RANK

0		Lowest		Inferior			Average			Superior			Highest	
	40	40		80	80	80		120	120	160	160		200	

Instructions: (4) Turn in the MANUAL of INSTRUCTIONS to the discussion of the LOWEST characteristics of the trait under consideration. Note carefully the typical characteristics and try to form as vivid an impression as possible of what gives one lowest rank in the possession of this particular trait. After doing this, select the names of two (and not more than five) students, of the fifty, who are entitled to lowest rank. Write their names at the head of this column.

Instructions: (5) Select the names of those who stand next to the lowest with respect to this trait. These should be unmistakably INFERIOR to the average. Write ten names in this column and not more than fifteen. Now proceed to column headed AVERAGE and follow instructions.

Instructions: (6) Place in this column the remaining names of the fifty.

(4) (cont) led to lowest rank. Write their names at the head of this column. Now proceed to column headed INFERIOR.

Instructions: (3) Select the names of those who stand next to the highest with respect to this trait. These should be unmistakably SUPERIOR to the average. Write ten names in this column and not more than fifteen. Now proceed to column headed LOWEST and follow instructions.

Instructions: (2) Turn in the MANUAL of INSTRUCTIONS to the discussion of the HIGHEST characteristics of the trait under consideration. Note carefully the typical characteristics and try to form as vivid an impression as possible of what gives one extraordinary rank in the possession of this particular trait. After doing this, select the names of two (and not more than five) students, of the fifty, who are entitled to highest rank. Write their names at the head of this column.

(2) (cont) Proceed to column headed SUPERIOR

461

The reader is invited to study Figure 14 closely and observe the following features of the plan:

(1) The rater must rate all pupils on a single trait rather than rating one pupil at a time on all traits.

(2) The rater must respect the normal curve in his distribution of the pupils along the rating scale.

(3) Features (1) and (2) prevent the "halo effect"—a term coined by Thorndike to designate the tendency of a rater to rate a subject on a specific trait according to his general impression of him. Figure 14 also forces both easy and hard raters to be discriminating and to use all intervals on the scale in normal-curve proportions. Figure 14 presents five divisions in the scale, which is the number that has been found to be most practicable. Seven scale divisions are used in some rating plans, but most raters find it difficult to make distinctions of that degree of fineness. A three-point scale is generally considered too coarse to be of much value.

(4) Directions for rating are so located that they are most certain to be read at the optimal time in the rating process.

(5) The traits are objectively defined—defined in terms of pupil behavior, conveying mental images of pupils who possess the trait in highest and lowest degrees. Research has shown that such definitions are necessary if raters are to be in agreement on the meaning of a trait.

(6) Hughes' plan called for the gathering of several ratings on each pupil and the averaging of the ratings, the latter a task which could be performed by a clerk. Research has demonstrated the validity of such an average rating to be greater than the rating given by a single judge. However, Hughes believes that the separate ratings should be kept on file for study because they are sometimes more significant and more revealing than a composite judgment. If, says Hughes, the pupil is co-operative in one classroom but not in another, if he is judged as possessed of high initiative in one situation and not in another, that may tell us considerable about him that ought to be known.[41]

To test the soundness of his method of rating, Hughes correlated intelligence and trait rankings with the results shown in Table 62.[42] The close correspondence of the two coefficients for each trait suggests that the two sets of raters, by virtue of the method employed and the behavioristic definition of the traits, achieved a high state of agreement in what they were doing. The reliability coefficient of .89 is evidence of this agreement. The coefficients are all low enough to signify that these character traits are relatively distinct from that which is measured by general intelligence tests. The first two traits,

[41] "Refining the Estimates of Personal Qualities," *Nation's Schools*, Vol. VII (February, 1931), pp. 55–60.
[42] "Organized Personnel Research and Its Bearing on High-School Problems," *Journal of Educational Research*, Vol. X (December, 1924), p. 389, Table I.

"Quickness of thought" and "Memory," are patently more characteristic of mentality than any of the others, and it is therefore not surprising to find them correlating more highly with intelligence than any of the others.

TABLE 62. Correlation of Intelligence and Trait Ratings in Two Schools

Traits	Senior High School Coefficients	Junior High School Coefficients	Senior High School Rank	Junior High School Rank
Quickness of thought	.42	.45	1	1
Memory	.38	.43	2	2
Force of personality	.37	.38	3	5
Capacity for leadership	.35	.41	4	3
Initiative-aggressiveness	.34	.40	5	4
Control of attention	.33	.37	6	6
Self-confidence	.31	.35	7	8
Sense of accuracy	.29	.36	8	7
Co-operativeness	.27	.28	9	10
Regularity-persistency	.24	.30	10	9
Trustworthiness	.22	.17	11	12
Respect for authority	.13	.23	12	11

Reliability coefficient 0.89

Hughes computed correlations between the traits and found coefficients ranging from .41 to .83, with a median of .68.[43] Thus, apparently, in this particular list of traits, there is considerable overlapping. In rating systems which give freedom for the halo effect to operate, evidence of much higher correlations—monotonously similar coefficients—have been found.[44]

The concluding topic of this section will refer again to Hughes' plan of rating, with suggestions for its adaptation in the interest of greater practicality.

The Graphic Rating Scale

This is perhaps the most widely used form of rating scale despite its violation of two or more of the established principles of rating. A good example is the scale constructed by Turney and shown here as Figures 15A and 15B.[45] As prepared by him, each rater had a sheet for each student, with the directions on the face and all the traits on the back. Seven scale divisions are in-

[43] "General Principles and Results of Rating Trait Characteristics," *Journal of Educational Method,* Vol. IV (June, 1925), p. 430, Table V.

[44] F. B. Knight, *Qualities Related to Success in Teaching.* Teachers College Contributions to Education No. 120 (New York, Teachers College, Columbia University, 1922).

[45] Austin H. Turney, *Factors Other Than Intelligence that Affect Success in High School* (Minneapolis, University of Minnesota Press, 1930), pp. 132–134. The entire scale included nine traits, but only the first four are here shown in Figure 15B.

dicated, with brief descriptive terms for each division and more extended descriptions at the extremes. Turney assigned numerical values to each division on the scale in descending order as follows: 130, 100, 80, 70, 60, 40, and 10. But then, as the rater was permitted to place his cross anywhere on the line (as stated in the directions), Turney assigned values at three more points on the scale between each vertical, so that ratings could be given numerical equivalents as follows: 130, 123, 115, 108, 100, 95, 90, 85, 80, 78, 75, 73, 70, 68, 65, 63, 60, 55, 50, 45, 40, 33, 25, 18, 10. Actually, this step transformed a 7-point scale into a 25-point scale.

With this rating instrument Turney measured the bearing of nine traits of character and personality on high-school achievement in the University High School of the University of Minnesota. Table 63 presents representative findings of the study.[46] The reliability coefficients (Column 1) were obtained by correlating the two ratings which were given in the year the study was made. Column 2 shows coefficients of correlation between ratings and marks which compare favorably with the *r* of .65 between I.Q. and marks. With I.Q. held

FIG. 15A. TRAIT RATING SCALE

Pupil's name . . . . Age . . . .
School grade . . . . Section (high, low, middle) . . . .
Name of rater . . . . Position . . . .
Length of time rater has known pupil . . . .
Date rating made . . . .

DIRECTIONS

1. Ratings should be made according to the following directions, which should be read very carefully before the rating is attempted. The ratings are to become a part of the permanent record of the school, and should, therefore, represent careful, conscientious judgments.

2. In each trait or characteristic named in the scale, compare the subject to be rated with the average child of the same age in the High School.

3. Try to make real distinctions. Do not rate a subject high or low on all traits simply because he is exceptional in some one or a few.

4. In rating more than one subject rate them all on one trait at a time. Then go through and rate them all on the next trait, and so on until the rating is completed.

5. In general it is not advisable to study too long over one trait. Make the best judgment you can and go to the next.

6. Do not omit any ratings.

7. Below each line underline the word that best describes how certain you feel about your judgment. Do this for each trait that you rate.

8. Make your ratings independently of other raters.

9. Locate the cross anywhere on the line. It need not fall at any vertical.

10. One extreme of the line is designed to represent the highest desirable amount of the trait; the other represents an extremely low amount of the trait.

[46] Data taken from Tables 19, 20, 21, and 26.

FIG. 15B

TRAIT 1. SELF-CONFIDENCE

Extreme self-confidence and self-reliance. Relies on own judgment. Courts responsibility.	Decidedly self-reliant	Rather self-confident	Average for age	Rather self-distrustful	Decidedly self-distrustful	Extreme lack of self-confidence. Distrusts own judgment. Avoids responsibility.

Was your judgment on the above trait very certain, fairly certain, rather uncertain, very uncertain? (Underline.)

TRAIT 2. INDUSTRY

Extremely industrious. Constantly and steadily engaged in any activity undertaken.	Decidedly industrious	Rather industrious	Average for age	Rather lazy or negligent	Decidedly lazy or negligent	Extreme lack of industry. Negligent. Quickly leaves task.

Was your judgment on the above trait very certain, fairly certain, rather uncertain, very uncertain? (Underline.)

TRAIT 3. LEADERSHIP

Extraordinary qualities of leadership. Gets others to follow.	Decidedly a leader	Tends to be a leader	Average for age	Tends to follow	Decidedly a follower	Always a follower. Never takes initiative. Suggestible.

Was your judgment on the above trait very certain, fairly certain, rather uncertain, very uncertain? (Underline.)

TRAIT 4. CO-OPERATIVENESS

Extremely co-operative. Always ready to join in common task. Works well in a group.	Decidedly co-operative	Rather co-operative	Average for age	Rather indifferent to group activities	Decidedly opposed to group activities	Extremely un-co-operative. Obstinate. Utterly unable to work in group.

Was your judgment on the above trait very certain, fairly certain, rather uncertain, very uncertain? (Underline.)

constant, as in Column 3, the correlation of industry, perseverance, dependability, and ambition with marks is indeed notably high. In these same traits "achievers" rated very much higher than "non-achievers," as shown by Column 4, these two groups being selected by the comparison of accomplishment with ability.

A first weakness of the graphic scale is the opportunity it gives for the halo effect to assert itself. With a sheet or card for each pupil, the most natural thing to do is to rate a pupil on all traits, then do the same with the

TABLE 63. Evaluation of Ratings of Certain Traits of Character and Personality as Shown by Measures of Reliability, and Relationship of Ratings with Achievement

Trait	(1) Average Reliability Coefficient (20 Raters)	(2) Correlation with Marks (68 Freshmen)	(3) Correlation with Marks (I.Q. Held Constant) (68 Freshmen)	(4) Mean Rating Achievers	Non-Achievers
Self-confidence	.80	.61	.46	80.3	71.5
Industry	.79	.66	.75	92.5	66.5
Leadership	.76	.53	.36	74.6	66.6
Co-operativeness	.65	.64	.57	90.0	73.8
Originality	.75	.69	.42	78.3	73.0
Perseverance	.74	.73	.74	91.1	66.4
Dependability	.77	.71	.73	91.8	68.7
Ambition	.80	.78	.79	92.3	68.9
Personal attractiveness	.81	.17	−.14	75.4	73.7
Total rating score	.88	.81	.74	764.4	627.4
Mental test (I.Q.)	....	.65	....	110.0	121.9

next pupil, and so on. With such a form as Figure 15B, having the "good" end of each scale at the left and the "bad" end at the right, it would be the path of least resistance for a rater who is hurried, lazy, or careless to say to himself, "Harry is a fine boy," and rapidly check down the left hand side of the sheet. Of Joe he might reminisce, "Joe has made a lot of trouble for me," and rapidly check down the right side.

A second weakness of the graphic scale is that it does nothing to compel the rater to distribute his ratees in accordance with the normal curve, or to use all the scale divisions. The tendency of some raters to rate too high and of others to rate too low is unchecked.

Turney apparently recognized these inadequacies of his rating plan and tried to guard against them in the directions which he gave (See Figure 15A) for his raters. In particular, the directions numbered 2, 3, and 4 constitute an effort to thwart the halo tendency and induce the rater to use the whole scale, keeping in mind the average child as a point of reference. Turney's rapport with his raters—a faculty of superior quality, well oriented to the idea of the normal curve—probably induced them to make a conscientious effort to rate their pupils according to his directions.

The Man-to-Man Rating Scale

Frequently the number of persons to be rated is too small for distribution approximating the normal curve. That was true in World War I, when the major was called upon to rate the officers of his battalion on qualities which had to be taken into account for the determination of promotions. To meet that problem Walter Dill Scott originated the man-to-man rating scale. Briefly, the rater was required, first, to create a five-point "master scale" for a given trait by writing on a horizontal line the five officers among all his acquaintances who exemplified the trait in the highest degree, in the lowest degree, in average degree, and in above-average and below-average degrees. Then he compared each ratee with each member of the human scale he had created and wrote his name below the scale name to which he most closely compared. For each additional trait the procedure was the same, first making the master scale, then comparing the ratees with the scale members.

Young employed the man-to-man scale to find the relationship of character traits to success in high-school French.[47] The one hundred students who took beginning French in the eleventh grade had come from three four-year junior high schools. Young procured ratings on certain character traits from their tenth-grade academic teachers. As no teacher had known more than twenty of the ratees, any plan of distribution in accordance with the normal curve was out of the question. Hence, the man-to-man scale was employed. Part of Young's directions to the rating teachers were as follows:

1. Read the first rating sheet. Study especially the "description of trait." Note that this description implies possession of the trait in high degree. Notice that a *Master Scale* is called for.

2. Look over the names of pupils listed in your class book. Select the one who you think possesses this trait in highest degree. Write his or her name under "Highest" on your *Master Scale*. Look through your class book again and select the pupil who you think possesses this trait in lowest degree. . . .

3. You are now ready to rate each of the students on the list given you, as regards *their possession of the trait* for which you have just completed the *Master Scale*. Compare the first student with each of the students of the *Master Scale* as regards *possession of the trait*. . . .

[47] Josephine A. Young, *Deriving Practical Instruments for Predicting Success in High-School French*. M.A. Thesis (Pittsburgh, University of Pittsburgh Library, 1933).

The composited ratings on the trait "Industry" were found to correlate with first-year French marks to the extent of a coefficient of .83.[48] This is marked evidence of the high relationship between this character trait and achievement. The man-to-man scale rating system has much to commend it from the standpoint of logic. As its theory is supported by this small study, its more extended employment may well be recommended.

Suggested Practice for a High School

Too little attention has been paid to character-trait rating. Satisfaction over the objective data derived from the testing of ability and achievement has absorbed guidance workers to such a degree that rating on character traits has been done hurriedly and inadequately, and the results have not been carefully collated and interpreted. Some of these deficiencies in rating practice were brought to light in a study by Masoner of the rating methods employed in one hundred of the best high schools of the country.[49] Of the 345 schools canvassed, 130 replied that they had no plan for personality rating, 115 sent insufficient data or did not reply, while 100 sent copies of the forms they used and fully answered the questionnaire concerning their practice. Of these 100 schools, 75 provided no definitions for traits, 98 made no attempt to obtain any degree of conformity to the normal curve, and only three directed raters to rate all pupils on one trait, then proceed to the second trait, and so on.

To avoid halo, to obtain a distribution of ratees somewhat in conformity to the normal curve, to endeavor to have a common understanding among raters of the meaning of each trait, the writer recommends that a high school adopt a rating plan closely comparable to that devised by W. Hardin Hughes, as described early in this section. Teachers would rate all of their pupils once a year, at the end of the year, when they have had the maximum time to become acquainted with them. They would not be asked to rate the pupils on more than five or six carefully chosen and defined traits. The ratings for each pupil would be averaged, but the separate rating sheets of each teacher would be placed on file.

The major criticism of the Hughes plan of rating is that it is cumbersome and time-consuming to use. The reader can grasp the dimensions of the job Hughes had the Pasadena teachers do, if he will imagine a typical departmentalized teacher who met 150 pupils in his classes every day. Such a teacher distributed his first fifty pupils on a rating sheet for "regularity and persistency," used a second sheet for the second fifty, and a third sheet for the third fifty. Then he proceeded in the same way to rate his pupils for "trustworthiness." By the time he had completed the rating on all twelve of Hughes' traits, he had written 1800 names and made 1800 judgments. He

---

[48] *Ibid.* Based on Table XXII, p. 36.
[49] Paul H. Masoner, *A Critique of Personality Rating Scales.* Ph.D. Thesis (Pittsburgh, University of Pittsburgh Library, 1949).

might endure such an ordeal once as a contribution to the scientific study of education, but the imposition of such labors as normal semester routine would seem to place an undue strain on the professional spirit. The reduction of Hughes' plan proposed in the preceding paragraph might hold the project within feasible and acceptable limits. To be sure that its importance is made evident to the faculty and that it is done well, probably a special time—one half-day—should be set aside for it, and the counselor should supervise its performance to answer questions and to help teachers with exceptional problems.

Because the principal and counselor are called upon in the spring of the year to furnish many references for seniors to colleges and employers, the trait rating for the senior class might well be done in January. A small convenient form could then be devised on which the composite trait profile could be drawn. A brief explanation on the form to inform its reader that the profile represents the composite judgment of the student's teachers on how he ranks in comparison with all the members of the class, and that the ratings were made as part of the school's program of pupil evaluation, would convey an impression of the same objectivity which characterizes the figuring of the pupil's scholastic rank.

At present, the principal is continually called upon to give trait ratings under duress. He receives a reference blank from a college; it calls for the rating of one of the school's graduating seniors on several traits. Under the pressures of such circumstances it is almost inevitable that the rating will be biassed in the direction of leniency. Colleges should much prefer the method described in the two preceding paragraphs, but it would be necessary for high schools and colleges to agree on the five or six traits for rating. At present wide variation prevails on that score. Perhaps agreement might be found in the six traits appearing on the ACE Cumulative Record Folder, reproduced in the next chapter.

A foundation for such improvement of rating practice as is here advocated is to be found in a recently completed research by Gardner.[50] This investigator canvassed the rating forms used by 75 colleges and universities and found that the traits on which ratings were asked could be adequately represented by the following designations: Reliability, Industry, Co-operation, Initiative, Efficiency, and Accuracy. He defined these traits in terms of the behavior of high-school students and obtained ratings by their teachers of all members of the senior classes in eight high schools—a total of 722 students—using a normal curve rating scale similar to that shown in Figure 14. Giving numerical evaluations of 1, 2, 3, 4, and 5 (minimum to maximum) to the intervals on the five-point scale, he found the mean rating to be 3.08 and the mean standard deviation of the ratings to be .8218. These

[50] M. E. Gardner, *Prediction of Academic Success in College from Personality Trait Ratings Obtained for High School Graduates.* Doctoral Dissertation (Pittsburgh, University of Pittsburgh Library, 1958).

data suggest that the rating system forced a spread approximating the normal curve. Intercorrelations of the trait ratings ranged from a coefficient of .743 between Co-operation and Initiative to a coefficient of .907 between Efficiency and Accuracy, with an average of .828. The coefficients of correlation between trait ratings and high school quality point average ranged from .578 for Co-operation to .740 for Accuracy, with an average of .672.

Of the 722 high school seniors thus rated, more than 200 went to college. Gardner was able to obtain college transcripts showing the college records of 190 of these students for a full semester or quarter, and of 119 for a full year. The high school trait ratings of these students were notably higher than those of the entire 722, averaging 3.66 for the 190 and 3.71 for the 119. The coefficients of correlation between the ratings on each trait and the college quality point average of the 119 students were as follows: Reliability, .570; Industry, .574; Co-operation, .355; Initiative, .550; Efficiency, .648; Accuracy, .664. Coefficients were slightly lower for the 190 students.

Gardner's study suggests that character-trait rating can be highly predictive of college success, for the coefficients of all his traits with the exception of Co-operation compare favorably with those obtained for other measures reported in Chapter 12. Furthermore, it is apparent that a useful rating scheme might be made with still fewer traits than he used. Further research may enable us to rescue character-trait rating from its present badly neglected and misused state as a method of pupil analysis. Actually, however, the immediate problem seems to be the improvement of practice to correspond to the level of existing knowledge of rating.

QUESTIONS, PROBLEMS, INVESTIGATIONS

1. With what you have learned from Chapters 12 and 13 as a beginning, proceed through further study to plan the total program of testing for a given school or college.

2. In a senior high school homeroom, search out each pupil's vocational interests by using the methods of observation and inquiry described in Chapter 11. Then use the Kuder Preference Record to ascertain their interests, and compare results.

3. Krathwohl's evidence cited in this chapter denies the existence of a generalized trait of industry. Does this imply that a person's industry is just a function of his interests? Discuss this issue in class. Discuss it with a senior high school homeroom group.

4. Draw up a form or forms, which could be mimeographed, for the valid rating of pupils on the six traits shown on the ACE Cumulative Record Folder.

5. Examine and evaluate the rating forms used by colleges in obtaining judgments on their applicants for admission.

6. Examine Falk's *Your High School Record—Does It Count?* with a view to summarizing frequencies of mention of certain character and personality traits.

7. With a group of pupils who have been rated by several judges using a sound method, test the theory of a generalized trait by measuring the degrees of dispersion of judgments for each pupil.

SELECTED REFERENCES

ANASTASI, Anne, *Psychological Testing* (New York, Macmillan, 1954), Chs. 20, 21.

ANDERSON, Rose G., "Do Aptitudes Support Interests?" *Personnel and Guidance Journal,* Vol. XXXII (September, 1953), pp. 14–17.

BRADSHAW, F. F., *American Council on Education Rating Scale.* Archives of Psychology, Vol. CXIX (1930), pp. 1–80.

BRAYFIELD, Arthur H., "Clerical Interest and Clerical Aptitude," *Personnel and Guidance Journal,* Vol. XXXI (February, 1953), pp. 304–306.

BUROS, Oscar, *The Fourth Mental Measurements Yearbook* (Highland Park, N.J., Gryphon Press, 1953).

———, *The Third Mental Measurements Yearbook* (New Brunswick, N.J., Rutgers University Press, 1949).

CARTER, Harold D., *Vocational Interests and Job Orientation—A Ten-Year Review.* Applied Psychology Monographs No. 2 (Stanford, Cal., Stanford University Press, 1944).

CHRISTENSEN, Thomas E., "Some Observations with Respect to the Kuder Preference Record," *Journal of Educational Research,* Vol. XL (October, 1946), pp. 96–107.

CRONBACH, Lee, *Essentials of Psychological Testing* (New York, Harper, 1949), Chs. 13–15.

CROSS, Orrin H., "A Study of Faking on the Kuder Preference Record," *Educational and Psychological Measurement,* Vol. X (Summer, 1950), pp. 271–277.

DARLEY, John G., *Clinical Aspects and Interpretation of the Strong Vocational Interest Blank* (New York, The Psychological Corporation, 1941).

———, "Tested Maladjustment Related to Clinically Diagnosed Maladjustment," *Journal of Applied Psychology,* Vol. XXI (December, 1937), pp. 632–642.

———, and HAGENAH, Theda, *Vocational Interest Measurement: Theory and Practice* (Minneapolis, Minn., University of Minnesota Press, 1955).

ELLIS, Albert, "Recent Research with Personality Inventories," *Journal of Consulting Psychology,* Vol. XVII, No. 1 (1953), pp. 45–49.

———, "The Validity of Personality Questionnaires," *Psychological Bulletin,* Vol. XLIII (September, 1946), pp. 385–440.

FEDER, D. D., and BAER, L. Opal, "A Comparison of Test Records and Clinical Evaluations of Personality Adjustment," *Journal of Educational Psychology,* Vol. XXXII (February, 1941), pp. 133–144.

FRYER, Douglas, *Measurement of Interests in Relation to Human Adjustment* (New York, Holt, 1931).

GUILFORD, J. P., *Psychometric Methods* (New York, McGraw-Hill, 1936), Ch. 9.

HAHN, Milton E., "Notes on the Kuder Preference Record," *Occupations,* Vol. XXIII (May, 1945), pp. 467–470.

HUGHES, W. Hardin, "General Principles and Results of Rating Trait Characteristics," *Journal of Educational Method,* Vol. IV (June, 1925), pp. 421–431.

———, "Organized Personnel Research and Its Bearing on High-School Problems," *Journal of Educational Research,* Vol. X (December, 1924), pp. 386–396.

———, "A Rating Scale for Individual Capacities, Attitudes, and Interests," *Journal of Educational Method,* Vol. III (October, 1923), pp. 56–65.

———, "Refining the Estimates of Personal Qualities," *Nation's Schools,* Vol. VII (February, 1931), pp. 55–60.

———, "Why Intelligence Scores Are Not More Highly Predictive of School Success," *Educational Administration and Supervision,* Vol. XII (January, 1926), pp. 44–48.

KRATHWOHL, Wm. C., "Effects of Industrious and Indolent Work Habits on Grade Prediction in College Mathematics," *Journal of Educational Research,* Vol. XLIII (September, 1949), pp. 32–40.

———, "Specificity of Over- and Under-Achievement in College Courses," *Journal of Applied Psychology,* Vol. XXXVI (April, 1952), pp. 103–106.

KUDER, Frederic, "The Use of Preference Measurement in Vocational Guidance," *Educational Record,* Vol. XXIX (January, 1948, Supplement 17), pp. 65–76.

LONGSTAFF, Howard P., "Fakability of the Strong Interest Blank and the Kuder Preference Record," *Journal of Applied Psychology,* Vol. XXXII (August, 1948), pp. 360–369.

MALLINSON, George G., and CRUMRINE, Wm. M., "An Investigation of the Stability of Interests of High-School Students," *Journal of Educational Research,* Vol. XLV (January, 1952), pp. 369–383.

ROTHNEY, John W. M., and SCHMIDT, Louis G., "Some Limitations of Interest Inventories," *Personnel and Guidance Journal,* Vol. XXXIII (December, 1954), pp. 199–204.

STRONG, Edward K., Jr., "Interest Scores While in College of Occupations Engaged in 20 Years Later," *Educational and Psychological Measurement,* Vol. XI (Autumn, 1951), pp. 335–348.

———, "The Role of Interests in Guidance," *Occupations,* Vol. XXVII (May, 1949), pp. 517–522.

———, *Vocational Interests Eighteen Years after College* (Minneapolis, Minn., University of Minnesota Press, 1955).

———, *Vocational Interests of Men and Women* (Stanford, Cal., Stanford University Press, 1943).

SUPER, Donald E., *Appraising Vocational Fitness by Means of Psychological Tests* (New York, Harper, 1949), Chs. 14–19.

SYMONDS, Percival M., *Diagnosing Personality and Conduct* (New York, Century, 1931).

TURNEY, Austin H., *Factors Other Than Intelligence that Affect Success in High School* (Minneapolis, University of Minnesota Press, 1930).

WATSON, Goodwin B., "The Measurement of the Less Tangible Qualities," *Vocational Guidance Magazine,* Vol. IV (March, 1926), pp. 281–289.

WITTENBORN, J. R., TRIGGS, Frances O., and FEDER, Daniel D., "A Comparison of Interest Measurement by the Kuder Preference Record and the Strong Vocational Interest Blanks for Men and Women," *Educational and Psychological Measurement,* Vol. III (Autumn, 1943), pp. 239–257.

CHAPTER 14

Synthesis, Diagnosis, and Prognosis

THE PRECEDING THREE CHAPTERS have been devoted to analysis of the individual, with special reference to performance of the guidance function. The gathering of personal data, the utilization of school marks, the measuring of the pupil's achievement, abilities, and interests with standardized tests, and the rating of his traits of character and personality—these procedures have been described as major steps in getting to know the pupil as an individual person. Meanings of the various items of evidence thus accumulated have been stressed—meanings for the choice of educational and vocational opportunities, and meanings for the various types of adjustment.

The meaning of any single item, however, even though it has been made the object of searching scientific investigation, is limited. It is not the same for any two individuals. It plays its role in the life of the individual only as an element in the mosaic pattern which is unique for that individual. Hence, the information which we have in bits and pieces must be assembled and synthesized for each pupil so that we see him as a whole person dynamically related to and influenced by his own peculiar environment. This chapter is concerned with the processes and devices of such synthesis and with the ensuing diagnosis and prognosis which are then made possible.

The first section of the chapter describes what may be termed a sub-assembly in the task of synthesis, namely, the testing program. While Chapters 12 and 13 presented the different types of tests and cited selected researches to define their values, no program of testing was outlined. So numerous are the tests available and so important is the role of tests in a modern guidance program that thoughtful consideration must be given to their selection and administration.

THE TESTING PROGRAM

Testing Not Exclusively a Guidance Feature

As pointed out in the introduction to Chapter 11, understanding the pupil is an essential condition for the discharge of the whole educational undertaking. The selection and administration of standardized tests, and the recording of results, will not, therefore, be conceived of as solely serving the guidance function. The counselor, as guidance specialist, will not bear sole responsibility for the testing program. While it is true that some tests, among the types described in Chapters 12 and 13, are more specifically designed to serve the guidance function than any other purpose, to a major extent the same tests which are used for guidance must be thought of as serving instruction and curriculum making as well. Through the study of standardized test results, the teacher is the better able to adapt instructional procedures. School and departmental curriculum committees obtain major cues for curriculum revision from the revelations of pupil capacity which they derive from analysis of test results. "Maid-of-all-work" is Bingham's characterization of the testing program,[1] a concept which may be given the following simple schematic representation:

$$
\text{Testing}
\begin{cases}
\text{to serve } \textit{Instruction} \\
\text{to serve } \textit{Curriculum Making} \\
\text{to serve } \textit{Guidance}
\end{cases}
$$

With this view of functional relationships it becomes apparent that the formulation of the testing program is a matter of concern to the whole faculty. Leadership might well be vested in a faculty member who has specialized in educational and psychological measurements in his graduate study. Or, it might be assumed by a committee composed of the principal, counselor, and two or three teachers. Leadership, in any event, should be interpreted to mean consultation with the faculty to ascertain the kinds of measurements they feel are needed, orientation of the faculty to the possible values in the different types of standardized tests, and helping the faculty to understand and interpret test results. To build a defensible testing program and to use it for the maximum advantage of pupils—that is the goal.

Selecting Tests

Within the limits here permissible for the treatment of the function of test selection, only a few general pointers can be given, only a few words of caution recorded. Actually, the selection of tests should be performed by someone who has considerable expert knowledge of test construction, standardization, and validation. He needs to be able to read, comprehend, and evaluate the researches which have been made to measure the validity and reliability of various tests, and such abilities depend largely on a command of educational statistics. Very often the school counselor is better trained for this task than any other member of the faculty.

Fortunately, in the work of Oscar Buros, test consumers now have a most helpful guide in test selection. Beginning in the late '30s, Professor Buros

---

[1] Walter V. Bingham, "A National Perspective on Testing and Guidance," *Educational Record*, Supplement No. 12, Vol. XX (January, 1939), pp. 137–150.

has issued a series of "yearbooks" which are compilations of reviews of the various tests. The reviews are especially written for the yearbooks, and written by authorities who are widely known and accepted for their competence. The candor of their evaluations signifies the objectivity of the scientist. With each test is listed a bibliography of the researches concerning it. A growing effect of Buros' yearbooks should be the raising of the quality of tests, as commercial publishers will be increasingly hesitant about placing a shoddy product on the market, when they know it will be impartially and expertly evaluated. But still true, it seems, is the remark of the sage that "what the country needs is fewer and better tests."[2]

Tests and a testing program planned for a senior high school have been described by Andrews[3] as a "basic testing program." Tests were selected to serve the following purposes: helping pupils with subject elections for the eleventh and twelfth grades, vocational planning, and personal adjustment. With due regard for these purposes, the following general factors were also taken into account: (1) the grade level at which tests should be administered; (2) the essential areas to be measured; (3) the fewest measuring devices that would yield adequate basic information for counseling purposes; (4) the extent to which the program would disrupt regularly scheduled classes; and (5) the extent to which the program would interfere with the counselor's other duties. The tests chosen were the *Differential Aptitude Tests,* the *Kuder Preference Record,* and the *Bell Adjustment Inventory.* They were administered in Grade 10B, the DAT battery being given in one afternoon and the following forenoon.

Minimum testing in the elementary and junior high school years should include the administration of general intelligence tests at three-year intervals, perhaps in Grades 1, 4, and 7, and some achievement testing. It is particularly essential to measure periodically the progress each child is making in the fundamental processes, so that adaptations can be made in the curriculum and instructional procedures. A general achievement battery should be employed at two or three intervals in the child's progress through these years. In a 6-3-3 school system, a crucial time for such achievement testing would seem to be at the end of the sixth grade, so that somewhat definitive information about each child can be transferred with him as he enters the junior high school. Other tests which may well be considered for the minimum program in these years are prognostic tests for measuring aptitude for the study of algebra and foreign language. Described in Chapter 12, noteworthy predictive value was cited for such tests. They would be administered early in Grade 8A, so that their results would be available for curricular counseling for Grade 9B.

[2] Recent Buros' yearbooks are: *The Third Mental Measurements Yearbook* (New Brunswick, N.J., Rutgers University Press, 1949); *The Fourth Mental Measurements Yearbook* (Highland Park, N.J., Gryphon Press, 1953).

[3] E. Brenneta Andrews, "A Basic Testing Program in Guidance," *Pittsburgh Schools,* Vol. XXVI (January-February, 1952), pp. 72–82.

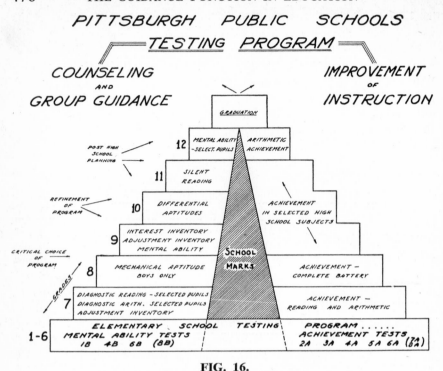

FIG. 16.

Figure 16[4] depicts a comprehensive testing program for a school system which is organized partly on a 6-3-3 basis and partly on an 8-4 basis. Readers may be critical of some elements of the program, but the comprehensive planning is in welcome contrast to the piecemeal and fragmentary arrangements which prevail in many school systems. Showing school marks in the drawing is indeed a desirable recognition of their importance as measures of the pupil's ability and achievement.

Not only should tests be selected for their individual soundness and their possibilities of service to guidance, instruction, and curriculum making, but each should fit into a planned program. Unnecessary duplication should be avoided. It is the impression of this writer that some schools are testing excessively. For example, the reader is requested to turn forward a few pages in this chapter to the facsimile reproduction of an American Council on Education Cumulative Record Folder, shown as Figures 17A, B, C, and D. On Figure 17A it is noted in the "Previous School Record" of Mary Margaret Anderson that she had earned "mental test scores which indicate intelligence quotients above 130." Yet in her secondary-school years it is recorded that she was given the Henmon-Nelson in the seventh grade and the

---

[4] Obtained through the courtesy of Oscar Schwarm, Director, Division of Guidance and Child Accounting, Pittsburgh Public Schools.

Kuhlmann-Anderson in each of the succeeding years. Nothing new was learned about the girl, and the testing authorities must have known that nothing new would be learned about her. Such practice is wasteful of tests and wasteful of time spent in administering, scoring, and recording. The loss of instructional time is irritating to teachers.

Further examination of Figures 17A and B shows the Stanford Achievement Tests to have been given in each of the junior high school years, the Iowa Reading examination in the tenth and eleventh grades, and the Co-operative Mathematics Test in Grades 10, 11, and 12. While it may be argued that these repetitions are justified as measures of progress, the administering of the tests in September, October, and November indicates that they were not a substitute for the usual teacher-made, year-end tests of achievement. To the mind of this writer the situation represents an excessive employment of standardized tests. (It is not the purpose here to offer any general evaluation of the testing program indicated in Figures 17A and B. That program was carried out in the years 1936–41.)

Administering Tests

While the selection of tests should be accomplished by procedures which are democratic and deliberative, the program of giving the tests to the children is definitely an administrative function, a task to be closely directed by a competent person and executed with exactitude by him or by those who work under his direction. Standardized tests must be given precisely according to the conditions laid down in their manuals, if the results are to be valid and comparable to the norms furnished with them. The directions to be given the pupils are carefully stated and must not be deviated from. Most tests are exactly timed as a whole and sometimes in subordinate parts. These characteristics of standardized testing are common knowledge to the readers of this book, but careful planning is needed to be sure that they are meticulously observed.

This writer will hazard the opinion that many test scores of the high-school pupils across the country are invalid. In those schools in which selected test-givers are carefully coached for the giving of a test—even to the extent of taking the test themselves under the direction of the coach—and a serious effort is made to prepare them for every detail, test results will generally be dependable. But in too many schools the testing is done by some broad class of teachers, such as homeroom teachers or English teachers. Preparation is haphazard. Sometimes the tests are stuffed in the teachers' postoffice boxes. Sometimes the teachers have no coaching but are simply expected to read over the manual.

Common sense should tell us that teachers vary a great deal in their capacity for rigorous adherence to standardized test conditions. Some are careless. Some are poor disciplinarians. Some are young and inexperienced. And a small percentage are congenitally inaccurate. While the giving of the

Anderson | MARY | MARGARET | MAE | BAPTIST | Amden, Mass. Feb 12, 1923 | M (F) (W) C Y

LAST NAME | FIRST | MIDDLE | NICKNAME | RELIGION | DATE AND PLACE OF BIRTH | SEX | COLOR

ADDRESS AND TELEPHONE: 11 Irving Terrace Circle 5600 | Same | Same | Same | Same | 2104 Maple Ave. East 0413 | Same

PREVIOUS SCHOOL RECORD: Names and Types of Schools Attended, Achievement in Subjects and Activities, School Difficulties Encountered. Summary of Test Results

Attended Paramount elementary school including Kindergarten. Very good record throughout. Citizenship always marked excellent. Work has always been commensurate with mental test scores which indicate intelligence quotients above 130. Tested reading performance above eighth grade level while in sixth grade. Superior performances in Art, Music, and Arithmetic. Family very cooperative with school and much interested in achievements of children. Excellent health and attendance records. Mary should wear her glasses in school.

Names and Type of School Attended	West Jr. High	Same	Same	Amden Sr. High	Same	Same
COUNSELOR	Miss Watson	Mr. Robinson	Mr. Robinson	Mr. Rones	Mr. Rones	Miss Cowan	Miss Cowan
AGE (As of Sept. 1)	12-7	13-7	14-7	15-7	16-7	17-7
SCHOOL YEAR AND GRADE	1936 7	1937 8	1938 9	1939 10	1940 11	1941 12

ACADEMIC ACHIEVEMENT

English:
- Lit. and Comp.
- Oral
- Grammar

Lang.:
- French
- Latin — Dropped

Math:
- Arithmetic
- Algebra
- Geometry
- Advanced Math.

Science:
- Chemistry

Social Studies:
- Soc. Studies
- American Hist.

Other Subjects:
- Practical Arts
- Drawing
- Music — Chorus
- Spelling

Physical Education

TEST RECORD

ACADEMIC APTITUDE (Sex, H. A. and I. Q. If Preferred)	TEST	Min. Score	%
Grade 7	Henmon-Nelson	S 113	98
Grade 8	Kuhl-Anderson	S (IQ-131)	
Grade 9	Kuhl-Anderson / Stan-Binet (L)	S (IQ-131) / N (IQ-142)	
Grade 10	Kuhl-Anderson	S (IQ-130)	
Grade 11	Kuhl-Anderson / ACE Psych.	S (IQ-130) 95 / N 117	
Grade 12	Kuhl-Anderson / ACE Psych. (College Form)	S (IQ-130) / N 154	96

READING	TEST	Min. Score	%
Grade 7	Stanford Ach. Paragraph M / Word Meaning / Spelling	S 113 98 / S 105 77 / S 102 85	
Grade 8	Stanford Ach. Paragraph M / Inglis Vocabulary	S 115 81 / S 76 92	
Grade 9	Stanford Ach. Paragraph M / Word Meaning	S 115 84 / S 109 74	
Grade 10	Iowa Reading Comprehension / Speed / W. Vocabulary	S 140 83 / S 39 85 / S 43 78	
Grade 11	Comprehension / Speed / W. Vocabulary	N 185 94 / N 43 89 / N 46 80	
Grade 12	Coop. Reading Level / Speed / W Vocabulary	O 66 90 / O 68 93 / O 60 89	

FIG. 17A.

478

FIG. 17B.

ACHIEVEMENT AND OTHER TESTS				Minnesota Clerical																
				Names	N		Coop. French	N	66	74	Minnesota Clerical	O			148	85				
				Numbers	N		Coop. Chemistry	N	64	77	Numbers	O		16A	87					
Language Usage	S	107	71	History-Civics	S	93	53					Coop. Am. History	O		53	51				
History-Civics	S	100	65	Geography	S	96	36					Coop. Math	O		51	95				
Geography	S	89	32					Coop. French	S	52	76									
Phys.-Hygiene	S	95	80					Coop. Latin	S	65	61									
Arith-Reasoning	S	105	70	Arith-Reasoning	S	110	77	Coop. Math	O	30	80									
Arith-Computation	S	100	72	Arith-Computation	S	105	54													
Arith-Competation	S	95	47	M-S Art Judgment	S	42	79	Minn. P. Form Board	N	47	75									

INTERPRETATION OF TEST RECORD AND ITS RELATION TO ACADEMIC ACHIEVEMENT (In the interpretation of test scores consider differences in scores used. In converting records to service bases of norms indicate kinds of norms.)

Superior in ability to do school work and frequently finds that work is not challenging enough for her. When this occurs she keeps busy with so many out-of-school activities that she neglects some school assignments.

Enthusiastic and exceptionally efficient reader. Can work accurately and fast on objective tests but finds teachers' tests based on cumulative drill work vary difficult. Could do much better in languages if she could see more reason for doing them.

Although Mary continues to make high scores on objective tests of ability she has difficulty with cumulative subjects where her background work is irregular and spotty. Finds it hard to settle down to drill which teachers recommend. French teacher says she could be an "A" student if she would do assignments. Performance in advanced Math very good despite fact that she had not covered all prerequisites. Mother advised her to carry on all co-curricular activities and have a full pleasant senior year.

ATTENDANCE (Excuses if irregular)

Absent 10 days - colds | No Absences | Same | Same | Same | Missed occasional classes for rehearsals and clubs

SIGNIFICANT ACTIVITIES AND ACCOMPLISHMENTS THAT GIVE EVIDENCE REGARDING INTERESTS AND POWERS

INTERESTS REPORTED BY STUDENT
Art. Lettering, drawing / Group sports / Vocal music | Art. Copy / Baseball + hockey teams / Music | Art / Copy / Any activity which brought contact with other people | Art / ← Same / Said she had read "all" the books in the library | Any opportunity to work or play with others | ← Same / clubs, dates, games.

EXPERIENCES IN SCHOOL
Choir | Art editor school paper / Glee club / Chorus | Art editor school paper / Designed cover for annual / Glee club / Chorus | Glee club | Glee club - president / Lead in Gilbert-Sullivan | Glee club - chorus / Duchess in Gondoliers

OUT OF SCHOOL AND SUMMER EXPERIENCES
Sunday school regular attendance / Scouts / Played at home in summer | Church choirs | Church choir / Designed original greeting cards | Church / Church choir / Leader church student group | Church choir / ← same | Church choir / chairman missionary group in church

NOTE TYPE, DURATION, HOURS PER WEEK, EARNINGS AND OTHER SIGNIFICANT FACTS

WORK EXPERIENCES
NONE | NONE | NONE | Assistant to secretary of school. No pay. Efficient worker | NONE | Cares for children in evenings. Paid $4 for evening. / 12 to 16 hours per month / Demonstrator-food show one week $15 | Secretary in position where math is used and then statistics. / Paid $6 monthly 20 hours.

FINANCIAL AID (Type and Amount)
NONE | NONE | NONE | NONE | NONE | N.Y.A. clerical $6 monthly 20 hours | NONE

Educational / Pupil
Go to college-then get married | Many vague ideas | Commercial artist / Rather discouraged choice of career in comm. art | Commercial artist | Teaching, math. or work in statistics. / Free choice own career but interest not yet limited | Secretary in position where math is used and then statistics.

Occupational / Parents / Plans / Counselor
Wait till school performance observed | None stated / Encouraged to continue may consider any career requiring college training | consider any career requiring college training | ← Same / ← Same | Further study of college and further training recommended | Parents agree with above Good compromise

HEALTH AND PHYSICAL CHARACTERISTICS (Vigor or limitations; assets, disabilities or limitations)
Should wear glasses for reading / No evidence of presence or absence of vigor / Rather plump | Vigorous - peppy / Radiant health / Beautiful blonde hair and fine color of complexion | Stopped wearing glasses because she thought they detracted from appearance. Nurse says she should wear them. Same | Will not wear glasses. / Excellent health and much vigor | SAME | Same / Same / Same

DISCIPLINE
Academic / Personal
NONE | NONE | Some make-up time required to get home-work done. | NONE | NONE | NONE | NONE

NOTE SIGNIFICANT ITEMS: Health, decease of either parent, birthplaces, citizenship, changes in type of occupation of parents, language spoken, type of community, study conditions or other factors such as "broken home".

All members of family appear to be in good health. Comfortable home in good residential area. Seems to be exceptionally pleasant home life. Both parents are anxious to give the children good educational opportunities but could not afford college training for all without great sacrifice. Family active in all affairs of their church and show great interest in community activities. Excellent study conditions are provided for the children and both parents cooperate effectively with the school.

10/40 Mother president of P.T.A.

Family	Type of Occupation	Education Degree and Kind	Religion	
Father Charles L.	Cabinet-maker	High school-Evening School-instructed Study	Baptist	
Mother Nora M.	Housewife	High and Secretarial school	Baptist	
Step-Parent or Guardian				
Sibling	Sex			Birthdate
Dorothy	F	Housewife	High school graduate	1918
Ruth	F	Secretary	High and secretarial	1921
Leslie	F	Student	One grade below Mary	1924

DESCRIPTION OF BEHAVIOR (Made by all those who have had sufficient opportunity to observe the pupil)

Key to persons making the descriptions below: Ad-Advisor, Ag-Agriculture, Ar-Art, D-Dramatics, E-English, F-French, G-German, HR-Home Room teacher, HE-Home Economics, L-Latin, M-Mathematics, Mu-Music, NS-Natural Science, SS-Social Science, Others,

		8	9	10	11	12	
RESPONSIBILITY	Responsible and Resourceful: Carries Through Whatever it Undertakes, and Also Shows Initiative and Versatility in Accomplishing and Enlarging Upon Undertakings.	SS-M-MU H.R.	SS H.R.	M	M-D	M-D-E HR-MU	Apparent decrease in responsibility in ninth grade due to increased assumption of duties out of school so that her assignments were hurriedly done or neglected.
	Conscientious: Completes Without External Compulsion Whatever is Assigned But is Unlikely to Enlarge the Scope of Assignments.	E	E-L	H.R.	H.R.	SS	
	Generally Dependable: Usually Carries Through Undertakings, Self-Assumed or Assigned by Others, Requiring Only Occasional Reminder or Compulsion.	SS	E-M	L	E		
	Selectively Dependable: Shows High Persistence in Undertakings in Which There is Particular Interest, But is Less Likely to Carry Through Other Assignments.		L	L	E		11th grade - Class work fairly well done but laboratory exercises neglected seriously.
	Unreliable: Can Be Relied Upon to Complete Undertakings Only When They Are of Moderate Duration or Difficulty and Then Only With Much Prodding and Supervision.				N.S.		
	Irresponsible: Cannot Be Relied Upon to Complete Any Undertakings Even When Constantly Prodded and Guided.						
CREATIVENESS	General: Approaches Whatever He Does With Active Imagination and Originality, So That He Contributes Something That is His Own.	SS H.R.	SS H.R.	M	M	E	7th grade: Other pupils say she is "full of ideas".
	Specific: Makes Distinctly Original and Significant Contributions in One or More Fields.	AR-E-MU	M	HR	HR	HR-M-SS	9th - Much of her art work is now copy but occasionally she does original.
	Promising: Shows a Degree of Creativeness That Indicates the Likelihood of Valuable Original Contribution in Some Field, Although the Contributions Already Made Have Not Proved to Be Particularly Significant.	AR-M-MU		E	E	MU	
	Limited: Shows the Desire To Contribute His Own Thinking and Expression to Situations, But His Degree of Imagination and Originality is Not, in General, High Enough to Have Much Influence on His Accomplishments.	L-SS	L-E				11th - Creativeness best shown in her management of groups.
	Imitative: Makes Little or No Creative Contributions, Yet Shows Sufficient Imagination to See the Implications in the Creation of Others and to Make Use of Their Ideas or Accomplishments.			L-E			
	Unimaginative: Has Given Practically No Evidence of Originality or Creativeness in Imagination or Action.				N.S.		
INFLUENCE	Controlling: His Influence Habitually Shapes the Opinions, Activities, or Ideals of His Associates.	SS-M H.R.	E-L HR	L-M HR	M HR	M-E-MU HR.	9th - Mary is frequently chosen by others to carry out ideas which she presents. She can win others to her cause by her logic and by her effectiveness in getting things done.
	Contributing: His Influence, While Not Controlling, Strongly Affects the Opinions, Activities, or Ideals of His Associates.	SS-M-E-MU H.R.	SS-M	E	HR	SS	
	Varying: His Influence Varies, Having Force When Particular Ability, Skill, Experience or Circumstance Gives it Opportunity or Value.	E-MU	L	E-NS			
	Co-Operating: Has No Very Definite Influence on His Associates, But Contributes to Group Thinking and Action Because of Some Discrimination in Regard to Ideas and Leaders.				N.S.		
	Passive: Has No Definite Influence on His Associates, Being Carried Along by the Nearest or Strongest Influence.						
ADJUSTABILITY	Secure: Appears to Feel Secure in His Social Relationships and is Accepted by the Groups of Which He is a Part.	SS-M-MU-E HR	SS-M-MU-E HR-L	M-E-L HR	M-E-NS HR	SS-M-MU-E HR	8th - At ease with any group of students or adults.
	Hesitant: Appears to Have Some Anxiety About His Social Relationships Although He is Accepted by the Groups of Which He is a Part.						
	Neutral: Shows the Desire to Have an Established Place in the Group, But is, in General, Treated With Indifference.						Described in senior year book as "most popular".
	Withdrawn: Withdraws From Others to an Extent That Prevents His Being a Fully Accepted Member of His Group.						
	Not Accepted: Has Characteristics of Person or Behavior That Prevent His Being an Accepted Member of His Group.						

FIG. 17C.

	GRADE	7	8	9	10	11	12

CONCERN FOR OTHERS

- **Generally Concerned:** Shows Balance in Considering Welfare of Himself and Others and Does What He Can About it.
- **Selectively Concerned:** Shows Concern by Attitude and Action About Certain Problems of Welfare of Persons.
- **Reactive:** Not Strongly Concerned About the Welfare of Others Unless a Situation Materially Affects Him.
- **Inactive:** Professes Concern About Welfare of Others But Does Nothing.
- **Unconcerned:** Shows Little or No Concern For the Welfare of Others.

Note (col 12): This trait takes its form most frequently in her religious activities and action, but she thinks and acts in what might be described as an altruistic manner very frequently

SERIOUS PURPOSE

- **Purposeful:** Has Definite Purposes and Plans and Carries Through to the Best of His Ability Undertakings Consistent With This Purpose.
- **Limited:** Makes Plans and Shows Determination in Attacking Short Time Projects That Interest Him But Has Not Yet Thought Out Goals for Himself.
- **Potential:** Takes Things as They Come, Meeting Situations Somewhat on the Spur of the Moment Yet May Be Capable of Serious Purpose if Once Aroused.
- **Vacillating:** Makes Plans That Are Fairly Definite, But Cannot Be Counted on for the Determination to Carry Them Through.
- **Vague:** Is Likely to Drift Without the Decisiveness and Persistence That Will Enable Him to Carry Out His Vaguely Conceived Plans.

Note (col 12):
- 8th grade: Seems to have lost sight of her goals.
- 11th grade: Drifting along. Needs help.
- 12th when future educational and vocational decision was made in February she regained her seriousness of purpose.

EMOTIONAL STABILITY

Describe Typical Behavior and Significant Variation in It With Respect to Such Factors as Apathy, Excitability, Over-Sensitiveness, Stability

- Grade 8: Bubbles over with enthusiasm about her activities
- Grade 9: Mary's many activities are carried through with serious intent. She is not frivolous. She enjoys them and gets things done.
- Col 11: Rather steady companionship with some introverted tendencies but an outstanding student in academic work.
- Col 12: Worked through serious problem of choice of further education and vocation in a calm and objective manner

Additional Comments About Behavior

- Grade 9: Mother attempts to supervise her reading but she gets in a few mystery stories of her own selection
- Grade 10: Some narrowing of activities needed now. She is working on list of activities, to decide on deletions
- Col 11: Parents gave her choice of and for college if she should seriously intend to go but she drifted into too many activities to find time for serious study.
- Col 12: Enrollment in good secretarial school is satisfactory

Tentative Synthesis and Suggestions for Guidance Made During, or at Close of Each School Year

- Grade 7: Encourage continuance of many co-curricular and community activities as try-out experiences / Elect college-preparatory courses.
- Grade 8: SAME / Tried to arrange for more challenging experiences in school.
- Grade 9: SAME / Continue college-preparatory course in senior high with Latin elective. Some help in budgeting time needed
- Grade 10: Continue college preparatory Latin this year. Elect chemistry as tryout in science field.
- Col 11: Attempt to win competitive college scholarship failed. Refused suggestions about electives and chose advanced mathematics without prerequisites
- Col 12: ...compromise with financial problem and waning enthusiasm for academic study. Advise secretarial school or the record of her entrance and remind about mathematics ability at time of placement.

NOTES: 7th grade— Early reputation as an artist keeps her interested and working in this field. She promised to keep scrap-book record of her work.

8th Check on scrap-book indicates that much of her work is copy from magazines.

9th Chorus and choir directors say she has a good voice, but say it is not strong enough to warrant serious consideration of a career in music. Discontinued piano lessons this year because she thought she knew enough to meet avocational needs and time for practice limited

10th Mother says Mary is not, and never will be, a real student. Mary may have chosen the kinds of activities which provide the best kind of education for her.

12th Counselor predicts satisfactory work in secretarial school, easy placement on a job, a short working period, and early marriage.

POST SCHOOL AND FOLLOW-UP INFORMATION

	Dates
College	
Other Schools Secretarial School	Entered Smith Sept. 1941
Work	
Marriage	
Civic Activities	

FIG. 17D.

tests that have been presented in these chapters does not require a specialist, to delegate test-giving to the general run of teachers is not wise.

Testing should be performed by a limited number of teachers who are selected for their known capacity for doing the job. They know the importance of following the conditions prescribed; they easily command the pupils' attention and effectively give directions. An important element in their competence is their ability to call forth the pupils' best efforts. They help pupils to feel that the test is important and that the results will be used for pupil advantage. They cultivate intense concentration but without excessive tension or anxiety. They take care of emergencies with the minimum of disturbance.

Scoring Tests and Recording Results

These functions are clerical. They should be performed under professional direction and planning, with a view to the most effective professional use. As the trend toward machine scoring of tests is advancing, and more and more tests are offered in alternate forms for machine scoring *or* hand scoring, the cost and the facilities for each method should certainly be investigated and compared before ordering tests.

The reference already made to Figures 17A and B has made it evident that test results should be recorded in the cumulative record folder of the pupil. The form provided in that folder does not allow for the recording of all the items that were indicated on page 381 of Chapter 12 as desirable in the case of an intelligence test, but by using an extra line, all items could be recorded.

It is difficult to provide, within the practical limits of a record folder, for all the alternative forms of reporting that may be desired with the different tests. For example, Figures 17A and B provide for four items on all tests, namely, test, month (year is shown above), score, percentile. But on many tests it would be desirable to compute and record the *local* percentile, so that a teacher or counselor can quickly see how an individual compares with his fellow students in his own school. Another form of expressing test results which is widely used and certainly very meaningful is that of "grade level" or "educational age." It applies to many achievement tests, particularly in the elementary and junior high school years, but not to intelligence or prognostic tests.

To help solve the problem of recording, many test publishers provide forms for the individual pupil's test results. Such a form is shown as Figure 12 in Chapter 12. The graphic representation conveys a near-instantaneous assessment of the individual. Raw scores and percentile ranks, however, are also recorded, as also the form of the battery, the norm used, and the date of testing. The well-known "profile sheet" for the Kuder Preference Record is another example of an individual report form which is effective representation of test results.

These forms should be filed in the individual pupil's cumulative record folder, so that all test results on a pupil will be assembled in the one place which is the repository for his school marks and all other data concerning him. For the most part, these profile sheets provided by the test publishers are so organized that they simply give a snapshot view of the pupil as of a given date rather than conveying any concept of growth or change, and the persons who consult them should recognize this limitation.

In concluding this abbreviated treatment of the school's testing program, the writer expresses the hope that enough has been said to make it evident that school authorities should "look before they leap" into a testing program. They must be sure, in the first place, that they have a program, and are not just vaguely "giving some tests." They must anticipate the problems of administering the tests and recording results, and above all, the modes of getting maximum use of test results. Possible values are great, but costs in money, time, and energy must be thoughtfully reckoned with, and each school is so individual that state-wide or county-wide solutions still leave many questions to be answered.[5]

THE CUMULATIVE RECORD

Characteristics and Values

Sir Francis Galton advocated that every child should have a cumulative record to follow him through school.[6] A recent survey of the departments of education of the 48 states by David Segel[7] brought out the information that 38 of those departments are giving positive recognition to the cumulative record by making available or requiring the use of a state-wide form, requiring or recommending the use of cumulative records (not a state-wide form), or serving schools by sending out packets of sample forms on request.

This widespread acceptance of the cumulative record as a guidance tool has come about during the past two or three decades. One may safely say that the big impetus to the growth of interest in this instrument was furnished by the publication in June, 1928, of the report of the Committee on Personnel Methods of the American Council on Education.[8] That report, prepared for the committee by Ben D. Wood, presented the record form which came to be known as the American Council Cumulative Record Folder, ex-

[5] The following reference offers a thoughtful treatment of many of the problems taken up in this section: Arthur E. Traxler, Robert Jacobs, Margaret Selover, and Agatha Townsend, *Introduction to Testing and the Use of Test Results in Public Schools* (New York, Harper, 1953).

[6] Helen M. Walker, *Studies in the History of Statistical Method* (Baltimore, Williams and Wilkins, 1929), p. 45.

[7] "Cumulative Records: State Laws and State Department of Education Regulations and Services," *Guide Lines* No. 5, May, 1955, U.S. Office of Education, Washington, D.C.

[8] "Personnel Methods," *Educational Record,* Supplement No. 8, Vol. IX (July, 1928).

plained its values and attributes, and gave concrete illustrations of its use. The report included a form for high schools and a form for colleges. Since 1928 the American Council has issued folders for the primary grades and for the middle grades, and has revised (1941) the folder for the secondary school.

Figures 17A, B, C, and D show this latter folder as revised in 1941. As may be judged, the folder is 9 by 12 inches in size, is made of the same tagboard as the common file folder, and is intended for the typical vertical office file. Figure 17 shows the form which is printed on its first, second, third, and fourth pages, respectively. We may examine this form in the light of the first of the criteria for a good cumulative record which Wood listed, namely: "The record form must show *trends of development* of abilities and interests."[9] To fulfill this requirement, the folder is organized by time sequence. The categories of information are listed down the left-hand side, and successive entries are made to the right of each item. Vertical lines mark off the folder in six columns to give space for entries for each of the six secondary years. The growth of the pupil during the elementary-school years is epitomized in free writing in a space near the top of Page 1. Provision is wisely made for the pasting in of two photos: pupils change notably in physical appearance between Grades 7 and 12. The general idea is that as one reads across the page the "trends of development" are most easily perceived. Pages 1 and 2 call for the record of such development as is evidenced by successive years of school marks, measures of ability and achievement, statements of interests, recordings of extra-curricular activities and out-of-school experiences, yearly reviewing of educational and vocational plans by pupil, parents, and counselor, descriptions of health and physical characteristics, and of disciplinary status or problems. Page 2 allows, also, generous space for the counselor's periodic evaluation of the pupil as regards the relation of his academic achievement to his standing in tests.

At the top of Page 3 a form is provided for the recording of certain family data, but in recognition of the wide variation in home and family conditions for which no form could possibly provide, a considerable space for free writing of "significant items" is made available.

The balance of Page 3 and part of Page 4 is given to space for a yearly "description of behavior" by each of the pupil's teachers. Under each of six character traits the teacher selects the ready-made description which he thinks most accurately characterizes the pupil. The gathering of these ratings involves the employment of supplemental blanks by means of which the teacher can make his ratings, uninfluenced by the ratings given by other teachers of the same year or preceding years. The manual provided with these folders has excellent suggestions for solving this problem.

As in the case of the evidence accumulated on Pages 1 and 2, this section on "description of behavior" is organized so as to show trends in develop-

[9] *Ibid.*, p. 17.

ment. How is the pupil's personality changing, forming, growing in the adolescent years which are so noteworthy as a period of self-exploration and self-finding? How does he react to the varied conditions and activities which the different subjects of the curriculum represent? What degree of consistency or inconsistency in behavior is to be perceived across the years? The answers to these questions which may be gleaned from the teachers' selections of descriptions are amplified by the remarks which teachers may volunteer for recording in the wide column next to the right-hand margin.

The assessment of "Emotional Stability," as called for on Page 4, is apparently regarded as best made by free writing, but the direction for such writing indicates that behavior is to be described, thus seeking a record of specific examples in contrast to abstract generalities. Presumably, the counselor would make such entries as he deemed significant, based upon his own contacts with the pupil and what he learns from teachers.

A yearly review of the case with a view to a kind of summation of the present state of development is called for by the heading, "Tentative Synthesis and Suggestions for Guidance . . ." near the foot of Page 4. Thus, synthesis is not an end event, a step to be taken after analysis is complete; it is a more or less continuing activity by which the counselor uses the evidence at hand to comprehend the unique individual which his client is.

Thus, this look at one cumulative record illustrates how this instrument serves the guidance function by bringing together the steadily accumulating body of evidence which progressive analysis makes available. In addition to a carefully planned form for recording information, if the cumulative record is a folder, as most of them are, it becomes a convenient depository for such profile sheets as Figure 12, for auxiliary cards or personal-data sheets, the autobiography, correspondence concerning the pupil, and other revealing evidence.

The American Council folder is the prototype of many cumulative record forms that have come to this writer's desk, of which the most recent is the product of a California state-wide committee. Their work took the form of a folder for elementary schools, a folder for junior-senior and four-year high schools, and a card for junior colleges.[10] The limitations of space here make it desirable to confine discussion and description to the American Council folder.

Synthesis, Diagnosis, and Prognosis Illustrated

To understand how the cumulative record functions as an instrument of guidance, the record of Mary Margaret Anderson, as shown in Figure 17, may be scrutinized closely. For the purpose in hand, we may well start with the 12th-grade entries of "educational and vocational plans" near the foot

[10] The publisher of these record forms is A. Carlisle & Co., 645 Harrison St., San Francisco. Issued by the California State Department of Education is a *Handbook on California Cumulative Records,* August, 1955.

of Page 2 and then work backwards to understand them. Mary's plan, as she was about to graduate from high school, was "Secretary in position where math. is used and then marriage." Her parents agreed, and the counselor said "Good compromise." How was that decision arrived at? What was the evidence which led to it?

When Mary entered junior high school it was known from elementary-school testing that she had an I.Q. in excess of 130—a measurement which was excessively verified in her secondary-school years. From the fact that her work in elementary school was always commensurate with her mental ability, she must have had a very successful, and therefore happy academic experience. Small wonder, then, that in the seventh grade she gave "Go to college" as her educational plan. The counselor must have realized as soon as Mary's elementary-school record came to his attention that she had plenty of intelligence to be successful in college, that, in fact, her general mental power corresponded fairly well with that of Ph.D.'s. But he withheld career suggestions until Mary was in the ninth grade, when he said, "consider any career requiring college training." Looking at Mary's interests and experiences, we note that she had many, of which art was prominent in the 7th, 8th, and 9th grades, but was fading out in the 10th grade. From her satisfactions in that area, however, she thought in the 9th and 10th grades of becoming a commercial artist. Evidence appears in the counselor's notes that both her artistic and musical interests and aptitudes were evaluated by teachers and found inadequate for consideration in her vocational plans. Mary turned to "Teaching math. or work in statistics" as her career choice in the 11th grade. Her school record shows marks of "A" in 10th-grade geometry and 11th-grade algebra; her standing on the "Coop. Math." achievement tests was at the 80th, 85th, and 95th percentiles in the 10th, 11th, and 12th grades, respectively. Hence, she found the success and presumably pleasure which caused her to think of mathematics as a vocational possibility.

Mary's over-all record in her subjects was good but not as high as her ability would lead one to expect. Especially it sagged in the 9th and 10th grades. In the "interpretation of test record and its relation to academic achievement" some explanations of the gap between achievement and ability are set forth. It seems that Mary's keen interest in outside activities caused her sometimes to neglect subject assignments and that cumulative drill work was particularly distasteful to her. A little corroborating evidence on this point is to be found in the "Description of Behavior" as regards the trait of "Responsibility." Her Latin teacher characterized her as only "Selectively Dependable," as did also her 11th-grade English teacher, while her chemistry teacher (N.S.) put her down as "Unreliable." Add to this picture the note made by the 10th-grade counselor at the foot of Page 4, "Mother says Mary is not, and never will be, a real student," and one is somewhat prepared for the notation concerning Mary's interests which the counselor found to be dominant in each grade beginning with the ninth, namely, "Any activity which brought contact with other people."

Emerging from the data thus far cited is the picture of a girl with a brilliant mind who has the *ability* to enter occupational life at the professional level, but whose *interest* is so strongly social and whose personality is so extrovert that the long period of study—a solitary activity—required for professional preparation, would be quite distasteful. In Barber's table of reasons why able high-school graduates did not enter college—cited here as Table 15 in Chapter 4—Mary would be classified under "Lack of academic interests" and probably also under "Preference for engagement or marriage." In this latter connection it is worthy of note that Mary's refusal to wear her glasses (see "Health and Physical Characteristics") signified her strong drive for social favor. Academic excellence was a secondary goal for Mary.

Other items in the analysis figured in the counselor's acceptance of Mary's final vocational choice as a "good compromise." The record shows that Mary's father was a cabinet maker. Mary was third in a family of four girls, rather closely grouped as to their ages. To give a college education to any member of such a family could only have been accomplished by great sacrifice. Furthermore, there was no tradition of college education in the family. Nevertheless, we are given a picture of family life in which the parents accorded fullest co-operation to the schools, and an 11th-grade counselor noted on Page 4 that "Parents gave her choice of aid for college if she showed serious intentions. . . ." It must be inferred, however, that the financial status and educational background of the family did not encourage college planning.

Attention is invited to one additional influence in the home environment. The mother's education, it will be noted, consisted of "high and secretarial school." The sibling Ruth, two years older than Mary, had the same education and was currently employed as a secretary. Thus, there was a family occupational pattern which no doubt played a part in Mary's final vocational choice.

Ability, interest, and *opportunity* all figured in the deliberations of Mary, her parents, and her counselors. She had the ability needed for college, but she lacked the interest, and the financial hurdle barred her from the opportunity. It was not difficult for the counselor to arrive at a prognosis of success either for college or for secretarial training and career. It is apparent from notes in the cumulative record that he also made unfavorable prognoses for careers in art and music.[11]

It is a temptation to speculate briefly on how a change in this factor or that

[11] Detailed illustrations of the use of the cumulative record in counseling individual cases are to be found in the following reference: Anna Rose Hawkes, "The Cumulative Record and Its Uses," Ch. 4 of *Guidance in Public Secondary Schools* (Arthur E. Traxler, ed.) (New York, Educational Records Bureau, 1939).

circumstance would have brought a different synthesis and a different decision. Suppose Mary had been a little less extrovertive, a little more responsible toward her assignments, and had had a strong desire to go to college, can we doubt that the opportunity would have been made available? Again, with either a strong college tradition in the Anderson family or a higher socio-economic level, Mary would doubtless have gone to college despite the dominance of her social interests over the academic.

The counselor's job is to study the balance of factors in each case, to define the synthesis and make the diagnosis and the prognosis. But, as is well illustrated in the case of Mary, he is not working at it alone: Mary, her parents, and the counselor were all interacting in the processes of understanding and deciding. The case also illustrates the unjustified presumptions of some writings about the interpretation of test results. The possibilities of interpreting any single measurement, factor, or condition are very much limited; it is the composite, or synthesis, of case data that provides the basis of interpretation.

The cumulative record of Mary well illustrates guidance as process rather than event. It depicts an individual in a succession of experiences, using them to find the self she wished to be, revealing herself progressively to teachers, counselors, and parents, carrying on the exploration of herself and her environment as a continuous activity. The cumulative record preserves that story and enables successive counselors to use the past as capital for interpreting the present. The record shows (Page 2) that Mary had four counselors in those six years. Without the orderly file of evidence accumulated in Grades 7 to 10, plus the succinct summation of Mary's elementary-school years, it is difficult to see how Miss Cowan, Mary's counselor in Grades 11 and 12, could have performed the functions of synthesis, diagnosis, and prognosis with any respectable degree of expertness.[12]

The argument for the kind of continuous evaluation and planning which is evident in Mary's cumulative record has been significantly buttressed by a recent report from the Wisconsin Counseling Study.[13] The authors studied the consistency of occupational choices of 347 students through the three years of senior high school and six months after high-school graduation. These students had fairly intensive counseling all three years. They indicated changes of occupational choice in any counseling interview, but for the purposes of this research the choice expressed in the last interview of each school year was defined as the vocational choice of that year, thus making three choices available for tabulations and for comparison with the occupa-

[12] Synthesis, diagnosis, and prognosis are admirably illustrated by a case described in the following reference: Donald E. Super, *The Psychology of Careers* (New York, Harper, 1957), pp. 92–100.

[13] John L. Schmidt and John W. M. Rothney, "Variability of Vocational Choices of High School Students," *Personnel and Guidance Journal*, Vol. XXXIV (November, 1955), pp. 142–146.

tion actually engaged in. The following is a quotation from the authors' approximate findings:[14]

1. One out of two students express the same choice for the first two years of high school.
2. One out of two students express the same choice for the last two years of high school.
3. One out of three students express the same choice all the way through high school.
4. One out of two students will change their choices at the end of each year of high school.
5. Two out of three students will change their choices at least once during high school.
6. One out of five students express the same choice all the way through school and follow through in their post high-school vocational activity.
7. One out of two seniors will follow through on their senior year choices.

Upon this evidence of variability in the vocational choices of counseled high-school youth the authors offer conclusions as follows:[15]

It appears that planning cannot be a "one-shot" process for all high school youth. For consistent students, vocational choices may have real meaning worthy of consideration and important in planning school programs. For others, they represent only statements that need much consideration at later dates. Since a method of early identification of the consistent ones is not yet available, planning services, continuous and personalized, appear to be needed over the whole high school period.

In such services the role of the cumulative record is undeniably important.

Some Considerations in Administration of the Cumulative Record

The arguments for an adequate cumulative record system are unassailable. Counselors, with their special responsibility for guidance, consider such records as absolutely essential to the performance of their function. And more and more, all school workers recognize the contribution that these records make to effective instruction and curriculum revision, as well as to guidance.

The installation, practical employment, and maintenance of this feature, however, calls for some sober thought. If the reader will turn back to the quotation with which the second section of Chapter 11 was introduced, he will note that teachers complained about the time required for keeping cumulative records and the slight value of them. It must be admitted that in many schools these records are poorly kept, or that they are kept at some cost in morale, or that so much professional time is consumed in *keeping* them that there is too little time left for *using* them. Probably a basic difficulty is that in many schools the records project is inaugurated without provision for any addition to the clerical and professional staffs.

[14] *Ibid.*, p. 145.
[15] *Ibid.*, p. 146.

The following are some considerations in the administration of a system of cumulative records:

1. The introduction of the system should come about through study by the school staff of their need for and the values in cumulative records. This point is especially emphasized by Allen in his monograph.[16] The major use for such records, as he sees it, is to help all members of the faculty do their work of educating children; they must therefore understand how records can help them. From such orientation, the faculty will go forward to clarify their own responsibilities in connection with the introduction, maintenance, and use of the system. Possibly a cumulative records committee could assist in launching the new system and be a continuous advisory body for the administrator.

2. Frequently it will be desirable to introduce the new system gradually. For example, a junior high school could initiate it in the seventh grade each year until it includes the whole school.

3. The record system should be so administered as to observe ethical and professional standards in the handling of personal information. Some of this information should be treated most confidentially. We have in our schools pupils who have served terms at correctional institutions, pupils whose fathers have committed crimes, pupils whose mothers have bad reputations. A knowledge of such facts frequently explains pupil behavior and needs, but should it be recorded? And if recorded, how shall it be guarded? On this point Ethel Kawin says,[17]

At least two alternatives . . . are possible. The confidential information may be kept in a file accessible only to professional guidance workers. Or a note may be made on the cumulative record to the effect that a certain person has additional information. That arrangement permits the person who has the information to use his discretion in giving as much or as little of it as he thinks the person who requested it will use for the good of the individual concerned.

In one school known to the writer an inconspicuous star or asterisk in a certain place on the folder indicates that the principal has additional information on the pupil.

This consideration of confidence has meaning for the use of student clerks to make entries on the cumulative records. Most writers on this subject condemn the use of such help. Quite properly they fear that persons of such immaturity and of so many friendships in the student body will gossip about what they learn from the records, even though the more discreditable items are not shown.

4. The location of the records and their custodial administration must be thoughtfully planned in the light of the use that is to be made of them, as well

[16] Wendell C. Allen, *Cumulative Pupil Records* (New York, Bureau of Publications, Teachers College, Columbia University, 1943).

[17] "Use of Records in the Elementary School," Ch. 3 of *Handbook of Cumulative Records* (Washington, D.C., U.S. Office of Education Bulletin No. 5, 1944), p. 18.

as to assure their safety and security. The California *Handbook* offers the following judgment:[18]

In general the central filing plan seems most feasible for the secondary school. The files should be located where they are as accessible as possible to administrative, counseling, health, and teaching personnel.

Such a viewpoint implies a compelling reason for locating counseling offices close to the administrative center of the school.

In the elementary school weightier reasons recommend housing the cumulative records for each class in its classroom. The teacher of the self-contained class will certainly be the principal counselor as well as instructor of the class. He will therefore be the main user as well as recorder of the records. Special teachers will have occasion to consult the records, but the classroom is as convenient for them to visit as is the principal's office. Besides, a visit to the classroom enables them to talk over the problem pupil with the one who knows the pupil best—his major teacher.

5. Maintenance of the record system must be planned for; it will not operate itself. Because the recording of test results is such an important item, some authorities have suggested that the tests-and-measurement person should also be designated as supervisor of the cumulative records. It is well to have certain times of the year when clerks make the entries which they are charged with making; if teachers are to make some entries, the job will be done better if it is planned for a certain week or month and if a memorandum of directions is issued, particularly for the orientation of new teachers. If folders are employed, the documents that have been filed in them should be sifted yearly, and some should be discarded after recording any important information they contain. Without a plan for such pruning, the folders become unnecessarily bulky and more difficult to use, because encumbered with dead wood.

6. When students drop out of school or graduate, their cumulative records should be streamlined thoughtfully and placed in an inactive file. For some years there will be occasions for consulting this file.

Some of the ideas expressed in the six administrative "considerations" set forth above are in contrast with points of view expressed or implied in the extended quotation in Chapter 10, pages 318–319 from the New Trier students' handbook. In that high school, with the homeroom teacher accorded paramount importance as the pupils' counselor, cumulative record folders are presumably in the custody of homeroom teachers instead of being centrally located. Furthermore, their confidential character is emphasized to the point that the pupils' subject teachers cannot consult them.

Clerk's 1926 manual for the New Trier advisory system, also cited in Chapter 10, specified that "These folders are in the custody of the advisers except during the Christmas and Summer vacations when they are left in

[18] California State Department of Education, *op. cit.,* p. 17.

the Registrar's office." Presumably, two purposes were thus served: first, the records were available for consultation and counseling in periods when teachers were not at the school; second, clerks could make certain entries. Supervision of teachers' maintenance of the records would also be effective: awareness of the semiannual scrutiny would stimulate the homeroom teachers to shoulder their responsibilities for the records.

The cumulative record is here to stay. Problems in the optimum management of it are being, and will be, solved as its values are more and more clearly understood.

THE CASE STUDY

Characteristics and Values

The recognition of individual variation, which received such an impetus after World War I, due primarily to the rapid spread of objective measurements, brought the case study into prominence. The 1920s witnessed the issue of a considerable body of educational and psychological literature on this subject. Increased acceptance of the concept that behavior is caused further popularized the case study, although it may well be said that the reverse is also true—namely, increased familiarity with the methods and results of case study have spread the idea that behavior is caused.

What is a case study? What kinds of skills and what level of training are necessary for the making of case studies? These questions are difficult to answer, for there really are no clear-cut, objective standards. Most people would agree that a case study is a detailed inquiry into all facets of an individual's life, eventuating in a diagnosis which forms the foundation for treatment. But their conceptions of the depth and range of the inquiry would vary widely. Some writings imply that it is entirely within the capacity of any well-trained teacher to make case studies; others definitely convey the idea that the case study requires the employment of techniques which are acquired by more advanced training than that possessed by the teacher.

What sorts of pupils and how many receive, or should receive, the benefits of case study? How shall we identify them? The answer to these questions awaits a more precise defining of case study than we have to date accomplished. It was said by a guidance worker in one of the large state universities some years ago that 40 per cent of the students enrolled in that institution should be case-studied. How he arrived at such a figure is unknown. Certainly the selection of individuals for case study is one more subjective factor.

In introducing reports of fifteen case studies made by high-school teachers, Anna Rose Hawkes argues that "it is as desirable for the normal child to be recorded and studied by the educational case worker as it is for the problem child to be so considered.[19] Thus, the view is set forth that *all* pupils should

[19] Arthur E. Traxler, ed., *Guidance in Public Secondary Schools* (New York, Educational Records Bureau, 1939), pp. 203–204.

have the advantage of case study and that teachers are competent to use the technique.

Smithies[20] quite evidently viewed the case study as too technical to be made by teachers. She called the functionary who makes case studies an "educational diagnostician or pedagogical case worker" and wrote of him as one who correlates information received from all the pertinent "experts," using a diagram to show the following:

Contributing Officers	Field of Material Contributed
Classroom teacher	Progress in academic work
Homeroom adviser	School attitude
Physical director	Present vitality—play life
Research worker	Tests and measurements
Vocational counselor	Aptitudes
Medical office	Health history
Visiting teacher	Home and neighborhood conditions

As regards training and qualifications, Smithies said,[21]

First and foremost, the case-worker should be a teacher with good training and adequate experience. . . . The best preparation for the work will include special training and extensive reading relative to tests and measurement, nutrition work with children, mental and physical growth, principles of social work, medical and social psychiatry, and psychopathology.

Personal qualifications which she enumerated as essential may be suggested by the following quotations:

. . . common sense . . . like and understand people . . . strong intuitive faculties . . . originality in questioning . . . keenness in detecting clews . . . alertness in following valid suggestions . . . accuracy in collecting data . . . using and interpreting the compiled data intelligently . . . a reasonably good memory . . . inspire confidence and create ease . . . impersonal, unbiased, and unemotional . . . close-mouthed.

To indicate the scope of information to be gathered Smithies gave a five-page outline under the following four headings:

I. Description of the Case as Presented
II. Investigation of Present School Life
III. Investigation of Life Outside of School
IV. Early History and Development

The completed case study required also the following:

V. General Diagnosis of the Case
VI. Treatment and Prognosis

The diagnosis has four steps: (1) the critical scrutiny and interpretation of

[20] Elsie M. Smithies, *Case Studies of Normal Adolescent Girls* (New York, Appleton, 1933).
[21] *Ibid.,* p. 10.

the evidence found in each field covered in the history; (2) the logical relation of each fact to the other; (3) the weighing of their mutual values, and (4) the unifying of the findings into a definite disorder with fundamental and contributory causations.[22]

The reports of the dozen cases which comprise the bulk of Smithies' book are of girls who were normal but who had problems which impeded their development and which ordinary school procedures could not cope with. It it quite clear that Smithies did not think of her technique of case study as being applied to all pupils. While her book was published a quarter century ago, it is probably as sound an exposition of case-study technique in education as has been written.

A general work in educational psychology, published in the same year as the Smithies volume, offers the following brief outline for the case study:[23]

I. History of the Child's Family
    A. Medical History
    B. Social and Emotional History
    C. Intellectual History
    D. Educational and Economic History
II. History of the Child's Life to Date
    A. Medical History
    B. Social and Emotional History
    C. Intellectual History
    D. Educational (and Economic) History
III. The Child's Present Condition
    A. Physical Condition
    B. Social and Emotional Adjustment
    C. Intellectual Development
    D. Educational Adjustment

The outline has the merit of being easy to remember, and it makes for logical recording, but the author points out that the most natural way to gather the information would be to work more or less backwards through the outline.

Reports of ten case studies constitute the first one hundred pages of Rothney and Roens' account of their experiment in guidance.[24] These reports give the highlights of five years' work in the analysis and counseling of high-school pupils who presented a variety of problems. Beyond the account of diagnosis and treatment (including success or failure), a distinctive feature of these studies is a brief concluding statement entitled "Eleven Years After Initial Counseling," which is a report of follow-up.[25]

[22] *Ibid.*, p. 23.
[23] S. L. Pressey, *Psychology and the New Education* (New York, Harper, 1933), p. 253.
[24] John W. M. Rothney and Bert A. Roens, *Guidance of American Youth* (Cambridge, Mass., Harvard University Press, 1950), pp. 3–101.
[25] The method of the case study is further illustrated in John W. M. Rothney, *The High School Student: A Book of Cases* (New York, Dryden Press, 1953).

Returning now to the first question raised in this section (what is a case study?), probably the majority of guidance workers would agree that it is an analysis, diagnosis, and treatment of the individual which considerably exceeds in depth, range, and complexity the same processes which are recounted in the story of Mary Margaret Anderson in Figure 17. In the present state of support for educational service, such a study and such a record of the great majority of pupils as is represented in Figure 17 seems to approximate the limit of expectations. The case study, as conceived by Smithies, Pressey, and other authorities listed in the selected references at the end of this chapter, is highly expensive. For baffling cases, however, it should indeed be available.

An Attempt to Objectify the Case Study

Already mentioned on page 360 in Chapter 11 is Hill's research which was designed to furnish case workers with a form for the collection of data which would assure uniformity in the items covered and would compel the evaluation of each item in standardized terminology.[26] His "Record of Problem Case" (RPC) consisted of 55 items, classified as follows:

Parental and family characteristics 8
Material factors in the home environment 8
Personal factors in the home environment 9
School records and tests 14
Developmental and personality history 16

For each item a descriptive rating scale was prepared. With the item, "Alcoholism and Use of Intoxicants," for example, the scale was as follows:

0. . . . . Chronic use by one or both parents (F. . . . M. . . .)
1. . . . . Frequent use in the home
2. . . . . Occasional use in the home
3. . . . . Occasional use outside the home
4. . . . . No use by either parent

Thus, the case worker checked the most suitable description, and it had a numerical equivalent. The best possible total score was 220, the average delinquent rated about 110, and the average normal child, about 165.

Hill tested the validity of the items by comparing 130 chronic school-behavior problem children—truants, incorrigibles, theft problems, etc.—with a matched control group of non-delinquents, obtaining the critical ratios of the differences between the means. With a ratio of 2.70 considered as representing approximate certainty of actual difference, 46 of the items showed critical ratios from 2.715 to 13.650.

[26] Arthur S. Hill, "The Use of an Objective Type of Case Study in the Analysis and Prognosis of Pupil Maladjustment Problems," *Educational Administration and Supervision,* Vol. XXI (November, 1935), pp. 611–618; also "A Statistical Analysis of Significant Factors in Pupil Maladjustment," *Journal of Educational Sociology,* Vol. IX (December, 1935), pp. 219–230.

Hill recognized that the total score on his RPC was prognostic rather than diagnostic, but pointed out that the RPC form made diagnosis possible because it presented the same evidence as would be found in the usual narrative case study. Because he realized that the individuality of every case would not be completely taken care of in his 55 items, he provided space for narrative material at the end of each subdivision.

To the mind of this writer, Hill's contribution offers at least a partial corrective for two of the major limitations of the traditional case study—its subjectivity and its high cost in time. While it may well be that the RPC is better suited to cases representing aggressive behavior than to withdrawing cases, that could only mean that the form would need more supplementation for some cases than for others. The extent to which this device has been accepted outside of Des Moines, where it was developed, is unknown to this writer.

The Case Conference

Many schools have found it advantageous to conduct the study of some problem pupils through groups of the faculty who are most concerned. Perhaps a most commonly found conference group would include the counselor, homeroom teacher, school nurse, school social worker, and the subject teachers of the pupil being studied. Two valuable purposes are served. First, the members pool the knowledge of the pupil which they have gained from their contacts with him, from their observations of his behavior and attitudes under varied conditions, and from their knowledge of his home environment. The group thinking builds an understanding of the pupil which has greater depth and fullness than would be possible for an individual worker to achieve. Evidence that may weigh heavily in the mind of one member is placed in proper perspective by the light which others shed upon the case. Thus, a better synthesis and diagnosis is attained. And if the treatment decided upon is to be administered by the members of the conference, they act more efficiently and intelligently because they have participated in the synthesis and diagnosis.

Second, the case conference constitutes a most valuable form of in-service training. The concrete situation of an individual case affords an excellent opportunity to grow in capacity for test interpretation, in understanding of human behavior and motivations, in sensitivity to the signs of maladjustment. It creates a consciousness of curricular and instructional inadequacies, and thus lays a foundation upon which a general school improvement program can be built. By bringing the individual sharply into focus, the case conference should be an antidote to the tendency toward mass-production, factory-type handling of pupils. And not only does the guidance specialist expose teachers to the spirit and techniques of the guidance function: he is himself stimulated by the reactions of teachers and by the necessity for clearly expressing himself on the synthesis, diagnosis, and treatment of the case.

A third purpose may well be served if the principal and assistant principal attend the conference, as is assumed by Strang in her dramatized example.[27] It is the opportunity to improve their understanding of teachers. In such professional conversations as the case conference, the members reveal themselves in the degree to which they possess such personal qualities as were quoted above from Smithies. When new appointments to counselorships are made, the teachers under consideration will need to be evaluated for their possession of these traits.

Hahn[28] has made concrete suggestions for the management of case conferences, or staff clinics, to use his terminology. He suggests a definite calendar for them throughout the year, meetings twice a month in the afternoon at the close of school, sessions held to approximately an hour, two cases taken up at each meeting. The regular guidance staff and the school nurse should attend; the homeroom teachers and the subject teachers of the cases should be invited, but their attendance should not be compulsory. The person in charge of the guidance program should usually act as the leader, but counselors and teachers should frequently be urged to present cases. The measurement data for the first case should be placed on the board before the beginning of the meeting, and for the second case, as it is being introduced. Care should be exercised in the selection of cases; they should represent some angle of interest, but they should not be so complex or baffling as to cause teachers to feel unable to understand them. "At all times the leader should avoid any appearance of the 'Jehovah' complex."

PREDICTION

Elements of the Predictive Process

The distinction between the terms "prediction" and "prognosis" is non-existent, in the opinion of many counseling specialists; others assert their relatedness but deny their identity, though not united on the distinctions in identity. Hence, this writer uses the terms interchangeably.

Guidance is not performed unless predictions are made. In making choices of education and vocation, the client must make predictions concerning his successes and satisfactions in the future. The counselor, by virtue of his diagnosis of the client and his understanding of educational and vocational opportunity, aids the client in evaluating the various facts and factors, in distinguishing the relevant from the irrelevant, and in estimating the chances of success.

[27] Ruth Strang, *The Role of the Teacher in Personnel Work* (New York, Bureau of Publications, Teachers College, Columbia University, 1953), pp. 444–448.

[28] Milton Hahn, "The Staff Clinic in the Pupil-Personnel Program," *School Review,* Vol. XLVII (January, 1939), pp. 32–36.

That prediction is basic to guidance has been implied throughout the first ten chapters of this book and at many points made explicit. Chapters 11, 12, and 13 have made the relationship manifest by describing numerous predictive factors and instruments, and presenting evaluative studies of them. It is pertinent in this chapter that the predictive process be briefly analyzed and its elements illuminated.

First, it is apparent that the activity for which success is to be predicted must be defined. As we commonly speak of the various activities, success in which we wish to predict, we convey no adequate conception of their complexity. Actually, the successful pursuit of a high-school elective subject, of college, of job, of life in family and community, involve hosts of factors which may be combined in varied weightings. Working in one of these complex situations, the prediction researcher seeks to discover differences in success or in level of performance. The measure of such differences which he accepts and employs as significant is called the criterion. Many difficulties impede the finding of a satisfactory criterion—a problem which was described at some length in Chapter 12. When a criterion is agreed upon—one that is feasible and significant, and one that differentiates in objective terms—the study by which it was found will often have revealed predictive factors most relevant to success or failure in the activity. The researcher then turns his attention to the predictive factors, constructs measurements of them, and tries out these measurements singly and in combinations to ascertain their predictive efficiency.

This abbreviated and overly simplified statement of the process basic to guidance has been described with clarity and fullness by Horst.[29] It has been illustrated extensively in earlier chapters of this book, particularly Chapter 12.

Clinical versus Statistical Prediction

This is the title of a recent book by Meehl[30] which is the most extended exposition to date of an argument of long standing among psychologists. The statistical predictor is essentially one who relies heavily upon actuarial data which show that the counselee, as a member of a given group, has such-and-such chances of attaining a given level of success. Statistical prediction was given extended illustration in Chapter 12. The emphasis is certainly on objective evidence.

The clinical predictor, on the other hand, focuses his study upon the individual as an individual and not upon him as a member of any class. He considers that each individual presents his own unique configuration of abilities and of character and personality traits. To identify that configuration and to

[29] Paul Horst and Others, *The Prediction of Personal Adjustment,* Social Science Research Council Bulletin No. 48, 1941.
[30] Paul E. Meehl (Minneapolis, University of Minnesota Press, 1954).

make a prediction concerning it, the clinician draws upon his theoretical training for the propositions, laws, and generalizations concerning human behavior which he deems applicable, upon his clinical experience, and sometimes upon such an obscure process as intuition, defined by Horst[31] as "a perception of factors or relationships in which the grounds of the perception are not known to the person [perceiving]." The clinician scorns the probability table as useless. If the statistician avers from his actuarial data that he has the evidence that there are eight chances out of ten that Billie Smith will become a delinquent, the clinician replies that such a fact still tells nothing about Billie. Billie will either become a delinquent or he will not, and the answer is still to be found in the boy's attitudes, his specific environment and similar factors which influence his individual behavior.

It seems likely that the reason for the greater intensity of this argument in psychological literature than in educational literature may lie in the fact that psychologists are so frequently in situations where they must predict with certainty. They examine children and decide whether or not to exclude them from school or to commit to an institution. Their judgments influence court orders in criminal law cases and in parole administration. Treatment for certain kinds of illness are determined by the psychologist's diagnosis and prediction. Another aspect of such predictions is that they are authoritarian —the client does not participate in the process. The situation resembles the physician's prognosis.

By contrast, school counseling is concerned largely with helping pupils to make choices, and those choices are to be made with full respect for the principle that most people can do a number of things about equally well. The counselor helps the pupil to weigh his chances of success in various fields and is under no obligation to predict with certainty. In adjustive guidance, actuarial data help the counselor to identify the pupils who are most likely to fail in their studies, to drop out of school, or to become delinquent. He then sets in motion the forces calculated to alter those pupils' attitudes or environment so that the trend to maladjustment is checked.

Among the authorities who have examined the issue of clinical versus statistical prediction is Theodore Sarbin.[32] It is his belief that the clinician really works on the basis of crude probabilities. As a hypothetical example, he cites the case of a student who wants to know his chances of succeeding in the University. He is given a probability statement based on his high-school marks and a college aptitude test, but the clinician has more data on the student for which no formal statistical evidence of significance is available. Perhaps the student works thirty hours a week or he is in love with a girl back home, or he just doesn't make a good impression in the interview. Actually,

[31] Op. cit., p. 224.
[32] "The Logic of Prediction in Psychology," Psychological Review, Vol. LI (July, 1944), pp. 210–228.

in considering these data, says Sarbin, the clinician is assigning the student to a class; he makes a prediction based on the idea that students in the past who have worked thirty hours a week made a poor scholastic showing, that love-sick boys did not do as well as their abilities would indicate, and that students who had not impressed him favorably in the interview had not succeeded.

Even if the judgment about the client did not involve any classification of him, it could be based upon his past conduct, the prediction being an extrapolation from his past behavior in similar situations. That would be operating from a probability table.

Well may one ask, Why not put the clinical and the statistical methods of prediction to the experimental test as a means of finding which one is superior? That has been done. Meehl evaluated all the studies of this character which he could find, and from his conclusions the following lines may be quoted:[33]

In spite of the defects and ambiguities present, let me emphasize the brute fact that we have here, depending upon one's standards for admission as relevant, from 16 to 20 studies involving a comparison of clinical and actuarial methods, *in all but one of which the predictions made actuarially were either approximately equal or superior to those made by a clinician.* . . . In about half of the studies, the two methods are equal; in the other half, the clinician is definitely inferior. No definitely interpretable, fully acceptable study puts him clearly ahead.

While the psychologists argue from a position which is different from that of school guidance workers in that they possess more advanced techniques for the study of human nature, and that their responsibilities are not the same, the latter group is constantly engaged in making predictions for the general run of children and youth, and the issue of clinical versus statistical prediction is fully applicable to their work. More and more statistical data are being made available. It certainly is the thesis of this book that guidance workers should possess the understandings of people and society which statistical studies contribute. At the same time, as was emphasized in Chapter 11, the average for a group may not be characteristic of a member of that group. The individual must be studied, as illustrated by the case of Mary Margaret Anderson in this chapter. There seems to be every reason for agreeing with a concluding remark by Horst, as follows:[34] "The statistician and the case-study investigator can make mutual gains if they will quit quarreling with each other and begin borrowing from each other." Similarly, support for joining the clinical and statistical approaches is found in the sentence with which Bingham concluded his chapter on the interpretation of test

[33] Paul E. Meehl, *Clinical vs. Statistical Prediction* (Minneapolis, University of Minnesota Press, 1954), p. 119.
[34] *Op. cit.,* p. 249.

results:[35] "When interpreting test results, ingenuity and fertility of insight as well as understandings of psychological statistics, are indeed to be desired, and richly informed common sense must hold the reins."

Methods of Expressing Prediction

Prediction is commonly expressed in the form of (1) a coefficient of correlation, (2) a critical score or scores, (3) a regression equation, or (4) a table of probability. In the footnote on page 388 the coefficient of correlation was briefly explained as a single numerical quantity for expressing the degree of agreement between two measures of a group. Because it is so exact and succinct, the findings of most prediction researches are expressed in this form. The chief advantage of the coefficient is that it facilitates the comparison of predictive instruments as to their effectiveness. In the exercise of the counseling function it is virtually useless because it affords no basis of prediction for any individual, and that is exactly the counseling problem.

Finding a critical score was illustrated in Table 56 from an early study by Johnston. The "threshold of ability" he called it. Its limitation was pointed out in connection with the table as being the very limited number of students for whom it afforded a prediction. Whereas Johnston used it only to predict lack of success in university studies, it can also be used to predict certainty of success, but again only for a few cases. The critical-score technique has been used more extensively for selection than for counseling. For example, a college may decide on a policy of admitting students only from the upper fifth of the high-school class. A graduate school may decline to accept any students whose undergraduate quality-point average is below a given level, or whose standing on the Miller Analogies Test is below a given score. The critical score is indeed the simplest of devices, but also a very coarse one. The selecting agency or authority will often use other measures or criteria in conjunction with it. That is, for example, the college says, "We select our students *from* the upper fifth."

The regression equation is a means of computing from prediction scores the exact achievement score which each individual is *most likely* to make. However, such pin-pointing of the most probable level of success is not particularly serviceable, because with the usual coefficients of correlation between the measures of prediction and achievement, the most likely score is still not very likely. The statisticians recognize this situation and therefore are prone to compute the standard error of estimate and then tell their readers that John has 68 chances out of 100 of scoring between ___ and ___.

All three of these methods of expressing prediction have their origins in the simple table of probability which was illustrated in Tables 47, 49, 50, 51, 55, and 56. For purposes of counseling, the table itself—variously called probability table, expectancy table, double-entry table, or scattergram—is

[35] Walter V. Bingham, *Aptitudes and Aptitude Testing* (New York, Harper, 1937), p. 264.

the most useful way to express prediction. Still applicable are the advantages stated by the writer in 1933, as follows:[36]

1. The double-entry table is not difficult to prepare. Any school worker, untrained and unskilled in statistical procedures, can construct one with only a brief explanation. On the other hand, the derivation of a coefficient of correlation is regarded as a formidable task by most students who have completed a course in educational statistics. . . .

2. The table of correlation gives facts which are intelligible to counselor, pupil, and parent. If the individual knows what level he himself has attained in the prognosis, he can know in simple arithmetical terms what the chances are that he will attain each of the various levels of success in the venture for which prediction is made. This is bringing science out of the Olympian clouds. . . .

3. The development and use of correlation tables should make counseling more possible and less dangerous for unspecialized workers to administer. . . . Correlation tables would be safe, practical instruments to put into their hands, thus promoting in a very real sense Thorndike's early vision of "exact and scientific study [in guidance] which . . . will give results whereby even a mediocre person in this field can do excellent work."[37]

4. Double-entry tables should make it possible to accomplish much guidance by group counseling. . . . Cannot the reader visualize homeroom group lessons centered about tables of prediction which have been placed on the board or mimeographed? . . .

Why pupils who have scored equally well on the predictive measurement vary as widely in achievement, as do the pupils in Table I [49, this text], for instance, is an appropriate topic for carefully guided speculation.

Bingham on numerous occasions vigorously advocated the computation and use of probability tables, and one of his last writings was entirely on this subject. Typical of his argument is the following:[38]

This concept of expectancy helps the counselor or the employer as well as the psychologist to think clearly about the meaning of a person's performance on a test battery, an aptitude index, or any other validated predictor. It helps also to communicate the facts to someone else, without ambiguity. Its value is most apparent when there is occasion to make clear to an individual the meaning of his own score.

At an earlier date Bingham's expressed dream of a scientific future for vocational guidance included the well-organized use of tables of probability, as indicated in the following quotation:[39]

[36] "Deriving Practical Instruments for Guidance," *Vocational Guidance Magazine,* Vol. XI (March, 1933), pp. 252–253.

[37] Edward L. Thorndike, "Vocational Guidance a Function of Public Education: A Forward Look" (Address given in 1913), *Occupations,* Vol. XIX (December, 1940), pp. 165–166.

[38] Walter V. Bingham, "Expectancies," *Educational and Psychological Measurement,* Vol. XIII (Spring, 1953), p. 47.

[39] "A National Perspective on Testing and Guidance," *Educational Record,* Supplement No. 12, Vol. XX (January, 1939), p. 141.

Data of the sort indicated conceivably might be compiled some day in a Counselor's Handbook of Ready Reference, like an engineering handbook, annually revised. . . . For instant reference when conferring with a student about his prospects, this handbook would contain, in addition to validity coefficients, simple tables of probability from which to read the individual's chances of achieving a favorable score in each criterion against which the test has been validated. . . . Counselors today do not have at their disposal even a remote approximation to such a Utopian handbook.

From this discussion it will be apparent that the method of expressing prediction can either tie the function of prediction into the activity of counseling in a very practical way, or make another small deposit in an ivory-tower bank. A coefficient of correlation cannot be unscrambled; this author pleads for the preservation *and use* of the table from which the coefficient was computed.[40]

QUESTIONS, PROBLEMS, INVESTIGATIONS

1. Plan the testing program for any school of your acquaintance—elementary, secondary, or collegiate—justifying your selection of tests by citations from Buros' yearbooks.

2. Compare and contrast a number of cumulative record cards and folders. (Instructor should have accumulated a representative sampling and made them available for student examination.) State your criteria, and write up your evaluation of several cards and/or folders.

3. For some school of your acquaintance—elementary, secondary, or collegiate—draw up plans for the essential details of administration and use of the cumulative records.

4. In the *Manual for Cumulative Records* of the American Council on Education, study the facsimile record of Philip Brownson (college student) and evaluate the counselor's final judgment on vocational plans, as was done in this chapter for Mary Margaret Anderson.

5. Survey the record system of some school or college and write a critique of its adequacy for serving the guidance function.

6. Read Smithies' *Case Studies of Normal Adolescent Girls* with this question in mind: Do these case studies justify the training and the personal qualities which the author describes on pages 10 and 11 as essential in the case worker? Illustrate abundantly.

7. Comparing Smithies' outline with her case reports, do you find some items of information that apparently need not have been collected? Do you find some that proved unexpectedly significant?

8. Define the activities involved in some school subject with which you are familiar. Find a basis for objectively measuring success in the activities. By what previous experiences in the pupils' lives may success in the subject be predicted?

[40] The point of view here expressed regarding the construction and use of local prediction tables is given vigorous endorsement in the following reference: Henry S. Dyer, "The Need for Do-It-Yourself Prediction Research in High School Guidance," *Personnel and Guidance Journal,* Vol. XXXVI (November, 1957), pp. 162–167.

9. As measures of achievement, compare teachers' marks and standardized achievement tests.

10. Discuss the factor of subjectivity-objectivity in the processes of synthesis, diagnosis, and prognosis.

SELECTED REFERENCES

ALLEN, Wendell C., *Cumulative Pupil Records* (New York, Bureau of Publications, Teachers College, Columbia University, 1943).

BINGHAM, Walter V., *Aptitudes and Aptitude Testing* (New York, Harper, 1937), Chs. 16–19.

——, "Expectancies," *Educational and Psychological Measurement,* Vol. XIII (Spring, 1953), pp. 47–53.

——, "A National Perspective on Testing and Guidance," *Educational Record,* Supplement No. 12, Vol. XX (January, 1939), pp. 137–150.

BRAYFIELD, Arthur H., *Readings in Modern Methods of Counseling* (New York, Appleton-Century-Crofts, 1950), pp. 13–114.

Committee on Personnel Methods, American Council on Education, "Personnel Methods" (Prepared by Ben D. Wood), *Educational Record,* Supplement No. 8, Vol. IX (July, 1928), pp. 1–68.

ELKIN, F., "Specialists Interpret the Case of Harold Holzer," *Journal of Abnormal and Social Psychology,* Vol. XLII (1947), pp. 99–111.

FLORY, Charles D., and WEBB, James F., "Cumulative Records for Elementary Schools," *Elementary School Journal,* Vol. XXXVIII (December, 1937), pp. 278–290.

HAHN, Milton, "The Staff Clinic in the Pupil-Personnel Program," *School Review,* Vol. XLVII (January, 1939), pp. 32–36.

——, and MACLEAN, Malcolm S., *Counseling Psychology,* Chs. 9, 12 (New York, McGraw-Hill, 1955).

Handbook of Cumulative Records, A Report of the National Committee on Cumulative Records, David Segel, Chairman (Washington, D.C., U.S. Office of Education Bulletin, No. 5, 1944).

HILL, Arthur S., "A Statistical Analysis of Significant Factors in Pupil Maladjustment," *Journal of Educational Sociology,* Vol. IX (December, 1935), pp. 219–230.

——, "The Use of an Objective Type of Case Study in the Analysis and Prognosis of Pupil Maladjustment Problems," *Educational Administration and Supervision,* Vol. XXI (November, 1935), pp. 611–618.

HORST, Paul, "Educational and Vocational Counseling from the Actuarial Point of View," *Personnel and Guidance Journal,* Vol. XXXV (November, 1956), pp. 164–170.

——, and others, *The Prediction of Personal Adjustment,* Social Science Research Council Bulletin No. 48, 1941.

HUTSON, P. W., "Deriving Practical Instruments for Guidance," *Vocational Guidance Magazine,* Vol. XI (March, 1933), pp. 247–254.

KVARACEUS, William C., "Prediction Studies of Delinquent Behavior," *Personnel and Guidance Journal,* Vol. XXXIV (November, 1955), pp. 147–149.

MEEHL, Paul E., *Clinical versus Statistical Prediction* (Minneapolis, University of Minnesota Press, 1954).

MORRISON, H. C., *The Practice of Teaching in the Secondary School,* rev. ed. (Chicago, University of Chicago Press, 1931), pp. 636–666.

ROTHNEY, John W. M., *The High School Student: A Book of Cases* (New York, Dryden, 1953).

————, and ROENS, Bert A., *Guidance of American Youth* (Cambridge, Mass., Harvard University Press, 1950), pp. 3–101.

SARBIN, Theodore, "The Logic of Prediction in Psychology," *Psychological Review,* Vol. LI (July, 1944), pp. 210–228.

SCHMIDT, John L., and ROTHNEY, John W. M., "Variability of Vocational Choices of High School Students," *Personnel and Guidance Journal,* Vol. XXXIV (November, 1955), pp. 142–146.

SEGEL, David, "Cumulative Records: State Laws and State Department of Education Regulations and Services," *Guide Lines,* No. 5 (May, 1955), U.S. Office of Education.

————, "Overall School Practice and Theory in Measurement," *Guide Lines,* Circular No. 474 (April, 1956), U.S. Office of Education.

SMITHIES, Elsie, *Case Studies of Normal Adolescent Girls* (New York, Appleton, 1933).

SUPER, Donald E., *Appraising Vocational Fitness* (New York, Harper, 1949), pp. 654–663.

TRAXLER, Arthur E., "Case-Study Procedures in Guidance," *School Review,* Vol. XLVI (October, 1938), pp. 602–610.

————, "The Cumulative Record in the Guidance Program," *School Review,* Vol. LIV (March, 1946), pp. 154–161.

————, ed., *Guidance in Public Secondary Schools.* Educational Records Bulletin No. 28 (New York, Educational Records Bureau, October, 1939).

————, JACOBS, Robert, SELOVER, Margaret, and TOWNSEND, Agatha, *Introduction to Testing and the Use of Test Results* (New York, Harper, 1953).

VITELES, Morris S., "A Dynamic Criterion," *Occupations,* Vol. XIV (June, 1936, Section One), pp. 963–967.

WATSON, Robert I., ed., *Readings in the Clinical Method in Psychology,* Part III (New York, Harper, 1949).

WILLIAMSON, E. G., *Counseling Adolescents* (Revision of Part I of *How to Counsel Students*) (New York, McGraw-Hill, 1950), Ch. 8.

CHAPTER 15

Counseling and Treatment:

Issues and Principles

THE FIFTH COMPONENT of distributive guidance (see Chapter 5) is "To help the child at times of selection and decision," and the fourth component of adjustive guidance is "To arrive at remedial treatment, administer it, and follow it through." This chapter and the one following will present the guidance activities and features which especially bear upon these components. Following analysis, synthesis, diagnosis, and prognosis comes the action of counsel and remediation as defined in form and scope by those prior processes.

To call these chapters simply "Counseling" seems to impose an inadvisable limitation. Strictly speaking, the word "counseling" connotes a one-to-one relationship between an adviser and client. In fact, Gustad has given the following definition:[1]

Counseling is a learning-oriented process, carried on in a simple one-to-one social environment, in which a counselor . . . seeks to assist the client . . . to learn more about himself and to accept himself, to learn how to put such understanding into effect in relation to more clearly perceived, realistically defined goals to the end that the client may become a happier and more productive member of his society.

But to act with good judgment upon the evidence revealed by the diagnosis will often involve much more activity than is represented by the interaction of counselor and client in an interview or series of interviews. A case may signify the need for conferring with parents, for counseling parents, for informing teachers of facts they need to know in their handling of the student, the utilization of special services of school or community for the benefit of

---

[1] John W. Gustad, "The Definition of Counseling," p. 17, in *Roles and Relationships in Counseling,* Ralph F. Berdie, ed. Minnesota Studies in Personnel Work, No. 3 (Minneapolis, University of Minnesota Press, 1953).

the student, school administrative action to change the situation of the student, or other alteration of the student's environment.

The major consideration in the process is that the welfare of the individual student is central. The wide range of ultimate action-steps to be taken in accomplishing his distribution and adjustment seems to be appropriately designated as "counseling and treatment."

THE COUNSELING PROCESS VIEWED AS TEACHING-LEARNING

Purpose of Counseling Is to Influence Behavior

As Frank Parsons envisioned the wise choice of a vocation, it was to be accomplished as the result of learning. The individual was to learn, on the one hand, all about his own abilities, interests, limitations; and on the other hand, he was to learn about the requirements and opportunities of the various vocations. Then he was to exercise true reasoning on the relations of these two groups of facts, so that vocational choice might be made on the basis of well-founded insights. Some of the means of accomplishing these understandings, as also the understandings contributory to adjustment, have been presented and explained in Chapters 6, 8, 9, and 10 of this book. As it was shown in Chapter 8 that teaching (in the sense of directing curricular activity, primarily for developmental purposes) is also performing guidance, so guidance in the form of individual counseling is also teaching—that is, it is an activity carried on for the purpose of changing present behavior (adjustment) or for giving direction and character to future behavior (distribution).

Thus, he who counsels must know what learning is and how it is brought about. Of recent books on counseling, two which have given extended attention to learning theory and experimentation are those by the Pepinskys[2] and by Shaffer and Shoben.[3] To understand how aberrant behavior in its multitude of forms was learned and how wholesome behavior can be learned to replace it, is indeed a field for long and intensive study.

The literature on the psychology of learning is both voluminous and discordant. Various schools of thought have developed to expound conflicting explanations of the learning process—explanations supported by both theory and research. Despite the divergence and lack of agreement, or probably because of it, great progress has been made in the refinement of our understanding of the learning process, although no generally acceptable and all-inclusive theory has been found. Some years ago (1942) leading psychologists in the field of learning collaborated in a yearbook on the subject,[4] devoting extended

[2] Harold B. Pepinsky and Pauline N. Pepinsky, *Counseling: Theory and Practice* (New York, Ronald Press, 1954).

[3] Laurance F. Shaffer and Edward J. Shoben, Jr., *The Psychology of Adjustment,* 2nd ed. (Boston, Houghton Mifflin Co., 1956).

[4] *The Psychology of Learning,* Part II of the 41st Yearbook of the National Society for the Study of Education (Bloomington, Ill., Public School Publishing Co.).

space to the exposition of three dominant theories, namely, conditioning, connectionism, and field theory. A chapter by the chairman, T. R. McConnell, attempted a reconciliation of the theories.

It seems likely today that we are prone to accept the point of view that learning takes place in different ways, that there is no simple, single explanation for it. Conditioning plays an important role in determining behavior patterns, but so do the development of motor skills and the development of perception with its attendant organization of impressions. The more consciously deliberative activities of acquiring understandings and solving problems also modify behavior. So likewise do appreciations, acquired by having experiences strongly affective in tone and calculated to arouse the emotions in support of the human values which are held in high esteem by contemporary society.

The undergraduate education of teachers acquaints them with these kinds of learning and with the varied methods to be used in acomplishing the learnings. They practice the methods in student teaching, and after graduation, as certified teachers. But as teachers or as counselors they need more intensive study of learning at the graduate level, for to bring about learning is the purpose of their professional existence.

A Contrast Between Curriculum and Counseling

Learning through counseling has greater possibilities of being accomplished than learning via the curriculum. If the reader will turn back to Chapter 3 he will note some of the obstacles to the accomplishment of behavioral change which sometimes characterize the school in its curricular activity: intrinsic motivation strangled by the disposition to think of education as an instrument for personal advancement; subject-centeredness compelling activity which is artificial and unrelated to pupil purposes and needs; systems of marking and credits which establish false values and divert the attention of teachers and pupils alike from the behavioral changes which are properly the goal of school activity.

By contrast, counseling is oriented to the pupil's needs and purposes. It starts with a problem felt by the pupil—the future course of his life, his present social relationships, his physical needs, his mental health—just to mention a few broad areas. The range and variety of the real problems of pupils was given some illumination in Chapter 10, as were also the means of taking inventory of the problems, in order to establish a sound foundation for life-like homeroom group-guidance programs. Now, counseling works directly to help the pupil solve his problems, acquire the strength to overcome the obstacles which oppress him, accomplish the growth which his nature compels him to strive for.

Counseling is unencumbered with subject matter. It is unimpeded by those artificial subject matter boundary lines which so often shatter and fragmentize the activity of the curriculum so that truly educative experience is impossible. It is free from the compulsions of having to instill into memory ill-understood rules and principles for which the pupil feels no need. Its intercommunications are not controlled by an organization of content which is extraneous to the purposes of the pupil's real life.

Subject matter there is in counseling. It is the content of the problem, of the background which clarifies and defines the problem, of possible solutions to the problem, and of the reasoned testing of the solutions. The organization of such subject matter must be found in the needs and experience of each individual counselee and in such knowledge as the counselor draws out of his experience file for its bearing on the case.

The purpose of making this rather obvious contrast between curricular experience and counseling experience is to suggest that the latter ought more surely to eventuate in true learning than the former. The conditions surrounding counseling are certainly more favorable. Nevertheless, the conditions cited are not just automatically present. The counselor needs to know the elements of the learning process and how to marshal them to take full advantage of his superior opportunity.

Motivation

Effective counseling depends upon the thorough understanding of the forces and drives that impel the learner to activity—that are responsible for his present behavior and that must be called upon to determine his future behavior. There are motivations that are characteristic of the various age groups; they drive the individual to accomplish the developmental tasks which are typical compulsions felt at the varying maturity levels. There are motivations that are characteristic of the various culture groups; a substantial and growing body of research is making us aware of the contrasting values held by the different social classes, ethnic and racial groups, occupational and geographical divisions of our people. Motivations vary also among individuals, so that what is broadly characteristic of a group must not be assumed of an individual in that group. Motivations vary in strength and in the tenacity with which they are held. Motivations vary in consciousness, presumably on a continuum from those which are in the brightest light of consciousness to those which are in the darkest corners of the subconscious.

Motives are learned. They are acquired from the environment, or, more accurately, from the dynamic relationships of organism with environment. Presumably, in Riesman's inner-directed man the influence of the organism plays the larger role in motivation: his directing forces were planted within him early in his life. With Riesman's other-directed man, environment is the major influence: he looks to his contemporaries for direction.[5] The trend of the times is toward increased other-directedness. The implications for the school counselor are that the individual is increasingly sensitive to and af-

[5] David Riesman, with Nathan Glazer and Reuel Denney, *The Lonely Crowd*, abridged ed. (Garden City, L.I., Doubleday and Co., 1954).

fected by the standards of his peer group. These standards may not be the best for a given individual, and then the counselor has the task of helping him acquire suitable motives.

In another writing[6] Riesman illustrates this problem by citing the hypothetical case of a girl who has marked potentialities for a career in music. If she is to develop her talent, she must put in long hours in practice. But such a schedule will deprive her of the opportunity to go to the movies with other girls of her age and otherwise to enjoy pleasant associations with them. Her mother is disturbed. She doesn't want her daughter to miss the friendships and good times of high-school life. Riesman suggests that such considerations are short-sighted, that the longer view would have the girl progress in her music so that she can surely gain admission to a fine musical conservatory where she will find a peer group with whom she will feel a much closer kinship than to the more heterogeneous companions of her high-school days.

Learning new motives is the major problem to solve in inducing youth of college ability in the lower classes of society to go to college and prepare for the professions. Beilin has effectively set forth the "psychological preparation" needed by such youth and their parents, saying in part,[7]

What is required, if larger numbers of lower-class youngsters are to go on to college is a clear-cut attempt to change the lower-class values, make faith in them less certain, and substitute middle-class goals for those relinquished. . . .

The most difficult aspect of the program suggested here involves generating the "drive" necessary to make the hard task before each youth worthy of sustained effort.

The whole work of such reconstruction of motives is complex, and Beilin's exposition suggests that he is quite aware of its dimensions.[8]

Let no guidance worker minimize the importance of motivation in inducing the counselee to set desirable goals and put forth energy to attain them. Properly and sufficiently motivated, the individual will uproot deep-set, long-standing behavior patterns and establish new ones with remarkable dispatch. But just as one of the most frequently found weaknesses of classroom teaching is the failure to arouse purpose in pupils, it is probably true that counselors often neglect—especially in adjustive guidance—to give sufficient thought to the motivation of their clients.

6 "How Different May One Be?" in *Individualism Reconsidered* (Glencoe, Ill., The Free Press, 1954), pp. 266–270.

7 Harry Beilin, "The Utilization of High Level Talent in Lower Socioeconomic Groups," *Personnel and Guidance Journal,* Vol. XXXV (November, 1956), p. 176.

8 Significant additions to the theoretical and scientific literature on motivation have recently been made by McClelland and his associates in the following two books: D. C. McClelland, J. W. Atkinson, R. A. Clark, and E. L. Lowell, *The Achievement Motive* (New York, Appleton-Century-Crofts, 1953); D. C. McClelland, *Studies in Motivation* (New York, Appleton-Century-Crofts, 1955).

A Simple Example of Learning from Counsel

Some years ago C. C. Ross reported[9] an experiment at the University of Kentucky for which forty pairs of freshmen were selected from the students who ranked in the lowest fifth of the class on intelligence tests. The pairing was done on the basis of sex and fraternity affiliation as well as intelligence.

The students in the experimental group were called together, and the purpose of the freshman tests was explained to them. They were told that it was felt they had a right to know that their scores had been comparatively low and that, while it was nothing to be particularly alarmed about, it was important for such students to recognize at the outset that they were up against a somewhat different situation from other students making better test scores. They were assured, however, that the experience at the University of Kentucky indicated that, if such students were really serious and willing to work hard and did not make the mistake of trying to carry too heavy a load or to undertake too many extra-curricular activities or outside work, there appeared to be no reason why they could not make a satisfactory record in college. When an opportunity for questions was given, considerable interest was shown, and a lively informal discussion followed. No information of any kind was given the control group. In fact, they never knew they were involved in an experiment at all.

A sample of Ross' data on the outcome of the experiment is shown here as

TABLE 64. Distribution, according to Average Quality Points, of Experimental and Control Groups of University Freshmen Taken from the Lowest Fifth in Intelligence

Average Quality Points	First Semester		Second Semester	
	Experimental	Control	Experimental	Control
1.8	1	...	...	...
1.6	1	1	2	3
1.4	3	1	2	1
1.2	5	2	5	2
1.0	9	2	5	...
.8	3	7	2	7
.6	7	8	8	4
.4	8	5	5	7
.2	2	10	1	7
.0	1	4	4	3
Total	40	40	34	34
No. earning 1.0 and more	19	6	14	6
Mean QPA	.94	.64	.85	.69

[9] "Should Low Ranking College Freshmen Be Told Their Scores on Intelligence Tests?" *School and Society*, Vol. XLVII (May 21, 1938), pp. 678–680.

Table 64.[10] The experimental group definitely excelled the control group in freshman scholarship.

The learning process which this brief counseling act set in motion is fairly self-evident. The counselor brought them to a more accurate self-perception; then he enlightened them on the dimensions and the demands of their main jobs as freshmen. Armed with such *understandings,* they must have imposed upon themselves a greater self-discipline and a more thoughtful use of their time than characterized the members of the control group. Probably, also, their learning expressed itself in the cultivation of *habits* which made for better time usage. The modification in their behavior was powered by their strong desire to be successful in the college venture. They were in a state of *readiness* to receive the counsel and to be influenced by it. A measure of anxiety was created in them; it generated the *drive* to protect their self-esteem and their vocational plans.

This explanation of the contrast which shows up in Table 64 is arrived at largely by inference. Behavior did change, and the inferences as to cause seem reasonable. The counselor will do well to measure the outcomes of his ministrations, but he is more certain to score successes if he knows the conditions and elements of the learning process and plans his procedure in the light of that knowledge.

THE INTERVIEW

Heart Process of Counseling

All of the counselor's knowledge of psychological and social processes, of educational and vocational structures, requirements, and opportunities, and of data concerning the ability, personality, and environment of the individual, are brought to a focus in the interview. It is true, however, that not all of the interchanges between counselor and individual counselee demand such a complete marshaling of the counselor's skill and knowledge. For example, Chapter 11 described such interviews as are held primarily for the obtaining of information when a pupil first enters a given school. Likewise, there may be interviews primarily for the purpose of giving information, of which an example just cited was the group interview held with forty university freshmen by C. C. Ross. Insofar as these types of interviews are restricted to the obtaining and giving of information, they are preliminary to the more crucial interviews which are held for the purposes of decision-making and adjustments.

The interview or series of interviews which are intended to help the individual decide upon a future course of action, or to influence his behavior, are the logical recognition of that uniqueness of the individual which has been emphasized in the preceding chapters on analysis, synthesis, diagnosis,

[10] *Ibid.* Adapted from Table 2, page 680.

and prognosis. It is an acknowledgment that the counselee is not identical with any other person. Performance of the counseling function demands, therefore, that each individual be given help in weighing the factors peculiar to his situation. Hence, the counseling relationship, as expressed in the interview, deserves the closest study.

When, however, it comes to knowing just what goes on in the interview, or what should go on, we are somewhat at a loss. Because it is so individual, the interview is a highly subjective process. It does not lend itself to the establishment of fixed procedures by scientific study. The interchange of thought and feeling between two personalities is heavily loaded with variables. Thus, the literature on the interview consists largely of descriptions of practice and the conclusions of experienced practitioners. In recent years, analyses of phonographically recorded interviews have somewhat illuminated interview techniques, especially the nondirective techniques which are described in the next section of this chapter. Most influential in the establishment of guide-posts for the conduct of the interview has been the expanding knowledge of the principles of mental health which has come to us in the past fifty years.

Some Governing Principles and Techniques

Rapport. Most prominent in the vocabulary which is used to describe the interview is the word *rapport*. First step in interview procedure, say the authorities, is to establish rapport, a contact which is friendly and understanding. Such a feeling of mutual trust is antecedent to the successful airing of the various angles presented by a problem in social or emotional adjustment, or to the frank expression of feelings, motives, and attitudes which affect educational and vocational choices.

Obviously, the creation of good rapport is dependent upon the personalities of counselor and counselee. If the latter is a stable, outgoing personality, it will not be difficult to get on friendly terms with him. If he is shy, withdrawn, and insecure, the establishment of rapport is a longer process and one which calls for all the skill the counselor can muster. On the other hand, variation in counselor skill and in personality type also profoundly affect rapport, making it easy or difficult to achieve this essential foundation for effective counseling.

With such numerous variables on each side in the relationship, rapport may be thought of as achieved in varying degrees. It may be nonexistent; it may be superficial, just an outward show of friendliness; or it may be warm and penetrating, a bond of acceptance and respect which permits the freest exploration and clarification of a problem.

Problems, likewise, make it difficult or easy to establish rapport. The girl who has been caught rifling a purse in the locker-room usually brings to the interview high protective barriers which must somehow be removed before her problem can be explored. On the other hand, there are usually no such emotional overtones, no involvement of the ego, in the case of a girl who is puzzled about choosing between French and chemistry.

The organization and administration of the counseling service greatly affect rapport. Sometimes schools and colleges manage this program in such fashion that they create problems for themselves. If Charles' homeroom teacher tells him, "You are to report to the counselor's office at 11:15 today," and the boy has no inkling of the purpose of the appointment, he is likely to report in quite a posture of defense. If Joe's grades slip badly because of his emotional turmoil over a broken engagement, and the dean sends him a note to report to the counseling center over on the other side of the campus, it isn't going to be easy for Joe to bring up his love life in his first conversation with a stranger—the counselor.

Insofar as possible, the problem of rapport should be circumvented. In Chapter 10 it was urged that the homeroom teacher, because of his daily availability and opportunity for continuous friendly contact, might have frequent casually scheduled interviews with the student in which rapport is always existent.

A basic method for avoiding the problem of rapport is to motivate an entire group of pupils to seek individual interviews with the counselor. A simple example of this procedure was cited by Wrenn[11] from his personal experience thirty years ago. In a small high school he administered the Stanford Achievement Test in six sections at six different assembly periods. The day after a section had been taken, he discussed results and gave interpretations in a general way.

At the close of the period of test administration the principal announced a certain hour each day when pupils could visit him and talk over test results. There was no hesitancy on the part of the pupils, and in this way practically the whole high school was reached. No compulsion was used at any time. The interviews ranged from ten to thirty minutes in length. . . .

The same technique was described by Hedge and Hutson.[12] During the autumn months a testing program was carried out with the 201 members of the junior and senior classes of a six-year high school. After the tests were scored, a test-record card was prepared for each student. The superintendent, who was directly in charge of the program of guidance, then announced that during a certain hour of each day, by making an appointment with his secretary, pupils could visit him and talk over the results of the tests. The ready response of almost every member was excellent testimony to the efficacy of this method of motivating interviews.

The problem of rapport was easily resolved, also, in Haines' experimental program centered about his "Graph of Occupational Potentials" which the

[11] C. G. Wrenn, "Initiating a Guidance Program in a Small School," *Vocational Guidance Magazine,* Vol. VII (October, 1928), pp. 36–37.
[12] John W. Hedge and P. W. Hutson, "A Technique for Evaluating Guidance Activities," *School Review,* Vol. XXXIX (September, 1931), p. 509.

reader will find described in Chapter 16.[13] His students were given some orientation as to the values of the tests they were taking and the questionnaires they were filling out, so that they looked forward with eager interest to their interviews.

But while doing all that can be done to eliminate or minimize the problem of rapport, the fact remains that it is still a hurdle to tax the counselor's skill in many an interview. In school or college, teachers are identifying students with problems or puzzling behavior and referring them to a counselor. Or, students are making such appointments on their own initiative. First task of the counselor is to put the counselee at ease so that he can express himself freely about his problem. Obviously, the counselor must meet the student in a welcoming and hospitable spirit. He must initiate the conversation, using his judgment as to the desirability of starting off with some small talk or immediately approaching the client's business with such a question as, "What did you want to talk with me about?" Davidian has designated these two alternatives as the "glad-hand" and the "get-wet-all-over" techniques.[14] She deplores overconsciousness of the rapport problem as sometimes actually causing difficulty in attaining it, and continues,

If we believe in the need for rapport, we must divorce ourselves from the idea of *consciously creating* this state. What, then, is a possible answer? The most effective method of attaining this feeling of ease might be in developing an aura which is conducive to rapport. Counselors can develop through their own actions and principles of living a healthy way of life which will prompt them to be sought after by clients with problems. Would this not be the best possible type of rapport? It is not superimposed, it is not artificial, it is not turned off and on at the counselor's door. This self is built by living a life which promotes respect, trust, and confidence. This self makes itself known in the lives of students, and rapport is established before there is any notion of the counselor-client relationship.

Plainly, then, the establishment of rapport for the infinite variety of counselees and their problems does not depend on the learning of any formula but primarily upon the counselor's sincerity and his basic regard for the worth of every individual.

Empathy. A quality essential to the effective practice of many professions and occupations which are concerned with interpersonal relations is a capacity for empathy. This term is used "to denote the imaginative transposing of oneself into the thinking, feeling, and acting of another, and so structuring the world as he does."[15] Certainly, in all phases of counseling, this ability is needed, for the counselor is trying to understand the inner life and experience

13 W. A. Haines, *A Study of the Application of Part IV of the "Dictionary of Occupational Titles" to the Occupational Counseling of High-School Seniors.* Doctoral Dissertation (Pittsburgh, University of Pittsburgh Library, 1956).

14 Elizabeth V. Davidian, "Rapport and the Human Element," *Personnel and Guidance Journal,* Vol. XXXIII (April, 1955), pp. 469–470.

15 Rosalind F. Dymond, "A Scale for the Measurement of Empathic Ability," *Journal of Consulting Psychology,* Vol. XIII (April, 1949), p. 127.

of the counselee. This cannot be done by viewing the counselee objectively and engaging in intellectual analysis of his problem. Nor is it desirable for the counselor to experience such emotional involvement that he takes over the counselee's problems and treats them as though they were his own. There is a certain neutrality about the process of empathy which gives the client a feeling of support as he faces his problem but without creating the expectation that the counselor will solve it.

Some highly important questions have arisen concerning empathy but have not been answered. Can the trait be isolated and measured? Is it inborn or can it be cultivated? Is it related to intelligence? to age? to intimate environmental experience, such as the family atmosphere in which one grows up?[16] Certainly people vary in depth and dimensions of empathic capacity. Some are keenly perceptive of the thinking and feeling of others; some are obtuse and insensitive, inwardly oriented and inflexible.

How to obtain counselors possessed of a capacity for empathy is a problem long recognized by discerning administrators. For example, some years ago a nationally known principal of a large high school,[17] on being asked, "How do you select a dean of girls?" replied,

When a teacher *is* a dean of girls, I give her the title, but not until then. Whenever there is in my high school a woman teacher to whom the girls seem naturally to go for counsel; whenever there is one to whom the teachers go to ask for advice about dealing with problems of girls; or whenever there is a teacher who becomes, in a broad sense, a professional spokesman in the interest of the girls of the school, that is the teacher I'll appoint as a dean of girls in case a vacancy occurs.

Empathy was surely in the mind of R. D. Allen, also, when he stipulated that two of his five screens for selecting counselors were "Superiority in Pupil-Teacher Relationships" and "Superiority in Teacher-Teacher Relationships.[18] A convenient one-word symbol for a quality that has profound importance in human relationships is this word *empathy*.

"Rules" for the conduct of the interview. From time to time thoughtful and experienced persons have formulated sets of rules or lists of techniques for the conduct of the interview. Because of the infinite variety of interview situations, such codes can have nothing like universal applicability. Anyone who assumes the counseling role must recognize the need for flexibility in the interview. Nevertheless, some canvass of these contributions to interview literature has great value. They spell out the activity, the conduct, and the

---

[16] Some studies have been made to enlarge our understanding of empathy, but they have not yielded conclusive results. They have been listed and interpreted in the following reference: Clyde A. Parker, "Empathy," *Personnel and Guidance Journal,* Vol. XXXIV (October, 1955), pp. 89–93.

[17] DeWitt Morgan, then principal of Arsenal Technical Schools, Indianapolis.

[18] "Selecting Counselors in Secondary Schools," *Vocational Guidance Magazine,* Vol. X (November, 1931), p. 69. Allen's contribution is more extensively drawn upon in Chap. 18.

attitudes of the counselor which are calculated to achieve and maintain rapport, to accomplish a state of empathy, and to exploit these conditions for realizing the purposes of the interview. Some of the "rules" are suggestions of positive and negative action on the part of the counselor to assure the counselee's right to, and responsibility for, self-discovery and self-resolution of his problems. Certainly most of the "rules" constitute implementation of the teaching-learning process as described in the first section of this chapter.

One widely quoted set of rules is that which grew out of the experimentation at the Hawthorne Works of the Western Electric Company in which 20,000 employees were interviewed under conditions designed to promote fullest expression of thought and feeling. This was not a school situation, but if the reader will question the applicability of each rule to counseling in schools, he will find it partially or wholly acceptable. The rules are as follows:[19]

1. The interviewer should listen to the speaker in a patient and friendly, but intelligently critical, manner.

2. The interviewer should not display any kind of authority.

3. The interviewer should not give advice or moral admonition.

4. The interviewer should not argue with the speaker.

5. The interviewer should talk or ask questions only under certain conditions:

a. To help the person talk.

b. To relieve any fears or anxieties on the part of the speaker which may be affecting his relation to the interviewer.

c. To praise the interviewee for reporting his thoughts and feelings accurately.

d. To veer the discussion to some topic which has been omitted or neglected.

Just as World War II ended, John Darley prepared a pamphlet on interviewing, for guidance of the numerious agencies which were being set up to aid individuals in the various adjustments they were making as the nation returned to a peacetime economy. Selective quotation from a section entitled "Techniques during the Interview" may be made as follows by way of offering some concrete suggestions to the readers of this book:[20]

2. *Phrasing Questions.* One of the best ways to cut off any conversational flow from the client is to ask a question that can be answered "Yes" or "No."

4. *Overtalking the Client.* Many people in an interview may find it difficult to state what they mean concisely, and without some fumbling for words. Do not be in such a hurry that you override or overtalk the client. . . . A very frequent

---

19 F. J. Roethlisberger and W. J. Dickson, *Management and the Worker* (Cambridge, Mass., Harvard University Press, 1939), p. 287.

20 *The Interview in Counseling* (Washington, D.C., U.S. Department of Labor, 1946), pp. 14–19.

error of beginning interviewers is to put words in a client's mouth or talk faster than the client or in some way take the conversation away from the client.

5. *Accepting the Client's Attitudes and Feelings*. At various points in the interview the client may be trying to express the more deep-seated attitudes and feelings that control his behavior. He will bog down in the task simply because none of us finds it easy to put into words some of our more private attitudes, resentments, doubts, and uncertainties. He may also fear that the interviewer will not approve of what he says. The interviewer must indicate to the client that he has accepted but not passed judgment on these feelings and attitudes. Merely saying, "I see," or "I understand," or "Yes," will serve to bridge the conversational gap and to keep the client talking.

6. *Cross Examining*. Do not fire questions at the client like a machine gun. The interview is not a cross-examination . . . when questions are needed, space them out and phrase them in as neutral a manner as possible.

7. *Silences in the Interview*. Most people are embarrassed if no conversation is going on. . . . If it becomes necessary to break a silence, merely ask the client to tell you a little bit more about the point he has just finished covering. This will give him a chance to get in motion again.

8. *Reflecting the Client's Feeling*. If the client is attempting to put a deeply emotional attitude into words, it may be a difficult and awkward process. He may have a feeling of shame or guilt attached to this attitude, or he may hesitate to appear ridiculous. . . . Whatever his motivations, this flow of emotion will have been cut off beyond recovery if the interviewer passes moral judgment on the attitude or turns aside from the underlying feeling that is emerging. The interviewer will have turned aside from the underlying feeling if he asks a question that moves the interview off in another direction.

It is better to say, "You feel that people are being unfair to you," than to tell the complainer, "Everybody has trouble getting along sometime. . . ."

9. *Admitting Your Ignorance*. . . . The client is likely to have more confidence in the interviewer who does not hesitate to admit his ignorance. . . .

10. *Distribution of Talking Time*. Probably the greatest mistake of beginning interviewers is their tendency to talk the client into a coma. . . .

11. *The Vocabulary of the Interviewer*. . . . the interviewer must make some judgment of the level of verbal ability and understanding of the person to whom he is talking. . . .

12. *The Number of Ideas Per Interview*. It is unlikely that in the usual interview a major miracle can be wrought in the life style of another person. This means that the number of ideas and topics discussed might well be kept to a minimum in most interviews. . . .

13. *Control of the Interview*. If the interview is to have the continuity and the end results that will lead to a modification of the client's behavior, the interviewer must keep control of the interview. . . .

14. *Avoid the Personal Pronoun*. . . .

15. *Bad News in the Interview*. Not all the facts that the interviewer must give to the client are happy or favorable. It does no good in such situations to reassure the individual by saying that "everything will turn out all right,". . .

18. *Setting Limits on the Interview*. . . . It is better if the interviewer and the client realize from the beginning that the interview will last for a fixed length of time. . . .

19. *Plans for Action*. While it is not essential in all cases that the client rush out and do something as a result of the interview, it is generally true that he will complete the learning process about himself and about his particular world if there are certain things that he feels he has to do as a result of the interview discussion. . . .

20. *Summarizing the Interview*. . . . If possible the client should do the summarizing. . . .

21. *Ending the Interview*. This is not an easy task. . . . Quite often a phrase such as "Do you think we have done all we can for today?" or, "Is there anything more you would like to talk about today?" will be enough to end the interview. . . .

Darley prefaced his list of "techniques" with an appropriate warning against regarding them as a rigid set of rules. With such limitations they make sense, and while they were intended primarily as guideposts for interviewing adults in nonschool situations, their applicability in the counseling of secondary-school and college youth will be apparent to an experienced teacher at either of those levels.

That the interviewer, in practice, often violates some of these suggestions may be taken for granted, but a couple of surveys may well be drawn upon for the picture of malpractice which they afford. For example, Speer obtained the reactions—anonymously stated—of 200 students to the counseling they had experienced in 17 different colleges and universities. Some 45 of the 200 papers reported definitely negative feelings, and the dissatisfactions that were expressed were classified as follows:[21]

	Number
Interview unplanned	23
Recommendations vague	20
Counselor talked too much	19
Did not consider student	16
No purpose or goal	12
Pre-established pattern	7

As regards the second category, Speer said there was evidence that some students had expected and desired that the counselor would give them authoritative settlements of their problems. The third category is indeed an indictment. The fourth category comprised those comments of students concerning treatment so impersonal that they felt they were not regarded as individuals but just as "cases." "Just going through the motions," is the essential characterization of comments classified in the fifth category, while the

[21] George S. Speer, "Negative Reactions to College Counseling," *Occupations*, Vol. XXIV (November, 1945), pp. 99–100.

sixth category has reference to the counselors who had a favorite theory of human behavior into which they tried to fit every incident. Other scattered dissatisfactions concerned interruptions of the interview, counselor doing something else at the same time (such as correcting papers), and two cases in which the counselor expressed shock and disgust at presentation of sexual problems.

Hook[22] used a questionnaire with university freshmen to obtain their reactions to the counseling interviews they experienced in high school. Sixty per cent characterized their interviews as generally satisfactory, 40 per cent, unsatisfactory. Some criticisms written in were the following:

> Sometimes felt that he listened out of duty and not sincere interest.
> I felt he was rather arrogant.
> He was not personal enough.
> Counselor said, "You are not qualified to take these subjects." I didn't like that.
> I had a feeling that he was a sneak.

One question was, "During your interview were there any interruptions?" "Yes," was the answer given by 75 per cent. To the question, "Did you notice any occurrences which made you feel awkward, hurried, or unnecessary?" approximately one third wrote in such comments as the following:

> He talked directly at me all the time.
> Kept looking at his watch.
> Not interested, hurried conversation so as to get rid of me.
> Seemed not to be listening when I talked.
> Tapping pencil.
> Acted as if he were rushed for time.
> He made me feel that my questions were silly.

Quite evidently there is something to be learned from these unfavorable reactions of interviewees. Their comments support the ideal qualities which we have cited as properly characterizing the interview, because they serve to outline the ideals more sharply.

Recording the Interview

The counselor's memory of what transpires in the interview, what progress is made, what decisions are arrived at, is patently too unreliable to serve the purposes of counseling. Notes must be taken. Sarbin suggests the following six purposes to be fulfilled by the case notes of the psychological counselor:[23]

[22] Jeannette W. Hook, "Is Your Interview Showing?" *Occupations,* Vol. XXX (February, 1952), pp. 332–334.

[23] Theodore R. Sarbin, "The Case Record in Psychological Counseling," *Journal of Applied Psychology,* Vol. XXIV (1940), pp. 184–197; see the same writing in the following reference: Arthur H. Brayfield, ed., *Readings in Modern Methods of Counseling* (New York, Appleton-Century-Crofts, 1950), pp. 423–432.

1. They serve as a point of departure in a subsequent interview. By affording the counselor a chance to refresh his memory just before the counselee reappears, time is saved and the counselee surely identified.

2. If it should happen that the counselee must be turned over to a second counselor, the record of previous counseling contacts will be essential for the orientation of the latter. (Figure 17 in Chapter 14 shows Mary Margaret Anderson as having four counselors in her six years in secondary schools.)

3. Case notes are evidence of what the counselor is doing, and they thus facilitate supervision of his work.

4. Case notes are used in the training of counselors, for they help to acquaint interns with the procedures of diagnosis and treatment.

5. Case notes constitute documentation of interview conversations so that the erroneous impressions which a counselee may convey to his parents or teachers by distortion or misquotation may be corrected.

6. Case notes may be useful in personnel research.

Sarbin gives illustrative case notes under such headings as "clinical data," "diagnosis," "prognosis," "treatment," etc. They include not only evidence but the generalizations and interpretations at which the counselor had arrived. By contrast, Tyler[24] advocates limiting the notes to a report of points brought out in the interview conversation, without judgments, interpretations, and technical phraseology. It is her thought that the client should be permitted to see the notes when any question comes up concerning a previous interview. Such an opportunity contributes to the client's confidence. "Client and counselor are seen as partners working from the same data."

When shall notes be taken? Darley said,[25] "It is best to write your case notes *immediately after* the interview. Case notes during the interview may bother the client." But Tyler's view is that[26] "Whether or not they are taken during the interview itself seems not to make much difference. . . . Whichever practice is followed, there should be no secret about [it]." Presumably, the counselor who takes notes during the interview explains to the counselee, "I'd better take a few notes to help me recall our conversation," and manages the process in such abbreviated form and with such selectivity as not to interfere with the free flow of ideas.

The reader should understand the distinction between the counselor's case notes and the notes which appear on such a cumulative record as Figure 17. The latter is a record of summaries and interpretations of the former.

The interview is indeed the heart of the counseling process. It has not been adequately treated in this section, but the following section will contribute additional concepts. The remaining sections of this chapter, and also Chapter 16, will cast further light on the interview.

[24] Leona E. Tyler, *The Work of the Counselor* (New York, Appleton-Century-Crofts, 1953), p. 74.
[25] *Op. cit.,* p. 20.
[26] *Op. cit.,* p. 73.

DIRECTIVE VERSUS NONDIRECTIVE COUNSELING

Main Characteristics of Nondirective Counseling

Perhaps no event in the history of the guidance movement has had a greater impact on the principles and practice of guidance than the publication, in 1942, of Carl Rogers' *Counseling and Psychotherapy* (Houghton Mifflin). The influence of this book has been enhanced by the steady flow of writings of research, analysis, and description which has come from Rogers and his students in the years since 1942. These writings have served not only to refine and to a slight extent modify the originally stated viewpoint, but also to elucidate its wider applicability.

Rogers described his concept of counseling as nondirective. More recently he has preferred to call it client-centered. The basic assumption of this attitude in and toward counseling is that the individual has, within himself, the capacity for growth and change which enable him to solve his own problem. Accordingly, the client does not go to the counselor as to a physician to be diagnosed and to receive a solution to his problem. Rather, he enters into a permissive situation which allows for the full release of his energies and the employment of his own resources. The counselor facilitates the process by fully accepting the client as he is, creating a warm and understanding atmosphere in the security of which the client may be himself and freely express his deeper feelings and attitudes. The counselor utters no moral judgments or evaluations; he shows no evidence of shock or disgust at whatever may be revealed. He enters into the feeling of the client so that he can see the world as the client sees it, and he reflects the client's feeling back to him. Advice is not given; neither is any intellectualized interpretation of the client's behavior or feeling.

The focus is upon the individual, not the problem. The aim is to bring about such growth in integration and self-dependence in the client that he is strengthened and organized to cope with present and future problems. Emphasis is on the accomplishment of this growth during the interview hour or hours and not after he leaves the interview. Hence, the need for such a counseling relationship as described in the preceding paragraph.

The road to growth is through the process of catharsis—the pouring out of feelings, the free expression of fears, anxieties, hatreds, the loosening of repressions. The counselor encourages this process; his remarks indicate that he is following the thought, but also they often clarify the client's thought and feeling by the use of more exact language. Ambivalences are brought out plainly, but not until the client has already expressed them, though inadequately and clumsily. "You hate your father, and yet you really love him, too." From such unburdening, in an atmosphere in which he does not have to defend himself, life begins to look different. The client moves toward a new understanding of himself, a new perception of relationships. As insight grows, his feeling of competence for taking care of his own problem or problems increases, and he himself comes to the conclusion that he no longer needs the support of the counseling relationship.

Rogers' second book, *Client-Centered Therapy* (Houghton Mifflin, 1951), is a fuller and more penetrating exposition of his theory. As in his first book, he makes extensive use of phonographic recordings of interviews to illustrate the several stages of self-organization of clients and the correct and erroneous comments or questions of counselors. The book is not a revision of the 1942 book, but an extension and elaboration of it. To become acquainted with Rogers' viewpoint, the reader should begin with *Counseling and Psychotherapy*.[27]

Criticisms, Questions, and Argument

The cases cited by Rogers in illustration of the principles of client-centered therapy concern individuals who are emotionally disturbed. Even those of his cases who superficially present problems of vocational and educational choice are in reality troubled by problems of some deeper nature which constitute the fundamental reasons for their being served at the type of psychological clinic in which Rogers has had his experience. Obviously, such individuals are to be found in every school and college student body, and they need attention whether a psychological clinic is available or not. But they are a minority. One of Rogers' students, Arthur Combs, connected with a general university guidance center, reported in an address at the 1946 Regional Conference of the Council of Guidance and Personnel Associations, Hotel Pennsylvania, New York, that nondirective counseling seemed appropriate in about 20 per cent of the cases seen in that center.[28] Presumably, the other 80 per cent were sufficiently wholesome, integrated, and free from conflict that they did not need personality reorganization; they needed educational and vocational information, the self-understanding contributed by interpretation of their academic records and test scores, or aid in the establishment of study habits and schedules. Like the maladjusted minority, they, too, acquired insight from the counseling experience, but without having to overcome emotional obstacles.

But Rogers does not care to set limits on the applicability of the type of counseling he espouses.[29] He points out that it has been used with people ranging in age from two to sixty-five, with problems involving mild adjustment to "severe disorders of diagnosed psychotics," with individuals who

[27] Rogers uses the terms "counseling" and "psychotherapy" interchangeably, but the average school counselor will be disposed to make a distinction. Be that as it may, the first-year graduate student, with the minimum of general and educational psychology in his undergraduate background, finds Rogers' book both intelligible and pleasurable to read.

[28] Donald E. Super, *Appraising Vocational Fitness* (New York, Harper, 1949), pp. 3–4.

[29] *Client-Centered Therapy*, pp. 228–230.

are normal to those who are deeply neurotic, with persons who are healthy and with those afflicted with psychosomatic ailments. In all categories, noteworthy success has been attained with some individuals; with some, partial success; and with some, failure. "It is felt that there is no advantage to be gained by trying to set dogmatic limits to the use of such therapy."

The school worker in guidance will feel, however, that there are *practical* limits to the use of such therapy. The general school or college counselor who reads the literature of nondirective counseling will be troubled by what seems a most profligate expenditure of time on a case. Most of Rogers' interviews seem to be scheduled for one hour, and the counselee may have as many of such interviews as he feels that he needs. A decade of experience has greatly increased the number of interviews per counselee. Says Rogers,[30]

Thus, where ten years ago a nondirective counselor found that his cases tended to average five or six interviews each, and rarely to run longer than fifteen, this same counselor finds that his cases now average fifteen to twenty interviews, and that fifty or one hundred interviews are not unusual. Has this development occurred because of the greater skill of the counselor in building an understanding relationship? Or because of the fact that as a counselor becomes well established more seriously maladjusted individuals turn to him? Or because some subtle change has taken place in viewpoint or technique? Whatever the cause, the thinking about client-centered therapy has been enriched by this range of intensity of experience.

Considering the present practical difficulties in establishing counseling service in schools and colleges, this type of counseling could only be made available to a very small fraction of the student body. At present, therapy which takes so much time with an individual is apparently mainly confined to child guidance centers and to the institutional and private practice of psychiatrists. Occasionally, someone reports an attempt to employ nondirective counseling on a restricted-time basis.[31] Despite the seeming obstacle of impracticability, there is no denying the value of having counselors, principals, and teachers understand the principles of nondirective counseling insofar as possible.

Naturally, one of the major questions asked of Rogers has been, What about diagnosis, including especially the use of our extensive armament of psychological tests? How can you carry on counseling without prior diagnosis? His measured reply, in a series of "propositional statements," is as follows:[32]

Behavior is caused, and the psychological cause of behavior is a certain perception or a way of perceiving. The client is the only one who has the potentiality of knowing fully the dynamics of his perceptions and his behavior.

---

[30] *Ibid.*, pp. 10–11.

[31] Helen Sargent, "Nondirective Counseling Applied to a Single Interview," *Journal of Consulting Psychology,* Vol. VII (July–August, 1943), pp. 183–190.

[32] *Op. cit.,* pp. 221–223.

In order for behavior to change, a change in perception must be *experienced*. Intellectual knowledge cannot substitute for this.

The constructive forces which bring about altered perception, reorganization of self, and relearning, reside primarily in the client, and probably cannot come from outside.

Therapy is basically the experiencing of the inadequacies in old ways of perceiving, the experiencing of new and more accurate and adequate perceptions, and the recognition of significant relationships between perceptions. In a very meaningful and accurate sense, therapy is diagnosis, and this diagnosis is a process which goes on in the experience of the client, rather than in the intellect of the clinician.

From this line of reasoning—upon which his counseling has been practiced —Rogers avers that "psychological diagnosis as usually understood is unnecessary for psychotherapy, and may actually be a detriment to the therapeutic process.[33]

In another writing Rogers has commented as follows on the use of tests:[34]

Psychometric tests . . . do not stand up well as a technique for client-centered counseling. If the counselor suggests the taking of tests, he is both directing the conversation and is implying, 'I know what to do about this.' To administer tests routinely or to have them administered at the beginning of the contacts is to proclaim in the strongest possible terms, 'I can measure you, can find out all about you,' and this implies to the client that the counselor can also tell him what he should do. For the counselor to interpret tests to the client is to say, 'I am the expert, I know more about you than you know about yourself, and I shall impart that superior knowledge.' In other words, when tests are used in the traditional fashion, they contradict almost completely the principles of client-centered counseling.

Rogers has expressed similar views regarding the limitations of the case history.[35] He concedes the high value of the case history for diagnosis but feels that the gathering of the data definitely interferes with the treatment process. The information-getting attitude which is essential for the counselor to assume in compiling a case history makes the client feel that the counselor is taking over the responsibility for solution of his problem. Rogers agrees, however, that if the treatment indicated by the case history is the alteration of environment, such a mind-set on the part of the client does no harm, that in fact the client may be more willing to accept environmental changes because he realizes such changes are based on thorough study of his situation.

It will be evident that in drawing a picture of nondirective or client-centered counseling Rogers has made extensive use of contrasts which give a

[33] *Ibid.*, p. 220.
[34] Carl R. Rogers, "Psychometric Tests and Client-Centered Counseling," *Educational and Psychological Measurement,* Vol. VI (1946), p. 141.
[35] *Counseling and Psychotherapy,* pp. 80–83.

picture of directive or counselor-centered counseling. That so-called directivists would object to Rogers' portrayal of them may well be assumed by
the reader if he will turn back to Chapter 1 (pages 20–21) and read the
quotations from guidance leaders who made those quoted remarks before
Rogers came upon the scene. Certainly the concepts of respect for the counselee and for his responsibility for making his own decisions without coercion
or imposition from the counselor, were stated with vigor and clarity by those
leaders.

In the debates which have been precipitated by Rogers' vigorous presentations, the "Minnesota point of view" has been mentioned as presumably being in opposition to that of Rogers. The prominent leadership which Paterson, Williamson, Darley, Wrenn, and others at the University of Minnesota
have given to the development of knowledge of counseling is perhaps the
reason for their involvement. At any rate, one of the expressions of their
point of view, penned by Williamson, may be briefly drawn upon here.[36]

. . . counseling is a *mutual* process between counselor and counselee. Minnesota
counselors are not required to take the 'vows of silence.' . . . Our conception of
counseling as a learning situation and experience has been that the counselor
contributes information and helps the individual develop and become skilled in
using methods of thinking or in bringing valid information to bear upon the
solution of his own personal problems, as well as to accept emotionally himself
and his situation. . . .

In contrast with this point of view we may ask certain questions of the nondirectivists. Is the truth about the nature of counseling encompassed in a series
of opposites, or two-order values, with no tenable ground between them? e.g.,
'nondirective versus directive'; 'client-centered versus counselor-centered'; 'silence versus advice'; 'all or none,' etc., etc. Or is it possible that we are dealing
with continuous situations which may be appropriate or inappropriate, relevant
or irrelevant, for different conditions, times, and persons? (pp. 149–150)

Concerning the importance which Rogers and his associates accord to the
principle that the counselee must make his own evaluations, decisions,
choices, and adjustments, Williamson says that is not new to a Minnesota
man but is quite congenial. While disclaiming all compulsions, he says that

we at Minnesota don't hesitate to suggest, inform, contribute, participate, help,
and even advise (!) students in their attempts to understand themselves and the
demands made upon them by the world about them.

At this point one may legitimately ask certain corollary questions:—Is advice
identical with imposition? Can the counselor have his own judgment, express it,
and yet be neutral? Is counseling restricted to therapy, to cases of emotion and
confused orientation? Or is counseling also applicable to normal learning of adjustments such as choosing an occupation? (p. 150)

[36] E. G. Williamson, "Counseling and the Minnesota Point of View," *Educational
and Psychological Measurement,* Vol. VII (Spring, 1947), pp. 141–155.

Perhaps the questions raised by Williamson in these two extracts afford a clue to the difficulty of obtaining a clear-cut statement of the issue between so-called 'directivists' and so-called 'nondirectivists,' an issue on which there could be a true clash of arguments. Williamson thinks of counseling in the context of a general university counseling bureau, serving the guidance needs of a large student body in accordance with the definition of guidance upon which this book is based. Considering the wide variety of problems met in such an agency, he feels the need for a variety of counseling approaches and techniques. Rogers, on the other hand, has apparently had all of his extensive experience with clients who are emotionally maladjusted. None of his writings have implied that on the shelves of the interview rooms in the Chicago Counseling Center one would find well-thumbed copies of the *Occupational Outlook Handbook* or Blauch's *Education for the Professions*. Thus, a set of principles based upon the assumption that the function to be performed is personality reorganization—a task which certainly varies in complexity and magnitude from client to client—cannot be sufficiently comprehensive to serve the full range of counseling responsibilities. So, just as the first section of this chapter pointed out that we cannot find one single, simple explanation for the learning process, it seems likely that we cannot find one universally applicable body of rules for counseling. It is not necessary to reconcile schools of thought, but it does take wisdom to be eclectic in employing them.[37]

Is There a Directive-Nondirective Continuum?

In one of the extracts just quoted from Williamson he questions the assumption inherent in the language used by Rogers that counseling is "encompassed in a series of opposites, of two-order values, with no tenable ground between them." Combs, writing out of his experience at the Syracuse University guidance center, does not try to find a middle ground but says that nondirective and directive techniques are complementary practices, each having its unique usefulness, depending upon the type of counseling problem.[38] Bixler, likewise, does not try to reconcile opposing techniques, but believes that no one method is appropriate to the problems of all clients and that selection of the *appropriate* therapy from an "armament of therapies" must be relied upon for most effective results.[39] He says the difficulty is that we have no criteria by which to decide which technique to use, but that it should be done on the basis of diagnostic and case history data.

Combs advocates the use of directive techniques when the client's primary

[37] A noteworthy contribution by the Minnesota group to counseling by nondirective methods, of a certain type of maladjusted student, is recounted in the section on disciplinary problems in Chapter 16.

[38] Arthur W. Combs, "Non-Directive Techniques and Vocational Counseling," *Occupations,* Vol. XXV (February, 1947), pp. 261–267.

[39] Ray H. Bixler, "Counseling: Eclectic or Systematic?" *Educational and Psychological Measurement,* Vol. VIII (Summer, 1948), pp. 211–214.

need is for information, education, or clarification of thinking, and the use of nondirective techniques where the primary need is for social and emotional adjustment. He acknowledges that a case which was started directively might prove to need nondirective treatment. Since it is difficult, and confusing to the client, for the counselor to make such a shift, it has been found best to tactfully refer the client to another counselor. In the realm of vocational counseling Combs finds nondirective techniques to have particular applicability in the following situations:[40]

1. *As a preliminary interview technique . . .* leaves the client free to bring up any problems . . . counselors . . . reserve any directive questions to the end of the session. . . .

2. *When the level of aspiration shows marked variation from demonstrated ability or when there is a wide discrepancy between expressed and measured interests. . . .*

3. *When the pre-counseling information from testing, observation, or reports from others indicates a pressing social, emotional, or personal problem. . . .*

4. *Whenever it is necessary for the client to make decisions. . . .*

5. *Whenever it is necessary to deal with parents.*

Edward S. Jones,[41] from long experience in counseling at the University of Buffalo, objects to the "all or none"—either directive or nondirective—dictum of Rogers.

Why not various stages on a continuum? To read some of the material it would seem that a spell is cast, that one must not get away from that particular spell or everything will be lost. . . . artificially non-co-operative. Conversation is not like that, nor are friendly discussions of any sort. Even if there is a general emphasis on student thinking, or client-centered unraveling, there are so often opportunities to give specific information, to mention a clue, or to illustrate what someone else has done or considered.

So, Jones suggests flexibility, adaptability—directive at one point and nondirective at another—in the same interview. He gives illustrations of such gradations in directiveness.

Strang[42] hypothesizes a nondirective-directive scale on which counselors can take different positions for using vocational information in counseling.

Danskin and Robinson have reported a thoughtful research project which was designed to determine if and to what extent the actual practice of counselors reflects a directive-nondirective continuum.[43] They analyzed the ver-

[40] *Op. cit.,* p. 267.

[41] "Gradations of Directiveness in Counseling," *Educational and Psychological Measurement,* Vol. VII (Autumn, 1947, Part II), pp. 559–563.

[42] Ruth Strang, "Use in Counseling of Information about Vocations," *School Review,* Vol. LIII (November, 1945), pp. 526–529.

[43] D. G. Danskin and F. P. Robinson, "Differences in 'Degree of Lead' among Experienced Counselors," *Journal of Counseling Psychology,* Vol. I (Summer, 1954), pp. 78–83.

batim transcriptions of 230 recorded interviews held with 82 university students by 35 counselors in five university counseling centers. Except for about ten cases, in which the interviews were focused on study skills, practically all of these interviews dealt with problems of adjustment—presumably comparable to Rogers' cases. In the 230 interviews, 890 discussion topics were identified, and each of these was analyzed for "degree of lead," which was estimated from two characteristics, namely,

(a) the extent to which the content of the counselor's remark seems to be ahead of the content of the client's last remark, and (b) the degree of pressure or definiteness in the counselor's remark that is apparently used to bring about client acceptance of the expressed idea.[44]

A distribution of the 82 cases according to the degree of lead exercised with them—from least to most—showed "no marked dichotomy" among the counselors, but a continuum type of arrangement. Eight known nondirective counselors appear in the upper half of the table, as might be expected, but "others definitely known *not* to be nondirectivists are mixed in with them." The cases in which the interviews were primarily on study skills were mostly found in the lower, or most directive, half of the table.

Granting the adequacy of the measuring instruments employed by Danskin and Robinson, they have shown that counselors in university counseling centers *are doing* adjustive counseling with varying degrees of directiveness. How successfully, is another question. One can dream of ascertaining the correlation of directiveness with success, but to date the dream has not been actualized. In the meantime, Rogers and his students have for more than a decade been publishing studies which report attempts to evaluate nondirective therapy.[45] No other counseling "school of thought" has been more aggressive in research.

The issues of this section may be seen in larger perspective by the reading of Ellis' canvass and evaluation of recent literature on the various techniques of therapy being advocated for use with "neurotic," "disturbed," or "maladjusted" individuals.[46] He identifies 42 different major techniques in a literature which is frequently characterized by "enthusiastic advocacy" on the one hand and "caustic condemnation" on the other. The human equation, he suggests, is a major consideration in the effective or ineffective use of them.

Ellis senses an "increasingly frank avowal of eclecticism," some decline in the dogmatic espousal of specialized narrow techniques, a greater willingness to acknowledge the merit of flexibility in approach to the same and different clients, a realization that there are many well-defined, wide-ranging

[44] *Ibid.,* p. 79.
[45] See especially Carl R. Rogers and Rosalind F. Dymond, eds., *Psychotherapy and Personality Change* (Chicago, University of Chicago Press, 1954).
[46] Albert Ellis, "New Approaches to Psychotherapy Techniques," *Journal of Clinical Psychology,* Vol. XI (July, 1955), pp. 208–260.

differences among clients, therapists, and therapeutic conditions which justify varied approaches.

Such methods of treatment as giving the client advice, reassurance, and information; or actively focusing on his current reality problems; or forcing him, through greater outside activity, to become fear-deconditioned; or setting distinct goals or values for him to achieve through therapy—these supportive and directive techniques, frequently much despised in the literature, have lately gained a much wider advocacy.[47]

Another trend noted by Ellis is an increasing emphasis on collaboration between therapist and client. ". . . democratic acceptance [of client] by the therapist is necessary for his maximum gain."

How School Practice Profits by the Directive-Nondirective Discussion

Rogers' contribution to counseling has been in nomenclature as well as in substance. He has made "nondirective" and "client-centered" the symbols which stand for a counseling process which rests upon certain principles and is performed by certain techniques. These principles were not new with Rogers. The expanding knowledge of mental hygiene, of learning, and of the conditions favorable to good personal relationships in school, in industry, and family life were affecting behavior patterns in the direction of the application of these principles before 1940. But clarification and emphasis has been given to them by their synthesis in "nondirective" counseling. Rogers' extensive use of transcripts of phonographically recorded interviews have given us illustrations of the exercise of the principles of democratic relationships, catharsis, empathy, client responsibility, and so on, thereby facilitating the learning of these principles by school guidance workers.

Readable as Rogers' writings are, however, it is a mistake for homeroom teachers or the general run of school counselors to think that they can, by self-study, practice nondirective therapy. Extended psychological training, followed by a long period of practice under competent supervision, is essential preparation for such work. The role of the amateur in psychotherapy may perhaps best be illustrated by a comparison of hypothetical treatments of physical injury and of emotional maladjustment. If, for example, a child has an accident, such as running an ugly sliver into his hand, his teacher or parent may presumably take one of these four courses of action: (a) let it alone, in which case the signs of festering will soon appear; (b) dig for the sliver with inadequate tools (a jackknife?) and inept skills, which will exacerbate the injured part and enhance the possibility of infection; (c) get the case to an expert—the physician—as soon as possible; (d) apply a soft poultice—it will keep the flesh moist and soft, act as an antiseptic, and most fully utilize nature's own healing processes. Similarly, if the behavior of the school child or youth is atypical—excessively shy and withdrawn, lacking in emotional

[47] *Ibid.,* pp. 248–249.

control, antisocial, or just enigmatic—the teacher or counselor may treat him in one of these ways: (a) ignore the problem; (b) take decided notice of it, ask direct questions to "get to the roots" of it, and otherwise take measures which are clumsy, embarrassing, and therefore irritating; (c) refer the case to a psychologist or psychiatrist; (d) apply the soft poultice of considerate, friendly words and actions which assure the individual of his genuine worth and importance, which give him a sense of security in his relationship to this one adult, and which create the kind of stable, consistent social climate that releases the individual's own power for growth.[48]

In view of the shortage of experts in psychotherapy, and the extraordinary time expenditure involved in Rogerian nondirective therapy, "the soft-poultice treatment" must be our main reliance. Some teachers and counselors seem naturally endowed with the attitudes and skills for employing it. The rest must acquire such attributes, even if doing so requires their own decided personality reorganization.

CAUTIONS FOR THE COUNSELOR

The Counselor as a Personal Factor in the Counseling Process

If every counselee is individual and unique, as has been emphasized over and over in these pages, it must be acknowledged that the counselor is also individual and unique. With all that may be done to ground the counselor in certain understandings, to school him to the exercise of certain techniques, he will still be a variable quantity, contributing to the subjective character of the counseling process. Flexibility he must indeed possess, if he is to cope with the infinite varity of counselees and problems. But beyond flexibility, the counselor is still an individual with his own built-in set of values, his own interests, prejudices, blind spots. He is indeed the product of his own heredity and environment, the reflection of his peculiar experience.

Questions, therefore, arise concerning the stamp he places upon his counselees. Does he have the tolerance, the breadth of viewpoint, to appreciate the relativity of some values, possibly the absolutism of others? Is he so rigid in inner-directedness that he cannot appreciate the influence of the peer group upon the standards and behavior patterns of modern youth? Is he strictly middle class and academic? Would he accept Mary Margaret Anderson (see Figure 17) for the self she was or insist on reconstructing her to a pattern in his mind for IQ's of 130?

From the forty "suggestions for counseling" listed by Watson and Spence quite a number of years ago, the following are selected for quotation here because they especially warn the counselor that he is a personal factor in the counseling process and that he must beware of certain human frailties:[49]

---

[48] For this analogy the writer is indebted to a colleague, Professor George L. Fahey.

[49] G. B. Watson and R. B. Spence, *Educational Problems for Psychological Study* (New York, Macmillan Co., 1930), pp. 339–343. Quoted by permission of the publisher.

25. Avoid pet theories, cure-alls, standard suspicions. Hunt for exceptions to theories, especially to new ones.

26. Don't try to save your own face. In many respects you may be less well adjusted than the counselee. Grow with him, don't reach down a helping hand from too high up.

32. Watch for budding stereotypes. When you find yourself getting an "intuition" in advance of investigation, which classifies a certain person or type of behavior, note it. It may mislead you often if not discounted.

35. Occasionally overhaul your motives in the counseling. Give due weight to the vicarious thrill of hearing about misdeeds, the sense of mastery, the delight in secret intimacy, the desire for affection and trust from the young, the enjoyment of a reputation. Try to keep these in proper proportion to the desire for welfare of counselee.

To exercise such precautions the counselor would certainly need a sense of the dramatic, a capacity for self-detachment, the ability to get outside of himself so that he can see himself and other people as the characters of a story. Some may have to implore as did Burns,

> O wad some Power the giftie gie us
> To see oursels as ithers see us!

It is essential that the counselor keep in mind the principle that good adjustment allows for wide variation in personality, interest, activity; it does not mean conformity to some narrow conception, such as success in the peer group. Years ago, in his newspaper column, William Lyon Phelps told of a boy whose behavior was peculiar while he was in high school. He wore loud blue suits, he wrote notes to the girls, he did not seem to "belong" to the boy society of the school. When this boy got to college, the sophomores hazed him severely. He went to see the dean about it—not to seek protection but just to talk it over with someone. The dean said, "If you want to persist in wearing that loud blue suit, and in acting differently from everybody else, you'll have to expect to be hazed. If you decide to conform to the crowd in your appearance and manners, the hazing will probably stop." The boy decided he would just be himself. Now, said Phelps, that boy is one of America's most noted playwrights, and just the other day he showed a great actress how to walk across the stage so as to express the meaning of his lines. How fortunate that this boy was not pressured to grow up into some sort of well-rounded mediocrity!

One rather obvious area in which many who counsel have prejudices and blind spots is that of the curriculum. In the high school, pupils are often advised in their choice of subjects and curriculums, by homeroom teachers. College specialization to prepare for teaching has narrowed these people; they have inadequate and sometimes quite erroneous conceptions of some of the subject fields. School counselors, too, may suffer from this limitation. The writer recalls one estimable lady who aggressively used the power of her office to build up enrollments in foreign language—her field of undergraduate specialization and subsequent teaching.

He who counsels for educational choices must be truly catholic in his understandings and interests. A partial corrective for the narrowness which has just been described would be to require every high-school teacher and counselor, as part of his fifth-year program, to pursue the kind of course in high-school curriculum which would give him orientation in the values, goals, methods, and progressive curricular formulations of each of the subject fields. Of course, another corrective to apply would be the careful screening of people for counseling on the basis of breadth of understanding of educational opportunity.

Thus, while we must understand the counselor to be a personal and subjective factor in counseling, we must labor to improve and control that factor.

Adjustment of Environment

As guidance was defined in Chapter 1 it was pointed out that the exercise of the adjustive phase of guidance is often the adjustment of the environment, rather than, or as well as, the adjustment of the individual. This may mean placing the individual in a *new* environment. Social workers have studied this mode of treatment intensively, because of their responsibility for placing children in institutions or foster homes. Several years ago a psychiatrist, working in an Illinois reformatory which was characterized by a true spirit of rehabilitation, said that the practice of the institution was to try to place dischargees in a new environment; if they went back to the environment from which they came, their future was almost always one of recidivism.

The school guidance worker will be alert, first of all, to the possibilities of shaping the school environment to the special needs of various individuals. For that purpose he will confer with teachers frequently to apprise them of special needs of pupils in their classes or in their extracurricular groups. The teacher will help the child who has feelings of inferiority or inadequacy to experience the satisfactions of achievement; he will give a special measure of friendliness to the youngster whose home life is devoid of affection; he will channel the excess energies of the highly active pupil who is frequently a disturber.

Correcting an unhealthy community environment will always be a challenge to the counselor. Chapter 18 will explore practices and possibilities of co-operation between the school guidance department and various community agencies for the improvement of community life.

The pupil's major environmental influence is, of course, his family and his home. The significance of this factor was explored at length in Chapter 11. Presented here are some hints of what the school guidance worker can do about this factor and how.

Rich in suggestion for fruitful teacher-parent contacts concerning young children is the recent book by Leonard, Van Deman, and Miles.[50] Langdon and Stout[51] are authors of another work in the same field, but with application to children of both elementary-school and secondary-school age. Both of these books depict the teacher-parent interview as a *conference* for the purpose of sharing information which bears on a shared goal, namely, the best development of the child. Their illustrations properly take account of the wide variation in the contacts—some initiated by the school and some by parents, some casual and some arranged, some formal and some informal. These democratic conferences often point to needed adjustment of school environment as well as of home environment.

Major cautions for the counselor which these and other authors have stated from their experience may be summarized as follows:

Let parents have plenty of opportunity to talk. Be a good listener. Do not evidence shock at whatever may be said. Be permissive.

Be honest. Do not gloss over, sugar-coat, or otherwise misrepresent. On the other hand, if Henry has his good points, state them as well as his shortcomings.

Do not be authoritative or get into arguments or use pedagogical language. Let there be no evidence of feelings of superiority or of standing in judgment.

Be ready and willing to explain, but it will be better if a child's difficulties and weaknesses can come as insights to the parents, rather than as revelations from you.

Objective evidence of the pupil's scholarship and discipline is always important, but especially so when it is necessary to correct false impressions held by the parents.

Orleans[52] has pointed to the strategic position of the guidance person as the guardian of both the counselor-student relationship and the parent-child relationship. She believes that while, as a general proposition, the guidance of the child will be shared by the counselor and the parents, circumstances sometimes arise which make such sharing inadvisable. For example, if the child is temporarily using the counselor as a parent substitute, the wisest course is not to see the parent unless it is absolutely essential, and then not without the knowledge and consent of the child. Such a situation is but one of the infinite variety which challenge the tact and good judgment of the counselor in the field of parent relationships.

When we consider adjustment of the environment—home, school, or community—it must be frankly acknowledged that oftentimes nothing can be done. There is the impossible home situation that cannot be improved. There is the slum community, devoid of wholesome, healthy influences.

[50] Edith M. Leonard, Dorothy D. Van Deman, and Lillian E. Miles, *Counseling with Parents in Early Childhood Education* (New York, Macmillan, 1954).

[51] Grace Langdon and Irving W. Stout, *Teacher-Parent Interviews* (Englewood Cliffs, N.J., Prentice-Hall, 1954).

[52] Myra Orleans, "Problems Peculiar to Parent Conferences," *Journal of the National Association of Deans of Women,* Vol. XVII (October, 1953), pp. 3–7.

There is the teacher whose discipline is poor or assignments unreasonable, but whose subject is a required element in some curriculum. Much counseling service is devoted to helping pupils survive and grow in spite of such handicapping environment. The counselor assumes a strengthening, supportive role, his own confidence buoyed up by his adult knowledge of the hosts of people all around him who are living effective, wholesome lives despite unfavorable environments.

Overemphasis on Environmental Causes of Behavior

Years ago one's behavior was considered to be primarily the product of heredity. One was born to be "bad"; another was born to be "good." This conception was basic in the theory of Lombroso, noted criminologist of the nineteenth century, and it certainly is reflected in the remarks and attitudes of some teachers today.

In recent decades the role of environment as a determinant of behavior has been given increasing recognition. The problem behavior that the schoolmaster formerly tried to correct by harsh punishment is now first made the object of inquiry—"behavior is caused," we say. The punitive procedures of the truant officer have given way to the social worker's mode of investigation and environmental amelioration.

Has the environmental interpretation of behavior been overdone? Do some people consider that the individual has no freedom to choose his responses to stimuli, or to choose the stimuli to which he will respond? Is he so completely dominated by the elements of immediate environment that nothing within him can be expected to exercise any control over him? Apparently the answer coming from some sources is, "Yes." A few years ago a grand jury returned indictments against two youths accused of auto theft, but, noting that in both cases the keys had been left in the cars by the owners, reported as follows:

Parking the car on a public highway, particularly in the night season, with the keys in the ignition switch, is in our humble opinion, an open and tacit invitation to anyone who has the urge to get into the car and drive it.

By this careless act, the owner is an aider and abettor in the crime, from a moral standpoint at least, and future grand juries should refuse to indict when the circumstances are such as related above.[53]

Apparently, overemphasis on environmentalism must have impressed Lichty, the cartoonist, to cause him to caricature that trend of thought. Two of his cartoons may be described as follows: (*a*) Father to Mother (both watching Junior's savage attack on a toy automobile which did not yield to his destructive impulses as had his other toys): "You think Junior might acquire a severe frustration from that unbreakable toy he got for Christmas?"

[53] Quoted by Andrew Bernhard, Editor of the *Pittsburgh Post-Gazette*, June 19, 1949.

(b) Two boys walking home from school, comparing report cards: "Wow! Look at my report card! Bet teacher will have my parents in for a conference to try and figure out what's wrong with them."

And *The New Yorker,* always adroit in lampoonery, has the lawyer say to the plug-ugly who is his client behind bars, "My notion is this—we plead guilty, put the blame squarely on the comic books, and throw ourselves on the mercy of the court."

While it may well be that the attitudes of some people signify a magnification of the influence of environment, teachers are continually being impelled to note individuals who are overcoming unfavorable environments and others who are failing in spite of favorable environment. "Isn't it marvelous," they say, "that Helen has made so much of her life when you think of the environment from which she comes?" And again, "Strange, isn't it, that George should be such a problem, when every circumstance has seemed to favor him?"

Two modern novels suggest that environment may be the major determinant of behavior, or that it may not be. In *Studs Lonigan,* James Farrell has his main character reflect his sordid slum surroundings by sinking to lower and lower depths of degradation as he grows to maturity. On the other hand, in *A Tree Grows in Brooklyn,* Betty Smith's heroine rises above her environment to use her talents and live an effective life.

Ilg and Ames of the Gesell Institute of Child Development, in their column "Child Behavior,"[54] conclude their reaction to sweeping charges of the responsibility of parents for juvenile delinquency by saying,

> Thus, there is no one answer to the problem of what causes delinquency. As we say, a bad environment can push some over into it. A good environment can save some from it. Some are scarcely threatened by even the worst environment. Some can scarcely be saved, even by the best.

The explanation of human behavior is not simple. The counselor is cautioned not only against overemphasis on environment but against overemphasis on heredity, on organic factors, or on any other category of influences. He should beware of a tendency to jump to conclusions from inadequate data.

COUNSELING FOR ACCURATE SELF-CONCEPTS

Self-theory and Counseling

The idea of self-discovery runs all through counseling literature as a paramount, if not *the* paramount, goal to be sought by the guidance function. Frank Parsons, thinking of vocational guidance, listed knowing one's self as one of the three simple elements of the process of rational vocational choosing. Carl Rogers and his followers, ministering to clients who present prob-

[54] *Pittsburgh Post-Gazette,* March 18, 1955.

lems of emotional and social adjustment, more and more emphasize that in their therapy the heart of the process is self-exploration, self-reorganization, self-actualization. The climax of nondirective therapy is insight: it signifies the attainment of a new and more accurate perception of self, affording a vantage point from which environment is viewed in a new perspective. The changed perceptions alter behavior.

Raimy[55] analyzed the self-references of fourteen counseling cases, using as his source the transcripts of their phonographically recorded interviews, of which the median number was seven. All were nondirectively counseled. The purpose of the analysis was to determine the extent to which the self-references signified self-approval or self-disapproval at the beginning, in the middle, and at the end of the interviews. The method of the study assumed that self-approval and self-disapproval represent two ends of a continuum which may be viewed as one of the major dimensions of the self-concept.

The basic postulates of the study were as follows: The Self-Concept is the map which each person consults in order to understand himself, especially during moments of crisis or choice. The approval, disapproval, or ambivalence he "feels" for the Self-Concept or some of its sub-systems is related to his personal adjustment. A heavy weighting of disapproval or ambivalence suggests a maladjusted individual since maladjustment in a psychological sense inevitably implies distress or disturbance in connection with oneself. When successful personality reorganization takes place in a maladjusted individual we may also expect a shift from self-disapproval to a positive or self-approving balance. The adjusted individual may dislike or disapprove of certain aspects of the Self-Concept but in general he finds himself to be attractive and desirable. (p. 155)

The principal findings of the study can be summarized very simply. At the beginning of counseling the clients disapproved of and had ambivalent attitudes toward themselves. As counseling progressed fluctuations in approval occurred with mounting ambivalence. At the conclusion of counseling the *successful* cases showed a vast predominance of self-approval: the *unsuccessful* cases showed a predominance of self-disapproval and ambivalence. (p. 161)

The therapeutic significance of self-understanding is attested by a study reported by Rogers, Kell, and McNeil[56] which was in the nature of a follow-up of a group of delinquent children two years after they had been studied and diagnosed by the Bureau of Juvenile Research in Columbus, Ohio. From the adequate files of this institution, six clinician judges, using carefully drawn rating scales, rated the cases on the following eight traits: heredity,

[55] Victor C. Raimy, "Self-Reference in Counseling Interviews," *Journal of Consulting Psychology,* Vol. XII (May–June, 1948), pp. 153–163. Same reference is in *Readings in Modern Methods of Counseling,* Arthur Brayfield, ed. (New York, Appleton-Century-Crofts, 1950), pp. 400–413.

[56] Carl R. Rogers, B. L. Kell, and Helen McNeil, "The Role of Self-Understanding in the Prediction of Behavior," *Journal of Consulting Psychology,* Vol. XII (May–June, 1948), pp. 174–186.

physical condition, mental status, family environment, cultural background, social experience, educational experience, and self-insight. Reports were then obtained on the state of adjustment of these subjects—two years after the diagnosis. The adjustment was rated by the use of an elaborate scale. Correlations were then computed between each of the eight predictive factors and the later adjustment, and the factor of self-insight was found to afford by far the best prediction.

The authors point to this finding as "socially hopeful" because this is the factor which lends itself most readily to natural change or planned alteration. Whereas much money is spent on the effort to improve environment by moving children to foster homes and institutions, on probationary supervision the effectiveness of which is certainly open to question, and on the alleviation of physical deficiences, the direct approach to the problem of helping the child to know and accept himself is quite neglected.

Citing the often observed phenomenon of a person's feeling such satisfaction over success in one area as to more than compensate for his failure in many other areas, Allport says,[57]

Only in terms of ego-psychology can we account for such fluid compensation. Mental health and happiness, it seems, does not depend upon the satisfaction of *this* drive or *that* drive, it depends rather upon the *person* finding *some* area of success *somewhere*. The *ego* must be satisfied, not the hunger drive, nor the sex drive, nor the maternal drive, however temporarily insistent these segmental tensions may be.

Multiple drives there are, but the ego drive takes precedence over all others. Counseling must take full account of this overriding motivation to protect and enhance the self.

Super has written of vocational choice and vocational counseling in terms of self-theory.[58] He points to the inadequacy of judging the success of workers by such criteria as output, advancement, stability, and efficiency ratings. Success, he says, is a personal, subjective thing best judged by the person's feelings and attitudes. For the workers in Western Electric's Hawthorne plant, job success meant pleasant social relationships, attitudes of respect on the part of the boss, a chance to participate in planning their work. These are the conditions of ego gratification.

While one cannot select an occupation just in terms of obtaining such conditions for work, emotional factors must inevitably play a role in choice as well as the rational. The client thinks of the kind of person he is and the kind of person he wants to be. He thinks of the values that he holds, the use of his abilities and interests that will afford him greatest satisfactions,

[57] G. W. Allport, *The Nature of Personality: Selected Papers* (Cambridge, Mass., Addison-Wesley, 1950), pp. 128–129.
[58] Donald E. Super, "The Criteria of Vocational Success," *Occupations,* Vol. XXX (October, 1951), pp. 5–9, and "Vocational Adjustment: Implementing a Self-Concept," *Occupations,* Vol. XXX (November, 1951), pp. 88–92.

the kind of life he wishes to live. Vocational counseling, says Super, takes account of such elements in choice and proceeds in the full knowledge that "in choosing an occupation one is, in effect, choosing a means of implementing a self-concept."[59]

Students' Capacities for Accurate Self-estimates

With all the extended attention that has been given to the creation of instruments by which counselors can measure the aptitudes, interests, and adjustment of their counselees, some thought has been given to the capacity of the client to measure himself. He must make his own choices; he makes them in terms of some image he has of himself. To what extent does his self-image correspond to the reality of himself? Chapter 4 set forth a considerable body of evidence to show the lack of such correspondence. Hence, the need for guidance service.

The problem of the individual's capacity for self-estimate has, however, been attacked more directly in researches that have been made over the past several decades. Although such studies have been generally criticised for the validity of their techniques, they have shed considerable light on operational characteristics of the self. Older researches, for example, establish the following tendencies in self-estimate: (1) underestimation by university students of higher capacity and overestimation by those of lower capacity; (2) overrating on socially desirable qualities and underrating on socially undesirable qualities; (3) overrating on traits the subjects think are important and more accurate rating on traits they think are relatively unimportant; (4) certain *individuals* consistently overrating or underrating themselves.

Among later studies one often cited in the literature is that of Arsenian.[60] This author designed a research to determine the capacity for self-estimation of entering college students during Freshman Week. He had them estimate their scholastic aptitude just before taking the American Council on Education Psychological Examination and again after taking the test. Similarly, they estimated their aptitude in English composition just before taking the Co-operative English Test and just after taking the test. Before taking the Co-operative General Culture Test, the Strong Interest Inventory, and the Bell Adjustment Inventory, they rated themselves on the traits represented by those tests. Comparing these data of self-estimates with the measurements yielded by the tests, Arsenian found a notable lack of correspondence. The ratings made *after* the measurement were not as far out of line as were the ratings which were made before the measurement. Students who grossly overestimated or underestimated their abilities, knowledge, and adjustment were as a group found to be somewhat less intelligent and less well adjusted,

---

[59] This view of the process of vocational choice is the dominant theme of Super's recent book, *The Psychology of Careers* (New York, Harper, 1957).

[60] Seth Arsenian, "Own Estimate and Objective Measurement," *Journal of Educational Psychology*, Vol. XXXIII (April, 1942), pp. 291–302.

and more frequently than the others had to be placed on probation, dismissed from college, or given more time of faculty counselors.

Torrance[61] made a study at Kansas State College similar in design to that of Arsenian and yielding results essentially supporting Arsenian. He found also that women evaluated themselves much more accurately than men, but underevaluated themselves more frequently. Students ranking in the lowest 25 per cent in scholastic aptitude expect to make as high grades as do those in the top 25 per cent.

Torrance was especially interested in the practical use of the self-estimate data in the understanding and counseling of students. He reported finding that it is easier for a freshman to accept his insufficiency in some particular subject field or activity than to accept a lack of college ability or general ability. With some frequency he found the expectations of parents to be interfering with the students' development of more realistic self-concepts. "I know you can make good grades if you just try," they say.

Morris' three devices of self-deception—irrationalism, determinism, and sin —were found to operate in the case studies. First, the individual tries to cling desperately to his fair image of himself and ignores, glosses over, and minimizes evidence contrary to this fair image. When he is no longer able to delude himself in this way, he adopts the attitude that he can do anything he wants at any time. When this no longer helps, he resorts to sin. He says, "I know I could do college work if I would just study, but I just don't, or I am lazy." Understanding these processes, the adviser can do much to help his advisee uncover his defenses and face himself more realistically.[62]

Torrance finds it very important to the college counselor to understand the dynamics of underevaluation and overevaluation. The underevaluator is likely to present himself for vocational guidance. His vocational goals are either lacking or very vague. It is his uncertainty concerning his perception of himself that causes him to be fearful of making a vocational choice. On the other hand, the overevaluator is likely to be sent for vocational guidance, sent by the dean or his professors who become aware of the gap between his pretensions and his potentialities. Such a one is likely to indulge in the devices of ego protection which are outlined in the quotation above.

Another recent study of the accuracy of self-estimates by college freshmen may well be cited because it yielded results somewhat in contrast to those found by Arsenian and Torrance. In interviews with 100 randomly selected liberal-arts freshmen at the University of Wisconsin, held after the first six weeks of college classes, Young[63] had each student select the decile

[61] E. Paul Torrance, "Some Practical Uses of a Knowledge of Self-Concepts in Counseling and Guidance," *Educational and Psychological Measurement,* Vol. XIV (Spring, 1954), pp. 120–127.

[62] *Ibid.,* pp. 125–126.

[63] F. Chandler Young, "College Freshmen Judge Their Own Scholastic Promise," *Personnel and Guidance Journal,* Vol. XXXII (March, 1954), pp. 399–403.

of freshman achievement which he expected to attain in the current semester. This first self-prediction was made *before* receiving any information about his performance on the ACE Psychological Examination and on the Co-operative General Culture Test. *After* his standing on those tests had been given and interpreted to him, he was asked again to make a "final" predic-tion of his success. Likewise, he was asked to guess the highest possible letter grade he would receive in each course, and the lowest possible letter grades. After the close of each interview, the counselor made a prediction for the student, basing his judgment on the student's high-school rank, test scores, self-predictions, and impressions received during the one interview. The correlations of these predictive measures with first-semester achievement are shown in Table 65.[64] From these coefficients Young was quite justified

TABLE 65. Coefficients of Correlation between Various Predictions and the Actual Scholastic Achievement of First-Semester College Freshmen

SELF-PREDICTIONS:
First (before test interpretation) 68
Final (after test interpretation) 69
High (guesses of highest possible marks) 69
Low (guesses of lowest possible marks) 61
High-Low (average of high and low predictions) 71
OTHER PREDICTIONS:
Counselor's predictions 68
Ability and high-school rank 67
High-School rank 61
Ability test (ACE Psychological Examination) 50

in pointing out that freshmen can predict their scholastic achievement with considerable accuracy and that the counselor can do no better. He goes to some lengths, however, to point out that his results may well be a reflection of the particular conditions under which he obtained the self-appraisals. Among these conditions, not the least significant was the fact that the stu-dents made their predictions after their first six or eight weeks of college classes. They had thus had some opportunity to learn of their progress and of their capacity for coping with course requirements.

The last word has indeed not been said concerning the capacity of students for accurate self-estimates. Nevertheless, much has been learned from studies in this field which serve to reveal some dimensions of the counseling task.

The Level of Aspiration

Closely bound to the self-concept is the level of aspiration which one holds. While the term, level of aspiration, has been used in research only since about 1930, guidance, in its emphasis on the selection of goals which

[64] *Ibid.* Adapted from Table 1, p. 403.

are in harmony with abilities, has always been concerned with the level of aspiration. Of the not too numerous researches carried on in this area,[65] some have been done in artificially created situations, but their findings have had important implications for practical goal choosing, such as degree of success sought in school work, or occupational choice.

One of these researches, carried on in a somewhat natural situation, was cited in Chapter 3, pages 100–101, as a study reported by Hilgard. This experiment showed that children with a past record of success in arithmetic and reading set time goals for the performance of tasks in those subjects which were close to but slightly better than those they had just achieved. Children with a past record of failure tended either to set their goals so low that they could not fail or so high as to be quite unrealistic. Thus, it is apparently easy for pupils who are accustomed to the experience of success to be reasonably accurate in their self-estimates. Pupils with a past history of failure depart from reality in devious methods of protecting the self.

Child and Whiting[66] analyzed everyday incidents in the lives of undergraduate students in which there was complete frustration, early frustration followed by goal-attainment, and simple goal-attainment without any appreciable frustration. The following are major conclusions which they reached from their analysis: (1) "Success generally leads to a raising of the level of aspiration, and failure to a lowering." (2) "Failure is more likely than success to lead to withdrawal in the form of avoidance of setting a level of aspiration." (3) "Effects of failure on the level of aspiration are more varied than those of success." (4) "The stronger the success the greater is the probability of a rise in level of aspiration; the stronger the failure the greater is the probability of lowering." (5) "Shifts in level of aspiration are in part a function of changes in the subject's confidence in his ability to attain goals."

Naturally, also, great differences are to be found between individuals in the degree to which these general tendencies apply. For example, some persons are relatively easily influenced to lower their levels of aspiration, whereas others are stubborn and yield reluctantly.

Most of the studies of the level of aspiration have been made in a somewhat narrow context, assuming that one's level of aspiration is derived from within him and his immediate experiences, whereas at various points in this volume the influence of social class and a host of other environmental influences has been demonstrated. Nevertheless, the literature on this subject is most helpful in understanding the reactions of counselees in situations of

[65] See a summary and interpretation of the earlier ones by Kurt Lewin, Tamara Dembo, Leon Festinger, and Pauline S. Sears, as Chapter 10, "Level of Aspiration," in *Personality and the Behavior Disorders,* J. McV. Hunt, ed. (New York, Ronald Press, 1944).

[66] Irvin L. Child and John W. M. Whiting, "Determinants of Level of Aspiration: Evidence from Everyday Life," *Journal of Abnormal and Social Psychology,* Vol. XLIV (July, 1949), pp. 303–314.

ego involvement. It sheds light on some of the adjustive mechanisms to which the self resorts when threatened—mechanisms which are briefly described in the last division of this section.

Shall We Tell Students Their Intelligence Ratings?

This is a very practical question that has been with us since the objective measurement of intelligence began. In a consideration of counseling for accurate self-concepts, the question is indeed central. The discussion of it may well start with the most recent interchange of views on the subject.

Punke[67] has noted the "traditions, assumptions, and rationalizations" which he finds to underlie the practice of withholding test results from youth. First is the fear that such information may cause such dejection or ego inflation as to ruin the student. Second is the "censorship and protection complex" on the part of elders who assume that they have superior judgment as to the information which it is safe for youth to have. Third is the cultural tradition which has left an exaggerated impression of the capacity of academically educated persons to advise others concerning the entire gamut of vocational and life adjustments. In contrast with these attitudes Punke holds that

Test results should be used to help youth get a more objective picture of their interests, potentialities, and limitations and to plan their futures accordingly. If educators withhold test results, they withhold important information which youth should take into account in arriving at judgments affecting their futures.

Shoben[68] reacted to Punke's article because he felt that Punke had not faced the problem of *how* to report intelligence ratings so that they can be properly interpreted and evaluated. The real task, he says, is to impart to pupils the *implications* of their test scores in the course of a systematic *counseling* relationship. It is clear to Shoben that psychological training is necessary for the performance of this function. It is, he says,

highly desirable for counselor and pupil to think together about the strengths and weaknesses that the pupil possesses, about the courses of action that might prove most valuable for him in capitalizing on assets and minimizing liabilities, about tentative plans with respect to further training and vocational goals, and about further self-investigative procedures, including additional testing, that might be relevant to his welfare.

Both of these writers clearly believe that the rationale of guidance demands accurate self-concepts on the part of the counselee and that intelligence-test ratings should be used to contribute to that end. Shoben would help the student "arrive at a prognostic understanding of his test perform-

[67] H. Punke, "Tell Students Their Intelligence Test Rating," *School and Society,* Vol. LXXIII (June 30, 1951), pp. 407–409.

[68] Edward J. Shoben, Jr. "Tell Students Their Intelligence Ratings?" *School and Society,* Vol. LXXIV (September 15, 1951), pp. 169–170.

ance without reference to specific scores," and he fears the results of giving out uninterpreted information.

Views expressed and experiences related by Pullias[69] in 1939 afford significant support for Shoben. He gave three examples of college students whose personalities were "deeply and perhaps permanently altered by their attitudes toward their intelligence quotients." One was incapable of using his ability because of having received undigested knowledge of his intelligence quotient around which he had developed feelings of inadequacy and inferiority. A second one had been informed by his high-school principal that his I.Q. was 92 (which proved to be in error by about thirty points). He could do nothing in class or on campus without consciousness of his supposed mental inferiority. A third one explained that he had an I.Q. of 147 and was therefore a genius. He was a prig, greatly disliked by his fellow students, and was doing barely satisfactory work in the university.

Pullias expressed the view that with modern culture placing so much emphasis on mental ability

a person's opinion concerning his own mental ability is at, or very near, the core of his ego organization; that is, his concept of his own ability is dynamically related to every other aspect of his personality. (p. 281)

The assimilation into the personality of a fact or a belief which relates to an important aspect of the self is never a simple process. The dictum (frequently met in the literature) that a person should see and face the facts about his mental ability is, at best, probably a gross oversimplification of the problem. The achievement of a wholesome attitude toward the nature and the extent of our abilities is one of life's most important and difficult tasks. (p. 283)

Of the attempts which have been made to measure objectively the results, good and bad, of informing pupils of their intelligence ratings, two will be cited here. One study, by Snyder,[70] involved informing pupils at the time the tests were administered when and where they would be able to learn the results. At the appointed time and place each pupil received a slip of paper on which his score, the percentile rank, was written. When all the pupils present had received their slips, the scores were explained to them, all being required to remain for the explanation.

Some of the points brought out during the explanation were: (1) the varying amounts of study time needed by pupils with high and low ranks, (2) the probable effects of too much participation in extracurriculum activities, (3) the meaning of "percentile rank," (4) the ability of pupils with ranks of 40 to earn places on the honor roll by hard work and careful application, and (5) the occasional failure of a careless or indifferent pupil with a rank of 90 or better.[71]

[69] E. V. Pullias, "Should an Individual Know His Own I.Q.? A Mental Health Problem," *Elementary School Journal,* Vol. XL (December, 1939), pp. 277–283.
[70] Troy Snyder, "Reporting Intelligence-Test Scores to High-School Pupils," *School Review,* Vol. XLV (February, 1937), pp. 105–111.
[71] *Ibid.,* p. 107.

At a later date the pupils answered a questionnaire which was designed to ascertain their feelings about knowing their test results. In the tabulation of answers they were divided into two groups—those who had stood above the 50-percentile on the test, and those who had stood below that level. The first three questions and the percentage of pupils in each division answering "yes" were as follows:[72]

	Pupils Ranking above 50	Pupils Ranking below 50
Should intelligence-test scores be reported to pupils?	90	72
Would you do better work if you did not know your intelligence-test score?	17	35
Does your score make you feel that you cannot be a success in your school work?	6	33

This sample of the data suggests that the experiment made some of the low-ranking pupils unhappy. However, the method of the experiment and the method of measuring it—both inadequately reported here—had some limitations. Snyder expressed the opinion that his project was no more damaging to pupil morale than reports of failure in classroom work. More refined evidence, however, was needed.

The second study, reported by Rothney,[73] involved individual interviews in which the scores (all in terms of percentiles) made on a considerable battery of tests were reported and interpreted to an experimental group of high-school sophomores. The implications of the test results were considered in such a counseling relationship as quoted above from Shoben. As soon as the interview was completed, the counselors made notes concerning the reactions of the pupils to the scores and interpretations. At the end of the series of interviews 811 items of reaction from 340 pupils were available, and these were classified in fourteen categories. While showing the categories for the reader's own judgment, the author interprets five of them, totaling 60.4 per cent of the reactions, as positive or favorable; five, totaling 31 per cent, as not clearly positive or negative; and four, totaling 8.6 per cent, as possibly negative. He says that in only three per cent of the cases did the counselors note obvious disappointment. In the continued contacts of this longitudinal study no severe emotional disturbance was observed as originating in the information gained by students from these interviews.

Rothney's study is a rather convincing affirmative answer to the question, Shall we tell students their intelligence ratings? It is highly suggestive of what can be done in counseling for accurate self-concepts.[74]

[72] *Ibid.,* from Table II, p. 109.

[73] John W. M. Rothney, "Interpreting Test Scores to Counselees," *Occupations,* Vol. XXX (February, 1952), 320–322.

[74] As further evidence on this question the reader will include the study by Ross which was cited in the first section of this chapter.

Types of Behavior Which Obstruct the Formation of Accurate Self-concepts

It has been implied throughout this section that the soundest adjustment of the individual is based upon his accurate knowledge and acceptance of himself. Being free from conflict with himself, he is not hampered by tensions, but attains an integration of mind and emotion which is conducive to the highest level of productivity.

However, no one is completely normal; no one wholly faces reality. The individual is continually faced with adjustment problems of varying degrees of difficulty. From infancy to the grave he is confronted with frustrations and conflicts. As the ego is threatened he sometimes resorts to reactions in its defense which are called *adjustment mechanisms*. They represent forms of compromise with reality and are not unhealthy unless carried to extremes. There is a continuous gradation of adjustment from the best-balanced person to the most obviously disturbed, and this continuum is commonly described as ranging from normal to neurotic to psychotic, with no sharply drawn lines of distinction between these areas of maladjustment. School guidance workers, of course, limit their ministrations to maladjusted children who are sufficiently reality-oriented to be classified as normal.

The literature on the adjustment mechanisms and their treatment is enormous, but in a book of such scope as this one, space is available for only the briefest description of the major mechanisms.[75] Some of these have been successfully understood and discussed in group counseling sessions with pupils of the middle and grammar grades.

One of the most commonly used mechanisms is *compensation,* which designates the overdevelopment of one kind of activity as a substitute for real or imagined failure or deprivation in another kind of activity. For example, the child who experiences failure in his school work may react to his feelings of frustration by working with great intensity to experience success in athletics or in social leadership. School practice, in theory at least, increasingly favors granting such opportunity for compensation. Self-esteem there must be, and when rigid school rules deny to the boy legitimate opportunities for ego gratification in studies, sports, or club activities, he may seek to find feelings of importance in gang membership.

In *rationalization,* the subject sets forth socially acceptable reasons for behavior that is socially unacceptable. Or, he may allege reasons for a failure which serve to take the onus off the self: the pre-med student ascribes his poor record to his father's illness, to a lately discovered astigmatism in his vision, or to anything but his own aversion to study. Sometimes there *is* a cause external to himself, but he magnifies it greatly to hide his own culpability. People of all ages employ this mechanism extensively.

Projection is a defensive reaction by means of which an individual trans-

---

[75] A comprehensive textbook of recent issue in this field is *The Psychology of Adjustment,* 2nd ed., by L. F. Shaffer and E. J. Shoben, Jr. (Boston, Houghton Mifflin, 1956).

fers the blame for his own shortcomings, mistakes, and misdeeds to others, or at least attributes to others his own unacceptable impulses, thoughts, and desires. Thus, a girl caught cheating in an examination may try to put the blame on someone else, or, if that is impossible, try to lighten the burden of her guilt by charging that "everybody is doing it." In some circumstances the defenses of projection or rationalization may be used so continuously that a delusion is established, an obviously false belief so persistently held that logical arguments cannot break it down.

Attention-getting is a mechanism which shows up in many forms of behavior. It is especially troublesome when the subject employs it while he is a member of a school group, for it is difficult for such a group to do its work unless all members conform to a discipline internally or externally imposed. Teachers sometimes take severely authoritarian measures to submerge the attention-getter into the group, but over and over in the literature of mental hygiene one finds advocacy of the positive approach of giving such a child special duties which will bring him legitimate social recognition.

Regression is considered a withdrawing type of defense because the person retreats to some earlier and simpler form of behavior which is not in keeping with his present state of maturity. The little child who misses the attention of his parents when a new baby arrives may regress to babyish helplessness to regain that attention. Children of various ages may be retarded in maturation by overly protective parents; their behavior then will not correspond to their years.

Fantasy (day-dreaming) is the fulfillment of desires in imagination. It is adjustment by escape from the difficulties of real life, an effortless flight into a realm where success can be attained without fail. Since fantasy can be entered upon with so little effort, it is not surprising that investigation shows it to be a mechanism which is employed by practically every one. People day-dream of physical feats, vocational and financial success, sexual satisfaction, acts of heroism. It is a great source of satisfaction for people whose contact with reality is threatening or unsuccessful, but it is also employed by individuals who exercise their imaginations creatively and then try to realize their dreams.

Fantasy has real value when used in a limited way. Thoreau said it is commendable to build castles in the air, but then enjoined, "Now build foundations under them." But a great deal of time is wasted in fantasy by some children, high-school pupils, and college students. Their efficiency, their accomplishments in the world of reality, may be greatly and needlessly reduced by the habit of letting their minds wander into imagined pleasures or achievements.

Moralizing with the individual about his waste of time will not do any good. Most people desire *real* pleasures and *real* achievements. If the day-dreaming seems to be just a reaction to which a student resorts when his study tasks do not immediately claim his interest or he runs into a little difficulty, it may be that some help in establishing time goals for his work, a schedule for study and play, will set him on the road to a more satisfying life. If, on the other hand, the daydreaming is escape from frustrations, conflicts, or a self that he does not like to contemplate, the sources or causes of the subject's maladjustments should be ascertained, and counseling skill should be focused on them.

Repression is the refusal, basically unconscious, to admit the existence of a painful reality. It is the most undesirable of the major mechanisms of adjustment which have been named in this brief presentation, because it is tension-producing rather than tension-reducing. Therapy involves the dredging up of the repressed experiences and facing them. School guidance workers are typically not equipped to cope with this mechanism. Unless and until more expert treatment, as represented in psychologist or psychiatrist, is available, the baffling symptoms of anxiety and fear evinced by the repressed person are best met by the soft-poultice treatment.

Looking at the adjustive mechanisms generally, it seems that the number of students who resort to them would be far less if they felt sure that teachers and counselors would not attack their egos. If all school workers kept in mind always the basic needs of everyone for physical and emotional security, for status, and for mastery, if they would steadfastly convey to their pupils their respect for them as persons (though not admiring or condoning all that they *do*), it would be much easier for pupils to achieve self-insight and self-acceptance. And since much of the resort to the adjustive mechanisms stems from failure experiences, the role of teacher and counselor should be to offer positive guidance to offset the negative of failure. The pre-med who has to accept his failure to win admission to medical school can do so with less ego damage if his potentialities are carefully canvassed to help him find a field which enlists his interest and in which he can be successful. The self is not seen truly if the individual is only told what he can *not* do. And a negative self cannot be viewed confidently, trustfully.

What Behavior is Characteristic of Individuals with Accurate Self-concepts?

To close this section on an affirmative note, readers will find it useful to obtain an image of the person who is well adjusted and makes the minimum use of adjustive mechanisms. Of the many sources that might be cited, just two will be employed. One is the work by Langdon and Stout[76] already quoted in Chapter 11. The other is a recent helpful handbook for school guidance workers, by DeHaan and Kough, from which the following concise word picture is quoted:[77]

[76] Grace Langdon and Irving W. Stout, *These Well-Adjusted Children* (New York, Day, 1951).

[77] Robert F. DeHaan and Jack Kough, *Teacher's Guidance Handbook,* Vol. II, *Helping Children with Special Needs* (Chicago, Science Research Associates, 1956), p.11.

1. Children with sound emotional or mental health are able to accept themselves and are happy to be themselves. They estimate their ability realistically, having neither too high nor too low an opinion of themselves. They accept their shortcomings and try to correct those that can be corrected. They can even laugh at themselves.

2. They stand on their own feet; they are reasonably independent in deciding things as compared with other children of the same age.

3. They are confident of their ability to handle the situations that may confront them.

4. They are not constantly afflicted with strong feelings of fear, anger, jealousy, worry, or guilt. Generally they seem to be fairly relaxed.

5. They like and trust others and are able to form warm, lasting personal relationships. They have at least one close friend. They expect people to like them.

6. They consider the interests of other people and feel some responsibility for the welfare of others.

7. They consider themselves an integral part of the group.

8. They accept reasonable responsibility.

9. They improve their abilities, skills, and talents, and face new experiences eagerly.

COUNSELING ETHICS

Need for a Code of Ethics

This chapter has described the counseling relationship as a communion of mind and spirit in which the counselee releases his feelings, vents his emotions, bares his innermost conflicts, confides his ambitions. This can only happen when he feels secure. Such feelings of security rest upon and derive from fullest confidence that the counselor will not betray him.

The counselor's role is greatly complicated by virtue of his responsibility to society as well as to the counselee. Not only must he help his client to preserve and enhance the self, but also to carry on that function in such a manner as to support school, home, occupations, and the other social institutions. In these circumstances, plus the fact that he has a self of his own which he is trying to preserve and enhance, the counselor's every act has marked ethical implications.

Other professions, such as law, medicine, psychology, and social work, which are characterized by a one-to-one relationship between practitioner and client have recognized the problems of ethics by drawing up codes for the guidance of their members. With established rules for professional conduct, machinery has also been established by the organizations of these professions to punish violations of their codes.

Counselors have not yet attained this level of professional maturity, except for those who are psychologists.[78] A number of writings, however, which have appeared in recent years attest increased feeling of the need for such a code. Schwebel, in trying to find by analysis the reasons why unethical practice occurs, names and illustrates three basic causes, as follows:[79] (a) *Self interest*—the counselor may be tempted by opportunities for some form of personal profit, for self-enhancement, or for the maintenance of security and status. (b) *Unsound judgment*—the counselor discloses confidences, not with gossipy intent, but in response to a poor judgment of his responsibility to an institution or a group. (c) *Ignorance*—the counselor blunders because of a lack of technical information or because his set of values represent some bias of which he is not aware. With regard to such dangers as these, it seems that a code of ethics should help to eliminate unethical practice both by virtue of serving as a guide for the practicing counselor and by figuring as significant content in the pre-service education of counselors.

Examples of the Ethical Problems Which Confront Counselors

The ethical aspect of counseling has been taken into account at various points in this book, but especially in the preceding sections of this chapter. No attempt will be made here to offer a comprehensive inventory, but only to give illustrative problems. For example, Schwebel, in another writing[80] than the one cited above, suggests a hypothetical lunchtime conversation in which several teachers who are discussing pupil John Doe, problem case, turn to the counselor for information, as he joins them for lunch. It is a very typical problem that the counselor faces. How much should he tell them, assuming that all are sincerely interested in helping John? Should he tell them right there at the lunch table, with the possibility that the conversation may be overheard by other school personnel? And if he withholds some information, how can he do so without offending, or appearing superior? Schwebel builds up the answers from a paragraph in the code of the American Psychological Association.

A sophomore high-school girl tearfully tells the counselor just before the Christmas recess that she expects to drop out of school. Her English teacher had warned her, she says, that unless she earned a grade of 75 in her weekly quiz she could not possibly get a passing grade for the term. And now—"she gave me 70. It's not fair. Look at that paper. Do you think this is fair?" What should be the counselor's course of action? A fellow professional worker is involved. The student should be helped to remain in school. Again, Schwebel finds guidance for the counselor in the code of the APA.

---

[78] The code formulated and adopted by the psychologists appears as the following reference: *Ethical Standards of Psychologists* (Washington, D.C., 1953) Committee on Ethical Standards for Psychologists, American Psychological Association.

[79] Milton Schwebel, "Why Unethical Practice?" *Journal of Counseling Psychology,* Vol. II (Summer, 1955), pp. 122–128.

[80] Milton Schwebel, "Some Ethical Problems in Counseling," *Personnel and Guidance Journal,* Vol. XXXIII (January, 1955), pp. 254–259.

A boy who is desperately anxious to make good marks admits to the counselor as he leaves the office that he has crib notes which he intends to use in a chemistry exam. What is the counselor's responsibility and to whom?

The term "counselor" has been used in these examples, but here as at many other points in this book, it is used in a generic sense. In a school where counseling responsibility is vested in the homeroom teacher, that functionary may at any time meet problems like the ones cited. A code is needed for all guidance workers.

Helpful beginnings to the establishment of such a code were made a few years ago by the members of a seminar at New York University, most of whom were practicing counselors and professional members of the National Vocational Guidance Association.[81] They examined the ethical codes of the four professions of law, medicine, psychology, and social work, selected items which seemed to them to be applicable to counselors, and revised the items as they thought desirable. In the code which they thus produced they listed in parentheses with each item the profession to whose code they were most indebted for it. The five sections of this counselor's code are entitled as follows:

The Vocational Guidance Counselor in Relation to Himself
The Vocational Guidance Counselor in Relation to His Professional Activity
The Counselor and His Relationship to the Client
The Counselor in Relation to the Public
The Counselor in Relation to Research and Publications

For the third section the committee framed four paragraphs pertaining to the use of occupational information, which were not derived from any of the four professional codes. The 104 paragraphs drawn up by this seminar constitute a most provocative document meriting close study by all school workers who have counseling responsibilities.

Contemplation of the ethical principles of counseling takes one to the heart of the counseling process. Because this service is the upbuilding of individuals to be the most effective persons they can be, the techniques of the profession must be founded upon ethical concepts. All the theories, procedures, and activities of counseling must be evaluated in terms of their contribution to the highest good of counselee and of society.

QUESTIONS, PROBLEMS, INVESTIGATIONS

1. As homeroom teacher or counselor, take an informal inventory of what you have accomplished in individual counseling during the past semester. What successes have you scored? What failures? Interpret in terms of learning, as reflected in behavior patterns.

2. Evaluate counseling interviews in your school or college from the stand-

[81] Samuel Gluck and others, "A Proposed Code of Ethics for Counselors," *Occupations,* Vol. XXX (April, 1952), pp. 484–490.

point of rapport. Is the interviewing organized in such a manner as to make easy or difficult the establishment of rapport? Can you suggest or plan improvement?

3. Recall interviews you have experienced, either as counselor or counselee, and select the one or ones which were characterized by a high degree of empathy. What was the behavior of the counselee which signified the presence of empathy?

4. Is the quality of empathy innate? Or can it be acquired? Canvass literature on the subject and quiz some counselors to get an answer.

5. Make a survey, intensive or extensive, of the practice of recording interviews, on the part of several counselors, in several schools or colleges. Compare findings with the discussion of the subject in this chapter.

6. Poll the class for experience with the "soft-poultice" treatment. What are the characteristics of the cases they recall? Are examples reported in which the treatment brought the case to a "head" so that the superficial measures that the teacher-counselor could apply brought about restoration to normality?

7. If you are a teacher-counselor or a homeroom teacher, think over the counseling you have done with your pupils, and list in two columns the evidences of your directiveness and nondirectiveness.

8. Hold a session for a verbal exchange of cases of individuals who have seemed *not* to develop according to environment.

9. From your own experience and that of fellow teacher-counselors draw up a list of examples of changes which parents have made in their own behavior in order to remedy a child's maladjustment.

10. How many members of the class using this textbook have learned their I.Q.'s or their percentile ranks on an intelligence test? Under what circumstances, in what context, did they receive such information? Was it in such a counseling relationship as Shoben asks for? How did they feel about learning this fact about themselves?

SELECTED REFERENCES

ALLPORT, G. W., *The Nature of Personality: Selected Papers* (Cambridge, Mass., Addison-Wesley Press, 1950).

ARSENIAN, Seth, "Own Estimate and Objective Measurement," *Journal of Educational Psychology,* Vol. XXXIII (April, 1942), pp. 291–302.

BEILIN, Harry, "The Utilization of High Level Talent in Lower Socioeconomic Groups," *Personnel and Guidance Journal,* Vol. XXXV (November, 1956), pp. 175–178.

BIXLER, Ray H., "Counseling: Eclectic or Systematic?" *Educational and Psychological Measurement,* Vol. VIII (Summer, 1948), pp. 211–214.

BORDIN, Edward S., *Psychological Counseling* (New York, Appleton-Century-Crofts, 1955).

BRAYFIELD, Arthur H., ed., *Readings in Modern Methods of Counseling* (New York, Appleton-Century-Crofts, 1950).

BURTON, William H., *The Guidance of Learning Activities,* 2nd ed. (New York, Appleton-Century-Crofts, 1952), Chs. 1–10.

CALLIS, Robert, POLMANTIER, Paul C., and ROEBER, Edward C., *A Casebook of Counseling* (New York, Appleton-Century-Crofts, 1955).

CHILD, Irvin L., and WHITING, John W. M., "Determinants of Level of Aspiration: Evidence from Everyday Life," *Journal of Abnormal and Social Psychology,* Vol. XLIV (July, 1949), pp. 303–314.

COMBS, Arthur W., "Non-Directive Techniques and Vocational Counseling," *Occupations,* Vol. XXV (February, 1947), pp. 261–267.

DANSKIN, D. G., and ROBINSON, F. P., "Differences in 'Degree of Lead' among Experienced Counselors," *Journal of Counseling Psychology,* Vol. I (Summer, 1954), pp. 78–83.

DAVIDIAN, Elizabeth V., "Rapport and the Human Element," *Personnel and Guidance Journal,* Vol. XXXIII (April, 1955), pp. 469–470.

DEHAAN, Robert F., and KOUGH, Jack, *Teacher's Guidance Handbook,* Vol. II, *Helping Children with Special Needs* (Chicago, Science Research Associates, 1956).

DRISCOLL, Gertrude P., *Child Guidance in the Classroom.* Practical Suggestions for Teaching No. 13 (New York, Bureau of Publications, Teachers College, Columbia University, 1955).

DYMOND, Rosalind F., "A Scale for the Measurement of Empathic Ability," *Journal of Consulting Psychology,* Vol. XIII (April, 1949), pp. 127–133.

ELLIS, Albert, "New Approaches to Psychotherapy Techniques," *Journal of Clinical Psychology,* Vol. XI (July, 1955), pp. 208–260.

GLUCK, Samuel, and others, "A Proposed Code of Ethics for Counselors," *Occupations,* Vol. XXX (April, 1952), pp. 484–490.

HILGARD, Ernest R., *Theories of Learning,* rev. ed. (New York, Appleton-Century-Crofts, 1956).

The Interview in Counseling (prepared by John Darley) (Washington, D.C., U.S. Department of Labor, 1946).

JONES, Edward S., "Gradations of Directiveness in Counseling," *Educational and Psychological Measurement,* Vol. VII (Autumn, 1947, Part II), pp. 559–563.

LANGDON, Grace, and STOUT, Irving W., *Teacher-Parent Interviews* (Englewood Cliffs, N.J., Prentice-Hall, 1954).

LEONARD, Edith M., VAN DEMAN, Dorothy D., and MILES, Lillian E., *Counseling with Parents in Early Childhood Education* (New York, Macmillan, 1954).

ORLEANS, Myra, "Problems Peculiar to Parent Conferences," *Journal of the National Association of Deans of Women,* Vol. XVII (October, 1953), pp. 3–7.

PARKER, Clyde A., "Empathy," *Personnel and Guidance Journal,* Vol. XXXIV (October, 1955), pp. 89–93.

PEPINSKY, Harold B., and PEPINSKY, Pauline N., *Counseling: Theory and Practice* (New York, Ronald Press, 1954).

The Psychology of Learning, Part II of the 41st Yearbook of the National Society for the Study of Education (Bloomington, Ill., Public School Publishing Co., 1942).

PULLIAS, E. V., "Should an Individual Know His Own I.Q.? A Mental Health Problem," *Elementary School Journal,* Vol. XL (December, 1939), pp. 277–283.

PUNKE, H., "Tell Students Their Intelligence Test Rating," *School and Society,* Vol. LXXIII (June 30, 1951), pp. 407–409.

RAIMY, Victor C., "Self-Reference in Counseling Interviews," *Journal of Consulting Psychology,* Vol. XII (May–June, 1948), pp. 153–163.

ROGERS, Carl R., *Client-Centered Therapy* (Boston, Houghton Mifflin, 1951).

————, *Counseling and Psychotherapy* (Boston, Houghton Mifflin, 1942).

————, "Psychometric Tests and Client-Centered Counseling," *Educational and Psychological Measurement,* Vol. VI (Spring, 1946), pp. 139–144.

————, and DYMOND, Rosalind F., eds., *Psychotherapy and Personality Change* (Chicago, University of Chicago Press, 1954).

ROGERS, Carl R., KELL, B. L., and MCNEIL, Helen, "The Role of Self-Understanding in the Prediction of Behavior," *Journal of Consulting Psychology,* Vol. XII (May–June, 1948), pp. 174–186.

ROSS, C. C., "Should Low Ranking Freshmen Be Told Their Scores on Intelligence Tests?" *School and Society,* Vol. XLVII (May 21, 1938), pp. 678–680.

ROTHNEY, John W. M., "Interpreting Test Scores to Counselees," *Occupations,* Vol. XXX (February, 1952), pp. 320–322.

SARBIN, Theodore R., "The Case Record in Psychological Counseling," *Journal of Applied Psychology,* Vol. XXIV (1940), pp. 184–197.

SARGENT, Helen, "Nondirective Counseling Applied to a Single Interview," *Journal of Consulting Psychology,* Vol. VII (July–August, 1943), pp. 183–190.

SCHWEBEL, Milton, "Some Ethical Problems in Counseling," *Personnel and Guidance Journal,* Vol. XXXIII (January, 1955), pp. 254–259.

————, "Why Unethical Practice?" *Journal of Counseling Psychology,* Vol. II (Summer, 1955), pp. 122–128.

SHAFFER, Laurance F., and SHOBEN, Edward J., Jr., *The Psychology of Adjustment,* 2nd ed. (Boston, Houghton Mifflin, 1956).

SHOBEN, Edward J., Jr., "Tell Students Their Intelligence Ratings?" *School and Society,* Vol. LXXIV (September 15, 1951), pp. 169–170.

SNYDER, Troy, "Reporting Intelligence-Test Scores to High-School Pupils," *School Review,* Vol. XLV (February, 1937), pp. 105–111.

SUPER, Donald E., "The Criteria of Vocational Success," *Occupations,* Vol. XXX (October, 1951), pp. 5–9.

————, *The Psychology of Careers* (New York, Harper, 1957).

————, "Vocational Adjustment: Implementing a Self-Concept," *Occupations,* Vol. XXX (November, 1951), pp. 88–92.

TORRANCE, E. Paul, "Some Practical Uses of a Knowledge of Self-Concepts in Counseling and Guidance," *Educational and Psychological Measurement,* Vol. XIV (Spring, 1954), pp. 120–127.

TYLER, Leona E., "The Initial Interview," *Personnel and Guidance Journal,* Vol. XXXIV (April, 1956), pp. 466–473.

————, *The Work of the Counselor* (New York, Appleton-Century-Crofts, 1953).

WILLIAMSON, E. G., "Counseling and the Minnesota Point of View," *Educational and Psychological Measurement,* Vol. VII (Spring, 1947), pp. 141–155.

YOUNG, F. Chandler, "College Freshmen Judge Their Own Scholastic Promise," *Personnel and Guidance Journal,* Vol. XXXII (March, 1954), pp. 399–403.

CHAPTER 16

Counseling for Some

Common Problems

TEN COUNSELING SITUATIONS have been selected for discussion in this chapter. They are as follows: (1) choice of subjects and curriculums; (2) college-going; (3) length of stay in school; (4) vocation; (5) extracurricular activities; (6) quality of academic work; (7) discipline; (8) home difficulties; (9) part-time employment and personal finances; (10) emotional and social maladjustment. The first five are mainly in the distributive aspect of guidance; the last five, in the adjustive aspect.

These categories are not as discrete as they may seem. As one example, the first four are surely intertwined and therefore difficult to consider separately. As a second example, the pupil who needs guidance because his work is of poor quality may have been unfortunate in his choice of subjects, may have home difficulties, may be spending too many hours in part-time employment, may be distracted by a severe emotional disturbance. The overlapping and the interrelationships of these categories need no further illustration. Despite the imperfections of classification, use of these practical counseling situations will afford convenient pegs on which to hang some useful information that the years of study and experimentation have bequeathed us.

Inevitably, this chapter must refer the reader at many points to previous chapters. The problems have been touched upon; some principles pertinent to the problems have been elucidated; and some techniques and data essential to the counseling have been already set forth.

CHOICE OF SUBJECTS AND CURRICULUMS

The First (Main) Planning Interview

Counseling for the choice of subjects and curriculums is a recurring function throughout the period of secondary and higher education. It must be performed prior to entry upon diversified educational opportunity—which usually begins in the ninth grade—and at succeeding intervals as new educational vistas present themselves. Plans which are at first made tentatively and in rough outline are later confirmed, altered, or refined as the counselee accumulates experience and reveals himself more clearly to the counselor.

Some schools make an important occasion of the first planning interview, recognizing that the curriculum and the electives chosen for the ninth or tenth grades should be thought of in terms of long-range goals—vocation, post-secondary education, adult living. Such a school is Huntington Beach Union High School, California, the counselors of which have described their program of ninth-grade interviews.[1]

Between January and April each freshman has a conference with his parents and one of the school counselors to plan his next three years of high school. Extensive preparation precedes these interviews. The first semester in this four-year high school is given to the careful study of the freshmen pupils. They take tests of intelligence, achievement, personality, interests, and differentiated aptitudes. Their teachers fill out an aptitude rating sheet and register whatever they have learned about the individual's hobbies, interests, and personal adjustment. The pupils themselves answer a Personal Data Questionnaire and write an autobiography in their English classes. These data are assembled in the pupil's folder along with important health information from the nurse's office, the attendance record, and any correspondence with parents. The material is studied by the counselor before the interview.

The parents are invited by a double (reply) postcard, and every effort is made to accommodate them, even to the extent of offering two evenings a week for appointments. The conferences are conducted informally, with the counselor interpreting the data from the folder to the pupil and his parents. Often all sit in front of a screen on which test results are flashed by means of an opaque projector. (Apparently, exact scores are thus shown!) Sometimes during the conference the pupil arrives at a tentative choice of vocation. In all cases, he makes a choice of the five curricula offered by the school, and lists, on a printed form—his educational plan sheet—the subjects he will take in each of the high-school years. The plan, it is acknowledged, may be changed as future circumstances and considered re-evaluation may indicate. After the conference is closed the counselor dictates a report for transcription and filing in the folder.

In its second year of operation, some statistics were gathered on this program. It was found that 64 per cent of the conferences were attended by parents or other responsible relatives. The interviews varied from 20 minutes to two hours in length, with an average of 48 minutes. Evaluation cards filled out and returned by the parents indicated satisfaction with near unanimity. The counselors felt that there were many benefits for which they

[1] Wilma Hughell and Gerald G. Lance, "Student-Parent-Counselor Conferences," *Personnel and Guidance Journal,* Vol. XXXI (May, 1953), pp. 509–512.

could offer no measurement. Under pressure of carrying out the plan on schedule they saw themselves as improving their techniques and becoming more effective. They sensed a growth in teachers' interest in the individual pupil, an increased understanding of their children and of the school on the part of parents, and a better attitude toward their work on the part of pupils.

The educational plan sheet—promoted by a past state director of guidance services—has been widely adopted in the state of Utah, according to a recent statement.[2] Practices in filling it out vary from school to school, and no detailed description comparable to that just cited for Huntington Beach is offered.

Very similar to the student-parent-counselor conference employed at Huntington Beach is the practice which Ryden has described as prevailing at Niles Township Community High School, Skokie, Illinois.[3] He emphasized especially the value of the three-way partnership in educational planning. Parent estimates of their children's interests and abilities were found in a considerable number of cases to have differed materially from the results obtained by the school's program of objective testing. Therefore, without a conference for the meeting of minds, it would be altogether possible for the parents' counseling to be in contradiction to that of the school counselor. Indeed, the literature of guidance is filled with such cases, and whenever that conflict of counsels occurs, the pupil is in an insecure position. The kind of conference depicted by Ryden and by Hughell and Lance is calculated to achieve the much needed unity of advisers.

Illustrative Use of the Table of Correlation

In the discussion of methods of prediction in the final section of Chapter 14 the use of tables of correlation in distributive guidance was strongly advocated. For counseling pupils with reference to their choices of curriculums and subjects, such tables may advantageously be employed. They help the pupil to see his chances of success.

From the report of an experimental program by Hutson and Webster,[4] carried out with the 222 pupils of the tenth grade of the high school at Ellwood City, Pennsylvania, and in which the 249 pupils of the eleventh grade were used as a control group, illustrative data will be drawn. The program as a whole consisted of planned group and individual counseling to help pupils in their choices of vocation, in making the college decision, and in their choices of elective subjects for the eleventh grade—particularly French,

[2] Phelon Malouf, "The Plan Sheet, a Guidance Technique," *Personnel and Guidance Journal,* Vol. XXXIII (April, 1955), pp. 451–455.

[3] A. H. Ryden, "Including Parents in Counseling," *Occupations,* Vol. XXIX (May, 1951), pp. 587–590.

[4] P. W. Hutson and Arthur D. Webster, "An Experiment in the Educational and Vocational Guidance of Tenth-Grade Pupils," *Educational and Psychological Measurement,* Vol. III (Spring, 1943), pp. 3–21.

advanced algebra, and shorthand. In these several choices, the experimental group was compared with the control group, which differed in that it was virtually unguided.

Seventy-four members of the eleventh grade (control group) took up the study of French. On the first day of school in September they were given the Luria-Orleans Modern Language Prognosis Test. At the end of the first semester, Table 66 was drawn up,[5] showing the relationship between standing on the predictive test and semester marks.

During the second semester, the tenth grade (experimental group) as part of the program of counseling, were given the Luria-Orleans test. After the

TABLE 66. Relation between Scores Earned on Luria-Orleans Modern Language Prognosis Test by Members of the Control Group and Their Success in First-Semester French

Scores	Number of Cases	French Grades					
		E	D	C	B	A	Totals
170–179	7				71.4	28.6	100.0
160–169	12			16.7	41.7	41.7	100.1
150–159	10			60.0	30.0	10.0	100.0
140–149	8		12.5	25.0	62.5		100.0
130–139	10		10.0	50.0	40.0		100.0
120–129	11		63.6	18.2	18.2		100.0
110–119	2	100.0					100.0
100–109	4	50.0	50.0				100.0
90–99	4	75.0	25.0				100.0
80–89	1	100.0					100.0
70–79	4	75.0	25.0				100.0
60–69	1	100.0					100.0
Total	74						

tests were marked, each pupil was given a card on which was written his score, and with it a mimeographed copy of Table 66. In a homeroom group-counseling lesson they were taught how to read the table, the first illustrative reading being as follows: "Of the seven persons who scored between 170 and 179 on the test, about 71 per cent made B in French the first semester, and about 29 per cent made A." Then, every pupil took account of his own score and made the personal application of the table by such a reading as this: "If my French prognosis test score lies between 120 and 129, then according to the results achieved by those who have preceded me, I have about 18 chances in 100 of making a B, 18 chances in 100 of making a C, and 64 chances in 100 of making a D." While homeroom teachers helped the pupils to realize that the number of cases at each interval in the table

[5] *Ibid.,* Table 1, p. 9.

was so small as to render important the factor of chance in their distribution, they nevertheless called attention to the general pattern formed by the 74 cases in the table and helped each pupil to grasp its meaning for him.

Marks in English were used as another predictor. Table 67[6] was put on the board to show the tenth-grade pupils the relation between the English marks earned in the ninth and tenth grades by the control group and their French marks in the first semester of the eleventh grade. They were then directed in figuring out their own quality point averages in English, based on their marks earned in the ninth grade and the first semester of the tenth grade. Each pupil was helped to read the table and interpret its meaning for himself in the light of his own English quality point average.

Was this type of counseling effective? As measured by several criteria, yes. The pupils of the experimental group who elected French for their eleventh grade proved to have higher average aptitude for the study of that subject than did the corresponding pupils of the control group. This superiority was evidenced by the comparison of prognosis-test scores and by comparison of marks in ninth-grade English. More significant was comparison of marks actually earned in first-semester French by the two groups, of which distributions and summaries are shown in Table 68.[7] The two groups were

TABLE 67. Relation between Quality Point Average of Grades Earned in Ninth and Tenth Grade English by Members of the Control Group and Their Success in First-Semester French

Q.P.A. in English	Number of Cases	French Grades					Totals
		E	D	C	B	A	
A (3.5–4.0)	7				57.1	42.9	100.0
B (2.5–3.4)	39		10.3	33.3	43.6	12.8	100.0
C (1.5–2.4)	23	34.8	34.8	17.4	13.0		100.0
D (0.5–1.4)	5	80.0	20.0				100.0
E (0.0–0.4)							
Total	74						

taught by the same teacher, and she was not aware that a controlled experiment in guidance was being carried on in the school. Presenting approximately the same degree of contrast as is evident in Table 68 were the dis-

[6] *Ibid.,* Table 2, p. 10.
[7] *Ibid.,* Table 8, p. 18.

tributions of scores on a standardized achievement test, the medians being 84.7 for the control group and 90.5 for the experimental group.

For guiding the experimental group with reference to their election of shorthand and advanced algebra, also, predictive tables similar to Tables 66 and 67 were constructed and used. Similar favorable results were obtained.

TABLE 68. Percentage Distributions of Pupils of the Control and Experimental Groups in French, according to Marks Received at the End of the First Semester of Study

Marks	Numerical Values	Control Group (74)	Experimental Group (65)
A	3.5–4.0	10.8	16.9
B	2.5–3.4	32.4	33.8
C	1.5–2.4	23.0	26.2
D	0.5–1.4	17.6	15.4
E	0.0–0.4	16.2	7.7
Totals		100.0	100.0
Upper quartile		3.01	3.21
Median		2.16	2.47
Lower quartile		.95	1.52

There are many factors, conditions, and considerations that enter into counseling for choice of subjects and curriculums, in addition to those thus far presented. Space can be allowed here only for naming some of them, as follows:

(1) Interest as well as ability of the counselee must be taken into account. The first section of Chapter 13 developed the meaning and significance of interests and described the instruments for measuring them. It was made apparent that interests are more stable and more certainly ascertainable among college freshmen than among ninth-graders.

(2) Opportunity. A child's ability and interest may surely justify his choice of a straight college preparatory curriculum, but if his opportunity to go on to college seems to be severely strictured by his family circumstances and the prospects of his responsibility for his family, the counselor will have to think more deeply with the counselee. Though the opportunity to go to college appears dim, the selection and pursuit of a "soft" program by a pupil of high ability seems never to be justified. Such a pupil should be counseled to take courses which are worthy of his steel; if the college opportunity should come, or if he *makes* it come, he will be ready. And if he does not go to college, he will be the better able to make his way in the world of vocation if he has pursued a rigorous program of mathematics, science, and foreign language, as well as college-preparatory courses in

English and social studies. Acutely conscious of the shortage of trained personnel as we are today, the prospect of a talented pupil who takes "the easy road" should be abhorrent to us.

The obstacle of lack of opportunity is faced in the case of the college student who has undoubted ability for one of the more learned professions, but whose financial resources and responsibilities dictate the shorter period of preparation for one of the *less* learned professions. We compromise at as high a level as possible.

(3) The counselor's comprehension and equitable evaluation of all the studies is essential to give sound counsel for the choice of subjects and curriculums. This is one of the "cautions" laid down in Chapter 15.

(4) Counsel should be essentially positive rather than negative. The individual must be aided in seeing his assets as well as his shortcomings, and in finding the subjects and curriculums from which he can derive profit. This may be hard to achieve. If, for example, a pupil's DAT profile (See Figure 12 in Chapter 12) indicates that he is decidedly below the median on every test of that battery, the counselor must search elsewhere for some favorable information. Here we have a serious limitation of the interview which is simply devoted to test interpretation. The more extensive and broadly based knowledge of the individual with which Hughell and Lance (described above) entered upon their interviews, affords the counselor more chance for the positive approach. From another angle, however, it is sometimes difficult to make the positive approach. If the school's program of studies includes no curriculum or subjects which fit the pupil's abilities and interests, positive counsel seems impossible. That is why some realistic counselors help such pupils to leave the school as early as the law will permit.

(5) Acceptability of the subject depends on acceptability of the teacher. How shall a pupil be counseled when a subject for which he has ability and interest is taught by a teacher who generally gives the pupils an unhappy time? Corey and Beery[8] submitted an inquiry to university freshmen which required them to look back over their high-school experience and reflect upon the relationship between popularity of subjects and teachers. They reported twice as many popular teachers teaching unpopular subjects as there were unpopular teachers teaching popular subjects. This condition probably poses a more serious problem in the ninth grade than at the college-freshman level, for the reason that the younger the counselee the more the teacher's personality is fused with the subject. The older person makes a distinction between teacher and subject. Nevertheless, the readers of this book know full well from their personal experience that the selection of subjects has always been much influenced by what is known of the teachers of those subjects. The counselor has always had to grapple with this problem, and no one knows a formula for solving it.

Like all of the other problems of the ten to be taken up in this chapter, counseling for choice of subjects and curriculums must be adapted to each individual. While much may be accomplished in groups, every case must be given individual attention.

[8] Stephen M. Corey and George S. Beery, "The Effect of Teacher Popularity upon Attitude toward School Subjects," *Journal of Educational Psychology*, Vol. XXIX (December, 1938), pp. 665–670.

COLLEGE-GOING

Two Problems

Counseling students of elementary-school and secondary-school years with reference to college-going must be thought of as essentially two problems: first, choice of going to college or going to work, and, second, choice of specific college to enter. The first problem involves deciding whether one has the ability, interest, and financial resources essential for entering upon some degree-granting curriculum. The alternative in this problem is not merely immediate entry into the labor market, but also the pursuit of training for a technical occupation in a nondegree curriculum, concerning which some comment will be offered later in this chapter.

The second problem—choice of specific college—involves deciding on what type of degree-granting institution is best suited to the needs, goals, and circumstances of the individual student. Should it be a small, separate liberal-arts college—that peculiarly American institution—or should it be a large, multi-unit university? Should it be coeducational, or restricted to one sex? Should it be an institution of specific religious affiliation? Should it be, if possible, in such proximity to the student's home that he can live at home while attending? These questions suggest some of the major considerations. Frequently, even with the most painstaking advisement, they must be answered by some kind of compromise. But in practice, as will later be demonstrated, they are too often not even deliberated, with the result that ill-suited choices are made.

Counseling as Regards College Ability

Essential facts useful in counseling the pupil regarding his ability for college work have been recounted in Chapter 12. There it was shown that rank in senior high school class or in junior high school class is the best single indicator of college success. The predictive values of intelligence tests and achievement tests were also presented. The qualifying factor of variation in the intellectual caliber of high-school and college student bodies was illuminated by citation of researches on the subject.

The method of *expressing* measures of college ability in relation to college success was also illustrated. The last division of the section on Prediction, Chapter 14, set forth the argument for the use of the table of probability as the expression of prediction. The use and the worth of this device may be illustrated by drawing again on the experiment by Hutson and Webster cited in the previous section.

One of the objects of that experiment with tenth-grade pupils was to help them make the college decision. Group lessons were taught and individual counseling was freely available. As the first step, the pupils of the experimental group were asked to compute from the marks they had earned in academic subjects in the ninth and in the first half of the tenth grades their quality point averages, using the values 4, 3, 2, 1, and 0 for the letter grades A, B, C, D, and E, respectively. With teacher assistance and careful supervision this was accurately done. The quality point averages were then reported and ranked for the entire class [222] from the highest to the lowest, the distribution was divided into tenths, and each pupil was informed as to the tenth of his class in which he stood.

Second, to each pupil was given a chart from Johnston's report of his investigation of the relationship between the high-school success of graduates of the Minneapolis and St. Paul high schools in 1922, 1923, and 1924, and their success at the University of Minnesota.[9] The chart was a bar diagram showing, for each tenth of the high-school class, the number entering the University of Minnesota and the number who were successful. From this objective information the pupils were able to determine their approximate chances for success in college. Discussion revolved about the congruity of the analogy of Ellwood City pupils with those charted by Johnston, and also about reasons why the relationship between high-school and college success is no more perfect or imperfect than it is.[10]

For four weeks the weekly homeroom group-guidance programs and considerable individual counseling by homeroom teachers and school counselor were devoted to the problem of the college decision. At the end of the year these tenth-grade pupils filled out a blank stating their occupational preference and their educational plans. Table 69[11] shows a comparison of the college-going members of the experimental group with the college-going members of the control group. The comparison is in terms of rank in high-school class, and the evidence is clear that the members of the experimental group who had declared their intention of going to college were considerably better selected.

The choices of these pupils, of course, did not simply reflect their improved knowledge of their capacity for college education. Nor did the counseling bear solely on that point. The program naturally had to take into account the interest pupils felt in pursuing a life of study for four or more years beyond high school. It had to take into consideration, also, the financial burden of college education. The college decision of each pupil grew out of deliberations concerning all these factors.

While this counseling program did not involve calling in the parents, common sense tells us that the kind of student-parent-counselor conference described in the first section of this chapter is to be recommended in the strongest terms for counseling with regard to the college decision. College education is so generally a family enterprise that parents need a first-hand acquaintance with the evidence of their child's college ability, and the coun-

[9] J. B. Johnston, "Vocational and Educational Guidance in the High School and Its Relation to Higher Education," *Vocational Guidance Magazine,* Vol. VII (October, 1928), pp. 15–21.

[10] Hutson and Webster, *op. cit.,* pp. 6–7.

[11] *Ibid.,* adapted from Table 4, p. 12.

TABLE 69. Percentage Distributions of Pupils of the Control and Experimental Groups Who Stated the Intention of Going to College—Distributed according to Percentile Rank in Class as Determined by Quality Point Averages of Marks Earned in Academic Subjects Taken in Ninth and Tenth Grades

Percentile Rank	Control Group			Experimental Group		
	Boys (39)	Girls (27)	Total (66)	Boys (36)	Girls (28)	Total (64)
90–99	7.7	14.8	10.6	30.6	25.0	28.1
80–89	20.5	7.4	15.2	11.1	17.9	14.1
70–79	7.7	40.7	21.2	16.7	17.9	17.2
60–69	23.1	7.4	16.7	11.1	17.9	14.1
50–59	10.3	11.1	10.6	13.9	3.6	9.4
40–49	15.4	3.7	10.6	2.8	3.6	3.1
30–39	2.6	....	1.5	5.6	7.1	6.3
20–29	7.7	3.7	6.1	8.3	3.6	6.3
10–19	2.6	3.7	3.0	....	3.6	1.6
0–9	2.6	7.4	4.5	....	....	....
Totals	100.2	99.9	100.0	100.1	100.2	100.2
Upper Quartile	81.8	79.3	80.5	91.8	90.0	91.0
Median	64.1	73.2	68.2	75.0	75.9	75.4
Lower Quartile	45.9	55.9	49.3	56.0	62.0	58.2

selor can help them to obtain it. The child cannot be expected to adequately relay the evidence to his parents.

Counseling as Regards the Specific College

While this problem is here presented separately, counseling for the specific college or university to be attended is really a part of the college decision from the beginning. The question, "does the child have college ability?" brings up immediately, "ability for *what* college?" Does he have the ability required for an engineering college, such as Rensselaer or Brooklyn Polytech, or does his ability more nearly correspond to that required for success in a liberal-arts college, such as Wooster or Williams? Again, does the *degree* or *extent* of his ability justify his aspiration to enter one of the institutions listed in the top half of Table 58, or will he be barely able to succeed in one of the institutions represented in the lower half of that table? Unfortunately, we do not know the names of those schools. With experience, however, the counselor acquires considerable knowledge of the intellectual capacity required for admission to and success in various colleges and universities. He is able, perhaps, to inform the counselee that a certain college selects its students entirely from the highest tenth of the high-school class, or from the first fifth, or from the upper two fifths, as the case may be.

Harriger, whose study of college entrance requirements was cited in Chapter 7, has more recently described the practice of counseling for the specific college as carried on in the secondary schools of Butler, Pennsylvania.[12] Students are urged, he says, to make the choice of college in the ninth grade, and when the problem of variation in college entrance requirements is explained to parents, the early decision makes sense to them and they are glad to participate. If the specific college cannot be settled upon, the general type and geographic location is usually identified. Students procure catalogues, plan intensively, become aware of the wide variations in college offerings, opportunities, entrance standards, costs, social programs, and academic ratings, and realize that college entrance is an individual problem not met by some over-all pattern. Says Harriger,

No longer do students elect two years of a foreign language in the "College Preparatory Course" and then find that the college chosen requires three years' study in a foreign language. More engineering students now learn early that specific combinations of subjects are required, with others being highly recommended. Under this plan the student can tailor his high-school program to dovetail perfectly with the college recommendations.

Harriger estimates that with this plan of early decision more students of ability are going to college.

How well do students know the colleges they choose to enter? The last section of Chapter 6 describes at some length the investigation made by McLaughlin in seeking an answer to this question. His negative findings constitute a challenge to organize counseling service so that pupils study college catalogues with pertinent questions in mind. A poignant example of the need for some exact knowledge of the college one plans to attend is the story of the high-school senior girl whose struggle with trigonometry finally brought her to the attention of the counselor. "Well, just why are you taking this fourth-year mathematics, anyway?" he asked. "I have to have it to get into Carnegie Tech," she replied. "Are you planning to take engineering at Tech?" "Oh, no, I'm entering the drama school." One may speculate that this girl had relied upon conversation with male classmates rather than a study of Tech's catalogue.

The amount of group counseling for college choice that can be done through homeroom groups, as mentioned above in the experiment by Hutson and Webster, is quite limited in many high schools, for the reason that so many pupils in the homeroom group are not going to college. Occasionally, one hears of the formation of a College Club, as in the Westinghouse High School, of Pittsburgh, which serves the valuable purpose of bringing together those pupils who are planning for college. Nevertheless, it is in such individual interviews as were described by Hughell and Lance and by Ryden that the pupil's thinking on this important matter will be most stimulated and also evaluated.

Counseling as Regards Financial Aid

It seems sound practice to counsel the junior high school pupil to pursue in senior high school the subjects that correspond to his capacity, without regard for other considerations. If the pupil has college ability, though financial support for college education is not in sight, he should, in most instances, choose college-preparatory English and social studies as well as science, mathematics, and foreign language. Scholarships and loan funds for college education are available in increasing amounts. Self-help through part-time employment, with full time in vacation periods, is an American college tradition which has been fully operative since World War II. By such means the economic handicap has often been dissipated for American boys and girls. If, however, at high-school graduation the financial obstacle to college should prove insurmountable, the student who has partaken of a rigorous intellectual experience can advantageously enter employment in commerce or industry: in a few months he can add clerical skills to his excellent foundation; he will be eagerly accepted in apprenticeship programs for skilled trades.

However, the high-school counselor has a duty to help needy pupils become aware of the wide range of financial aids which are available. Such compendia as are mentioned in Section V of Ruth Anderson's long article[13] will be available in the library and in the counselor's office. The successive publications by S. N. Feingold (*Scholarships, Fellowships, and Loans,* Bellman Publishing Co., Cambridge, Mass., Vol. I, 1949; Vol. II, 1951; Vol. III, 1955) are useful references, as is also *Scholarships Available to Entering College Freshmen* (Chronicle Guidance Publications, Moravia, N.Y., 1955). The counselor will also gather information in his own geographic area which is of special interest to his own school. Best example of such practice to come to the writer's attention is the 1956 mimeographed book, *Scholarships and Student Aid: A Guide for Students and Counselors,* compiled by the Guidance Department of the Providence Public Schools.[14] For each of the degree-granting institutions of special interest to Providence pupils it gives pertinent information concerning scholarships, loan funds, and work opportunities. A second section gives similar treatment to post-secondary schools which do not grant degrees, and a third section lists the financial aids offered by various local and national organizations. This book is wisely made available in the elementary as well as the secondary schools of Providence.

[13] "An Annotated Bibliography of School and College Information," *Bulletin of the National Association of Secondary-School Principals,* Vol. XXXVI (October, 1952), pp. 170–208.

[14] Made available to the writer through the courtesy of Mary D. Basso, Supervisor of Guidance and Placement.

It has been the observation of this writer that some schools obtain many more scholarships for their pupils than do others, and that often this is not just attributable to the superior quality of their students but rather to alert, aggressive counseling. Sometimes such counseling involves teaching naïve and unsophisticated youth the details of making an effective appearance before a scholarship committee. On this point, Havighurst and Neugarten[15] give contrasting examples to show how a "diamond in the rough" from the lower class was at a disadvantage in scholarship competition with a boy of less ability but of middle-class suavity and polish.

While this section is concerned with counseling high-school students, it seems pertinent in this discussion of financial aid to point to the remarkable record of one college in helping its students to win scholarships and fellowships for graduate study. Lawrence R. Malnig[16] has described the techniques of gathering and organizing information about graduate scholarships and fellowships, identifying and counseling the students who have the potentialities of good applicants, making recommendations that are discriminating and precise, and conducting a follow-up study to learn how to improve the procedure.

In concluding this section on counseling for college-going, the reader is invited to re-read the portions of Chapter 4 which reveal the dimensions of this challenge. The percentage of high-school graduates who enter college is steadily increasing and is presently reported at approximately forty. Yet this percentage includes many who are not of college caliber and excludes many who would be excellent college risks. College selective procedures are too coarse and wasteful to solve the problem. High-school counseling of the individual student is the best immediate hope for improving college student bodies.

LENGTH OF STAY IN SCHOOL

Improving the School Experience

To increase the length of stay in school, the reasons for dropping out of school ought first to be examined. This was done in Chapters 3 and 4. There it was shown that early elimination from school especially stemmed from unsuccessful academic experience and unhappy social experience. The child who is frustrated in his studies and/or denied gratification of his need for satisfying social relationships is prone to escape from the school environment at the earliest opportunity. To improve the curriculum and instruction, to create a social life in the school which is geared to the needs of all, and to administer the school in the spirit of fullest respect for pupils as persons—

[15] Robert J. Havighurst and Bernice L. Neugarten, *Society and Education* (Boston, Allyn & Bacon, 1957), pp. 274–276.
[16] "Who Gets Those Graduate Scholarships?" *Personnel and Guidance Journal,* Vol. XXXIII (February, 1955), pp. 331–333.

these tasks are not elements of the guidance function. They are, however, basic determinants of the pupil's length of stay in school.

The counselor may play an important role in bringing about the school conditions which make pupils wish to remain in school. It is he who becomes aware of pupils' needs and of curricular inadequacies most promptly. His test data tell him that Harry is trying to do eighth-grade work with fifth-grade reading ability, that all the 90 IQ's are handicapped and frustrated because the required English is college-preparatory, and that the abilities and interests of many pupils are not recognized by an adequate offering in the practical and fine arts. The isolates and friendless come to his attention and impress him with the inadequacy of the social groupings of the school for giving all members the essential feeling of belonging. These shortcomings of the school the counselor is able to dramatize to principal and faculty. Thus the school's program may be improved, and that is the most fundamental step in achieving length of stay.

Group Guidance Lessons on Reasons for Remaining in School

The popularly expressed ideal of our society is for every child to remain in school and study diligently until he obtains a high-school diploma. Compulsory school attendance laws, however, generally set an age limit rather than a school grade limit; modal practice is to require attendance until the age of 16. As the sixteenth birthday overtakes some youngsters while they are in the ninth or tenth grades, they may and do drop out of school in those grades.

Reasons for remaining in school are conflicting. As pointed out in the first section of Chapter 3, our democratic society operates schools with public funds for the purpose of developing a trained citizenry, arguing that those who exercise the franchise should understand social issues and institutions, be oriented in the physical world, and have such control of the tools of learning that they can continually keep abreast of the changing times. The individual, on the other hand, thinks of the school as an instrument for helping him to gain a preferred position in the socio-economic order.

While fourteen-year-old boys and girls are not devoid of social responsibility, they have been raised in a world which sets great store by individual success, and they are well indoctrinated in that value. Hence, the strongest argument to induce them to stay in school is that of individual advantage. It is therefore suggested that group guidance lessons with that emphasis be taught in the seventh and eighth grades as a type of counseling to increase length of stay in school. Figure 18[17] summarizes some facts gathered by the United States Census Bureau showing the relation between extent of schooling and yearly earnings of middle-aged men. Such data, mimeographed and placed in the hands of each pupil so that he can take them home, may well

[17] *Guidance Newsletter,* Science Research Associates, February, 1956.

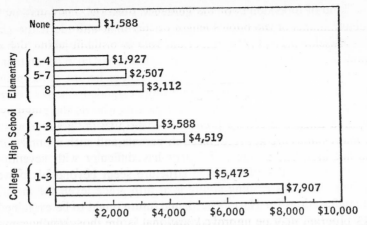

FIG. 18. Average (mean) income in 1949 for men 45 to 54 years old with different amounts of education.

cause some careless youth who are anxious to start self-exploitation to take second thought.

Study of the various occupations which are typically taken up by workers who have attained the several educational levels shown in Figure 18 could be carried on extensively. It would be social study, acquainting pupils with aspects of the occupational structure, but they would inevitably make personal applications.

Of course, one of the hazards of this kind of group instruction is that in such general employment of the goal of personal ambition, some members of limited ability will set their sights too high. In the present agitation over shortages of highly trained workers, we are prone to overlook this danger of wholesale salesmanship. There is no getting around the fact that just as some youth are dropping out of school before they have profited by it as much as they could, others try to remain for a longer period than is profitable for them.

Individual Counseling

Actually, length of stay in school will be a major consideration of the initial interview with the pupil and his parents, as depicted in the first section of this chapter. Educational and vocational plans assume a longer or shorter stay in school. As has already been pointed out, one of the pressing problems of the times is to induce those parents of low educational traditions who have a gifted child to accept the idea of extended schooling for their child. A counselor in a city high school was recently expressing to the writer her sorrow over the fact that the boy standing first in the graduating class and the girl standing third highest were not going to college. "My mother says that our kind of folks don't go to college," was the girl's explanation. There might have been a chance to alter such a parental attitude if the girl had been identified as a good prospect for college while still in junior high school years and the education of her parents to that idea had been begun that early.

In contrast to those who wish to leave school before developing their potentialities are the pupils who plan for more extended schooling than their abilities justify. Often, of course, it is the parents who do the planning; they are ambitious for their children, desirous to help them "get a good start in the world." It is no kindness to let such parents and such a pupil continue indefinitely in their illusions. If Harry has difficulty with seventh-grade arithmetic, if the rules of language structure seem beyond his powers of comprehension, if his reading ability is at fifth-grade level, the meaning of these manifestations for Harry's academic future ought to be explained, and his assets for further training and a vocational future thoughtfully canvassed. Topp[18] has well pointed out the unjustified strain that is sometimes imposed on a child by unthinking parents and teachers who urge him on with the easily voiced admonition, "You can do it if you try." Our vast knowledge of individual differences should tell us that such counsel must be given most discriminatingly.

The curricular and extracurricular opportunities of the school should be sufficiently wide and varied that every pupil can remain in high school with profit and enjoyment until graduation. But in case those conditions do not obtain, the counselor should recognize that some pupils will be better off if they leave school at the earliest legal age for quitting. They should be able to quit with his frank approval, counsel for the future, and aid in placement.

Plainly, the import of these paragraphs is that the counselor must deliberate this question in the case of every pupil: What is the optimum length of schooling for this individual, in consideration of his own and the social good? The same question applies to the counseling of college students, as will be evidenced in the next division of this section.

Counseling at College

From time to time data have been published showing the extraordinary erosion of student bodies in higher education. Most recent figures to come to this writer's attention are those cited in *Guidance Newsletter* (Science Research Associates), March, 1956, as being derived from a study by the United States Office of Education, which had not yet been published. The cumulative percentages of college dropouts found in this study were as follows: end of first year, 27½; end of second year, 42; end of third year, 48; end of fourth year, 55.

This wastage is a serious challenge to all who have responsibility for higher education, for it means that the majority of students spend valuable

[18] Robert F. Topp, "You Cannot Always 'Do It If You Try!'" *Elementary School Journal,* Vol. LIV (December, 1953), pp. 230–234.

time in pursuit of an educational goal which they do not attain. Their truncated curriculums and their excursion into "college life" are not wholly without value to them. Nevertheless the loss is great, and the possibility of increasing society's reservoir of trained personnel by saving some of these dropouts is deserving of urgent study and action. It is known that some were poor college risks to begin with; state-supported institutions are often under obligation to accept any graduate of a state-accredited high school. Other students, however, are unsuccessful in their academic work because they cannot adjust to the irregular schedule and the freedom from daily supervision. Many have poor study habits and use their time inefficiently. Some attempt too heavy a load of extracurricular activity or of part-time employment. Some get started on a curriculum which is ill-suited to their special interests and abilities. Numerous other causes appear with minor frequency in the case-study literature of college counseling.

It is relatively easy for the college student to drop out when the academic road becomes rough, when his social desires are not gratified, his life seems too circumscribed or the period of non-earning seems too long. His earning power is considerable and he is tempted to use it. There are no legal barriers. He is assumed to be an adult, competent to know his own welfare and make his own decisions.

Actually, he has not attained maturity. Ordway Tead has said,

The college years present a subtle problem of transition from adolescence to adulthood. The college does stand *in loco parentis*, more at the outset and hardly at all by the time of graduation. And the solicitous interest of someone who will care about how each student is unfolding, is a virtual must. How we can achieve that in huge student bodies it is not easy to see, unless a wholly new emphasis in relations with students is aggressively developed. . . . There is no escape from the psychic reality that if there is to be guided growth, some individual, warm of heart and wise of mind, should be the guide, counselor, and friend of every student.

The present expansion of personnel programs in higher education suggests that the colleges are accepting Tead's idea. The old policy of "Here's college education—take it or leave it—it's up to you" has proven too wasteful of human values. That the new guardianship can notably increase the numbers who remain in college until they attain the baccalaureate, is well demonstrated by Toven's experiment.[19]

Counseling at the college level for length of stay in school should not be confined to the salvage of young people who do not know how to study or who make poor judgments in the use of their time. It should be carried on in a context of vocational diagnosis and advisement which helps the student to a greater refinement of choice than was possible while he was in high school.

[19] J. Richard Toven, "Appraising a Counseling Program at the College Level," *Occupations*, Vol. XXIII (May, 1945), pp. 459–466. This study will be described in Chapter 19.

To the mind of this writer, the end of the freshman year is a most desirable time for the analysis and counsel of all students. By that time the college has had opportunity to test the student's general ability, special aptitudes, and interests. He has been observed for a year in the academic atmosphere. Two semesters of marks are on his record. Faculty members can be polled for their estimates of his traits and potentialities. The cumulative record has been initiated and contains its valuable lore of personal data. It is time to test the student's vocational and educational plans, to help him find them if he does not have any, to make prognoses of his possible and probable attainments along various lines. If the prognosis of his admission to law school or medical school—his objective—is unfavorable, more promising prognoses should be found and offered to him.

One accomplishment of this systematic canvass at the end of the freshman year should be the identification and counsel of the individuals who have the capacity to earn the Ph.D. Since it has been figured that only one in 25 who have such capacity do win the degree, and since the dire present and future need for workers with such advanced training to staff college faculties and commercial laboratories has been extensively publicized, college counseling bureaus clearly have a responsibility. To exercise this function in the senior year, as proposed in the *Association of American Colleges Bulletin* of March, 1953, is too late! By that time plans have been made for vocation and perhaps marriage; the student's family is unprepared for further deferment of his self-exploitation. To counsel graduate school at that late date is probably as ineffective as to counsel college in the senior year of high school. The idea of earlier counsel of the talented student is to give him *and his parents* time enough to raise their sights, to make plans for necessary sacrifices for the deferred gain.

The need for trained manpower, for the maximum use of those individuals who have the capacity to serve society in professional occupations, seems at this writing to be so critical as to justify a requirement that no one be registered for sophomore studies without the evidence in his folder that he has had the benefit of the kind of comprehensive counseling interview which is here advocated. Most students will eagerly seek the interview; the requirement is necessary to assure the inclusion of a minority who for various reasons would fail to avail themselves of it.

Some evidence of the practicability of such freshman counseling has recently been accumulated in Brooklyn College and is reported by Buckton and Doppelt.[20] They demonstrate noteworthy correlations between a battery of tests given at college entrance and a "Pre-Sophomore Battery" on the one hand, and the Miller Analogies Test (a test aimed at measuring scholastic aptitude at the graduate school level) and the Graduate Record Examina-

---

[20] LaVerne Buckton and Jerome E. Doppelt, "Freshman Tests as Predictors of Scores on Graduate and Professional School Examinations," *Journal of Counseling Psychology,* Vol. II (Summer, 1955), pp. 146–149.

tions on the other hand. They advocate counseling with the aid of expectancy tables and present two such tables, as follows: (1) students classified by entrance battery scores and Miller Analogies Test scores (r = .63), and (2) students classified by the Pre-Sophomore total reading scores and Law School Admission Test scores (r = .72). Graduate and professional schools make considerable use of tests in the selection of their students, but, of course, they also regard the student's academic record as very important in the estimation of his fitness.

Counseling for length of stay in school has many facets, some of which are inextricably interwoven with counseling for vocation, the subject of the next section.

VOCATION

Major Elements Briefly Stated

Counseling for vocational choice certainly assumes a knowledge of the counselee—his abilities, interests, opportunities, handicaps. Chapters 11, 12, and 13 presented the major instruments for acquiring such knowledge and gave an introduction to the literature on their value.

Second, counseling for vocational choice assumes knowledge of vocations —their nature and requirements, their demand and supply factors, their rewards and penalties. It assumes a knowledge of the sources of information so that they can be utilized for the instruction of the client. Sinick[21] has summarized a number of writings on how to use occupational information in the counseling interview. Mainly, they advocate deferment of the use of such information until after individual diagnosis, bringing it into the interview when the subject feels a need for it, employing printed materials in preference to the counselor's oral message, selecting materials appropriate to the client's reading level (unless the counselor reads and interprets), and devoting attention primarily to beginning jobs.

The importance of the counselor's being a thoughtful reader of occupational literature is illustrated by an exceptional case reported to the writer by a former student who was then a counselor in a veterans' guidance center.[22] The case was that of a young veteran who felt he *must* go to college. (It later developed that this was a reflection of parental pressure.) However, his score on the ACE Psychological Examination placed him at the eighth percentile of college freshmen. This was interpreted to him as auguring little chance of success in college. He desired to study music at college, and on the Seashore Tests his scores were all well above average. But he had had virtually no musical training, and the age of 26 seemed very late to begin. He was given tests of mechanical comprehension, finger dexterity, and spatial compre-

---

[21] Daniel Sinick, "Occupational Information in the Counseling Interview," *Vocational Guidance Quarterly,* Vol. IV (Summer, 1956), pp. 145–149.
[22] Courtesy of G. G. Santavicca.

hension, and stood very high on them. He said that he liked to work with his hands. Several trades were suggested to him. None appealed—and besides, that was not the way to go to college.

In pondering this discouraging conflict of interests, desires, abilities, and limitations, the counselor recalled having read and filed a few weeks before an announcement from the Conn Vocational School, of Elkhart, Indiana, and he asked the veteran if he would like to consider the trade of musical instrument repairman. He was shown the pamphlet, depicting a modern school situated upon a beautiful campus. It was illustrated with photos of the modern machinery used to repair musical instruments. A little study of entrance requirements showed the veteran to be qualified. At the end of six months the course would be completed, and because a need existed for musical instrument repairmen, the school probably would be able to place him on a job. Speaking as if a burden had been lifted from his heart, the veteran said, "That means I can go to school. And I won't have to go to college for four years, either."

At the end of four months a follow-up letter to the Conn school brought word that the young man was happily and successfully completing his course and that he was one of their best students. The example demonstrates how important it is for the counselor to study occupational information and to keep it adequately filed.

The third major element in counseling for vocation is a knowledge of the process of vocational choice. This is a subject which will be developed in the division of this section which immediately follows.

Theories of Vocational Choice

Efforts to state a single comprehensive theory of vocational choice have proven unfruitful. Perhaps the most ambitious attempt to do so is represented in the study of Eli Ginzberg and his associates.[23] These authors regarded occupational choice as a process which is developmental in character, taking place over a period of years, and achieved through three successive phases, as follows: fantasy, tentative choice, realistic choice. Compromises of such factors as abilities, interests, values, and opportunities are characteristic. The Ginzberg theorizing was based on research which has been so thoroughly criticized as inadequate that one may say the main contribution of the study has been to stir up interest in the process of vocational choice.

Small[24] has explored vocational choice with a limited but carefully designed study in which he compared well-adjusted boys, ages 15–19, with emotionally disturbed boys of the same ages. He found no evidence of a developmental progression towards greater realism of vocational choice, but

[23] E. Ginzberg, S. Ginsburg, S. Axelrad, and J. L. Herma, *Occupational Choice* (New York, Columbia University Press, 1946).

[24] Leonard Small, "Personality Determinants of Vocational Choice," *Psychological Monographs: General and Applied*, Vol. 67, No. 1, pp. 1–21, Whole No. 351, 1953.

much evidence that reality factors and elements of fantasy operate simultaneously. The well-adjusted boys made vocational choices which were more realistic than did the emotionally disturbed boys; the choices of the latter group were more reflective of fantasy. Small found the evidences of compromise in vocational choice and commented as follows on how compromise is achieved:[25]

Compromise implies that reality is perceived by the individual, who uses these perceptions to curb, mitigate, or redirect the impulses generating fantasies. The perception of reality and the control of impulses are ego functions; compromise is a function of the adequacy or strength of the ego. We find evidence for this point in the greater realism of choices made by the better-adjusted boys, and the environment-involvement nature of their job fantasies as contrasted with environment-avoidance fantasies of the disturbed boys.

A theory of vocational choice determination must take account of ego strength. With this factor as nearly constant as possible rather than an unknown variable, it would be possible to test the relative importance of developmental factors, interests, aptitudes, family traditions and pressures, environmental opportunities, and the host of other factors recognized as individual determinants but not yet integrated into a sound theory. Such a theory must encompass what goes into the choice, and the process by which the factors in play are consolidated into a choice.

As indicated in the paragraph just quoted, many constituents play a part in vocational choice. Some are unsound and irrational; there seems to be no point in integrating them; counseling seeks to rule them out.[26]

Distribution of Abilities Within the Individual

Progress toward a theory of vocational choice, as just presented, is further impeded by the fact that most people have the capacity to do many things about equally well. Kitson stated this principle many years ago,[27] and the wealth of information concerning the distribution of human ability which has since been collected, bears him out. For example, Reynolds' generalizations are as follows:[28]

The requirements of most jobs in modern industry are not very exacting: a minimum level of manual dexterity, reaction speed, and physical stamina; ability to understand simple instructions; and such personal traits as punctuality, attentiveness, and ability to adjust to personal contacts with fellow workers and super-

---

[25] *Ibid.*, p. 17.

[26] A summary of the literature is found in the following reference: Lloyd Meadow, "Toward a Theory of Vocational Choice," *Journal of Counseling Psychology,* Vol. II (Summer, 1955), pp. 108–112. For an extended treatment of this subject see the following reference: Donald E. Super, *The Psychology of Careers* (New York, Harper, 1957), Part II.

[27] Harry D. Kitson, "Suggestions toward a Tenable Theory of Vocational Guidance," in Meyer Bloomfield's *Readings in Vocational Guidance* (Boston, Ginn, 1915), pp. 103–108.

[28] Lloyd G. Reynolds, *The Structure of Labor Markets* (New York, Harper, 1951), p. 152.

visors. Given these traits, all but a small percentage of manual jobs can be learned quickly and performed competently. This amounts to saying that for most jobs there are a great many 'right' men and that which of these men gets the job is a matter of indifference from a production standpoint.

The point of this quotation is emphasized by Caplow's discussion of "horizontal mobility" among workers, a theme which he illustrates by citing the 22 varied jobs which had been held by a man in his thirties, a "not unusual" career.[29] Even in professional fields, Kitson "found that among 1,000 persons listed in *Who's Who in America,* 16 per cent changed one or more times to an occupation completely different from that held previously."[30]

The now classic research in establishment of principles of the distribution of ability within the individual is that of Hull.[31] Whereas innumerable studies have been made to show the variation among individuals on a given trait, Hull conducted an investigation to ascertain the variability within the individual. He sought the answer to such questions as the following: Does the distribution of talents within the individual correspond to the familiar bell-shaped contour? What is the extent or range of differences within the individual? (If they are all equal or approximately equal, he can do one thing about as well as another, and special aptitudes do not exist.) Are people all equally variable in the amounts of the various talents possessed by them? Or shall we find that the talents of one person will cluster closely together around one particular point on the scale while those of another may be scattered very widely over all parts of the scale?

Hull gave 35 tests to 107 first-year high-school pupils. The tests represented a variety of functions, some being parts of intelligence tests (this was before the day of differentiated aptitude tests). The scores on these tests were converted into equivalent values to facilitate comparison of the scores of individuals and comparison of scores on different tests for a single individual. On each of the 35 tests the scores of the group were such as to distribute the members in accordance with the normal curve.

But then when Hull gathered together the scores made by an individual on each of the 35 tests and represented them as a histogram, its shape showed an approximation to the bell-shaped curve. Studying the histograms for each of the 107 pupils, he was able to say,[32]

The indication seems to be pretty clear that the distribution of talent within an individual follows the normal law in exactly the same sense that distributions of individual differences do, and presumably with the same implications.

[29] Theodore Caplow, *The Sociology of Work* (Minneapolis, University of Minnesota Press, 1954). pp. 82–88.

[30] Review of Eli Ginzberg, *et al., op. cit.,* in *Occupations,* Vol. XXIX (May, 1951), p. 612.

[31] Clark L. Hull, "Variability in Amount of Different Traits Possessed by the Individual," *Journal of Educational Psychology,* Vol. XVIII (February, 1927), pp. 97–106. See also Hull's *Aptitude Testing* (New York, World Book, 1928), Ch. II.

[32] *Ibid.,* p. 102.

By computing the standard deviation of the 35 transmuted scores of each individual, it was possible to determine the extent of trait variability. The scores of the individual having smallest variability yielded a standard deviation of 4.3, whereas the one with greatest variability had a standard deviation of 9.09, and the great majority of the pupils had standard deviations of 6 or 7. It was found that such variability within the individual bore no relation to the average ability which he possessed. That is, an individual of high average ability was just as likely to vary widely in extent of variability as was an individual of low average ability.

Thus one may picture the abilities of one person as distributed in the form of a high narrow curve resting on the right or high end of the base line; he can do almost everything very well. One may picture another individual as having a high narrow curve resting on the left or low end of the base line; he does almost everything very poorly. A third individual may have a broad, relatively flat curve, which means that he can do some things relatively well and other things relatively poorly. Hull found the average trait variability of the entire group to be 6.33 points as compared with a variability among individuals of 7.00, which clearly indicates that the extent of trait differences within the average individual approaches rather closely the amount of difference found in a normal group in respect to any single trait.

Assuming that the functions tested by Hull are comparable to genuine vocational aptitudes, his research means that the average person has a great variety of occupational potentialities. It is the task of vocational guidance to help the individual choose one of the vocations corresponding to the traits or capacities which he possesses in highest degree and in which he will not be handicapped by the traits he possesses in low degree.

This last sentence might be interpreted as implying that people generally possess some traits in high degree which compensate for their deficiencies. Dressel[33] has appropriately called attention recently to the fact that some people will be found to stand below average on every measurable trait. And while they *may* have other unmeasured abilities in which they are above average, it cannot be assumed. The counselor should be cautious about conveying such unjustified assumptions to the client. The counseling of such persons may be difficult, but the cause of guidance will not be served by building up hopes that have little chance of fulfillment.

An Example of Practice

One of the tools of vocational guidance which can help the counselor to locate the vocations which correspond to the stronger traits of the counselee is the publication entitled *Entry Occupational Classification,* Part IV of the *Dictionary of Occupational Titles.* Since the Revised Edition of Part IV

---

[33] Paul L. Dressel, "Working with Youth Below Average Ability," *Personnel and Guidance Journal,* Vol. XXXIV (February, 1956), pp. 348–350.

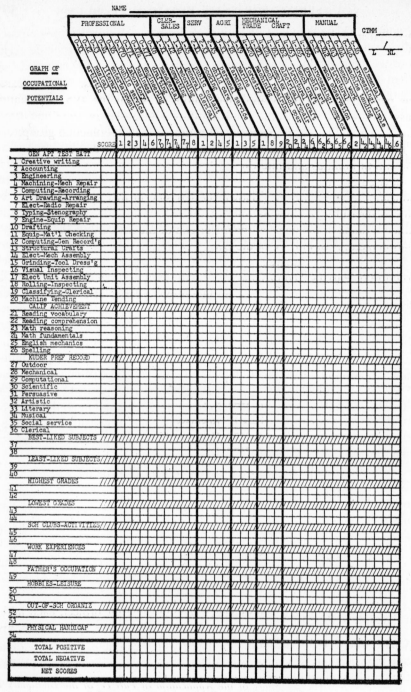

FIG. 19. Graph of occupational potentials.

appeared in 1944 this writer has felt that this publication has great possibilities of usefulness with subjects who have reached the level of maturity represented in high-school seniors. These possibilities were explored and measured in a controlled experiment carried out by Haines.[34] The research was performed in a Maryland high school in which the 1952 graduating class, numbering 57, was the control group. The classes of 1953 and 1954, numbering 86 and 89, respectively, constituted the experimental group.

For each member of the experimental group Haines expressed the relationship of abilities and interests to occupations in a counseling tool which he devised and named "Graph of Occupational Potentials," shown here in reduced size as Figure 19.[35] Down the left side in this figure are listed the various measures of capacity and interest which were employed with these subjects. Some of the items at the lower end of the list correspond to "classification factors" of Part IV of the D.O.T. Across the top of the grid are listed the broad areas and subareas which comprise the occupational classification structure of Part IV. To provide a uniform interpretation of the relations of vertical items to horizontal items in the Graph, a series of conversion tables were prepared. They were used as a constant source of reference in the plotting of each senior's Graph. For example, in following the appropriate conversion table, if a senior had a high score on the Mathematics Reasoning part of the California Achievement Test, an "x" was placed on the "Mathematics Reasoning" line of the Graph in each of these columns:

0–X70	Laboratory
0–X71	Business
0–X74	Engineering
0–X77	Drafting
1–X1	Computing
4–X20	Machining

Since negative results, as well as positive data, were deemed valuable for counseling purposes, the former were recorded in red and the latter in black. With test results, scores above the 70th percentile were considered positive, and those below the 30th percentile, negative; scores in the middle range were regarded as not significant. The tallies in each column were summarized at the foot of the Graph.

The counseling of the seniors was a second-semester project, each initial interview usually being completed within an hour. The student was first invited to state his post-graduation plans. After some discussion of them, the client's Graph of Occupational Potentials was introduced, explained,

[34] W. Ardell Haines, *A Study of the Application of Part IV of the Dictionary of Occupational Titles to the Occupational Counseling of High School Seniors.* Doctoral Dissertation (Pittsburgh, University of Pittsburgh Library, 1956).

[35] In its original size, 11 x 17, the Graph can be folded once to fit into a cumulative record folder.

and interpreted. Frequently, it confirmed his plans as reasonable and in harmony with his abilities and interests. At other times the data of the Graph constituted evidence which did not suport his plans. In either case the seniors were impressed with the detailed objective evaluation which they could examine for themselves. Self-guidance was thus fostered. Further discussion revolved about personal problems, such as financing, in the carrying out of plans. Availability of employment in the occupational potentials suggested by the Graph was a subject that came up in almost every interview. While the counselor was doing little in the way of conducting a placement service, he did help a number of seniors to find actual employment.

The Class of 1952—control group—had been measured with the same tests as were the Classes of 1953 and 1954, and had been individually counseled for their futures, but no use had been made of Part IV of the D.O.T.

Effectiveness of the counseling programs carried on with the three classes was measured, nine or ten months after graduation, by obtaining evidence of their job satisfaction from the counselees themselves and estimates of their state of job adjustment from their employers. (The numbers who went to college were too small to yield meaningful data for their group.) Questionnaires were specially constructed for these purposes, one for the counselees and one for their employers, and followed up sufficiently to obtain 95 per cent returns. The experimental group, on average, indicated in their replies a distinctly higher level of job satisfaction than did the control group, even though a few of them had not taken employment in the fields indicated by their Graphs as best suited to them. Employers rated the experimental group more highly than employers rated the control group on such characteristics as general performance on the job, closeness of fit of job to the individual's abilities and interests, ability to profit from instruction, absence and tardiness, quality and quantity of work turned out. Six of the questions asked of employers called for a rating on a five-point scale. Of the Class of 1952 (control) the average of the percentages given highest rating on these six questions was 15.5; the corresponding figure for the Classes of 1953 and 1954 (experimental) were, respectively, 27.8 and 20.8.

More definitive proof of the value of the analysis provided by the Graph of Occupational Potentials came to light when Haines partitioned his experimental group into what he called "high followers" and "low followers" for purposes of comparison. "High followers" were the counselees who entered an occupation indicated on their Graphs by net scores of 5 and higher. "Low followers" were those who took up occupations on which their net score was less than 5. The latter group included some individuals who could not have chosen better because they had no score as high as 5. The average percentages of each group who were given highest ratings on the six questions mentioned in the preceding paragraph were as follows:

Class of 1953
    High Followers   49.0
    Low Followers   20.3
Class of 1954
    High Followers   36.7
    Low Followers   17.8

Haines' study shows the way to a more precise vocational counseling of high-school seniors than has previously been demonstrated. The Graph of Occupational Potentials affords a plan for bringing together many of the elements involved in an analysis of the individual's abilities and interests and joining them to the occupational outlets with which they harmonize. From the study of such an orderly basic picture of the individual, counseling can proceed to the deliberation of additional considerations in occupational choice, such as financial requirements, worker supply and demand, training requirements and opportunities, and the personal opportunities of the counselee. The Graph offers the comprehensive view of the world of work which is embodied in Part IV of the *Dictionary of Occupational Titles;* it therefore brings vocational counsel to that large group of high-school seniors whom we typically serve most inadequately, namely, those who are not going to college and have not acquired skills for office work.

EXTRACURRICULAR ACTIVITIES

The values of the extracurriculum for distributive and adjustive guidance were set forth in the third section of Chapter 8 and somewhat in the fifth section of Chapter 3. Obstacles to the achievement of those values were also described, together with suggestions for a sounder administration of the extracurriculum. Just as the guidance worker has his hands tied by a rigid or inadequate curriculum, so he is thwarted if the extracurriculum lacks breadth and variety or is administered for the purpose of training a few specialists.

There are various reasons why extracurricular activities are insufficiently employed to serve both guidance and developmental purposes. Perhaps a major reason lies in the following attitude of many school workers: "These are *voluntary* activities. It's up to the student. If he wants to participate, OK. If he doesn't want to, OK." This viewpoint is true, in a literal sense. But it is negative, in that it assumes no counseling situation is involved. On the contrary, the student should have the benefit of mature advice; he should be counseled by one who knows his needs for exploratory experiencing and his state of social adjustment. Nor should it be left up to the student to *seek* advice; he may not know that he has problems or needs, and he may be quite ignorant of what extracurricular opportunity can do for him. A positive program of group presentations of the extracurriculum will indeed help, but beyond that, "the solicitous interest of someone who will care about how each student is unfolding is a virtual must," to quote again from the sage remarks of Ordway Tead. Such a "solicitous interest" was that of a physical education teacher who was sensitive to the girls in her classes who felt lonely, strange, and unwanted in the six-year high school to which they had just come from a contributing junior high school. This teacher gave those girls a friendly, personal, and individual invitation to join the after-school intramural sports program.

Another reason for the underemployment of the extracurriculum is the fact that the activities available for participation are often so limited in number and variety as to represent no reasonable correspondence to the diversity of student interests. Positive leadership within the faculty is required to correct such poverty in the educational program. A suggestion given in the third section of Chapter 8 was that the teacher in charge of a study hall during club period should deliberately seek to abolish his job by helping the pupils to form new clubs as well as join existing ones. This would require some thoughtful analysis of individuals as well as a capacity for making stimulating suggestions.

"Solicitous interest" must discover and offer counsel, also, to those students who are prone to overparticipation in the extracurriculum. Always there will be some who will exercise poor judgment in this phase of student life. Some schools have tried to regulate participation by assigning points to all the various activities and forbidding all students to carry more than a specified number of points. Such an over-all rule has been found to be too coarse an instrument to perform the function desired. Students vary so widely in their capacity, in their efficiency, in their home responsibilities, and in part-time employment circumstances, that each one should be individually advised. The challenge of this counseling problem simply illustrates again the importance of seeing the individual whole.

Not much literature exists on the problem of helping pupils choose extracurricular activities. This fact suggests that these educational media have not yet been fully accepted as such.

QUALITY OF WORK

The Problem

Counselors in colleges and high schools spend a great deal of time in counseling failing students. Homeroom teachers in secondary schools are commonly expected to accept the academic success or failure of their charges as a matter of major concern; as report cards go out, the "F's" are noted and constitute the objects of inquiry and counsel. In the colleges, a student's low quality-point average on his semester report automatically initiates an administrative routine of probation notification and an invitation to report to the dean's office or the counseling center for counsel or admonition.

How effective are these attempts to salvage academic careers? Certainly some members do change their ways sufficiently to meet scholastic standards, although how much of such change is attributable to the counseling program is problematic. The literature which defines nonachievers and the factors in nonachievement is much more extensive than that which tells what can be done about it, what procedures have been scientifically proven effective.

The most common practices in counseling for this problem are probably superficial and inadequate in the following respects:

1. Counsel is given only to those members who are failing to meet some standard of achievement that all are expected to meet. These may be high-school pupils whose report cards show F's or college students who are not earning quality points in sufficient number to be making satisfactory progress toward graduation. On the other hand, able students who are just "getting by," failing to perform according to their potentialities, are not thought of as needing counsel. This indefensible practice reflects the inadequate recognition of individual differences. The ideal in the utilization of human resources is to have each individual producing according to his ability; the capacity of the individual is the proper yardstick to use in measuring *his* performance.

2. The criterion of success and failure is often how well one stands among his fellows. When that is the case, counseling those at the lower end of the distribution can only be successful when such counselees compete effectively enough to outrank those who have been above them. Someone must always be bringing up the rear.

3. If failure is failure to meet some uniform standard which is common for all, the chances are that the standard will be high enough so that some can never meet it, especially in the lower schools where pupils are unselected. They just do not have sufficient ability.

4. If the case is one in which the trouble seems to be a lack of motivation, or of the effort that springs from motivation, the counselor is limited to the arousal of *extrinsic* motivation. He endeavors to stir the counselee to a feeling that his marks and credits are important, that he ought to be a "success" so that he can "graduate," make a "good record" so that he can get a good job or get into "med. school." When it comes to inducing the pupil to engage in the activities of his subject because the activities are satisfying in and for themselves—*intrinsic* motivation—it is the teacher who must be looked to. The counselor is essentially outside the learning situation; being so limited, his efforts to improve the quality of the pupil's work must be relatively superficial whenever the problem is basically one of motivation.

One source of extrinsic motivation that has been explored by a number of researches is the chosen vocation. That is, investigators have tried to determine whether or not the fact of having chosen a vocation influences the quality of scholarship of the student. Zorbaugh and Kuder,[36] for instance, studied Ohio State University women to compare college grades of those who had made a vocational decision with those who had not. After equating the two groups in intelligence and in length of college residence, they found no dif-

[36] Grace S. M. Zorbaugh and G. Frederic Kuder, "College Grades and the Vocational Motive," *School and Society*, Vol. XLVI (July 10, 1937), pp. 62–64.

ferences of statistical significance. In another study, Williamson[37] similarly partitioned 860 freshmen enrolled in liberal arts at the University of Minnesota and found no significant differences in scholarship record.

The reasons for scholastic work of poor quality are so numerous and so varied with each individual as to make the problem of counseling a constant challenge to the diagnostic powers of the counselor. Some of these reasons are as follows:

1. Low ability, general or specific. The counselor does well at the outset to check all measurements of ability in the student's record.

2. Insufficient and inadequate application. How does the counselee use his time? Is there evidence of excessive use of time in extracurricular life, recreatory pursuits, gainful employment? Is his time well planned, scheduled?

3. Ignorance of sound study procedures. So commonly is this condition found to exist that some colleges have how-to-study courses for freshmen. Certain it is that all who do counseling for quality of work need competence for diagnosing study procedures and the ability to do corrective teaching in this area.

4. Reading disabilities, general and specific. So commonly does poor academic performance stem from weakness in reading that every academic counselor should prepare to meet it with as much understanding of the reading process, of means of diagnosing, and of corrective measures as he can muster. The voluminous literature in this field has been recently given a comprehensive treatment in its diagnostic and corrective aspects.[38]

5. Inadequate background of skills and understandings for the subject in which achievement is poor.

6. Home environment negative—not encouraging to study, may be definitely discouraging.

This list is only partial and not intended to be exhaustive, but it is sufficient to be suggestive of the widely ramifying causes of low scholastic accomplishment. To that extent it defines the problem of counseling for quality of work.

Studies Made With Probationary University Students

A number of researches have tested various factors in underachievement in college and university. Two will be cited here chiefly because they suggest procedures in counseling. First is Klingelhofer's study, an experiment with probationers, designed to evaluate the effects of one hour of individual, directive, educational counseling as compared with four hours spread over the semester. The counseling activity is described as follows:[39]

[37] E. G. Williamson, "Scholastic Motivation and the Choice of a Vocation," *School and Society,* Vol. XLVI (September 18, 1937), pp. 353–357.

[38] Guy L. Bond and Miles A. Tinker, *Reading Difficulties: Their Diagnosis and Correction* (New York, Appleton-Century-Crofts, 1957).

[39] Edwin L. Klingelhofer, "The Relationship of Academic Advisement to the Scholastic Performance of Failing College Students," *Journal of Counseling Psychology,* Vol. I (Fall, 1954), p. 127.

Upon reporting for the initial interview, each student was told that the purpose of the conference was to help him to better his academic achievement. He was then asked to complete the *College Inventory of Academic Adjustment* [by H. Borow, Stanford University Press], a time budget, and an occupational preference sheet. These instruments were chosen since they provided direct information on the areas over which counseling was to take place. After the student completed the inventory and the information sheets the experimenter discussed and evaluated the individual's study practices and skills, health factors, class attendance, extracurricular activity, vocational choice, and personal problems, utilizing the data from the inventory and his permanent record. At the end of the first one-hour session the counselor summarized the interview and indicated *positive steps the individual might take* to improve his scholastic performance.

The second, third, and fourth conferences that were held with the more intensively counseled group dealt with the individual's progress in his subjects and his utilization of the habits and skills essential to good academic performance.

Klingelhofer demonstrated that counseling brought gains but that the more intensively counseled group did not gain any more than the group which was given the single, highly structured interview described above.

Jones[40] has recently reviewed some of his experiences with probationers at the University of Buffalo and cited an experiment. He estimates that about 80 per cent of these students are cases of poor motivation or not knowing how to study, but finds that it pays to work with them because the majority can be led to improve significantly. About 20 per cent of strictly probation students do graduate.

Jones analyzed a group of probationers in comparison with a control group of equal ability but satisfactory scholarship, on a number of factors, of which the high-school academic record was one of the most revealing. The percentage distributions according to high-school fifths were as follows:

	Probationers	Controls
1st fifth	12	55
2nd fifth	14	43
3rd fifth	43	3
4th and 5th fifths	31	0

Major differences between the two groups were also found in their methods of study.

Our data . . . seem to show that three points stand out as specially important: (1) The greater variety of studying methods characterizes the superior student; he uses more devices of note-taking and reviewing for exams. (2) The good student anticipates questions; at least, he studies continually with a questioning attitude. His note-taking is often the question-answer type. (3) The better stu-

40 Edward S. Jones, "The Probation Student: What He Is Like and What Can Be Done About It," *Journal of Educational Research,* Vol. XLIX (October, 1955), pp. 93–102.

dents are worriers and integrators; they constantly try to bring together textbook and lecture notes. There is a sense of urgency about their efforts.[41]

Jones urges that the interview with the probationer should be free from any signs of hurry or tension, that he should be given support in his main goals and helped to clarify them, and that he should be accorded ample time and encouragement to make his own verbal analysis. Jones further characterizes the interview as follows:

If this counseling in study habits would be called primarily *directive*, we see no harm in it so long as the student himself is interested and willing to try out a variety of suggestions. . . . Naturally, the motivational emphasis in counseling will be more *non-directive* in character. Here it is more a personal and emotional problem, in which the student must be led to talk earnestly about his situation, and during which discussion he will mention clues for further exploration.

To analyze and correct inadequate motivation, says Jones, is far more complicated than to discover and fill a need for study skills.

That colleges and universities have many students whose achievement is not as high as their ability, is patently clear and has been documented by research. Crawford, from his survey[42] of Yale's selected student body, reported that a considerable number of students who were able to make a good showing on relatively difficult entrance examinations did not exhibit any genuine intellectual interest.

Morgan[43] found 132 liberal-arts freshmen at the University of Minnesota stood above the 90th percentile on the ACE Psychological Examination, freshman norms. These students ranged widely in freshman scholarship, 43 having QPA's ranging from 2.1 to 3.0; 49, from 1.3 to 2.0; and 40, from .3 to 1.2. These data illustrate the problem, but, except for the probationers, programs for a systematic attack on the problem have not been described and evaluated.

Studies With Secondary-School Pupils

Serene[44] carried out an experiment with the eleventh grade in his high school to ascertain the effectiveness of a counseling program designed to raise the academic performance of the underachievers in the class. Assuming that the average of marks in academic subjects should approximate the level of general intelligence, Table 70[45] was drawn up to show the correlation of these two variables, the marks being those earned in the tenth grade and the

[41] *Ibid.,* p. 101.

[42] Albert Beecher Crawford, *Incentives to Study* (New Haven, Yale University Press, 1929).

[43] Henry H. Morgan, "A Psychometric Comparison of Achieving and Non-Achieving College Students of High Ability," *Journal of Consulting Psychology,* Vol. XVI (August, 1952) pp. 292–298.

[44] Michael F. Serene, "An Experiment in Motivational Counseling," *Personnel and Guidance Journal,* Vol. XXXI (February, 1953), pp. 319–324.

[45] *Ibid.,* Table 1, p. 321.

IQ's being obtained from the administration of the Henmon-Nelson test at the beginning of the tenth grade. The school was employing the sigma system for determining marks. With the line of expectancy in Table 70 outlined, a count of cases indicates that 93 pupils are on the line, 84 are 1, 2, or 3

TABLE 70. Scattergram Showing Correlation of Ability and Achievement of the Eleventh Grade at the Beginning of the Study (Experimental Group)

Average Marks	Intelligence Quotients							
	82 or Less (E)	83–89 (D)	90–96 (C−)	97–103 (C)	104–110 (C+)	111–117 (B−)	118–124 (B+)	125 or More (A)
A							2	4
B+				2	11	10	9	4
B−				10	20	23	13	4
C+			1	14	26	16	8	1
C	1	1	9	20	15	6	2	1
C−		2	11	10	8	6	1	
D	1		4	17	8			
E								

$$r = 0.566$$
$$PEr = \pm 0.026$$

steps above the line (overachievers), and 124 are 1, 2, 3, or 4 steps below the line (underachievers).

Early in the school year Serene initiated a schedule of interviews with the underachievers, beginning with those whose achievement was farthest below their potentiality. The program was carried on very quietly, so that neither the faculty nor the student body were aware of it. An average of approximately three interviews was held with each student in the course of the year, the first one usually being the most extended. At this first interview, rapport being established, the pupil was given a small card on which were shown his "grade average" and his "potential grade average." Those concepts were explained, and then the conversation was turned toward the causes of the discrepancy between ability and accomplishment. For the conduct of this joint effort at diagnosis the principal had prepared himself by advance study of the pupil's folder for such understanding of the pupil's life circumstances as it offered.

Following such diagnosis of the pupil's problem, he was given a copy of a small pamphlet on how to study,[46] and the paragraphs which seemed to have special pertinence for his case were pointed out. The elements of effective study were discussed with him.

The second step was to show the pupil Falk's _Your High School Record, Does It Count?_[47] This is a volume of letters received from many employers

[46] John V. Southworth, _How to Study_ (Syracuse, N. Y., Iroquois Publishing Co., Inc., 1947).

[47] Robert D. Falk (Pierre, S.D., South Dakota Press, 1949).

and a few college and university authorities in response to Falk's inquiry concerning the importance they attached to an applicant's high-school record. For each interviewee the letters selected were those which had most bearing on his interests and plans for his future.

To pupils following the academic curriculum was shown Johnston's table (See Table 56 in this volume) of correlation between success in college and combined ranking on psychological test and in high-school class standing. The data of this table are highly provocative to thought about the factors that may determine college success, factors that may well be pondered by the pupil preparing for college.

The motivation was extrinsic, for the reasons pointed out in the first division of this section. However, the challenge to the pupil was to measure up to his own capacity rather than to surpass others, and the soundness of such a course was calculated to appeal to the pupil's pride.

At the end of the year eleventh-grade marks were correlated with I.Q.'s as shown in Table 71.[48] The contrast with Table 70 is marked; it is summarized in the coefficients which have been noted in the lower right-hand corner of each table, as .566 and .760, respectively. Not only did underachievers move up to the line of expectancy, but overachievers dropped back in the ranking so that they tended to take up their proper positions on the line of expectancy.

TABLE 71. Scattergram Showing Correlation of Ability and Achievement of the Eleventh Grade at the End of the Study (Experimental Group)

Average Marks	82 or Less (E)	83–89 (D)	90–96 (C−)	97–103 (C)	104–110 (C+)	111–117 (B−)	118–124 (B+)	125 or More (A)
A							3	7
B+				1	6	6	20	5
B−				6	14	36	6	1
C+				14	39	11	6	
C			5	30	18	6		
C−	1	1	13	12	9			
D		2	4	8				
E								

r =   0.760
PEr = ±0.016

A second study of counseling for underachievement is that reported by Calhoun[49] as being carried on with eighth-grade pupils in a junior high school. He established control and experimental groups of underachievers—forty pairs equated as to age, sex, I.Q., and number of months of underachieve-

---

[48] *Ibid.*, Table 2, p. 322.
[49] S. Reed Calhoun, "The Effect of Counseling on a Group of Under-Achievers," *School Review,* Vol. LXIV (October, 1956), pp. 312–316.

ment. With the experimental group a program of individual counseling for academic success was carried through the year. Three interviews were rather definitely planned in advance and additional interviews with the pupils and/ or their parents were arranged as the experiment progressed. At the first interview each pupil was given an "underachievement card" showing graphically his standard scores for ability and achievement as well as the number of months of disparity in achievement and mental ages. As the next step the pupil filled out a data sheet, giving information about his home and family situation, school history, educational and vocational plans, study habits, etc. Besides yielding valuable information for the counselor, the data sheet served as a point of departure for the pupil in his search for possible causes of his underachievement. Typically, the first and later interviews involved making some notes on a "pupil plan sheet." In one section the pupil set down what he felt were possible causes of his relatively poor achievement; in another, he specified just what steps he thought he should take to alleviate the condition. In the great majority of cases the pupils themselves were able to work out plausible courses of action. Later interviews involved especially a review of the pupil plan sheet.

At the end of the school year another form of the achievement battery by which the underachievers had been identified was administered, and the results, together with school marks, were the bases on which the experimental and control groups were compared. The changes in mean achievement age, expressed in months, were as follows:

	Control	*Experimental*
Initial testing	153.34	153.86
Final testing	164.06	167.42

Although these means showed the experimental group exceeding the gain of the control group by more than three months, statistical treatment of the data indicated that the difference could have occurred by chance.

As compared in school marks, the difference between the two groups was statistically significant in favor of the experimental group. Of these results, Calhoun says:[50]

A possible explanation of the apparent inconsistency between these two criteria is that school marks represented chiefly an assessment of current performance in a subject area, while the test scores reflected total background. . . . Here, as in many guidance activities, more definite conclusions can be reached only through follow-up in later years.

Both the Serene and Calhoun studies make clear the importance of helping secondary-school pupils to a more accurate self-perception. Some had quite inadequate ideas of their potential and of the inappropriateness of their achievement. Pupils need to be given, and helped to interpret, information

[50] *Ibid.*, p. 316.

about their capacity and performance as a basis for realistic self-appraisal.

A third study has demonstrated certain approaches to the problem of underachievement to be ineffective. In his capacity as a home and school visitor in Youngstown, Ohio, Schoenhard[51] carried out a carefully planned experiment with a program designed to improve the academic performance of underachieving pupils in a four-year high school. The unique ingredient of the experiment was the work with parents—each home being visited in the first few weeks of the school year, the parents being given the evidence of the actual achievement and the potential achievement of their children, together with verbal and mimeographed suggestions for helping their children to more successful academic living. Contact was maintained with the parents through the year, by personal conferences, by telephone, and by correspondence. Pupils also were interviewed and given mimeographed suggestions for effective study and time utilization.

The parents were most pleased with the individual attention given their children and were highly co-operative. The pupils were outwardly co-operative and never showed hostility. But comparisons of the experimental and control groups yielded the results shown in Table 72.[52] Both groups made gains during the year, but *in Grades 10 and 11 the experimental groups did*

TABLE 72. Mean Number of Quality Points of Underachievement*

	Beginning of Year	End of Year
Ninth grade		
Control	3.33	1.91
Experimental	3.30	1.33
Tenth grade		
Control	3.52	1.63
Experimental	3.55	2.97
Eleventh grade		
Control	3.04	1.59
Experimental	3.06	2.31
Twelfth grade		
Control	2.63	1.35
Experimental	2.66	.25
All grades		
Control	3.18	1.62
Experimental	3.19	1.76

* The total "quality points" for each pupil were computed by equating A's with 5, B's with 4, C's with 3, D's with 2, and F's with 1, in keeping with the school's policy. Under this system, the pupil earning 4 C's was credited with 12 quality points. If his ability was such that he should have earned 4 B's, or 16 quality points, he was underachieving by 4 quality points.

[51] George H. Schoenhard, *Home Visitation as a Means of Raising the Academic Attainment of High School Students.* Doctoral Dissertation (Pittsburgh, University of Pittsburgh Library, 1957). See also Schoenhard's article, "Home Visitation Put to a Test," *Personnel and Guidance Journal*, Vol. XXXVI (March, 1958), pp. 480–485.

[52] *Ibid.*, adapted from Table XXII.

not gain as much as the control, and when all classes are taken together, the control pupils stood nearer to par achievement at the end of the experiment than did the experimental.

Schoenhard canvassed a number of factors to find an explanation for the unexpected results of his experiment, but finally concluded that working on parents to induce them to exercise greater surveillance and supervision over their adolescent offspring was an unfortunate approach. Just at the age when youths are inwardly driven to perform their all important developmental task of shaking off the shackles of parental control, the counselor was stirring up parents to increase their control. Support for this interpretation is to be found in the most recent Gesell report,[53] in which the age of fifteen is described as the height of the rebellion.

In closing this section on counseling for quality of work, it must be conceded that in respect to no other problem area is the need for careful diagnosis more urgent. And while the research here cited deals with the labors of counselors, it should be plain that the improvement of the curriculum and of teaching is the more rational approach, one which should be the more fruitful and influential.

DISCIPLINE

Counseling disciplinary problem cases has no basis in scientific studies. The literature on the subject consists of expressions of points of view, descriptions of practice, and case studies. Prevalent until recent years was the idea that discipline and counseling must be kept far apart. It was asserted to be impossible for a counselor to operate effectively in a counseling situation and at the same time be responsible for administering discipline. The rapport necessary for effective counseling was said to be destroyed by having disciplinary problems delegated to the counselor. This charge was indeed justified by the philosophy of discipline commonly held and practiced.

For discipline was conceived to be the imposition and arbitrary application of external control, "direct authoritative control of pupil behavior by punishment and/or reward . . . punishment for the sake of training, correction, chastisement, etc. . . . discipline for all practical purposes . . . synonymous with punishment."[54] True it is that if discipline tends to destroy rapport, it must merely mean punishment to the student. The emphasis is on conformity with some requirement of the social order and not the growth and development of the student.

The modern view is that the disciplinary case desparately needs counseling. One who early accepted this view was Fred Clerk, from whose manual

[53] Arnold Gesell, Frances Ilg, and Louise B. Ames, *Youth, the Years from Ten to Sixteen* (New York, Harper, 1956).

[54] Otis D. Froe, "The Negative Concept in Discipline and Its Relation to Rapport in Counseling," *Educational Administration and Supervision,* Vol. XXXIX (December, 1953), p. 471.

for the homeroom advisory organization of the New Trier Township High School, Figure 10, in Chapter 10, was drawn. In that manual Clerk included a section entitled "Discipline of Advisees" in which he avowed his philosophy of counseling and quite specifically outlined its implementation, as indicated in the following quotation:[55]

The adviser is the one officer of the school who has the responsibility for the disciplinary control of his advisees. His relationship, however, is that of a counselor for the defense always. It is his duty, *not to punish*, but to advise and counsel. All disciplinary reports of a student should be sent in written memorandum form by the teacher concerned in the case to the adviser, and the adviser should report back by the same method what disposition of the matter has been effected. In the event of three such reports to an adviser about the same student the status of the student should be then reported to the adviser chairman. The adviser chairman should then write a letter to the home of the student, suitable to the occasion, *urging* the parent of the student to visit the school and discuss the matter with a view of making a friendly, sympathetic adjustment in the hope of preventing further breaches of discipline. When the matter has been thus referred to the adviser chairman the adviser should do all he can legitimately to defend the advisee, but not to the extent that the status of the disciplinary control of the school is jeopardized. The object is justice to both the school and the student, with the best interests of the student uppermost. No punishments will be inflicted in the school by anyone except deans.

Feingold, who was for years principal of the Bulkeley High School, in Hartford, strongly expressed his conviction that disciplinary problems are a challenge to the counseling function.[56] He deplored the punitive attitude toward such behavior as truancy, insolence to teachers, cheating, and smoking in the school building. He pled for thoughtful diagnosis, rehabilitative counseling, and environmental changes.

At the university level Williamson and Foley[57] have described the joining of counseling and discipline in a practical manner to conserve human values. Their attitude is that individuals who violate university regulations or the moral code are a challenge to adjustive guidance, and they give examples of their restorative procedures.

In a more recent writing Williamson has declared[58]

It is to discover the correctible causes of misbehavior that I believe discipline must be infused with counseling. Discipline as punishment is no corrective of misbehavior unless it is part or a consequence of a counseling relationship. Alone, punishment is repressive and growth-arresting. With counseling it can become educative, corrective, and growth-producing.

[55] *Op. cit.*

[56] Gustave A. Feingold, "A New Approach to Guidance," *School Review*, Vol. LV (November, 1947), pp. 542–550.

[57] E. G. Williamson and J. D. Foley, *Counseling and Discipline* (New York, McGraw-Hill, 1949).

[58] E. G. Williamson, "The Fusion of Discipline and Counseling in the Educative Process," *Personnel and Guidance Journal*, Vol. XXXIV (October, 1955), p. 75.

Williamson points out that whereas many counselors accept a consultant role in cases of misbehavior, they are so anxious to maintain a position completely divorced from authority that as a result the principal is made to stand as "a repressive and threatening authority symbol." This is not a desirable outcome, and it can be modified, says Williamson, if the counselor has a larger vision of the possibilities of his office.

It seems to me that, in addition to the consultant role, there are three other functions that counselors properly have in disciplinary situations: first, counseling as active rehabilitation of misbehaving offenders; second, the prevention of misbehavior through counseling to achieve normal development of inner control of self; and, finally, counseling as a way of aiding students to perceive and to accept that external authority which influences inner development and modifies unbridled individualism.[59]

Such a definition of the task of counseling accords to discipline an affirmative character which makes it a type of re-education. It tests the counselor's knowledge of how learning occurs, his command of counseling techniques, his orientation to the principles of mental hygiene. And, obviously, the implementation of such a definition calls for the intelligent participation of all school personnel in the creation of a healthy social and emotional climate.

HOME DIFFICULTIES

The following twelve cases taken from a 9A homeroom of 38 pupils in a city junior high school illustrate home situations which are mostly inimical to a child's wholesome development:

1. Andy, both parents dead, lives with a married sister and her husband in a duplex apartment. Another sister and her husband live in the other apartment. The boy is overweight and has normal adolescent distaste for neatness. A disciplinary problem in all his classes because of a constant tendency to distract and disturb, Andy has been given numerous paddlings at school and more at home. Homeroom teacher has diagnosed this boy's behavior as signifying a dire need for recognition and resorting to disturbing activities to obtain it. "The remedy lies with those members of his family who are immediately around him and are in the best position to help him. A series of conferences has been arranged with his sisters. . . ."

2. John, transferred from another school, continues his favorite pastime of doing nothing, fails all tests. Family consists of father, who is a bus driver, mother, a housewife, and a younger brother and sister. Because of John's academic failure (plus absences) his parents have been called into the school several times. They always pledge their whole-hearted support, but their interest is feigned. Mother writes excuses for his absences, although he has been caught in truancy several times. ". . . the boy is a very heavy smoker and is morally degraded, his parents again refusing to keep a check on his after-dark habits."

[59] *Ibid.,* p. 76.

3. Ed, a large, well-developed Negro boy, "will not do a stitch of work for his teachers." His mother is a career woman who has made a remarkable success as a cateress, far outdistancing her eighth-grade education. Divorced from her first husband; second husband is a truck driver, passive, not influential with Ed. Mother is highly conscious of the color line. She has instilled into the boy an outward show of respect for all members of the white race, while actually breeding a seething hate inwardly. Ed expresses his feeling by refusing to do the lessons assigned by white teachers.

4. Frank's parents are divorced. He lives with his mother and maternal grandmother. Father, remarried twice, has "the habits of a 20-year-old hot-rodder." Frank greatly admires his father and is "beginning to pick up some of his habits." Mother has low-paying employment on a 4 P.M. to midnight shift and cannot get employer to give her other hours. Grandmother cannot check Frank, and so he is out every night until 12 or 1 o'clock.

5. Henrietta, 4′ 11″ in height, weighing 98 pounds, enjoys perfect health, but of late has been showing signs of fatigue. Father, a chef, invested his money in a small restaurant ten years ago, and has done reasonably well until recently stricken with a fatal disease. Henrietta has had to spend much time in helping run the restaurant, and her school record is suffering. Financial condition of the family is becoming precarious.

6. Jane's mother and father are divorced and both have remarried. She lives in comfortable circumstances with her mother and stepfather in a six-room apartment. Her appearance is striking. "She uses much make-up to enhance a job already well done by Mother Nature. Although her hair is already blonde, she has bleached it in order to put the icing on the cake." Entering the school in the 8A grade, Jane did not know how to make friends, but with the counsel of her homeroom teacher she acquired attitudes of friendliness and amiability. Her mother was co-operative in bringing about this transformation.

7. The problem is simple—Tom doesn't like school. Family consists of father, foreman on a construction gang, mother, a housewife, and three younger brothers. Contact with the family has been sketchy because of a lack of interest on the part of the parents. Truancy developed, in the course of which Tom and his buddies stole a car. Mother regularly lied when the school called to inquire about Tom's whereabouts. Father claimed that he knew nothing of all this.

8. Bill's mother is about 60 and very impatient with an adolescent. Bill's real father is dead, but he has a stepfather who is blind. An older brother is in the Navy. A blind uncle lives with the family. It was Bill's job to guide the two blind men on a tour of saloons every evening begging money. When he protested, his stepfather threshed him soundly. Later, as the blind men found other guidance, Bill became a paper boy's helper on a night newsstand, then a pin-boy in a bowling alley, turning his paltry earnings over to the family.

9. Katharine, very attractive and very bright, comes from a home in which the father is a laborer in a steel mill and the mother is a housewife. There are two younger sisters. Making a good school record, Katharine was not particularly noticed in the 7th and 8th grades, but in the 9th grade she came to the attention of her teachers because of her venomous criticisms of the dress and appearance of girl classmates, which brought on fighting, accompanied by vile language on

the part of Katharine. Her mother then became involved, and she proved to be the instigator of Katharine's belligerancy. Conferences revealed the mother as having acquired a rough exterior through having had a tough childhood in a tough neighborhood, growing up with a chip on her shoulder, determined "not to take any guff from anyone."

10. Both of Helen's parents are dead, the father having died this year after a lengthy illness. She lives with her grandmother who also took care of her father while he was ill. Little or nothing is known about the family background. The attendance department does have some information but refuses to divulge it. Although average in ability, Helen is barely passing. For her 30 to 40 absences a semester, she brings excuses that are obviously phony. This girl never attempts to speak to anyone and says little or nothing when someone speaks to her.

11. Gerald comes from a home at a very low economic level in which both parents are illiterate. His I.Q. is 68 and he cannot read. He is the ringleader of a group which is using minor extortion methods to obtain money from other boys of the school.

12. Little is known about Glenn's family except that his father is an army officer stationed away from home, that his mother works, and that he has an older brother and sister. Glenn is a normal, well-adjusted boy, making an academic record which is consistent with his ability, exercising leadership in school activities, making sound plans for his future.

Most of these pupils had home difficulties of varied sorts and types. The reader's attention is invited to the somewhat extended treatment of the home as an all-important factor in the child's life, which features the latter half of Chapter 11. For some specific suggestions on principles to be observed and techniques to be employed in counseling for home difficulties, the reader is referred to "Adjustment of environment," a division of the fourth section of Chapter 15.

The utmost of delicacy and tact is required in meeting those situations which involve or stem from inadequate home environment. Every case is unique. Sometimes, indeed, the child by himself is surmounting the handicap of a poor home and is then embarrassed at having teacher or counselor know about his home. As Kornegay[60] has pointed out, the pupil from an inadequate home may have taken the values of the peer group in his school as his own. He will feel that he has been "found out" if the teacher comes to call on his parents. For such reasons, a uniform rule requiring the visitation of all homes seems to be unwise.

Very helpful as preparation for meeting the counseling problems to which this section is devoted is the most recent work of Langdon and Stout.[61] These writers have taken stock of the extraordinary variety of situations that occur

[60] William G. Kornegay, "Another Look at Home Visiting," *High School Journal,* Vol. XL (January, 1957), pp. 166–168.

[61] Grace Langdon and Irving W. Stout, *Teacher-Parent Interviews* (Englewood Cliffs, N.J., Prentice-Hall, 1954).

in parent-child-school relations in the general run of homes. Most of the home difficulties represented in the twelve cases which have been cited above, however, are more pathological than the cases cited by Langdon and Stout. Several of them are types that call for teacher-counselors who assume a supportive role, acting as substitutes for parents who are remiss or missing. And so it was that the homeroom teacher of Bill, Case No. 8 cited above,

decided what he needed most at that time was a chance to talk over with someone his problems and conflicts. I began a series of informal conferences with him at odd moments during the day, and it wasn't long before Bill was coming to me with every little problem that arose at home and at school. Seeing that someone was genuinely interested in him did the trick. His grades, while they didn't set the world on fire, did improve to enable him to pass on to the next grade with a safe margin. I had Bill help me paint the scenery for the Variety Show and this increased his confidence in himself. Along about the same time he began arriving at school more and more often on time.

Space precludes elaboration of the manifold problems of counseling pupils with home difficulties (let it be remembered that college students are in this category as well as children of elementary and secondary years), but when we think of this group, Ordway Tead's plea for "the solicitous interest of someone who will care" has an extraordinary poignancy of meaning.

PART-TIME EMPLOYMENT AND PERSONAL FINANCES

At two previous points, namely, in the second sections of Chapter 7 and Chapter 11, the values and problems of work experience have been given considerable treatment. When part-time employment is closely regulated by the school, as in the Four-Four Plan cited in Chapter 7 from Marion Brown's description of Oakland practice, counseling is acknowledged to be important —in fact, education is accepted as the dominant purpose to be served by the experience. The pupil is counseled in his choice of employment and he is counseled on the job.

Such educational control of the employment of either secondary or college students, however, is rare. Uncontrolled and unguided employment of students, on the other hand, represents a problem of enormous proportions involving millions of American youth. For the most part, high schools and colleges evince little concern for or awareness of the way that students put in their time outside the compulsory hours of school and classes. It is all the same whether the pupil is studying geometry, playing basketball at the YMCA, or setting up pins in the bowling alley. This attitude is defended on the grounds that the regulation of the pupil's life outside the school day is the responsibility of the parents. Furthermore, who is to say that it is more educative for John to play football after school than to put stock on the shelves in the supermarket?

Only when the working pupil shows signs of being trapped in academic quicksand has he become the object of counseling attention. Then his daily and weekly schedule is inquired into, and he is advised to spend less time in gainful employment. Such advice is quite similar to that given the failing student who is in such a dizzy whirl of extracurricular activity that he does not have time enough for his studies.

On the level of higher education, "working one's way through college" is an honored tradition, honored because such a phenomenon is deemed symbolic of American democracy and opportunity. Typically, we have admired the working student. We have also felt sorry for him—he had to miss so much of the good college life. But without the job he couldn't go to college.

Now there are signs that attitudes of some students—both college and high school—are changing. They work from choice rather than necessity. They work to maintain a high standard of living. They work to be independent of parental control. From the vantage point of his position in the office of the dean of men in a large urban university, Sherwood conducted an investigation to obtain evidence of the 1956 attitudes.[62] By individual interview he gathered pertinent data from 126 single, nonveteran, male undergraduates (aged 17–22) in the engineering school, living with their families. Seventy-two of these students had gainful employment for at least 20 hours per week during the academic year; the remaining 54 were not working. As the first step in the interview each student filled out a financial survey form which included data about his family as well as himself. Then came the interview proper, the interviewer following a schedule, so as to insure uniform data on each pupil. The object of the whole procedure was to obtain a sufficiently clear picture of the circumstances and activities of the student and his family to reveal the degree to which they adhered to the *basic assumption* that insofar as possible the student should give full time to the college experience during the academic year. A case report was prepared on each student.

The case reports were then rated according to the following scale, separate evaluations being made for each student and for his family:

Rating 1. Behavior shows a disposition to make material sacrifices in acceptance and support of the assumption.

Rating 2. Behavior shows thorough acceptance and support without material sacrifice.

Rating 3. Behavior shows some acceptance and support of the assumption.

Rating 4. Behavior shows recognition of the assumption but an absolute minimum of support.

Rating 5. Behavior shows no recognition or support of the assumption.

Table 73 shows the percentage distributions of these ratings. They make it clear that the nonworking students and their families were considerably

62 Paul M. Sherwood, *Student and Family Attitudes toward Financing the College Experience.* Doctoral Dissertation (Pittsburgh, University of Pittsburgh Library, 1956).

more devoted to the ideal of college as a fulltime job than were the working students and their families. Sherwood had a large sample of his case reports rated by three competent judges. They substantially verified his judgments.

Counseling should take account of the work activities of students and help them and their parents make sound judgments in that connection. Both colleges and high schools can do something toward the cultivation of good judgments by circulating attractive brochures which set forth the values of varied kinds of educative experience— courses, group living, the wide range of extracurricular activity. Students and parents need to learn that school means much more than attending classes and picking up credits.

TABLE 73. Percentage Distributions of Students and Their Families according to Ratings on the Degree of Their Acceptance of the Ideal that College is a Fulltime Job

Ratings	Working Students	Nonworking Students	Working Students' Families	Nonworking Students' Families
1	2.8	40.7	4.2	35.2
2	5.6	57.4	19.4	59.3
3	41.7	1.9	52.8	5.5
4	50.0	. . . .	19.4	. . . .
5	. . . .	. . . .	4.2	. . . .
Total	100.1	100.0	100.0	100.0
Median rating	3.50	1.65	3.00	1.75

One of the areas in which pupils need to be counseled to exercise good judgment is in their expenditures. A city teacher one day observed a boy from one of her classes driving a new auto. The next day she met the boy in the hall and said, "I saw you driving down the street yesterday. That's a very nice car your folks have." "Folks, nothing! That's *my* car," was the boy's reply. He had earned the down payment and had a job in a warehouse for earning the future payments. This is a story which is heard with considerable frequency.

The counseling of parents with reference to the part-time employment of their children varies with every case. Guidance workers may well report apparent effects of gainful employment which they observe, but their conferences with parents on this as on other matters may well be characterized by a humble spirit and an open mind; they are not in a position to take over parental responsibilities. They will find some parents in the lower social classes who feel such pride in their son's weekly earnings that they are oblivious to the educational values he is missing. Another parent who has more or less lost control may say, "If the boy didn't have a job, he'd be out with a gang every night." Still another may not realize that his son's job is a declaration of independence from a parental rein so tight that adolescent needs could not be met.

Some school people and some parents take the narrow point of view that if the student's school marks are not jeopardized by his employment, all is well. Rather, they must ask, "What is the well-rounded life for this young person whose main business at this stage should be self-development?" If he uses 20 or 30 hours a week for self-exploitation, he takes that time from some developmental activity. Plenty of case studies show that the time is sometimes taken from sleep, sometimes from study, sometimes from recreational and aesthetic activity, sometimes from socializing experience. Counseling will be constantly cultivating an awareness of the full range of developmental opportunities in high school and college life.

And to the rejoinder that gainful employment is or may be developmental, the answer is, "Yes, within limits, and let us utilize it during *vacation periods* for both the students who need the money and those who do not." Of necessity, some will have to have term-time employment as well. It is not desirable, however, to make a virtue out of that necessity.

EMOTIONAL AND SOCIAL MALADJUSTMENT

Legion are the problems which may be classified in this category. They range in severity from the relatively simple but unsatisfactory behaviors with which teachers and guidance workers may be expected to cope, to the neurotic and psychotic adjustments which challenge higher levels of training in the healing arts. They arise when people meet obstacles in attempting to satisfy their psychological and physical needs and fail to employ the constructive methods of deliberate, conscious, objective analysis and intelligent judgment. Instead of such reasoned reaction to frustration, they adopt one or more of the many adjustive mechanisms, several of which were briefly described in the fifth section of the last chapter.

These reactions which we call maladjustments are learned. Probably in early experiences of frustration in trying to satisfy a need, a person's responses will vary. As he continues to encounter that frustrating situation, he tends to work out a somewhat standard mode of meeting it, a mode of which he is pretty much unconscious. Obviously, the longer and the more frequently that pattern of behavior is employed, the more difficult is the task of displacing it with another.

Diagnosis is complicated by the circumstance that a given symptom or type of maladjusted behavior may arise from very different causes. Hammer[63] has sketched several cases to illustrate the wide variety of psychody-

---

[63] Emanuel F. Hammer, "Functions of a Psychological Consultant at a High School," *High Points,* Vol. XXXVI (November, 1954), pp. 5–15.

namics uncovered behind the symptom of truancy. They may be briefed as follows:

1. Jane, a 14-year-old girl, feigned illness in the morning so she would not have to go to school. The difficulty proved to be the complete shift of parental attention from her to a baby brother. She wished to stay at home to protect her interests and gain some attention.

2. Albert's mother was a perfectionist. She was not satisfied with 99. She wanted 100. By playing hooky Albert had an excuse for imperfect achievement. It was easier on his ego to be considered delinquent than stupid.

3. Tom feared older children. His timidity was rooted in certain circumstances of his earliest years which made him cling to home and mother.

4. Miriam's truancy was a revolt from overstrict and overdemanding parental control. Such behavior gratified her desire to punish her parents.

5. Donald was of dull-normal intelligence. He played truant to get away from course content which did not interest him.

A second complication confronting diagnosis resides in the fact that the same set of circumstance may find expression in different overt behavior in two people or in the same person at different times. Thus, the same or substantially similar treatment of two children may result in withdrawing behavior on the part of one and aggressive behavior on the part of the other.

The schools deal with persons who are in the developmental, formative years, who are attempting to do things they never did before, who are ever striving to attain new standards as they enter successive stages of growth. The uncertainties which they face—uncertainties concerning the kind of physical person they will be, the economic role they will play, their membership in social groups of the present and future—these and the many other problematical conditions of growth and change impart to life a precarious, adventurous character which can bring emotional strain.

A small but provocative study by Angelino and Mech[64] illustrates the pains and worries of growing up in just the physical sense. These authors asked 32 women university students, with a mean age of 20.3 years, to "write a brief anonymous account of some aspect of physical development which disturbed you either during childhood or adolescence." All complied. Twelve mentioned height (too tall or too short); 10, weight (overweight or underweight); 3, teeth defects; 2, speech defects; 5, menstruation or puberty. In all cases, emotional and social concomitants figured; the subjects never related their physical development or change to school work in any academic or intellectual sense.

The authors did not report any analysis of the emotions declared or implicit in the papers written by these subjects, but since the students reported conditions which had "disturbed" them, one may assume that feelings of

[64] Henry Angelino and Edmund V. Mech, "Fears and Worries concerning Physical Changes: A Preliminary Survey of 32 Females," *Journal of Psychology,* Vol. XXXIX (January, 1955), pp. 195–198.

anxiety, fear, shame, dejection, and inferiority must have been experienced. Case-study literature is filled with examples of individuals who experienced these emotions concerning their physical development or condition.

In concluding this sketch of the tenth of "some common problems" for counseling chosen for inclusion in this chapter, it seems to this writer that the major suggestion to be offered the teacher or guidance worker is the following: When confronted with pupils who are noticeably shy or seclusive, aggressive, stubborn and negativistic, dishonest, impertinent, lazy, or truant, one should ask oneself such questions as: What fundamental need of this individual is unfulfilled? Is it security, affection, status, a sense of mastery? What developmental tasks may he be frustrated in accomplishing? Is it the acceptance of his physique, the achievement of his proper sex role, emancipation from parental control? These are questions with which the abundant literature of mental hygiene is concerned, and no better advice can be given the reader than to refer him to that resource.

QUESTIONS, PROBLEMS, INVESTIGATIONS

1. Choose any high-school elective subject and canvass a dozen high schools to ascertain practices in counseling pupils with reference to the choice of that subject. How are the values and the nature of the subject made known to the pupil? Do you find any evidence of recruitment pressure?

2. How will you counsel a pupil with reference to the choice of a subject which you know to be poorly taught?

3. To what extent are the pupils of your school influenced in their choice of vocation by the proximity of a given type of employment? How will counseling policy take notice of this circumstance?

4. Learn how to use Part IV, *Entry Occupational Classification,* of the *Dictionary of Occupational Titles.* Then employ it in the counsel of one or more high-school and college youth of the age of 16 or more.

5. Draw up plans for group and individual counseling in your school or college in regard to extracurricular activity. Take account of the obstacles stated in the section on Extracurricular Activities in this chapter.

6. In many high schools the vice-principal is the "disciplinarian." Draw up a list of suggestions for his practice of that function.

7. Analyze and criticise the theory and practice of discipline in your school. Is it growth producing or growth arresting?

8. Make a survey of your high-school homeroom or a subject class to gather such essential facts about their part-time employment as nature of jobs, hours per week, schedule, pay.

9. Interview two students who work twenty or more hours per week to ascertain how the following aspects of life are affected: (1) sleep and rest, (2) school work, (3) extracurricular participation, (4) recreation, (5) home duties and chores, (6) eating habits and schedule, (7) participation in church activity.

10. Plan counseling policy for two or three of the cases that are briefly described in the section on Home Difficulties.

SELECTED REFERENCES

Counseling for Distribution

ANDERSON, Ruth, "An Annotated Bibliography of School and College Information," *Bulletin of the National Association of Secondary-School Principals,* Vol. XXXVI (October, 1952), pp. 170–208.

BUCKTON, LaVerne, and DOPPELT, Jerome E., "Freshman Tests as Predictors of Scores of Graduate and Professional School Examinations," *Journal of Counseling Psychology,* Vol. II (Summer, 1955), pp. 146–149.

COREY, Stephen M., and BEERY, George S., "The Effect of Teaching Popularity upon Attitude toward School Subjects," *Journal of Educational Psychology,* Vol. XXIX (December, 1938), pp. 665–670.

DRESSEL, Paul L., "Working with Youth of Below Average Ability," *Personnel and Guidance Journal,* Vol. XXXIV (February, 1956), pp. 348–350.

GINZBERG, E., GINSBURG, S., AXELRAD, S., and HERMA, J. L., *Occupational Choice* (New York, Columbia University Press, 1946).

HARRIGER, Guy M., "College Entrance Requirements Need Not Be a Problem," *Educational Leadership,* Vol. X (May, 1953), pp. 481–485.

HAVIGHURST, Robert J., and NEUGARTEN, Bernice L., *Society and Education* (Boston, Allyn & Bacon, 1957).

HUGHELL, Wilma, and LANCE, Gerald G., "Student-Parent-Counselor Conferences," *Personnel and Guidance Journal,* Vol. XXXI (May, 1953), pp. 509–512.

HULL, Clark L., *Aptitude Testing* (New York, World Book, 1928).

———, "Variability in Amount of Different Traits Possessed by the Individual," *Journal of Educational Psychology,* Vol. XVIII (February, 1927), pp. 97–106.

HUTSON, P. W., and WEBSTER, Arthur D., "An Experiment in the Educational and Vocational Guidance of Tenth-Grade Pupils," *Educational and Psychological Measurement,* Vol. III (Spring, 1943), pp. 3–21.

JOHNSTON, J. B., "Vocational and Educational Guidance in the High School and Its Relation to Higher Education," *Vocational Guidance Magazine,* Vol. VII (October, 1928), pp. 15–21.

MALNIG, Lawrence R., "Who Gets Those Graduate Scholarships?" *Personnel and Guidance Journal,* Vol. XXXIII (February, 1955), pp. 331–333.

MALOUF, Phelon, "The Plan Sheet, a Guidance Technique," *Personnel and Guidance Journal,* Vol. XXXIII (April, 1955), pp. 451–455.

MATTINGLY, Richard C., *Scholarships and Fellowships: A Selected Bibliography* (Washington, D.C., U.S. Office of Education, 1957), No. 7.

MEADOW, Lloyd, "Toward a Theory of Vocational Choice," *Journal of Counseling Psychology,* Vol. II (Summer, 1955), pp. 108–112.

Occupational Information for Counselors: An Annotated Bibliography (Washington, D.C., U.S. Department of Labor, 1956).

RYDEN, A. H., "Including Parents in Counseling," *Occupations,* Vol. XXIX (May, 1951), pp. 587–590.

SINICK, Daniel, "Occupational Information in the Counseling Interview," *Vocational Guidance Quarterly,* Vol. IV (Summer, 1956), pp. 145–149.

SMALL, Leonard, "Personality Determinants of Vocational Choice," *Psychological Monographs: General and Applied,* Vol. 67, No. 1, pp. 1–21, Whole No. 351, 1953.

SUPER, Donald E., *The Psychology of Careers* (New York, Harper, 1957).

Counseling for Adjustment

ANGELINO, Henry, and MECH, Edmund V., "Fears and Worries Concerning Physical Changes: A Preliminary Survey of 32 Females," *Journal of Psychology,* Vol. XXXIX (January, 1955), pp. 195–198.

BOND, Guy L., and TINKER, Miles A., *Reading Difficulties: Their Diagnosis and Correction* (New York, Appleton-Century-Crofts, 1957).

BRATTON, Dorothy, "Classroom Guidance of Pupils Exhibiting Behavior Problems," *Elementary School Journal,* Vol. XLV (January, 1945), pp. 286–292.

CALHOUN, S. Reed, "The Effect of Counseling on a Group of Under-Achievers," *School Review,* Vol. LXIV (October, 1956), pp. 312–316.

CRAWFORD, Albert Beecher, *Incentives to Study* (New Haven, Yale University Press, 1929).

DREIKURS, Rudolf, *Psychology in the Classroom* (New York, Harper, 1957).

FEINGOLD, Gustave A., "A New Approach to Guidance," *School Review,* Vol. LV (November, 1947), pp. 542–550.

FROE, Otis D., "The Negative Concept in Discipline and Its Relation to Rapport in Counseling," *Educational Administration and Supervision,* Vol. XXXIX (December, 1953), pp. 470–477.

GESELL, Arnold, ILG, Frances, and AMES, Louise B., *Youth, the Years from Ten to Sixteen* (New York, Harper, 1956).

HAMMER, Emanuel F., "Functions of a Psychological Consultant at a High School," *High Points,* Vol. XXXVI (November, 1954), pp. 5–15.

JONES, Edward S., "The Probation Student: What He Is Like and What Can Be Done About It," *Journal of Educational Research,* Vol. XLIX (October, 1955), pp. 93–102.

KLINGELHOFER, Edwin L., "The Relationship of Academic Advisement to the Scholastic Performance of Failing College Students," *Journal of Counseling Psychology,* Vol. I (Fall, 1954), pp. 125–131.

KORNEGAY, William G., "Another Look at Home Visiting," *High School Journal,* Vol. XL (January, 1957), pp. 166–168.

MORGAN, Henry H., "A Psychometric Comparison of Achieving and Non-Achieving College Students of High Ability," *Journal of Consulting Psychology,* Vol. XVI (August, 1952), pp. 292–298.

ROGERS, Dorothy, *Mental Hygiene in Elementary Education* (Boston, Houghton Mifflin, 1957).

SCHOENHARD, G. H., "Home Visitation Put to a Test," *Personnel and Guidance Journal,* Vol. XXXVI (March, 1958), pp. 480–485.

SERENE, Michael F., "An Experiment in Motivational Counseling," *Personnel and Guidance Journal,* Vol. XXXI (February, 1953), pp. 319–324.

SHAFFER, Laurance F., and SHOBEN, Edward J., Jr., *The Psychology of Adjustment* (Boston, Houghton Mifflin, 1956).

TOPP, Robert F., "You Cannot Always 'Do It If You Try!' " *Elementary School Journal,* Vol. LIV (December, 1953), pp. 230–234.

WILLIAMSON, E. G., "The Fusion of Discipline and Counseling in the Educative Process," *Personnel and Guidance Journal,* Vol. XXXIV (October, 1955), pp. 74–79.

———, "Scholastic Motivation and the Choice of a Vocation," *School and Society,* Vol. XLVI (September 18, 1937), pp. 353–357.

———, and FOLEY, J. D. *Counseling and Discipline* (New York, McGraw-Hill, 1949).

ZORBAUGH, Grace S. M., and KUDER, G. Frederic, "College Grades and the Vocational Motive," *School and Society,* Vol. XLVI (July 10, 1937), pp. 62–64.

Distribution and Adjustment

BRAYFIELD, A. H., *Readings in Modern Methods of Counseling* (New York, Appleton-Century-Crofts, 1950).

LANGDON, Grace, and STOUT, Irving W., *Teacher-Parent Interviews* (Englewood Cliffs, N.J., Prentice-Hall, 1954).

LOFQUIST, Lloyd H., *Vocational Counseling with the Physically Handicapped* (New York, Appleton-Century-Crofts, 1957).

ROTHNEY, John W. M., *The High School Student: A Book of Cases* (New York, Dryden Press, 1953).

———, and ROENS, Bert A., *Guidance of American Youth* (Cambridge, Mass., Harvard University Press, 1950).

TOWNSEND, Agatha, *College Freshmen Speak Out* (New York, Harper, 1956).

TYLER, Leona E., *The Work of the Counselor* (New York, Appleton-Century-Crofts, 1953).

WILLIAMSON, E. G., *Counseling Adolescents* (New York, McGraw-Hill, 1950).

CHAPTER 17

Placement and Follow-Up

EARLY IN THE HISTORY of the guidance movement one of the leaders described placement as "the alpha and omega of vocational guidance."[1] In the broadening of the guidance concept and in the development of the idea that guidance is a process rather than an event, placement has been reduced from this dominant position. Authorities frequently say today that placement is neglected. They point out that no guidance program is adequate which does not have placement as one of its features serving every pupil. This latter position seems logical, for, if the school is to get its charges ready for life, placement is the final evidence that the school is carrying out its responsibility.

Placement is both educational and occupational. This chapter will primarily emphasize the latter. On the other hand, procedures in the follow-up of graduates and school-leavers for both research and service will be taken up without distinction between those who are extending their education and those who are at work.

PLACEMENT

Need for Placement Services

From an interview survey of two samples of workers in a New England city of varied industries, Reynolds presented some facts about placement which are reproduced here as Table 74.[2] The absence of any mention of the service of a placement agency is to this writer the most striking observation to be offered concerning this table. The methods by which these workers learned about their first jobs were predominantly personal. If qualifications were weighed, it was done by employers. The thoughtful analysis of the individual and the objective, rational matching of man and job which might be

[1] Anna Y. Reed, *Junior Wage Earners* (New York, Macmillan, 1920), pp. 162–164.
[2] Lloyd G. Reynolds, *The Structure of Labor Markets* (New York, Harper, 1951), Table 19, p. 129.

expected from a placement service operating from a professional viewpoint, is not in evidence.

TABLE 74. Method of Learning about First Job

Method	Sample 1 (Per Cent)	Sample 2 (Per Cent)
Through Relatives or Acquaintances: in Same Plant	35	34
Through Relatives or Acquaintances: Not in Same Plant	11	8
Working for Relatives or Acquaintances	9	11
Previous Part-time Work in Plant	9	7
Direct Application	29	29
All Others	7	11
Total	100	100

Because Table 74 shows that workers *do* find jobs without benefit of placement service, someone may venture the idea that placement service is unnecessary. Such thinking amounts to an assertion that chaotic, haphazard, unplanned occupational affiliation results in the individual job satisfaction and the social utilization of human energies which are the goals of guidance. It is to deny the significance of the knowledge of human ability and job requirements which we have created in this twentieth century. It is to assume that the placement depicted in Table 74 is *sound* placement.

More detailed studies of the experiences of youth in achieving occupational affiliation may well be cited for the light they shed on the function of placement. One such study is that made by Leonard,[3] who interviewed 123 graduates of Pittsburgh trade schools. These youth had graduated from six trade curriculums in June, 1947, and the interviews took place in the summer of 1948. The intervening year had been characterized by strong labor demand. Distributed according to their occupational status, 43 per cent of the group were found to be working in the trade or trade field for which they had been trained, 50 per cent in other fields, and 7 per cent unemployed. Of the members who were working in the trade or trade field for which they were trained, 40 per cent gave "school personnel" as the source responsible for their placement, while the other 60 per cent named relatives, personal applications, friends, newspaper ads, and labor organizations in decreasing order of frequency. Of the entire group of 123, it could only be said that about 17 per cent had placement service. While many reasons undoubtedly played a part in this substantial failure of such service, it is nevertheless shocking that graduates of vocational curriculums should have had their occupational affiliation so irrationally and haphazardly accomplished.

[3] Regis J. Leonard, "Occupational Experiences of Trade School Graduates," *Occupations*, Vol. XXVIII (October, 1949), pp. 28–31.

The interview study of 524 Louisville youth made by the United States Department of Labor[4] brings one very close to the painful realities of transition from school to work in a situation in which immature individuals mainly fend for themselves. Interviewed were 113 youths aged 14 and 15 years, 217 youths aged 16 and 17 years, and 194 youths aged 18 and 19 years. The data gathered were their reasons for leaving school, their employment history and present status, their vocational plans and satisfactions. Although the Kentucky school-attendance law at the time of the study required children under 16 to attend school full-time unless they were working at a job for which they had a work permit, 46 per cent of the out-of-school youth aged 14 and 15 were found to be unemployed, as also were 36 per cent of those aged 16 and 17, and 21 per cent of those aged 18 and 19. Jobs were obtained mainly through such sources or methods as are named above in Table 74. However, about 1 in 10 had at some time been placed in a job by the state employment service, though less than 3 per cent had had the assistance of that agency in obtaining their latest job.

The Louisville story was one of young people working out their problems of occupational adjustment by themselves. Trial and error, much shifting about from one job to another, aimless drifting, idleness, waiting for the 16th or 18th birthday to bring some desired opportunity—these were major characteristics of a process that was unsupervised and unguided. The waste in human values represented by thus suddenly throwing young people on their own resources to cope with a competitive labor market which is operated for profit rather than for human development—this deplorable waste could be minimized by the use of a placement service which, in a true counseling spirit, would bridge the gulf between school and successful job adjustment.

The situation disclosed in Louisville appears not to be unique. Landy found only 3.9 per cent of the youth in the six schools of his study to be obtaining their first jobs through school authorities.[5] The others were employing such methods or sources as are listed in Table 74 above.

The later evidence reported by Andrews is that[6]

A survey of 227 high schools in 1951 revealed that while 86 schools provided placement services to assist graduates in obtaining suitable additional education, only 14 provided placement services to assist graduates in obtaining suitable employment.

Thus, there is reason to feel that one feature of the guidance program very commonly missing is that of placement.

[4] *Hunting a Career: A Study of Out-of-School Youth in Louisville, Kentucky,* Bulletin 115 (Washington, D.C., U.S. Department of Labor, 1949).

[5] Edward Landy, "Occupational Adjustment and the School," *Bulletin of the National Association of Secondary-School Principals,* Vol. XXIV (November, 1940), p. 55.

[6] Margaret E. Andrews, *Providing School Placement Service* (Chicago, Science Research Associates, 1957), p. 6.

Instruction in Job-Finding and Progress

So much testimony to the awkwardness and crudities of job applicants has come from employers that the desirability of training students for job seeking can hardly be questioned. Application blanks filled out inaccurately, incompletely, and untidily are an old story. Poor manners, ill-favored appearance, and a lack of poise too often characterize the applicant in his interview. These inadequacies constitute obstacles to obtaining employment, and it is highly necessary to remove them or minimize them. Their existence in the untrained person should not be surprising; coaching, or instruction, is commonly necessary to prepare people for meeting new situations.

While many schools and colleges make few or no provisions for this essential feature of a guidance program, a great deal of helpful literature is available from which counselors and students can obtain aid. As a relatively complete list has recently been assembled in an annotated bibliography which should be available in all schools and colleges, no selection will be presented here. Under the caption "Seeking the Job," Forrester gives an eight-page list of these writings.[7] In another work Forrester devotes a chapter to the theme "Instruction in Job Finding."[8] It is an exposition of the practical activities by which a school may well carry out that theme. Suggestions are given for reading, radio programs, phonograph recordings, motion pictures, dramatization, talks, posters, letters of application, practice interviews, practice in filling out application forms.

At the college level, a recent bulletin gives pointed directions on "Job-Finding Techniques."[9] They are organized under the following headings:

1. Preparing a personal folder
2. Canvassing the possibilities
3. Submitting an application
4. Making the most of the interview
5. Choosing your job
6. Reaching an agreement with the employer

A program involving such elements was that described a number of years ago by Josephine Hammond,[10] as being carried on at Hunter College. In this plan, seniors in their last semester were offered the opportunity to register for a course conducted by the counselor in charge of placement, in which they studied, first, the occupational opportunities of New York City, second, their individual problems in good grooming, and third, interviewing for jobs. For this last section, 500 women, each well established in her own work,

---

[7] Gertrude Forrester, *Occupational Literature: An Annotated Bibliography* (New York, H. W. Wilson, 1954), pp. 417–426.

[8] *Methods of Vocational Guidance,* Ch. 25 (Boston, Heath, 1951).

[9] *Job Horizons for the College Woman,* Women's Bureau, Pamphlet One (Washington, D.C., U.S. Department of Labor, 1956), pp. 32–38.

[10] "Bridging the Gap," *Occupations,* Vol. XIX (May, 1941), pp. 570–572.

agreed to act as consultants for one or two graduating girls. Interviews by each girl with five of these women materially helped them to feel at home in the employer's world. The group approach was an economical mode of preparing students for job hunting. However, each student had individual counseling in the concluding weeks of the course.

A program of instruction in job-finding has such full support in logic that there seems to be every reason for its establishment in the guidance program. Youth must be prepared for entry into the labor market. To depend upon the assistance of friends and relatives is undesirably limiting. As the market is competitive, whether it is private industry or government service, the individual should be prepared to make a sale. The little experiment described by Reed[11] many years ago demonstrated the value of such preparation. She gave every alternate youth who came for placement brief instructions on job application. Checking up on results after 200 cases, she found that 90 per cent of those who had been given instruction on how to apply were successful in obtaining the positions they sought, while only 60 per cent of the others were successful.

Organization for Placement

Most recent data on the organization of placement service is the survey reported by Lerner.[12] He canvassed the 92 cities having populations of 100,000 or more, using questionnaires, direct correspondence, and personal interviews, received complete data from 82, and incomplete information from 4. He found the following three types of public-school placement services:

1. *Centralized Public School Placement Service.*
Here, placement activities are centered in a single location, where the personnel directly engaged in youth placement have their records and headquarters. Interviews are conducted here.

2. *Decentralized Public School Placement Service.*
Here, placement activities are carried on in more than one location, usually in the high schools where placement personnel have their headquarters; youth desiring help in job placement usually apply to the office in the high school they attend, or to the one nearest their homes if they are dropouts; all relevant records are held in the corresponding office.

3. *Centralized-Decentralized Public School Placement Service.*
Here, placement activities go on both in a central location and in other locations, usually in high schools; operating personnel have their offices either in a central location or in other locations. Applicants apply at either location or at both; all placement activity in the city is co-ordinated in the central location which itself actually engages in youth job placement.

[11] Anna Y. Reed, *op. cit.,* p. 88.
[12] Leon L. Lerner, "Placement by Public Schools," *Occupations,* Vol. XXVII (February, 1949), pp. 322–325.

Of the 86 cities reporting, 10 were classified as of the centralized type, 34, the decentralized, 6, the centralized-decentralized, while 36 cities were conducting no placement service at all.

Lerner identified the following ten elements of functioning in a placement service:

Full time is devoted to placement work by personnel.
Placement service is extended to high school graduates.
Placement service is extended to high school dropouts.
Job openings are solicited by telephone.
Job openings are solicited by personal contact.
A special office, or room, is set aside for placement work.
Active files are kept of students seeking jobs.
Specific forms are used in job placement activity.
Follow-up is made of youth referrals.
Close co-operation is indicated between placement and school personnel.

He found that the greater the tendency toward centralization, the larger was the number of the elements involved. Listing the elements here has the value of giving the readers of this book a concise set of criteria by which to judge or to build a placement service. Most of these elements are to be thought of as desirable features of the placement service in all sizes of school systems. Organization to achieve them, however, must vary with size and complexity of school system, as also with other factors to be presently mentioned.

Andrews[18] has presented advantages and disadvantages of the three types of organizations found by Lerner. Naturally, aspects which favor the centralized plan do not favor the decentralized, and the reverse is also true. In such cities as were canvassed by Lerner, each having a number of high schools, a central placement bureau makes the whole youth labor supply of the city more readily available to employers and makes the whole job market available to job seekers. It is more feasible to use well-trained placement workers, to adopt stream-lined office procedure, to collect city-wide statistics, and to work out effective relationships with the state employment service and other community agencies. On the other hand, if placement is carried on by each high school, the student will more readily seek placement assistance because he is in familiar surroundings; information about students can be easily kept up to date.

As examples of the centralized-decentralized type, Andrews cites Minneapolis and Newark. In these cities, students file their applications at their own schools, whereas employers file their requests only with a central office. The requests are reviewed and then referred to particular schools. If one school has no suitable applicant, other schools are called.

This plan tends to combine most of the advantages of the centralized and decentralized plans. A clearinghouse is maintained without the expense of a full-

13 *Op. cit.*, pp. 12–16.

fledged employment office. The central office serves as a strengthening link between employers and students.[14]

In smaller school systems the plan of organization employed must vary with the numerous conditions which make each system unique. In general, the smaller the system the less specialized can personnel be. The function of placement may be part of the duty load of the general school counselor; it may be delegated to a teacher who has contacts with trade and industry, especially a teacher of shop or business subjects; or it may be that the principal will operate the service.

Another factor affecting the organization of placement service is the presence or absence of a state employment service office. These offices, numbering 1500 or more across the land, are obviously located in close proximity to some schools and more remotely from others. They offer free placement assistance to teen-agers as well as counseling. These agencies have a knowledge of the labor market which the schools cannot and probably should not duplicate. On the other hand, they do not know their youthful registrants as well as do the schools. It may also well be true that the employment offices may be more interested in taking care of manpower shortages than in long-range planning for the good of the registrants.

Many advantages would seem to accrue from co-operative planning on the part of the schools and the employment service in the organization of placement activity. Lerner found that of the 86 cities which replied to his inquiry, 69 averred that they co-operated with the local office of the state employment service, but only four claimed "close" co-operation. In illustration of the latter, Lerner quoted the following description received from one of the cities:[15]

"The placement of pupils is done co-operatively by the State Employment Service and the schools. The State Employment Service provides four interviewers and the schools four. The former spend part of their time at the State Employment Service offices receiving job orders and developing jobs. They then go to the schools where, in co-operation with the vocational counselors, they fill these job orders. The school interviewers spend part of their time at the State Employment Service office interviewing out-of-school youth, receiving job orders, and developing jobs. They spend about one month each summer as full-time interviewers at the offices of the State Employment Service. All interviewers of both groups work in the schools during the year and so have the school records available at all times. The actual interviewing of in-school youth is done in the schools. With the exception of Continuation School, all of our high schools operate through the State Employment Service office. These job orders are then picked up daily by interviewers—both school and State Employment Service interviewers—who go on regular schedules to our high schools and try to fill the orders."

[14] *Ibid.*, p. 16.
[15] *Op. cit.*, pp. 323–324.

Thus, as Lerner points out, close co-operation contains the following elements:

> Interchange of personnel
> Offices in both agencies available to each
> Interchange of records
> Interchange of occupational information

The advantages of such organization of placement should be readily apparent. Considering the school's control and influence over the clientele of placement, it seems that school personnel should take the initiative in working out the co-operation with the state employment service.

Another factor in placement organization is the migratory character of the American people. Large sections of our country are exporting workers to other sections. This phenomenon is significantly illuminated by the study of Harrison County, West Virginia, which is being conducted by the United States Department of Labor.[16] Out-migration is occurring among school dropouts and graduates. To assist these adolescents in occupational placement and adjustment in distant labor markets calls for more organization than presently exists. Suggestions for meeting this challenge cannot be offered here, but the widespread need must be admitted.

The Employment Certificate

The function of occupational placement of minors must be performed within the limits and the restrictions of the child-labor laws and standards of each state. These have been helpfully summarized for each state by a Department of Labor publication.[17] For the enforcement of these standards, the procedure usually calls for the issuance of an employment certificate for each employed minor as the evidence of legal compliance. Fuhrman[18] has pointed out that the idea of the employment certificate antedates the vocational guidance movement by some decades, being an outgrowth of nineteenth-century efforts in Massachusetts to make certain that children complied with school requirements before going to work. Gradually, the issuance of the certificate came to hinge upon school record (extent of schooling), proof of age, and promise of employment, and these three elements are basic to present-day practice in employment certification. An additional feature required in some states is a certificate of physical fitness. In New York the examining physican can refuse to authorize issuance of a *regular* employ-

[16] Naomi Riches, "Background for Work—A Study of Young People Leaving School in Harrison County, West Virginia," *Occupational Outlook,* Vol. I (May, 1957), pp. 6–10.

[17] *State Child-Labor Standards:* A State-by-State Summary of Laws Affecting the Employment of Minors under 18 Years of Age. Bulletin 158, Bureau of Labor Standards (Washington, D.C., U.S. Department of Labor, 1952).

[18] Miriam Fuhrman, "The Employment Certificate as an Aid in Vocational Guidance," *Occupations,* Vol. XXV (March, 1947), pp. 317–320.

ment certificate, and he may authorize a *limited* certificate for employment which is suitable for the child's physical condition.[19]

In many states employment certificates are required to the age of 18; certificates may be granted to 14-year-olds and 15-year-olds only for out-of-school hours and nonfactory work; certificates for 16-year-olds and 17-year-olds may be granted for work during school hours, but limited to certain nonhazardous occupations. The details of practice in the issuance of employment certificates in the city of Philadelphia are described in a bulletin of the Federal Government.[20]

Fuhrman says that the following "administration procedures characterize the better certificate systems:"[21]

1. The certificating officer is a responsible public official, usually the superintendent of schools.

2. The child is required to apply in person for the certificate and signs that certificate in the presence of the issuing officer so that the person using the certificate may always be identified as the person to whom it was issued.

3. The employer retains the certificate in his files for the duration of the child's employment and returns it to the issuing officer when the employment is terminated.

4. A new certificate is issued for each new job.

5. Duplicates of all certificates are sent to one central reporting agency, usually the department charged with enforcing the state child-labor law, for the purpose of review for legality of employment and uniformity of issuance practice.

Many authorities have pointed out that the issue of employment certificates should not be carried out in a spirit of clerical routine but should be administered as an occasion for professional counseling. Leaving school to go to work is a most important decision. Fuhrman suggests that a device for automatically channeling the student to the counselor at the time he plans to leave school is to require that he obtain his school record from his school counselor when applying for his first certificate, instead of having the form filled in by a clerk. Such procedure gives the counselor the needed opportunity to review with the student the problems and pressures which are impelling him to leave school. Perhaps the decision has been ill-advised. Perhaps adjustments can be made to make school more palatable, practicable, or valuable to the pupil. And if the decision to leave school seems justifiable or unavoidable, some advice on employment may be helpful. The counselor is face-to-face with the problem of helping the pupil make the most favorable transition from school to work. Total life plans, the longer view, opportunities for further training—these are typical of the considerations that should

[19] Regina K. Stix and Arthur Lenz, "For the Health of Working Boys and Girls," *Child,* Vol. 16 (April, 1952), pp. 118–122.

[20] *After Teen-Agers Quit School: Seven Community Programs Help Would-Be Workers,* Bulletin No. 150, Bureau of Labor Standards (Washington, D.C., U.S. Department of Labor, 1951), pp. 11–14.

[21] *Op. cit.,* p. 318.

enter into counselor-client deliberations at this interview. No great exercise of the imagination is required to see how the issuance of the employment certificate may be and should be closely linked to counseling.

Placement Techniques

Among the ten elements of functioning in a placement service named by Lerner are several items of technique in job placement. Kleiner[22] urges that schools should adopt the sales methods of business houses for the marketing of their product. Since every placement agency measures its success by the number of registrants it places in employment, why should it not use sound promotional practice for making "sales"? In addition to the solicitation of job openings by telephone and by personal contact, as mentioned by Lerner, Kleiner advocates the direct-mail approach, responding to "Help Wanted" advertisements, and using the "Situations Wanted" columns. He would invite representatives of industry to the school, employ co-operative and work experience programs to help students acquire practical experience to enhance their value, and utilize the trade connections commonly possessed by shop teachers.

One school's practice in acquainting employers with its product was described by Cocklin.[23] This school puts out a brochure giving information about individual graduates and has appointed a staff member to act as an employment agent. Data included in the brochure are the class-yearbook photographs of the graduates, the courses taken by each one, activities engaged in, and work experience. The employment agent helps the pupils to make good job choices. He also visits them on the job (with employer's permission) and talks with the employer.

Further examples of promotional practices in placement are to be found in one of Forrester's chapters.[24]

A placement technique of another type is the planning and use of an interview sheet, of which a good example has been described by Sue Mechtersheimer of the Chicago Public Schools.[25] Jointly developed by business and school personnel, the sheet used by placement counselors in the Chicago high schools is a repository for the information concerning the pupil which is needed by the counselor in performing placement. It also gives the student experience with the kind of information which is important for placement, and, finally, it serves as a permanent record depicting the pupil as he was in

[22] Julius Kleiner, "Some Techniques for Better Placement," *Personnel and Guidance Journal,* Vol. XXXIII (September, 1954), pp. 34–35.

[23] Warren H. Cocklin, "Upper Merion High School Finds the Right Job for Its Graduates," *Nation's Schools,* Vol. LIV (November, 1954), pp. 82–83.

[24] Gertrude Forrester, *Methods of Vocational Guidance* (Boston, Heath, 1951), Ch. 26.

[25] *Chicago Guidance Newsletter,* April 13, 1954, pp. 4–5. Obtained through the courtesy of Isabel G. Lassen.

his final semester in the school. Although much of the information is contained in the pupil's cumulative record folder, that instrument is clumsy to work with in placement. The interview sheet presents a kind of summary of the pupil's development, picturing him in the potentialities, preferences, and limitations with which he is emerging from the school's guardianship. It summarizes what has been learned about him and what he has to offer the world of work.

A Special Problem: the Mentally Retarded

In vocational advisement the occupations which involve the minimum of skill and training receive scant attention, as do also the individuals whose abilities correspond to those occupations. In vocational placement it is the same. Occasionally, however, there comes to attention an example of serious, thoughtful consideration to the problems of the mentally retarded in making the transition from school to work. For instance, some of the activities of Chicago teachers of special classes for educable mentally handicapped children in giving this kind of help to their charges, have been reported by Mullen.[26] These activities are not the work of placement specialists, but of teachers who specialize in helping low-ability children meet all their needs for successful living. One of these needs is that of occupational adjustment. They recognize it by organizing units of instruction which give pupils specific information about and practice in the skills needed in a number of the jobs most frequently reported by former pupils. A co-operative relationship has been established with the Youth Counselors of the Vocational Rehabilitation Division of the Chicago Welfare Department. Some teachers actively seek part-time work opportunities for the youngsters now in their classes and full-time jobs for those who leave. Into the classroom for all pupils they bring a realistic understanding of the jobs available to them. They teach a unit the object of which is to see that every pupil has a birth certificate and a social security card. The process of obtaining the employment certificate also receives instructional attention.

Andrews[27] has described an example of a more specific placement program for the over-age, ill-adjusted pupils in junior high schools. A co-ordinator selected the pupils for the program, enrolling only those who were 16 or would become 16 before the end of the semester, and obtaining the parents' consent. He gave several aptitude tests, and on the basis of these and the pupil's cumulative record, talked to employers and gained placement for the pupils. No pupil was sent out on a job, however, until the co-ordinator felt that his appearance and attitudes were such that he could succeed. All

26 Frances A. Mullen, "Mentally Retarded Youth Find Jobs," *Personnel and Guidance Journal,* Vol. XXXI (October, 1952), pp. 20–25.
27 Margaret E. Andrews, "Minneapolis' Successful Junior High Work Program," *Clearing House,* Vol. XX (October, 1945), pp. 106–109.

pupils were scheduled to full time in school until they were placed; then they went to school for three hours in the forenoon, taking English, an elective, and a course in Occupational Relations taught by the co-ordinator. Andrews submitted various evidence of the effectiveness of this program in improving pupil appearance, morale, industry, attendance, and citizenship.

This section has shown occupational placement to be a feature of the guidance program which is a logical extension of the services of analyzing and counseling clients. It bears upon the fifth component of distributive guidance, namely, "To help the child at times of selection and decision." It implements in a concrete way the role of the school as an agency for bringing about optimum occupational adjustment.

FOLLOW-UP

Need for Follow-up Studies and Service

After the school-leaver or graduate has been placed in his first job, two other important subfunctions of guidance remain to be performed. One is the conduct from time to time of a follow-up study, which is in the nature of research. It is designed to collect information from the former students of the school and from their employers or college teachers, from which the work of the school in guidance and instruction may be evaluated. The other function—follow-up service—is that of counseling former students with a view to helping them to achieve such occupational and educational adjustment as to make the most of their potentialities and to experience the fullest self-realization.

How generally activities to perform these functions have been incorporated into guidance programs is not known with any degree of accuracy, but there is reason for believing that the number of such schools is relatively small. A bit of evidence on this point appears in a recent study of status by Vassalo and Kindred.[28] These authors sent out a questionnaire to the high schools of a five-state area—Delaware, Maryland, New Jersey, New York, and Pennsylvania—to which 339 schools (75 per cent) replied. Concerning follow-up, they found that "Fewer than 25 per cent of the schools . . . make any effort to find out what happens to those who leave school before graduation." They did not report practice in the follow-up of graduates.

A decade ago Myers,[29] from close contact with guidance practice, called follow-up "the step-child of the guidance family," an aspect that, like Mark Twain's weather, everybody talks about but does nothing about. The literature of the field suggests that follow-up studies are made sporadically and of-

---

[28] Theodore P. Vassalo and Leslie W. Kindred, "How Counseling Can Be Improved," *Nation's Schools,* Vol. 59 (April, 1957), pp. 58–60.

[29] George E. Myers, "Follow-Up: The Stepchild of the Guidance Family," *Occupations,* Vol. XXVII (November, 1948), pp. 100–103.

ten ineffectually, that very few schools have incorporated such activity into their guidance programs as a regular feature.

Yet the need for follow-up studies is amply attested by a canvass of the outcomes of the Occupational Adjustment Study made under auspices of the Implementation Commission of the National Asociation of Secondary-School Principals in 1939–41. These outcomes make it clear that the follow-up study is much more than a feature of the guidance program: it has great significance for curriculum and instruction as well as guidance. Landy[30] and his co-workers described the outcomes of their Study—a follow-up participated in by two hundred schools—under the following captions:

Changes in the regular curriculum
    Inauguration of new courses
    Modification of established courses
    Provision of direct-learning experiences
Changes in the counseling program
    Making educational and vocational decisions
    Group counseling in the homeroom
Changes in placement policy
Evaluation of practices
Improved public relations
Professional growth of the faculty
Service to former students

From this list it is evident that much light is shed on the effectiveness of school functioning when the product is evaluated by employers and colleges and when the former students themselves evaluate their preparedness for the post-school situations in which they find themselves.

The need for follow-up *service* for school-leavers and graduates should be transparent. Many young people, after placement on their first jobs, need counsel on a variety of problems in order to achieve occupational adjustment. How to work harmoniously with fellow-workers, how to find and accept one's proper role in a union, how to profit by supervision which may be less sympathetic and kindly than that which was exercised by teachers, how to prepare one's self better for the job and for promotion, when to leave one job and seek another—these problems only illustrate the point that the beginning worker needs a counseling resource upon which he can draw. The transition from school to work is not accomplished at one fell swoop. Some, it is true, will find themselves in the world of work with little or no difficulty; others will need much help. And no institution is as favorably situated as the school for the exercise of sound supervision over this process.

[30] John R. Beery, Byron C. Hayes, and Edward Landy, "The School Follows Through," *Bulletin of the National Association of Secondary-School Principals,* Vol. XXV (November, 1941), pp. 9–28.

Techniques of the Follow-up Study

Probably no better example of a plan for follow-up studies has appeared than that described by R. D. Allen in the 1930's.[31] The plan was comprehensive for the schools of Providence; it was continuous, a regular feature of the guidance program; and it was about as universal in its coverage as any of such studies reported. Since it was learned by this author in a recent visit to Providence—1957—that the guidance plan established by Allen still stands in most of its features, the follow-up procedure may be described in the present tense.

As was pointed out in Chapter 10, the class counselor is the key person in the Providence guidance service. It is therefore planned that he should conduct the follow-up studies of his own classes. Having built up a three-year acquaintanceship with his counselees in school, he is in a position to conduct a very personal follow-up, in contrast with the more impersonal inquiry that would be made by the central office of the school system or even by the principal of the school. The class counselors in the senior high schools make one-year, three-year, and five-year follow-up studies, following a calendar which gives them only one such study to make each year.

While still in school the pupils are prepared for participation in their own follow-up surveys. In their group guidance conferences they study the follow-up reports that have been made of previous classes and are thus made conscious of the value of such data and of the confidential manner in which they are handled. By creating a favorable, co-operative attitude, the counselor paves the way for future successful follow-up studies.

In Providence the class counselor usually starts the follow-up by enlisting the help of the class officers and continuing to utilize their contacts and acquaintanceships to win responses. About two weeks after the first letter goes out, a second letter, containing another copy of the questionnaire, is sent to all who have not responded. The telephone is then resorted to for rounding up the delinquents. Finally, personal calls are made as may be necessary. Many one-year studies, says Allen, show 100 per cent returns and seldom fall below 97 per cent. In the three-year studies the percentage of replies generally ranges from 92 to 95, and in the five-year studies 85 to 90 per cent respond. Providence technique aims to account for all members of the class. Replies are treated statistically, the findings are mimeographed by the central office and sent to all advisers, principals, and staff officers, and later the data from all the high schools of the city are combined. The studies are utilized to achieve such outcomes as those listed above from the Occupational Adjustment Study.

Allen's insistence on obtaining replies from every member of the class was indeed sound—a highly essential characteristic of a follow-up study. Through the years that he has been reading reports of follow-up studies, this writer

[31] *Organization and Supervision of Guidance in Public Education* (New York, Inor Publishing Co., 1937), pp. 297–308.

has felt that the many which report their findings as based on returns from 25, 40, 60, or 75 per cent of the cases must yield distorted and untrue pictures. This impression has been verified by the important contribution to our knowledge of sampling techniques made by Rothney and Mooren.[32] These investigators sent a double-postcard follow-up inquiry to 690 graduates of four Wisconsin high schools six months after graduation. In one month replies were received from 56 per cent. A second card, identical with the first, brought replies from another 23 per cent. For the third mailing a form letter was used to accompany the reply card. It brought another 10 per cent, raising the total percentage of responses to 89. To the remaining 11 per cent was sent a personal, hand-written letter asking the subjects to return the card. It brought the percentage of returns to 95. The fifth and final step, which brought in replies from the final 5 per cent, was the visitation of the homes.

Partitioning their cases according to steps which brought their replies, Rothney and Mooren proved that follow-up studies based on incomplete samples are deceptive; they give a more favorable picture than do studies based on complete returns. Major findings from their study are as follows:[33]

Graduates of high schools in industrial communities tend to respond faster to follow-up requests for information than graduates of schools located in agricultural areas.

Subjects who have received intensive individual attention respond faster than those who have not.

Subjects who have been interviewed frequently in a counseling program and those who have sought out further counseling respond more quickly than those who have not.

Girls respond faster than boys.

Subjects who rank highest in their graduating classes tend to respond faster than the lower ranking subjects.

Subjects who score high on intelligence tests respond faster than the lower scoring students.

Those subjects who are continuing education beyond high school respond more quickly than those who enter employment.

Of employed subjects, those who are in the higher level jobs respond faster than subjects who are unemployed or employed at unskilled jobs.

Those subjects who report satisfaction with their post-school activity respond more quickly than those who are dissatisfied.

Youth who had been uncertain about their vocational choice during the last month of senior high school did not reply as quickly as those who had indicated definite plans for post-school activity.

Youths from broken homes tend to be slower in response than others.

[32] John W. M. Rothney and Robert L. Mooren, "Sampling Problems in Follow-up Research," *Occupations,* Vol. XXX (May, 1952), pp. 573–578.
[33] *Ibid.,* p 577.

In a more recent writing, Rothney reports that later studies have confirmed these findings and that if such follow-up studies stopped with the 60 per cent responses that are usually obtained,

they missed the subjects who were in prison, whose marriages had been broken, who were considered failures by themselves and society, who had been the lowest ranking students in their high-school classes, who held grudges against school and school personnel, and who were dissatisfied with their current status.[34]

The content and form of the follow-up inquiry vary widely. Perhaps the double postcard is the form most widely used; it is the most economical, and the brevity of the response it calls for encourages recipients to reply. A limitation is the impossibility of giving a complete guarantee that the response will be held in confidence; a postcard is unlike a sealed letter in that respect. Whether the inquiry is as brief as is required by a postcard or is more extended, care is necessary in deciding on its form and content. Any questionnaire should be checked in every detail to see that it is adequate in space, form, and intelligibility for the responses it is expected to elicit. A trial with a dozen typical respondents will help to avoid mistakes or weaknesses.

As to content, the most common items of inquiry are for the exact address of the addressee, marital state, post-secondary education, employment (kind of work, remuneration, how obtained, name and location of employer, etc.), satisfactions with work, evaluations of high-school experience, plans or desires for the future. Lorenzen reviewed 18 unselected high-school follow-up studies that were made in the 1940s and reported that in the main they called for data that could be objectively verified.[35] Only six, he said, reported any investigation of the opinions of the subjects, and for the most part only one or two questions were of that character. It is Lorenzen's contention that the opinions of young adults who have been out of school one or more years and have had a little time to reflect on their school experiences can be very enlightening. He suggests that the follow-up study should contain questions designed to elicit their views on such subjects as the basic goals of education, degree of student freedom for running their extracurricular activities, homework, the daily schedule, the merits of work experience. A "noteworthy exception" to the general run of follow-up studies, according to Lorenzen is the Occupational Adjustment Study by Edward Landy and others, a research already cited in this section.

This latter study[36] was not an example of the practical follow-up study

[34] John W. M. Rothney, "Follow-up Services in the Small Secondary School," *High School Journal,* Vol. XL (May, 1957), p. 275.

[35] Stanley H. Lorenzen, "Opinion Reactions in High School Follow-up Studies," *Bulletin of the National Association of Secondary-School Principals,* Vol. XXXIII (January, 1949), pp. 119–126.

[36] Reported in two issues of the *Bulletin of the National Association of Secondary-School Principals,* as follows: Vol. 24 (November, 1940), pp. 1–154; and Vol. 25 (November, 1941), pp. 1–131.

that a school might incorporate into its guidance program as a regular feature. It was a subsidized research into occupational adjustment. However, from the methods of the study and the findings which accrued much may be learned concerning the techniques and the values of the follow-up study.

More than 900 youth who had been graduated or withdrawn from six high schools for from 1.5 to 5.5 years were the subjects of this study. Data were obtained mainly by interviews with them and their employers, by questionnaires from principals, and by consultation of school records. The forms and schedules were reproduced as appendices in the reports of the study; a canvass of them reveals the detail with which the process of occupational adjustment was analyzed. If a school were to conduct such a probe once in five years and each time take action in accordance with the findings, it could indeed become a sensitive, serving instrument of society.

Follow-up Service

By what age in the life of a school-leaver or graduate has the school completed its service? The answer for most schools is that they render little or no service except to their active enrollees. As was pointed out in the first section of this chapter, schools are generally negligent of even the first placement in gainful employment, to say nothing about performing a follow-up service. Yet, as pointed out at the beginning of this section, there are numerous occupational adjustments that the beginning worker must make and for which he needs mature advisement. Myers has given a word picture of the existing situation and offered a solution in the following passage:[37]

. . . school systems as now organized cannot possibly provide adequate follow-up service. They operate on the theory that their responsibility ends when a youth graduates or legally leaves school without graduating. Members of the high-school staff then say, figuratively if not literally: "Good-bye and good luck. You're on your own now. Come back and see us sometime." This done, they turn their already crowded attention to a new crop of students. Nor can an overburdened high-school staff be expected to do more.

A new unit in the school system, as distinctive as the high-school unit, is necessary if an adequate follow-up service is to be provided. The names and records of all who graduate or leave school without graduating, including all information gathered by the guidance department, should be turned over to this new unit. In fact, students should be transferred to the new unit as they are now transferred to senior high school. This unit might be called the Occupational Adjustment Center or Vocational Induction Agency, except that it is concerned with other needs besides vocational. Perhaps Community Life Induction Agency, or Orientation Center, would be better. By whatever name it is known, its responsibility would be to serve the orientation needs of every youth who goes out from the high school. To be sure, some would require much help, others little, but the needs of each one should be studied and then served as well as possible.

Obviously, the duties of the new unit would be many and varied. Contacts

[37] George E. Myers, *op. cit.*, pp. 102–103.

would have to be made with each youth . . . calling his attention to the help the unit was prepared to give him. A great number of counseling interviews would be necessary. Frequent conferences and much correspondence with employers, colleges, employee organizations, and numerous social agencies would be essential. Much information regarding colleges and other educational institutions should be brought together for ready reference. A list of educational facilities available to those who do not go on with a full-time educational program—evening classes, extension courses, correspondence courses, etc.—should be prepared and kept up to date. It may be necessary to provide educational facilities in addition to those already available. Familiarity with the recreational facilities of the community, and with the opportunities for engaging in voluntary community service activities, would be necessary. A continuing inventory of full-time and part-time jobs in the community would be required. There would be referrals to employers and records kept of the results. . . .

Prior to the writing from which the above quotation is made, Myers had imaginatively developed his idea of a post-school adjustment service in a chapter of his book,[38] elaborating upon the following six "needs": "in connection with a second or later placement," "for help in leaving a job that is no longer desirable," "for help in removing causes of dissatisfaction," "for additional vocational preparation," "for help in planning cultural, recreational, and community-service activities," and "in case of prolonged unemployment."

Follow-up counseling is described by the United States Employment Service in a recent bulletin,[39] but it is not conceived on the comprehensive scale described by Myers. Some approach to Myers' idea is evident in the brief report by More'li on a youth center for school-leavers and graduates between the ages of 16 and 21.[40] Close collaboration was developed between schools and the state employment service.

It is evident that follow-up service, as also placement, is intended to be the practical implementation of the guidance ideal. Both bear upon the ultimate goals of distribution and adjustment. When their development is neglected, as shown in this chapter, guidance programs are truncated, and the full value of other features is therefore not realized.

QUESTIONS, PROBLEMS, INVESTIGATIONS

1. Make an investigation of the youth placement program of the state employment service office which is nearest to you.

2. Describe and evaluate the placement activities and program of any high

[38] *Principles and Techniques of Vocational Guidance* (New York, McGraw-Hill, 1941), Ch. 16.

[39] *Counseling and Employment Service for Special Worker Groups,* Ch. VIII (Washington, D.C., U.S. Department of Labor, August, 1954).

[40] Emery A. Morelli, "Salt Lake City's Youth Counseling and Placement Center," *Vocational Guidance Quarterly,* Vol. I (Spring, 1953), pp. 10–11.

school or school system in which you have an opportunity for investigation, making use of Lerner's ten elements of functioning in a placement service.

3. Help a high-school senior to plan his job-finding campaign, making use of such a book as Edlund's *Pick Your Job—and Land It* and any other materials.

4. What are the dimensions and extent of the labor market for the youth of your community?

5. Study the employment opportunities of your community. To what extent do they affect favorably or unfavorably the occupational placement of your school-leavers or graduates?

6. If graduates and school-leavers of your school are leaving the community to obtain employment, make a study of their problem and draw up plans for helping them to attain occupational adjustment.

7. Study the rules and procedures of employment certification which apply to your community and find out how well they are being observed.

8. Make a study of the part-time employment of pupils in your school. How did they obtain placement? What should be the role of the school as regards the placement of such pupils?

9. Interview the director of a college or university placement bureau to learn its procedure.

10. For a school or college with which you are associated, plan a follow-up study in the light of what you have learned from this chapter; if possible or feasible, carry out the plan.

SELECTED REFERENCES

After Teen-Agers Quit School: Seven Community Programs Help Would-Be Workers, Bulletin No. 150, Bureau of Labor Standards (Washington, D.C., U.S. Department of Labor, 1951).

ALLEN, R. D., *Organization and Supervision of Guidance in Public Education* (New York: Inor Publishing Co., 1937), pp. 297–308.

ANDREWS, Margaret E., "Minneapolis' Successful Junior High Work Program," *Clearing House,* Vol. XX (October, 1945), pp. 106–109.

———, *Providing School Placement Services* (Chicago, Science Research Associates, 1957).

BAER, Max F., and ROEBER, Edward C. *Occupational Information,* rev. ed. (Chicago, Science Research Associates, 1958), Ch. 10.

COCKLIN, Warren H., "Upper Merion High School Finds the Right Job for Its Graduates," *Nation's Schools,* Vol. LIV (November, 1954), pp. 82–83.

Counseling and Employment Service for Special Worker Groups (Washington, D.C., U.S. Employment Service, Department of Labor, August, 1954), Ch. 8.

FORRESTER, Gertrude, *Methods of Vocational Guidance* (Boston, Heath, 1951), Chs. 25, 26.

———, *Occupational Literature: An Annotated Bibliography* (New York, H. W. Wilson, 1954), pp. 417–426.

FUHRMAN, Miriam, "The Employment Certificate as an Aid in Vocational Guidance," *Occupations,* Vol. XXV (March, 1947), pp. 317–320.

HAMMOND, Josephine, "Bridging the Gap," *Occupations,* Vol. XIX (May, 1941), pp. 570–572.

HAYES, Byron C., LANDY, Edward, and BEERY, John R., "The School Follows Through," *Bulletin of the National Association of Secondary-School Principals,* Vol. XXV (November, 1941), pp. 1–131.

Hunting a Career: A Study of Out-of-School Youth in Louisville, Kentucky, Bulletin 115 (Washington, D.C., U.S. Department of Labor, 1949).

Job Horizons for the College Woman, Women's Bureau, Pamphlet One (Washington, D.C., U.S. Department of Labor, 1956).

KLEINER, Julius, "Some Techniques for Better Placement," *Personnel and Guidance Journal,* Vol. XXXIII (September, 1954), pp. 34–35.

LANDY, Edward, and others, "Occupational Adjustment and the School," *Bulletin of the National Association of Secondary-School Principals,* Vol. XXIV (November, 1940), pp. 1–154.

LEONARD, Regis J., "Occupational Experiences of Trade School Graduates," *Occupations,* Vol. XXVIII (October, 1949), pp. 28–31.

LERNER, Leon L., "Placement by Public Schools," *Occupations,* Vol. XXVII (February, 1949), pp. 322–325.

LORENZEN, Stanley H., "Opinion Reactions in High School Follow-up Studies," *Bulletin of the National Association of Secondary-School Principals,* Vol. XXXIII (January, 1949), pp. 119–126.

MULLEN, Frances A., "Mentally Retarded Youth Find Jobs," *Personnel and Guidance Journal,* Vol. XXXI (October, 1952), pp. 20–25.

MYERS, George E., "Follow-Up: The Stepchild of the Guidance Family," *Occupations,* Vol. XXVII (November, 1948), pp. 100–103.

———, *Principles and Techniques of Vocational Guidance* (New York, McGraw-Hill, 1941), Ch. 16.

REED, Anna Y., *Junior Wage Earners* (New York, Macmillan, 1920).

———, *Occupational Placement* (Ithaca, N.Y., Cornell University Press, 1946).

REYNOLDS, Lloyd G., *The Structure of Labor Markets* (New York, Harper, 1951).

RICHES, Naomi, "Background for Work—A Study of Young People Leaving School in Harrison County, West Virginia," *Occupational Outlook,* Vol. I (May, 1957), pp. 6–10.

ROTHNEY, John W. M., "Follow-up Services in the Small Secondary School," *High School Journal,* Vol. XL (May, 1957), pp. 274–279.

———, and MOOREN, Robert L., "Sampling Problems in Follow-up Research," *Occupations,* Vol. XXX (May, 1952), pp. 573–578.

"Services to Young Workers and Employers through Employment Certification: Two City Programs." Bureau of Labor Standards, U.S. Department of Labor (Reprinted from *Newsletter,* The National League to Promote School Attendance, June and September, 1955).

State Child Labor Standards: A State-by-State Summary of Laws Affecting the Employment of Minors under 18 Years of Age. Bulletin 158, Bureau of Labor Standards (Washington, D.C., U.S. Department of Labor, 1952).

STIX, Regina K., and LENZ, Arthur, "For the Health of Working Boys and Girls," *Child,* Vol. XVI (April, 1952), pp. 118–122.

VASSALO, Theodore P., and KINDRED, Leslie W., "How Counseling Can Be Improved," *Nation's Schools,* Vol. LIX (April, 1957), pp. 58–60.

CHAPTER 18

Organization and Administration

of the Guidance Program

To PERFORM A function of some complexity requires the making of thoughtful arrangements of many sorts, the selection and direction of essential personnel, the marshaling of materials, the co-ordination of energies. Such activities are components of the organizing and administrative process. They are of interest and concern to all who have interest in and concern for the performance of the function. Let no one assume that the practices of organization and administration are the prerogative and the mystery of some demigod who operates in remoteness from the battlefield. The ways and means of getting a program carried out with economy, efficiency, and orderliness should be the object of constructive appraisal, if not creation, by all who have responsibility for the function.

Viewed in this light, all teachers need orientation in the organization and administration of the guidance function. They are workers at the professional level, just as are counselors, deans, and principals. They are not to be "master-minded." They have too much to offer to be ignored in organizational decisions. And full respect for their talents is the best assurance of their enthusiastic participation in the program.

At numerous points in preceding chapters problems in organization and administration have been pointed out and discussed. Practices have been described and evaluated. Features of the guidance program could not be adequately presented without such treatment. Now, in order that this chapter may not be unnecessarily repetitive, the reader will be referred to the pertinent prior treatments as occasion justifies.

BASIC CONSIDERATIONS

The Need for Organization and Administration

The study of the preceding chapters of this book makes evident the need for this chapter. With a function so pervasive and so continuous as that of guidance, performed through the media of so many activities and processes, and involving so many workers of varying degrees of specialized training, chaos and failure are only to be avoided by careful planning for all elements. Such planning is complicated by the fact that many of the features of the guidance program, as well as many of the personnel of guidance, also serve the major purpose of the school—development. Co-ordination, then, must characterize the activities of the personnel. Administration is more than a list of activities to be carried on; it is "an organized arrangement of interdependent parts."[1]

No current surveys are available to show how completely schools and colleges have established guidance programs which are adequate for the implementation of the components of distributive and adjustive guidance. It seems safe to assume, however, that programs vary widely in the number and strength of their guidance features. Partially developed programs are no doubt the rule, but the increasing number of specialized guidance workers strongly suggests the steady advance in the number of guidance features to be found in a school and the approach to completeness in guidance programs.

The day of well-rounded guidance services will be hastened as the need for organization is appreciated and met. To institute the activities and the features which perform the guidance function through each of its components, to educate the unspecialized guidance workers to their roles, to staff the school with specialized workers, and to co-ordinate the efforts of all to the end of giving unified assistance to the child—these tasks make obvious the need for planning and for building an organization.

Some General Principles

It will be well for the planners to have certain guiding principles in mind. Some are axioms to be followed in the organization and management of various types of complex enterprises. Some have been stated or implied in previous chapters of this book as peculiarly important for the discharge of the guidance function. With no claim to completeness the following suggestions are offered:

1. The total guidance task must be understood and divided into its elements. This is no chore for a novice. The leader, the creator, in guidance organization should have studied the field and gained experience in it.

2. Responsibility for the various elements of the program should be allocated to qualified personnel. This involves a knowledge of the skills and understandings that are required for each job. Naturally, limited financial resources will often determine the extent to which specialized personnel can be employed.

[1] Edward H. Litchfield, "Notes on a General Theory of Administration," *Administrative Science Quarterly,* Vol. I (June, 1956), p. 10.

3. Each member should be working at the highest level of which he is capable. No one should be assigned a job which can be done by someone of lesser training. As an example, counselors and teacher-counselors must be protected from a burden of clerical work.

4. The question of whether guidance is exclusively a job for experts or can be entrusted to nonexperts has already been well answered in this book. It is this writer's philosophy that guidance is so pervasive a function that all teachers are responsible for it, but that experts in several degrees of gradation are also absolutely required. It is precisely this factor of diffusion of responsibility among personnel so numerous and so varied that makes organization both necessary and difficult.

5. Specialists should function in such a manner that their work is educative for teachers, causing them to grow in their capacity to meet the needs of children. The service of the experts will be organized so that by precept and example they will play a significant role in the plan for continuous training and growth of guidance personnel.

6. All the guidance workers of the school should be appropriately oriented to the responsibilities of each of the others. This understanding is basic to a proper respect for the role each one plays, and such respect contributes to that sense of worth which is the foundation of high morale and job satisfaction.

7. Guidance is a function to be performed for *all* children. It is not to be limited to "trouble-shooting," to problem cases, to times of crisis.

8. Essential to the performance of guidance is such organization that each child or student has one faculty person who is closely interested in him and who naturally keeps in contact with him from day to day or from week to week. This arrangement contributes to the maintenance of a unified influence on the counselee and to the co-ordination of the efforts of specialists.

9. The economies of group instruction should be utilized. This applies not only to educational and vocational information but also to the understanding of the mental mechanisms and the principles of mental hygiene in their common applications. Thus, insofar as good distribution and adjustment rest upon a base of knowledge, group methods may be used for guidance as they are for the developmental purpose.

10. Line action and staff service should be recognized and provided for. Line activity consists of the actions which are taken to directly influence the behavior of the pupils—the choices they make, the steps they take to achieve the best academic, social, emotional, physical adjustment. Staff service consists of the investigations made, the knowledge collected, and the research performed in order that line action may be intelligent, informed, effective. In schools or school systems that are large enough to afford it, there may be specialized personnel to perform staff service. But in schools of all sizes the two types of service should be rendered. As illustrations of staff service in guidance, one may point to the administering of standardized tests, the preparation and maintenance of the cumulative record, the selection of occupational literature for the library, and the gathering of local occupational information. These are activities which make line action possible; they give it direction and substance, so that it accomplishes the distribution and adjustment of pupils. Whether or not a school system has special

functionaries for staff duty, all line workers, such as teachers, homeroom advisers, and counselors, render some staff service. They write anecdotal records, they identify problem pupils, they note improvements that might be made in the annual career conferences, they observe and report the weaknesses in various policies. If the school is democratic in spirit, such staff work will be performed with enthusiasm and intelligence.

11. Organization and administration must necessarily vary with size of school or school system, financial support, character of community, and numerous other factors. Such uniqueness challenges the creative powers of all who are called upon to organize and administer. Blind imitation will not do.

CO-ORDINATION OF FORCES WITHIN THE SCHOOL

Suggested Organization of Guidance Services in a City School System

One advantage of thinking first about the organization of guidance activities in a large city system is that the analysis of the function can be suggested more clearly. Figure 20, taken from Sears,[2] shows the elements of the function but only hints at functionaries. The single executive head, "Director of Guidance," is directly responsible to the superintendent of schools, and is significantly placed in the same echelon as the assistant superintendent in charge of instruction and the director of research. Responsible to the director of guidance are three main subordinates. The one at the right is in

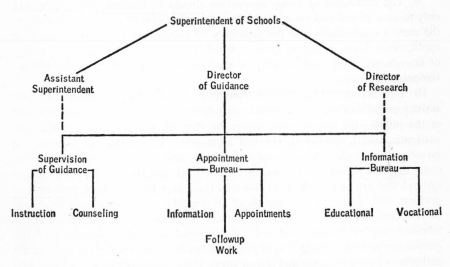

FIG. 20. Plan of organization for guidance service.

[2] J. B. Sears, *The School Survey* (Boston, Houghton Mifflin, 1925), Fig. 11, p. 328.

charge of the information bureau, which is the agency for rendering staff service. It accumulates essential information about children, about local and national vocational opportunities, and about educational opportunities. This information is *used* by the other two subordinates. The one at the left is in charge of line service for children as long as they are in school. He assigns counselors, directs group instruction for guidance purposes, and plans the system of individual advisement. The third subordinate, in charge of placement, receives requests for workers from employers and helps school-leavers and graduates to obtain jobs. He renders follow-up service to them.

A broken line joins the assistant superintendent to the "supervision of guidance." It signifies co-ordination. One cannot conceive of counselors working in the schools solely under the direction of the director of guidance and independently of the straight line of authority and responsibility which extends from the assistant superintendent to the principals and from the principals to the teachers. Another broken line connects the director of research with the "information bureau" of guidance. Here again, co-ordination is desired. If the staff service for the guidance function were carried on independently of the staff service for the system as a whole, needless and wasteful duplication would result. As has been pointed out in the first section of Chapter 14, the measurements of pupils which serve guidance also serve the functions of curriculum making and instruction. The same point holds for occupational studies; if a survey of local job opportunities reveals extensive employment in oil production and refinement, the school not only uses the facts in vocational counseling but also institutes a Smith-Hughes curriculum to train boys for those occupations.

Figure 20 is theoretical. It shows only major functionaries. The numbers and types of lesser functionaries would depend on local conditions, size of school system, and various other factors, but one of the desiderata of organization, as stressed throughout this book, would certainly be the close integration of guidance service with the over-all task of the school.

As an illustration of a procedure involving this criterion, consider the appointment of counselors. If it is authorized that each school should have a counselor, or a head counselor, it would be unsound to have such an appointment made solely on the nomination of the director of guidance. It would violate the widely accepted tenet of school administration that the principal should be responsible for his school and should be given opportunity commensurate with that responsibility. On the other hand, for the appointment to be made by the principal and assistant superintendent without consulting the director of guidance would deny to the latter a fair opportunity to carry out a program. The solution to this problem is to have the counselor appointed on joint nomination of the principal and director of guidance. Similar co-operation would have to prevail in the direction and supervision of the counselor.

The Providence Plan

No one has thought more creatively about the organization and administration of guidance than did R. D. Allen a generation or more ago. He built up the guidance program at Providence, publicized it widely through numerous articles on its various elements, and finally brought out the complete explanation of his work in book form.[3] As indicated in Chapter 17, the structure reared by Allen was found in 1957 to be virtually intact.

As already related in the fifth section of Chapter 10, the key personnel in the Providence plan are the class counselors in the junior and senior high schools, one assigned to each semester grade and remaining continuously with that grade for the three years of their enrollment. Both group and individual guidance is done by the class counselor. He meets his pupils two periods a week in groups of classroom size for instruction in vocations and vocation choosing, for educational orientation, and for deliberation on such problems of adjustment as may be effectively handled in group discussion. As the basis for individual advisement, the class counselor carries on the testing of his class and initiates and maintains the personnel records of each student. Follow-up studies are made by each counselor with the classes he has counseled. The techniques and the results were recounted in the second section of Chapter 17. The reader is requested to turn back to Chapter 10 and 17 to reread those descriptions of elements in the Providence plan.

One of Allen's notable contributions was his plan for selecting counselors. His perception of the difficulties and the importance of this step in building a guidance program was most impressive. He chose to sift the high-school faculty through successive screens to find those who were superior in (1) subject teaching, (2) pupil-teacher relationships, (3) teacher-teacher relationships, (4) records and research, and (5) professional attitude.[4] Each screen was defined in terms of behavior. For example, superiority in pupil-teacher relationships was deemed evident in the teacher

1. whom pupils seek for advice and help.
2. who seeks contacts with young people outside the classroom.
3. who leads clubs and activities.
4. who has social-service interests.
5. who has made home contacts.

Allen was quite aware that the counselor needs certain personal qualifications as well as professional training to do his work, and that it may be difficult to find counselors who are satisfactory on both counts. His screens assume some combination of the two, as revealed in the behavior of the teacher, but

[3] Richard D. Allen, *Organization and Supervision of Guidance in Public Education* (New York 3—207 Fourth Ave.—Inor Publishing Co., 1937).

[4] *Ibid.,* pp. 150–155. (Same may be found in R. D. Allen, "Selecting Counselors in Secondary Schools," *Vocational Guidance Magazine,* Vol. X (November, 1931), pp. 68–72.

they do not represent any criterion of professional counselor training. Allen felt that much of such training would be acquired on the job and that the individuals who would be selected by his screens would be capable of the needed growth in knowledge.

It is the opinion of this writer that no better formula for selecting counselors has been devised. One other screen might be added, namely, executive capacity. Since the counselor to a large degree makes his own schedule and creates his own job, he needs the ability to mark out his own time thoughtfully, to use his time efficiently, to organize clerical and professional associates for productive effort—all to the end of getting things done.

Someone may demur against Allen's screens on the grounds that only a nonexistent paragon could be superior in all five of the characteristics he named. The answer seems to be to admit the probable truth of the charge and to agree to accept as counselor the teacher who is rated, let us say, as superior by two screens, as above average by two, and as average on one, provided such standing is the best of any of the candidates. The screens would at least have forced an evaluation on each of the important criteria and prevented the selection of someone who is definitely weak on any of them. Such weakness, though limited to just one characteristic, might make the counselor a practical failure on the job.

Allen's rotating scheme for the training of class counselors was another unique feature of his administration.[5] It should be thought of as a supervisory device. According to this plan, the junior high school class counselors held bi-weekly conferences on the following themes:

7B — Group Guidance and Library
7A — Educational Tests and Records
8B — Placement, Follow-up, Employment Certification
8A — Attendance, Discipline, Home Visiting
9B — Occupational Research
9A — Psychological Tests, Mental Hygiene

Thus, in a three-year cycle, the counselors canvassed recent developments in the several aspects of the guidance field. Considering how the constant accretions to scholarship are altering the possibilities of guidance service, this rotation of topics constitutes a quite logical and much needed stimulus to growth.

New Trier

In the fourth section of Chapter 10 one division was given to a description of the counseling organization of the New Trier Township High School, Winnetka, Illinois. Readers are asked now to review that account and especially to note Figure 10 which charts the personnel. There is little to add here. The homeroom plan of New Trier is one of the best known in the country, and

[5] *Ibid.,* pp. 278–286.

the long quotation from the school's handbook cited in Chapter 10 suggests how soundly the details of organization have been thought through. Some readers will object to the separation of girls and boys, and this writer would not argue for such bifurcation.

Role of the Counselor[6]

Allen made quite clear the role of the class counselor in the Providence secondary schools. And across the country some schools—we know not how many—have followed the Providence pattern. Probably a much larger number have one or more counselors and place more or less dependence on home-room teachers to carry the burden of counseling, with more or less supervision. Without a thoughtful allocation of duties, together with common understanding of the allocation, the guidance program may be seriously deficient.

Consider the secondary school of 500–1000 pupils which is staffed with one full-time counselor. He has much freedom to schedule his own day, week, and semester. He is the guidance expert of the school. The principal may or may not know what to expect of him; the principal may have to be educated by the counselor to play a principal's role in guidance.

If the counselor proceeds to mark out his work strictly according to his title, he will not be assuming responsibility for the guidance program of the school. The word "counselor" has reference to the function of personal advisement, of a vis-à-vis session with one counselee, then with another, and so on. The word does not connote managing, directing, administering, coordinating the energies of a group of people who are properly concerned with the exercise of the guidance function. Yet considering the emphasis throughout this book on the guidance roles of all teachers, it is evident that leadership, stimulation, and organization will be needed. It will be helpful if the principal furnishes much of this, but the task properly calls for guidance skill and specialized knowledge, a contribution which the counselor should be considered as equipped to make. With one guidance specialist in the school, it seems ill-advised, in the light of all that is to be done, for him to devote his energies solely to individual counseling.

With a more fitting title than "counselor," there is more likelihood that the larger job will be done. Some schools have acknowledged this need by entitling the guidance expert "director of guidance." This term signifies an administrative or managerial relationship, with connotations of authority. While it does imply that guidance is much more than individual counseling, it also threatens teachers with a duality of direction—the principal for instruction and the guidance director for guidance—which detracts from their serenity. More consistent with the concept of the principal as responsible for his school—a postulate of sound administration vigorously advanced by

---

[6] Cited in Chapter 1 was the well-known job-analysis of the counselor, *Counselors and Their Work,* by Rachel D. Cox (New York, Archives Publishing Co., 1945).

Cubberley a half-century ago—is the idea that the real director of guidance is the principal himself. That point of view is definitely conveyed in several of Allen's writings[7] and in a more recent statement by Christensen.[8] The latter authority, city-wide director of guidance in Worcester, Massachusetts, thinks of the principal as having responsibilities in (1) procurement of facilities for counseling, (2) selection of counselors, (3) development of favorable attitudes toward the guidance program on the part of teachers, pupils, parents, and citizens, (4) clarifying the guidance functions to be exercised by himself and by the counselor, (5) distribution of guidance duties, *e.g.,* building the guidance library, operating the testing program, etc., (6) the plan for collecting and disseminating occupational information, (7) planning time for guidance activities, and (8) planning the pupil interview program with full respect for the daily schedule of instruction.

Accepting the principal as "director," the role of the counselor may more properly be described as "guidance consultant." The practice of using this title prevails in Minneapolis. It was recommended in the survey of the Pittsburgh schools, and the post was defined as follows:[9]

In every high school there should be one person who has a broad view of the guidance program and who will co-ordinate all the services within a particular school. . . . In addition to his co-ordinating function, he has two other major responsibilities—working with and through teachers and working directly with pupils on their special problems.

This title of guidance consultant has much to recommend it. Presumably it implies one who is a specialist, an expert, in the guidance function, one who will advise the principal in establishing and directing the guidance program, one who will be consulted by homeroom and classroom teachers for assistance in rendering guidance services. The title conveys no impression of authority. Rather, the consultant is a resource person. Perhaps at first the teachers seek his advice and help because the principal has directed them to do so, but presently it is to be hoped that they do so because they have found him to be a valuable source of assistance.

Assuming that homeroom teachers, either because of the principal's orders or because of faculty decision, feel an obligation to become counselors to their pupils, the consultant is the person to whom they will turn for assistance and training in the counseling function. He will educate them in the sound interpretation of test results, to a true evaluation of the various items

[7] R. D. Allen, "Delegating the Guidance Functions within the Secondary School," *Vocational Guidance Magazine,* Vol. X (October, 1931), pp. 14–19; "A Guidance Program that any High-School Principal May Undertake," *Vocational Guidance Magazine,* Vol. XI (February, 1933), pp. 199–205; "How a Principal Can Direct Guidance," *Occupations,* Vol. XVI (October, 1937), pp. 15–20.

[8] Thomas E. Christensen, "Responsibilities of the High-School Principal in the Guidance Program," *School Review,* Vol. LVII (March, 1949), pp. 149–154.

[9] *The Report of a Survey of the Public Schools of Pittsburgh, Pennsylvania* (New York, Teachers College, Columbia University, 1940), p. 241.

on the cumulative record, and to an increasing sensitivity to the many forms of pupil behavior, healthful and unhealthful. The consultant will help teachers to build a wholesome group consciousness in their homerooms; he will help them to lead their pupils in the identification and attempted solution of their problems. He will build up files of useful suggestions for group guidance programs.

In his role as educator of the teachers, the consultant should not limit himself to individual conference. The economy of counseling teachers in groups should be as apparent as the economy of counseling pupils in groups. But the practice should be based upon the felt need of the teachers just as in the case of the pupils.

The possibilities of aiding homeroom teachers through the use of the mimeograph should be transparent. Up-to-date information about educational and vocational opportunities may thus be brought to their attention. The probability tables which have been so strongly advocated in previous chapters as instruments for guidance may be made generally available by such duplication. In short, if the consultant is to be an effective resource person for homeroom teachers, he must keep in communication with them, and the mimeograph is an invaluable aid.

One of the methods by which the consultant cultivates the "guidance-mindedness" of the teachers and improves their skill is by his handling of problem cases. As one who is more expert through experience and training than any one of the teachers, the consultant may expect to have problem cases referred to him for his personal study and counsel. He should manage this matter so that teachers do not wash their hands of all responsibility, but are inspired to greater interest and competence in their advisory work. If the consultant will fully utilize teacher observations of a problem pupil, employ teachers in the administration of remedial treatment, and let teachers know his procedures, the case may well be an object lesson. There is no better way to promote the growth of teachers in their power to discover, diagnose, and resolve pupil problems, and that indeed is the consultant's main objective.

An important caution should be urged in this connection. In the direct handling of cases, the consultant will always take pains to uphold and protect the homeroom teacher in his role as pupil counselor. To belittle or ignore the homeroom teacher's responsibility in connection with these cases will do great damage to the whole desired structure of confidential and friendly relationships between homeroom teachers and their pupils. Respect for the homeroom teacher will especially be expressed by keeping him fully apprised of all developments in a case study, and by such evidences of deference as the medical specialist pays to the family doctor who has called him in on a case.

As pointed out above, the guidance consultant will be employed by the principal as well as by the teachers. The guidance expert can help in organizing the school for guidance and in the allocation of guidance responsibilities. As pointed out in the fourth section of Chapter 10, the consultant may be expected to be a close student of the faculty in their potentialities for guidance. He will be able to advise the principal in the selection of homeroom sponsors and in their assignment to the age groups with which they can work most effectively.

In closing this discussion of the role of the counselor, it may not be amiss to offer a word of evaluation of those school organizations in which the work of counseling is apparently divided along sex lines, as indicated by the designation of a boys' counselor and a girls' counselor. The assumption of such a division seems to be that the work of a counselor is simply that of individual advisement, rather than that of responsibility for the school's guidance program, as has just been depicted. In practice, the division works out awkwardly and uneconomically, because in most schools the groupings of pupils in most of their classes and in their homerooms do not divide the sexes. Lloyd-Jones offers the following criticism of the bifurcation and a resolution of the issue:[10]

In a family it would be abnormal for the mother to think of herself as the mother of only the girls; similarly for the father to be interested in only the boys of the family. On the other hand, a family of boys and girls which has *only* a father or *only* a mother is seriously deprived. . . . both men and women personnel workers are needed, working closely together, with some specialization of functions cooperatively worked out, but with both men and women personnel workers concerned with both boys and girls, to see that the needs of all students are adequately met.

Role of the Homeroom Teacher

In describing the role of the school counselor, much has been said to imply the role of the homeroom teacher. And since the homeroom was given a somewhat extended treatment in Chapter 10, space need be taken here only for a brief addition.

In many school guidance organizations the homeroom teacher is, or is expected to be, the principal line-worker: he works directly on the pupils, conducting group instruction and giving individual counsel to influence their behavior. However, schools vary so widely in their reliance on the homeroom teacher that no standards exist and the responsibility is undefined, except as individual schools have acted on the problem. Two investigators have made studies to find out what homeroom teachers *ought* to do, by obtaining a consensus from competent judges of what homeroom teachers ought to *know*. One investigator[11] presented to a jury of ten college teachers of guid-

---

[10] Esther Lloyd-Jones, "Some Current Issues in Guidance," *Teachers College Record,* Vol. XLIX (November, 1947), p. 88.

[11] G. G. Santavicca, *An Inventory of the Concepts in Distributive Guidance Which Should Be Possessed by the Homeroom Teacher.* Doctoral Dissertation (Pittsburgh, University of Pittsburgh Library, 1951).

ance and a jury of fourteen selected secondary-school counselors a list of 268 concepts of distributive guidance. Fifty per cent or more of the members of the combined juries designated 202 of the concepts as desirable for homeroom teachers to possess. In a brief article, the author has presented the 47 concepts on which 80 per cent or more of the jurors agreed, together with a table—presented here with slight modification as Table 75—which gives some idea of how the 268 concepts covered the field of distributive guidance.[12]

TABLE 75. Classification of the Concepts of Distributive Guidance

Categories of Concepts	Number of Concepts
1. Major characteristics of the process of distributive guidance	17
2. Need for distributive guidance	19
3. Educational information	16
4. Occupational information	35
5. Pupil analysis	22
6. Statistics	33
7. Tests and measurements (general)	19
8. Measuring ability	19
9. Measuring intelligence	17
10. Measuring interest	15
11. Measuring personality	15
12. Prediction	22
13. Counseling techniques	19
Total	268

The second study[13] reported a consensus from two juries—11 college teachers and 11 counselors or supervisors of counselors—of concepts of adjustive guidance which homeroom teachers should possess. The concepts voted upon were classified as shown in Table 76. Of the 257 concepts, 240, or 93 per cent, were accepted by more than 50 per cent of the jurors as desirable for homeroom teachers to possess.

In both of these studies, the jurors were instructed to mark each concept

H — if you think the homeroom teacher should possess the concept.

C — if you think the concept is properly held by the counselor but too specialized to expect of the homeroom teacher.

D — if you doubt the truth or accuracy of the concept.

[12] "What Homeroom Teachers Should Know," *Occupations,* Vol. XXX (February, 1952), pp. 351–355.

[13] Charles E. Lyle, *An Inventory of the Concepts of Adjustive Guidance Which Homeroom Teachers Should Possess.* Doctoral Dissertation (Pittsburgh, University of Pittsburgh Library, 1956).

TABLE 76. Classification of the Concepts of Adjustive Guidance

Categories of Concepts	Number of Concepts
UNDERSTANDING ADOLESCENT BEHAVIOR	
1. Origins and development of personality	25
2. Human adjustments	33
3. Adjustment mechanisms defined	10
4. Human emotions	24
5. Adolescent development	17
6. The developmental tasks of youth	15
7. Characteristics of the well-adjusted person	8
GUIDING THE ADOLESCENT	
8. Adjustive guidance—general concepts	14
9. Preventing maladjustment	11
10. Identifying (discovering) maladjustment	18
11. The counseling process—general concepts	28
12. Diagnosing maladjustment	16
13. Remedial treatment and follow-up	22
14. Discipline and juvenile delinquency	13
15. Evaluating homeroom guidance	3
Total	257

Among the jurors for distributive guidance, 70 per cent of all the responses made by college teachers and 54 per cent of all the responses made by counselors were *H* responses. The corresponding percentages of responses among the jurors for adjustive guidance were 76.9 and 82.2, respectively.

While it would be necessary for the readers of this book to make their own canvass of these concepts in order to judge their simplicity or complexity, the writer will advance his own estimate that the results of the two studies amply justify his assertion in the preface that this is a book for all school workers. Its contents teach a great many of the concepts that the jurors accepted for homeroom teachers.

The Organization of Guidance in Small Secondary Schools

For the many small schools which have no guidance specialist, but are staffed only with a principal, or teaching principal, and teachers, the following organizational suggestions are offered. The task of organization may well be thought of as concerned with the performance of these major functions:

1. Testing and recording (accumulating information about pupils).
2. Gathering and making available information about occupations and educational opportunity.
3. Instruction of pupils in groups about occupational and educational opportunity.

4. Counseling at times of decision, for adjustment, etc.

5. Articulating pupils (*a*) with employment or (*b*) with advanced education when they leave or graduate from the school.

Suggested Allocation of Functions in a High School Enrolling 100–250 Pupils. Let the principal administer the testing program (1), probably giving the tests himself, and recording scores, percentile ranks, etc., for guidance purposes. Let him utilize clerical assistance insofar as available and feasible, or perhaps have some assistance from teachers, but assume detailed responsibility for accumulating information about pupils and making it accessible. (This work serves the instructional and curriculum-making functions as well as that of guidance.)

Let the principal do individual counseling (4).

Let the principal directly exercise function No. 5.

Let a teacher perform functions No. 2 and No. 3.

In the above plan, as in the one which follows, it is assumed that the principal has more extended professional training than most of his staff; it is assumed that in the small school he knows more about the guidance function in the large, and perhaps in most of its details, than do his teachers. But the personal factor should be given full consideration in the assignment of guidance functions. It is quite conceivable that the principal of a school may not be able to meet the pupils in the counseling relationship as well as one of his teachers; or that it may be desirable for him to carry a heavy burden of direct sponsorship of athletics and other extracurricular activities; or that he may partially alienate pupils through his exercise of the disciplinary function—a function which can seldom be delegated. Under such circumstances, he will do well to assume teaching duties to relieve a teacher for counseling duty. Good administration requires a careful survey of the abilities of all members of the staff in the light of the varied work to be done, and then "utilizes all the brains of the organization." The total load of the teachers and of the principal (instructional and extra-instructional) must be adjusted and equalized to achieve the best allocation of all the functions to be performed.

Figure 21 offers an organization of guidance for high schools enrolling 250–500 which do not have a guidance specialist. Many such schools now are staffed with a counselor, and the others would certainly do well to acquire at least a part-time counselor.

How Shall Guidance Service be Organized in the Elementary School?

The provision of specialized service in guidance at the elementary-school level is a recent development and a growing one. Presumably, the fact that elementary-school children are not facing the problem of making educational and vocational choices has made guidance seem less necessary for them than for secondary-school pupils. But the study of the guidance problems which exist in secondary schools has convinced more and more people that the best chance of solving many of the problems depends upon their early identifica-

FIG. 21. Suggested Allocation of Functions in a High School Enrolling 250–500 Pupils

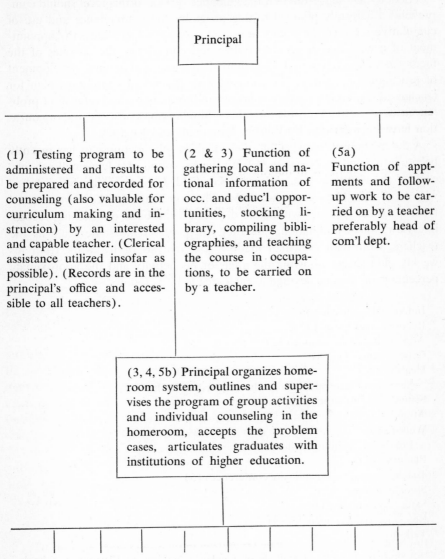

Principal

(1) Testing program to be administered and results to be prepared and recorded for counseling (also valuable for curriculum making and instruction) by an interested and capable teacher. (Clerical assistance utilized insofar as possible). (Records are in the principal's office and accessible to all teachers).

(2 & 3) Function of gathering local and national information of occ. and educ'l opportunities, stocking library, compiling bibliographies, and teaching the course in occupations, to be carried on by a teacher.

(5a) Function of apptments and follow-up work to be carried on by a teacher preferably head of com'l dept.

(3, 4, 5b) Principal organizes home-room system, outlines and supervises the program of group activities and individual counseling in the homeroom, accepts the problem cases, articulates graduates with institutions of higher education.

(3 & 4) Homeroom teachers

Each homeroom group homogeneous as to grade. Homeroom teachers of each grade constitute a committee, of which one member is selected by the principal as chairman. In addition to working as a committee on guidance problems and programs of their class, they sponsor the social life of the class and give it educational direction; they foster wholesome class loyalties.

tion, diagnosis, and remediation. Hence, the urge to organize guidance, particularly in its adjustive phase, in elementary schools.

Traxler[14] has suggested that the guidance service at this level should comprehend a carefully planned testing program, the maintenance and use of cumulative records, the timely appraisal of personal qualities, the appointment of a guidance director to utilize and co-ordinate the energies of the faculty as well as to counsel some individual pupils and parents, development of procedures for cultivating contacts with parents, a continuous plan for teacher education in guidance concepts and techniques, and referral of problem cases to agencies outside the school. Similar views of scope and organization have been written by Wilson, Krugman, and Kearney.[15]

A description of the work of an elementary-school counselor has recently been contributed by Newman.[16] With the exception of a few small schools, each of the elementary schools of Bakersfield, California, has been staffed with a full-time counselor since 1954. These guidance workers are selected from qualified teachers within the district on the basis of teaching record, interview, and examination, and they are paid on the same scale as the teachers. Counselor Newman made a job analysis of his work from his weekly plan sheets, showing the areas of his activity and the approximate percentage of his time devoted to each area to be as follows:

Individual counseling (12)
Records and reports (12)
Administrative assistance (12)
Group counseling (8)
Health (8)
    Screens all referrals from teachers regarding health
School-wide guidance programs (5)
Attendance (5)
Welfare (5)
    Food and clothing problem cases
Planning (5)
Teacher consultation and case conferences (5)
Student activities (5)
Safety committee (3)
Referrals to other agencies (3)
Talks to classes (3)

[14] Arthur E. Traxler, "Essentials of Guidance Services in Elementary Schools," *Elementary School Journal,* Vol. LIII (December, 1952), pp. 207–210.
[15] Frances M. Wilson, "Guidance in Elementary Schools," *Occupations,* Vol. XXIX (December, 1950), pp. 168–173.
    Morris Krugman, "Why Guidance in the Elementary School?" *Personnel and Guidance Journal,* Vol. XXXII (January, 1954), pp. 270–273.
    Milo E. Kearney, "Making Guidance Effective in Elementary Schools," *Elementary School Journal,* Vol. LVI (April, 1956), pp. 348–353.
[16] William H. Newman, "A Full-Time Counselor in an Elementary School," *Elementary School Journal,* Vol. LVI (April, 1956), pp. 354–357.

Testing (3)

Enrollment (3)

   Pupils enrolling after the beginning of the school year

Informal contacts and observations (3)

This list conveys a clear impression that a guidance specialist may find ample need for his services in the elementary school. Organization, however, must take into account the contrast of the teacher's position in the elementary school with that of the teacher's position in the secondary school. The elementary teacher has a far closer and more broadly based relationship to pupils than is true of either subject or homeroom teachers in the high school. Elementary teachers typically know their pupils much better than do high-school teachers. They will therefore play a more active role in identifying, diagnosing, and treating maladjustment. In these and other distinctions, the organization of guidance in the elementary school presents special problems.

Guidance Services in the Junior College

The guidance features to be provided in the junior college are similar to those needed in the high school. Instruction is the basic purpose of the institution—instruction in common learnings, instruction in differentiated learnings. The students are to be distributed to curriculums which correspond to their abilities and interests and appropriate vocational goals. They need adjustive service to remove impediments to development. For some, as in high school, junior college education is terminal; for others, it is preparatory.

Guidance programs seem to have developed more slowly in junior colleges than in high schools, probably for several reasons: the institutions themselves are new, having had their beginning in 1910; their students may be supposed to have undergone such self-exploration and such exploration of education and vocation as to have found their life goals; their students are beyond the compulsory school age, are assumed to be mature, self-directive, not needful of such guardianship as guidance represents, and not to be "mollycoddled."

However belatedly, junior colleges are accepting the guidance function and are organizing features to perform it. Johnson sees the following six elements to be provided:[17]

1. Assemble information regarding students—their background, interests, abilities, needs, problems, and goals.

2. Make information regarding students available for use by staff members and by students themselves.

    a. In counseling and guidance.

    b. In teaching.

    c. In curriculum building.

[17] B. Lamar Johnson, "The Advising, Guidance, and Counseling of Junior College Students," *Bulletin of the National Association of Secondary-School Principals,* Vol. XXXVII (February, 1953), p. 31.

3. Aid the individual student to understand himself—his strengths, weaknesses, problems, and interests.

4. Aid him to establish valid goals and to develop realistic plans to achieve these goals.

5. Aid him to evaluate his progress toward his goals and adjust them and his plans to new conditions and situations.

6. Aid him to bridge the gap between the high school and junior college, and between the junior college and post-junior college life, whether that consists of employment and/or further schooling.

In his survey of California junior colleges, Johnson found three general categories of guidance programs which he designated as (1) instructor-adviser programs, (2) counselor and administrator-counselor programs, and (3) basic courses as a vehicle of guidance.[18] As an illustration of the first category, he describes the program at San Mateo Junior College in which approximately two thirds of the faculty have the students divided among them for advisement. "Counseling records on each student are centralized in a folder kept in the adviser's possession." Serious problems are referred to a dean.

Compton College is cited as an example of the second type of program. Here, a student personnel office, centrally located and accessible to all students, administers counseling through a dean and a small group of teacher-counselors who are on duty for general counseling approximately three hours a day. An in-service training program by means of counselor meetings, case studies, and sessions with a consultant helps to assure continued growth of the counselors.

For the third type of program, Johnson cites San Diego Junior College, among others. The chief guidance feature is a psychology course required of all students during their freshman year at the college. It is group guidance, emphasizing orientation to the junior college, vocational guidance based upon an analysis of each student's interests and abilities in relation to possible occupational fields, and personal and social adjustment. Other elements of the San Diego program are a testing program, from which a guidance profile or psychograph is drawn, advisement by instructor-advisers, with trained counselors available to all students, and remedial instruction for students who are handicapped in reading and other study skills.

At Stockton College, a four-year unit comprising Grades 11–14, group guidance is a significant element in a core course of English and history taught in the eleventh and twelfth grades.

In such scattered examples of practice as have here been cited, junior college staffs may find the elements from which guidance programs are built. Organization will come as the optimally effective arrangement of features becomes evident, along with the need for supervision.

[18] *Ibid.*, pp. 23–30.

Guidance Services in Colleges and Universities

Counseling programs have been developing rapidly in institutions of higher education within the past few years. Their growth has no doubt been spurred by the many surveys showing the country's need for workers in the various professions, while the wastage of human talent due to drop-outs has also been brought to the public attention. Counseling services to conserve human resources at the level of higher education are badly needed. Most typically, central counseling bureaus are established, being, in some cases, converted Veterans Administration Guidance Centers.[19] They operate the testing program for the measurement of the aptitudes and interests of the student body and give additional tests to individuals as a need is indicated in counseling interviews. The bureaus are staffed with professionally trained personnel, especially counseling psychologists, and the scope of their service runs the gamut of problems in distributive and adjustive guidance.

In numerous institutions, however, the need for faculty participation in the identification, diagnosis, and treatment of student problems is recognized. In addition to the utilization of faculty-student contacts in the classroom, systems of faculty advisers are established, by which a considerable fraction of the instructional staff is assigned to be the advisers of groups of students frequently ranging from 10 to 25 in number. These are not departmental advisers, but counselors for the whole student, concerned with helping their counselees to attain the fullest growth from the college opportunity. As envisaged by Koile,[20] the adequate working of such a counseling plan involves several conditions and features, as follows:

1. Recognition in load. This means a reduction in the normal full-time teaching schedule to compensate the faculty-adviser for the time necessary for careful study and counsel of each of his advisees.

2. A program of in-service training, by which advisers grow in their knowledge of the dynamics of human behavior, of the nature of human abilities and interests, of the interpretation of psychological tests, of interview techniques. This program of training would be carried on by the professionally trained personnel of the central counseling bureau, who would also receive referrals from faculty advisers and act as consultants to them. The bureau would perform the staff service of collecting, organizing, and interpreting information about counselees.

3. Selection of faculty members who are best suited to advisement by virtue of (a) a knowledge of human behavior and skill in counseling techniques (or a willingness to acquire them), (b) a suitable personality, and (c) a genuine interest in working in a counseling relationship with students.

To find faculty members who have this "genuine interest" is indeed a problem at all school levels. It may well be most severe in the university, for

[19] As an example, see George D. Barahal, *Converting a Veterans Guidance Center* (Stanford, Cal., Stanford University Press, 1950).

[20] Earl A. Koile, "Faculty Counseling in Colleges and Universities," *Teachers College Record,* Vol. LV (April, 1954), pp. 384–389.

while the major purpose of elementary schools, secondary schools, and colleges is the growth of the student, the major purpose of the university is the growth of knowledge. An eminent professor of physics was said to have told a young instructor in his department, "Why are you fooling away so much time with students? Your business is to get on with your research." To the extent to which the faculty is dominated by the research ideal, interest in the student is inhibited.

Koile has made a contribution to the solution of the problem of selecting faculty advisers who are interested in students.[21] He has constructed and validated an instrument for the measurement of such interests, called the *Professional Activity Inventory for College Teachers*. Certainly the selection of faculty members to carry a part-time counseling load is a task worthy of much careful thought.

COUNTY ORGANIZATION AND SERVICES

School services are being expanded. They are being differentiated to correspond to the differentiated needs of children. These trends are attributable to the increasing value our society attaches to each individual and to the progressive refinement of our perception of individual need.

To provide the school services which our ideals call for, school districts are being enlarged. The larger aggregations of pupils thus created make it economically possible to assemble the building facilities, the equipment, and the specialized personnel essential to the satisfaction of our educational ideals. However, in many sections of our country, population is too sparse and scattered to make feasible the creation of districts as large as desired. Such circumstances have caused attention to be focused on the county as a possible school unit. While some states have created county districts to completely displace the former local districts, other states have tended to utilize the county as an "intermediate unit," standing between the state and the local districts. Whether the county currently has authority over local schools and their personnel or is limited to a consultative and co-ordinating role, the trend is indeed toward greater county participation in school control and service.

This discussion points to the question, "What is or should be the role of the county in performing the guidance function?" Langston gathered some facts a few years ago to determine trends in California.[22] He reported the number of guidance personnel employed by county offices to have increased steadily from 1928 to 1943 and rapidly since World War II. Prospective demand for the decade of the 1950s was estimated to be greatest for psy-

---

[21] Earl A. Koile, "A Measure of Interest for Selecting Faculty Counselors," *Educational and Psychological Measurement*, Vol. XV (Spring, 1955), pp. 47–57.

[22] Daniel W. Langston, "Trends in County-Level School Guidance Services," *Occupations*, Vol. XXIX (May, 1951), pp. 579–583.

chologists, guidance co-ordinators, psychiatric social workers. The number of counties offering guidance service grew from none in 1929 to 70 per cent in 1949. As county-level workers in California do not have legal jurisdiction over local-school guidance workers, the emphasis is on local-school responsibility for establishing and maintaining the guidance program. Other than providing certain specialized services by personnel of advanced training, the county serves mainly in a consultative role. A measure of county influence was the fact that 82 per cent of the counties had a county-wide uniform cumulative record system in operation in 1949.

In a state in which the county is developing as an intermediate school unit, Bowman sought to determine by jury technique what guidance services *ought* to be performed by the county superintendent's office.[23] To the county superintendents of Pennsylvania, to a random sample of local school administrators, and to a number of guidance experts he submitted an "opinionnaire" listing 115 guidance services. These juries were asked to designate the services that should be performed by the county office. Generally, they indicated indirect guidance services as appropriate for the county to perform, while the direct counseling of pupils, individually and through group instruction, was regarded as the responsibility and the privilege of the local school. It was felt that the county office staff could advantageously (a) plan and participate in programs for training teachers to carry on guidance activities, (b) advise district administrators in drawing up their plans for acquiring and recording information concerning their pupils, (c) serve as a referral agent for children needing clinical services, (d) help high schools to build up their guidance materials, (e) promote follow-up studies and projects for appraisal of the effectiveness of guidance programs. In short, the county should be looked to for leadership, stimulation, and staff service. It means that every county office should have a guidance expert, one who is also possessed of administrative skill, a high level of ability in communication, enthusiasm, and adroitness in human relations.

The county seems destined to play an important role in guidance. The next decade will witness noteworthy clarification of that role.

CO-OPERATION WITH OUTSIDE AGENCIES

An important element in the task of organizing and administering guidance service is the utilization of agencies outside the school for the distribution and adjustment of youth. Through governmental action and through voluntary philanthropy, instrumentalities for human conservation have been created with which schools should co-operate. To a marked degree they have the same objectives as school guidance programs. The executive head of the

[23] Douglas Bowman, "Guidance Services Appropriate to the County Superintendency," *Personnel and Guidance Journal,* Vol. XXXIV (November, 1955), pp. 154–158.

school guidance program is surely the person who is mainly responsible for creating the bonds and the spirit of co-operation with these outside agencies. All teachers and teacher-counselors should, however, be acutely aware of such sources of aid to their pupils.

First of the outside organizations to be mentioned is the state employment service. The part it may play in placement was described in Chapter 17, pages 611–612, and an excellent example of thoroughgoing co-operation with the schools in the exercise of the placement function was cited. To that description may well be added a brief exposition of the counseling activity of the state employment service. Since 1945 this agency has had a counseling division represented in all or most of its offices. It administers the General Aptitude Test Battery—described in the first section of Chapter 12—and offers counsel on the basis of the test results plus such other data as it may gather or as may be made available. A canvass of the series of articles published a few years ago under the general title "Services to Youth Entering the Labor Market,"[24] indicates that in many communities across the nation it has become customary to give the GATB to high-school seniors who are not going to college and who are not acquiring the skills required in clerical positions.

The test battery is usually administered in the school by employment service personnel with the school staff assisting. The subsequent counseling apparently varies somewhat in its effectiveness. Generally it is done by employment service counselors who come to the school with GATB scores. If they have no other data, they can merely indulge in "test interpretation" and make pronouncements for which the thin support is obvious. Some schools, however, give them access to the cumulative records of the counselees, and if these have sufficient detail which the counselor studies carefully, the interview may be more fruitful. As Ruth E. Potter, of the Minnesota Division of Employment and Security, says, "our best counselors know how to *relate* properly the GATB test results and other counseling information."[25]

In a few states, at least, the co-operation of the employment service has consisted of giving and scoring the GATB, then turning the test results and interpretations over to the school's staff for their use in counseling. Experts from the employment service have also conducted conferences or workshops of school counselors to train them in the kind of vocational counseling which inclusion of GATB results makes possible. This practice has the merit of recognizing the extensive knowledge of the counselee which is possessed by the school counselor. It has the disadvantage of the school counselor's limited knowledge of the labor market and occupational opportunity, as compared with the employment service counselor's.

Staff service to build up the fund of occupational knowledge of school counselors and students is a noteworthy co-operation rendered by the Michi-

[24] *Employment Security Review,* Vol. XX (April, 1953), pp. 3–32.
[25] *Ibid.,* p. 11.

gan State Employment Service.[26] It publishes and makes available to high schools and colleges *The Michigan Occupational Guide Series.* At the time of this description of the practice, the *Series* consisted of 55 different booklets, each covering one occupation or field of work and characterized by information of special interest to residents of Michigan. Other publications of this state agency are job surveys of various communities, a monthly called "Michigan's Labor Market," and a local "Labor Market Letter" issued for each major area. Considering the economic handicap of the individual school in compiling local occupational information, this kind of aid from the offices of the state employment service could be extremely helpful.

The future in all likelihood will witness closer co-operation between the schools and the state employment service. This agency can have more expert knowledge of occupations, more skill in the accumulation of such knowledge, more facilities for the testing of occupational aptitudes, and more competence for occupational placement than can the schools. Guidance workers should recognize these realities, sense their own limitations, tap this resource.

A second outside agency with which co-operation should be planned is a group of organizations which may be designated as welfare societies. The possibilities of their service to human conservation by rendering guidance in its adjustive phase are so transparent that the schools should welcome the closest liaison. Identifying these organizations and stating their purposes as they exist in Buffalo, is the following statement from a report by Sielski:[27]

. . . it is important to know that the function of the Family Service Society is that of strengthening family ties and that this is accomplished through parent-child counseling, family life education, and counseling for personality and emotional problems. The Children's Aid Society on the other hand is concerned with neglected children, child protection, foster care homes, and adoptions. The Ingleside home has the function of assisting with the problems of unmarried parents, while Catholic Charities and the Jewish Community Service Society offer family and child services with the added emphasis of a religious setting.

To make the most of the co-operation between the school and these welfare organizations Sielski urged the exchange and sharing of pertinent case history information. He expressed the view that the classroom teacher plays a key role in this co-operation by utilizing his opportunity to sense early behavior or environmental problems and taking the responsibility for initiating a referral to a social agency.

Many schools now have a specialized personnel worker known as the school social worker (formerly home-and-school visitor) who visits the homes of pupils who are excessively absent, whose academic performance is inexplicably low, who are maladjusted in health, personality, or social

---

[26] *Ibid* (Sherrill C. Passage), pp. 25–27.

[27] Lester M. Sielski, "Developing Principles of Public School and Social Agency Cooperation," *Personnel and Guidance Journal,* Vol. XXXV (December, 1956), pp. 247–248.

relationships. He acts as a counselor to parents and child, employs such meliorative measures as he can, and refers the case to the proper welfare agency when necessary. At times a law-enforcement agency must be called in. In a large city system the school social workers are frequently responsible to the director of guidance, and that seems to be their proper organizational connection.[28]

A third outside force with which the school's guidance service should be closely co-ordinated is the group of agencies which is particularly concerned with law enforcement, the prevention of law violation, the rehabilitation of law breakers, the safety of life and property. The police, the juvenile court, and correctional schools are the principal organizations in this category. Few are the school systems which have created really well-organized plans for co-operation with these agencies—that is, co-operation for the prevention of delinquency. An outstanding example of such organization is the Passaic (N.J.) Children's Bureau, described at length by Kvaraceus[29] a few years ago and briefly in a more recent and more comprehensive work.[30] This agency has as its director the assistant superintendent of schools in charge of guidance and special services. His staff consists of three plainclothes policemen and one policewoman, one social worker, one psychologist, one reading specialist, three attendance officers, and three secretaries. The Bureau maintains close contact with the juvenile court and with all youth-serving agencies of the community. It is housed in the school administration building. Its police personnel are carefully selected from the regular police force of the city and specially trained for their work in the Bureau. They are in close touch with the regular police who promptly convey to the Bureau knowledge of violations by minors and information that identifies incipient delinquents. However, the police unit of the Bureau works under the direction of the professional social worker or the psychologist, and with such supervision they participate in the study and treatment of cases as well as in apprehension.

Naturally, this Passaic agency receives cases from the schools as well as from the police. Pupils who are troublesome in the classroom are referred to the Bureau for diagnosis and treatment. Pupils whose withdrawing behavior baffles the analytical powers of teachers may be understood and restored by social worker or psychologist or psychiatrist. While the Bureau does not have psychiatric service within its own organization, it can call in such specialized assistance as it may be needed.

The Passaic Children's Bureau represents a pioneer adventure into a field

[28] For an excellent portrayal of the role of the school social worker, the reader may turn to the following reference: Grace Mitchell, "When to Prescribe the School Social Worker," *Elementary School Journal,* Vol. LVIII (May, 1958), pp. 439–444.

[29] Wm. C. Kvaraceus, *Juvenile Delinquency and the School* (New York, World Book, 1945).

[30] *The Community and the Delinquent* (New York, World Book, 1954), pp. 232–34, 286–288, 420–421.

of co-ordination that has been too little explored. It is a recognition that the individual's adjustment is influenced by community, home, part-time job, and the society of his peers. The school does not carry on its work in a vacuum. The initiative for achieving teamwork with other youth-serving agencies may well be taken by the school.

This section, which merely introduces the reader to a theme of crucial importance to the cause of human betterment, may well be concluded by calling attention to Havighurst's vision of a co-ordination of educational forces which is more comprehensive, more all-embracing, than any conception we have cited.[31] It is his thought that the pupils of a community might well be thoughtfully screened at about the level of Grade 4 for the identification of two general classes, as follows: (1) the gifted children, those having special abilities or talents, and (2) the maladjusted, both aggressive and passive. The program for developing the children thus discovered would involve helping the community to make a more efficient use of the people and the facilities it already has for work with children. Havighurst envisioned a nine-months' program of training for such people as school and church-school teachers, public health nurses, scout leaders, YMCA and YWCA staff members, social workers, and parents. Teams of these people would then have children assigned to them for study and assistance.

Essentially, this program is one of discovering children with needs which might otherwise go unnoticed and putting them "on the conscience" of a small group in the community, who will keep on studying and trying to help them until they grow up.[32] An experiment with this plan was initiated in a Midwestern city in 1951 and its progress reported in three monographs to date.[33] It is an ambitious attempt to co-ordinate energies and to focus them sharply on the individual problem.

RELATION OF GUIDANCE FEATURES TO COMPONENTS OF THE GUIDANCE FUNCTION

This chapter has been devoted to the exposition of principles that should be observed in building programs of guidance. The numerous features, as they have been described in Chapters 6–17, must be fitted together into a

[31] Robert J. Havighurst, "A Community Youth Development Plan," *School Review*, Vol. LIX (November, 1951), pp. 457–466.

[32] *Ibid.*, p. 460.

[33] Robert J. Havighurst, *et al.*, *A Community Youth Development Plan*, Supplementary Educational Monograph No. 75 (Chicago, University of Chicago Press, June, 1952).

————, *Studying Children and Training Counselors in a Community Program*, Supplementary Educational Monograph No. 78 (Chicago, University of Chicago Press, June, 1953).

Paul H. Bowman, Robert F. DeHaan, John K. Kough, and Gordon P. Liddle, *Mobilizing Community Resources for Youth*, Supplementary Educational Monograph No. 85 (Chicago, University of Chicago Press, October, 1956).

FIG. 22. THE BEARING OF THE FEATURES OF THE GUIDANCE PROGRAM UPON THE COMPONENTS OF THE GUIDANCE FUNCTION.

Features of the Guidance Program

Components of the GUIDANCE FUNCTION	School Publications to Orient and Inform	Organization of the school and the offering	Curriculum and Extra-curriculum	Study of Occupations	Homeroom Group and Individual Guidance	Testing and Analysis	Counseling	Placement	Follow-up
DISTRIBUTIVE:									
1. Acquaint pupil with educational and vocational opportunities	Very important	Important	Very important	Very important	Very important	Little or no importance	Very important	Little or no importance	Important
2. Acquaint pupil with his own powers, interests, and limitations	Little or no importance	Important	Very important	Important	Important	Little or no importance	Very important	Little or no importance	Important
3. Keep the school acquainted with educational and vocational opportunities	Important	Little or no importance	Little or no importance	Very important	Very important	Little or no importance	Little or no importance	Little or no importance	Important
4. Acquaint the school with pupil's powers, interests, and limitations	Little or no importance	Important	Very important	Important	Important	Very important	Very important	Little or no importance	Important
5. Help pupil at times of decision and selection	Important	Little or no importance	Little or no importance	Little or no importance	Very important	Little or no importance	Very important	Very important	Important
ADJUSTIVE:									
1. Prevent maladjustment	Important	Important	Very important	Little or no importance	Very important	Very important	Important	Little or no importance	Important
2. Identify cases of maladjustment	Little or no importance	Little or no importance	Important	Little or no importance	Important	Very important	Very important	Little or no importance	Important
3. Diagnose cases	Little or no importance	Little or no importance	Important	Little or no importance	Important	Very important	Very important	Little or no importance	Important
4. Arrive at remedial treatment and administer it	Little or no importance	Little or no importance	Important	Little or no importance	Important	Little or no importance	Very important	Little or no importance	Important

Legend: Very important; Important; Little or no importance

unified, logical plan which is in harmony with the over-all purpose and program of the school. Single features do not discharge the guidance function. A feature bears upon one or more of the components of the function, as they were defined in Chapter 5. As each feature has been described, its bearing on the components has been pointed out. To summarize these relationships and attempt to represent the strength of each, Figure 22 has been drawn. It expresses the subjective judgments of the author, and readers are therefore fully privileged to offer their own judgments. Indeed, it is hoped that this schematic arrangement of goals and means will provoke the reader to test each relationship shown and to discuss it with fellow students.

QUESTIONS, PROBLEMS, INVESTIGATIONS

1. Evaluate the guidance program of any school of your acquaintance:
   a. Describe and evaluate the role of the principal.
   b. Describe and evaluate the role of the counselor or counselors.
   c. How does the role of the homeroom teacher compare with that of the homeroom teacher in New Trier?
2. Evaluate the guidance service in a school which has separate counselors for boys and girls.
3. Survey the guidance program of a college or a junior college of your acquaintance to estimate its adequacy.
4. Canvass the co-operation of your high school and the state employment service. How could the co-operation be improved?
5. Read the full account of the Passaic Children's Bureau in Kvaraceus' *Juvenile Delinquency and the School* and then study the co-operation of police and schools in your town.
6. Find out just what the school social worker does. How does he work with the school counselor?
7. Make a study of Havighurst's "Community Youth Development Plan" by reading the three Supplementary Educational Monographs of the University of Chicago Press cited at the end of the fourth section.
8. Make an extended list of guidance activities classified as "line" and "staff."

SELECTED REFERENCES

ALLEN, Richard D., "Delegating the Guidance Functions within the Secondary School," *Vocational Guidance Magazine*, Vol. X (October, 1931), pp. 14–19.

———, "A Guidance Program that Any High-School Principal May Undertake," *Vocational Guidance Magazine*, Vol. XI (February, 1933), pp. 199–205.

———, "How a Principal Can Direct Guidance," *Occupations*, Vol. XVI (October, 1937), pp. 15–20.

———, *Organization and Supervision of Guidance in Public Education* (New York 3—207 Fourth Ave.—Inor Publishing Co., 1937).

————, "Selecting Counselors in Secondary Schools," *Vocational Guidance Magazine,* Vol. X (November, 1931), pp. 68–72.

ARNOLD, Dwight L., "Time Spent by Counselors and Deans on Various Activities," *Occupations,* Vol. XXVII (March, 1949), pp. 391–393.

BARAHAL, George D., *Converting a Veterans Guidance Center* (Stanford, Cal., Stanford University Press, 1950).

BOWMAN, Douglas, "Guidance Services Appropriate to the County Superintendency," *Personnel and Guidance Journal,* Vol. XXXIV (November, 1955), pp. 154–158.

BOWMAN, Paul H., DeHAAN, Robert F., KOUGH, John K., and LIDDLE, Gordon P., *Mobilizing Community Resources for Youth,* Supplementary Educational Monograph No. 85 (Chicago, University of Chicago Press, October, 1956).

————, et al., *Studying Children and Training Counselors in a Community Program,* Supplementary Educational Monograph No. 78 (Chicago, University of Chicago Press, June, 1953).

CHRISTENSEN, Thomas E., "Responsibilities of the High-School Principal in the Guidance Program," *School Review,* Vol. LVII (March, 1949), pp. 149–154.

COX, Rachel D., *Counselors and Their Work* (New York, Archives Publishing Co., 1945).

FAILOR, Clarence W., "Two Jobs That Don't Mix," *Nation's Schools,* Vol. XXIII (January, 1939), pp. 22–24, 54.

HAVIGHURST, Robert J., "A Community Youth Development Plan," *School Review,* Vol. LIX (November, 1951), pp. 457–466.

————, et al., *A Community Youth Development Plan,* Supplementary Educational Monograph No. 75 (Chicago, University of Chicago Press, June, 1952).

JOHNSON, B. Lamar, "The Advising, Guidance, and Counseling of Junior College Students," *Bulletin of the National Association of Secondary-School Principals,* Vol. XXXVII (February, 1953), pp. 19–36.

KEARNEY, Milo E., "Making Guidance Effective in Elementary Schools," *Elementary School Journal,* Vol. LVI (April, 1956), pp. 348–353.

KOILE, Earl A., "Faculty Counseling in Colleges and Universities," *Teachers College Record,* Vol. LV (April, 1954), pp. 384–389.

————, "A Measure of Interest for Selecting Faculty Counselors," *Educational and Psychological Measurement,* Vol. XV (Spring, 1955), pp. 47–57.

KRUGMAN, Morris, "Why Guidance in the Elementary School?" *Personnel and Guidance Journal,* Vol. XXXII (January, 1954), pp. 270–273.

KVARACEUS, William C., *The Community and the Delinquent* (New York, World Book, 1954).

————, *Juvenile Delinquency and the School* (New York, World Book, 1945).

LANGSTON, Daniel W., "Trends in County-Level School Guidance Services," *Occupations,* Vol. XXIX (May, 1951), pp. 579–583.

LITCHFIELD, Edward H., "Notes on a General Theory of Administration," *Administrative Science Quarterly,* Vol. I (June, 1956), pp. 3–29.

LLOYD-JONES, Esther, "Centrifugal and Centripetal Guidance Programs for Children," *Teachers College Record,* Vol. LI (October, 1949), pp. 7–13.

————, "Some Current Issues in Guidance," *Teachers College Record,* Vol. XLIX (November, 1947), pp. 77–88.

MITCHELL, Grace, "When to Prescribe the School Social Worker," *Elementary School Journal*, Vol. LVIII (May, 1958), pp. 439–444.

NEWMAN, William H., "A Full-time Counselor in an Elementary School," *Elementary School Journal*, Vol. LVI (April, 1956), pp. 354–357.

REAVIS, William C., *Programs of Guidance*, U.S. Office of Education Bulletin (1932), No. 17, Monograph No. 14 of National Survey of Secondary Education.

ROSECRANCE, Francis C., "The Staff Needed for the Development of an Effective Guidance Service," Chapter 10 of *Guidance in Educational Institutions*, 37th Yearbook, Part I, National Society for the Study of Education (Distributed by University of Chicago Press, Chicago, 1938).

SANTAVICCA, G. G., "What Homeroom Teachers Should Know," *Occupations*, Vol. XXX (February, 1952), pp. 351–355.

SEARS, J. B., *The School Survey* (Boston, Houghton Mifflin, 1925), Ch. XIII.

"Services to Youth Entering the Labor Market," *Employment Security Review*, Vol. XX (April, 1953), pp. 3–32.

SIELSKI, Lester M., "Developing Principles of Public School and Social Agency Cooperation," *Personnel and Guidance Journal*, Vol. XXXV (December, 1956), pp. 247–248.

SYMONDS, Percival M., "A Plea for the Integration of School Guidance Activities," *Teachers College Record*, Vol. XXXVIII (May, 1937), pp. 686–710.

The Team Approach in Pupil Personnel Services. A Report by the Advisory Pupil Personnel Committee Dealing with the Role of School Social Workers, School Psychologists, and School Counselors (Hartford, Conn., State Department of Education, June, 1955).

TRAXLER, Arthur E., "Essentials of Guidance Services in Elementary Schools," *Elementary School Journal*, Vol. LIII (December, 1952), pp. 207–210.

WILSON, Frances M., "Guidance in Elementary Schools," *Occupations*, Vol. XXIX (December, 1950), pp. 168–173.

WRENN, C. G., "Initiating a Guidance Program in a Small School," *Vocational Guidance Magazine*, Vol. VII (October, 1928), pp. 36–37.

WRIGHT, Barbara, "Minneapolis School Counselors Analyze Their Jobs," *Occupations*, Vol. XXIV (January, 1946), pp. 214–219.

CHAPTER 19

Evaluation

THE MEASUREMENT OF THE OUTCOMES of instruction has undergone marked development in the past forty years. The instruments and the techniques of this function have won wide acceptance, a state which is attested by the financial support now accorded to them in most school budgets. In contrast, the measurement of the outcomes of guidance is a function concerning which little is known and less is practiced. Most of the schools and colleges which have guidance programs carry on guidance activities with no plans for testing their worth. The values of guidance are simply assumed.

To become firmly established, any social function needs objective evidence of its merit. The case studies which conclude happily are heart-warming to read. And the individual boys and girls whom we have helped to make good adjustments or choices constitute a source of satisfaction. Such subjective data and isolated instances, however, are not enough. Statistics are needed—data which will portray the effect of a guidance program on a whole group. Specific procedures and techniques need testing on a broad scale so that those which are found ineffective can be modified or discarded and those which prove valid can be confidently recommended for wider usage.

In the present immaturity of guidance measurement, it is impossible to offer a suitable program of guidance evaluation for a school or college. The best that can be done in this chapter is to cite the fragmentary literature which describes attempts to objectively appraise guidance programs, features, or devices. Since previous chapters have drawn upon many of these evaluative studies, the reader will be referred to them and asked to reread them in the context of this chapter.

MEASURING THE EXTENT TO WHICH COMPONENTS OF THE GUIDANCE FUNCTION ARE PERFORMED

Are Pupils Acquainted with Educational and Vocational Opportunities?

Figure 22, with which the last chapter was concluded, shows how guidance is performed by indicating the bearing of various features and activities on the components of the distributive and adjustive phases of guidance. Evaluation, then, may well have its beginning with the question, "Are each of the components being performed?" And, specifically referring to the first component of distribution guidance, "How adequately are pupils being made acquainted with the educational and vocational opportunities of the world?" A horizontal reading of Figure 22 shows many features to bear upon that component.

To measure the attainment of this first component, numerous investigators have created instruments of measurement and applied them. Presumably the reason for the greater activity in measuring this component than any other lies in the fact that it deals with the acquisition of information, an educational objective which school people are quite accustomed to testing.

In the 1930s a number of researches were carried on for the purpose of measuring the educational and vocational information possessed by junior high school pupils. Most of these studies were intended to evaluate, by the criterion of knowledge possessed, the effects of a course in occupations. They were seriously limited in accomplishing that purpose because of the fact that school children are busily acquiring educational and vocational information through so many media other than the course in occupations. Only to look at Figure 22 and see how many features bear on this guidance component helps one to understand the handicap of such research. Thus, while Mildred Lincoln's experimental groups earned median end scores which were statistically higher than those of the control groups, the difference was not large. And the initial scores of both groups were of such magnitude as to indicate the possession of considerable educational and occupational information before the experiment began.[1]

Williamson reported the measurement of gains in educational and occupational information which were made by classes in a one-quarter course entitled "Vocations," taught in the General College, University of Minnesota.[2] The measurement was made by means of a test of 203 questions given at the beginning and at the end of the course—a test which had been standardized for use with the course. A summary of the simpler data submitted for experimental and control groups is shown here as Table 77.[3] The mean pretest scores show that both the experimental and control groups had a considerable grasp of the content of the course before it was given. Both made gains during the quarter the course was given, but the experimental groups gained much more than did the control groups.

These examples of the measurement of this component suggest that we are enveloped in considerable fog as to the information basic to life planning

[1] *Teaching About Vocational Life*, Chapter 9 and Appendix, (Scranton, Pa., International Textbook Co., 1937), pp. 466–477.

[2] E. G. Williamson, "A College Class in Occupational Information," *School Review*, Vol. XLV (February, 1937), pp. 123–129.

[3] *Ibid.*, Table II (adapted), p. 127.

for education and vocation. Yet such studies as McLaughlin's, described in the fourth section of Chapter 6 and revealing the extreme ignorance of high-school seniors concerning the colleges they had elected to attend, attest the dire need of students for knowledge of educational and vocational opportunity. Studies cited in the second section of Chapter 4 likewise bear testimony to this need. To leave the acquisition of such knowledge entirely to features of the guidance program *other* than the study of occupations may prove adequate if such other features are properly exploited for that purpose. Sachs' comprehensive comparison of guidance outcomes in two junior high schools pointed to this possibility.[4] As described briefly in the concluding pages of our Chapter 10, one of these schools operated on a guidance-teacher

TABLE 77. Scores on Pretest and Retest on Occupations Made by Three Experimental Groups Receiving Instruction in Occupations and Two Groups of Control Students

	Number of Students	Mean Pretest Score	Mean Retest Score	Average Gain
Groups receiving instruction in Occupations:				
Autumn quarter	27	103.17	117.28	14.11
Winter quarter	35	93.30	120.20	26.90
Spring quarter	50	95.28	120.64	25.36
Control groups:				
Students in Writing				
Laboratory	87	92.61	100.06	7.45
Freshmen in Arts College	72	103.83	111.17	7.34

plan (resembling the Providence class-counselor plan), and the other relied upon homeroom teachers for group and individual guidance. Sachs included among her measuring instruments tests of educational and occupational information. She summarized her comparisons on these tests as follows:[5]

Although final scores and gains on a test of educational guidance information slightly favored the homeroom groups, no consistent differences were found between the two schools with respect to initial scores on this test.

Mean gains and final scores on the occupational information test favored the homeroom groups. Mean initial scores, however, favored the School A guidance groups at the lower grade levels and the homeroom groups at the higher grade levels.

The outcomes with which Sachs was concerned in stating these findings are commonly referred to as educational and vocational "orientation." Look-

[4] Georgia May Sachs, *Evaluation of Group Guidance Work in Secondary Schools.* Southern California Education Monographs No. 14 (Los Angeles, University of Southern California Press, 1945).

[5] *Ibid.*, p. 38.

ing for the results of the various types of orientation programs or courses which schools and colleges administer, one may well ask, "When is one oriented?" or, "What is it to be oriented?" Some years ago, in recognition of the low visibility of orientation outcomes, Wolf described his attempt to measure the orientation of students graduating from high school.[6] He devised a test to measure understanding of the nature of three subject fields, namely, economics, psychology, and sociology. Sample test items were included in his article. On a scale on which the arbitrarily selected score intervals were designated as "Excellent," "Fair to Good," "Doubtful," and "Very Poor," he found two thirds of his subjects to rate as "Doubtful." Wolf's contribution is well worth reading for the questions it raises as well as for the answers it gives. He pointed to the desirability of determining the orientation of individuals at all levels of the school system.

Costolo constructed a test[7] to measure the educational and occupational orientation needed by junior high school pupils for choosing a curriculum and elective subjects in a comprehensive senior high school. The 200 items of the test were grouped to determine the pupil's knowledge of the following relationships:

School subjects and occupations
Subjects and high-school curriculums
Curriculums and occupations
Subjects, and ideas, abilities, or appreciations which are educational outcomes
Subject fields and statements defining their nature and scope
Occupations and the level of training required

These relationships are patently essential in the pupils' understanding if they are to face the choices of the senior high school in a knowledgeable state. The categories represent something of an analysis of educational and vocational orientation.

In conclusion, it must be said that no standards are available by which to judge the achievement of this component of distributive guidance, and the tests which have been used in researches to date are of uncertain validity. From a common-sense standpoint, however, schools can profit greatly by applying such measures as have here been cited to see if pupils have the enlightenment and realistic knowledge of their educational and vocational opportunities which are basic to well-reasoned choices.

Are Pupils Acquainted with Themselves—Their Powers, Interests, and Limitations?

Considering guidance as a service devoted to helping people acquire the capacity for accurate self-estimate, we should be deeply concerned with the

[6] Lyle H. Wolf, "The Measurement of Orientation," *School Review,* Vol. XL (October, 1932), pp. 577–586.

[7] Herbert L. Costolo, *Measuring the Educational and Occupational Orientation of Junior High School Pupils.* M. A. Thesis (Pittsburgh, University of Pittsburgh Library, 1933).

measurement of the adequacy with which we are achieving that goal. There is no evidence that schools and colleges have systematic programs for measuring attainment of this component. If any instrument were available for this measurement, it is apparent that no common key could be applied in its scoring. The self-knowledge possessed by each individual can only be appraised for its adequacy by comparing it with the individual himself as he actually is. Nevertheless, when the members of a counseled group who choose to elect French or who choose to go to college represent a higher degree of aptitude for those choices than do the members from an uncounseled (control) group who make those choices, we *assume* gains in self-understanding. (See the first and second sections of Chapter 16 for quotations from the study of Hutson and Webster.)

While large-scale evaluation of the realization of this component seems quite restricted, the research which represents attempts to measure directly the individual's capacity for self-estimate is noteworthy. If the reader will turn back to Chapter 15, he will find that the entire fifth section is devoted to the subject. Especially are the contributions of Arsenian, Torrance, and Young calculated to stimulate thought concerning the creation of practical instruments for evaluating self-knowledge in certain limited aspects.

Regardless of the possibilities of surveying a whole class of high-school or college students for their self-understanding, the real counselor looks for evidence of how each counselee perceives himself. Sometimes the evidence stands forth plainly in speech and behavior; sometimes it is so obscure or camouflaged as to challenge all the interpretive skill of a sensitive and well-trained specialist.

Measuring Attainment of the Remaining Components of Distributive Guidance

Distributive components 3 and 4 in Figure 22 refer to the school's preparedness for giving assistance to the pupil in his tasks of understanding himself and the array of educational and vocational opportunities. Table 9 in the sixth section of Chapter 3 suggests quite plainly that teachers in secondary schools know relatively little about their pupils. The author of the table created it as a summation of a research in which he submitted to a group of teachers an extended questionnaire to be answered concerning each one of a random sampling of their pupils. The inquiry form was never published. How well do homeroom teachers, teacher-counselors, and counselors know their pupils? No published study has come to this writer's attention to indicate that anyone ever tried to obtain an answer to that question. And therefore no measuring instrument exists by which the attainment of this component could be ascertained.

As to the other component, how well the school keeps fully and continuously acquainted with the world of educational and vocational opportunity, and reflects that world to the pupils, no mode or instrument of evaluation is known to exist. School surveys, such as the New York Regents' Inquiry, which was quoted in the second section of Chapter 3, give descriptive appraisals which bear upon the component, but that is as near to measurement as we have come. That the component is necessary to realize, however, is transparent. A young woman who was teaching occupations in a bookish, artificial manner knew she was failing in this component. She said, "Mr. Blank is the person who should be teaching this course." And who was Mr. Blank? He was a fifty-year-old veteran then teaching problems of democracy. But he could teach any subject and through it help students to understand the world of reality. Not only did he have a conventional college education, but he had also graduated from the "university of hard knocks," for every summer he had worked in widely ranging clerical, sales, and manual jobs. Thus, the realization of the component may depend in large degree upon the experience and the attitudes of the teaching staff. Chapter 8 gave many illustrations of activities bearing upon the component. Comprehensive and objective evaluation of their effectiveness, however, is unknown.

The effectiveness with which the school performs the fifth component of distributive guidance, namely, "to help pupils at times of selection and decision," is perhaps mainly to be judged by such measures as are applied to appraise the entire state of distributive guidance. These will be described in the next section. It is true, of course, that follow-up studies have sometimes sought the testimony of graduates or school leavers on this point. But the subjective character of such evidence, plus the lack of valid standards for rendering judgments which must characterize such respondents, causes a lack of confidence in appraisal by such methods. This fifth component is so bound up in the first four, so dependent for its effectiveness on the adequacy with which the first four have been performed, that it can hardly be judged by itself.

Measuring Attainment of the Separate Components of Adjustive Guidance

Is the school preventing maladjustment? Is it identifying the cases of maladjustment, diagnosing them, administering remedial treatment? These are the evaluative questions which are implicit in the components. Readily applicable tests to answer them do not exist. Researches, of course, have been made to determine the extent of maladjustment. One of these, by Carl Rogers, designed to locate the individuals in an elementary school who are socially and emotionally maladjusted, was described in the third section of Chapter 4. The procedure of Rogers' study impresses this writer as eminently practical for the identification of pupils who need help, but its employment does not seem to have come into any general practice.

Cited in the first pages of Chapter 11 were several manuals for the study of children, by the use of which teachers would be enabled to identify members with various sorts of maladjustments and to some extent to diagnose their troubles. To measure the effectiveness, however, with which a school is rendering this service to its children, would necessitate the use of some such instrument of survey as that of Rogers. Eventually—probably with the increased staffing of schools with guidance specialists—the use of discriminating school surveys to measure the state attained must become more common.

MEASURING THE PERFORMANCE OF DISTRIBUTIVE GUIDANCE

To measure the attainment of a component of guidance is not to measure guidance. Pupils may, for example, be well acquainted with educational and vocational opportunities and still not make wise choices. Basic testing of the guidance program is the measurement of the attainment of satisfactory distribution and adjustment. These are the really important questions: Are pupils' choices of vocation, curriculum, and elective subjects in harmony with their abilities and with society's needs for differentiation? Are pupils scholastically, emotionally, socially, and volitionally adjusted to the situations in which they find themselves so that their development goes forward at a rate truly consistent with their abilities? Instruments for ascertaining the accomplishment of these ultimate goals, crude though they are, may be called achievement tests in guidance.

In taking up the first of these questions, the reader is first referred to some of the researches quoted in Chapter 4 as "evidences of the need for guidance." The early studies by Johnston in Minnesota and the recent national studies by Wolfle, both showing that many students were unwise in choosing to go or not to go to college; the studies of vocational choice in Western Pennsylvania, Nebraska, and other localities, showing choices made without regard to ability or social need—these are measurements of guidance. They are not measurements of any particular programs of guidance, but the criteria accepted and the instruments employed are the same as one would use in measuring a specific program.

The earliest study known to this writer as the measurement of a specific program was one made by Proctor, pioneer in guidance, at the time the Stanford-Binet and the Army Alpha intelligence examinations first became available.[8] The question for which his investigation sought answer was, "Does curricular counseling of pupils just entering high school pay dividends in decreased failure and decreased elimination?" Upon those criteria he compared a "guided" group and an "unguided" group, the former being advised by a counselor who had before him intelligence test data, elementary school records, teachers' estimates, and vocational and educational plans of

[8] William M. Proctor, *The Use of Psychological Tests in the Educational and Vocational Guidance of High School Pupils,* Journal of Educational Research Monographs No. 1 (Bloomington, Ill., Public School Publishing Co., June, 1921), pp. 23–31.

the pupils. The results showed that the "guided" group had chosen their subjects more wisely. While the number of cases involved in Proctor's study was too small to preclude the possibility that the outcome of the experiment was influenced by chance, the method was sound and the objective was practical.

Hedge and Hutson[9] reported the measurement of a guidance program with high-school juniors and seniors. At the beginning of the school year these students filled out blanks indicating their occupational choices and educational plans. They were given intelligence tests and tests of achievement and aptitude. The student's rank in class on each of the tests and on his academic record was recorded on a card, together with the occupational choices he had designated. The card was the basis of an interview which the counselor held with each student for the purpose of considering the counselee's plans for the future. Other procedures of the program included carefully planned homeroom group-guidance lessons centered about objective data calculated to stimulate thinking about abilities and aspirations. In May, the students again responded to an inquiry concerning their educational and occupational plans.

The method of evaluating the guidance program was that of comparing the abilities of the groups which in May made certain choices, with the abilities of the groups which in September had made the same choices. Table 78 shows the improvement in the quality of the college-going group, as measured by rank in class. This desirable change was accomplished almost entirely by the subtraction of students of low college aptitude and very little by the addition of students of high college aptitude. This fact may be taken as evidence for the need of centering guidance for the college decision more sharply in the junior high school years; the high-school juniors and seniors who have proceeded so far in pursuit of objectives which do not include college education cannot easily change their course.

Supporting the assumption of this study that the changes of intention shown in Table 78 were due to the guidance program was the college-going

TABLE 78. Summary of Class Rank of Students Who in September before Guidance and in May after Guidance Expressed Intention of Entering College or University

	Seniors		Juniors	
	September	May	September	May
Total number of students	79	79	122	122
Number planning to go to college	20	14	32	27
Percentage in upper half of class	50	71	72	78
Percentage in lower half of class	50	29	28	22

[9] John W. Hedge and Percival W. Hutson, "A Technique for Evaluating Guidance Activities," *School Review,* Vol. XXXIX (September, 1931), pp. 508–519.

record of the class that had just graduated from that high school. The median of the ranks in high-school class of those who entered college was 55.0; from the highest quarter of the class—a class of 108—24 per cent entered college, and from the lowest quarter, 27 per cent.

For a study with a more experimental design which illustrates the measurement of the performance of distributive guidance, the reader is referred to the research of Hutson and Webster[10] which was quoted at some length in Chapter 16. Both the method and the results are described in the quotations.

Various studies have been made to measure a particular device or procedure in distributive guidance, although in the practical situation it is difficult to isolate a single simple variable and test it. Haines' experiment, which was described in the fourth section of Chapter 16, was, for example, a plan for measuring the effects of a counseling program built mainly around the studied use of Part IV of the *Dictionary of Occupational Titles*. Because the guidance of the pupils was the major concern, the counselor did not hesitate to use whatever skills he possessed and which seemed to be needed in each case. Haines' criteria for sound distribution were, it will be remembered, the degree of job satisfaction experienced by his control and experimental groups, and the degree of their job adjustment as rated by their employers.

How does group counseling for educational and vocational choices compare in effectiveness with individual counseling? To answer this question a group of counselors in the Los Angeles City School Advisement Service[11] experimented with the senior boys of two successive classes of one of the city high schools. The class of 1950 was given individual counseling, and the class of 1951, group counseling. After counseling, folders containing extensive data on each student were submitted to four counselor-psychologists for the rating of the student's vocational objective as to its realism. A three-point scale was used, as follows: *unrealistic,* of *doubtful realism,* and *realistic*. No differences were found between the methods of counseling. Approximately 58 per cent of the choices of each group were rated as realistic, 4 per cent as unrealistic, and 38 per cent as of doubtful realism. The study is indeed a recommendation for the use of the time-saving group guidance, although even this brief resume should not omit the fact that the group counseling method included one individual interview as the concluding element in the program.

Another experimental study with one of the techniques of guidance has been reported by Cuony and Hoppock.[12]

[10] Percival W. Hutson and Arthur D. Webster, "An Experiment in the Educational and Vocational Guidance of Tenth-Grade Pupils," *Educational and Psychological Measurement,* Vol. III (Spring, 1943), pp. 3–21.

[11] David Bilovsky, William McMasters, Joseph E. Shorr, and Stanley L. Singer, "Individual and Group Counseling," *Personnel and Guidance Journal,* Vol. XXXI (March, 1953), pp. 363–365.

[12] Edward R. Cuony and Robert Hoppock, "Job Course Pays Off," *Personnel and Guidance Journal,* Vol. XXXII (March, 1954), p. 389.

Cuony . . . taught a course in Job Finding and Job Orientation to an experimental group of high-school seniors in Geneva, N.Y. One year after graduation he compared them with an equated control group from the same class of the same school. The students who had had the course were better satisfied with their jobs than those who had not had the course. The combined annual earnings of the experimental group exceeded those of the control group by $7,719; the course cost $1,542.

A unique element in this experiment was the method of equating groups. The authors rejected the usual bases of age, intelligence, achievement, etc., for equating, because they considered that equation on the basis of such characteristics as personality, motivation, and work habits—attributes that are practically impossible to measure—was just as important. Instead, they first eliminated all seniors who intended to go to college, then divided the remaining students by sex, arranged each sex group alphabetically, numbered them consecutively, and put the even-numbered students in the experimental group and the odd-numbered in the control group. They tested the assumption that this method gave equated groups by employing it with the preceding three classes who had graduated, and comparing those groups as to job satisfaction and earnings. They found the two groups in each class —none of whom had had the course in Job Finding and Job Orientation—to be approximately equal on both criteria. Thus tested, the method of equating groups for the experiment was considered valid.

The work that has been done in the development of methods for the measurement of distributive guidance is not inconsiderable. The great need is for the widespread use of our existing knowledge of such measurement.

MEASURING THE PERFORMANCE OF ADJUSTIVE GUIDANCE

The measurement of programs or of techniques in adjustive guidance has been mainly confined to academic adjustment. No doubt the reason for this is the fact that school marks or achievement tests can be employed as criteria. By contrast, objective criteria for appraising emotional or social adjustment are hard to find.

The measurement of guidance programs designed to improve the state of academic adjustment has been well illustrated. In the first section of Chapter 15, Ross' experiment with low-ability university freshmen was described and the major results shown in Table 64. The study is remarkable for the brevity and simplicity of the guidance variable. The sixth section of Chapter 16, which is devoted to counseling for quality of work, reports evaluative studies by Klingelhofer, Jones, Serene, Calhoun, and Schoenhard. The guidance variable in these experiments was, for the most part, complex and involved. They may well be reread in connection with this section.

Two additional examples of the measurement of a program for academic adjustment will be presented. One is a study of counseling in higher education reported by Toven.[13] Two groups of freshmen in a large liberal-arts college were matched person to person on the basis of general intelligence, sex, age, college class, race, religion, and curriculum chosen. They constituted 188 pairs. One group was counseled systematically throughout their four years by faculty advisers appointed by the dean. Six interviews were required in the freshman year, four in the sophomore year, and two in the junior and senior years. At the end of the four-year period the two groups were compared on the basis of the following factors: (1) graduation from college, (2) persistence in college, (3) scholastic action by the faculty, (4) cumulative college grade averages, (5) college grades A to F, and (6) numbers of points completed. In all the comparisons the counseled group excelled. The differences between the two groups are typified by the fact that 101, or 53.7 per cent, of the counseled group were graduated; comparable figures for the non-counseled group were 68, or 36.2 per cent.

Toven characterized the faculty advisers as individuals chosen with extreme care for their recognized teaching ability, good judgment, sensitivity to student problems, willingness to serve as advisers, and familiarity with the organization of the institution. They kept a confidential folder on each student.

A study similar to that of Toven was reported by Faries.[14] From the freshmen who entered City College of New York an experimental group of 140 students was made up of those who sought assistance from a counselor, plus a few who were referred by academic deans because of poor scholarship. Paired with them on the basis of high-school average, composite score on entrance tests, and the degree for which the student chose to work were students who did *not* seek counseling assistance. Both the experimental and control groups had attended the freshman orientation classes in which the counseling service was described and its availablity made known to them. Thus the main difference between the groups was the disposition to seek counseling assistance.

Of the experimental group, 108, or 77.1 per cent, graduated; of the control group, 72, or 51.4 per cent graduated. The number of interviews per student which they had had ranged from one to seven and averaged 1.9. Speculating on reasons why her counseling was more effective than that of Toven, Faries offered the following explanations:

1. In Toven's study, faculty members, presumably without specialized training, did the counseling, while in the Faries' study all the counseling was done by one person, one who had specific training for the work of personal counseling.

[13] J. Richard Toven, "Appraising a Counseling Program at the College Level," *Occupations,* Vol. XXIII (May, 1945), pp. 459–466.
[14] Miriam Faries, "Short-Term Counseling at the College Level," *Journal of Counseling Psychology,* Vol. II (Fall, 1955), pp. 182–184.

2. The counselor in the Faries' study undoubtedly had better tools, more individual data on students, than did the Toven counselors.

3. The voluntary nature of the counseling in the Faries' program meant that the counselees were strongly motivated. They had to ask for appointments and then maintain their motivation for a period varying from a few days to two weeks until the time of the appointment.

The Faries' experiment and interpretation seems to support the contention of Cuony and Hoppock, cited above, to the effect that some of the imponderables, such as personality, drive, and work habits, may count for more in an individual's achievement than traits which are more measurable.

COMPREHENSIVE EXPERIMENTATION

Described at some length in the concluding pages of Chapter 10 and again briefly in the first section of this chapter, Sachs' comparison of two junior high school guidance organizations is noteworthy for the comprehensiveness of its measurement, as indicated by the 27 criteria, organized under eight areas of study, which she employed. They are as follows:[15]

Adjustment to the School
1. Extent and accuracy of pupils' information concerning library usage and study skills
2. Extent and accuracy of pupils' information concerning the school program and school activities
3. Degree of pupils' understanding of the purposes of school subjects
4. Degree of pupils' adjustment to school, as measured by personality inventory

Adjustment in Social Relationships
5. Extent and accuracy of pupils' information concerning etiquette or social usage
6. Degree of pupils' adjustment to home and family life, as measured by a personality inventory
7. Degree of pupils' general social adjustment, as measured by a personality inventory

Personal or Self Adjustment
8. Degree of pupils' personal or self adjustment, as measured by a personality inventory
9. Degree of pupils' understanding of mental hygiene principles

Self-Appraisal
10. Degree to which pupils make *reliable* estimates of their own personality traits and abilities
11. Degree to which pupils make *accurate* estimates of their own personality traits and abilities

Information Basic to Life Planning

[15] Georgia May Sachs, *op. cit.,* pp. 19–22.

12. Extent and accuracy of pupils' information concerning false or pseudo guidance
13. Extent and accuracy of pupils' educational guidance information
14. Extent and accuracy of pupils' information concerning opportunities for vocational education at Pasadena Junior College
15. Extent and accuracy of pupils' information concerning the world of work
16. Extent and accuracy of pupils' information concerning the occupation in which he is most interested

Effectiveness of Life Planning

17. Extent to which pupils have made vocational plans
18. Extent to which pupils have made educational plans
19. Appropriateness of pupils' vocational plans
20. Appropriateness of pupils' educational plans
21. Degree to which pupils show evidence of critical thinking in the area of educational and vocational planning

Teacher-Pupil Relationships

22. Adequacy of information possessed by guidance teachers concerning their counselees
23. Degree to which information about pupils is pooled as a basis for guidance
24. Rapport between guidance teachers and pupils

Evaluative Reactions of Teachers and Pupils

25. Teachers' and pupils' reactions concerning outcomes
26. Teachers' and pupils' attitudes toward the group guidance programs
27. Teachers' reactions concerning the strong and weak points of the group guidance programs

With each criterion Sachs stated briefly how and with what instruments she measured its attainment. A study of these criteria makes it plain that the author aimed to measure guidance in all its aspects.

A research of similar breadth, but with the added factor of being longitudinal, is the experiment which Rothney and Roens carried on in the schools of Arlington, Massachusetts.[16] They started a special guidance program with a group of 129 pupils in the eighth grade and carried it on to high-school graduation. Then, by means of follow-up reports obtained from the students eight to eighteen months after graduation, some appraisals of their state of adjustment and distribution were made. A control group was also carried all the way, and the measurements made compared the control and experimental groups.

Interviews with a guidance specialist constituted the basic technique, and they were used with the fullest flexibility and variation demanded by each case. Both distributive and adjustive guidance as defined in this text were the goal of the counselor's activity, and the aim of the counselor was not only to influence the choices and adjustments of a group of pupils, but also

[16] John W. M. Rothney and Bert A. Roens, *Guidance of American Youth* (Cambridge, Mass., Harvard University Press, 1950).

to instruct parents, teachers, and principals in techniques of assisting pupils. The authors speculate on the probability that in attaining this latter goal, some of the control pupils might have benefited, for there was an apparent growth in guidance consciousness on the part of the faculty. Undoubtedly, the variable in this experiment was complex and composed of many elements, with variation in the treatment of the pupils being perhaps most important.

On most measures of school progress and success, the guided group excelled the unguided group. In the follow-up reports after graduation, the general pattern of responses showed the guided group to have matched themselves with educational and vocational opportunities more accurately than the unguided group, to have attained greater stability, and to be better equipped for grappling with future problems of educational and vocational progress.

The Rothney and Roens experiment significantly follows its subjects over such a period of time as to permit a test of the enduring value of the counseling program. They were able to show in the post-school behavior of their subjects that school counseling paid off. Their report is rewarding to read for its account of the development of the guidance program and for the 100-page section devoted to the reporting of ten case studies.[17]

In the evaluations of guidance described in this chapter, or referred to as described in preceding chapters, are to be found something of satisfaction, more of challenge. While the measurement of guidance presents many difficulties, research has given us many yardsticks for this purpose. It seems to this writer that the main reason why guidance measurements have not been incorporated into common school practice is that no one expects guidance to have to prove itself. It is a service which lingers long in the promotional stage—currently riding high in the public favor—a ministry too largely accepted on simple faith in the unsupported assertions of its protagonists. A great university leaps into a counseling program without first establishing bench marks of the present state of adjustment and distribution of its student body, against which later gains—or losses—can be measured. A high school establishes guidance personnel and activities because the standards of an accrediting association call for them. Elementary schools are currently awakening to an ill-defined "need" for guidance, but without taking steps to measure the extent to which guidance fulfills that need.

In all educational institutions administrators and guidance workers must become imbued with the sort of healthy skepticism which is continuously seeking evidence of the worth of guidance procedures and techniques. Such an attitude is the best assurance that the features of guidance will always be

---

[17] A recent significant addition to the literature of evaluation is John W. M. Rothney's report of an eight-year study of the effects of a guidance program, published under the title, *Guidance Practices and Results,* by Harper and Brothers.

vital and dynamic, will be harnessed to worth-while purposes, will bear upon one or more of the components of the guidance function.

QUESTIONS, PROBLEMS, INVESTIGATIONS

1. Because junior high school pupils face the differentiated program of senior high school, it is highly important that they have educational and vocational orientation. Follow these suggestions for building tests of orientation:
   a. Study the nature and scope of senior high school subjects.
   b. Using the *Occupational Outlook Handbook,* select occupations on which to test pupil's knowledge of extent and kind of education which is required or advantageous for entering and carrying on each occupation.
   c. Which high-school curriculum would be best to follow in preparing for, or looking toward preparation for, each of the occupations?
   d. Test pupil's knowledge of the experiences of elementary and junior high school years from which they can judge their ability for and interest in senior high school subjects.

2. Make a study of last year's high-school graduating class and prepare a graph similar to Figure 3 in Chapter 4.

3. Gather data from this year's high-school seniors similar to those shown in Table 78.

4. Make a comparative study of Sachs' *Evaluation of Group Guidance Work in Secondary Schools* and Rothney and Roens' *Guidance of American Youth* for such purposes as the following:
   a. Comparison of criteria employed.
   b. Guidance features employed.
   c. Comparison of measuring instruments used.

5. In your homeroom, select one or more major guidance goals to be attained in the course of the semester or year. Measure the position of the group with reference to the goal at the beginning and at the end of the period.

SELECTED REFERENCES

ARSENIAN, Seth, "Own Estimate and Objective Measurement," *Journal of Educational Psychology,* Vol. XXXIII (April, 1942), pp. 291–302.

BILOVSKY, David, MCMASTERS, William, SHORR, Joseph E., and SINGER, Stanley L., "Individual and Group Counseling," *Personnel and Guidance Journal,* Vol. XXXI (March, 1953), pp. 363–365.

CALHOUN, S. Reed, "The Effect of Counseling on a Group of Underachievers," *School Review,* Vol. LXIV (October, 1956), pp. 312–316.

CUONY, Edward R., and HOPPOCK, Robert, "Job Course Pays Off," *Personnel and Guidance Journal,* Vol. XXXII (March, 1954), pp. 389–391.

FARIES, Miriam, "Short-Term Counseling at the College Level," *Journal of Counseling Psychology,* Vol. II (Fall, 1955), pp. 182–184.

HEDGE, John W., and HUTSON, Percival W., "A Technique for Evaluating Guidance Activities," *School Review,* Vol. XXXIX (September, 1931), pp. 508–519.

HUTSON, P. W., "Testing the Guidance Program," *Nation's Schools,* Vol. XV (June, 1935), pp. 21–23.

——, and WEBSTER, A. D., "An Experiment in the Educational and Vocational Guidance of Tenth-Grade Pupils," *Educational and Psychological Measurement,* Vol. III (Spring, 1943), pp. 3–21.

JONES, Edward S., "The Probation Student: What He Is Like and What Can Be Done about It," *Journal of Educational Research,* Vol. XLIX (October, 1955), pp. 93–102.

KLINGELHOFER, Edwin L., "The Relationship of Academic Advisement to the Scholastic Performance of Failing College Students," *Journal of Counseling Psychology,* Vol. I (Fall, 1954), pp. 125–131.

LINCOLN, Mildred E., *Teaching About Vocational Life,* Ch. 9 and Appendix (Scranton, Pa., International Textbook Co., 1937), pp. 466–477.

PATTERSON, Russell L., and FOTIU, P. G., "The Effectiveness of Guidance Center Counseling," *Journal of Educational Research,* Vol. XLVI (January, 1953), pp. 359–363.

PROCTOR, W. M., *The Use of Psychological Tests in the Educational and Vocational Guidance of High School Pupils,* Journal of Educational Research Monographs No. 1 (Bloomington, Ill., Public School Publishing Co., June, 1921), pp. 23–31.

ROSS, C. C., "Should Low Ranking Freshmen Be Told Their Scores on Intelligence Tests?" *School and Society,* Vol. XLVII (May 21, 1938), pp. 678–680.

ROTHNEY, John W. M., *Guidance Practices and Results* (New York, Harper, 1958).

——, and ROENS, Bert A., *Guidance of American Youth* (Cambridge, Mass., Harvard University Press, 1950).

SACHS, Georgia May, *Evaluation of Group Guidance Work in Secondary Schools.* Southern California Educational Monographs No. 14 (Los Angeles, University of Southern California Press, 1945).

SCHOENHARD, G. H., "Home Visitation Put to a Test," *Personnel and Guidance Journal,* Vol. XXXVI (March, 1958), pp. 480–485.

SERENE, Michael F., "An Experiment in Motivational Counseling," *Personnel and Guidance Journal,* Vol. XXXI (February, 1953), pp. 319–324.

TORRANCE, E. Paul, "Some Practical Uses of a Knowledge of Self-Concepts in Counseling and Guidance," *Educational and Psychological Measurement,* Vol. XIV (Spring, 1954), pp. 120–127.

TOVEN, J. Richard, "Appraising a Counseling Program at the College Level," *Occupations,* Vol. XXIII (May, 1945), pp. 459–466.

TRAVERS, R. M. W., "A Critical Review of Techniques for Evaluating Guidance," *Educational and Psychological Measurement,* Vol. IX (Summer, 1949), pp. 211–225.

WILLIAMSON, E. G., "A College Class in Occupational Information," *School Review,* Vol. XLV (February, 1937), pp. 123–129.

——, and BORDIN, E. S., "Evaluating Counseling by Means of a Control-Group Experiment," *School and Society,* Vol. LII (November 2, 1940), pp. 434–440.

——, "The Evaluation of Educational and Vocational Counseling: A Critique of Methodology of Experiments," *Educational and Psychological Measurements,* Vol. I (1941), pp. 5–24.

WOLF, Lyle H., "The Measurement of Orientation," *School Review,* Vol. XL (October, 1932), pp. 577–586.

WRENN, C. Gilbert, "The Evaluation of Student Personnel Work: A Critique of the 'Guidance Movement,'" *School and Society,* Vol. LII (November 2, 1940), pp. 409–414.

YOUNG, F. Chandler, "College Freshmen Judge Their Own Scholastic Promise," *Personnel and Guidance Journal,* Vol. XXXII (March, 1954), pp. 399–403.

Index